FOUNDATIONS of PARAPSYCHOLOGY

FOUNDATIONS of PARAPSYCHOLOGY

Exploring the Boundaries of Human Capability

Foreword by T.X.Barber

HOYT L. EDGE ROBERT L. MORRIS
JOSEPH H. RUSH JOHN PALMER

Routledge & Kegan Paul
London and New York

First published in 1986
Reprinted in 1987
by Routledge & Kegan Paul Ltd.
11 New Fetter Lane, London EC4P 4EE

Published in the USA by
Methuen Inc. in association
with Routledge & Kegan Paul Inc.

Set in Times 10 on 11 pt
by Input Typesetting Ltd, London SW19 8DR

Printed and bound in Great Britain by
Robert Hartnoll [1985] Ltd., Bodmin, Cornwall

Library of Congress Cataloging in Publication Data

Foundations of Parapsychology.
Bibliography: p.
Includes index.
I. Psychical research. I. Edge, Hoyt L.
BF1031.F598 1986 133 85–20486
British Library CIP data also available

ISBN 0–7102–0226–1
ISBN 0–7102–0805–7 (pbk.)

Contents

Plates

Acknowledgments

In addition to the careful help that the editors at Routledge & Kegan Paul have given us, we would like to acknowledge the following: the Parapsychology Laboratory at the Royal University of Utrecht for the support of John Palmer and Hoyt Edge in important stages of writing and editing the text; the University of Syracuse for support of Robert Morris; the Parapsychology Foundation for financial assistance in the research of chapter 4; our present institutional affiliations; and our wives – Jean Edge, Joanna Morris, and Juanita Rush – for their understanding and personal support.

Foreword

A striking theme that pervades the history of intellectual and scientific endeavors is that, with few exceptions, theories, assumptions and even 'facts' that were deeply accepted at one period are viewed later as either erroneous, misleading, or limited. An interrelated theme is also omnipresent in the history of science: as investigators probe more intensively into cosmology, physics, biology, psychology and other compartments of inquiry, the accumulating data increasingly indicate the resounding conclusion that reality, or everything we can possible know and possibly experience, is much broader, deeper and richer than is dreamed of in our philosophy. The more we probe, the more we realize that there are levels of complexities and depths in every aspect of every phenomenon. If we glance at the biological sciences, for instance, we see that, as research expanded, more complex and richer organization or orchestration was found at every biological level – in cells, in cell organelles, in macromolecules, etc.

Careful consideration of these pervasive historical themes broadens our horizons; by deeply accepting the idea that virtually all of our present-day assumptions and theories will be discarded later as they are shown to be either mistaken, misleading, or severely limited, we become more open to new (*really* new) data, assumptions and conceptualizations. We become more open, for instance, to anomalous data that seem to contradict 'official' viewpoints, such as the data presented by parapsychologists, while, at the same time, remaining aware that many of the assumptions and theories which are tightly bound to both 'official' and 'nonofficial' viewpoints will one day be discarded and replaced by wider understandings.

For many years parapsychology has needed a wide-spectrum text that attempts to integrate the vast amount of data which have accumulated around the phenomena traditionally labeled as telepathy, clairvoyance, psychokinesis, precognition, apparitions, etc. This text admirably fills the need. The authors can be commended for their in-depth survey of the field and also for their awareness, implicit throughout the text, that the assumptions and theories of both proponents and critics are, at best, severly limited.

In reading the text we will have to consider once again important questions that are asked by all thinking men and women. What are the potentials of the human species? Are we in contact with each other in ways that are not bound by our known senses? Do our thoughts, images and feelings influence other people by processes that exceed our present understanding? Is the future knowable or influenceable by means which lie outside of our present awareness?

This text will also guide the reader to ask very specific questions. Why is the accumulated evidence in parapsychology (as in many other areas of human endeavor) convincing to some and totally unconvincing to others? To what extent and in which way does conviction depend on prior basic judgments or philosophical assumptions about what can exist in what way? Why do some investigators in this area rather consistently find positive evidence for the existence of the phenomena whereas others consistently fail to find supporting evidence? To what extent are the positive and the negative results due to malobservation, deception, misapplication of statistics, or misinterpretation, and to what extent are they independent of such human error?

The data and analyses presented in this broad-ranging text also lead us to ask whether the phenomena are multifaceted and possibly due to a variety of causes. Could some of the phenomena be due to 'senses' or 'awarenesses' that are utilized by human beings but which have not as yet been categorized and understood, somewhat in the same way as the echolocation sense in bats, the magnetic sense in bees, and the electric sense in mormyrid fish were not understood until relatively recently? Could some of the phenomena be due to 'psychic experts' who have acquired a level of knowledge and awareness that is potentially available to all human beings in somewhat the same sense as any expert in any field of endeavor – e.g. an entomologist, a nematologist, a physician, or a clinical psychologist – has special knowledge of his animal or human subjects and appears to others, who are unaware of his special expertise, to be able to 'read the minds' of his subjects and to predict or 'precognize' some of the specifics of their future experiences? Could some of the phenomena be due to something much less tangible; for instance to more basic limitations in our unquestioned philosophical assumptions, possibly pertaining to such categories as space, time and causality? Finally, are some of the phenomena simply not what their name implies; for instance, could psychokinesis and recurrent spontaneous psychokinesis (poltergeist phenomena) be due simply to tricky subjects who are able to fool investigators?

The critical analyses presented in this text will also stimulate us to ask which of the phenomena now included under parapsychology will be viewed as part of normal psychology in the near or distant future. We might expect that the same fate will befall some of the present-day topics of parapsychology as befell mesmerism and hypnotism; during part of the nineteenth century, these phenomena were viewed by many respected scholars as subfields of 'psychical research' and many years elapsed before they were clearly seen to involve normal but neglected psychological processes occurring in a unique social psychological situation. Similarly, faith healing, which was at one time classified with paranormal phenomena, is now associated with intensified normal psychological processes, such as strong expectancies, profound convictions, and believed-in suggestions, working through intensified normal psychophysiological processes that have been or are being elucidated. More recently, Kirlian photography was being classified by some investigators among the paranormal but it has now become clear that it also is due to known physical principles.

I recommend this text to all scholars but I especially recommend it to research scientists who may be stimulated to conduct further investigations. Researchers will find a rich source here especially in the chapters which critically review the following topics: the 'hard' research data and the criticisms that have been leveled at studies yielding the data; the many methods that can be used selectively to conduct rigorous research in the area; the methods of statistical analysis that are especially useful for experiments in parapsychology; and the skills that are needed to detect sleight of hand, deception and other pitfalls in research.

Theodore Xenophon Barber, PhD
Cushing Hospital
Framingham, Massachusetts

Preface

Few topics arouse the passions of scientists as much as does parapsychology. Students who wish to understand this complex field find themselves bombarded by a bewildering assortment of claims and counterclaims. Some parapsychologists attempt to persuade them that psychic (psi) phenomena are an established fact, while some of their critics assert with equal assurance that there is no evidence for psi at all! Such polemical treatises are often warmly received by those already committed to the polemicist's viewpoint, but they are apt to be unsatisfying to those who are simply curious about the subject and feel capable of drawing their own conclusions if presented adequate and unbiased information with a minimum of rhetorical overlay. It is to readers with this mentality that our book is addressed.

Some readers may feel that it is premature to write a textbook in a preparadigmatic field like parapsychology in which there are no findings that are universally accepted by the scientific community. We respectfully disagree. Even if one accepts that psi is not an established fact, that is not the same as saying there are no facts in parapsychology. It is a fact that a large percentage of people have had 'psychic' experiences which if taken at face value imply that they are interacting with the outside world in ways that cannot be explained by orthodox scientific theory. It is a fact that a substantial number of qualified scientists have repeatedly reported anomalies in the more controlled context of scientific experiments which likewise seem to defy such explanation. Are these facts all to be explained as human error or credulity, or will they ultimately require additions and perhaps even modifications to our current scientific laws and theories? Whatever the answer, the question is important, both for science and for society generally. *Ad hoc* explanations of these anomalies are cheap and abundant. However, definitive explanations can only come from more and better research, and this research will be most effective if it is informed about what has happened in the past. Hence the need for a comprehensive text.

This book is primarily a summary of the methods, research findings and theories of those whose orientation has been to try to establish that the anomalies *do* require explanations transcending known scientific laws and theories. Those who favor conventional explanations for the most part have chosen to make their case by attacking the research of the psi proponents rather than by putting their own hypotheses to test in independent research. Although we agree that the burden of proof falls on psi proponents to demonstrate the paranormal nature of the anomalies, conventional explanations must likewise be verified on a broad scale and not just assumed a priori. We hope that when the next textbook of parapsychology is written there will be greater balance in the empirical contributions from the two sides (or, better yet, that the two sides will merge into one side capable of adopting either perspective).

Although the authors of this book can fairly be described as parapsychologists, we all maintain strong identities with the orthodox fields in which we were trained: psychology (Morris, Palmer), physics (Rush), and philosophy (Edge). None of us considers psi to be an established fact, but we are united in the conviction that the research to be described in this book is sufficiently suggestive of the paranormal nature of some of the relevant anomalies that the pursuit of continued research from a paranormal perspective is not only justified but should be actively encouraged. At the same time, we value the critical role played by those who favor more conventional explanations of the anomalies, and we have tried to remedy the deficiency of several previous parapsychology books by giving a fair summary of the skeptical viewpoint. The only attitude we condemn is the tendency of certain fanatics and opportunists to mislead the public with oversimplifications, exaggerated claims, and sensationalism in the media. This behavior used to be the exclusive province of some radical psi proponents, but recently certain elements of the skeptical community have been trying very hard to catch up.

Each chapter or chapter section has been written by only one of us, as identified at the beginning of the chapter. We have tampered little if at all with each other's material. Thus our differences in persepctive remain. Occasional disparities in interpretation may be found, and there may be duplications of material where such material is an integral part of the subject matter of more than one chapter.

Although we hope to reach a wide audience with our book, it is intended primarily as a college text. We believe that the enigma of psi will be solved only when a responsible parapsychology is fully integrated into academic life, a parapsychology that combines a firm commitment to the basic principles of rigorous scientific methodology with a sincere openness to heretical as well as conventional hypotheses. If our book makes some small contribution to this outcome, we will consider it to have been well worth the effort.

Hoyt L. Edge
Robert L. Morris
John Palmer
Joseph H. Rush

Part I
Parapsychology: an overview

Note: In most of the chapters, each important term that is introduced or defined in the chapter will be followed by an asterisk (*). All such terms are listed at the end of the chapter in the order they appear in the text.

Most of the chapters conclude with sets of questions which invite the reader to think more deeply about the material presented in these chapters.

Chapter 1
What is parapsychology?

Joseph H. Rush

1 Characteristics of parapsychological events

A woman writing a letter to her daughter suddenly feels a severe pain in her right hand, at the same time that the daughter suffers a burn on her right hand. A man is visited in his bedroom by a lifelike apparition of his father, just before he receives a telegram telling of his father's unexpected death in a distant city the same evening. A young man is discharged from his job in a warehouse because merchandise falls off shelves or flies across the room when he is about. A woman hears an airplane in the clatter of her sewing machine and suddenly 'knows' that an airplane has struck the Empire State Building. Several persons in Britain dream of children being killed in the destruction of a schoolhouse, days before a pile of coal-mine waste slides down a hillside and buries a school.

All of these varied incidents are reported examples of what commonly are called *psychic experiences.* They are typical of the kinds of claims that parapsychologists are concerned with investigating. Yet such spontaneously occurring experiences are highly varied, ranging from the trival to the tragic, from simple to complex, from ill-defined forebodings to lifelike visions or audible messages. They occur in the sleeping or waking states, to young and old, to visionaries and business executives. They involve both sensory (subjective) and motor (external) effects that mimic those of ordinary experience.

What, then, are the common characteristics that relate such experiences and justify treating them as a single class? What are the boundaries of parapsychology?

The prefix *para* means beside or beyond. Psychic phenomena are not isolated anomalies. They merge into the mystery of mind in all its aspects. Parapsychology is conceived as being, not outside and distinct from the field of psychology, but on its unexplored borders. Psychology ultimately must be concerned with the mind-body problem that has baffled philosophers through the ages, the riddle of the relation between consciousness and the objects of its awareness. The subject matter of parapsychology is a portion of this continuum of experience and awareness. However, a fairly consistent distinction can be drawn between the more familiar modes of experiencing and influencing the world and those called psychic.

1.1 Independence of known physical mediation

Ordinarily, interaction between the human or any other organism and its environment (which includes other organisms) is mediated by identifiable, observable physical agencies. A falling object excites vibration in the surrounding air that sets an eardrum vibrating in unison with the object. The resulting excitation of sensitive nerves registers in consciousness as a characteristic sound. An analogous, though more complex, train of physical events relates vision to the thing viewed. Conversely, the subjective intention or 'will' to pick up an object somehow initiates neural processes that excite contractions in the appropriate muscles to execute the action. Such ultimately physical mediations have been identified for almost all of the sensory and motor modes of interaction between organisms and their environments (including the internal environment of the organism), except for the persistent hiatus between neural processes and subjective experience.

Psychic phenomena depart sharply from this pattern. Through a psychic event, a person typically gains information about a situation that is quite beyond the range of the physiological senses. More rarely, one may influence a physical situation that is outside the normal physical range of action. Authenticated reports of spontaneous psychic experiences, as well as experimental findings, consistently exhibit this indifference to familiar physical constraints. Information apparently is transferred despite great distances, massive material barriers, even (in glimpses of future events) time itself. It is this ostensible independence of physical factors that is at once the most distinctive characteristic of psychic experiences and the most difficult to accept or explain. It is clear that the term *parapsychology* is somewhat arbitrary, for the phenomena it comprehends ramify into biology and physics as well.

Parapsychology*, then, is the scientific field that is concerned with interactions, both sensory and motor, that seem not to be mediated by any recognized physical mechanism or agency.

1.2 Rarity and strangeness of psychic experiences

Psychic experiences, in modern Western culture at least, are relatively rare. Typically a person of stable personality, dreaming or engaged in some ordinary activity, is suddenly involved in an 'impossible' experience that is likely to be associated with danger or death. The experient is shocked and bewildered, and returns as quickly as possible to normal activities; but the memory of that extraordinary incident persists. Most people are never aware of experiencing psychic events at all. A few, commonly called *psychics,* experience them repeatedly. Most such people, at least those we hear about, learn to accept and even to encourage and develop their unusual talents. Some live in fear of them and try to suppress them.

Another notable characteristic of psychic experiences is their strangeness. This quality is felt and commented on by almost everyone who reports such an incident, in such terms as 'weird,' 'uncanny,' 'unnatural,' 'unreal.' Frequently cold sensations and 'gooseflesh' are reported, together with strong emotions of awe and sometimes terror. Though rarity itself contributes to such feelings, rarity alone does not always evoke them. The element of strangeness, of the lack of a rational framework to encompass an experience, is an essential factor in the typical reaction to a psychic episode.

2 An evolving science

Parapsychology began a century ago with the collection and analyses of spontaneous psychic experiences as reported by participants and witnesses. However, experimental approaches to the investigation of psychic phenomena soon developed, so that the investigation of spontaneous experiences is now a subordinate phase. As in any developing field, emphases shift and boundaries are flexible. Psychical research, as parapsychological investigations originally were termed, was preoccupied with the question of survival of bodily death and with simply establishing that psychic phenomena actually occur. The survival question has dropped out of prominence because of logical and methodological difficulties and changing cultural attitudes. More recently, proof of the validity of parapsychology has been subordinated to the effort to discover relations between ostensible psychic phenomena and psychological or other factors.

Some phenomena are provisionally considered parapsychological, though they may be susceptible to other explanations. On-site dowsing or 'water-witching,' for example, usually is regarded as parapsychological (if indeed it is a valid phenomenon). However, alternative hypotheses that assume sensitivity to electric or magnetic field variations or other subtle physical cues are difficult to eliminate. Conversely, the weight of evidence indicates that the migratory and homing behavior of birds and other animals is mediated by physical senses; yet some aspects of such behavior, particularly 'trailing' feats by abandoned pets that find their way to their owners' new locations, suggest a psychic component. Some anecdotal evidence, supported by a small but growing body of experimental data, indicates that certain persons can induce physiological 'healing' of injuries or infections without the use of medical techniques. Is such healing to be regarded as a paranormal influence of the healer on the body of the patient, and therefore parapsychological? Or does the healer influence the mind of the patient to do its own healing through its psychosomatic capabilities?

To clarify what parapsychology is, it may be helpful to point out some superficially related activities that are not parapsychological. Astrology, palmistry, Tarot-card reading and other systems for divination are not parapsychology, since they depend upon prescribed rules, rather than subjective insight, for interpreting patterns. Kirlian photography, the production of aura-like corona patterns by high-frequency electric discharge, may prove to be useful as a clinical and research tool; but nothing yet reported justifies placing it in the realm of parapsychology. Such distinctions will be developed more fully in later chapters.

2.1 The technical language of parapsychology

A science, like any other specialty, develops its own peculiar vocabulary. In the beginning, it uses common words to express the familiar concepts and observations out of which the science has arisen. But the meanings of commonly used words tend to become fuzzy as usage changes and multiple meanings evolve. Such words are not suitable for expressing the precise, unambiguous concepts that are essential to scientific discourse. Common words also accumulate emotional associations that interfere with objective discussion. The ambiguity and richness of association that appeal to the poet only present difficulties for the scientist.

New ideas and discoveries therefore require new words for clear communication. During the past century the technical terms used in parapsychology have evolved from beginnings in folklore and spiritualism, becoming more numerous and more esoteric as the field has advanced.

Just how important neutral, noncommittal terminology may be to objective thinking is open to question. To an active worker in a specialized field, any word quickly comes to mean just whatever complex concept it symbolizes in that field; any prior associations that are irrelevant to that context are lost. Conversely, a neutral term can become the symbol of a preconceived idea. Such a term is unidentified flying object, which was devised to avoid the implications of such a prejudiced expression as flying saucer. Yet its acronym, UFO, has become a popular word, ufo, which signifies an extraterrestrial space ship!

Much of the parapsychological terminology now in use has grown out of the research at Duke University in the 1930s under the direction of J. B. Rhine. He adopted the word parapsychology from the German *parapsychologie* as a scientific term for the field that had been called psychical research. He also introduced the term extrasensory perception (ESP)* for all psychic phenomena that are analogous to sensory functions (but to many people ESP has come to mean any kind of psychic ability or manifestation).

Prior to the research at Duke University most investigators had tacitly assumed that any psychic transfer of information must involve two minds, a 'sender' and a 'receiver,' so that the term telepathy* was applied loosely to any situation that lent itself to that interpretation. After experiments had indicated that paranormal access to information sometimes occurs even if the information is not in the mind of anyone, clairvoyance* was strictly redefined to mean this phenomenon only. Telepathy was limited to situations in which the target information exists *only* in someone's mind, with no opportunity for clairvoyance. Communication under such conditions as had been common in most experiments, which had permitted the possibility of both telepathy and clairvoyance, Rhine termed general extrasensory perception (GESP)*.

As experiments were developed to test the possibility of prevision of future events, traditionally called prophecy, this manifestation was termed precognition*. Note that this is not a third category, parallel to telepathy and clairvoyance. Rather, it is a modifier expressing time relations. Either telepathy or clairvoyance, used alone, implies communication of currently existing information, whereas precognition implies either telepathic or clairvoyant awareness of information that does not yet exist.

The Duke University laboratory also investigated the possibility that a person may affect a physical event or situation by mental influence alone. Rhine named this effect psychokinesis (PK)*, literally mind movement. However, any attempt to define subcategories comparable to telepathy, clairvoyance, or precognition reveals logical difficulties and ambiguities that will be dealt with later.

Scientists prefer to use neutral words for phenomena they do not yet understand, in order to avoid subtly prejudicing their thinking. Thus they do not like the spiritualistic term medium, which has been applied without much discrimination to persons who show exceptional psychic ability. Yet no term for such a person has come into general acceptance. Sensitive, paragnost, gifted subject, psychic are terms sometimes used.

To avoid the ambiguity and undesirable associations of such terms as psychic phenomena or psychical research, the word psi* (for the Greek letter ψ) has been widely adopted to represent the unknown factor in psychic experiences. It is short and noncommittal, as befits a good scientific term. Thus, we may speak of psi phenomena, of a psi experiment or psi subjects, or simply of psi.

The scientific terms that have been mentioned have evolved in Western Europe and the United States. Despite efforts toward linguistic neutrality, they imply to some extent the assumptions about psi phenomena that have been current in Western society. Meanwhile, in the USSR and Eastern Europe, a vigorous development of interest in these phenomena has evolved a technical vocabulary that reflects the materialistic philosophy that is prevalent in those societies. Instead of parapsychology or ESP, such terms as psychotronics or biocommunication are current. Psi phenomena are attributed to bioenergy, the aura and some other manifestations to bioplasma. Such terms imply the firm rejection of dualism and the attribution of all the phenomena of life unequivocally to the biochemical mechanism.

Summary of terms

parapsychology
extrasensory perception (ESP)
telepathy
clairvoyance
general extrasensory perception (GESP)
precognition
psychokinesis (PK)
psi

Chapter 2
Parapsychology: a historical perspective

Joseph H. Rush

1 The cultural background: antiquity to 1882

All science grows out of the application of reason and imagination to ordinary experience. The root experiences of parapsychological science are as old as human records and traditions. Almost every culture has had its lore of veridical dreams, of miraculous healing of disease, of telepathic and clairvoyant communication, of various forms of divination, and of mystical guidance or revelation. Some knowledge of these traditions is useful in understanding the emergence of parapsychology as a scientific discipline. In particular, it will illuminate the peculiarly ambivalent attitude of Western society toward psi phenomena, essentially a reaction to the spiritistic vs. naturalistic dilemma that derives from the more fundamental mind-body problem.

This brief historical summary will trace some antecedents of parapsychology in the Greek, Roman and Judaeo-Christian cultural heritage of Europe and North America, the area in which the scientific investigation of psi phenomena first evolved. The rich mystical and religious traditions of the East are omitted because they were not directly involved in the development of psychical research in the West. It is impossible to make any scientifically satisfactory judgment as to the reality of the phenomena that are reported in these old records. The purpose rather is to demonstrate a consistent and enduring pattern in the accounts of those human experiences that are the subject matter of parapsychology (Dodds, 1971; Inglis, 1977; Podmore, 1902/1963).

1.1 Ancient Greece and Rome

Both the Greek and Roman cultures evolved elaborate mythologies, and the latter were further enriched by the cosmopolitan influences of the empire. It is difficult to estimate how much of these theological systems reflected common beliefs based on experience and how much was invention. Various records indicate belief in clairvoyant and sometimes in precognitive dreams, even among philosophers; E. R. Dodds mentions several such cases. Apparently such dreams were commonly accepted as communications from the gods. The belief system did not admit of their being communications from spirits of the dead, who were confined to the limbo of Hades.

Even at this early period, however, there is evidence of the dilemma mentioned above. Though clairvoyant and precognitive dreams generally were believed to be divinely inspired, certain of the philosophers, notably Democritus and Aristotle, speculated that such dreaming probably was a natural function of the mind.

The oracle, a kind of institutionalized 'psychic reader,' was common. The Delphic oracle became famous, in part as the result of its performance in perhaps the first parapsychological experiment. King Croesus of Lydia (c. 550 BC) wanted a divine opinion of his plan to conquer Persia. First, however, he put a test question to several oracles: what would he be doing at a specified date and hour? Only the oracle at

Delphi answered correctly. Croesus then confidently submitted his real question. The oracle told him that if he invaded Persia he would 'destroy a great empire.' He did. It was his own!

Even as now, the apparently genuine psi experiences inspired imitation. Various methods of divination flourished, especially among the Romans. The flights of birds, the entrails of sacrificed animals, the behaviour of smoke and other irrelevant patterns were solemnly analysed by priests and soothsayers for divine auguries of personal affairs, politics, or war. And even as they do today, some of the philosophers (notably Aristotle) denounced the occult practices but accepted the spontaneous evidences of psi.

1.2 The Judaeo-Christian tradition

Accounts of paranormal phenomena occur frequently in the Bible. Many of these are remarkably similar to modern reports of such experiences. They include clairvoyant and precognitive dreams, apparitions, paranormal healing, spirit mediumship, physical phenomena, 'speaking in unknown tongues,' and prophetic visions. It is notable that the Hebrew King Saul had a 'witch' (psychic practitioner or medium) call up the spirit of the dead prophet Samuel to foretell Saul's fate (1 Samuel, chapter 28). Evidently the Hebrews, unlike the Greeks, believed in the possibility of communicating with spirits of the dead. This belief was not carried over into Christianity but was revived in the eighteenth century by the teachings of Immanuel Swedenborg.

The Roman Catholic Church through many centuries developed its own policies for evaluating and dealing with claims of paranormal phenomena. Cases of hauntings, poltergeist disturbances, or 'demonic possession' of individuals were dealt with by rituals of exorcism. Reports of miracles experienced by or in the presence of various saints presented a more difficult problem. The Church did not consider every paranormal phenomenon a miracle (i.e. evidence of divine grace). In fact, it assumed the contrary unless certain theological criteria were met. These phenomena often involved human apparitions, traveling clairvoyance, levitations, and other types of experience that appear frequently in the literature of psychical research.

Investigations of such reports by Church officials led to a remarkable study in the eighteenth century by Prospero Lambertini (later Pope Benedict XIV). As the chief investigator of alleged miracles and other paranormal phenomena, Lambertini probed many such claims and reached some remarkably astute conclusions (Haynes, 1970). He observed that psychic experiences were not peculiar to religious devotees but were experienced by all kinds of people and even animals. He further noted that such experiences occurred more often in dreams than in the waking state and frequently were perceived symbolically rather than literally. He concluded that most such phenomena, even apparitions of living or dead persons, should not be attributed to either divine or demonic agencies, but to innate capabilities of the persons experiencing them. Thus even within the spiritistic orientation of the Church we find a precociously naturalistic interpretation of psi phenomena.

1.3 The naturalistic approach

1.3.1 Mesmerism

Dr Franz Anton Mesmer, finding no welcome for his radical doctrine in Vienna, came to Paris in 1778 and soon had instigated one of the most remarkable movements on record (Ellenberger, 1970). He proclaimed a theory of 'animal magnetism' as the basis for healing therapy and put it to clinical use by procedures that appear no less bizarre today than they did to the medical profession of his time. Initially Mesmer 'magnetized' his patients by passing magnets over their bodies. Soon the hands alone were used, and a ritual of 'magnetic passes' developed. Typically the patient would respond by going into a 'magnetic crisis,' exhibiting convulsions, swooning and other hysterical behaviour. Many reported improvement or cure of their ailments, but it is impossible now to assess the validity of these claims.

The controversial course of mesmerism is not directly relevant to parapsychology. What does concern us is the fact that its practitioners soon noticed paranormal manifestations by some patients that appear to have been psi phenomena (Dingwall, 1968). Some patients responded to the magnetic influence by going into a deep abnormal sleep. In this somnambulistic or trance* state they exhibited the behaviour now familiar in hypnotic subjects: obliviousness to all sensory input except the practitioner's instructions; and on waking, no memory of what happened during the trance. Further, some responded to *unspoken* instructions, even when the practitioner was in another room, or identified concealed objects. Others sometimes accurately diagnosed diseases of persons they had not seen before or described correctly the activities of distant persons. Though allowance must be made for possible sensory cues, some of these early accounts nevertheless suggest the occurrence of psi communication. Whether valid or not, they were so interpreted. They thus contributed substantially to the developing interest in paranormal communication that led to the emergence of parapsychology.

1.3.2 Naturalistic antecedents

Actually, Mesmer's theoretical concepts were not original but were borrowed from earlier mystical philosophers whose speculations already had inspired a 'sympathetic' system of medicine. Pioneering investigations of the lodestone, a natural magnet, had stirred philosophers' imaginations. The magnet, with its opposite poles and its mysterious ability to point north-south and to influence bits of iron at a distance, seemed a prototype of opposed tendencies in general. It suggested invisible influences that were believed to interpenetrate stars, earth and living organisms. The sixteenth-century physician-philosopher Paracelsus had used actual magnets in his practice, but later he apparently evolved a metaphorical concept of magnetism.

'Magnetism' came to mean any vaguely conceived influence that could act at a distance, much as 'vibrations' is used by occultists today. This magnetic influence was conceived to be almost unimaginably subtle and tenuous. Such speculation led to the idea that one's material body is coexistent with an 'ethereal body' that is immersed in the magnetic medium and can communicate with other ethereal bodies at great distances, a concept that still is popular among occultists.

For our purposes, the important point is that Mesmer and his predecessors were essentially naturalistic. They did not invoke spirits or demons to account for what they observed but attempted to discover explanations through universal natural principles. Podmore (1902/1963, vol.1) comments that these men,

> though their methods and results differ superficially from those of modern science, were still animated by something of the scientific spirit. They essayed to relate phenomena to one another by comparison, observation, and analysis, and to subsume them under universal laws. The main difference [between them and scientists] would seem to be that the mystics, with an impatience, and even contempt, for the mere brute fact . . . lacked both the inclination and the means to wait for the slowly maturing results of experimental investigation. . . . The mystical philosophy, in fact, was an attempt at a short cut to knowledge, a premature synthesis of the universe. But it was, nevertheless, a synthesis on rationalist lines. . . . (p.47)

As noted earlier, even a high official of the Church considered many psi phenomena to be expressions of natural capabilities. Even some mesmerists came to believe that certain phenomena of the somnambulistic trance were manifestations of spirits. These opposed concepts of the paranormal are interwoven throughout the history of the subject and are evident even today.

1.4 The rise of spiritualism

In 1848 the spiritistic concept that had been implicit in many earlier interpretations of paranormal phenomena abruptly emerged in a remarkable religious movement (S. Brown, 1972; G. K. Nelson, 1969; Podmore 1902/1963). Spiritualism became a craze that swept through the United States and Western Europe, exciting devotion and scorn, enthusiastic acceptance and bitter controversy. Quite incidentally, it aroused the serious interest of scientists and other intellectuals and thus inspired the emergence of psychical research.

1.4.1 Historical antecedents of the spiritualist movement

Despite the ancient belief in the intervention of various spirits in human affairs, the idea of communication with spirits of dead humans arose in Europe only with the teachings of Immanuel Swedenborg (1688–1772). He was a respected Swedish savant who apparently developed clairvoyant abilities and also reported many experiences of communication with surviving spirits. Podmore (1902/1963, vol. 1, p. 76) mentions records of experiments in 1787 by members of a small Swedenborgian society in Stockholm in which spirits of deceased relatives 'spoke' with them through the voice of an entranced medium. This is possibly the earliest record of a phenomenon that was to become the central practice of spiritualism.

Though Continental thinking was dominated by the naturalistic doctrines of Mesmer and others, spiritistic interpretations and mediumistic practices became common in Germany early in the nineteenth century, and a few such experimenters emerged even in France before mid-century. All of their experiments appear to have depended upon mesmeric somnambulism, the deep hypnotic state induced by the experimenter. Voluntary 'going into trance' by the medium developed later.

The American society of the mid–1800s was a fertile medium for the propagation of novel doctrines and philosophies. The democratic spirit and geographic isolation from Old World culture, together with the limited education of most people, loosened the hold of tradition and encouraged social and religious experimentation. Mesmerism, phrenology and allied practices had found their way into the culture and expressed themselves in characteristically innovative ways. Itinerant mesmerists amazed their audiences with somnabulistic demonstrations, and clairvoyants diagnosed diseases or uttered inspired revelations, some of which were published.

The most notable of these literary oddities were produced by Andrew Jackson Davis, a young seer of Poughkeepsie, New York. His first serious work, *The Principles of Nature* (A. J. Davis, 1847), was received with such popular enthusiasm that it went through 34 editions in less than 30 years. Davis's work drew heavily on Swedenborg's teachings. Despite its many faults, it provided an appealing folk philosophy that created widespread receptivity and probably even a demand for evidence of spirit communication.

1.4.2 The Fox sisters

Evidence was not long in appearing. In March 1848, the John D. Fox family in the village of Hydesville, New York, began hearing mysterious rapping noises. The raps occurred in the family bedroom, seeming to come from chairs, bedsteads and other sites. They seemed to be associated with the adolescent daughters, Kate and Margaretta. (See Plate 1.) The girls soon discovered that the raps would respond to their clapping or finger snapping. It was but a step, then, to begin questioning the rapper, with a code of two raps for 'yes,' and silence for 'no.' A few weeks later Kate went to stay with a sister in Rochester, and Mrs Fox and Margaretta followed. There the rappings continued. By calling out the letters through the alphabet until the raps responded, the sisters enabled the raps to spell out messages. These disclosed that a growing number of spirits were seeking to communicate with earthbound friends and relatives. Many persons who attended these seances discovered afterwards that they also could produce rapping communications. A public lecture on the phenomena in November 1849 led to investigations of the Foxes by a series of committees, none of whom was able to explain the rappings. These events aroused widespread interest, and the cult of spiritualism was launched.

Was the whole strange enterprise founded on fraud? Much evidence indicates that the Fox sisters practiced trickery, the favorite explanation being that they made the rappings by unusual manipulations of knee or toe joints. An investigation by three physicians appeared to verify this theory, and a relative of the sisters stated that Kate had shown her how the trick was done (Podmore, 1902/1963, vol. 1, p. 184). Forty years later Kate and Margaretta publicly confessed to fraud and then recanted the confessions. Yet many witnesses maintained that the rappings often were much louder or more rapid than any that ever were demonstrated by manipulation of joints. Further, though most of the accurate answers to personal questions could have resulted from acute attention to the questioners, not all are so easily disposed of, nor were all witnesses credulous believers. E. W. Capron, for example, took a handful of small shells from a basket, without counting, and twice the raps told the number correctly (Gauld, 1968, p. 8).

1.4.3 The movement grows

The new religion found eager followers and spread rapidly throughout the country. Curiously, the ability to elicit raps and other phenomena proved to be so common that almost any earnest group could develop such mediumship in one or more members. Thus the movement was not hindered by any lack of practitioners. Many of these became professionals, providing their clients with the communications they sought and charging fees for their services.

Demand stimulated supply; the phenomena proliferated. Table tipping*, automatic writing*, speaking with 'spirit' voices in trance, clairvoyant diagnoses of illnesses, all became commonplace. Phantom hands or entire figures sometimes were seen. Tales of physical marvels progressed from raps to movements of tables and other objects and even levitation* (lifting) of the medium, disembodied 'direct voices*,' 'spirit writing' on slates*, and 'apports*' of objects from remote places into the seance room. As the new art of photography became popular some mediums began to discover spirit faces or figures in their photographs of clients (Carrington, 1907/1920).

Spiritualism did not catch on immediately in Britain; but the American developments inspired on the Continent a craze for 'table tipping' that swept Britain about 1863. To practice table tipping, several persons sit around a small table with their palms resting lightly on it. Questions are answered by rocking movements of the table. The renowned scientist Michael Faraday had sitters place their hands on a small wooden platform that rested on several layers of waxed cardboard on the table. (Some accounts say he used small rollers under the board.) The direction of creep of the cardboard layers showed that the platform, not the table, always moved first. Thus he demonstrated that the movement was caused, not by some mysterious external influence, but by unconscious muscular effort. But the spiritualists, nothing daunted, laid paper on the table and fastened a pencil to a movable platform. *Voila!* – the *planchette,* ancestor of the ouija board.

1.4.4 D.D. Home: the mediums and the scientists

The wave of enthusiasm for spiritualism inspired in Britain by the table-tipping fad soon ebbed, but in 1859 two diverse events contributed to a broad and enduring revival. The publication of Darwin's *Origin of Species* and the ensuing controversy had climaxed a naturalistic trend that challenged the prevailing belief in the divine nature of humankind and troubled many serious minds. To some of these, the spiritualist claims offered the possibility that the challenge might be met by direct evidence of a spiritual component of personality that could survive death.

The other event was the arrival in Britain of the most famous American medium, Daniel Dunglas Home (Beloff, 1977, p. 7; J. Burton, 1948). Home was primarily a physical medium*. Though he sometimes gave messages through writing or in trance, he produced a staggering variety of ostensibly paranormal physical effects. He really had evolved a repertoire analagous to that of a stage magician, in which spirit agency was only weakly implied. In his presence, on the word of a large number of intelligent and ordinarily reliable witnesses, tables moved or were levitated without human touch, an accordion floated in the air and played unearthly music, and Home himself was levitated. (See Plate 2.) He appeared to handle glowing coals without injury, affect the reading of a weighing scale without touch, and cause a pencil to write spirit messages. He never charged fees, relying for support on his numerous hosts and patrons. There is no good evidence that he was ever caught cheating.

Genuine or not, Home's feats gained wide and favorable notice. They also encouraged imitators, so that patrons of seances came to expect the spirits to manifest through paranormal physical effects (telekinesis*), as well as verbal messages. Such claims aroused the interest of scientists, conjurers and other critics who had paid little attention to the reports of spirit communications. Thus, the increasing audacity of the mediumistic performers was countered by increasing sophistication on the part of the investigators. The result within a few years was the exposure of a succession of fake physical mediums and a sharp decline in the credibility of the rest. But both spiritualists and some other investigators began to distinguish between the largely discredited physical phenomena and the evidences for paranormal communications, which in many instances continued to defy rational explanation.

Because of the readiness of spiritualists to attribute all sorts of unlikely happenings to spirits, spiritualism served to consolidate the known or claimed paranormal phenomena that hitherto had not always been considered to be related. Mediumistic communications and telekinesis, thought transference, 'possession*', haunts* and poltergeists*, automatisms*, 'psychometry*', some hypnotic effects, all went into the common bag. By thus organizing paranormal phenomena as elements in a superficially rational, even though basically faulty, system, spiritualism prepared the way for the obvious next step – the serious scientific investigation of these claims. Inevitably, it also impressed upon many of the early scientific investigators a strongly spiritistic bias.

2 The emergence of psychical research: 1882–1900

One of the earliest attempts to investigate psi phenomena impartially and scientifically was undertaken by the London Dialectical Society in 1870–71 (Podmore, 1902/1963, vol. 2, p. 147). Several subcommittees were set up to conduct various studies, but only two reported any significant work. Their favorable conclusions were severely compromised by weak procedures, inadequate descriptions of conditions and inconsistencies in reporting.

A much more impressive report came from William Crookes (1889; Podmore, 1902/1963, vol. 2, p. 237), a member of the Royal Society and a physicist of some renown. In this and earlier reports, Crookes detailed experiments he had done about 1872 with Home and with a nonprofessional medium, Mrs Clayer. He had observed a force on a spring balance and movement of a stretched parchment under conditions that he was satisfied precluded any normal influence on the instruments by the medium. Crookes's reports provoked much unfavorable criticism, but they led a few scientists to take the spiritualists' claims more seriously.

One of those so influenced was another physicist, William F. Barrett. In 1876 he reported experiments he had conducted with hypnotized subjects that he believed demonstrated paranormal communication. He also attested to raps and other lesser physical phenomena that he had observed under good test conditions; but his appeal for a learned committee to investigate these phenomena went unheeded.

2.1 The Society for Psychical Research

In 1882 Barrett called a conference of interested persons, to whom he proposed the formation of an investigative organization of scientists and spiritualists. The Society for Psychical Research (SPR) was formally launched on 20 February with Henry Sidgwick, a professor of philosophy at Cambridge, as president (Gauld, 1968; Haynes, 1982).

The first Council of the SPR included Barrett, Lord Rayleigh and Balfour Stewart (all prominent physicists), several leading spiritualists, and two close associates of Sidgwick – Frederic W. H. Myers and Edmund Gurney. Within a few years internal conflicts led to the disgruntled withdrawal of most of the spiritualists. During its first 20 crucial years the standards and policies of the society were determined largely by the influence of Sidgwick, his wife Eleanor M. Balfour, Myers and

Gurney. However, the organization did not lack other notable and highly capable members. During those early years it counted among its company several Fellows of the Royal Society, a past and a future prime minister, and many professors. That the SPR could attract such people to so unpopular an enterprise says much for the esteem in which its founders were held.

Henry Sidgwick, Myers and Gurney had become friends during their student days at Cambridge. Sidgwick was a philosopher, Myers a classical scholar, writer and poet. Sidgwick was quiet, judicious, disciplined, Myers emotional, energetic, given to transient enthusiasms. Their complementary qualities, together with Eleanor Sidgwick's quiet persistence and Gurney's dedicated energy, made for a team of rare competence and integrity. The SPR under their leadership carried out the first sustained rational investigations of what had come to be called psychic phenomena.

The intellectual quality of the SPR leaders was reflected in their conception of their subject matter. Almost all earlier investigators had concerned themselves only with the phenomena of spiritualism. Sidgwick and his associates saw these as merely one aspect of a quest for nothing less than the understanding of human personality, a new approach to the ancient mind-body problem. Accordingly, they established committees to investigate a wide range of phenomena: thought reading (which Myers termed *telepathy*); hypnosis; clairvoyance; apparitions and hauntings; and physical phenomena. Finally, a Literary Committee was charged with collecting and organizing all materials relating to these subjects.

The investigations and experiments that the early SPR carried out in these areas brought into prominence several new investigators: Frank Podmore, Richard Hodgson, Oliver Lodge, Alice Johnson. They included experiments in telepathy and investigations of spirit mediums. Communications through some mediums, notably Leonora Piper of Boston, were so impressive that Myers and several others became convinced of survival of death.

The SPR investigators also gave some attention to the phenomena produced by physical mediums. These efforts, in their judgement, amounted to an education in the methods of fraud. One episode of this period is so salutary that it deserves particular notice. A young man, S. J. Davey, became suspicious of the spirit writing obtained on slates by William Eglinton, a fashionable and impressive medium. For several months Davey practiced conjuring to produce effects similar to Eglinton's; then, with Hodgson as sponsor, he 'came out' under an assumed name as a slate-writing medium. He completely deceived his clients, principally by distracting their attention so subtly that they did not notice that they were being distracted. The reports of his methods (Gauld, 1968; Hodgson, 1892) compared step-by-step with the clients' reports of what they thought had happened afford some of the most entertaining and chastening lessons in the annals of psychology.

Ironically, the work that probably is of most enduring value was done by the innocuous-seeming Literary Committee. Under the leadership of Gurney this group became involved in collecting personal accounts of spontaneously occurring psychic experiences. They were so impressed by the numbers of such reports, the underlying similarities among them, and the contrast between them and popular notions of 'ghost stories' that they were impelled to collect and verify a large number of such incidents. These were reported in two monumental works: *Phantasms of the Living* (Gurney, Myers, & Podmore, 1886/1970; abr. and ed., E. M. Sidgwick, 1918/1975); and 'Report on the Census of Hallucinations' (H. Sidgwick, Johnson, Myers, Podmore and E. M. Sidgwick, 1894). These studies indicated that psi experience is much more widely distributed than the investigators had imagined. They thus encouraged the dependence upon ordinary persons as experimental subjects that has become customary in parapsychology.

The *Journal* and the *Proceedings* of the SPR have recorded during a century of publication many of the important developments in psychical research, particularly during the earlier years when responsible periodicals were few. Myers was a man of enormously fertile imagination and insight; his wide-ranging work on human personality (Myers, 1903/1975) has become a classic. Gurney was principally responsible for *Phantasms of the Living;* and the books of Podmore (1897, 1902/1963, 1908/1965, 1910/1975), though perhaps over-cautious, nevertheless are valuable records of much early work. They are salutary reading for the credulous.

The early SPR investigators made their share of mistakes and were biased in some of their judgments, despite their uncompromisingly rational approach. Nevertheless, these pioneers of psychical research set standards, developed methods and accumulated data that departed significantly from the fumbling, sporadic efforts of almost all of their predecessors. They established the scientific study of psi phenomena. In the words of Alan Gauld (1968, p. 341), 'They amassed in favor of paranormal phenomena evidence which would in the case of almost any other kind of natural event have been unhesitatingly and almost universally accepted.'

2.2 Continental and American research

The rapid and productive rise of psychical research in Britain was not matched by any comparable development on the Continent. However, a few serious investigators left records of scientific interest.

One of these was a French physician, Pierre Janet, whose brief experimentation with telepathic induction of hypnotic trance produced some of the most remarkable results on record (Myers, 1886; J. B. Rhine, 1947a). In 1885 he and a colleague, a Dr Gibert, took turns 'willing' their hypnotic subject to go into trance while she was in her home a kilometer distant. Sixty trials* were attempted at arbitrary times known only to Janet and Gibert; they judged 27 to be completely successful. Unfortunately, Janet apparently considered it imprudent professionally to continue these studies.

Charles Richet (1923/1975), Nobel-prize physiologist at the University of Paris, devoted many years to investigations of paranormal phenomena. From our perspective his most remarkable innovation was, in 1884, a successful card-guessing experiment in which he applied probability theory to calculate the scores to be expected by chance.

Almost all of these Continental investigations were sporadic individual efforts. In 1890, however, occurred a development that brought together at intervals almost all of the leading psychic investigators in the world. Cesar Lombroso, an Italian psychiatrist, discovered Eusapia Palladino, already a veteran of some sixteen years as a physical medium. Her seances soon drew the attention of Richet and other Continental investigators, Myers and Lodge. Later Hodgson and the Sidgwicks, Pierre and Marie Curie and other notables became involved. Throughout her long professional career, Palladino frequently was caught cheating; but whether *all* of her phenomena were fraudulent is still controversial (see section 3.2).

A visit by Barrett to the USA resulted in the organization in Boston in 1885 of a society on the pattern of the SPR. Harvard philosopher-psychologist William James soon became its leading member. In 1887 Hodgson went to Boston as manager of the work there. The society became a branch of the SPR two years later (Gauld, 1968).

Hodgson was energetic and dedicated. Under his direction the Boston society engaged in various investigations; but its work with the mental medium Leonora Piper became by far the most significant. Unlike Palladino, Piper survived many years of intensive investigations without ever being found cheating even by that nemesis of fake mediums, Hodgson.

3 A time of transition: 1900–1930

The progress of psychical research during the first three decades of the new century was not marked by any such salient development as the founding of the SPR 20 years earlier. The period was one of slow, tentative evolution, but the end result was a fundamental shift of investigative methods and emphasis. The quest for evidence of survival of death raised more questions than it answered. Investigations of physical mediums were so beset by resistance to effective controls and by evidence of fraud that interest in such phenomena declined, and many investigators came to doubt the genuineness of all physical phenomena. Evidence of paranormal communication from spontaneous case reports and mental mediums proved to be impressive but inconclusive. All of these unsatisfactory developments emphasized the need for better evidence. Inevitably, research interest shifted toward controlled experiments, and reports of such efforts appeared with increasing frequency.

The reader should be reminded that this chapter is a historical survey only. Much material that is briefly summarized here or omitted entirely will be dealt with more fully in later chapters.

3.1 Mental phenomena

A psychic* is the common term for a person who produces verifiable information apparently without sensory access to it. The term medium*, derived from spiritualism, means a psychic who produces such information ostensibly from spirits of dead persons. A few claimants to such capabilities have been studied intensively by parapsychologists. Only enough will be mentioned here to indicate the general character of these practices (Gauld, 1977, p. 579).

3.1.1 Psychics and mediums

One procedure commonly used by psychics is token object reading* – commonly miscalled 'psychometry' – in which the psychic gives images and ideas associated with an unfamiliar test object. Gustav Pagenstecher, a physician in Mexico, reported a series of such tests (1923; Prince, 1921) with a hypnotized subject, Maria Reyes de Zierold. Many detailed responses were verified.

Another notable psychic, Stefan Ossowiecki of Poland, was studied between the wars by Richet and other investigators (Rogo, 1975, p. 149). He gave many demonstrations of clairvoyant perception of concealed writing or drawings, even when some were sealed inside a lead tube.

Most psychics who practice what we now call ESP, like those above, work in an apparently normal or near-normal mental state. Mediums, however, almost always show obvious evidence of dissociation. A frequently used technique is automatic writing, in which the hand writes independently of conscious control or even awareness. More commonly the medium goes into a self-induced apparent sleep, or trance, and another personality – the control – speaks with the medium's voice, though in its own characteristic tones and manner. The control then mediates between the inquiring sitter* and the ostensible spirit communicator*. Sometimes the communicator displaces the control personality and speaks directly.

The first medium to attract sustained scientific attention was Leonora Piper, mentioned earlier. From 1885 to 1911, working through both trance voice and automatic writing, she continued to produce veridical communications that indicated, at the very least, remarkable telepathic or clairvoyant ability. Despite sometimes extreme precautions against fraud, none of her investigators ever found cause to doubt her integrity (Heywood, 1959, p. 53).

Gladys Osborne Leonard (Heywood, 1959, p. 95) also maintained an impeccable lifelong reputation as a trance medium. Her best-known patron was Oliver Lodge, the SPR pioneer scientist who became convinced of the reality of communications with his son, Raymond, killed in World War 1.

Another of the many mediums who developed during that war was Eileen Garrett (Angoff, 1974; Gauld, 1977, p. 584). Working usually in trance, her best-known exploit involved communications from crewmen killed in the crash of the dirigible R–101 that included many unlikely technical details. Objective and skeptical of her control personalities, she cooperated repeatedly with British and American investigators.

It may be worth noting that not all mediums are otherwise commonplace persons. Mrs M. de G. Verrall, who led the cross correspondence project (below), was a professor of classics. 'Mrs Willett,' an automatic writer also deeply involved in that project, was the pseudonym of Winifred Coombe-Tennant, long active in British politics. Eileen Garrett founded the Parapsychology Foundation in New York, with its associated publishing ventures.

The bizarre mediumistic dialogues between sitters and spirits produced much detailed, responsibly verified information. In some instances, they were strongly persuasive of a surviving personality, particularly to witnesses who sometimes attested to a compelling but incommunicable sense of presence and character. Yet the difficulties of scientifically evaluating such material are great. The language often is fragmentary or ambiguous. Inferences by the medium from a sitter's questions or comments must be considered, and the role of chance is very difficult to assess. Only about 1930, when scientific interest was shifting to controlled experiments, were serious attempts begun to develop quantitative methods for evaluating mediumistic messages (Pratt & Birge, 1948; Roll, 1982).

There is also the question of the control personality. Enough is known of dissociation and multiple personalities to indicate that the control is an alternate personality of the medium that manifests only when the normal personality voluntarily withdraws. Controls identify themselves as surviving spirits; but the details they offer of their former lives are rarely if ever verifiable.

3.1.2 The survival dilemma

The motives of the founders of the SPR went far beyond scientific curiosity. Reared in a religious tradition that lately had been shaken to its depths by Darwin's evolutionary theory, they saw in the claims of the spiritualists a possibility of salvaging something of the unique spiritual status formerly accorded to humankind. Proof of personal survival of bodily death would have weighed heavily in supporting the traditional view. They and their successors therefore gave high priority to survival research (see chapter 13, section 3; Gauld, 1968, 1977; Roll, 1974).

Among other approaches, investigators sought evidence bearing on survival through mental mediums. But even before the turn of the century the evidence for telepathy and clairvoyance as innate capabilities of living persons had become clear enough to create logical difficulties for survival evidence. Many spontaneous experiences indicated such ability, and much mediumistic material could be attributed more plausibly to telepathic contact between medium and sitter, or other persons, than to spirit agency.

Thus the survival hypothesis reached a dilemma. The very investigations that had sought evidence for survival had developed information that made all such evidence ambiguous. To be verifiable, information must exist in a living mind or some kind of material record. Consequently it must then be accessible, at least in principle, to paranormal cognition by the medium. Direct demonstration of survival then becomes impossible. Further evidence must be sought indirectly, in communications so complex and so remote from the knowledge of medium or sitters that spirit agency may appear more plausible than 'super ESP.'

Some such evidence developed through cross correspondences* (see chapter 13, section 3.3.2; Saltmarsh, 1938/1975). In the best of such cases a communicator gave cryptic, obscure messages through one or more mediums independently. Another medium then independently produced a message that, together with the others, formed an intelligible pattern. From about 1900 to 1930 the SPR was deeply involved in a series of such communications, in some of which Hodgson and others in the United States participated. However, the cross correspondences accumulated some 3,000 scripts and required complex, esoteric interpretations. They, too, proved inconclusive. By 1930, because of the evidential dilemma and lack of fresh approaches, interest in survival research had declined (Murphy, 1945; Roll, 1974).

3.2 Physical phenomena: the battle of wits

After its investigators had detected Palladino in fraud during sittings at Cambridge in 1895, the SPR lost interest in claims of paranormal physical phenomena. Continental investigators were not deterred, however. A series of spectacular reports continued into the 1930s, and interest revived for a time even in Britain (see chapter 10; Nicol, 1977; Rush, 1977, pp. 17–28).

Many favorable reports of Palladino's phenomena (Carrington, 1954) moved the SPR in 1908 to sponsor another investigation. Three experienced and skeptical investigators, Everard Feilding, W. W. Baggally and Hereward Carrington, conducted eleven sittings with Palladino while a stenographer recorded their continual comments on control conditions, effects they observed, and other details (Feilding, 1963; Feilding, Baggally and Carrington, 1909). They detected attempts at deception but became convinced that some well-observed phenomena had been paranormal.

Yet, despite these sustained and painstaking efforts, no consensus resulted. Expert opinions ranged from Hodgson's conviction that all of Palladino's phenomena were fraudulent to Richet's acceptance of most of them as paranormal. Investigations of later claimants to physical phenomena usually led to similar results: dubious evidence and often bitter controversy. Control methods that depended crucially upon sustained vigilance and accurate interpretations of sensory impressions simply were not good enough.

During the heyday of spiritualism, many mediums had produced substantial objects that purported to be the 'materialized' forms of hands, heads, or even entire bodies of spirit visitants. Reports of materializations* during Palladino's seances, sometimes under apparently strict control, aroused renewed interest in such claims. This phase culminated in the person of a French girl, Marthe Beraud ('Eva C.' in some reports).

Richet (1923/1975) discovered Beraud in 1905 and published reports that stand among the most spectacular claims ever to have come from reputable investigators. He described various phenomena, climaxed by the emergence of a tangible robed and helmeted figure. Despite the absence of trustworthy controls, Richet professed his conviction that it was a genuine materialization. He named the alleged materialized substance ectoplasm*. However, the test conditions that he and other investigators found acceptable hardly bear comparison with some of the better conducted and meticulously reported sittings with Palladino. Later, more scientifically conducted studies of Beraud were done by an SPR committee (SPR, 1922) and by a committee of the Sorbonne. Manifestations were minimal and conclusions uncertain.

An English investigator, Harry Price (1925/1973; Rush, 1977, p. 25), studied phenomena produced by a young woman, Stella Cranshaw. She worked usually in trance, her hands and feet being controlled by the sitters in the usual manner. Price, however, devised instrumental tests that further reduced the possibility of fraud. A recording thermometer showed drops of several degrees in air temperature during levitations or other strong effects, and an electric switch in a container sealed by a bubble film was operated without the film being broken. Later, Price (1930) conducted sittings with another medium, Rudi Schneider, under apparently the strictest controls that had been used for such phenomena. The half-dozen sitters all were selected by Price. All, including the medium, were fitted with metallic shoes and mittens. Holding hands and touching feet closed electrical circuits to several indicator lights. If anyone in the circle freed a hand or foot the broken contact would cause one of the lights to go out. Nevertheless, movements of objects and apparent materializations of hands and arms were witnessed. In 1931 Osty conducted further sittings with Schneider at Paris in which phenomena were obtained in the presence of instrumental controls (Rush, 1977, p. 26). Yet this promising physical mediumship ended indecisively. The electrically controlled test by Price ostensibly demonstrated paranormal effects beyond reasonable doubt, but Price's later behavior cast a shadow on all his work (chapter 10, section 2.1).

One physical mediumship remains to be noted for its climactic dramatization of the devious motivations and the complex interplay of personalities that have seriously compromised most such investigations (Tietze, 1973a). In 1923 'Margery' Crandon, wife of a prominent Boston surgeon, began her trance developments in a home circle. During the ensuing decade her sittings drew in such diverse investigators as psychologists E. G. Boring and William McDougall, poet W. B. Yeats, master magician Harry Houdini, and psychical investigators Hereward Carrington, W. F. Prince, and J. B. and L. E. Rhine, among others.

Early reports told enthusiastically of movements and materializations, plus the 'direct voice' (i.e. not vocalization by the medium) of the spirit control, Margery's dead brother Walter. Prince and the Rhines, and later Houdini and others, reported evidence of fraud; but they were overwhelmed by the chorus of believers until a spirit thumbprint that 'Walter' had impressed on a piece of dental wax was found to match that of Margery's dentist. The Margery fiasco signalled a climactic end, for a time, to the long and frustrating battle of wits between investigators and physical mediums. Possibly its most significant result was its influence in turning J. B. Rhine resolutely from mediumistic seances toward controlled experiments.

3.3 Haunts and poltergeists

Most spontaneous psychic episodes are nonrecurrent, once-in-a-lifetime experiences. For centuries, however, tales of recurrent manifestations have excited fear and wonder. Investigators soon recognized that these fall generally into two classes: haunts and poltergeists. A haunting is characterized by subjective visions ('ghosts') and sometimes noises in a particular location, usually an old house. These phenomena typically recur sporadically for years (e.g. Morton, 1892). Poltergeist manifestations usually are associated with a person rather than a place. They consist principally of noises and violent movements and breakage of objects, supplemented sometimes by intelligible communication through raps or mediumistic means. An outbreak typically begins abruptly and fades out in a few weeks or months (A. R. G. Owen, 1964; Roll, 1977).

Several studies of collections of haunting and poltergeist cases were reported during this transition period (e.g. Bozzano, 1920; Flammarion, 1923/1971). Barrett (1911) carried out an extensive study of poltergeist cases, a few of which he personally investigated. He reached several conclusions: usually the disturbance was associated with a child or adolescent; most outbreaks were sporadic and soon declined; and, perhaps most significant, the effects appeared to be very similar to the physical phenomena reported from spiritualistic seances.

3.4 The evolution of controlled experiments

Lightning, the aurora, even sunlight are all electromagnetic phenomena. Yet electromagnetic science grew from investigations, not of these marvels, but of strange forces exerted by the lodestone (a natural magnet) and by rubbed amber. These phenomena were weak and apparently trivial, but they could be subjected to controlled experiments*. Similarly, the predominant concern of psychical research has shifted gradually from unmanageable marvels to relatively minor but more controllable phenomena.

The distinction is one of degree. The vexing mediumistic sittings involved various degrees of control against fraud and misinterpretation of observations. However, the medium almost always imposed conditions that compromised the controls, in the judgment of critics if not of the investigators who were present. A controlled experiment is understood to mean a situation in which the essential conditions for validity of the observations are fully controlled by the experimenter. Even this criterion is not clearcut. Frequently investigators of seance phenomena have thought they had control when in fact they did not. Thus, a further condition for satisfactory controls is simplicity. A complex situation is difficult to control.

3.4.1 Types of controlled experiments

The concept of experiments in 'thought transference' (telepathy) developed early in psychical research. Only a few of the more significant reports will be mentioned here; summaries of many more appear in works by J. B. Rhine (1934/1973, 1977; Richet, 1923/1975), and others. In most such tests, someone acting as agent* would concentrate on a target* object, idea, or sensation, while a percipient* (often called the subject) would try to get a mental impression of the target.

In principle, controls against sensory cues between agent or target object and percipient were simple. If the two were in closed rooms some distance apart sensory contact would be eliminated. Yet few early experiments provided this degree of control. Usually both parties, plus several witnesses, were in the same room, so that the bare possibility of sensory cues rendered the results dubious. Also, most experimenters used drawings or other arbitrary targets; consequently, responses that were not obvious hits* were difficult to evaluate.

The advantages of using card suits or numbers, a set of prescribed digits, or other restricted-choice targets* were appreciated very early by some experimenters. Responses to such targets could be scored simply as hits or misses. Further, as Richet had recognized as early as 1884, probability theory could be applied to restricted-choice test data to estimate the score that should be expected by chance alone. A few years later methods were developed to calculate how improbable a particular score might be. Nevertheless, drawings and other free-response* target material appealed to many investigators for psychological reasons.

It is important to note that almost all experiments before 1930 were intended to test for telepathic ability (but actually were open to clairvoyance also). Mind-to-mind communication was suggested by spontaneous psychic experiences and by mediumistic data, and it was superficially plausible. Clairvoyance, the nonsensory perception of information not normally known to anyone, appeared so implausible as to be almost ignored even by professional investigators. Yet in 1888 Richet had conducted a brief, highly successful experiment with cards in sealed envelopes as targets, and several more clairvoyance tests were reported during the transition period (e.g. Fukurai, 1931/1975; Kotik, 1908; Tischner, 1925).

3.4.1a *Experiments with free-response targets*

Even in the early period of psychical research some experimenters were wondering whether telepathic or clairvoyant ability might be improved by training. A French engineer, René Warcollier (1938/1975), worked for several years with a select group of volunteers in 'telepathy' (i.e. telepathy/ clairvoyance) experiments. His approach was unusual, being not to prove telepathy but to understand its operation. Having first studied *Phantasms of the Living* and other accounts of spontaneous psychic experiences, Warcollier recruited twenty persons who had had such experiences, reasoning that they should be superior percipients in experiments.

Warcollier's experiments probably are the most varied on record. He explored the effects of personality and sex of agent and percipient, of various mental states and subjective techniques, of a wide variety of target objects, thoughts and sensations, and of physical conditions. He also carried out detailed analyses of the results in relation to what was known of the psychology of memory, association, suggestion and other factors. The techniques did not produce large numbers of trials, nor were the results (usually drawings) readily adaptable to statistical treatment. Evaluation of each trial depended on subjective judgment. Nevertheless, many cases strongly indicated paranormal communication, though they could not distinguish between telepathy and clairvoyance. These results, together with Warcollier's extensive analyses and comments, are still a valuable source of ideas for further research.

One of the most significant experiments of the period was reported, not by a scientist or engineer, but by a popular novelist, Upton Sinclair (1930/1962). The percipient was Mrs Sinclair, who had read reports of telepathic ability and determined to develop it herself. She evolved a subjective technique of relaxing, 'blanking' her mind, and passively noting any spontaneous imagery that appeared. While her husband in another room concentrated on a simple drawing, she wrote or sketched her impressions. The close correspondences they obtained obviously exceed what might be expected by chance. The principal value of the report, however, is in Mrs Sinclair's lucid account of her subjective technique and how she developed it.

3.4.1b *Experiments with restricted-choice targets*

Another remarkable 'telepathy' experiment was done by psychologists at the University of Groningen in the Netherlands, H. J. F. W. Brugmans and a Dr Weinberg under the direction of M. Heymans (J. B. Rhine, 1977, p. 28; Schouten and Kelly, 1978). Their percipient, a young man, sat blindfolded behind a screen in front of which was a board bearing 48 numbered squares. The experimenters, in a darkened upper room, could watch the board through a glass-covered opening; but the percipient could not see them. For each trial the percipient reached through a hole in the screen and tried to point to the randomly selected target square while the experimenters watched and 'willed' him to point correctly (Pratt, 1964, p. 41).

They performed only 187 trials; but 60 of these were successful.

About four would be expected by chance. The probability of such a score as was obtained is infinitesimal. However, critics have suggested that the decisions on some ambiguous pointings may have been biased and that the choices of targets favored the central region of the board.

Another 'telepathy' experiment was carried out by a Harvard University psychologist, George H. Estabrooks (1927/1961). After more than a year of exploratory work to develop an effective experimental design, he reported a series of 1,660 card-guessing trials with mainly student volunteers as percipients. The resulting scores for color and for suit far exceed chance expectations.

The significance of Estabrooks's experiment lies both in these results and in the remarkable insights he developed as to psychological conditions for success. He preferred subjects who showed little interest in the experiment ('The very best type is the one who regards both you and the experiment as a nuisance. . . . The very worst type . . . is the instructor in psychology.'). He stressed the importance of a casual, friendly atmosphere, and he limited each subject to 20 trials to minimize declines in scoring that appeared in long runs*.

A notable experiment in clairvoyance was performed unwittingly by a psychologist at Stanford Univeristy. John E. Coover (1917/1975) carried out a long series of card-guessing trials that he intended as a definitive test for telepathy. In the 'telepathy' tests he looked at each card in turn as the subject tried to call its number and suit. Instead of comparing the resulting scores with those predicted by probability theory, Coover compared them with the scores he obtained in 'control' tests in which he *did not* look at the faces of the cards during the run. Though he was aware of the hypothetical possibility of clairvoyance, apparently he considered it too implausible to be taken seriously. Consequently, he in effect compared the scores of a general ESP test and a clairvoyance test and, finding them similar, concluded that both were attributable to chance coincidences.

Yet, as Richet (1923/1975, p. 93) noted, Coover's results were 'not negative whatever he may say.' Comparison with the results predicted by probability theory for random (chance) events reveals that Coover's combined score for both 'telepathy' and clairvoyance conditions is to be expected no more than once in 200 such experiments. Despite his laborious and persistent experimenting, Coover's interpretations showed no enthusiasm for positive results.

The British investigators were so much influenced by their traditional emphasis on telepathy that they did no test exclusively of clairvoyance until the late 1920s. Ina Jephson (1929) administered 6,000 guessing trials for suits of playing cards with 240 percipients. She obtained a total score of extremely low probability. Most of the tests, however, had been done by mail without adequate safeguards against sensory cues or other irregularities. A second experiment of 'approximately fraud-proof' design yielded results near chance expectation (Besterman, Soal and Jephson, 1931).

3.4.2 Unusual experiments in the Soviet Union

Meanwhile, unknown to the outside world, a sustained program of psychic experimentation was proceeding in the Soviet Union. V. M. Bechterev, director of the Leningrad Institute for Brain Research, about 1921 found evidence of telepathic ability in some performing dogs (Ryzl, 1961). He also carried out some exploratory experiments with a young woman subject and set up a commission to continue these and related investigations. One of its members was L. L. Vasiliev (1963/1976; Pratt, 1977), who directed the work after Bechterev's death in 1927 until the program ended in 1938. But Vasiliev's work, which produced interesting and significant results, was unpublished and unknown outside the USSR until 1963.

The Soviet investigators approached the subject from a standpoint markedly different from then-current tendencies in the West. Not surprisingly, they ignored the spiritistic and 'nonphysical' tradition that still pervaded British and American psychical research, following instead in the naturalistic tradition that had dominated earlier Continental thought. Instead of adopting the fashionable trend in experimentation, however, they took up where Janet and a few others had left off forty years earlier. They worked with good hypnotic subjects, selecting those who showed promise in preliminary trials. Some experiments involved perception of drawings or other imagery; but most required involuntary motor responses of the percipient (e.g. swaying) or induction or termination of hypnotic sleep at the hypnotist's silent command.

Most of these experiments produced results that are statistically signficant. Their primary purpose, however, was to discover the physical agency or mechanism of telepathic communication, which Vasiliev assumed to be electromagnetic (radio) waves. Some contemporary investigations by an Italian neurologist, F. Cazzamalli, had claimed detection of such radiation from a person's head, and Vasiliev and his associates confidently expected to verify this work and carry it further. Yet they were unable to confirm Cazzamalli's results. Further, they did several experiments to compare telepathic success with the agent or percipient, or both, inside or outside of electromagnetic shields that would effectively block radio waves. They found no significant difference in scoring between shielded and unshielded conditions.

3.4.3 Beginnings of experiments with physical phenomena

It is notable that all of the controlled experiments of this transition period that have been mentioned were mental tests, usually for 'telepathy.' Some studies of the physical phenomena of Tomczyk, Cranshaw, and Rudi Schneider approach qualification as controlled experiments* (see section 3.2; Nicol, 1977, p. 320). Another investigation of physical phenomena that compares with the better telepathic experiments was a study of paranormal photography by T. Fukurai (1931/1975; Eisenbud, 1977, p. 416) of the Imperial University of Tokyo about 1910–20. Fukurai experimented with several persons who, without dimming of lights or any spiritistic implications, were able to imprint symbols or letters he prescribed as exposures on sealed photographic plates. Though his experiments were not faultless in execution (the battle of wits again!), the concept of his investigations meets reasonably well the criteria for a controlled experiment.

3.5 Trends in the transition period

By 1930 psychical research still was carried on sporadically by individuals or special associations, with few exceptions. The SPR continued an active program. Its American branch, after the death of Hodgson in 1905, had been reorganized independently as the American Society for Psychical Research (ASPR). Under the leadership of James H. Hyslop, it carried on a modest investigative program until controversy over the Margery mediumship disrupted its ranks. One of its former research officers, W. F. Prince, then led the formation of the Boston Society for Psychical Research. The publications of these and other societies, together with books by individual investigators, constituted nearly all of the serious literature of psychical research.

On the Continent, Richet, Geley and others founded the Institut Métapsychique International about 1914. It sponsored investigations and published the *Revue Métapsychique,* replacing the *Annales des Sciences Psychiques.* An Institut für Parapsychologie was founded in Berlin in 1928. (*Parapsychologie* was a new term for psychical research that had been proposed by Max Dessoir.)

The universities generally had kept aloof from mediumistic research. Faculty members such as Sidgwick, Richet, or James who engaged in such work did so as an outside avocation. With the rise of controlled experimentation the campuses became a bit more hospitable. Coover worked at Stanford University under an endowment for psychical research that the university had accepted, not without embarrassment, from the brother of its founder. Brugmans carried out his famous experiment as a graduate student at the University of Groningen, as did Estabrooks at Harvard. Gardner Murphy did his transatlantic telepathy experiments with Warcollier and other parapsychological studies at Columbia University. Harry Price's laboratory was transferred to the University of London.

These instances of active or tacit support by universities were exceptional. Most intellectuals continued to react to psychical research with indifference, embarrassment, or hostility. The Royal Society had denied Crookes publication of his experiments with Home. Fukurai was dismissed from his university position. William James (1901/1960) commented sourly on the evasiveness and even dishonesty of his Harvard colleagues when confronted with his evidence. Stanford University has used its psychical research endowment almost entirely for work that has been negatively motivated or irrelevant (Dommeyer, 1975). Nevertheless, by 1930 a trend to university sponsored professional experimentation in parapsychology was beginning to be evident.

4 The Duke University period 1930–c.1960

When William McDougall came from Harvard to head the Psychology Department of Duke University at Durham, North Carolina, in 1927, Joseph B. and Louisa E. Rhine came with him. This young couple already had gained some experience in psychic investigations, notably with the dubious physical medium Margery. These experiences had impressed them with the difficulties in developing scientifically satisfactory evidence from such ill-defined situations (Brian, 1982: Mauskopf and McVaugh, 1980).

McDougall, a staunch dualist, no doubt saw in parapsychology some prospect of empirical evidence against behaviorism. He therefore hoped to establish psychical research as a legitimate field for university studies; but he recognized that a better approach was needed than the mediumistic investigations. J. B. Rhine, when he joined the psychology faculty, also was ripe for a new approach to the investigation of what he soon renamed extrasensory perception (ESP). The exploratory program undertaken by Rhine and his colleagues emphasized three principles:

(1) dependence upon undistinguished subjects, usually student volunteers:
(2) simple, easily controlled restricted-choice test procedures;
(3) rigorous statistical evaluation of results.

Rhine's Laboratory of Parapsychology at Duke University marked a sharp departure in psi research, and its influence dominated the field for a generation. Yet nothing in Rhine's experimental approach was essentially new. Richet and others had used statistics, and various investigators had tested ordinary subjects with cards and similar materials. Even the term parapsychology was borrowed. What was new at Duke was the persistent use and improvement of these experimental techniques in a sustained series of investigations by a regular research staff under university sponsorship. And, one must add, the implacable zeal of J. B. Rhine.

4.1 ESP card tests: telepathy, clairvoyance and precognition

Most earlier experimenters had used drawings or ordinary playing cards as guessing targets in their 'telepathy' experiments. Rhine and his colleagues soon adopted cards as the most convenient target material, but they felt that playing cards imposed a confusingly large number of choices. They adopted instead a set of five symbols: circle, cross, star, wavy lines and square. Twenty-five cards bearing five sets of these symbols made up the standard ESP deck that was used by most experimenters during the next 40 years.

Hand shuffling was superseded in some experiments by a simple machine. Any of several test procedures might be used. Rhine recognized that the traditional 'telepathy' test admitted also of clairvoyance, so that pure telepathy tests were methodologically difficult. He therefore concentrated on clairvoyance tests, in which no one looked at a target card before the subject called it, and general ESP (GESP) tests, in which the experimenter looked at each target card before the subject's call. Manual matching procedures and other variations were developed (see chapter 5).

Accounts of these early Duke experiments emphasize the informal, playful atmosphere that the experimenters tried to maintain (e.g. Pratt, 1964; J. B. Rhine, 1934/1973, 1937, 1977; J. B. Rhine and Associates, 1965). Experimenter and subject usually were in the same room, sometimes without adequate safeguards against sensory cues. In some experiments, however, they were separated by distances ranging from the next room to many miles. The strongest of these was conducted between graduate assistant J. G. Pratt and a remarkable student subject, Hubert Pearce. Using a refined clairvoyance procedure between rooms in separate buildings, they produced highly significant scores. This experiment will be discussed more fully in chapter 7, section 2.1.

Subjects usually performed about equally well in clairvoyance and GESP tests. Further experiments achieved some success in precognition, in which a subject called the future order of symbols in a deck not yet shuffled. These findings led to an impasse in attempts to test for pure telepathy. To exclude clairvoyance, a sender or agent might imagine each target symbol but record it only after the subject's call. Precognition, however, opened the possibility that the subject might get a precognitive clairvoyant impression of the not-yet-written target record. Ingenious methods were devised to avoid this difficulty (Birge, 1948; McMahan, 1946; Rush, 1976), but the developing psychokinesis (PK) experiments introduced further logical difficulties, so that telepathy tests were abandoned as being unavoidably ambiguous.

4.2 Psychokinesis (PK) experiments with dice

The ESP card experiments grew directly out of sporadic experiments dating from the 1880s or earlier; but experiments with physical psi effects had no such pedigree. The movements of objects and other physical effects reported from mediumistic seances and poltergeist incidents apparently were so bizarre that no one thought of looking for them in small-scale experiments with ordinary subjects. J. B. Rhine had considered such a possibility during the early ESP research; but it was an interested visitor to the Duke laboratory, a professional gambler, who inspired a practical method. The gambler believed that he sometimes could 'will' dice to do what he wanted. True or not, the claim suggested to Rhine that dice might be a good medium for tests of telekinesis – for which he adopted a new term, psychokinesis (PK). Dice were like the ESP cards in presenting a few easily evaluated targets, and they excited the mood of playful challenge that he believed made for success in psi tests.

The PK experiments, begun in 1934, evolved similarly to those for ESP (J. B. Rhine, 1946b, 1947b; L. E. Rhine, 1970: L. E. Rhine and

J. B. Rhine, 1943). Dice were thrown by hand, then from a cup, and later by a simple machine. The subject's task was not to *predict* the fall of the die, but to will or wish the prescribed target to turn up. Usually a single die was thrown, or two for 'high dice' or 'low dice;' but sometimes close to 100 were tossed at once.

The dice experiments never produced the phenomenally high scores that were observed in some of the ESP tests, and the early procedures were open to more serious criticisms. However, the scores indicated that in many instances a non-chance influence was affecting the dice.

4.3 Criticisms of the Duke experiments

J.B. Rhine's (1934/1973) monograph report of the early ESP experiments set off a lively controversy. Psychologists had not shown much concern for the earlier sporadic reports of psi phenomena; but Rhine's claim of sustained and consistent success, coming from a professor of psychology in a university laboratory, aroused strong and sometimes bitter criticism (Honorton, 1975a; J.B. Rhine, Pratt, Stuart, B.M. Smith and Greenwood, 1940/1966).

Since the claims of ESP rested upon statistical evidence rather than directly observable effects, many criticisms were directed to Rhine's statistical methods. A few of these were valid in principle but of little practical significance. The others were soon disposed of. The controversy nevertheless led statisticians to refine the methods and to clarify some mathematical questions.

The most serious criticisms applied to the experimental conditions and procedures, principally to the possibility that subjects might be getting subtle sensory cues. While these criticisms were of only limited application, being irrelevant if target cards and subject were in separate rooms, they did raise legitimate questions as to the reliability of much of the early exploratory work. Other procedural criticisms related to insufficient shuffling of cards and to inadequate safeguards against errors in recording target and call sequences. The controversy accelerated the adoption of more sophisticated experimental procedures at the Duke laboratory.

Publication of the first reports of the PK experiments with dice (L.E. Rhine and J.B. Rhine, 1943) resulted in another round of criticisms and rebuttals (e.g. Girden, 1962a; Murphy, 1962b; Rush, 1977, p. 39). This exchange, less vehement than the ESP controversy, focused on the effects of imperfections in the dice that would favor certain faces, on recording procedures, and on the legitimacy of some of the statistical analyses. It also led to refinements in the experimental designs used at Duke and elsewhere.

Critics also attacked both the ESP and the PK reports on more fundamental grounds. Some argued that the claimed psi phenomena were a priori impossible because they appeared to be independent of physical laws (G.R. Price, 1955). Others insisted that the phenomena, if genuine, ought to be demonstrable by any experimenter on demand.

These arguments raise basic questions as to the nature of scientific evidence and method. They will be dealt with in chapter 12.

4.4 Repetitions of the Duke research: further developments

Rhine's experiments excited widespread interest and many attempts to replicate them. By 1937 students or staff members at a dozen American colleges had reported successful ESP card experiments; a few had reported failures. Many independent experimenters also reported card tests of varied quality and reliability.

The Duke reports aroused considerable interest abroad, particularly in Britain. Here, however, a quite different situation developed as the experimenters met almost complete frustration in trying to repeat Rhine's results. Chance-level scores became so familiar that they led to speculations as to possible effects of differences in climate, temperament, and other factors between America and Britain. They led also to sometimes caustic British skepticism and criticisms of Rhine's claims (e.g. Mundle, 1950; Soal, 1948).

Meanwhile a few experimenters were developing ESP test methods somewhat different from Rhine's. G.N.M. Tyrrell (1938), a British engineer, devised an apparatus that turned on a light randomly in one of a set of closed boxes. His subject scored a hit if she opened the box that would be lighted a moment later. These experiments were highly successful. Whately Carington (1940), also in Britain, carried out many successful trials in which he used pictures as targets and compared them with response drawings by his subjects. Publication of the Duke PK experiments in 1943 similarly excited many experimenters, some of whom reported impressively successful scores. Another notable exception to the usual British experience was that of A.M.J. Mitchell and G.W. Fisk (1953), who gave their subject, 170 miles distant, the task of throwing dice for targets known only to the experimenters. She was successful.

Of a variety of novel test devices that were developed during this period, the most used was the PK placement test (see chapter 9, section 2.1.2, and chapter 10, section 3.1.2). In this procedure, cubes (i.e. dice without spots) slid down a chute on to a horizontal board. The object was to influence the cubes to tumble toward the right or the left of a center line, whichever side was the target area.

The experiments we have been considering were designed primarily to demonstrate that psi phenomena actually occur. Mingled with this purpose, however, was a persistent interest in discovering something about the psi process itself, what variables might influence it and how it relates to psychology and other fields. These process-oriented* studies included tests of physical parameters, particularly time and distance, and of such psychological variables as experimental environment, subject's personality, mood, or attitude toward ESP, and personality of the experimenter. Gertrude R. Schmeidler, for example, found that subjects ('sheep') who believed ESP to be possible under the conditions of the experiment generally scored higher than those ('goats') who were highly skeptical (Palmer, 1977, p. 193; Schmeidler and McConnell, 1958/1973). Margaret Anderson and Rhea A. White (1956) found that schoolchildren's individual scores on ESP tests conducted by their teachers were higher if teacher and child liked each other. Such findings have been confirmed by other experimenters; but still others have failed to confirm, so that the worrisome difficulty remains of establishing consistent relationships involving psi phenomena.

4.5 Declining scores: summary of experimental findings

During the first few years of Rhine's program at Duke University a series of remarkable ESP and PK subjects had appeared. As these left Duke or declined in scoring ability, few were found to replace them. Rhine believed that the unique conditions of novelty and pioneering enthusiasm during the early years enhanced his subjects' psi scores. Skeptics argued that tighter experimental procedures brought them down. Whatever the cause, almost all experimenters found increasing difficulty in getting statistically significant scores. This lack of exceptional subjects led to increasing dependence, as in psychological experiments, upon composite scores by groups of ordinary subjects. By 1960, for reasons that are not clear, reports of PK experiments had almost ceased.

What did these three decades of psi experimentation accomplish? Several findings appeared in the research with enough consistency and strength to justify at least tentative acceptance:

(1) The reality of psi phenomena. The cumulative evidence for *clairvoyance, precognition* and *psychokinesis* is impressive:
(2) Certain internal *signs of psi** (J.B. Rhine's term): a *decline effect**, or tendency for a subject's scoring rate to decrease during a test run or session, or over longer periods; *psi-missing**, a tendency sometimes to score at significantly less than chance level; *scoring in opposite directions* on different types of targets; and abnormal values of statistical *variance,* indicating sporadic psi-hitting and psi-missing:
(3) Some *correlations of psi performance* with subjects's attitudes and personality traits, though these are weaker than (1) and (2) above.

4.6 Spontaneous psi: case collections and field investigations

The new vogue for experimental research dominated parapsychology during the entire period 1930–60, and interest in spontaneous psi experiences declined. Only a few investigators persisted in collecting case reports and in pursuing these elusive phenomena in active field studies.

The Duke research itself led to the principal case collection and studies of the period. Reports of the experiments encouraged many persons to send accounts of strange experiences to Rhine's laboratory; but the busy staff took little notice of them.

In 1948 L.E. Rhine began a sustained study of the growing case collection that led to a series of reports (e.g. L.E. Rhine, 1965, 1967, 1981). Her approach departed sharply from that of the earlier SPR studies, following instead a philosophy enunciated by J.B. Rhine (1948). In this view, the legalistic type of evidence in even the best case reports inevitably must fall short of scientific demonstration. Such reports rather must be seen as suggestive prototypes for experimental designs and as continuing reminders to specialized experimenters of the root phenomena of parapsychology.

L.E. Rhine therefore treated the case reports statistically, looking for consistent patterns and relations. Any false elements, whether deliberate inventions or unintentional distortions, should be inconsistent and essentially random and therefore should drop out of prominence in an assessment of many cases. Her studies generally have confirmed the principal findings of the SPR studies and revealed some additional tendencies (see chapter 3). However, they have not had their anticipated effect of stimulating novel experimental designs. (See Plate 3.)

Of several additional case studies (e.g. Murphy, 1962a; Nicol, 1961), the most notable was Tyrrell's (1942/1962) landmark study of reports that involved apparitions. He concluded that these visible figures must be hallucinations rather than substantial entities. Several case collections and analyses dealt with physical manifestations (poltergeists). One of these, the first extensive study since Barrett's (1911) work, was compiled by Hereward Carrington and psychoanalyst Nandor Fodor (1951). This and other studies generally supported Barrett's findings.

Almost all field investigations of spontaneous psi effects deal with poltergeists. Only a few such investigations were reported during the period 1930–60. The principal new development was Fodor's (1948, 1959/1968) attempt to apply psychoanalysis to the interpretation of several poltergeist cases.

4.7 Institutions and publications

The fresh interest in parapsychology that was aroused by the experiments at Duke University stimulated new organizations and publications as well as research. The first such consequence was the establishment of the Laboratory of Parapsychology at Duke University in 1935. Its publication, the *Journal of Parapsychology,* was founded two years later.

The American Society for Psychical Research (ASPR), which had been disrupted by dissension over the Margery mediumship, overcame its organizational problems and in 1941 resumed its function as a leading educational and research organization. The ASPR resumed publication of its *Proceedings* and transformed its *Journal* to a more experimental orientation.

The British SPR continued its program and publication of its *Proceedings* and *Journal.* Various other publications and research nuclei developed, though the Duke laboratory continued to dominate the experimental field. These other research activities usually reflected the influence of a dedicated individual rather than an institutional commitment.

American parapsychologists took a significant step in 1957 by organizing the Parapsychological Association as an international professional society.

5 Recent developments: 1960–present

The division of a historical sequence into discrete periods is largely a matter of convenience. However, several developments in parapsychology define rather clearly a new phase that began to be evident in the 1960s. The Duke cards-and-dice techniques were giving way to more varied and sophisticated apparatus. A series of remarkable performers revived interest in studies of exceptional individuals, especially those claiming strong PK effects. New theoretical proposals by physicists and others began to appear. A wave of popular interest resulted in the offering of psi courses in many schools.

5.1 Return of the 'stars': renewed interest in macro-PK

5.1.1 Exceptional PK performers

The interest in physical mediums that had lapsed about 1930 was revived by several new claims of macro-PK: i.e. directly observable physical effects. Jule Eisenbud (e.g. 1967/1969, 1977), a psychoanalyst, experimented for three years with Ted Serios, whose specialty was the paranormal production of photographs. A Russian woman, Nina Kulagina, was studied by both Soviet and Western investigators (Pratt, 1977). She moved small objects without contact and produced other effects. Uri Geller, a professional entertainer, attracted much attention by both ESP and PK demonstrations, notably metal bending (Rush, 1977, p. 45; Schmeidler, 1977, p. 115); but his claims have not been subjected to sustained experimentation. Ingo Swann, an artist, has worked with several investigators and gained a reputation for producing a variety of strong effects in controlled experiments (Puthoff and Targ, 1974a, p. 537; Schmeidler, 1977, p. 100).

These and several other exceptional performers have contributed substantially to the serious reports of strong PK effects. These recent investigations contrast markedly with the trances, dark rooms and spiritistic overtones of the earlier periods. They have been conducted in normal light, usually with sophisticated electronic and other apparatus. Yet these demonstrations have contributed little toward understanding of psi processes, and most of them remain controversial even among parapsychologists. They thus raise anew the question of what would serve as convincing evidence for the reality of rare, isolated physical effects.

The revival of interest in PK contrasted sharply with the relative neglect of such phenomena during the 1950s. A similar, though less marked, interest in exceptional ESP subjects developed about 1970. Several such 'stars' – notably Keith Harary, a remarkable experimenter-subject, Lalsingh Harribance, a professional psychic, and Bill Delmore, a law student – worked with a series of investigators (Palmer, 1978b, p.62). The resulting experiments, more conventional in design and inherently less spectacular than the macro-PK demonstrations, are more generally accepted.

5.1.2 New light on poltergeists

Several new studies of poltergeist case reports appeared (e.g. Cox, 1961; Zorab, 1964). A.R.G. Owen (1964) of Cambridge University produced the most comprehensive work, including some cases he had investigated in person.

In the difficult area of direct field investigations of poltergeist phenomena, two leaders emerged: William G. Roll (1976, 1977) in the United States and Hans Bender (1974; Rush, 1977, p. 48) in West Germany.

As in other parapsychological investigations, they have used tape recorders, cameras and other instrumentation. In several cases they or their associates observed movements of objects and other physical effects.

5.1.3 Tape-recorded voices

Claims have come from several sources that voices and other sounds have been recorded paranormally on magnetic tape (see chapter 9, section 3.2.5; Rush, 1977, p. 54). Raymond Bayless (1959), an American painter, first reported such recordings in work with a direct-voice psychic. Extensive further reports were published by Friedrich Jürgenson in Sweden and Konstantin Raudive of Latvia. However, criticisms have been severe, and professional parapsychologists have shown little interest in the phenomenon.

5.1.4 Experimental sitter groups

Several experimenters have reported obtaining psi effects in group sittings inspired by the spiritualistic seances of an earlier time but conducted without spiritistic implications (Rush, 1977, p. 51; Schmeidler, 1977, p. 111). Kenneth Batcheldor, a British psychologist, conceived the idea that group participation might facilitate psi funtioning by relieving the sitters of feeling individually responsible, and that darkness and distracting conversation might moderate the shock of confronting 'impossible' events. He and several others have reported strong PK effects in such sessions, some in full light.

5.2 The new look in statistical experiments

5.2.1 New apparatus and designs

Rhine's use of standardized ESP cards and dice for PK experiments had been a distinct advance over earlier target materials for statistical experiments. However, these and other mechanical devices involved disadvantages, and experimenters began to look to electronics for more sophisticated techniques. The naturally random disintegrations of radioactive atoms suggested the possibility of using such events as psi targets, and during the 1960s several investigators reported experiments using this principle (Rush, 1977, p. 55). Helmut Schmidt, a physicist on J.B. Rhine's staff, developed a versatile, highly reliable apparatus of this type, which with minor variations has largely supplanted cards and dice.

Improvements in experimental procedures and judging techniques have led also to a revival of interest in statistically evaluated free-response ESP tests, in which the subject typically tries to report significant details of a picture. Montague Ullman and Stanley Krippner (1970; Van de Castle, 1977b, p. 485) reported successful picture experiments with dreaming subjects; and 'remote viewing' of real scenes was reported by Harold Puthoff and Russell Targ (1979) and others.

In the better-equipped laboratories sound and video recorders, electronic REG machines, and on-line computers are commonplace. These facilities have made possible more flexible experimental designs and varied target displays that are psychologically appealing to subjects. They also have largely eliminated the tedious and error-prone manual recording and analyses of data.

5.2.2 Trends in statistical research

Almost all of the early psi research was concerned simply with demonstrating that paranormal effects occurred. By the 1950s, however, as parapsychologists gained confidence in their results, an increasing number of experiments were designed to explore the psychological processes that are involved in ESP and PK. The new electronic techniques greatly extended the possibilities for such process-oriented research, and experimenters have responded with experimental concepts and designs of great subtlety and variety.

The renewed interest in PK has been expressed in a sharp rise in the frequency of statistical PK experiments. These have been encouraged both by the intriguing effects attributed to the remarkable PK performers mentioned earlier and by the new facilities for highly varied and rigorously controlled statistical experiments (Stanford, 1977c).

Prominent among these recent research efforts have been investigations of altered states of consciousness upon psi performance, of precognition and PK by animal subjects, of retro-PK (the PK analogue of precognition, influencing a past event), and of covert psi intervening without conscious intent or awareness. Some of these experiments will be described in later chapters.

5.3 Recent theoretical trends

Two major needs in parapsychology are more consistent replications of psi experiments and a testable theoretical model. Unfortunately, these defects reinforce each other: efforts to improve psi performance suffer from lack of theoretical insight, and variability of results makes theory testing difficult.

Since the recent PK revival aroused renewed interest among physicists, several have proposed tentative theoretical approaches to psi phenomena. Prominent among these are adaptations of quantum theory, which still is afflicted by paradoxical implications and ambiguous interpretations even within the framework pf physics. New extra-physical theories also have emerged, such as Lawrence LeShan's 'clairvoyant reality' and Stanford's concept of covert psi as a goal-seeking agency in everyday life. These and other theoretical approaches will be dealt with in chapters 11 and 13. They are mentioned only briefly here because none has been clearly validated or has led to any fundamental understanding of psi.

5.4 The new generation of critics

Henry Sidgwick (1882), first president of the SPR, once proposed a goal for the Society's research. Its methods, he said, should be made so rigorous, its results so unassailable, that critics of positive findings would have no alternative but to charge the experimenters with fraud.

Rational criticisms of the early card and dice experiments were concentrated on methodological details such as sensory leakage, recording errors, and inappropriate statistical analyses. Fraud, when it was suggested, almost always was imputed to the subjects. In many instances these specific criticisms were justified. More recently, however, with the advent of electronic apparatus and more sophisticated procedures, the stronger experiments have attained Sidgwick's goal. The consequence is as he foresaw: the rational critics, whenever they have confronted such experiments at all, have increasingly concentrated on experimenter fraud or delusion as a preferable alternative to psi. Usually they have been careful not to allege that fraud occurred, but only to point out that it could have. G.R. Price (1955) had argued for this interpretation of the stronger psi experiments. A British psychologist, C.E.M. Hansel (1960, 1980), applied similar arguments to several important ESP experiments. Similar a priori arguments ('ESP didn't occur because it's impossible') have been regularly advanced by other critics.

Unfortunately, fraud by scientific investigators in parapsychology and other fields is not unheard of (Markwick, 1978; Palmer, 1978b, p. 67; J.B. Rhine, 1974). A rare case of proven fraud obviously does not justify condemning an entire professional field. However, the prominence of such charges by critics emphasizes the need for more consistently predictable results in psi experiments and for a perusasive theoretical model. Meanwhile some critics, notably Ray Hyman, have eschewed the allegation of fraud in favor of the more customary methodological and statistical criticisms of the sort that parapsychologists typically employ in criticizing each other's work.

Not all criticisms are rational. Some reveal personal bias by attacking relatively weak experiments or demonstrations while ignoring the stronger ones, by exhibiting only superficial knowledge of the work that is criticized, and by generalizing an alleged flaw in one experiment to the entire field. Even personal ridicule and slander are not unknown (Morris, 1982; Rockwell, 1979; T. Rockwell, R. Rockwell and W.T. Rockwell, 1978a).

The skeptics, under the leadership of philosopher Paul Kurtz, recently have organized as the Commitee for the Scientific Investigation of Claims of the Paranormal (CSICOP), which publishes a semi-popular journal, *The Skeptical Inquirer.*

5.5 Institutions and publications

Academic acceptance of parapsychology as a legitimate field of investigation has made little progress. In 1969 the Parapsychological Association was admitted to membership in the American Association for the Advancement of Science (AAAS). This testimonial to the legitimacy of parapsychology probably has facilitated the increase in psi research and courses at American colleges and universities during the past decade. However, the concurrent wave of student interest in occult and metaphysical subjects also has increased the demand for psi courses.

This academic involvement with parapsychology still follows the pattern that has been evident for a century. Only rarely has a university institutionalized parapsychology (e.g. Duke University, the University of Utrecht, and recently the University of Edinburgh). Almost always the field is represented by a lone parapsychologist financed by an outside grant or teaching in a related discipline. Consequently, the pattern of university-related psi courses and research is continually shifting as individuals come and go. Courses or research, or both, currently are conducted at: St John's University in New York; John F. Kennedy University in California; Washington University in St Louis, Missouri; Princeton University; the University of Virginia; Andhra University in India; the University of Utrecht; the University of Edinburgh; and a few other schools.

Other institutional and financial support for psi research has improved somewhat. J.B. Rhine in 1963 transferred his research organization from Duke University to a new Foundation for Research on the Nature of Man (FRNM) at Durham, North Carolina. The Mind Science Foundation in Texas and the Psychophysical Research Laboratories in New Jersey are devoted to psi research, and SRI International in California has for several years supported a psi research program. The Parapsychology Foundation in New York continues to support research, and the late industrialists Chester F. Carlson and James S. McDonnell,

Jr, contributed generously to the field. Yet, despite these and other sponsors, lack of funding and institutional stability continues to retard the development of parapsychology.

In addition to the journals mentioned earlier (section 4.7), several new ones have recently appeared. The *Parapsychology Review* is published by the Parapsychology Foundation. The *European Journal of Parapsychology* is published at the University of Utrecht; and the Institute for Border Areas of Psychology at the University of Freiburg publishes the *Zeitschrift für Parapsychologie und Grenzgebiete der Psychologie.* Sociologist Marcello Truzzi publishes the journal *Zetetic Scholar,* which is intended to promote dialogues between proponents and critics of the paranormal.

The wave of popular interest mentioned earlier has spawned a glut of books on all aspects of paranormal phenomena, real and imagined. Most of these appear to be designed more for sensation than for enlightenment. However, an impressive number of reliable works on parapsychology have appeared. Two of these merit particular notice, because they are the most authoritative and comprehensive surveys of parapsychology to appear in a generation. They are the *Handbook of Parapsychology,* edited by Benjamin B. Wolman (1977), and *Advances in Parapsychological Research* (4 vols), edited by Stanley Krippner (1977, 1978, 1982). Three useful references, especially for the pre–1930 periods, are Fodor's (1933/1966) *Encyclopedia of Psychic Science,* D. Scott Rogo's (1975) *Parapsychology: A Century of Inquiry* and Rosalind Heywood's (1959) *Beyond the Reach of Sense.* Finally, since 1972 abstracts of papers delivered at the annual conventions of the Parapsychological Association have been published in book form in the series *Research in Parapsychology.*

Summary of terms

[1]Because a large number of new terms are introduced only briefly in this overview chapter, the terms followed by an asterisk in the text are listed here in alphabetical order and will be defined rather than merely listed.

Agent The 'sender' in a telepathy or GESP test, or the person who is the ostensible source of PK influence.

Apport An object that ostensibly has been transported by psi agency, usually through walls or other barriers.

Automatic writing Writing without conscious intention or effort, usually in a dissociated state.

Automatism Any pattern of meaningful activity done unconsciously, usually while in a dissociated state.

Communicator An ostensible spirit personality that communicates through a medium, automatic writing, or other means.

Controlled experiment An experiment in which significant variables are either held constant or compensated for.

Cross correspondences Fragmentary communications through two or more mediums, which make sense only when brought together.

Decline effect The tendency of extra-chance scoring in psi tests to regress toward chance expectation during a session or series of trials.

Direct voice Voice sounds produced in a mediumistic seance ostensibly independently of the medium's vocal organs.

Ectoplasm A substance purportedly issuing from the body of a physical medium, of which materializations are composed.

Free-response target In ESP tests, a target, usually a picture, that does not restrict the subject to prescribed responses.

Haunt A recurrent spontaneous manifestation, often involving an apparition, associated with a particular place.

Hit In a psi experiment, a successful trial.

Levitation Purported lifting of an object or person without known physical means.

Materialization The purported production of material forms or objects by a physical medium.

Medium A person who purports to produce communications from spirits (mental medium) or paranormal physical effects by spirit agency (physical medium).

Percipient A person who experiences spontaneous ESP or is the subject in an ESP experiment.

Physical medium See Medium.

Poltergeist Recurrent spontaneously occurring physical psi phenomena, associated usually with a particular person.

Possession Abnormal behavioral condition interpreted as displacement of normal personality by a spirit or other alien entity.

Process-oriented research Investigations designed primarily to explore the variables that affect a phenomenon.

Proof-oriented research Investigations designed primarily to demonstrate the occurrence of a specific phenomenon.

Psi-missing Scoring significantly less than chance expectation in a psi test. Contrast with Psi-hitting.

Psychic A person who exhibits exceptional psi ability. Also, pertaining to psi.

Psychometry See *Token object reading.*

Restricted-choice target In an ESP test, a guessing target that is limited to a few prescribed possibilities.

Run A group of successive trials in a psi test.

Signs of psi In psi test data, internal statistical evidence of non-random patterns other than overall scores.

Sitter A participant, other than the medium, in a seance.

Slate writing Ostensibly paranormal writing on slates in the presence of a physical medium.

Table tipping A spiritualistic practice in which several persons place their hands on a table and, by a code, read messages spelled out by the tipping of the table. Largely if not entirely motor automatism.

Target In an ESP test, the information that the subject is trying to perceive; in a PK test, the physical effect that the subject is trying to achieve.

Telekinesis Earlier name for psychokinesis.

Token object reading The use of an object associated with a target person as a focus for efforts at ESP.

Trance A dissociated, hypnotic state, usually self-induced by a medium.

Trial A single attempt to guess a target (ESP) or influence a target (PK).

Thought questions

(1) Similar odd 'psychic' experiences have been reported from all times and places. This uniformity of human experience sometimes is cited as evidence for psi. Can you think of an alternative explanation for the uniformity?

(2) Richet used statistics in evaluating a restricted-choice card guessing experiment in 1884. Why do you suppose investigators were so slow to adopt this kind of experimental method?

(3) The experimental ESP techniques that J.B. Rhine used were not essentially new, and many of his experiments were deficient in design or execution. Yet his work initiated a major departure in parapsychology and his influence dominated the field for a generation. How can you explain this apparent contradiction?

(4) Early psychical research was strongly influenced by spiritualistic concepts. Can you identify any remnants of that influence in the concepts or terminology of recent parapsychology?

(5) Which five experiments or other investigations before 1940 do you consider most impressive as evidence of psi? What are your reasons?

Part II
Research methods and findings

Chapter 3
Spontaneous psi phenomena: case studies and field investigations

Joseph H. Rush

1 Introduction: case collections

The raw materials of parapsychology are the strange, seemingly impossible 'psychic' experiences that have been reported in all times and cultures (see chapter 2). Such experiences include: dreams that contain verifiable information not otherwise known to the dreamer; waking visions, voices, or intuitive impressions that include such information; movements of objects and other physical effects without normal explanation; 'miraculous' recoveries from diseases or injuries; and some other effects. Many such incidents have been published in the parapsychological literature, especially in the *Proceedings* and *Journals* of the SPR and early ASPR. Reports of such experiences were speculated upon even in antiquity, but only during the past century have sustained efforts been made to collect and verify large numbers of spontaneous cases of psi phenomena or to investigate them while they were occurring, and to subject them to scientific analyses.

Most spontaneous psi experiences occur as isolated incidents; they are non-recurrent*. Even when someone reports more than one such experience, these usually appear unrelated. Some types of phenomena, however, are recurrent*. Of these, the most commonly reported are poltergeists (i.e. noisy ghosts). These are physical disturbances, associated usually with a particular person, that may persist for weeks or months. More rarely, hauntings are reported. In these cases visible phantoms, noises and sometimes other perceptual effects are associated with a place rather than a person and may recur for months or years.

Obviously an investigator's chance of being present when a non-recurrent psi incident occurs is nearly zero. The first approach to the investigation of a rare phenomenon is to collect reports by persons who have witnessed or experienced such a phenomenon and try to interpret them. Practically all investigations of non-recurrent spontaneous psi events and many of recurrent phenomena have been done by means of such case collections*. However, many instances of recurrent spontaneous psi have been observed directly by experienced investigators. Such cases, in which the investigator goes where something is happening and observes the events, will be referred to as field investigations*.

The advantages of spontaneous case reports as material for psi research are limited but important. They reflect the involvement of psi in everyday life, in a great variety of situations and subjective modes. To the extent that they are valid accounts, they provide the investigator a sampling of the natural range of psi phenomena without the restrictions on their variety or their physical and psychological contexts that experimental procedures necessarily impose. Like all natural phenomena, they embody the ultimate criteria by which scientific theories must stand or fall.

However, spontaneous case studies involve the investigator in several difficulties. Most obvious, of course, is the uncertain accuracy of a case report. Even with the utmost integrity and the best intentions, one's ability to observe and remember the details of even an ordinary experience is surprisingly limited. If an experient learns of the event to which a vision apparently relates before recording it, then any later record of it is severely compromised by the inevitable tendency to tailor the memory to fit the event. If the accuracy of the report be granted, there is still the possibility that it represents a mere chance coincidence.

All of these difficulties derive from the fact that spontaneous psi experiences rarely are repeated, and none can be repeated on order for the benefit of the investigator. Without repetition or the opportunity to experiment, the scientist is seriously handicapped.

In the discussions that follow, the non-recurrent and recurrent types of phenomena will be treated separately. Because of the great variety of spontaneous experiences and investigative approaches, it is not practicable to discuss all of the significant studies. We can only mention the more important collections and their associated investigative methods, and indicate some additional sources. The findings from these and other types of investigations will be summarized in the final section.

1.1 Non-recurrent experiences: principal case collections

1.1.1 The SPR and ASPR collections: treatment and criticisms

The first and most thorough effort to collect and verify spontaneous psi experiences was conducted by the SPR soon after it was organized in 1882. In response to public appeals, the SPR received many reports of spontaneous experiences. These became the subject of a monumental two-volume study, *Phantasms of the Living,* by Edmund Gurney, F.W.H. Myers and Frank Podmore (1886/1970). This work detailed 702 cases classified and arranged to demonstrate the authors' concept of a continuum of telepathic phenomena from experiments (which also were included) to the more complex types of spontaneous incidents. Despite the title, the cases were not limited to apparitions. Eleanor M. Sidgwick (1918/1975) produced a one-volume edition of *Phantasms* and (E.M. Sidgwick, 1923/1975) extended the case record by publishing in similar arrangement about 200 cases that had appeared in the *Journal* of the SPR since 1886.

These case collections by the SPR staff, strengthened as they are by much supporting testimony, still are one of the most impressive bodies of evidence for psi that have been developed from non-recurrent spontaneous experiences. They were undertaken at a time when such investigations offered the most immediate prospect for demonstrating and to some extent understanding psi phenomena. They therefore were pursued with a degree of enthusiasm and thoroughness that has not seemed justifiable since the experimental approach became dominant.

In 1950 the ASPR published a magazine article that brought many reports of spontaneous experiences. Analysis of nearly 400 of these and a later lot were published; the results supported generally the earlier SPR findings (Dale, 1951; Dale, White and Murphy, 1962). These ASPR investigators followed the SPR practice of trying so far as practicable to verify and authenticate the more interesting cases.

Response to a similar public appeal by Hans Bender at Freiburg resulted in a detailed analysis of 1,000 verified reports (Sannwald, 1963). Among other interesting findings, the results indicated that precognitive information was perceived usually in a waking state. Feelings of meaningfulness also were more frequent in the waking experiences.

Besides these major collections, many less ambitious case collections have been reported. Some of these are comparatively recent (e.g. Crookall, 1961; Green, 1960, 1968; Palmer, 1979; Stevenson, 1970b). In another type of case study, an investigator selects published cases of a certain type – precognition, poltergeists, or other limited class – and subjects them to intensive analysis. An outstanding study of this kind is G.N.M. Tyrrell's (1942/1962) treatise on apparitions, in which he examined in detail the reported appearances and behavior of these phantoms and concluded that they are not substantial objects, but hallucinations. Two other recent works of this kind concern poltergeists (Gauld and Cornell, 1979; Roll, 1977).

1.1.1a *Qualitative analysis of case records*

Spontaneous case reports are diverse and complex. Studies of them necessarily must begin with qualitative examination and intuitive judgment. The investigator looks for features that are common to many cases and from these tries to establish classifications and tendencies. One will note, for example, that psi experiences occur both in dreams and in waking states, and may then look for any consistent differences between these classes of experiences. Or, noting that some experiences relate to past or current events while others pertain to the future, the investigator will look for differences in the personalities or circumstances involved in these categories.

Myers and Gurney, in examining their reports of spontaneous experiences, appear to have been most impressed by the consistency among their cases and by the differences between them and traditional or fictional notions of ghosts. Further, they noted that popular mythology included ghostly appearances or messages from the dead, but not such manifestations of persons near death or in imminent danger as appeared frequently in the SPR case collection. Above all, they were impressed by the continuity between the spontaneous experiences and the 'telepathic' experiments of the day. They saw these as varied manifestations of a single basic principle, 'a natural group of phenomena which differ far more fundamentally from all other known phenomena than they can possibly differ among themselves' (E.M. Sidgwick, 1918/1975, p. 130).

1.1.1b *Evidential evaluation of spontaneous cases*

The evidential status of spontaneous psi experiences is ambivalent. Many persons, even skeptics, have been convinced by personal experiences of this kind. In fact, a substantial number of professional parapsychologists first became seriously interested in the field through such experiences. However, such conviction is private; it cannot be converted into scientifically convincing evidence. Nearly all serious investigators now consider spontaneous case reports to be useful but definitely accessory aids to parapsychological research.

When the SPR began its work it appeared that the study of non-recurrent spontaneous experiences might conclusively demonstrate the occurrence of telepathy and possibly other phenomena. For this purpose, the reliability of reports of such experiences had to be established with all the care applied to establishing a case in court. In either situation, the primary incident cannot be observed, so conclusions must be drawn from eyewitness testimony, documents, testimonials and sometimes circumstantial evidence.

Gurney's legal background no doubt emphasized this concept in his approach to case investigations. In his great work on 'telepathic' cases (Gurney *et al.*, 1886/1970) each primary report of a strange experience typically is followed by supplementary information from the same person, supporting statements by others who had knowledge of the incident, and sometimes by contemporary letters or other documents.

In many cases an investigator interviewed persons who had been involved in the experience.

However, critics were not convinced that chance coincidence was not an adequate explanation for even the stronger cases. Accordingly, the SPR carried out a Census of Hallucinations-(H. Sidgwick *et al.*, 1894) to determine the frequency, in a general population, of recognizable apparitions of persons within twelve hours of their deaths. They found 80 such reports among the 17,000 persons they queried. Compared with the contemporary death rate, the data – even after some conservative adjustment – indicated that death-related apparitions were occurring nearly 500 times as frequently as should have been expected by chance alone.

The methods and arguments developed by Gurney and his associates are typical of those that have been used in most studies of spontaneous case reports. Later investigators (e.g. West, 1948), with the advantage of much more sophisticated statistical methods, have noted sampling defects and other faults in the SPR survey, so that the impressive numerical result has been discounted. In retrospect, the Census of Hallucinations is significant as an indication of a dawning awareness of the necessity for quantitative methods in parapsychological research.

1.1.2 The Duke-FRNM collection: treatment and criticisms

Publication of the early ESP experiments at Duke University in the 1930s resulted in many unsolicited reports of spontaneous psi experiences. These have continued to accumulate, more than 14,000 cases being on file at the Foundation for Research on the Nature of Man (FRNM), successor to the Duke University Parapsychology Laboratory.

In 1948, when more than 100 such reports had been received, Louisa E. Rhine undertook a systematic study of them. Her work resulted in numerous papers and several technical books (L.E. Rhine, 1965, 1967, 1981).

1.1.2a *Statistical evaluation*

L.E. Rhine's studies took a direction radically different from that of the authors of *Phantasms.* Experience had shown that even the strongest case reports never could be wholly convincing, and research interest had turned decisively to controlled experiments. The spontaneous case investigations therefore were guided by a new concept of the use of such data, a concept undoubtedly inspired by the statistical philosophy that guided the Duke experiments.

This approach was summarized by J.B. Rhine (1948). He noted that the necessities of controlled experimentation had taken the attention of parapsychologists far from the spontaneous experiences that were their natural subject matter. To balance this tendency, he recommended that experimenters study case reports to renew their familiarity with these basic phenomena and to discover fresh ideas and clues to be tested in experiments. He recognized that a collection of unverified reports necessarily would include much distorted and even false material, but he argued that the spurious elements would not be systematically repeated throughout a large number of cases. Only the genuine phenomena would emerge as consistent patterns and tendencies. 'A spontaneous case can serve to contribute a hypothesis, raise a question, or furnish a possible insight, but it cannot go far beyond this . . .' (p. 232).

As an example of the application of this approach, L.E. Rhine (1951) found that in more than half of 1,600 reports the percipient had felt convinced that the experience was not a fantasy, but that it related to a real situation. This feeling of certainty appeared not to depend upon the amount of information in the experience, but upon an indefinable emotional quality that in many cases impelled the percipient to immediate action.

Both J.B. and L.E. Rhine emphasized that the results of spontaneous case studies are necessarily inconclusive and that they therefore should be regarded only as clues and suggestions for further experimentation. Later L.E. Rhine was so impressed by the consistency and other aspects of the many unverified cases she had studied that she broadened somewhat her conception of the usefulness of such research. In a review of her work (L.E. Rhine, 1969) she found the case reports to be generally consistent with experimental findings and came to regard these diverse types of research as complementary efforts in the quest for understanding of psi phenomena. She recognized, however, the necessity of ultimate experimental confirmation.

Her reliance upon statistical analyses of unverified case reports has been criticized as unreliable (e.g. Stevenson, 1970a). The principal argument is that an unverified collection is so diluted by unreliable information and omissions of essential details that it cannot yield reliable results. In response, L.E. Rhine reiterated the argument that, under statistical treatment, consistently reported features will become conspicuous while sporadic, inconsistent features will not emerge significantly. She emphasized also that insistence upon witnesses and other means of verification must result in a biased collection, because some kinds of experiences are inherently easier to verify than others. An unverified collection therefore should more nearly represent the full range of psi experiences.

1.1.3 Comparative analyses of case collections

These difficulties and justifications of the early SPR case studies and of the Duke-FRNM studies apply generally to case investigations of these respective types. If we consider extremes, it is obvious that accurate, ideally verified reports would need no confirmation and that no analysis of a collection of completely false reports could yield any reliable findings. Actual reports range between these extremes. It seems clear that statistical evaluations of such reports can yield useful information, but that its reliability must depend upon the prevailing level of reliability of the reports.

How reliable are reports of spontaneous cases? Sybo Schouten (1979, 1981, 1982) at the University of Utrecht used computer techniques to carry out a series of comparative analyses of case data from *Phantasms of the Living*, from Sannwald's study, and from the Duke-FRNM collection. He scored each case with respect to 32 categories of information: e.g. sex of percipient, age of percipient, type of experience, seriousness of event, etc. He then performed literally hundreds of correlation analyses among these categories to discover consistent relationships and to distinguish between genuine relations and artifacts. For example, noting a strong preponderance of female percipients in the *Phantasms* cases, he found that this preponderance persisted in the subgroup of cases in which percipients and target persons were spouses, thus disposing of the possibility that the effect might simply reflect a preponderance of females in the population. Several such comparisons showed that, though certain reporting artifacts contributed to the effect, earlier workers' finding of a preponderance of female percipients and male target persons was confirmed as a real phenomenon.

The later studies were designed to test in detail the consistency of the three case collections from different places and periods. Schouten included 562 cases from *Phantasms*, 789 from Sannwald's collection, and 1,630 representative cases from the massive Duke-FRNM file. Three-fourths of the analyses of Sannwald's data and two-thirds of those of the Duke-FRNM cases agreed quantitatively with the *Phantasms* analyses. The discrepancies were related to certain reporting artifacts and to two principal effects that were attributable to real cultural differences: whereas experiences of waking imagery predominated in *Phantasms*, intuitions and dream experiences were more prevalent in Sannwald's cases; and relatively more positive or trivial experiences appeared in the Sannwald collection. Analyses of the Duke-FRNM data also differed from those of *Phantasms* in the predominance of intuition and dream experiences, and they showed fewer death cases and more slight and serious accidents.

What is impressive in the results of these three meticulous studies is the high degree of consistency observed among reports of spontaneous psi experiences collected during diverse periods from different populations and by different methods. The significant quantitative differences are a minor portion of the findings, and qualitative agreement is almost total. Analyses of a group of the best-witnessed cases in *Phantasms* agree with the overall results. Such consistency, together with the analytical elimination of some of the commonly suggested artifacts, does much to enhance confidence in the principal characteristics of spontaneous experiences. It also appears to vindicate the Rhines' reliance on statistical treatment of unverified data. Schouten's own evaluation of his studies is in preparation.

1.2 Recurrent experiences: principal case collections

Most spontaneous psi experiences occur sporadically. Even if a person has several such experiences, usually they pertain to unrelated events. But in rare instances apparitions or other effects are observed repeatedly in a particular place (hauntings), or physical disturbances occur in the vicinity of a particular person (poltergeists); and repeated healing miracles are claimed for certain shrines and other sites.

1.2.1 Haunts and poltergeists

Ghost stories are perhaps the most familiar references to psi effects in folklore, but well attested reports are rare. Consequently, original case collections are few and usually meager. Most studies have been based upon collections of published cases, sometimes supplemented by the investigator's own observations. Though haunts and poltergeists are conceived as distinctly different categories of effects, essentially the ESP and PK aspects of recurrent phenomena (chapter 2, section 3.3), actually the distinction is blurred. Phantoms and physical effects sometimes manifest together, as when an apparition really opens a door or a poltergeist disturbance is accompanied by a visible phantom. Many studies therefore treat haunts and poltergeists as an intermingled complex of phenomena.

Alan Gauld and A.D. Cornell (1979) took this approach. In examining 500 cases – old, recent and original – by both qualitative and statistical methods, they concluded that the distinction between haunts and poltergeists is a misleading convenience and that the phenomena are more complex than parapsychologists have recognized. Another such collection (Salter, 1938) includes also some non-recurrent apparitions.

Several investigators have limited their collections to essentially poltergeist cases. The first such comprehensive study was done by physicist and SPR founder William F. Barrett (1911). He assembled all of the credible case records he could find, together with some personal observations, and made a comparative analysis of them. His principal findings are still valid: the central role of a child or adolescent in most cases; the brief duration of the disturbances; and their similarity to the effects observed with physical mediums.

One of the most comprehensive poltergeist studies is that of A.R.G. Owen (1964). Among his own cases is one of the best examples of the possibilities of an investigation that must depend upon the testimony of witnesses. This 'Sauchie poltergeist' developed around an 11–year-old-girl who, through unfortunate circumstances, had been abruptly separated from her home and family and sent to live with an older brother. The movements of objects and other effects, which occurred both at home and at school, were attested by the child's teacher, three physicians and a minister, besides her family.

Investigator William G. Roll (1977) assembled 116 of the stronger cases from published reports. His statistical analysis, too extensive for brief summary, ranged over many aspects of the phenomena, including the physical effects themselves, geographical distribution of cases and personal characteristics of the agent persons.

1.2.2 Paranormal healing

'Faith healing' and 'miraculous cures', like ghost stories, occur frequently in folklore, but scientific study of such claims is extraordinarily difficult. Consequently, not many collections of reliably witnessed healings exist. Probably the most extensive and impressive is the records of the Catholic shrine at Lourdes, France, where miraculous cures have been reported for more than a century. For many years the Church has kept records of medical examinations made before and after each apparent cure and tried to determine in each case whether the healing was genuine and whether it could be attributed to known medical or psychological processes. A very few cures have been officially pronounced miraculous.

Two books published in the same year illustrate the difficulties of investigating such cases. Two Catholic physicians, Francois Leuret and Henri Bon (1957), wrote an evaluation of some of the more impressive case reports from Lourdes, concluding that some were paranormal. But psychologist D.J. West (1957) also evaluated eleven cases that had been pronounced miraculous, examining all available documents, and came to the opposite conclusion.

1.2.3 Introspective observations

Some especially interesting and significant accounts of recurrent spontaneous paranormal experiences come from persons commonly called psychics or sensitives. Their accounts provide valuable clues to the kinds and variety of psi experiences.

Eileen J. Garrett (1949; Angoff, 1974) was orphaned in infancy by the suicides of both parents and was reared by strict, emotionally withdrawn relatives in rural Ireland. Isolated and lonely, she accepted spectral 'playmates,' saw luminous auras around people, and repeatedly witnessed smokelike emanations from persons or animals at death. Continual rejection and punishment for her fanciful 'lies' apparently reinforced her isolation and receptivity to such experiences. She saw a lifelike apparition of an aunt and infant about the time both died. During World War I she similarly witnessed the death of her husband in battle. She became a notable professional medium, but continued to experience spontaneous psi events.

Matthew Manning (1974) presents quite a different account. He says nothing of his early childhood in an English middle-class family. But when he was 11 years of age a series of poltergeist incidents persisted for nearly a month, with noises and movements of objects. Four years later a more violent series of disturbances began in the Manning home and continued in Matthew's dormitory after he had returned to boarding school. Some of these events were witnessed. After several weeks the disturbances subsided, apparently as Matthew began to try to divert them to automatic writing and other more orderly manifestations. He noted that both series of disturbances occurred when he was under stress because of important upcoming examinations.

Ingo Swann (1975), an artist, grew up in a small Colorado mining town in circumstances comparable to Eileen Garrett's. An understanding grandmother was the only person who did not reject his tales of clairvoyant dreams and other experiences. Like Garrett, he saw 'fluttering forms of color' around people and objects; and a spontaneous out-of-body experience during ether anesthesia led him to develop that ability. But about age 8 he decided that alienation and loneliness was too high a price to pay for being 'different.' Only many years later did he resume the deliberate development of his psi capabilities.

Rosalind Heywood (1964) produced a remarkably thoughtful and observant account of a lifetime of odd experiences. As a child in a middle-class family in Edwardian England she endured continual suppression of feelings and frustration of her venturesome, inquisitive nature. Most of her apparent psi experiences were of two general classes: passive awareness, ranging from intuitive 'knowing' to apparitions, and insistent urges to specific actions that proved to be appropriate despite their sometimes appearing absurd. Though she dreamed freely, psi dreams were rare. She never tried to develop her psi abilities, simply accepting such experiences as normal events in an active life; but she wondered continually about their implications.

Heywood's account is not limited to events that clearly imply psi. Rather, the broad range of incidents she reported suggests a continuum of experiences ranging from creative insights and intuitions to apparitions and precognition. Her book is not merely an account of curious experiences, but also a thoughtful classification and examination of them in an effort to discover meaningful clues and relationships.

1.2.4 Criticisms of recurrent-experience studies

Recurrent psi events, such as hauntings or RSPK disturbances, can hardly be attributed to chance coincidences; but other criticisms of non-recurrent case studies generally apply. Witnesses may be deceived by fraud or the shock of a strange experience. Studies of anomalous healings are plagued by dubious diagnoses. Personal accounts by psychics of their experiences usually are uncorroborated, and they are subject to distortion by the experients' personal beliefs.

Formal criticisms of recurrent case reports have been sporadic, perhaps because few critics have taken them seriously. Criticisms usually have concentrated on fraud; Podmore (1902/1963, vol. 1, p. 10) attributed all poltergeists to 'tricky little girls or boys.' G.W. Lambert (1955, 1960) attributed many English haunting and RSPK cases to noises and vibrations caused by underground streams coupled with excessive imagination; but he took no account of the many situations to which this explanation could not apply. Eric J. Dingwall and Trevor H. Hall (1958), both highly critical investigators, analysed several well-known haunting and poltergeist cases. From these examples they developed a manual of procedures and precautions for investigators of such phenomena.

1.3 Some specialized case collections

Though all collections necessarily are specialized to some degree – the great collection in *Phantasms* is limited to cases suggesting telepathy – all of those that have been mentioned are concerned with rather broad classes of phenomena that appear in relatively large numbers of cases. Some investigators, however, have developed much smaller collections that deal with more specialized classifications of apparent psi manifestations. Because of their diverse types and limited scopes, both the methods and results will be included in this section.

1.3.1 Dying and near-death experiences

Though spontaneous psi experiences frequently relate to persons who are dying or in imminent danger of death, few case collections are primarily concerned with death. The case studies mentioned earlier have been concerned primarily with evidence of psi in such situations, rather than with the experience of dying as such. Yet much folklore testifies to remarkable deathbed experiences, usually involving peaceful and even happy moods, visions of dead relatives or religious figures, and sometimes paranormal knowledge. A few parapsychologists have turned their attention to such experiences (e.g. Barrett, 1926; Hyslop, 1908).

Karlis Osis (1961; Osis and Haraldsson, 1977) of the ASPR directed three surveys of deathbed observations by physicians and nurses. The first two surveys were conducted in the United States. The third, designed to examine the influence of patients' cultural background upon their dying experiences, was done in India. Altogether, the investigators followed up 1,067 reports by further correspondence or interviews.

Some dying patients saw hallucinatory visions of light and beauty, but most saw apparitions of religious figures or of dead persons, principally the latter. The outstanding finding, confirming the earlier studies of Hyslop and Barrett, was that apparitions of the dead and of religious figures were far more frequent than those of living persons. This finding contrasts sharply with the results of comparable surveys of apparitions seen by persons in normal health, in which apparitions of living persons predominate.

In most cases, patients felt that the apparitions had come to take them away, to escort them into another existence. Not all welcomed this prospect, and in this attitude the investigators found the only significant difference between American and Indian patients' experiences. Almost all of the American patients welcomed the personages, usually relatives, who had 'come for them,' but one-third of the dying Indians showed anger or terror.

Nowadays it is not unusual for a person to 'die' by drowning, heart failure, or other cause and then be revived after having been clinically dead. The experiences of such persons, who have been apparently as near death as one can be and yet return to tell about it, constitute a category that some believe is related to psi phenomen and at least obliquely to the survival question. A psychiatrist, Elisabeth Kübler-

Ross (1969, 1975), has accumulated and analysed many cases of such experiences. Another such collection and commentary has been published by physician Raymond A. Moody, Jr (1975). Many such persons report no experience during the 'dead' period. Among those who do, many report somewhat similar experiences, typically involving a sense of traveling through a dark passage, emerging into brilliant light, and in many such accounts meeting a luminous, godlike person. However, it must be emphasized that these features are by no means uniform. Michael Sabom (1982), a physician, analysed 116 near-death crisis cases objectively and in detail. His findings differed somewhat from those just mentioned, in that the dark-passage and luminous-person impressions were less prominent. Further, each of the 43 percent of his cases who remembered experiences while near death reported an out-of-body experience (OBE*), a subjective experience of being out and away from one's body. Half of these described watching the efforts to resuscitate them; many details were later verified.

1.3.2 Reincarnation

Reincarnation, whereby the spirit of a dead person may enter the body of a newly conceived child, is an ancient belief in some cultures. Sometimes a young child takes on a strange personality, insisting that it really is another person and that its true home and family are in another community. Names, place descriptions and other details may lead to investigation and verification. Psychiatrist Ian Stevenson of the University of Virginia has collected data on several hundred cases of this kind. In many instances, in Turkey, India, Sri Lanka, Europe and the United States (most notably Alaska), he has personally investigated the circumstances by visiting and talking with persons and trying to authenticate his cases. However, it obviously is very difficult to verify the testimony of family members and other witnesses and to eliminate the possibility that information given by the child was not picked up in ordinary ways. Stevenson has recognized these difficulties, but believes a residue of reliable evidence supports the possibility of reincarnation. His investigations have been reported in papers in the *Journal* of the ASPR from 1960 and in several books (e.g. Stevenson, 1974a, 1975, 1977).

1.3.3 Psi-trailing

The cat's homing instinct is proverbial, and stories are fairly common of lost or abandoned dogs, cats, or other pets finding their way back home. It is another matter if an animal is left when a family moves, sometimes hundreds of miles, and some weeks or months later rejoins its 'family' at the new home where it never had been before. The most serious study of such cases was made by J.B. Rhine and Sara R. Feather (1962).

In assessing many such reports that came to the Duke laboratory, they applied the usual criteria for evaluating spontaneous cases. They considered the completeness, consistency, and apparent sincerity of the report (usually by a pet's owner), any supporting statements, and all the individual circumstances (distance involved, condition of the animal on arrival, evidence of its identity, etc.) of each case.

After applying these criteria, Rhine and Feather retained 54 cases, involving 28 dogs, 22 cats, and four birds, that they considered offered credible evidence of psi-trailing: i.e. of homing achievements that they could not plausibly explain.

1.3.4 Premonitions

Many spontaneous experiences appear to be precognitive: i.e. to be previews or prior knowledge of future events. Nearly all such incidents concern personal misfortunes or larger disasters. Very few premonitions of happy events have been reported. Whether the particular emotions that accompany disturbing events facilitate psi experiences is not clear. As any newspaper editor knows, bad news makes a stronger impression than does good news. It may be that people simply do not notice or remember premonitions of pleasant events.

1.3.4a *The* Titanic *disaster*

Ian Stevenson (1960, 1965) collected 17 case records that appeared to involve premonitions of the sinking of the steamer *Titanic* in 1912, in which about 1,600 persons perished. Seven of these experiences occurred the night of the disaster, four less than ten days earlier, and six from one to ten months preceding the event. A woman watching the ship putting out to sea was overcome with a feeling of certainty that it would sink. A marine engineer refused an attractive position aboard the *Titanic* because he had a foreboding of disaster. In 1898 Morgan Robertson had published a novel, *Futility,* that involved the sinking of a supership, the *Titan,* also by collision with an iceberg (Eisenbud, 1982, p. 88). As in the case of the *Titanic,* the accident occurred in April, there were not enough lifeboats, and many lives were lost. The list of coincidences between *Titan* and *Titanic* is remarkable; however, as Stevenson recognized, some of them were predictable by anyone with a good knowledge of shipping.

Stevenson found no comparable records of premonitions of the sinking of the *Lusitania* by a submarine in 1916, also with great loss of life. He noted that the *Titanic* disaster had been a terrible shock: there was no war, and that greatest of ships was believed to be unsinkable. The sinking of the *Lusitania,* in a war zone following specific warning, was hardly surprising. A 'premonition' of so predictable a disaster would have been trivial.

1.3.4b *Unconscious psi intervention*

W.E. Cox (1956) applied the principle of statistical assessment of spontaneous psi to situations that did not involve reports or probably even awareness of paranormal experience. Noting that spontaneous experiences range from realistic apparitions to vague feelings of foreboding, he suspected that such paranormal promptings might sometimes influence a person's actions without ever coming to conscious awareness. Seeking a practical test of this hypothesis, he studied records of occupancy of passenger trains on the days of serious accidents versus occupancy on comparable days preceding each accident. These data showed a distinct, statistically significant reduction in occupancy of trains on the trips that ended in serious accidents. This reduction was greater for coach occupancy than for sleeping cars, correlating with the more immediate and flexible planning involved in coach travel. Cox interpreted these results as evidence that some persons must have been motivated, probably unconsciously, to avoid the disastrous runs by either cancelling their trips or choosing other days to travel.

This study by Cox appears to have been the earliest attempt to investigate the possibility of an unconscious psi component in ordinary activities. This concept was later proposed by Eisenbud (1963b) and Rush (1964) and elaborated by Rex Stanford (1977b, p. 839) in his hypotheses of psi-mediated instrumental response (PMIR) and of conformance behavior (see chapter 13, section 5.3).

2 Field investigations of spontaneous psi

Field investigations of psi phenomena generally are limited to recurrent effects (but note section 2.3 below). Field investigations are a miscellaneous lot, so that classification is sometimes difficult. This discussion is concerned only with investigations of spontaneous occurrences. Certain experiments and quasi-experimental investigations conducted under field conditions are considered in other chapters.

The investigator of an active poltergeist or other recurrent phenomenon enjoys the great advantage of personal observation of many aspects of the situation that might not be noticed by an inexperienced witness. The investigator sometimes can establish quasi-experimental conditions by introducing controls and aids to accurate observation and may even experience the reported phenomena. But recurrent psi manifestations are rare. Field investigations necessarily imply working under improvised conditions wherever something interesting is happening. Many such efforts end up as case studies because the investigator arrives only after the reported phenomena have ceased.

Nor is it always easy to gain the confidence of an affected family. Tired, harassed, frightened people are likely to be edgy and suspicious. Moreover, they rarely are interested in research – they simply want to get rid of the disturbances. Sometimes religious preconceptions cause further difficulties (Roll and Stump, 1971).

Claims of paranormal healing are particularly difficult to assess. To appreciate the problem, consider how difficult it is even to establish the medical value of a new drug. Healers do not claim success in every case, and apparent cures are so complicated by medical and psychological uncertainties that frequently it is impossible to determine whether a cure has occurred, to say nothing of the means of healing.

2.1 Haunts

Since hauntings involve reports of recurrent sounds or sights at a particular place, meaningful investigation should be possible. However, the results of such efforts have been meager. Evidential reports of haunts are rare, and there is no system for bringing such events promptly to the attention of qualified investigators, who also are rare. Frequently nothing happens while the investigator is present, or the investigator cannot see or hear the effects that other witnesses claim to be aware of. The investigator may question witnesses, check the consistency of their reports, and inspect the premises for clues to any normal explanation of the manifestations. Cameras, strings across the ghost's accustomed path, or other devices have been tried, but such investigations have produced little reliable data.

Folklore has long attributed haunts to emotionally troubled spirits who are unable to let go of the scenes of their tragic deaths. It has remained for modern psychiatrists to suggest that the troubled spirits are still in the flesh, that the ghosts they see are in some sense reflections of their repressed conflicts. Psychoanalyst Nandor Fodor's (1959/1968, p. 91) account of the 'Ash Manor ghost' offers a remarkable example of such a psychodynamic situation. A couple and their adolescent daughter, living in an old manor house, were troubled by the lifelike apparition of a repulsive-looking man of an earlier time. They reported that the ghost had appeared repeatedly at the husband's bedroom, being seen sometimes by the wife also, and that loud footsteps had been heard. Fodor observed none of these phenomena, but he recognized signs of severe tensions in the family. His impression was confirmed by the psychic Eileen Garrett when Fodor brought her to Ash Manor to try to evoke the ghost personality. She went into trance and almost at once exhibited the personality and expression of a confused and frightened man who the residents said resembled the phantom they had seen. Fodor's questioning of the 'ghost' developed a dramatic tale of betrayal and murder several centuries earlier. None of the information could be verified, however. Eventually Fodor led the couple to acknowledge their secret problems, centered in the husband's sexual conflict, and to recognize that they had in effect evoked the ghost as a distraction. The apparitions then ceased.

Several other investigators have taken mediums or other psychics into haunted houses (Maher and Schmeidler, 1975). Some of these have shown possibly significant reactions, such as identifying the room where manifestations have been reported; but the historical information they have given concerning the house or the haunting personality has not proved to be evidential.

2.2 Poltergeists: RSPK

Poltergeist phenomena have been investigated with more success than hauntings (e.g. Bender, 1974). The typical poltergeist outbreak is briefer than the course of a haunt, being usually weeks rather than months or years; and the physical effects facilitate more varied observations. Cameras, tape recorders and other instruments have been used with some success. Usually, however, the phenomena appear to evade the instruments or even damage them.

Among contemporary investigators of poltergeists, the best known are Hans Bender in Germany and William G. Roll of the Psychical Research Foundation in North Carolina, who introduced the technical term recurrent spontaneous psychokinesis (RSPK*) for poltergeist phenomena.

Roll's most effectively investigated case, the Miami poltergeist (Roll and Pratt, 1971) offers an example of the factors that influence such an investigation and of the adaptation of methods to a specific situation. The paranormal effects were unusually simple, being the almost monotonous flight of one small glass or ceramic novelty item after another from its place on a warehouse shelf to the floor, where it usually broke. As a well-known investigator, Roll was promptly informed of the situation. He invited J.G. Pratt to join him, thus facilitating the work and making the report more credible.

The investigators soon recognized that the disturbances appeared to be associated with a young male employee, Julio. To preclude fraud, an ever-present possibility in such cases, they continually observed the locations of the several employees in the room, particularly Julio. When they heard an object strike the floor (they rarely saw these flights), they immediately recorded the location of each person and of the beginning and end points of the object's flight. These records not only minimized the possibility of fraud in most instances, but also provided data relating the distances and directions of the flights to Julio's position. (See Plate 4).

Roll and Pratt noticed that, when an object had flown from a shelf and been replaced by another, the second object also frequently flew or fell. Certain types of items were affected more often than others. By 'baiting' active locations on the shelves repeatedly with preferred objects and keeping them under close surveillance, the investigators both improved their controls and encouraged more phenomena. They observed ten events under such test conditions. The disturbances ceased when Julio's employers dismissed him.

Bender and his associates (Bender, 1971a, 1974; Karger and Zicha, 1971) reported a bizarre case of RSPK in a lawyer's office at Rosenheim. The apparent agent was a young woman employee. When she was in the offices, pictures and light fixtures swung, light bulbs exploded, telephones were dialed or rung erratically and circuit breakers kicked off. The investigators videotaped some movements. However, their attempts to study the electrical disturbances were largely frustrated by the RSPK influence itself. Technicians trying to monitor the power line with a recording voltmeter found that their instrument was making anomalous traces that were unrelated to the actual line voltage. However, interpretation of the case is complicated by the fact that on another occasion the agent was caught producing effects fraudulently (Resch, 1969), a not uncommon occurrence in poltergeist cases. As in Roll's Miami case, the disturbances stopped when the young woman was dismissed.

Investigators of poltergeist phenomena have long suspected that the physical disturbances are somehow related to unresolved emotional stress in the agent person. A Swedish pioneer psychoanalyst, Paul Bjerre (1947; A.R.G. Owen, 1964, p. 111) reported that RSPK effects attending a hysterical young woman seemed to be associated with a secondary personality. He noted that the hysterical symptoms subsided about the time the secondary personality and RSPK began to manifest. John Layard (1944), a British psychologist, also proposed that RSPK phenomena provide a covert form of release, and thus a curative function, for repressed conflicts. Fodor, as noted earlier, was a strong exponent of this psychodynamic approach. However, psychologist Alfonso M. Taboas (1980) sharply criticized this interpretation, arguing that the incidence of psychiatric problems in RSPK agents is not significantly greater than in the general population.

Roll (1977, pp. 400–1, 405–7) noted that the records of 92 RSPK agents showed dissociative states or seizures in about one-fourth of them, with diagnoses of epilepsy in several cases. He proposed that RSPK may be associated with epileptiform disturbances in the brain; Roll and Elson de A. Montagno (1983; Montagno and Roll, 1983) explored this possibility in more detail. However, the hypothesis must be considered highly speculative, since it rests almost entirely on analogies between epileptiform symptoms and RSPK manifestations, such as emergence usually in adolescence or triggering by stressful experiences.

Roll, Bender and some other contemporary investigators treat the psychological aspects of their cases as being comparable in significance to the RSPK effects themselves. Wherever possible, they include psychiatric examinations of the apparent agent and others in the situation.

2.3 Psychoanalytic observations

Sigmund Freud himself was the first psychoanalyst to comment on incidents in his clinical practice that seemed to require paranormal explanations, but he was persuaded that publication of such matters would only hinder the acceptance of psychoanalysis. Jung gave much attention to paranormal phenomena, and later practitioners have continued to report clinical evidence for telepathy and other effects.

Jan Ehrenwald (1977a) has summarized these developments, to which he has been a major contributor (Ehrenwald, 1955/1975b). George Devereux (1953/1971) edited a collection of the earlier reports. Most incidents have involved apparent ESP, usually manifesting in patients' dreams. Typically, the patient may report a dream that reflects in specific detail contemporary incidents in the analyst's private life or relation with another patient. Sometimes the material is precognitive.

The analyst may, for example, dream of details that are repeated shortly afterward by a patient.

Jule Eisenbud (1970) has written extensively on psi manifestations and the attendant psychodynamics in the therapeutic situation. In addition to the analyst-patient interactions mentioned above, he has commented also on highly improbable incidents in a patient's private life that appeared to have been timed to serve specific neurotic needs. In one such instance, a man – a bird watcher – afflicted with a mother-dependent tendency finds himself 'abandoned' when his wife is away, the housemaid doesn't arrive, and his secretary quits. Walking in the park, aimless and depressed, he suddenly feels sure that he soon will see a certain rare bird, though its season is past and it is seldom seen anyway. He does see the bird, with witnesses (Eisenbud, 1955). Noting that birds are ancient and intercultural mother-symbols, Eisenbud suggested that the patient's emotional need motivated a psi process that made him aware of the bird and led him to it, thus providing consolation by this 'miraculous' appearance of the symbolic mother.

Applying similar reasoning to paranormal dreams and other interactions with his patients, Eisenbud (1963a) advocated an alternative approach to spontaneous psi material. He noted that practically all earlier case studies had evaluated case reports almost entirely in terms of their weight as evidence for paranormality. The alternative he proposed, particularly for clinical cases or others occurring in a known psychological context, is to treat an anomalous incident as any other emerging information in psychotherapy. The significant question is not whether the incident was really paranormal, but why that particular incident occurred at just that time in the therapy. In short, what psychological need did it serve?

Montague Ullman (1959, 1975) also recognized telepathic elements in some patients' dreams, which he believed represented unusually urgent emotional needs seeking expression. He further noted that such dreams were reported mainly by withdrawn, schizoid patients and suggested that in such cases telepathy may serve as an alternate mode of communication. Ullman's clinical observations led him and his associates to carry out an extensive study of experimental induction of telepathic dreams (see chapter 7, section 3.1). He observed that telepathic dreams occurred most frequently in patients who were on the verge of psychosis but were rational enough to be aware of imminent breakdown. He viewed such dreams as desperate efforts to communicate when normal verbal communication had become blocked (Ullman, 1952).

In addition to reporting observations of telepathic dreams and other apparent evidence of psi intervention in his clinical work, Ehrenwald (1977b) proposed a fundamental distinction between the low-level psi manifestations found in statistical experiments and the rarer but much stronger spontaneous experiences. He believes that psi is a primitive function which we are evolving away from and that the mental mechanism normally blocks any intrusion of psi information. On this view, experimental psi is evidence of accidental leakage due to imperfect blocking, but spontaneous manifestations indicate regressions to need-serving, psychodynamically meaningful evocations of psi capability.

3 Spontaneous psi phenomena: summary of findings

The following summary of spontaneous phenomena is highly condensed. Most details and many odd effects have had to be omitted. Some good sources for more detailed information are: Gauld and Cornell, 1979; Gurney et al., 1886/1970; L.E. Rhine, 1969, 1981; Roll, 1977; E.M. Sidgwick, 1918/1975.

3.1 Variety and consistency of spontaneous phenomena

The range of spontaneous *subjective* (ESP) experiences has been suggested already. Such experiences may involve information relating to past, present, or future situations, near or far. Every cognitive mode has in some instances served as a channel for psi information. Spontaneous *objective* (PK) effects also are reported in great variety, most notably in RSPK disturbances. However, many non-recurrent physical manifestations also have been reported: clocks stopping, pictures or other objects falling (usually coincidentally with a related death), or objects being broken.

The consistency with which tales of psychic experiences recur in various times and cultures is not in itself evidence of paranormality; but it does suggest that such experiences cannot be attributed solely to fads or local traditions. The remarkable internal consistency of spontaneous case reports, noted by the early SPR investigators, has been abundantly confirmed by Schouten's more sophisticated analyses.

West (1960) noted that the visionary and hallucinatory experiences of the spontaneous case reports differ consistently from those of persons affected by psychosis, drugs, starvation, or sensory deprivation. These abnormal states evoke hallucinations that generally are not integrated with the experient's surroundings or interests. Osis's study of deathbed visions (section 1.3.1) confirmed this distinction. He noticed particularly that four-fifths of these apparitions, like those reported in spontaneous cases, were seen as if present in the experient's actual room. Only the apparitional figures were hallucinated, in contrast to psychotic hallucinations that characteristically replace the actual surroundings.

3.2 Frequency of spontaneous experiences

Jan Kappers (1964) conducted a sampling of spontaneous psi experiences among residents of Amsterdam. Of 8,000 questionnaires, 1,329 were returned; 408 of these claimed spontaneous experiences. After evaluating these reports, the investigators estimated that probably between one and three percent of the sampled population would experience at least one incident of spontaneous psi in a lifetime. Palmer (1979), in a mailed survey of 1,000 randomly selected persons in a community, obtained 622 responses. Of these, nearly 40 percent claimed waking or dreaming ESP in addition to some who reported other types of psi experiences.

Publicized requests for reports of spontaneous experiences always bring in large numbers of anecdotes, and any lecturer on the subject who asks how many in the audience have had such an experience can count on an impressive show of hands. Even after allowing for misconceptions or distortions in many instances, it appears that odd experiences of the kinds we are considering are unusual but not rare. They evidently are normal experiences of normal people.

Non-recurrent subjective (ESP) experiences have been reported much more frequently than objective (PK) incidents. L.E. Rhine (1969), for example, found in more than 10,000 case reports only 178 that included apparent PK effects. This disparity between the ESP and PK experiences is at least partially attributable to selection. Since a simple physical event, such as an anomalous stopping of a clock or falling of a picture, conveys little information, it is rarely possible to relate it to a specific past or future situation. Usually only a close time coincidence between the event and, for example, a relative's death can suggest a significant relation. An inherently meaningless physical incident need not excite much wonder – it is easily shrugged off with any plausible explanation. Thus many trivial PK events may go unrecognized.

Recurrent spontaneous psi experiences appear to be much rarer than the non-recurrent types. Although the number depends upon the criteria for credibility that are applied, probably no more than a few hundred recurrent cases worth considering are on record.

3.3 Circumstances of experiences; process-oriented research

Most spontaneous psi experiences occur in dreams or when the experient is relaxed or engaged in some monotonous activity. Such observations suggest that psi manifestations may be facilitated by certain kinds of situations and states of mind. The exploration of such relations is an aspect of process-oriented research, i.e. research that is primarily concerned with discovering the principles or processes by which psi manifestations occur. Unfortunately, most experients are so preoccupied with the psi experience itself that they give only scanty information about the circumstances in which it occurred.

3.3.1 External circumstances

Almost all subjective phenomena seem to occur without regard to barriers, distance, or even time. The case is not so clear for the nonrecurrent objective effects, because the person or agency that is responsible for the effect cannot be determined.

The tendency of RSPK disturbances to occur almost always near an identifiable agent suggests a limited range of action of the psi influence; but this limitation could be psychological. Roll found in several RSPK cases an approximately exponential decline in frequency of events with distance from the agent (e.g. Roll, Burdick and Joines, 1973).

Sparse data suggest, but by no means demonstrate, that precognitive experiences become more probable as the time of the target event approaches. Both Stevenson (section 1.3.4a) and J.C. Barker (1967), in their studies of premonitions of two shocking disasters, found that the experiences became more frequent as the time of the event approached. Most of them clustered within the week preceding the event. However, such a distribution obviously is distorted by psychological factors. One is more likely to remember a dream or other impression and relate it to a later event if the time between impression and event is not great.

Most nonrecurrent experiences relate to emotionally disturbing events: public or private disasters, deaths, or personal misfortunes. Many reports, however, relate to trivial situations, and many more of these may not be reported or even noticed. Evidently no sharp boundary can be drawn between ordinary subjective experiences and those involving a psi component. Several studies cited earlier (section 1.3.4b, 2.3) suggest that in ordinary activities psi and sensorimotor functions may blend in a complementary relation.

Some evidence also suggests that spontaneous psi experiences can be facilitated, at least in some instances, by an external situation that is somewhat similar to the scene that emerges paranormally (Rush, 1964). In one example, a woman was moved by a vague impulse to go outdoors and sit beside a garden pool, in which she then saw an accurate vision of her brother drowning. Or the experient's situation may provide only an ambiguous stimulus that, as in crystal gazing, encourages subjective imagery.

3.3.2 Psychological circumstances

Even a cursory survey of nonrecurrent spontaneous cases suggests that both subjective and objective experiences are associated with certain states of consciousness. L.E. Rhine (1969) noted that about half of her cases, and practically all of those that involved imagery, had occurred in dreams or waking reverie. Those that occurred while the experient was actively awake manifested in less obvious forms, ranging from diffuse uneasiness to explicit intuitive knowledge. Few such experiences have occurred to persons who were actively involved with others or were engaged in mental concentration. Frequently experients were either quietly relaxed or busy at simple, habitual tasks that required little conscious attention.

The significant incidents that occur during sleep are not limited to ESP experiences in dreams. Some persons have reported that they were awakened by the sound of a picture or other object falling, or some other physical event, at a time that proved to be significant. Generalizations about the psychological conditions attending recurrent experiences are more difficult because of the rarity of such cases. Many incidents of haunting phenomena have been reported by observers who were nearly asleep or were awakened; but many others apparently were fully awake. RSPK disturbances usually cease when the agent is asleep. Again, however, the records report many exceptions to these tendencies.

Evidence concerning the psychological contexts of hauntings and poltergeists has been presented earlier (see sections 2.1, 2.2). Although RSPK effects usually appear to depend upon one person as agent, recent investigators have recognized that the agent's relations with others are significant. Rogo (1980) reported some evidence supporting the concept of a hostile, deeply disturbed 'poltergeist family' in which the RSPK effects emanate from their conflicted situation rather than from an individual agent.

Motivation is a fundamental aspect of spontaneous psi experiences, but little is known beyond conjecture. Many nonrecurrent incidents formerly were thought to have been initiated by the person in crisis trying to convey a message to the experient. The preponderance of evidence now appears to indicate that the experient is also an active element in such a case – if, indeed, such a designation has meaning. Psychoanalytic theories of motivation in need-serving psi experiences have been discussed (see section 2.3). Similar reasoning applies plausibly to some crisis cases, in which a wife, for example, concerned for her soldier husband, would be motivated to seek information about him. But what of the many crisis cases in which the experient had no normal reason for apprehension, or the cases that involve only trivia? The motivation for nonrecurrent psi experiences remains obscure; possibly it is not even a meaningful concept.

As to recurrent phenomena, similar considerations apply with even greater force to hauntings, since the agency is not clear. However, the observations and theories concerning the psychodynamics of RSPK phenomena cited earlier (sections 2.1, 2.2) suggest that the underlying motivations in these cases may be more accessible.

Summary of terms

nonrecurrent
recurrent
case collection
field investigation
out-of-body experience (OBE)
recurrent spontaneous psychokinesis (RSPK)

Thought questions

(1) A man tells you that ten years ago he and his wife saw an apparition of a woman in the room where she had been murdered. Would you consider this a credible report? If not, what additional evidence would you require?

(2) In what respects are findings concerning haunts and poltergeists similar? How do they differ?

(3) Many persons have reported experiences (OBEs) in which they felt they had left their bodies. Is the OBE a testable hypothesis? How would you propose to distinguish between an actual OBE and ESP/PK effects?

(4) Spontaneous case studies have involved testimony concerning great numbers of cases. Field investigations have been relatively few, but they have permitted direct observations by the investigators. Which of these approaches do you believe has yielded the more impressive evidence for spontaneous psi phenomena? What are your reasons?

(5) Do you believe that the subjective experiences of dying persons or some who have almost died are of any evidential value with respect to the question of survival of death? Explain your reasoning.

Chapter 4
What psi is not: the necessity for experiments

Robert L. Morris

1 Introduction

When we consider the evidence for psi, we must bear in mind that there are many ways we can be misled into thinking that we have witnessed or experienced an instance of psychic functioning. In some cases, we naturally mislead ourselves because we are not fully aware of all the factors involved. Unfortunately, we can also be deceived by deliberate fraud perpetrated by those who would fool us for their own purposes. In this chapter we survey some of the factors involved in producing events that may seem to be psychic but are not. We need to understand these factors so that we can better evaluate the likelihood of true psychic occurrences in our daily lives and in controlled laboratory research. As the next section indicates, there are also some socially important reasons why we must be aware of the strategies of deception.

2 The social context of psychic fraud

Psychic fraud has been around a long time. Anthropologists supportive of psi research acknowledge that many nonindustrial societies incorporate fraud techniques in their rituals and demonstrations of powers (e.g. Reichbart, 1978). It seems likely that such techniques have flourished in any society that supports claims for special mental powers in select individuals.

Although the exact social context may vary from society to society, generally the practitioner is using fraud to manipulate the belief systems of audiences and followers to facilitate greater social control by one of the society's religiously linked institutions or to consolidate a personal power base (including financial power).

The Rev. Jim Jones apparently relied extensively upon fraud to attract followers to his American church, to persuade them to follow him to Guyana, and to keep them at Jonestown despite its obviously repressive social structure. In the United States an important part of his services was the diagnosis and treatment of illness through the psychic power that God had supposedly conferred upon him. On one occasion a parishioner was attacked outside her home, beaten and left dying by the street. Shortly a team of paramedics drove by, saw her, and gave her first aid. They noted she had a broken arm and placed a cast around the arm. The next night at church, Rev. Jim spotted the cast, called the woman forward, administered healing, removed the cast, and had the woman move her arm to show all that it was no longer broken. It was later learned that Rev. Jim had a cadre of intimates who aided him in such matters. They had beaten her up, had then come by dressed as paramedics, had declared her arm to be broken (it was not), and had sealed it up in the cast. His followers had some parishioners 'spit up harmful tumors' by opening their mouths as part of the healing service, then inserting foul-tasting masses into their mouths by sleight of hand, then recapturing the 'tumors' as the healees gagged and spit them out. Rev. Jim also upon occasion 'raised the dead' (generally confederates, but sometimes drugged parishioners), administered mild poison to a recalcitrant parishioner to simulate God's wrath, and even faked a gunshot attack from which he 'miraculously' recovered. When in Guyana he made it a special point to simulate all the standard miracles of Christ. Walking on water had been unusually difficult; the river was deep by their camp and stepping stones hidden just beneath the water's surface were not conveniently available. Thus Rev. Jim had to improvise: he went to the other side of the river by boat, then walked very close to the water's edge while in full view of his parishioners. One of them (a confederate) shouted that Rev. Jim was now walking on water; the other viewers readily agreed, and Rev. Jim's track record was intact. Description of some of the above incidents can be found in *Six Years with God,* by Jeannie Mills, a former lieutenant of Jones's; the remainder was conveyed to the author personally by Ms Mills.

Exploitation can occur at the individual level as well. Consider the following. A man with stomach cancer diagnosed as incurable goes to a psychic surgeon in the Philippines. After suitable ritual, the man is placed on a flat surface and his stomach bared. The surgeon draws his finger across the stomach and a thin incision line appears. The surgeon reaches down into the now-bloody incision and pulls out a tumor. The incision is closed, the blood mopped up, and the body is left without a scar. The man sits up and declares he never felt better. Here is one way such an apparent miracle can be accomplished. The psychic starts by palming a small flesh-colored bladder containing cow blood. A slight squeeze produces a small rupture in the bladder allowing blood to trickle down the inside of a finger and off the fingertip, thus making a thin red line of blood as the finger is moved across the stomach. The psychic then ruptures the entire bladder, spilling all the blood out, at the same time pushing down on the skin of the stomach. This provides a cavity for the blood to gather in and, when done skillfully, creates the impression that the skin has been pulled aside to reveal the bloody interior of the abdomen. The accompanying distraction allows the psychic to palm a piece of animal tissue, then reach into the blood-filled cavity with the tissue in hand and either leave it there for awhile or withdraw it immediately, for public inspection. The blood is then mopped up and the skin slowly kneaded. This creates the appearance of slowly closing the wound. There are many variants on the specific procedures just mentioned, but when done skillfully they create a powerful impression, on onlookers as well as on the patient. Whether or not such powerful experiences occasionally contribute to genuine remission of the illness is beyond the scope of this chapter.

Another group frequently exploited comprises those whose relatives, lovers or friends have died. Such people may need companionship, contact with loved ones, and advice, both spiritual and practical. The ideal prey for a fake medium is a recently widowed spouse of someone who was of considerable wealth and who made all the financial decisions in the family.

Keene (1976) describes his life as a full-time professional fake medium, both in the famous enclave for mediums, Camp Chesterfield, and as head of his own spiritualist church. He describes a variety of techniques for faking darkroom seance phenomena such as levitating tables, spirit voices that speak through trumpets, and apparitions that float through the air. He also describes an elaborate system of sharing data from medium to medium and spiritualist camp to spiritualist camp on the personal affairs and vital statistics of wealthy repeat patrons of such camps. Other topics covered are revealed in chapters with titles such as, 'The name of the game: money, or The spirits and Swiss banks,' and 'Sex in the seance, or How to lay a ghost.'

Other people potentially exploitable include those whose usual means of communication have been diminished by accident, illness or age, and who therefore are eager to explore alternate means of communication that are not so limited by one's own physiology. Those whose abilities to control their own destinies are impaired are eager to reacquire such abilities, or at least to know what the future holds so they can adapt.

An additional area of need that can affect people from a wide variety of walks of life can be the need for meaningful religious experience. Many churches no longer provide experientially rich religion and rely more on assertion by authority to persuade. How often have the spiritually and/or materially troubled cried out, 'Show us a sign – any sign – that God exists!' We have already seen how Rev. Jim helped meet the needs of these people.

Addressing the social ethics of psychic fraud is not necessarily easy, however. If we burst into a mediumistic camp and grab great handfuls of cheesecloth to show that Aunt Joan is not really available in spirit form, have we necessarily made the world a happier place? The needs will still be there, now no longer being met. With disillusionment may come despair and worse. If we are to unmask systematically the psychic frauds, we may need to do so with considerable thought addressed to the provision of alternative support for those who may be hurt. And suppose a friend returns from the Philippines apparently cured by a psychic surgeon who gets caught in the act later on; do you tell the friend about it and insist upon an X-ray to see what's really still in the friend's body?

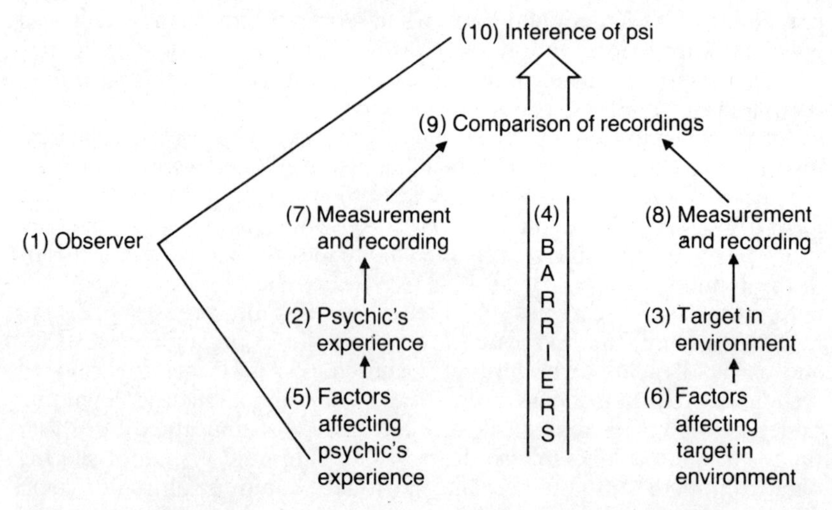

Figure 4.1: A model of factors affecting an observer's assessment of the likelihood that psi has occurred

Some self-confessed fradulent practitioners claim to have started their careers using genuine psychic ability, but then learned to augment their natural talents with tricks so that the faithful followers would be kept happy and the world would be a better place. Do the ends justify the means? In the long run, I think clearly not, else I would not write this chapter. In the short run, however, I would encourage the reader to proceed with sensitivity in introducing the material that follows into any given social situation.

A model for assessing psi

To organize our understanding of the many factors involved, we need a model of what goes on when we interpret a set of events as indicating psi. Figure 4.1 presents such a model. It has ten components, any or all of which may contribute to an observer's assessment of whether or not psychic functioning has taken place.

3.1 The observer

The observer is the person(s) who forms a judgment about whether or not something is psychic, on the basis of information available from some or all of the other components. For a magician, the observer is the audience.

3.2 The psychic's experience

The psychic is whatever organism, generally human, is being regarded as potentially displaying psychic ability. (Although in this chapter we will frequently use the term 'psychic' as equivalent to 'fraudulent psychic,' this is not meant to imply that all psychics are in fact fraudulent.) If the psychic is being evaluated for ESP, then we are asking whether the psychic has acquired information about a target aspect of the environment, through some new means. To do this, we attend to the psychic's experience, generally as reflected in the psychic's behavior. Sometimes the observer and the psychic are the same person, as when we are trying to decide whether or not we ourselves are psychic. In those cases we may pay attention only to our internal thoughts and feelings. If we are interested in whether someone else is psychic, however, we pay attention to their behavior. This can include asking them to show or tell us what they are thinking or feeling, so that we can compare it with the target. Comparably, if we are looking for evidence of PK abilities, then we are asking whether the psychic's needs and intentions have had some sort of direct impact upon a target aspect of the environment. If we are evaluating ourselves, then we judge for ourselves what our needs and intentions are. If someone else is the psychic, we infer their needs and intentions from what information we have about them. Often, especially in an experiment, we have deliberately requested a person to exert a psychic influence on a specific target.

3.3 The target in the environment

The target is any aspect of the environment with which the psychic is hypothetically interacting. For ESP, the target is the aspect of which the psychic appears to have knowledge. Information appears to have been conveyed from the target to the psychic. For PK, the target is whatever the psychic appears to have influenced. Information (or influence, as most prefer) appears to have been conveyed from psychic to target.

3.4 The barriers

In order for us to regard any apparent exchange between psychic and target as indicating psi, we must be sure that no presently understood means of information transfer between the two could have been responsible. Thus we look to see if adequate barriers to such means were present. Much of the problem in assessing the presence of psi concerns the adequacy of the barriers to ordinary communication. The barriers may involve large distances, or time differences (as in precognition); or they may involve physical barriers, like walls, between target and psychic. The barriers are essentially whatever appears to block any relevant, known means of conveying information or influence.

3.5 Factors affecting the psychic's experience

If we are to understand the relationship between the psychic's experience and the target in the environment, we must understand as best we can all the factors that might affect the nature of that experience, to assess whether any of those factors might bias the experience to resemble the target. For ESP, we must consider whatever might influence the psychic's behavior, or experiential content. For PK, we must consider the psychic's needs and intentions specifically. Certainly, the psychic's entire history is capable of exerting some influence, including the psychic's knowledge of, and expectations toward, the target and factors affecting the nature of the target. In general, psychics can be influenced by whatever information or influence comes their way.

3.6 Factors affecting the target in the environment

We must understand all the factors affecting the target in the environment, for similar reasons. Any information about the specific nature of the target or its determinants should not be available to the psychic. Likewise, any information about the psychic's behavior or its determinants should not be known to those in a position to determine the final nature of the target. In general, there should be no common factors contributing to the psychic's experience and the target. In daily life circumstances, this can be very difficult to assess. Fortunately, there are a variety of devices available to research scientists to help them isolate the factors controlling the nature of the target, as can be seen in later chapters describing experimental studies.

3.7 Measurement and recording of the psychic's experience

Ideally, the psychic's experience should be measured in some objective way, and then permanently recorded, such that its measurement and recording are not influenced by knowledge of the nature of the target. Such measurement can include monitoring of the psychic in a variety of ways, including having someone present to note what the psychic is saying or doing.

3.8 Measurement and recording of the nature of the target

The nature of the target should also be measured objectively and recorded permanently, in a manner not influenced by knowledge of the nature of the psychic's experience. For either kind of measuring and recording, occasionally the observer may be the measurer and recorder. If the same person does both, this must be done such that each measurement is still objective. In good experimental research, such measurements are either taken by two separate people or else at least one is done automatically.

3.9 Comparison of recordings

Some representation of the psychic's experience and the target's nature must be brought together and compared for their degree of similarity, if we are to assess whether psychic functioning took place. Sometimes this comparison is very informal and is based on purely subjective impressions, especially when the measurements and recordings themselves have been taken informally, with little precision. Such informal comparisons readily allow bias. In experimental research, there has generally been systematic manipulation of the nature of the target, involving a statistically random process of some sort, such that the relatively precise tools of statistical analysis can be applied to evaluate the degree of correspondence between psychic and target.

3.10 Inference of psi

Once a comparison between psychic and target has been made, the outcome can be evaluated as evidence for psi. Such an evaluation is generally conducted by people aware to varying degrees of what has gone on before. The more they know, the better they can evaluate the likelihood that nonpsi factors contributed to any correspondence between psychic and target. Generally those performing the evaluation are functioning as observers, in the sense described earlier. Occasionally, however, they are people who are themselves biased and are attempting to mislead observers about what has happened. In such cases, they are generally working with observers who have had little if any direct knowledge of what has happened between psychic and target.

3.11 Summary

The ten components listed above and represented in Figure 4.1 show the main sets of factors that are involved when someone attempts to decide whether psychic functioning has taken place. By bearing them in mind, we can now consider some of the main ways that people can be misled to think that psi has occurred, when in fact it has not. Of course, many of these same ways can be used to mislead people to underestimate the occurrence of psi as well. Bias can extend in both directions.

From the above model, we can derive three general sets of ways that people can be misled about psi. One set involves the relationship between the psychic and the target for ESP, when information appears to be transferred from target to psychic. A second involves the relationship between psychic and target for PK, when information/influence appears to be transferred from psychic to target. The third involves the ways that information about what has happened is conveyed to the observer, especially when the observer is not an active participant.

4 The relationship between psychic and target for ESP

4.1 Psychics can take in and process more information than we generally realize

4.1.1 The range of our senses

We normally regard ourselves as having five senses. Yet recent textbooks on sensation and perception may run the list well over thirty (e.g. Geldard, 1972). Our skin contains a variety of sensing devices (the cutaneous senses) that convey specialized information about temperature, pressure, touch, vibration and pain; there are even sense receptors in our skin whose functions are not yet completely understood (Brown and Deffenbacher, 1979). Inside our bodies we have kinesthetic sensors in our muscles and around our joints that provide a constant stream of feedback about the positions of our limbs and our bodily movements. Our vestibular sense provides information about balance. Additional sensors in our internal organs provide crude temperature, pressure and pain information. Highly specialized sensors monitor the delicate balance of chemicals in our bodies. These are all devices that monitor information close to or inside our bodies. We often tend to forget about them and the wealth of information they can provide, including good 'intuitions' about our state of health. When we turn our attention to unfamiliar sensory input, we may not be able to interpret it properly; ordinary visceral feedback may seem like 'psychic energy' building inside the body, especially if that's what we are told.

Other senses convey information from more distant sources. In addition to smell, sight and hearing, there may be additional remote sensing devices. We know all too well that human and animal tissue can be affected by large-scale atomic radiation. Apparently our experience can even be affected by very low levels of radiation. McNulty, Pease and Bond (1975) found that when charged particles such as pions and muons pass through the eyeball, they produce visual sensations through Cerenkov radiation. Such sensations were first noted as mysterious flashes of light by astronauts. Presman (1970) summarizes evidence for the responsiveness of tissue from a variety of species, including humans, to electromagnetic radiation ranging from very high radio frequencies down to frequencies so low that they basically represent static electric and magnetic fields. Barnothy (1964) surveys additional evidence for tissue responsiveness to strong and weak magnetic fields and to changes in field strength. More recently, Adey (1981) and Becker and Marino (1982) extended these findings to include influences upon behavior. Becker and Marino specifically relate electromagnetic field effects to the healing of tissue and describe their usage in medicine. Baker (1980) presented evidence that humans may be able to 'home,' like homing pigeons, by using a primitive magnetic sense to compare geomagnetic differences between their present location and their actual home. Gould and Able (1981) were not able to replicate Baker's findings, and the issue remains open.

We do not as yet have a firm picture of human capabilities for sensing in each of the above areas, as research findings are not consistent. Subtle differences in experimental procedure may be responsible; one would expect people to do best when given extensive training in the detection of faint and unfamiliar stimuli, yet little effort has been devoted to exploring such training techniques. For present purposes, we must acknowledge that people may have sensitivity to a wide range of weak physical information coming from the environment, that such information may not be readily interpreted or even consciously noticeable, and that it may account for many unusual feelings that we have around certain pieces of equipment or geographic locations. Those who train themselves or who have naturally greater sensitivity may seem to us to be psychic, in that they are processing and responding to information not available to the rest of us.

4.1.2 Hyperacuity of the senses

For all our sense modalities, the level of sensitivity varies considerably, depending on a variety of factors, particularly those that affect our distribution of attention. When we attend selectively to input from a specific sensory source, we amplify the strength of the signal and are thus more likely to notice faint signals or changes in intensity. For each modality we have a sensory threshold, representing the smallest amount of stimulation necessary to produce a conscious sensation when we are paying close attention.

Repeated experience and training can heighten one's sensitivities in most sense modalities, producing hyperacuity. Such heightened sensitivity may provide us with much more information than we usually obtain, thus allowing us to perform mental and physical feats that seem impossible and thus potentially psychic in nature. The closeup magician can, through practice and diligent care of the surface of the hands, manipulate ordinary objects with great precision and with sufficient speed to escape notice. One skill mastered by many skilled practitioners is to be able to cut a deck of cards manually to any specified depth just by feel and dexterity. Training for such manual dexterity is described in detail in Hugard and Braue (1974).

4.1.3 Information processing wonders

Information that we acquire may not always become consciously available to us. Dixon (1971) summarizes evidence that information presented to us below our threshold of awareness (subliminal perception) can nevertheless influence our verbal behavior, dreams and other mental processes. Even when we are aware of the arrival of information, we may still forget that we have been exposed to it, only to have it surface in our awareness later on as apparently new information. This phenomenon, known as cryptomnesia or 'buried memories,' has been suggested as an explanation for cases in which people appear to remember details of having lived before (e.g. Kline, 1956). Tales told to us as youngsters remain hidden and forgotten until, years later, they may reemerge as components of a set of experiences that seem to be related to a lifetime in other times and other lands.

Yet another area of uncertainty is the range of human information processing and memory skills. We know of various kinds of 'idiot savant,' people who seem to have unusual specialized musical, mnemonic or mathematical skills, yet remain less than competent in a variety of other mental areas. Luria (1968) has described the life of a skilled 'mnemonist' – a man who, through practice, had developed extraordinary powers of memorization. His skill later became detrimental in that he came to memorize out of habit rather than necessity and found his consciousness crowded with daily life trivia. Various writers (e.g. Higbee, 1977) have described memorization techniques that appear to be usable by most people. Many stage magicians and fake psychics have incorporated such abilities into their acts.

4.1.4 Summary

The important point in this section is that we have far more ability to acquire, process and store information than we ordinarily realize,even in ourselves, without necessarily being aware of it. We must bear this in mind when we are evaluating the potential role of ESP in any unusually insightful behavior we notice in ourselves or in others.

4.2 Targets can emit more information than we realize

4.2.1 Natural information available from the target

Events and the objects that comprise them generate a constant stream of information about themselves. Much of this information is obvious. Some of it may affect our less-familiar senses, such as physical fields surrounding certain kinds of equipment, vibration carried along floorboards from inaudible footsteps in an adjoining room, and so on. Some of it is available only to the skilled detective who knows where to look. If I enter an empty room, I can tell where a person was sitting by feeling which chair is warm; my nose can tell me whether they were smoking or drinking, wearing cheap or expensive cologne/perfume, and so on. Sherlock Holmes seemed psychic at times; Doyle showed us time and again that much of his acumen was due to effective use of his senses and an extraordinary knowledge of the characteristics of events and things in the world around him.

Of especial interest is the information that people emit through subtleties of behavior and appearance. Suppose for instance that a psychic comes to your home and gives you a psychic reading which you find to be astonishingly accurate. You are then the target and you are emitting information.

Straight physical appearance conveys considerable information. Age, sex, certain medical problems (e.g. poor sight or hearing, arthritis and so on), general ethnic background, physical beauty (both natural and acquired), neatness of appearance, and a host of other characteristics can be observed and can often be combined with other information to be useful to the psychic reader. Clothing can provide additional information, including aspects of socioeconomic status, occupation, attitudes toward self and (often) the kinds of groups or trends with which the person identifies. Clothing can occasionally provide quite specific information. Many people forget that articles of clothing or other possessions may bear their initials. A belt with the buckle through the tightest hole and with wear marks across the other holes indicates that the wearer has recently lost considerable weight.

In addition to matters of appearance, people send out information about themselves through their behavior. Some of this revealing behavior occurs at the physiological level, as signs of emotional arousal such as perspiration, blushing or paling, muscle tension, growling stomach, and so on. Some is through body movements such as posture, gait, body position (e.g. legs crossed or arms folded) and customary social gestures. If the psychic can engage the target person in conversation then dialect and general speech patterns become available. Skilled frauds can become skilled questioners, prompting answers that allow other answers to be inferred. A favorite strategy is changing the topic when crucial information is given so that the target person forgets that the information has come out; then the information is reintroduced much later on in modified form, such that the target person never really makes the connection.

Perhaps the most striking example is the fine art of muscle reading (also known as Cumberlandism or Hellstromism, after two of its outstanding practitioners). A muscle reader is someone who makes use of fine muscular movements by a target person to become aware of some aspects of the target person's thoughts. Observation of the muscle movements can be done either tactually or visually.

Washington Irving Bishop (as described in Christopher, 1970) once located a diamond brooch hidden in Manhattan while blindfolded and relying upon the cues provided by a single newspaper journalist. Stuart Cumblerland would do psychic readings for people seated on the other side of a door; the only point of contact was a string extending through the door's keyhole with the target person at one end and Cumberland at the other. Cumberland would make a series of statements, leading off with an obviously correct one and an obviously incorrect one to enable him to learn how the target would signal correctness. From then on, Cumberland could rely on patterned changes in the tension exerted on the string to cue him as to the accuracy of his statements. That plus an extensive knowledge of the behavior and habits of upper-class Europeans enabled him to be a favorite and successful entertainer of the wealthy in nineteenth-century Europe (see Cumberland, 1888/1975, for a first-person description of his exploits).

It should be noted that even animals can learn to respond to the subtle movements of humans. A famous 'intelligent' horse, Clever Hans, was found to be relying upon slight changes in the body posture of knowledgeable observers for cues as to when to stop tapping (if asked to tap out the answer to a math problem) or which lettered block to press with the nose (if asked to 'type' out answers to verbal questions on a specially designed keyboard). The feats of this horse mystified investigators for years until some clever detective work by an investigator named Oskar Pfungst revealed the specific cues in use (Pfungst, 1965).

In summary, people reveal their thoughts and feelings in a variety of nonobvious ways. These ways illustrate the more general point that targets of all kinds can emit information about themselves in many ways that can be capitalized upon.

4.2.2 Artificial information available from the target

A deliberate fraud may arrange for the target or target environment to be modified such that it transmits information that the fraud knows to look for. Some modifications, such as specially marked cards, can be obtained commercially. Or, the fraud can make the modification personally, such as by slightly bending or 'crimping' a card or nicking it with a fingernail, then replacing it in the deck so that it can serve as an indicator.

Other people in the environment of the target may intentionally or inadvertently provide cues about the target's nature. Confederates are often used in mind-reading acts or provide subtle signals to the psychic. These can be in the form of physical cues left behind by the confederate, behavioral cues when the confederate is actually allowed contact with the psychic, or even electronic signaling systems between confederate and psychic. Many stage acts have involved elaborate verbal codes by which an assistant can convey considerable coded information via the words used, their order, and the duration of the interval between words. Even nonconfederates who know the nature of the target may inadvertently provide cues. In any formal evaluation, therefore, information about the nature of the target should not be available to anyone in a position to communicate it, until after the psychic's impressions have been clearly and objectively registered.

4.3 Barriers can be skirted in advance

As described in the model presented earlier, generally there is a barrier of some sort between psychic and target, a barrier that impresses us because it seems to prevent the transfer of information from target to psychic. In this section we consider circumstances in which the barrier was ineffective because transfer of information took place before the barrier came into play. A check of Figure 4.1 shows two sets of factors that can have effects before any barriers are in place: factors affecting the nature of the target, and factors affecting the psychic's experience. Interactions between these sets of factors can lead to a correspondence between target and psychic that has nothing to do with psi.

4.3.1 Factors affecting the nature of the target become known to the psychic

When we are dealing with naturally occurring events, rather than controlled experimental studies, we must bear in mind that the world is basically fairly well organized and that most target events can be anticipated with proper knowledge of the precursor events leading up to them and the rules that tend to relate those events to the target event. As we go through life, most of us build up a fairly good understanding of 'the way the world works,' which enables us to generate inferences, consciously and unconsciously, about what is likely to happen next. Often what appear to be psychic hunches are really the product of considerable unconscious synthesizing of information based on a variety of past experiences, most long forgotten.

Psychics who make popular predictions about politics, economics, the love lives of famous people, and so on, of the sort so nourished by the supermarket tabloids, generally maintain rather extensive information-gathering networks. They often specialize, and keep very well read within their areas of claimed psychic expertise. Some maintain small information-gathering staffs, subscribe to newspaper clipping services, and so on. Once known for an area of expertise, they may develop a gradually increasing circle of acquaintances within that area, generally people who have come seeking psychic advice. In order to get information, such seekers often provide considerable information as they pose their questions, chat informally, explain their interests, offer their own interpretations of the psychic's statements, and so on. Thus the psychic comes to build up a storehouse of information that can be drawn upon for predictions, often including very detailed inside information. An observer who knows little about the area of expertise can often be quite impressed by predictions that utilize common knowledge and would not be at all impressive to a specialist. There are general trends in business, politics and so on that professional analysts (nonpsychic) draw from routinely.

If a psychic can learn a client's identity in advance, it is easy to acquire background information that allows commentary on the client's present and likely future circumstances. As Lamar Keene (1976) describes in *The Psychic Mafia,* spiritualist camps would often share files on clients that were known to frequent such camps. Thus no advance scouting is necessary; one need only learn who is visiting the camp on a given day, and identify each individual in person. A related point is that if the psychic comes to learn about a particular client, he can generally infer much about that client's needs and can tell the client what the client wants to hear. Most of us wish to hear good things about ourselves and that the future will be favorable; the skilled psychics know how to tell us these things but in ways tailored to individual clients. They also learn to sense when they are 'laying it on a bit too thick,' expressing themselves so completely positively that they start to arouse suspicion.

We should not assume from the above that the client has received no service. It could be argued that someone who combines the psychologist's skills with those of the business advisor may often provide valuable, insightful advice tailored to the unique individual, that might not be readily available elsewhere. But it wouldn't be psychic advice, and the client should be wary of any sudden psychic hunches that result in the client giving large sums of money either to the psychic for investment or to 'a new company that is sending out very good vibes.'

In addition to the above, there are also a variety of mentalism techniques in which the psychic learns the nature of the target before the barriers are in place. For instance, in a recent demonstration at a Committee for the Scientific Investigation of Claims of the Paranormal Conference, Cornell psychologist Darryl Bem asked in advance that a staff member unknown to him take four unusual items from her home and place them in a container to be sealed and brought to the conference. He then had her come out on stage, with the container, to help him demonstrate characteristics of the mentalist arts of muscle reading and skilled questioning. After a few general questions and social interaction, he was able to identify each of the items. The audience applauded. Dr Bem then informed them that he had not accomplished his feat by muscle reading and skilled questioning; rather, he had simply gone backstage beforehand, gotten access to the container at an unguarded moment, and examined its contents directly.

4.3.2 Knowledge of factors affecting the psychic's experience may influence selection of the target

Our experiences, especially our guessing behavior, occur in patterned ways, more so than we realize. If others wish to persuade us that we are psychic, they can draw from knowledge of how we pattern our behavior and experiences to help them select a target that we are likely to respond to, guess, or match with our behavior in some way. If asked to think of a European city, we will likely say Paris; if thinking of a vegetable, carrot is most popular. When asked to make a 'random' guess about numerical information, most of us will studiously avoid anything that doesn't look quite random. If asked to select from a row of five objects, we tend to choose the second or fourth. Choosing the one at either end or in the exact middle seems to us too nonrandom. If asked to select a number between one and a hundred, a surprisingly large proportion will select thirty-seven. Any number ending in a zero or five looks nonrandom, as does any number that is very low, very high, or very close to the middle, or any number with the same digit repeated. When guessing through a series of items such as a deck of cards, we tend not to repeat ourselves, e.g. call the same suit twice in a row. Yet by chance the same suit will be repeated once every four times. Marks and Kammann (1980) present an excellent discussion of such general patterns in our behavior and how they can be used to make us seem psychic. Each of us may also have very idiosyncratic patterns to our behavior, which can be exploited by someone who takes the trouble to learn them. And on any given occasion, the events that have just been happening to us may further bias our behavior toward some specific pattern.

4.3.3 Common factors may influence both the psychic's experience and the target nature

As noted above, human behavior can be influenced by specific environmental events. Thus certain similarities between the actions and experiences of two or more people may be due to shared recent experiences rather than evidence of telepathy. If it's a hot day, or there's a tragedy in the news, peoples' thoughts, daydreams and so on may focus on heat or death, respectively. Shared specific experiences such as seeing the same movie can contribute to commonalities in thoughts, feelings and behavior for some time afterward. This can be a problem in interpreting evidence for telepathy drawn from daily life events in which the thoughts of two people seem to correspond to a striking extent. Even in controlled laboratory research there can be a problem if the 'sender' or experimenter chooses the target in any nonrandom way that allows his own biases or preferences to contribute. Ullman, Krippner and Vaughan (1973,p. 86) describe two dream telepathy sessions with Eileen Garrett in which correspondences between her dreams and the thoughts of the sender involved famous movies being shown at the time. These were exploratory sessions not using the rigorous target selection methodology later employed in psi dream research; any interpretation of them as evidence for telepathy is compromised by the possibility that the availability in the public eye of these movies contributed to the similarities between psychic's experience and nature of the target.

The above involves naturally occurring common factors. However, someone wishing to persuade you that you are psychic may both determine the target and 'force' you to make a choice that matches the target. The most frequent forces involve selecting from among a set of alternatives. Suppose your target is the identity of a concealed playing card and I know that the target is a ten-spot, because I arranged to have it be the target. I can now try to force you to choose the ace of diamonds from among other cards in a variety of ways. One way is to fan the cards in front of you, with their backs to you, and ask you to pick one. If selecting from among cards fanned in front of them, people will select cards that stand out perceptually in some way, such as being raised slightly or having the cards on either side spread more widely apart. If you seem to be ignoring the desired card, then I can (with skill) just watch you, determine the moment at which your choice is about to be made and your hand is about to move toward the cards, then shift the fan slightly so that the desired card is directly in front of your hand. Even though you may have had another card in mind, you will go ahead and take the card that is most conveniently in reach. Triplett (1900) used this as an example of the 'law of economy of effort,' used in many forces, which states that in general people will do whatever is easiest for them to do. If one wishes to force a particular action or decision, one merely needs to make sure the desired decision is the easiest to make.

This kind of force can take great skill and a keen observational eye, and it often doesn't work. Suppose, in our example above, that you instead select a card of lesser value, say a seven. I then say, 'Fine, let's set that card aside.' I then ask the chooser to choose another card and this time force the choice of a three. Three plus seven is ten, and the trick somehow seems even more amazing. If you had chosen a value higher than ten, say a king (valued twelve), I may ask you to choose another card and announce, 'Now we'll try a little subtraction,' or 'Now we'll invoke the mystical principle of opposites.' Then I force a two. The point here is that as of the first force attempt, I have not really stated what the rules of the game are. I am thus free to modify or reinterpret them as the trick proceeds, until the proper force has succeeded. Such shifts or additions to the rules of the game after the fact are frequently referred to as 'outs.' They enable a fraud to get 'out' of a situation that has not yet developed favorably.

Some forces involve linguistic ambiguities. For instance, suppose I have two cards in opaque envelopes side by side in front of me, with you standing opposite. The envelope with the ten of diamonds is the one on my right and, therefore, on your left. I ask you to say whether the envelope on the right or the left is to be chosen. If you say 'right,' I say, 'The envelope on my right; very good,' and pick up the one on my right. If you say 'left,' I say, 'The envelope on your left; very good,' and pick up the same envelope. If you protest, I may then go ahead and take the envelope on my left and state, 'Okay, now we've eliminated this one. There's only one remaining. Let's open it up and see what it is.' If done skillfully and in front of supportive observers, a good fraud with a silver tongue can generate (force) whatever outcome is desired.

4.3.4 Implications for controlled research

The problems considered in this section can be dealt with effectively in controlled research in two ways. First, target selection must not transpire until adequate barriers are clearly in place. Second, targets must be selected from among a set of equally likely alternatives by some adequately random process. The ways of doing this properly are discussed later in the book.

4.4 Problems with the barrier itself

4.4.1 A good barrier can often be circumvented by special means

In some cases, what seems like a perfectly good barrier to information transfer is rendered ineffective by special circumstances. As noted earlier, people have access to more sensing capabilities than we ordinarily realize, and targets can give off information in many ways that we ordinarily do not consider. A barrier that is perfectly good against the usual channels of sensory input may be completely ineffective for targets that happen to emit information that we are not ordinarily aware of. Some psychics may train themselves to have heightened sensitivities in certain sense modalities, such as smell, which are little used in our society. Also, someone from another society that emphasizes different senses than our own may seem to have unusually acute awareness.

Robert Van de Castle has described to me his experiences with the Cuna Indians in the San Blas Islands off the coast of Panama. They use body odor as a source of information about each other's feelings. When greeting, they will often clap each other under the armpits and sniff their hands to see if the other party has been feeling anxious, working hard, or whatever. In our society we spend literally millions yearly to suppress such olfactory information flow between people.

Some psychics make use of specialized signaling devices to convey information about targets, especially in telepathy demonstrations in which sender and receiver are in active collusion. Hansel (1980) has suggested that high-pitched whistles may have been used in the 1950s to signal in a study conducted by older experimenters whose hearing at such high frequencies was likely impaired. Today's electronic sophistication provides countless ways for sender and receiver to exchange information over considerable distances using very small transmitters and receivers. To avoid being noticed by observers, a small receiver can be inserted in a shoe, for instance, and transmit information to the person by pulsed vibrations against the surface of the skin. Detection of such devices can be done through electronic monitoring, resulting in a high-tech cat and mouse game. Many researchers prefer to avoid investigations of sender-receiver teams that they do not know, offering instead to have one of their own staff members serve as sender if indeed one is needed.

4.4.2 A barrier to information transfer can be temporarily removed: the glimpse

All that a psychic generally needs is a brief peek, a 'glimpse,' of the target. The barriers between psychic and target need only be lowered for a second or two, if the psychic is in proper position to observe. There are a few basic strategies for providing glimpses. In sleight of hand, the psychic diverts the observer's attention while performing some brief manual manipulation. In the present case, the manipulation generally involves the dextrous opening and closing of a target concealment device. This means any relevant mechanism must be understood. Sleight of hand artists may practice extensively with a variety of containers, clasp mechanisms and so on. Such sleights may involve manipulating target materials at the time of opening a container rather than manipulating the container itself. An example is the famed 'one ahead' trick for billet reading. In a standard billet reading act, members of the audience are given envelopes, pads and pencils and asked to write out questions of importance that they wish the psychic to answer. The question (the 'billet') is then sealed in the envelope. All envelopes are collected and brought up to the psychic, who takes an envelope and holds it, collecting impressions. Then he states a question and asks whose question it is. Someone in the audience responds. After answering the question, the psychic opens the envelope, removes the question, and displays it to the audience so they can see that it resembles his statement. Following verification, another envelope is selected and the procedure is repeated with complete accuracy, until all envelopes are gone.

This effect can be accomplished as follows: as soon as the envelopes are brought to the psychic, he palms a folded question which he himself wrote on paper like that given to the audience. He then takes up an envelope and speaks out loud the question. A confederate in the audience claims that the question is his. The psychic then tears open the envelope and removes the question but palms it (or lets it drop to his lap) and shows the audience the pre-prepared question instead. The observers thus are impressed with the response to the first envelope. Now the psychic prepares for the second envelope. He spreads open on his lap (out of sight of the audience) the question from the previous envelope, takes another envelope, holds it to gain impressions, and reads aloud the question in his lap from the first envelope. That question came from a genuine naive observer in the audience, who will then acknowledge the question is accurate. The psychic then palms the 'real' question in his lap and substitutes it for the question in the second envelope as he opens that envelope. The question from the second envelope drops to his lap; the question from the first envelope is displayed to the audience as though it had just come from the second envelope, thus verifying the accuracy of the psychic's statement about the second envelope's contents. This process is repeated: the psychic will now read aloud the question in his lap from the second envelope, pretending that he is psychically responding to the contents of the third envelope, and so on until all the envelopes have been used. The last envelope held aloft, of course, will either be empty or contain a blank sheet of paper, prepared in advance by the psychic. This trick and the many refined variants on it have been popular in psychic demonstrations.

There are many optical tricks for rendering a physical barrier temporarily ineffective, without recourse to sleights to remove the barrier. Three examples illustrate the scope. First, one can make use of reflections. People wearing sunglasses and looking at a card will often reflect the face of the card in their glasses, such that it can be glimpsed by a properly positioned psychic. Small mirrors hand-held by the psychic or a confederate can be put to good use, as can mirrors prepositioned elswhere in the room. Second, backlighting can also be used. In backlighting, the psychic arranges for a light source to be placed behind an object inside a partly translucent container such that the object's outline can be observed. A psychic given a line drawing inside a sealed envelope could cup a small light source in his hand and illuminate the envelope briefly from behind, long enough to glimpse the features of the drawing. A third strategy is to apply some substance to an opaque barrier to render it transparent, either temporarily or permanently. For example, a quick-evaporating odorless alcohol can be used to make an envelope containing a drawing temporarily transparent. In one procedure, the alcohol is stored in a vial in a pocket and fed by a tube to a small sponge near the pocket opening. The psychic has a second, flesh-colored sponge attached to the inside of his thumb; when he wants to use the alcohol, he presses his thumb sponge against the other sponge to soak up the alcohol. He then takes up an envelope containing a target and, with his thumb, smears alcohol across the face of the envelope facing him. This renders the envelope transparent, allowing the glimpse. In a few seconds the alcohol has evaporated and the envelope appears normal again.

The placement of barriers may focus on the psychic rather than on the target. In such cases obtaining a glimpse is a matter of temporarily weakening barriers blocking the psychic's senses. The most common example is the use of blindfolds. One blindfolding procedure involves the placing of a large coin over each eye, then a wad of dough over each coin to seal all the openings around its edges, then wide cotton strips placed diagonally across each eye, then a hood of some sort placed over the entire head. The psychic can arrange to see through all of this by a set of fairly simple maneuvers. Dough will tend to stick more to cotton strips than to an oily face. Thus once the hood is in place, the psychic can work the coins and dough loose from their position over the eyes either through movements of facial muscles or by a brief manual adjustment of the hood. When the hood is put on, the assistant (or an observer) may naturally ask the psychic whether or not the hood is on 'all right', in some way. He responds in some way, making a small adjustment with the hands at the same time. If this gesture is done naturally, in concert with the verbal exchange, observers will not readily notice the gesture. Once the coins and dough are lifted off the eyes, they can be allowed to sag down the face. The psychic can then see through the hood by one of several devices. A dab of clear gauze on the tip of the nose can be smeared on the inside of the hood. Gauze on the psychic's fingertip can be applied to the outside during the adjusting gesture. Either will render the hood transparent at that spot. Alternately, some hoods have either a loose weave at the front or a double layer that can be made single by an adjustment inside. If the cotton strips are fairly tight, then the psychic just tries to create a peek hole down the sides of the nose or the outer corners of the eyes, peering through the hood at an angle rather than looking straight ahead. There are many more strategies for seeing through blindfolds, and analogous strategies can be used for devices that attempt to block other senses as well.

Concealment devices may have special properties allowing glimpses. For the sake of completeness, it should be noted that some devices used for concealing a target may have false bottoms, hidden compartments, detachable parts, and so on, such that the targets can be temporarily removed, inspected and replaced.

4.4.3 Barriers can be deceptively weak

Many physical devices for concealment are simply less effective than they may seem, as is the case with many simple cloth blindfolds. Some barriers that screen information in some sense modalities allow its passage in other modalities that simply may not occur to us, such as odor. Short distances may only block information for those with weak senses. In general, we should test out any barriers that we regard as important, to see if they really function as we assume they will, and we should not rely on others' assessments especially if they have reason to be biased.

4.4.4 Some barriers in fact are not present at all

Often when we are reliant upon another's description of what happened, we may get an exaggerated version which implies or states that barriers were present when in fact they were not.

A special circumstance involving implied barriers that aren't really there involves certain kinds of evidence for precognition. In precognition, the barrier is the passage of time and relies upon the assumption that the target future event will be determined in ways that are not influenced by events related to the psychic's experience. Two problems may arise.

First, a psychic may deliberately bias various determinants of a psychic event in order to validate a prediction. Some confidence games require only that the psychic be labeled as an accurate predictor for a short period of time, in which case he needs only to make his prediction temporarily appear to come true. For instance he may predict for an investor that a certain area will yield gold; then he 'salts' the area with small lumps of actual gold; the investor checks out the land, finds the gold, has it assayed, and pays the psychic a handsome finder's fee; the psychic then departs before the investor learns that the prediction was bogus all along. Comparably, a psychic may hire someone to steal an object from a wealthy potential patron, then predict where the object will be found, then hide the object in that location to be discovered later.

Second, people aware of a given prediction may innocently act of their own initiative to bring about the success of the predictions (self-fulfilling prophecy). An obvious example is the good advice found in astrology columns in the newspaper. Many people read the columns not with the sense that the advice is truly dictated by the stars but rather because it gives a convenient 'excuse' to follow some good advice. If one is told to be open and friendly to newcomers because this will be profitable, then one is likely to derive more value from what newcomers one does meet. If one is told that Leos will be incompatible but Sagittarians very compatible, one will likely treat Leos with caution and little interest; more energy and self-confidence will go into one's interactions with Sagittarians, and the predictive statement will start to ring true. If a psychic predicts election outcomes publicly, he may actually influence the election outcomes, since many will want to vote with the psychic, or vote for a winner, or not bother voting if they prefer the predicted loser. The psychic who wishes to have self-fulfilling prophecy work for him simply makes prophecies that observers will be motivated to validate and whose validation lies within the observers' capabilities.

As a closing note, we should remember that self-fulfilling prophecy can work in negative directions as well, and can lead people to act against their own interests. A particularly nasty version was described to the author by law enforcement agents in California. It goes as follows. Some new psychics move into a poor but religious neighborhood. They spread word of their availability for psychic counselling very informally, and work out of private homes. When someone comes for a reading, the reading is general and positive, with some specific accuracy, drawing from strategies as described earlier. It ends with a hint that there may be some minor interpersonal difficulties developing in the observer's life. A candle is lit, there is a short prayer, and a donation of five dollars is humbly accepted. Within perhaps a week, the client is back for a second reading, and is concerned because he or she has started to notice problems in dealing with one or more other people. This time the reading is more intense and more negative; there are enemies marshalling forces against the client, and only the psychic can help. Many candles must be burned, and the donation is correspondingly greater. The client is now hooked, and can be relied upon to return repeatedly for help. Self-fulfilling prophecy is well underway; the client is looking for suspicious behavior by others and is sure to find it. Others are treated with suspicion and will modify their end of the interactions accordingly, thus making the situation worse. Often the psychics will simply suddenly leave the neighborhood and move on to new territory, leaving people with their newly acquired problems. Some psychics may gradually announce that the situation is now getting better, that the candles and prayer are working, and the evil is being vanquished. If the psychic is skillful enough in handling his clients, he may be able to orchestrate the development and defeat of a quiet crisis that never is communicated to one's friends and acquaintances, such that the observer never takes overt actions strong enough to make permanent enemies (and thus make the crisis harder to fix). There are many ways the game can be played, but all involve rather cruel exploitation of people's abilities to find trouble when they take steps to look for it.

Such problems can be dealt with in controlled research by proper safeguarding of the processes of target selection in precognition research.

4.5 Problems in the measurement and recording stage

In this section we consider problems that arise in the measurement and recording of the psychic's experience and the target nature. At this stage the barriers often are no longer in operation.

4.5.1 The measurement and recording of the psychic's experience is influenced by the recording of the target

Sometimes the measurement and recording of the target takes place before the psychic's experience is actually measured. If information about the target becomes available to the psychic or those measuring and recording the psychic's experience, they could be biased to produce a recording that more closely resembles the target.

One aspect often overlooked is that recording an event can create additional sources of information about the event. Three points are important. First, the act of recording itself may provide information. For instance, if someone is making a simple line drawing on a sketch pad, a psychic nearby could gain information both by the sounds made by the drawing implement and by glimpsing the movements of the upper tip of the implement as the basic movements are made. Large movements are obvious to everyone; smaller movements take practice to decipher.

Second, the record itself of a target event can serve as a source of information. If the identity of a target is recorded or represented elsewhere, then that record must be kept from the psychic just as completely as the target event itself.

Third, the production of a target record in turn can produce secondary effects capable of providing information. For instance, another strategy for accomplishing billet reading involves collecting all the pads of paper used by the audience for writing questions. These pads are taken backstage by an assistant and then lightly shaded by a stick of graphite (the side of a pencil point will do). This shading will emphasize the marks made on the pad by the pressure exerted in writing the question. The questions written can thus be easily read. Their contents can then be passed on to the psychic, perhaps verbally into a receiver behind his ear.

Sometimes, the psychic gets access to information about the recording of the target through carelessness by observers and investigators or through one of the ploys mentioned above. If none of these is likely to work, then a response can be simulated and held concealed until the barriers are down; then the correct response is made and substituted for the simulated prediction. Two examples will illustrate this strategy. A psychic claims to be able to predict the outcome of elections. But 'just to make sure that knowledge of my prediction doesn't affect anyone's vote,' the prediction is sealed in an envelope only to be opened after the election is over. The envelope is given to a trusted town official for safe keeping; the day after the election, the official opens the envelope with great ceremony, revealing a correct prediction. What happened was that the psychic placed either a blank sheet of paper or nothing at all in the envelope, at the start. After the election was over, he wrote the correct result upon a piece of paper and inserted the paper inside a compartment in a special letter opener. This opener was given to the town official who used it to open the envelope. The opener was specially designed such that when held in a normal way, inserted into an envelope and pressured across the blade, it would eject its contents (the correct prediction) into the envelope, thence to be discovered by the official. To run less risk, the psychic could handle the opener himself. Of course, given access to the sealed envelope after the outcome is known, he could arrange to substitute another envelope containing the correct outcome or else to steam the envelope open, insert the prediction, and seal it again.

In a related procedure, a psychic claims to be able to guess the sum of two numbers being thought of by members of the audience. He jots his prediction on a pad of paper and sets his pencil down. Two members of the audience are then selected and asked to think of a number between one and one hundred. They comply; they announce their numbers; another member of the audience adds the numbers together; the psychic immediately shows the pad to the audience, with the correct number written on it. Here's how it could have been done. The psychic initially wrote nothing on the pad, simply dragging a fingernail across the paper for acoustical effect. He set his pencil down to indicate that he was done writing. The two numbers were then thought of and announced. As soon as they were announced, the psychic added them in his head and wrote the sum on the pad of paper using a sliver of graphite attached to the thumb of the hand that holds the pad. Devices known as thumbnail writers are available commercially for this purpose at magic shops; they are flesh-colored and not noticeable unless one is very close. Once the sum has been thus written, the pad can be set down or handed to an audience member who then announces the psychic's success.

A variant on this theme is often practiced by well-known psychics who are constantly alluding to the future in daily conversations. If they have made enough statements that have not been recorded and are only vaguely remembered by those involved, then such psychics can simply wait until a timely event comes along and forcefully persuade the others that in fact the event had been predicted with precision. Essentially they are guaranteeing that effective measurement and recording will take place only after a worthwhile event has transpired. That event is thus declared to be the target, which is now registered officially, at the same time as a particular past statement, suitably modified, is now registered as the official record of the psychic's experience.

Although such a set of assertions after the fact may seem rather brazen, it can be made to work if presented to a sufficiently supportive set of observers (often including reporters looking for a story). Also, it is easy for us to use a milder version of such a procedure, in all innocence. Upon encountering a striking event in our daily life, we may recall having had a dream that resembles it. We then decide that the dream was psychic. Yet we had not written the dream down, or declared it in advance to be a psychic dream. And in truth we have picked it out from among many other dreams, such that we are now conveniently ignoring all the dreams, remembered or not, that did not strike us as resembling any later events in a meaningful way. Also, after the fact it is easy for us to embellish our memories of the specific dream, omitting erroneous or inconsistent details, thereby making the correspondence to the target closer and closer. This can take place equally easily for any nondream experience as well – once we notice a correspondence with an external event, we may begin to shape our recall of the experience in accordance with our biases.

4.5.2 The measurement and recording of the target is influenced by the recording of the psychic's experience

The reverse of the above can take place as well, in situations in which the psychic's experiences have been recorded and can be accessed by those responsible for determining and/or recording the target. If I have a very vivid experience, a powerful dream or a sudden strong mental impression, I may record that impression, especially if I think I'm psychic, and then go looking for target events to match with it. If I'm creative, I won't have too much trouble. Or if I have a specific target in mind, such as the thoughts of a friend or spouse, I may call up that person and ask what they were thinking about at that time of day. Once I've declared my experience, to myself and to the other party, we have the opportunity to decide for ourselves which of that party's thoughts were most like my own. It will be hard to keep our biases from intruding.

If someone else wishes to persuade me that I am psychic, they may conceal a dummy target for me, then wait until I have declared and recorded my experience, and then insert covertly, in any of several ways, a target that matches my experience. The logic is very similar to that developed in the above section.

4.5.3 Implications for research

As usual, the above problems can be avoided by adequate research procedures. A hard copy record of both the target nature and the psychic's experience should be made immediately, while experimental safeguards such as adequate barriers are still in effect, and duplicate copies made if possible. If the recording must be made by people rather than automatically, then the person who measures and records the target should not be the person who measures and records the psychic's experience. Ideally, a record of the target is prepared at the time the target is selected, and then treated as though it were the target itself.

4.6 Problems in comparing recordings

Once measurements have been recorded, they are compared to assess their similarities. In daily life events, the process of measurement and recording tends to be informal and less precise. Often there is no objective record at all, and evaluation relies upon memory. The less precise the recording, the more difficult it is to compare similarities and, therefore, to asses the likely contribution of psi. In this section, we are focusing on situations in which some form of objective recording exists, however imprecise and informal.

One problem arises when in fact many recordings have been made, involving many potential psychic events. The problem can be illustrated by attempts to evaluate multiple predictions. Predictions can be made in abundance, with attention called later only to those that are likely to be regarded as accurate. As we shall see later, people easily forget information that never becomes relevant for them later on. A psychic may make many predictions, recording them all but discarding those recordings that are inaccurate. Evaluation is only encouraged for the remainder, with those doing the evaluation being either unaware of the existence of the other recordings or having forgotten their existence. An alternate strategy is to make predictions in front of many separate observers, following up only on those observers who were given predictions that worked out. For example, in areas that are sparsely settled with little communication between towns, a psychic might select sixty-four small towns spread over several states as potential targets. He writes to the newspaper editor in each town; for half he predicts one outcome of a binary event such as a sports contest, and for the other half he predicts the second outcome. He then waits until the event takes place; those editors who received a false prediction are ignored, but the remaining thirty-two are all sent follow-up letters with half predicting one outcome of a second event and the other half predicting the other outcome. The process is repeated a third and fourth time, which now yields four communities whose editors have received four straight correct predictions. By this time some local interest has usually been generated, and the psychic can visit the town to ply his trade amidst much fanfare.

Even if we are not consciously trying to confuse the issue with an abundance of recorded psychic experiences, it can be easy for us to lose track of how many times we have written something down, perhaps in a dream diary, and then ignored it when it did not come true. Having a recording in itself helps us to do a better job of evaluating daily life events, but it is most effective if incorporated into an orderly logbook of some sort that does not permit the omission of unfavorable items.

Another set of problems with recordings and their comparison concerns the ways in which they are worded. Once again, examples drawn from precognition can illustrate. The exact wording of predictions can increase the likelihood that they will later be regarded as correct. Words must be chosen to be flexibly interpretable after the fact. One strategy is to make general statements, likely to be true. 'There will be an international tragedy tomorrow.' Of course; there always is, if you monitor the news thoroughly. One can also emphasize vague or ambiguous statements. 'There will be a major international tragedy in the East.' How major is major? Does a small bomb in a warehouse that injures a night watchman count? And where is the East? Japan and China? The American Eastern seaboard? A third strategy is to use symbolic statements. 'I see a book with the pages slowly turning – this generally means change, such as travel.' But if the observer receives a much-desired book as a gift in the mail a day later, will the psychic's imagery still be regarded as purely symbolic? Also, by their very nature symbolic statements tend to have a general nature to them and to be easily reinterpreted after the fact.

The two important features of the above kinds of statements are:

flexible initial interpretability and amenability to reinterpretation after the fact. Often the psychic becomes actively involved in reinterpretation. This can either be public reinterpretation, aided by the media, or private reinterpretation, through later meetings between psychic and a particular observer. Whatever reinterpretational strategies the psychic prefers (e.g. extensive use of ancient symbols) should be taken into account in the initial phrasing of the prediction. With polished wording and manner, the psychic can generally present the reinterpretation as an explanation instead, often leading the observer to assume responsibility for having misinterpreted the psychic's original remarks.

4.6.1 Pattern recognition: detection or imposition

A major component of the problem lies in the very nature of the act of making comparisons. When we compare two items or events, we are looking for similarities between them. If the items are complex. as they often are in daily life situations, then we are comparing sets of characteristics, looking to see if there is a pattern in one that resembles the pattern of the other in some way. We also assess whether the separate items seem to fit together in an overall pattern that has meaning for us of some sort. The characteristics compared may be sensory, as in colors or shapes; or they may be content-laden, such as people who don't necessarily look like each other but who look like our close friends. 'Today I saw an incredible number of people who looked like my old friends.'

We are very good at this skill; since birth and perhaps before, we have been constantly organizing our environmental inputs into patterns, building an understanding of the way the world works. Objects and events that occur close to each other in space and/or time naturally get grouped together; we tend to assume they have commonalities, such as common causes, and thus are components of a meaningful pattern. Often that assumption is valid. We have detected a pattern that is there and does reflect commonalities of some sort among the separate elements. At least equally often, however, our assumption may be invalid; we have imposed a pattern upon unrelated events, events having no meaningful commonalities. Sometimes we can notice this process in ourselves. For example, as we walk through a crowd at the fair, thinking of love and being in love, we look up and see several couples close to each other, smiling, we may say, 'Aha! I was thinking of love and now love is around me. I was probably psychically tuning in on it.' But then the couples split up – they were only isolated individuals emerging from a fairly narrow passageway. For a while we were imposing a pattern that wasn't really there, just as we were when we temporarily thought that strangers were old friends.

Expectations, moods and needs play an important role. They may bias our perceptions; when we are lonely we may see more people who resemble old friends. Or, they may affect our organization of events into larger patterns. If we expect ourselves or a certain other person to be 'psychically active,' we may look very hard to impose pattern wherever we see any two events or objects with vague similarities.

Marks and Kammann (1980) have noted that one way we impose pattern as a result of expectation is by selectively noticing similar pairs and ignoring dissimilar pairs. Thus we can extract an overall pattern from a diversity of information. They give two examples: the 'clustering illusion,' that objects and events that are similar seem to cluster in space and time; and the 'gremlin illusion,' that bad things seem to happen all at the same time. Once we notice such a pattern developing, we then scan for further examples and ignore all exceptions. Patterns involving several objects and events can emerge when we are comparing a complex internal event such as a dream with equally complex external target events. Such patterns can also emerge when we are considering a psychic's claim that, 'Because I'm psychic, things just occur in synchronized patterns around me. Today will be a day for anger and for orange.' Of course, it is possible to carry our concerns to an extreme, such that we become overly cautious and run the risk of ignoring some important patterns in our daily lives. Much of creative problem solving involves becoming aware of patterns around us and looking for information that others have missed or ignored.

In psi research, these problems can be handled with proper experimental procedure, measurement, and statistical techniques for comparing measurements and evaluating their degree of similarity. Specific rules for data analysis are employed, drawing from hypotheses about the data stated clearly in advance.

4.7 Problems in inference from similarity

This section conceptually is a continuation of the previous one. Once we have noted a pattern and have confidence that the similarities between target nature and psychic experience are real, we must then decide whether or not such similarity indicates psychic functioning. Several factors may operate to lead us to overestimate the significance of the evidence. First, there may be social pressure on us, from the psychic or from others around us. The art of interpersonal persuasion can be practiced with considerable effectiveness. Second, we ourselves may have strong needs to regard ourselves or others as psychic. As noted at the beginning of the chapter, we can be powerfully motivated by a need to contact deceased loved ones or improve our failing health. Third, unless we have a thorough knowledge of all that has previously transpired, we may be unaware of sets of hidden factors that artificially produced the similarity between target and psychic. Correlation does not imply causation. Finally, as Tversky and Kahneman (1973, 1974) have illustrated, people in general have a very poor intuitive grasp of probability theory, of the likelihood of occurrence of various classes of coincident events just by chance. The classic example is the birthday problem. How many people do you need in a group before there is a fifty-fifty chance of two of them sharing the same birthday? That seems like an unlikely correspondence, and we tend to declare that a large number would be necessary. Yet the correct answer is only twenty-two.

In general, we have a tendency to be impressed by coincidences and to overestimate their rarity. When we see strong coincidences, it is thus easy for us to decide that they couldn't have arisen 'just by chance.' Alcock (1981) presents a useful summary of factors that can bias judgment; they can, of course, also be applied to the biased critic who refuses to acknowledge any evidence for psychic functioning.

As in the previous section, experimental research relies upon proper statistical analysis and rules of statistical inference to avoid these problems, as discussed later in the book.

5 The relationship between psychic and target for PK

5.1 Psychics can emit information capable of influencing targets in more ways than we generally realize

In addition to the physiological and behavioral information that we emit into our environments, there are additional outputs we generate that can have influence upon aspects of our environments. All living tissue seems capable of producing weak magnetic fields (e.g. Cohen, 1975) as well as electromagnetic radiation and electrostatic fields (e.g. Presman, 1970). These outputs are weak, decay rapidly with distance, and are generally masked by background noise. Their strength can vary with small changes in tissue, including in some cases changes in mental activity. Brenner, Williamson and Kaufman (1975) found that visual stimulation in humans could produce changes in the brain's magnetic field. Perhaps the most common of such effects involves the movements we can induce in small, light objects by building up static electric charges on ourselves.

Heat from our bodies can affect objects both directly and indirectly. An example of a direct effect involves starting stopped watches. Some watches will cease functioning when lubricants congeal in the workings. Holding the watch in your hand while psychically trying to start it may melt the lubricants and start the watch. Indirect heat effects can be produced by convection currents around the body, since warm air rises. Holding your hands around an open cylinder causes warm air to rise out of the cylinder, thus inducing small movements in any materials above that are light enough to be sensitive to breeze. We also create breeze effects as we walk, move parts of our bodies, move air in and out of our mouths and noses, and so on. These effects are not major, but they can produce small movements in our immediate vicinities and they can affect sensitive physical measuring instruments placed near us.

5.2 Target objects can be influenced in more ways than we realize

As noted above, some stopped watches can be started by melting congealed lubricants. Others can be started, at least temporarily, simply by shaking them; if shaking jars loose a small piece of dirt that had jammed the workings, the watch may run for quite some time. In general, there are so many physical ways that target systems can be influenced that it would not be feasible to attempt to organize and list them here. If we are to interpret anomalous physical effects as evidence of psychic functioning, e.g. if we are to link them to the mental activities of potential psychics, then we must bring to bear a full knowledge of the laws of physics and how they may apply to the target system in question. In experimental research, this means working with a target system whose properties are well understood.

5.3 Barriers can be skirted in advance

5.3.1 The target and/or factors affecting it are influenced in advance

Probably the most prevalent strategy for faking psychokinetic powers is to prepare a target in advance in some nonobvious way. Once the barriers are up, e.g. the psychic's abilities to interact with the target appear to be sufficiently constrained, advance preparation allows the target to behave in ways that seem to be under the direct mental control of the psychic.

Some impressive physical effects involve objects, including written messages, that appear to have been materialized out of thin air, or to have been suddenly transported from one location to another. This can be done in several different ways. One strategy involves concealing the target object in its new location in advance, then suddenly revealing it. In a slate writing effect, for example, a psychic prepares a blank slate in advance by writing a message on it with an odorless, invisible chemical. Later this slate is given to an observer/researcher for inspection. The observer then seals the slate in a packet and places it on a table. Unknown to the observer, the table has a hidden source of heat in it. The psychic turns on the heat source just long enough to produce a chemical reaction that turns the chemical message a chalky white. By the time the observer opens the packet and examines the slate, it has cooled again and seems to the observer to be exactly as it was before, save for the mysterious message in chalk.

The specific means of revelation to the observer depends in part upon the means of concealment. Basically, a covering is removed or the optical properties of the object in its environment are changed, and the change goes unnoticed by the observer. The most frequent means of concealing an uncovering is through temporary physical shielding. For instance, the psychic passes between the observer and the concealed object or passes something else temporarily between observer and object; while the observer's view is blocked, the covering is removed from the concealed object. A second method is to uncover the object with great speed, generally while distracting the observer.

If the above strategy is inconvenient, the target can be concealed close to its place of appearance, then brought to its place through means undetected by the observer. Two major ways of doing this are: by rapidly snapping the target into place via an invisible thread or similar device; or by conveying the target into place concealed in something else.

In a third general strategy for materialization, the target object is concealed near the receiver system and remains in its location; through optical or acoustic devices, it is made to appear to be within the system. Many darkened seance-room apparitions are accomplished through use of a light source behind a transparency such as a slide, all concealed in a small box. The transparency is projected upon artifically created smoke or mist. By varying the density of smoke or mist, the image can be made to fade or grow stronger. Many outstanding stage appearances or vanishes have been accomplished by mirrors onstage which reflect the presence of an object that in truth is offstage, out of view of the audience. By changing the incidence of light upon the offstage object or on one side of the mirror or the other, the object can be made to appear or disappear, rapidly or gradually as desired. A pane of glass lit from one side but not the other acts as a mirror. A pane lit equally from both sides essentially reflects nothing. A pane of glass silvered at the back is a standard mirror of the sort we are all familiar with. By grading the silvering of a mirror along its length, one can manipulate the mirror to produce some very effective gradual appearances and vanishes.

Objects can be made to vanish by reversing the processes described above; if desired they can be made to reappear elsewhere, through means described above, or through the use of duplicates. The reader may respond that such means would clearly be obvious to the unaided eye; yet when done properly, they are not at all obvious. Such deception is part of an art that has developed over the centuries and, with proper handling of the observer, may go undetected even by colleagues in the magic arts who know roughly what to expect. If a change in optical conditions is necessary, such as a change in level or direction of illumination that will negate some form of camouflage, this can be accomplished by providing a sudden distraction for the audience timed to synchronize with the optical change.

Other effects are less dramatic than materializations, and involve anomalies in the behavior of target obects. For such effects, the object may be modified in advance, in a way unknown to the observer, and the modification concealed until the proper time. In some metal bending performances, the psychic gets access in advance to the materials to be bent, then pre-bends them back and forth to create many tiny fractures in the metal. The object, such as a piece of cutlery, is then straightened and replaced. Later on, an observer is forced by the psychic to select the pre-bent item. After some 'psychic' rubbing or stroking, the metal bends and, if gently but firmly worked, will even snap in two. When held at one end and wiggled, it will become pliant at the bend and may break off. James Randi has demonstrated this effect publicly on many occasions. In many analogous situations, the psychic or a confederate gains access to the materials in advance and manipulates them in some way such as to make them amenable to minor physical influences later on.

5.3.2 The psychic's intentions are influenced by knowledge of factors affecting the target

As noted earlier, we are good at detecting patterns in our environments and at learning rules for how things work. Such knowledge may enable us to anticipate how targets will behave, such that we can develop our intentions accordingly. For instance, someone familiar with weather patterns or stock market behavior can study the situation, then announce that they are going to 'make' the next week be rainy, or bullish, and so on. If I know that a certain friend always looks in a mirror whenever he passes by it, I can announce to you that I am going to 'make' my friend look in a mirror the next time we are together in his presence. In similar fashion, if I want to persuade you that you are psychic, I can point to my friend (whom you may not know at all) and suggest that you try your psychic skills by seeing if you can 'make that person over there look in the mirror when he walks by it.'

In general, we should not employ any target system whose characteristics are easy to infer, to avoid the problems just noted. Earlier we discussed strategies for inferring the target nature in advance as a means for simulating ESP. We have now seen how the same strategies can be used to simulate PK.

5.4 Problems with the barrier itself

5.4.1 A good barrier can often be circumvented by special means

As with ESP, many techniques for simulating PK involve special devices or procedures that at least temporarily render a good barrier useless. Influence is actually taking place at the time the psychic claims it is, but via normal means, often facilitated by advance preparation of the target. Movement in a remote object can be induced by magnets, both naturally magnetic objects and objects that have had a small magnet placed inside them in advance. Invisible threads, generally clear or black, can be attached to an object by a small wad of gum such that when snapped quickly the thread and gum will come loose, leaving the object free to be inspected. A thread looped between the two thumbs can be used with the hands placed on opposite sides of a small target to enable that target to seem to be psychically pushed forward or back. In today's high technology world, a variety of small electronic devices can be bought or constructed to induce remote physical action in ways that seem completely mysterious.

5.4.2 Barriers can be deceptively weak

Often barriers of distance or physical coverage are not as effective as they may seem. We have already noted how the body can be used to produce air currents over fairly short distances. Likewise heat-related effects can transcend physical shields that would seem to be good covers.

5.4.3 Some barriers in fact are not present at all

Various procedures for producing psychokinetic effects employ strategies that eliminate even needing to cross the barrier. Functionally, no barrier is really there. In one strategy, the target object is removed secretly from its location, modified, and then returned with its modification revealed to the observer at the appropriate time.

Consider the following key bending procedure. The observer provides the psychic with a housekey. The psychic presses the key into the palm of the observer, then closes the observer's fingers over the key, concealing it. After some 'psychic thoughts,' the psychic opens the observer's hand and reveals the bent key. This effect can be accomplished as follows. When the psychic presses the key into the observer's hand, he either substitutes another key via sleight of hand, or else simply removes the target key by sleight, relying upon the sensations produced by pressure to persuade the observer that the key is still in place. While all attend to the observer's hand, the psychic bends the key, perhaps inserting it into a gap between two well-anchored, solid objects and applying enough leverage to produce a bend. When the psychic reopens the observer's hand, a resubstitution by sleight takes place. There are many variants on this strategy; in each case the target object is removed from the observer's view for a brief period prior to or during the apparent psychic influence.

In adhesion and levitation effects, gravity seems to be suspended at the will of the psychic. In adhesion effects, an object is seen to stick or adhere to the surface of another object, without any observable explanation. Adhesion can be produced by a variety of physical means, including glues, resins, physical attachers such as hooks or velcro, devices that utilize atmospheric pressure such as suction cups, and electromagnetic effects such as the use of small magnets concealed in the target object and/or surface to which the object adheres.

Such devices can also be used to simulate levitation, if used to cause adherence to an invisible support of some sort. A support used with adhesives can be quite simple in structure: a single thread or rod will do. If such a support system is used without adhesives or mechanical attachments, the support structure must be able to balance and control the object supported by itself. Some support frames are rigid, can be locked into place, and can be mechanically manipulated by a power source out of the observer's view. The frame itself must also not be apparent to the observer. Concealment of the frame can be accomplished either by covering it or by camouflage.

5.4.4 Summary

The last two sections, on barrier problems and skirting barriers in advance, have described a variety of strategies for simulating PK, drawn largely from the literature of stage magic effects. This literature is extensive; the present overview has been very superficial, deliberately avoiding detailed description of the mechanics of the tricks by which professionals amuse and amaze us. In general, a physical manipulation is concealed from the observer by a psychological manipulation. In the final section of the chapter, we will cover the logic of the deception of observers in more detail. For a good discussion of the basic organization of the physical effects and their accomplishment, see Fitzkee (1944).

As far as the researcher is concerned, it is hard to rule out magicians' tricks in uncontrolled environments. Even in the laboratory environment, one must be careful when investigating claims of unusual psychokinetic abilities, relying on target systems that by their nature can be safeguarded from manipulation in advance or direct influence by hidden means.

5.5. Problems in the measurement and recording stage

As considered above for ESP evidence, various problems arise for PK evidence in the measurement and recording stage. These problems are quite analogous to those for ESP. Since we have already discussed factors affecting bias in measuring, recording, comparing and interpreting similarities between psychic's experience and target nature, this discussion will not be repeated. Instead we will present examples illustrating the application of these concepts to PK evidence.

5.5.1 Measurement and recording of the target event is influenced by measurement/recording of the psychic's intentions

Once we know what the psychic's intentions are, we may selectively look for target events that match these intentions and ignore information that does not support it. For instance, if I announce that I have been meditating in a certain city in order to increase the well-being of all inhabitants of that city, then all observers can sift through the various kinds of data about the city to pick out those that most clearly support my claim. Observers in this case can be myself, researchers, close followers, the media, city officials, and so on.

This bias can also occur with regard to individual lives. If I announce that I am putting a curse on you, then two things may happen. First, you may act in such a way as to bring about negative events in your life (analogous to self-fulfilling prophecy). Second, once I have announced my curse, you and others will be on the lookout for negative events, worrying about them and emphasizing them while ignoring positive events. Neutral events may be reinterpreted as negative events. A particularly nasty hoax can be perpetrated by a curser and a savior, working as a team. The curser curses you in your presence. After a day or so, the savior approaches you, announces that you appear to have problems, and offers to rid you of them for a fee.

In general, there is much similarity between the problems that occur when: (a) a psychic announces a prediction about a future event, and (b) a psychic announces an intention to influence that future event.

5.5.2 Measurement/recording of a psychic's intent is influenced by measurement/recording of a target event

Once we know what events are going on in the environment, we are free to decide that the psychic indeed intended for those events to happen. If I wish to persuade observers that my meditation causes the quality of life to improve in a city, I may either go to a particular city and not announce myself until things are going very well; or I may select a city where I have good reason to believe that things are going well now or are likely to start going well in the near future. If someone dies, I can then announce that I recently put a curse on that person.

A variant on the above is that a third party wishing to persuade you that you are psychic may arrange to bias both your assessment of your intentions and your (or others') assessment of related events in the environment.

As is the case for ESP, the above problems can be avoided by adequate research procedures, including specification in advance of the psychic's intentions and a target system whose determinants are well understood and not amenable to biased external influence, with outcomes that are objectively measurable.

These issues are identical to those raised in section 5.3.2, except that now we are dealing with measurement and recording of the psychic's intentions rather than initial determination of those intentions.

5.6 Problems in comparing records and evaluating them

The set of problems and solutions that exist here for PK evidence are conceptually the same as those that exist for ESP evidence.

6 Strategies for controlling the information processed by the observer

In this section we consider the strategies that a fraudulent psychic can use to control the information that reaches the observer about the interaction between psychic and target. Although we are specifically considering deliberate control, it should be noted that these strategies can also describe naturally occurring processes, by which we can be misled without any conscious intention to deceive. Five separate levels of control are involved.

6.1 The observer may be given inaccurate information

The first level of control employed is control over the physical information that arrives to be sensed by the observer. An effective psychic limits the physical information coming to the observer, allowing through only the information that tells the observer what the psychic wants, and screening out information that tells too much. Where convenient, the psychic arranges for deceptive physical signals to be sent to the observer, signals which, when processed accurately by the observer's peripheral and central nervous system, will produce a false impression. The use of mirrors, other optical devices, echoic acoustical devices and so on, are examples.

6.2 The observer may be led to misperceive the information

We have learned through the study of the laws of sensation and perception that our mechanisms for processing information can deceive us. The physical signals arriving at our sense receptors adequately represent the external world but our peripheral and central nervous systems will themselves distort the information. Three kinds of examples will illustrate.

6.2.1 Camouflage, or 'black art'

In camouflage, a figure is made to resemble its background such that our senses no longer detect the boundaries or substance of the figure and we thus do not know that a figure is present. Some camouflage techniques rely upon the use of complex patterns on figure and ground, such that our senses follow the lines of the patterns more than the lines that mark the boundaries of an object. Other camouflage techniques, known often as 'black art', employ figure and ground covered with material that absorbs light and emits so little light that the eye has almost no information to work with. Black or very dark purple colors on nonreflective materials such as velvets and velours are very good for this. Many fake mediumistic performances involve assistants dressed totally in black who manipulate trumpets and other objects undetected in a darkened seance room. Many stage acts involve similar performances against a very dark backdrop. Although camouflage generally involves a figure vs. a ground, it can also involve concealing any boundaries indicating where one object stops and another begins, as well as holes, openings of various sorts, and so on. Camouflage can occur in other sense modalities besides vision, of course.

6.2.2 Inadequate information from a key event itself

Camouflage involves inadequate information about an object/event in relation to its background. Yet the important object/event itself may emit too little information, regardless of the background. Examples include black or clear threads, so thin and nonreflective as to be invisible; objects moving too rapidly to be seen by the eye; and the simple strategy of lighting a room dimly.

6.2.3 Sensory overload

A burst of very strong sensory stimulation can greatly reduce the effectiveness of processing what happened just before or just after the stimulation. A light glaring in one's eyes, even briefly, can prevent the visual system from efficient information processing. In some vanishing acts, it is necessary to shift the direction of illumination from in front of a one-way mirror to behind it. This can be accomplished without the audience noticing that one bank of lights has just been turned off and another turned on. One way is for the psychic to fire a blank cartridge from a gun at just the moment the change takes place, perhaps using an acoustically activated light control. The audience is so busy being startled, first by the gun's sudden appearance and then by its noise, that it doesn't notice the dramatic change in lighting. And finally, of course, the audience is stunned to see that the elephant has just disappeared. Christopher (1970) describes such a procedure in full, which mystified thousands over many performances.

6.2.4 Advantageous use of the laws of perceptual organization

As we grow, we build up an organized picture of the way the world tends to work. This organization entails learning to make various generalizations/assumptions about what causes what, how things tend to be shaped, and so on. Such assumptions can readily be exploited by the psychic. Familiar objects such as top hats, canes, and so on, tend to be used as props because we have many assumptions about how they work. If we are shown a container that is quite unfamiliar to us in general shape and structure, we will make few assumptions about what compartments it has, how heavy it is, what's inside, whether it is solid, etc. Thus we are more likely to suspect tricks with it, even if we cannot specify exactly how they were done.

More generally, we tend perceptually to group things according to similarities. We assume regular laws of motion, we assume that what happened once will recur, and we assume things come in organized wholes. We tend to experience what we expect to experience, as shaped by the laws of perception. We may see the blade of a sword protruding from one side of a box and the handle protruding from the other end; if when the psychic pushes in on the handle the blade moves out at the same rate, we assume that there is a single sword sticking through the basket. But the sword blade inserted into the basket may have collapsed into the handle, and a person in the basket, well rehearsed, may have pushed a second blade out the other side. A psychic gestures to toss a coin with one hand and catch it with the other. An observer will assume that the coin was indeed tossed; yet it may merely have been palmed by the first hand, with the second hand remaining empty.

6.3 The observer's attention may be diverted

The psychic sometimes cannot avoid some information getting through to the observer that would reveal too much. Thus it becomes necessary to divert the observer's attention elsewhere. Or, the psychic may need to guarantee that the observer is building up the picture of the trick that is desired. Such techniques are well understood by practicing magicians; the discussions in the present and following section draw heavily from Nelms (1969).

As Nelms sees it, each step in an act is conveyed to an observer by a source of information. These sources can be actions or words. They make points to the observer and are ideally interpreted by the observer as the psychic wishes. The center of interest (C of I) is what the audience wants to watch; the source of information (S of I) is what the psychic wants the audience to watch. The psychic must make sure that the C of I and the S of I coincide. This can be done either by making the S of I inherently interesting, such as the body of an attractive assistant or a very unusual and interesting object; or, it can be done by inducing interest in the S of I.

There are various tactics for focusing attention. (1) Pointing. An observer looks where you are pointing. One can point with finger, hand, elbow, nose, other 'pointed' body parts or articles of clothing, direction of gaze, direction and content of voice, and so on. (2) Contrasts. An object containing sharp contrasts or which contrasts strongly with its background will be attended to. (3) Movement. Observers pay attention to movements, even small ones. (4) Variety. Observers become bored with anything that stays the same. Thus the S of I should be undergoing change, while places that the psychic doesn't want the observer to experience should stay the same. (5) Casualness. If the psychic treats something casually, he implies that it is unimportant and the observer is less likely to attend to it. (6) Diversion of attention to something apparently outside the routine. If a major distraction is needed, an assistant can seem to be about to spill water, for instance. Yet distractions away from the S of I should be avoided. An assistant striking a sensuous pose during a crucial part of the act may cause observers to miss a crucial point that the psychic wishes to make. In general, Nelms advises the performer to be fixing the observers' attention at all times, so that they do not miss any important points, and so that the observers' attention continues to be easy to direct.

Attention can be redirected in time as well as space. One may lead the observer to anticipate that a crucial action will be done at a later time, then perform the action in advance before the observer is paying attention properly. Conversely, one may pretend to do a crucial action at one moment, so that the audience will relax its vigilance; the action can later take place unnoticed.

6.4 The observer may be led to misinterpret the information perceived

Often the psychic cannot really divert the observer's attention effectively. Thus the psychic may need to create a false frame of reference for the observer, so that what is experienced is placed in a misleading context. Nelms refers to this as mental misdirection. He suggests various tactics, as outlined in sections 6.4.1 to 6.4.4.

6.4.1 Provide erroneous explanations and motivations for the nature and purpose of your act

This will help break up the observer's logic and lead him to misunderstand key factors. He thinks you are trying to do one thing but in fact you have a different goal or effect in mind. For instance, a muscle reader may describe himself as having a psychotronic target detector, a hand-held empty black box which is 'powered' by contact with another person. This provides a false frame of reference for the muscle reader's need to touch the observer's body. All such touches are now placed in a totally different context and can be observed quite directly without their true function being revealed.

6.4.2 Change familiar props or procedures frequently
Thus a repeat observer will not be able to construct a consistent picture of what is going on. Similarly, routine actions should be carried out in unconventional ways, e.g. with an extra flourish here and there. This makes them temporarily mildly baffling to the observer who must then put extra effort into interpreting exactly what he just saw.

6.4.3 Introduce devices or elements in the routine at illogical moments
This also breaks up the observer's ability to create a well-organized picture of what is going on and how to interpret what he sees.

6.4.4 Confuse the natural sequence of events and have alternate modes of procedure
Thus the observer does not know what will happen next. For example, consider 'Annemann's Force,' as described by Nelms. The observer is presented with three containers, A, B and C. The psychic wishes to force the selection of B and does so by asking the observer to choose two. If he chooses A and C, then his attention is called to B, the remaining one, which he is now told he has 'chosen.' If the observer chooses B plus either A or C, he is asked to hand one of them to the psychic. If he hands over B, he is told that this is his choice. No matter what he does, the observer is shown that he has chosen B. It works because the observer has no adequate frame of reference for interpreting what is happening when it happens. He has not been told about the timing and procedural rules of the game. As a result, the observer's attention is not under his own control, e.g. he has no firm expectation of where to attend to next and thus is less likely to spot some information that would only be noticed with concerted attention. Also, this strategy allows the act to continue if things don't go well the first time (see discussion of 'outs' earlier).

6.5 The observer may be led to misremember the information perceived

The psychic's last line of defense, so to speak, is to induce a misremembering of what has previously happened. One strategy is simply to insert a very strong stimulus into a routine just after something has happened that the psychic does not want the observer to remember. The observer's attention will be bound up in the new event and the old one will not get properly consolidated. Another strategy is to provide later information which strongly conflicts with the earlier perceptions. This can take place within the act, e.g. the observer saw the ball enter container A but later is shown that the ball is in container B. Or it can come after the encounter with the psychic, if other witnesses present a conflicting account to the observer or if the psychic in a skilled way later gently but firmly insists that things happened differently. The observer may later even be shown something such as a doctored photograph 'proving' how things really happened. A related strategy, assuming the psychic has continued access to the observer, is to suggest a different context for the event after the fact to the observer, to lead the observer to reinterpret his memories in line with the psychic's wishes. Often this happens when the psychic has failed in some way and the observer is starting to raise questions. It can involve changing the description of a session from being a true test to being purely informal and exploratory, and thus not to be counted in evaluation. Or it could be as specific as suggesting that a room was too dark for the observer to see anything and that the dark humanlike figures that seemed to be blowing through the trumpets at the seance table must have been only the observer's imagination. Likewise, a confident, skilled psychic may talk observers into remembering things that never happened, e.g. suggesting that a specific event had been predicted at an earlier meeting when in fact no such prediction had been given at that meeting.

Thus each of the psychological strategies aims at a slightly different level of information organization and processing in the observer, with each successive level serving as a device to deal with situations that cannot be handled adequately at earlier levels.

7 Conclusion

As we have seen, there is endless variety to the strategies for being misled about the presence of psychic skill in ourselves and others. Unfortunately, parapsychological research must take into account such strategies, as they have been employed in the past to fool researchers as well as laypeople. Guidelines are needed both for detecting deception and for eliminating it. The chapters in this book on research methodology detail the attempts made by researchers themselves to minimize the likelihood of being misled, deliberately or unintentionally, while still maintaining the psychological comfort of the research participant. It is not easy.

Thought questions

The first four questions pose general situations which may arise. Feel free to make the situation more specific in ways that interest you.

(1) A person you have apparently never met before walks up to you and starts telling you about yourself. Name as many sources of information available to that person as you can.

(2) A friend claims to be able to make political predictions. Design a fair test of your friend's claim that rules out alternatives.

(3) A dear friend has just returned from undergoing psychic surgery

for lung cancer, claims to feel great, and wants to avoid further medical expense. How would you respond, and why?

(4) You are in charge of a consumer protection task force assigned to investigate an organization that claims to teach anyone psychic powers in two weeks. How would you proceed?

(5) Has your overall impression of the validity of psychic claims been affected by this chapter? Why?

Chapter 5
Experimental methods in ESP research
John Palmer

1 Introduction

The purpose of this chapter is to introduce you to the wide variety of methods parapsychologists have developed over the years for testing ESP in controlled laboratory situations and to serve as an introductory guide to those of you who may wish to attempt such tests yourselves. For an additional discussion of contemporary methods, see Morris (1978).

In order to choose intelligently which method to use in a particular experiment, it is first necessary to specify as clearly as possible the objectives of your research. Then you must determine what characteristics your test must have to meet these objectives and, finally, which available procedure includes the greatest number of these characteristics.

Alternatively, you may choose to develop a technique of your own which embodies these characteristics better than ones already in existence. This chapter will assist you in these latter steps, but choosing a good research objective depends on your own insight, common sense and knowledge of previous research. Good research always begins with asking the right question.

2 Illustration: a card guessing test

2.1 Basic procedure

Although many of the basic principles of ESP testing have been alluded to in the preceding chapters, a systematic review of them at this point will help to set the stage for some of the more complicated considerations to follow. A simple example which illustrates many of these basic principles is card guessing. A good way to get a feel for them is to conduct such a test yourself with a friend. Take a deck of ordinary playing cards and shuffle it thoroughly. Place the deck face down on the table and cut it once. Every five seconds (or some other agreed upon time interval) tap on the table, pick up the top card, and look at its face while attempting to 'send' the identity of its suit to your friend. Then place it face down on the table, beginning a second pile.

Your friend should be seated at a location where he or she can't see you, preferably in another room. Every time your friend hears you tap, he or she should try to get an image or impression of the card you are sending and then record on a sheet of paper which suit he or she thinks it is. This procedure should be repeated for each of the 52 cards in the deck.

After the test is completed, record the order of the cards from the second pile and match up this record with the list of responses made by your friend. Count up the number of times your friend's response was correct. This total is your friend's score on the ESP test.

Each of the 52 episodes in which you looked at a card and your friend responded constitutes a trial. Each correct response is called a hit. Thus your friend's score is the total number of hits. Your friend is the percipient or, more generally, the subject. You are identified as the agent, because you were trying to send the target to the percipient. You were also the experimenter, because you were in charge of conducting the test.

2.2 Measurement of ESP

An important principle of scientific research is measurement. Measurement implies quantification, which means that we want to express ESP as a number on some kind of scale. In our card test, the measure of ESP is your friend's score. Theoretically, this score could range from 0 to 52. We would like to be able to say that this score is a true measure of the amount of ESP your friend demonstrated in the test. Unfortunately, the situation is not quite so simple.

2.2.1 The need for statistics

As you no doubt have already realized, your friend is likely to get a certain number of hits just by chance. This expected number of chance hits is called mean chance expectation or MCE*. It can be defined mathematically as the number of trials divided by the number of target alternatives, which in this case is four; i.e. the four suits. Thus MCE is 52/4, or 13. Now if we knew that every time subjects took our ESP test they would get exactly 13 chance hits, we could easily compute their 'real' ESP scores by subtracting 13 from their total number of hits in the run. However, MCE is only the average (or mean) number of hits subjects will obtain by chance if we give them a very large number of such tests. On any given run, a subject may get slightly more or slightly fewer than 13 chance hits. An estimate of how much, on the average, the number of chance hits is likely to deviate from MCE is reflected in the term *standard deviation*.

So how do we know whether the number of hits a subject obtains is enough greater than 13 to allow us to say that any of the hits can be attributed to ESP? If the subject gets a very high score, say 40 hits, it would be obvious that at least some of the hits were ESP hits. However, in current ESP research the score will almost certainly be much lower than that. Thus we must use statistics to tell us whether a score is high enough to reflect ESP. More precisely, statistics tell us the likelihood or probability that a score as high as we obtained could occur by chance. Following a somewhat arbitrary convention adopted by psychologists, we reject the chance or null hypothesis if the probability of your friend's score being as far away from MCE as it was is less than one in 20, or .05. This is often expressed as $p < .05$. If the probability is much lower than .05, it is customary to express the 'p-value' as reflecting this lower level; e.g. $p < .01$. In our card test, if your friend scored 20 hits or more, we would conclude (based on appropriate statistical analysis) that he or she obtained a significant* score and had demonstrated ESP. This is because a score that high will occur less than one in 20 times by chance. If your friend obtained only 18 hits, we would conclude that the 'extra' five hits were due to chance or 'good luck.'

It of course is possible to get fewer than 13 hits. This will occur by chance a little less than half the time, but if the score is low enough (in our test, six or less) we would attribute it to ESP operating in a negative direction, somehow causing the subject to consistently avoid the target. This form of ESP, called psi-missing, occurs rather frequently.

If we were able to predict in advance the direction of scoring, we would be entitled to apply a so-called one-tailed statistical test*, which would allow us to divide the normal two-tailed p-value by two. Ideally, one should only use a one-tailed test when one is willing to ignore a significant outcome in the 'wrong' direction, but there is some disagreement among parapsychologists (and statisticians) about how strictly this rule should be applied.

2.3 Eliminating alternative interpretations

Actually, it would be a bit premature to conclude that a score of 20 or higher (or six or lower) on our card test means that your friend necessarily demonstrated ESP. Strictly speaking, a statistically significant score only tells us that the score probably cannot be entirely attributed to chance. We must be able to rule out other reasonable alternate interpretations of the extra-chance scoring before concluding with confidence that ESP has been demonstrated.

2.3.1 Sensory cues

The most common alternate interpretation of ESP results is sensory cues*. We must be sure that subjects have no sensory contacts with the targets, or with persons having knowledge of the targets, prior to making their responses. Elimination of sensory cues is primarily common sense, but that is not to say that such cues are always apparent. In our card test, for example, it is obviously important that your friend not be allowed to see the faces of the cards while you are looking at them. But it is also important that your friend not even be allowed to look at the backs of the cards: what if one of the cards had a slightly bent corner and your friend knew from examining the deck beforehand that it was the jack of clubs? One 'hit' due to sensory cues!

It is also important that subjects be sensorially shielded from the agent or experimenter during the test if the latter knows the target order. Visual shielding is not always adequate. In our card test, you could unwittingly transmit sensory cues through differences in the loudness or form of your taps. For example, you might unconsciously tap louder if the target is a club, and your friend might unconsciously pick up on this difference and associate the louder tapping with clubbing, thus being more likely to respond with 'club' on such trials. Such hypotheses might sound far-fetched but, as was noted in chapter 4, people can be quite sensitive to subtle environmental stimuli. In a rigorous ESP test, the tapping would be done either by a third person unaware of (or 'blind*' to) the target sequence, or by the subject signaling the agent when to look at the next target. The latter alternative has the advantage of allowing subjects to proceed at their own preferred pace.

2.3.2 Nonrandom target sequences

It is also important for the target sequence to be unpredictable, or as random* as possible. This is particularly crucial if the test is designed such that the subject is informed after each trial what the target for that trial was. If this modification were to be introduced into our card test and the target sequence had some nonrandom feature (e.g. no suit ever turning up twice in a row), your friend might use this information to help improve his or her score. In other words, as soon as your friend caught on, he or she would avoid calling the same suit twice in a row. This would effectively increase the probability of a hit on each trial but the first from one-fourth to one-third.

Although logical inference is not usually a serious problem in tests without such trial-by-trial feedback, a related problem can occur if a bias in the target sequence happens to match a bias in the sequence of the subject's responses. For example, if our card sequence had an excess of hearts at the beginning of the deck and your friend called a large number of hearts early in the run and then tried to compensate by calling few hearts toward the end of the run, an artifactual (i.e. illegitimate) excess of hits could result simply by a matching of the corresponding biases in the target and response sequences.

Randomness and techniques for assuring randomness will be discussed further in section 2 of the next chapter.

2.3.3 Summary and conclusions

In summary, if (1) our ESP score were statistically significant, and (2) we could rule out with reasonable certainty alternate interpretations based upon sensory cues and nonrandom target sequences, we would be entitled to conclude that ESP had been demonstrated in our card test. But what does this mean? Although the term 'ESP' suggests that some form of perception or at least acquisition of information has taken place, we really don't know this for a fact. All we know is that your friend was somehow relatively successful in duplicating the target sequence by some unknown means. We have discovered what scientists call an anomaly, and ESP is nothing more than a label we apply to our ignorance of this anomaly. Much of the challenge of modern psi research is trying to discover what the anomaly means. But at the same time it is important to recognize how little we have learned by simply demonstrating that ESP has occurred.

2.4 Some basic distinctions and choices

A researcher confronted with the task of designing an ESP test faces a number of choices. In section 3, these choices will be outlined in a more or less chronological order. However, there are several major choices germane to our card guessing example that it is appropriate to introduce at this point.

2.4.1 Modes of target presentation

2.4.1a Telepathy, clairvoyance and precognition

In chapter 1, we drew the distinction between telepathy, clairvoyance and precognition as subcategories of ESP. Telepathy and clairvoyance distinguish the apparent source of the information, whereas precognition refers to its locus in time. These are philosophical or, more precisely, metaphysical distinctions which derive from the often implicit assumption parapsychologists have traditionally made that ESP is a quasi-perceptual process. In practice, it is impossible to isolate fully these subspecies of ESP. In our card test, your friend could get information either from your mind (telepathy) or from the card (clairvoyance). In either case, your friend could access the information as it existed at the time of the response or as it would exist at some future time (precognition).

Parapsychologists have occasionally attempted tests of 'pure' telepathy or clairvoyance (e.g. McMahan, 1946; Schmeidler, 1964). Strictly speaking, pure telepathy* is impossible to demonstrate, because there must be some objective record of the target sequence (even if it is coded) for purposes of scoring. Telepathy is also impossible to isolate for another reason if we assume that any mental image is represented by some state of the agent's brain. Apprehension of the latter is considered clairvoyance; telepathy thus literally assumes the existence of mind as distinct from brain.

Pure clairvoyance*, on the other hand, can be isolated from telepathy if the targets are generated and scored by a machine, such as a computer, which destroys the target sequence after the test has been scored and before anyone has seen it. Precognition can be isolated from contemporaneous ESP if the target sequence does not exist and cannot be inferred from information available at the time the subject makes the response, but it is not possible to rule out the subject using PK to create a future target matching the response. The subject could use PK in the same way to succeed in a clairvoyance test.

Because of these problems, it has become increasingly common for parapsychologists to define the types of ESP operationally rather than metaphysically. If a test involves an agent sensorially observing a target and trying to send it to a percipient, we call it telepathy or, more precisely, general extrasensory perception (GESP). Thus our card test was a telepathy or GESP test. If no one is trying to send the targets to the subject, we call it clairvoyance. If in either case the target is not generated until after the subject makes the response, we call it precognition.

There is no clear evidence that subjects score better on one kind of test than the other, so the choice often depends on the personal taste of the researcher. Precognition tests have the advantage of eliminating sensory cues, since the target does not exist at the time of the response. Telepathy tests are the most difficult to control against sensory cues because of the need to prevent sensory contact with the agent. On the other hand, telepathy is more likely than precognition to seem plausible to research subjects.

*2.4.1b Trial-by-trial feedback**

Another choice faced by the researcher, a choice alluded to previously, is whether or not to inform the subject after each trial that the response was a hit or a miss and/or the correct identity of the target. Such feedback might be useful if the objective is to train ESP 'ability.' Some parapsychologists suggest that such feedback heightens subjects' motivation and interest in the task (Tart, 1966) while others contend that it is likely to be distracting, frustrating, or anxiety-arousing (J. E. Kennedy, 1980b; Sondow, 1979). There is some evidence that scoring rates are less likely to decline over time when feedback is used (Tart, 1976), but you should feel free to use whichever approach seems useful for your particular situation. The evidence that feedback enhances ESP scoring will be critically examined in chapter 8, section 5.

2.4.2 Modes of response: restricted-choice and free-response

In our card test, your friend was required to choose from among the four suits of a standard deck of playing cards. Testing procedures in which the subject's responses are limited to a fixed set of alternatives are called restricted-choice tests or forced-choice tests. However, parapsychologists are turning increasingly to another kind of procedure in which the subject is allowed to report any impression that comes to mind. These free-response tests commonly employ more complex targets than playing cards to capitalize on the richness of the subject's impressions. For example, the target might be a picture of a horse race and the subject asked to report anything and everything that comes to mind. To score free-response tests, judges are asked to match or to otherwise assess the correspondences between a series of targets and responses. We will examine these procedures in more detail later in the chapter.

Free-response tests have several advantages. By allowing subjects to explore their minds freely, free-response tests capture the spontaneity characteristic of ESP as it usually occurs in real life. They are generally more appealing to subjects than restricted-choice tests, which tend to get tedious after a while. They are especially appropriate if you want to study complex mental imagery in relation to ESP.

On the other hand, restricted-choice tests are much easier to score and evaluate statistically than are free-response tests. Because a large number of trials can be accumulated over a short period of time in restricted-choice tests, they are ideal for comparing a subject's performance on two or more sets or types of trials, or for assessing changes in scoring rate over time. In free-response tests, it is customary to conduct only one trial per session.

2.4.3 Duration or length of test

In determining the length of a restricted-choice test (i.e. the number of trials), you must strike a balance between competing considerations. If the test is too long, the subject is apt to become fatigued and scores might decline. Such 'decline effects' have often been noted in ESP tests (Palmer, 1978b). On the other hand, enough trials must be accumulated to provide a relatively reliable measure of the subject's ESP. As a general rule in psychological testing, the longer the test the more reliably and accurately it measures the ability or trait tested. In ESP tests, this is especially true if the number of target alternatives is large, say ten or greater. (For example, 52 trials would be too short in our card test if your friend guessed the ranks of the cards instead of their suits.)

Parapsychologists have adopted no strict convention regarding the length of restricted-choice tests, but tests of between 50 and 100 trials per session are common, with a pause of a couple minutes between each 25–trial run. The important principle, though, is to give as long a test as possible without fatiguing the subject. But always be sure to set the number of trials in advance and stick to it. Otherwise an artifact due to optional stopping* may result; i.e. stopping the test at a point which just happens to coincide with a high chance score.

As mentioned earlier, free-response tests usually consist of one trial per session. They have been known to last anywhere from five to 45 minutes each. The principle here is to allow subjects enough time to fully develop their impressions of the target. Such impressions do not always pop up right away, so both the experimenter and the subject need to be patient.

3 Steps in an ESP test: decisions and tradeoffs

In the remainder of the chapter, we will consider in more detail and roughly in chronological order the steps a researcher must follow in designing and executing a good ESP test and the decisions he or she needs to make along the way.

3.1 Selecting the subjects

One of the first decisions a researcher must face after deciding upon the purpose and rationale of the experiment is which potential subject or group of subjects to test. There are several alternatives.

3.1.1 Psychics or 'gifted subjects'

The most obvious choice would seem to be to test someone who is 'psychic.' But this is a trickier business than it seems. A person who has had many psychic experiences may not necessarily be able to produce ESP on demand under laboratory conditions. Fortunately, there are a small number of people who seem to have at least some control over their ESP faculties, and some of them are willing to explore these apparent talents with scientists. Several are among the leading figures in psi research because of their success in controlled ESP tests.

However, working with psychics is not always an easy task. Psychics are often very sensitive people who have been ostracized by 'straight' society because of their 'gift'. As a result, the researcher may need a great deal of tact and interpersonal skill to do research with them effectively. Many psychics have strong feelings about the kinds of tests in which they are willing to engage, and the researcher must be able to accommodate these preferences while still maintaining rigid experimental controls.

On the other hand, some people who claim to be psychic are deluded or are charlatans out to exploit the field for fame and fortune. Such 'psychics' may seek credibility by 'triumphing' in scientific tests. Some may be hybrids: people with genuine psi abilities who supplement real ESP with pseudo-ESP when the situation requires it. As discussed in chapter 4, these charlatans employ standard magic or mentalist tricks to mimic ESP. Thus the parapsychologist should have some familiarity with these techniques and be willing to consult with skilled magicians or mentalists when appropriate. If a professed psychic is a stage performer or is known to have a magician's skills, particular caution is required. Results with such persons are likely to be suspect regardless of how well controlled the test appears to be. Such extreme skepticism may not always be logically justified, but it is a good reason to consider whether research with such subjects is worth the effort. Finally, some psychics, particularly those who earn a living at it, may be tempted to seek publicity that might misrepresent or exaggerate the outcome of the research, or otherwise embarrass the investigator or the field of parapsychology.

3.1.2 Special subject populations

An alternate approach for obtaining talented subjects is through mass screening. Tart (1976), for example, gave a short card guessing test to hundreds of students in classes at a large American university. Recognizing that a few would obtain significant scores by chance, he retested the 'successful' students on another restricted-choice test. Those students who continued to score significantly were then chosen for more extensive investigation.

Yet another approach is to work with subjects who may or may not appear to be psychic but who have other skills or attributes that would make them especially suitable for ESP research. Examples are persons who have engaged extensively in mental disciplines such as brainwave biofeedback training or meditation, or persons highly susceptible to hypnosis.

3.1.3 Unselected subjects

Although research with 'gifted' subjects captures most of the public attention, the bulk of the research in parapsychology is in fact conducted using ordinary folk – mostly high school and college students – who volunteer out of curiosity or interest in psi. This research strategy is predicated on the assumption made by most – but not all – parapsychologists that psi is an ability common to all of us and distributed in the population much like intelligence. Thus although few if any such persons are likely to be psychic enough to score significantly on their own, collectively the total or average of their scores may be high (or low) enough to achieve significance. Because of the large number of scores obtained in such group experiments, a lower total or average score is required for statistical significance than ordinarily is the case in research with a single subject. Working with unselected subjects requires patience, as the magnitude of the results is likely to be small and studies don't replicate as consistently as we would like. On the brighter side, unselected subjects are readily accessible, relatively easy and pleasant to work with, and the results we obtain with them can be generalized more readily to other people than can those obtained from more specialized populations.

3.1.4 Animals as subjects

A final option available to the researcher is to use animals as subjects. This choice assumes, of course, that animals are capable of manifesting psi. The evidence we have suggests that if psi exists, animals probably have it as well as humans (Morris, 1970). There is no intrinsic reason to choose one species over another, but most 'anpsi' research has been conducted with rodents and cats, largely for reasons of convenience.

The reasons for using animals in ESP research are similar to the reasons for using them in other behavioral science research. The most obvious reason is an interest in exploring ESP in a particular species. Second, a researcher may wish to examine the relationship between ESP and relatively simple motivational or cognitive factors without having to deal with the complexities of these characteristics in humans. Finally, certain studies involving drugs or noxious stimulation (e.g. electric shocks) might be prohibited with humans for ethical reasons, but not with animals. On the other hand, many people (including many scientists) consider such studies to be unethical even with animals unless substantial and tangible benefits from the research can be forseen. Parapsychologists tend to be a rather humane lot, so one finds very little research of this type in the parapsychological literature, although there are a few exceptions.

3.2 Selecting the target material

The choice of target material for ESP tests is limited only by the creativity of the researcher. Although the exercise of such creativity is often beneficial, the use of standardized targets has the important advantage of allowing greater comparability of results across experiments. In this section we will examine some of the various types of target material that have been used in ESP experiments.

3.2.1 Restricted-choice tests

3.2.1a Types of targets

In restricted-choice tests, the standard targets for many years consisted of a deck of 25 cards containing five of each of five symbols: circle, cross, waves, square, and star. J. B. Rhine (1934/1973) selected these symbols after consulting with a perceptual psychologist, because they were simple, easily discriminable and emotionally neutral. Discriminability, at least, is still considered an attribute of good restricted-choice targets, but they need not be dull. In one successful experiment, for example, the target cards were elaborately drawn African masks incorporating the ESP symbols (Rao, 1964). Most parapsychologists nowadays believe that the capacity to evoke emotional responses is a desirable characteristic of ESP targets.

A novel means of covertly introducing emotionality into ESP targets is to enclose neutral targets such as the standard ESP cards into individual opaque envelopes along with emotionally arousing pictures. In one such experiment, pornographic pictures were used for this purpose. Subjects were not told that these pictures were involved in the experiment at all; they simply were asked to guess the ESP symbol in each envelope (Carpenter, 1971).

It sometimes may be advantageous to use targets with multiple attributes, each of which can be scored independently. These are called multiple-aspect targets* (J. E. Kennedy, 1980a). An example is the deck of playing cards in our earlier example, where the independent attributes are suit and rank. The multiple-aspect nature of such targets can be capitalized upon by having subjects respond to each attribute on each trial. We can then compare the results on the different attributes and also assess whether subjects obtain more exact hits* than we would expect by chance given their rate of success on the component attributes.

Cards, however, have given way for the most part to machines, called random event generators (REGs)* or random number generators (RNGs), which automatically select a target for each trial and then record the targets, responses and hits (Schmidt, 1970c). In some of these machines, the targets are simply different colored light bulbs on the machine's face. More recently, researchers have either attached these machines to computers or substituted computers outright. Many small computers have graphics capabilities, including color graphics, which give the researcher tremendous flexibility in creating appealing target displays which can be shown on the computer's screen (Honorton and Tremmel, 1980). Commercial home video games can occasionally be adapted for ESP testing using the computer, thereby making the restricted-choice test even more involving for the subject.

Finally, ESP targets need not be visual. In one study, the targets were five musical selections recorded on tape (Keil, 1965), while in another the target on a given trial was whether or not the experimenter received an electric shock (Tart, 1963). In short, any discriminable stimulus is a potential ESP target.

3.2.1b Number of target alternatives

The number of target alternatives in a restricted-choice ESP test generally ranges from two to ten. A smaller number of alternatives are easier to keep track of and may be more reinforcing or encouraging to subjects because they provide a greater proportion of hits. They also may decrease the possibility of subjects confusing their impressions of one target symbol with those of another. Tests with a smaller number of alternatives are also easier to evaluate statistically if the number of trials is small, because the distribution of scores more readily approximates the normal curve*, a mathematically defined, bell-shaped distribution of numbers required for the application of many statistical tests.

A large number of alternatives have the advantage of reducing the proportion of chance hits relative to ESP hits. This is especially important in training projects where the subject receives feedback after each trial and is asked to try to discriminate which internal sensations or impressions are associated with correct as opposed to incorrect responses (Tart, 1976): chance hits in such a context provide the subject with false feedback that makes such discrimination difficult.

In practice, most researchers split the difference and use tests with four or five target alternatives.

3.2.2 Free-response tests

3.2.2a Types of targets

Free-response targets are generally richer and more complex than restricted-choice targets. Examples from past experiments include line drawings (e.g. Stuart, 1945), magazine photographs (e.g. Stanford and Palmer, 1975), postcard prints of famous paintings (e.g. Ullman *et al.*, 1973), View-Master slide reels (Honorton and Harper, 1974), and geographical or architectural sites (Targ and Puthoff, 1977). Charles Honorton and associates painstakingly created a set of 1,024 slides each containing a montage of images of varying complexity, often juxtaposed in creative ways suggesting primary-process associations, e.g. an ear superimposed on a picture containing musical instruments (Honorton, 1975b).

Researchers agree that free-response targets should be motivating or arousing to subjects, but they disagree on how best to accomplish this. Some believe that the targets should represent emotional or archetypal themes likely to stimulate unconscious mental processes and bring latent imagery to the surface. Such targets are especially appropriate when studying ESP in dreams (Ullman *et al.*, 1973). Researchers who use geographical sites as targets, on the other hand, stress that their realism and the potential practical application of identifying real targets is an important motivating factor that is absent when the targets are pictures or slides (Targ and Puthoff, 1977). As a general guideline, choose targets that best complement the situation or context in which your experiment is to be conducted.

3.2.2b Size and structure of the target pool

Whatever type of target material is selected, it is good to have a large pool of potential targets to draw from, so that the full range of content is represented. If possible, a pool should consist of at least 50 pictures. (Although for convenience free-response targets will often be referred to as 'pictures,' it should be kept in mind that they can take many other forms.) Since free-response tests are usually evaluated statistically as if they were restricted-choice tests (see chapter 6), it is often desirable to divide the pool in advance into sets of from two to ten pictures each. The members of each set should be as discriminable as possible in terms of semantic content, geometric form of objects, and type of emotion the picture is likely to evoke. Getting a group of judges to make similarity ratings of all possible pairs of pictures is a time-consuming but effective way of helping to assure that sets meet this criterion.

3.3 Determining the sequence of targets

As noted earlier in discussing our card guessing example, it is important that subjects not be able to infer the order of the targets. Such inference is less of a problem in free-response experiments with only one trial per subject, but it is still important that each picture have an equal opportunity of being selected as the target for each session. The best way to assure that this condition is met is to select the sequence of targets in as random a manner as possible.

3.3.1 Methods of randomization

3.3.1a Shuffling

In card tests, the traditional method of obtaining a random sequence of cards is simply to shuffle the deck thoroughly and cut it. Whereas five good dovetail shuffles is an adequate method in principle (Epstein, 1967), its adequacy in practice may vary with the skill of the shuffler and how ordered the deck was to begin with.

3.3.1b Random number tables

A more reliable method which has been used extensively in card tests since the 1950s employs random number tables (J. B. Rhine and Pratt, 1957). An entry point is selected to a sequence of random digits in any of several published tables. You need to be sure that the numbers in the table have been checked to assure randomness. Most parapsychologists use the table published by the RAND Corporation (1955). The digits are then translated into the corresponding targets according to a predetermined code. For example, if the targets are the standard ESP symbols, the code might be: 0 or 5 = star, 1 or 6 = circle, 2 or 7 = cross, 3 or 8 = waves, 4 or 9 = square.

3.3.1c Random event generators and computers

REGs generate outcomes electronically, often at a very rapid rate, most commonly using either white noise (like radio static) and/or the emission of electrons from a very weak radioactive source (e.g. strontium 90) to assure random selection (e.g. Schmidt, 1970c). The researcher can cause the machine to select a single target or a whole sequence of targets by simply pressing a button. The machines are generally built to choose from among two to ten possible targets.

Alternatively, most microcomputers and even many pocket calculators have the capacity to generate pseudo-random sequences of numbers. The researcher enters an arbitrary 'seed number' into the computer which activates a complex mathematical formula which generates each number in sequence. Although not random in the strict sense, the sequences are usually unpredictable enough for ESP tests. Nonetheless, all sources (whether pseudo-random or random) should be checked periodically to assure that the sequences they generate approximate true randomness to an adequate degree. (See section 2 of the next chapter for a further discussion of this point.)

3.3.2 Contamination by experimenter psi*

All of the above procedures have to a greater or lesser extent one potential drawback which becomes an issue whenever it is important to isolate the source of psi in an ESP experiment. The problem is this: might the experimenter, or whoever else generates the target sequence, use his or her own psi to produce a sequence that happens to match the subject's response sequence to a greater than chance degree?

In the case of card shuffling, this process is called the psychic shuffle*, and some research suggests that it actually can occur (J. B. Rhine, B. M. Smith and Woodruff, 1938). It would appear that either the shuffler uses PK to influence the shuffle or (more likely) stops shuffling when by chance the sequence of cards optimally matches the subject's response sequence – a special example of the optional stopping artifact mentioned earlier. In either case, we must assume that the shuffler has unconscious precognitive knowledge of the subject's responses.

Theoretically, at least, the likelihood of a psychic shuffle can be minimized by stipulating in advance the number of times the deck is to be shuffled and how it is to be cut.

Sequences selected from random number tables seem more immune from contamination by experimenter psi, but not entirely so. The researcher could theoretically use ESP or PK to select an entry point that gives a finite sequence of targets which happens to match the subject's response sequence to a greater than chance degree. Again, there is evidence that this can happen (Morris, 1968). In order to minimize this possibility, parapsychologists have devised complex procedures for determining entry points to random number tables (J. B. Rhine and Pratt, 1957). These same principles apply to the selection of seed numbers to be used in generating pseudo-random target sequences from computers.

Target selection by REGs is the method most susceptible to this potential bias, because the selection mechanism is very sensitive to minute physical forces, and thus to PK as well. In fact REGs are designed specifically for use in PK experiments.

In summary, there is no known way to completely eliminate contamination of ESP experiments by psi from the person who selects the target sequence. Nonetheless, it behoves the careful researcher to select procedures that theoretically minimize this difficulty as much as possible in those cases where the source of psi in an experiment is at issue.

3.3.3 Forms of target dependency

Random selection of targets generally guarantees that the targets will be independent of one another, i.e. no target can be predicted from knowledge of the others. However, certain research designs impose limits on this target independence even when the selection procedure is otherwise random. We will now discuss the two most prevalent of these research designs.

3.3.3a Open versus closed decks

The most common procedure which limits target independence is the use of the so-called closed deck*. A closed deck is a target sequence in which the number of times each target appears is stipulated in advance. The standard ESP card deck is a closed deck because each symbol appears exactly five times; only the order of the cards is randomized. Our deck of playing cards in the initial example is also a closed deck. In contrast, sequences based upon selections from a random number table or an REG are generally open decks*; each alternative can appear any number of times, although in most situations they will tend to appear with about equal frequency.

In free-response tests, a closed deck target sequence is one in which each picture is the target for one and only one trial. This procedure is sometimes called selection without replacement*, because once a picture is selected for a trial it is not put back in the pool and thus is not available for subsequent trials. On the other hand, an open deck is generated by selection with replacement*; once a picture is selected it is put back in the pool and has as much chance as any other picture of being selected for a subsequent trial. The concept of target dependency in closed decks can be readily grasped by considering a standard ESP card guessing test in which the subject is informed of the target after each trial. By keeping track of how many of each symbol has appeared, the subject can identify with certainty the target for the last trial of the run; in other words, the 25th target is predictable from knowledge of the preceding 24.

This could only happen in a free-response test if subjects knew in advance which pictures were to be included in the target set. But if the targets in the pool are highly diversified (as they should be) and subjects receive trial-by-trial feedback of targets, they could increase their chances of getting a high score on the test by avoiding mention of characteristics present in earlier targets. For example, if the target picture on trial 1 included a bridge, subjects could improve their scores artifactually by not mentioning bridges in their responses on later trials.

The upshot of all this is that closed decks should be avoided in experiments where subjects are given trial-by-trial feedback of targets. Closed decks can be used when such feedback is not given, but corrections may need to be applied to the statistical evaluation of the results. (See section 4.2 of the next chapter for a discussion of such corrections.) As a general rule, use open decks unless you have a good reason not to (Burdick and Kelly, 1977; J. E. Kennedy, 1979).

3.3.3b The stacking effect

Another kind of target dependency occurs when more than one subject responds to the same target sequence. In parapsychological jargon this is called the stacking effect*. It is most likely to occur when subjects are tested in a group setting such as an academic class. The target sequence in effect is being duplicated for each subject in the experiment, hence the dependency. The bias is relatively minor in restricted-choice tests with relatively long target sequences (J. W. Davis, 1978), but it can be a serious problem in free-response testing where the target 'sequence' might consist of only one trial. Say, for example, a test is given to a class of 30 students in which the target happens to be a scene of a lake with trees near it. Since many people automatically think of such things when asked to spontaneously generate mental imagery, you could end up with a lot of 'hits' having nothing to do with ESP. (Likewise, if the target happened to be something obscure, you might get pseudo psi missing). As more targets are included in the test, such biases eventually wash out.

To be safe, it is best to avoid the stacking effect whenever possible, even in restricted-choice tests. In group clairvoyance or precognition tests, the best solution is to simply generate a separate independent target sequence for each subject. This becomes more of a problem in telepathy or GESP tests, because you would need a separate agent for each percipient.

3.4 Preparing the subject

3.4.1 Putting the subject at ease

Experimenters' interactions with their research subjects should be conducted in a friendly and supportive manner that puts the subject at ease and inspires confidence. Such an approach is not only mandated by humanistic considerations, but it is also likely to help subjects score at the maximum level of which they are capable. The idea of psi can be threatening to people, perhaps at an unconscious level, and most parapsychologists believe it can be suppressed if the social and (to a lesser extent) the physical environment is not supportive.

The only exception to this advice would be experiments in which the social or physical situation is to be manipulated to test an experimental hypothesis about the effect of such a manipulation on ESP scores. But even in this case a humanistic approach should be adopted to the extent possible, and the experimenter should explain to the subject at the end of the session why the manipulation was necessary.

3.4.2 Inducing altered states of consciousness

In some experiments, the researcher may wish to further prepare the subject for the ESP test by inducing an altered state of consciousness (ASC)*. Such inductions are particularly common prior to free-response tests, where ASCs may help the subject to access complex imagery or impressions that might be relevant to the target.

Not all ASCs are considered to be psi-conducive. Those commonly induced by psychedelic drugs such as LSD, for example, are generally considered too extreme and disorienting for ESP testing (c.f. Cavanna and Servadio, 1964). The subject must be able to maintain enough alertness and self-control to orient toward the test while at the same time being free from the constraints of overly structured thought processes. This is a delicate balance that can best be achieved through less extreme ASCs induced without chemicals.

3.4.2a Types of ASC inductions

Traditionally, the most common procedure used to induce an ASC in ESP research has been hypnosis. However, the two most popular procedures in recent years have been progressive relaxation* and the ganzfeld*. Progressive relaxation was developed by a psychologist named Edmund Jacobson (1938/1974) to help people cope with stress. The client is asked to alternately tense and relax a sequence of specific muscle groups (e.g. toes, calves, thighs, etc.) and to notice the contrast between the feelings of tension and relaxation. The body is extremely relaxed following this procedure. A modification of the procedure that is sometimes used in ESP experiments is to have subjects simply imagine relaxing their muscles without actually doing so. This procedure is similar to a set of exercises called autogenic training. Progressive relaxation was introduced into parapsychology by William and Lendell Braud (1973) who customarily follow this exercise with suggestions for stilling the mind by having the subject imagine relaxing scenes.

The ganzfeld procedure was introduced into psychology by Herman Witkin (Bertini, Lewis and Witkin, 1969) and into parapsychology simulataneously by Charles Honorton (Honorton and Harper, 1974) and William Braud (W. G. Braud, Wood and L. W. Braud, 1975). It is based on the principle of perceptual deprivation, i.e. eliminating sources of patterned or meaningful stimulation from the external environment. Patterned visual stimulation is eliminated by affixing acetate hemispheres (halves of ping-pong balls) over the subject's eyes and shining a moderately bright white or colored light (red is generally preferred) through them. Patterned auditory stimulation is eliminated by playing white or, preferably, pink noise (something like soft radio static) through comfortable headphones. No formal attempts to exclude tactile stimulation are usually included, but the subject should either by lying down or seated in a comfortable reclining chair (see Plate 5.) The subject is left in the ganzfeld between 20 and 45 minutes. Sometimes subjects are asked to observe and/or report their imagery during the reception period, whereas in other experiments the ESP trial does not begin until afterward.

Other common induction procedures include meditation (e.g. Osis and Bokert, 1971; Roll and Solfvin, 1976) and brainwave biofeedback (Honorton, Davidson and Bindler, 1971). The important thing, though, is not the particular technique used but the appropriateness of the ASC obtained. If you plan to use ASCs in psi research, you may need to experiment to find the one you are most comfortable with and that seems most effective. ASC inductions also can sometimes be dangerous if not handled properly, and you should be supervised by a trained professional until you become proficient with them.

3.4.2b Are ASCs necessary?

Not all parapsychologists are sold on the value of ASC inductions. Advocates of a procedure called 'remote viewing,' for example, insist that equally good results can be obtained in normal waking consciousness (Targ and Puthoff, 1977). It might be that ASCs are most effective when the target material is abstract, archetypal, or 'dreamlike,' whereas they may be less psi-conducive when the targets are realistic.

The research on ESP in altered states will be discussed critically in chapter 7, section 3 and chapter 8, section 2.2.

3.5 Testing and response procedures

3.5.1 Traditional card guessing methods

A variety of standardized methods was developed for administering card guessing tests by J. B. Rhine in the 1930s (J. B. Rhine, 1934/1973; J. B. Rhine and Pratt, 1957). Although such tests are not used as frequently now as in the past, the student who wishes to understand the experimental research in the field prior to 1965 should be familiar with them, and they have been used in some important research since that time.

3.5.1a DT tests

The simplest of the card guessing procedures is the 'down-through' or DT* method, applicable to tests of clairvoyance. The deck of cards is shuffled, cut, and placed face down on the table. The subject's task is to guess the order of the cards from top to bottom. Subjects can either record their own responses on a record sheet or call them out to the experimenter. In the former case, subjects need not record their responses in order, but this departure from the standard protocol is rather uncommon.

An adaptation of the DT procedure which is particularly useful in group or classroom testing is called the envelope test*. The procedure is to record the target order on a record sheet, sandwich this sheet between two sheets of heavy construction paper, and seal the sandwich inside a manila envelope with the record sheet facing up. A blank record sheet is then taped on the front of the envelope. The packets are then distributed to the subjects, who record their responses on the blank sheets.

3.5.1b BT tests

A second clairvoyance procedure is the 'basic technique' or BT*. The experimenter picks up each card from the top of a shuffled deck, holds it for a predetermined number of seconds without looking at its face, and then places it face down on a second pile. You may have noticed that this is very similar to the GESP technique used in our card guessing example at the beginning of the chapter, except that in that case the experimenter/agent looks at the faces of the cards. Thus the GESP procedure can be considered as an adaptation of BT. As with DT, subjects can either write down or call out their responses. Especially if in a GESP test the agent is to be someone other than the experimenter, the latter should make a record of the target order in advance.

3.5.1c Matching tests

The third class of procedures, used exclusively in clairvoyance tests, are the matching procedures. In addition to the deck of target cards, matching procedures employ key cards*, one for each target alternative. In the 'open matching' or OM* test, the key cards are placed in a row in front of the subject, face up and in random order. The order of the key cards should be changed from run to run. The subject is given the shuffled deck of cards and asked to place each card face down (without looking at it) in one of five piles in front of the key card corresponding to the perceived target. For example, if the subject thinks the target is a star, he or she would place it in front of the 'star' key card. Because the subject handles the target cards and might accidentally see their faces, it is customary and highly desirable to enclose each target card in a small opaque envelope for open matching tests.

In 'blind matching' or BM* tests, the procedure is the same as OM, except that the key cards are either face down or concealed in opaque envelopes, their order unknown to the subject. This procedure is more complicated for subjects than OM, because they must correctly identify both the target card and the key card to make a correct match. Most subjects cope with this problem by simply placing the target in the pile that 'feels right.' Thus the BM procedure encourages a less cognitive and more 'automatic' approach to ESP responding.

An adaptation of the standard matching test that gives the experimenter control of the target cards is the 'screen touch matching' or STM* procedure. The subject and experimenter sit on opposite sides of a table separated by a wooden screen with an aperture at the bottom. The key cards are placed on pegs on the subject's side of the screen, their faces either exposed or concealed. Blank cards designating the piles are placed under the aperture. The subject points with a pencil to the appropriate blank card on each trial, and the experimenter then places the top card of the target deck in the corresponding pile on his or her side of the screen. (See Plate 6.)

The most famous ESP experiment conducted using this rather uncommon procedure will be discussed in chapter 7, section 2.2.

3.5.2 Random event generators

The various card guessing methods just discussed serve as prototypes that can be and have been adapted in the more modern machine test. In most REG tests, subjects indicate their responses by pressing buttons on the device itself or keys on a computer terminal attached to the device, and these responses are stored along with the targets in the memory of the REG or computer for later analysis. In contrast to card tests, subjects in REG experiments customarily receive trial-by-trial feedback which can be either visual or auditory.

A unique feature of REG tests in comparison to card tests is that the targets are generated on a trial-by-trial basis rather than all at once before or after the test. The implications of this feature are greatest in precognition tests, because the time interval between response and target designation is considerably shortened.

An REG can be adapted for GESP testing by connecting it to an auxiliary device which is located in the agent's room. In the AQUARIUS machine described by Tart (1976), for example, each time the REG selects a target one of four lamps is automatically lit on the agent's console illuminating a slide of that target for sending. The agent can also be given immediate feedback of the subject's subsequent response.

Portable REGs such as those developed by Schmidt (1970c) have the advantage of allowing subjects to be tested at home while still maintaining the necessary security and controls. On the other hand, attaching the REG to a computer provides researchers the capability to utilize a wide variety of tests and test protocols by writing their own programs. Some REGs are simply 'boards' that can be inserted inside modern microcomputers by the researcher.

3.5.3 Physiological response methods

In most ESP tests, such as the card guessing tests discussed in the preceding section, the subject makes an overt, behavioral response representing some conscious impression of the identity of the target. However, many parapsychologists theorize that ESP information may exist unconsciously but fail to reach consciousness because it is repressed or because it is distorted upon interacting with other mental processes (e.g. L. E. Rhine, 1962). Can such information be retrieved?

One solution is to tap the involuntary physiological processes of the subject. More often than not, the choice has been momentary or 'discrete' responses of the autonomic nervous system. This system, among other things, controls our physiological reactions to stress or danger. The autonomic measures most commonly used by parapsychologists are the plethysmograph* (a measure of changes in blood volume in the finger due to constriction or dilation of blood vessels) and the galvanic skin response, or GSR* (measures of the activation of sweat glands). Because these responses reflect emotional arousal, the target sequence must consist of a random ordering of emotionally arousing and emotionally neutral targets. Examples of emotional target stimuli are index cards containing names of significance to the percipient mixed in with blank cards or cards with neutral names (e.g. Dean and Nash, 1967; Schouten, 1976), and momentary electric shocks received by an agent interspersed with trials where the shock is diverted to a resistor (Tart, 1963). The design of the experiment is thus basically the same as in any restricted-choice test; the subject's score is a function of the degree of physiological response on the emotional trials as compared to the neutral ones.

Less frequently, brainwaves (measured by the electroencephalograph, or EEG*) are used as the response measure. In one GESP study, a strobe light was flashed into the eyes of an agent on randomly selected trials, disrupting her normal resting EEG pattern. The researchers found that in corresponding trial periods a similar effect was noted in the EEG record of the percipient, who was seated in a different room (May, Targ and Puthoff, 1979). The average evoked potential*, a small momentary EEG response to a brief sensory stimulus which is revealed when a series of EEG records obtained under identical stimulus conditions are superimposed on one another, has also been used in ESP tests but without significant results (Hartwell, 1978).

3.5.4 Free-response methods

Free-response testing methods are more uniform than their restricted-choice counterparts. The subject should be located in a nondistracting environment and encouraged to relax while carefully observing whatever impressions come to awareness. These include sounds, bodily sensations and emotions as well as visual images. Most parapsychologists recommend that subjects avoid censoring their impressions and minimize interpreting them. Often, for example, a subject will correctly apprehend the shape of a target object but be led astray by an improper interpretation or labeling of it. It also is best to allow images to come independently of one another and to avoid trains of logical associations. Subjects can either write down their impressions or report them orally. In the latter case, the experimenter can either transcribe them directly or record them on tape for later transcription. It sometimes is a good idea to have subjects draw their impressions, particularly in remote viewing studies.

The researcher must decide whether to have subjects give ongoing reports of their impressions during the reception period or wait until afterwards. Ongoing reporting helps to assure that the subject will not forget to report some impressions, but it also can be distracting and interrupt the flow of imagery, especially if the subject is inexperienced.

Another decision the researcher faces is whether to be present in the room with the subject during the reception period. Some subjects may find the experimenter's presence reassuring while others may find it uncomfortable or distracting. The most common procedure is to have the experimenter in another room monitoring the subject via intercom.

It is often desirable for the experimenter to ask subjects to elaborate on their impressions or to describe them more precisely, either during or after the reception period. In the latter case, the experimenter should read the initial reports back to the subjects in order to jog their memories. Obviously, if the experimenter interacts with subjects in any such way, he or she should not know the identity of the target.

Ideally, the experimenter should not even be aware of the target pool. For example, if the subject accurately apprehends one aspect of the target, a careless experimenter who knows the target pool might guide the subject to elaborate this imagery in such a way as to artifactually increase its degree of correspondence to the target. Thus a modest hit comes to look like a striking hit. Subjects, of course, can do the same thing on their own, and this is one reason for keeping even subjects unaware of the target pool in free-response experiments (C.

P. Irwin, 1980). A second reason is that the less subjects know about the target pool, the less their responses are likely to be biased by logical constraints; one key to successful performance on ESP tests seems to be spontaneity (Stanford, 1975).

3.5.5 Covert test* methods

One characteristic shared by the tests we have considered so far is that the subjects are quite aware that they are being tested for ESP. However, this often is not the way ESP operates in the real world. For example, a person may dream of an airplane crash and not realize that the dream may have been psychic until reading about the crash in the newspaper the next day. Rex Stanford (1974) suggests that we might be using psi a great deal in our daily lives without realizing it. In addition to not accurately modeling how ESP often seems to function outside the lab, conventional ESP tests also may engage conscious or unconscious psychological defenses capable of blocking ESP.

Recognizing these difficulties, parapsychologists have devised ingenious procedures for testing ESP covertly. These procedures rely on other kinds of tests structured in such a way as to be scorable for ESP. For example, Martin Johnson (1973) adapted the envelope test described above to an exam in a psychology class. Instead of a sequence of ESP symbols, each envelope contained answers to a randomly selected half of the exam questions. The exam itself was taped to the outside of the envelope. The students had no idea that their exam was a covert ESP test. Their scores were the differences between their test scores on the items 'answered' inside the envelopes and their scores on the other items. As predicted, students scored significantly higher on the answered items. In a followup experiment, Johnson supplied incorrect answers inside the envelopes. This time students scored significantly *lower* on the 'answered' items!

A disadvantage of covert tests is that they require the experimenter to deceive the subject about the nature of the study. Some researchers consider such deception to be a breach of ethics. With Johnson's method an additional question arises: if the test scores really did reflect in part ESP, should the test be considered a fair measure of the students' mastery of the course content? Covert tests have provided good evidence of ESP, so these considerations are real ones that must be weighed against the advantages of such tests.

3.5.5a Test methods with animals

ESP tests with animals can be considered examples of covert tests. In this case, parapsychologists have borrowed procedures from experimental psychologists who study animal learning. For example, rats can be taught to discriminate levels of brightness by placing them in boxes containing two adjacent bars with an illuminable disk above each one. On each trial the two disks light up. One is brighter than the other, which one being determined randomly on each trial. The rats must learn to press the bar under the brighter disk. If they do so, they receive food pellets as a reward.

To turn this into an ESP test, it is only necessary to equate the brightness of the two lights, forcing the rat to use ESP to determine which bar to press. (Note that we now have a restricted-choice ESP test with two target alternatives.) It can even be made into a GESP test by having an 'agent' rat in another box outfitted with disks but no bars. On each trial, the disk corresponding to the correct bar in the percipient's box lights up in the agent's box. If the percipient presses the correct bar, both rats get a food pellet (Schouten, 1972).

Another example is avoidance learning. In an ordinary psychology experiment, the experimenter might place a rat in a cage with an electrified grid floor and a short barrier dividing the cage into two equally sized compartments. The rats must learn that whenever they hear a certain sound stimulus they have five seconds to jump the barrier to the other compartment. If they fail to do so, they receive 'punishment' in the form of shocks.

To make this an ESP test, the floor of the box can be attached to an REG which randomly chooses one of the two compartments to receive shock on each trial (Duval and Montredon, 1968). The rats must use precognition to locate themselves in the other compartment. Again we have a restricted-choice ESP test with two target alternatives.

Both of these procedures have been used successfully in ESP research (e.g. Duval and Montredon, 1968; Parker, 1974; Schouten, 1972; Terry and Harris, 1975), and they seem to produce comparable results. Since the avoidance learning procedures involve pain to the animal, it would seem advisable to use procedures in which the reinforcements are positive unless the researcher is interested in avoidance learning *per se*.

3.6 Scoring the ESP test

3.6.1 Restricted-choice tests

Scoring of restricted-choice ESP tests is usually a straightforward matter. If the test is conducted with an REG or computer, the machine can do the scoring itself. All the experimenter has to do is read off the score from the dial or screen. It is desirable, however, to attach the machine to a printer, which provides a 'hard-copy' record. It is also important to be sure that scores are transferred properly to all data sheets during data analysis.

In tests where machines are not used, it is often necessary to match up written target and response sequences. Although this can be facilitated by folding the record sheets lengthwise such that the target and response sequences on the respective sheets are lined up adjacent to each other, human error can still conceivably result in an incorrect counting of hits. Skeptics have suggested that a scorer who believes strongly in ESP might be biased to count too many hits (J. L. Kennedy and Uphoff, 1939), whereas it could be argued with equal force that a hardened skeptic might count too few.

A simple way to remove all doubt is to record the target and response sequences in duplicate. This can readily be accomplished for each sequence by inserting a piece of carbon paper between two record sheets before the test. One person then scores the original sheets while another independently scores the carbon copies.

Finally, in precognition tests, the person who generates and records the target sequence after the test should have no knowledge of the subject's responses.

3.6.2 Free-response tests

Scoring of free-response tests unfortunately is much more complicated than scoring of restricted-choice tests. Most free-response scoring methods require that a judge, who may or may not be the subject, assess the degree of correspondence between the subject's impressions on a given trial and the target for that trial. If a closed deck target selection procedure is used, the judge may be asked to match up the targets and responses over a series of trials. If an open deck procedure is chosen, the judge might be asked to pick out the target for each trial from among the members of a set of potential targets for that trial. If the responses consist of psychic readings for a group of individuals, each reading may be broken down into component phrases and the judge asked to determine whether or not each phrase applies to each individual. These methods will be discussed more fully in the next chapter.

No one really has any clear idea what specifically to look for in judging free-response correspondences, and the nature of the correspondence is likely to vary depending upon the individual subject and the nature of the targets and test procedure. This is a problem that can only be solved by more research. In the meantime, common sense is the best guide for the prospective judge.

3.6.2a Subject judging versus independent judging

A controversial issue among parapsychologists is whether it is better to have subjects serve as judges of their own responses or to employ independent judges* not otherwise involved with the experiment. As usual, each alternative has its advantages. One obvious advantage of having subjects be the judges is that they are the ones most intimately familiar with their own impressions. Even if they describe their impressions in great detail for independent judging, something is bound to be lost in the translation. Moreover, only the subject is likely to be able to evaluate symbolic correspondences, especially if the symbolism is personal. For example, an independent judge is unlikely to give a high score to a response with a religious theme if the target was a bluebird. Yet the subject might give this correspondence a very high score if the bluebird happened to be the symbol of a religious sect to which he or she belonged.

But independent judging also has its advantages. Persons can be selected who seem to have particular skill in judging or who have been trained to look for particular things in the protocols. If a group of subjects are being tested and each subject is the judge for his or her own trial, the differences in the scores are likely to be influenced by differences in the styles or skill of the judges. These judging idiosyncrasies are eliminated when the same judge scores all trials. In scoring methods which require the subject as judge to examine pictures in the target pool other than the target, some parapsychologists have suggested that these other pictures might serve as unintentional precognition targets that could influence the subject's impressions. In other words, the subject might look ahead precognitively to the judging task during the reception period. If independent judges are used, the subject need be shown no other picture except the target.

Finally, in studies where it is important to identify the specific source of ESP, there exists the problem that ESP might contaminate the judging process *per se.* If the subjects are the judges, there is little the investigator can do to detect this. If independent judges are used, persons can be selected who seem to have minimal ESP ability themselves. The possibility of contamination can be reduced further by using several judges and averaging the scores they assign to each trial. Not only does this procedure improve the reliability of the final scores, but if the scores assigned by one judge are contaminated by ESP in the judging process, this effect is likely to be washed out by the scores assigned by the other judges.

3.6.2b Sources of judging bias

It is obviously essential that the judge have no information about the identity of the target for each trial during the judging task, i.e. the judge must be 'blind.' One potential source of such information is available in GESP studies in which the subject handles a target picture that is later included among the set of materials given to the judge. For example, the picture might reveal extra signs of handling (e.g. bent edges, fingerprints) or the odor of a perfume or cologne that the agent was wearing. The best way to avoid such contamination is to have duplicate sets of target materials, one set to be handled only by agents and the other set only by judges. It is also important that the judge receive the targets in random order.

When the judge is someone other than the subject, careful attention must be paid to how the transcripts of the subject's responses are edited. As a general rule, the transcripts should not be edited at all; even remarks that on the surface might seem to be irrelevant to the task might reveal emotions or attitudes that have something to do with the target.

On the other hand, transcripts sometimes contain comments that could bias the experiment, especially when the same subject is completing more than one trial. In remote viewing experiments, for example, a subject might refer to 'that lake which was the target yesterday' or comment that 'I can't see the target very well because it is raining.' An alert judge could use such information to help identify the target. For example, the judge could rule out a lake as being the target in the first example if he or she knew that a closed deck target selection procedure had been utilized, and the judge could at least narrow down the choice of possible targets in the second example if photographs of the target sites taken by the agent at the time of the trial constituted the target material given to the judge. The researcher or some person not otherwise involved in the experiment should carefully examine transcripts to eliminate potentially biasing statements prior to the judging.

As we shall see in chapter 7, failure to pay sufficient attention to the kinds of factors discussed in this section has led to much controversy about the evidential status of some prominent ESP experiments.

3.7 Analysing the data

The final step in an ESP experiment is to apply statistical analyses to the ESP scores to determine if they differ significantly from what would be expected by chance or from ESP scores obtained under other conditions or from different subjects. Statistical analysis is by far the most complicated phase of the research process, so we have devoted the entire next chapter to a discussion of the range of options available.

Summary of terms

mean chance expectation (MCE)
significant (statistically)
one-tailed test
sensory cues
blind
random
pure telepathy
pure clairvoyance
trial-by-trial (immediate) feedback
optional stopping
multiple-aspect target
exact hit
random event generator (REG)
normal curve
experimenter psi
psychic shuffle
closed deck
open deck
selection without replacement
selection with replacement
stacking effect
altered state of consciousness (ASC)
progressive relaxation
ganzfeld
down-through (DT)
envelope test
basic technique (BT)
key cards
open matching (OM)
blind matching (BM)
screen-touch matching (STM)
plethysmograph
galvanic skin response (GSR)
electroencephalograph (EEG)
average evoked potential
covert test
independent judge

Thought questions

(1) In section 2.4.1 it was stated that there was no direct way to demonstrate 'pure telepathy' experimentally. Can you think of an experiment that would nonetheless provide indirect evidence of telepathy (as distinct from clairvoyance)?

(2) You are given an opportunity to test a 'gifted' psychic for one hour and you want to demonstrate as conclusively as possible that he or she has genuine psychic talent. The psychic is equally comfortable with all of the tests described in this chapter applicable to humans. What kind of test would you choose, and why?

(3) Closed decks normally include an equal number of each target alternative. However, sometimes a closed deck is set up intentionally to include a large number of some targets and a small number of other targets. Can you think of a hypothesis that such a deck would be ideal for testing?

(4) Altered states inductions are most commonly used in conjunction with free-response ESP tests, but occasionally they have been used with restricted-choice tests also. Which of the kinds of restricted-choice test procedures discussed in section 3.5.1 do you think would be most compatible with an ASC, and why?

(5) You plan to do a free-response ESP test comparing the efficiency of ESP in dreams (in which the targets are paintings rich in symbolism) with remote viewing (in which the targets are geographical sites). Assuming you wish to use independent judges, would you use the same set of judges to evaluate both the dream and RV protocols? Why or why not? Can you see reasons for choosing the opposite?

Chapter 6
Statistical methods in ESP research

John Palmer[1]

1 Introduction

Once data have been obtained from a properly conducted ESP experiment, it is usually necessary to apply a statistical analysis to determine whether it is reasonable to rule out the hypothesis that the results were due to chance or random variation of hits. The statistical methods parapsychologists use are based upon, and often identical to, those used generally in the social and behavioral sciences. The methods discussed in this chapter are adaptations of these more general methods to the unique challenges posed by parapsychological data. Although this chapter is oriented toward the evaluation of ESP data, many of the techniques discussed are equally applicable to PK research.

Your comprehension of this chapter will be greater if you have completed an elementary course in statistics. In particular, some knowledge of statistical notation is necessary for understanding the formulas which will be introduced from time to time. On the other hand, some of the less technical material will be within the grasp of most readers and will enrich your understanding of the research to be described in subsequent chapters.

Before we can consider the scoring and analysis of ESP tests, it is necessary briefly to discuss another important matter: determining the randomicity of target sequences.

2 Testing randomicity of target sequences

Before any ESP test involving a sequence of targets can be properly evaluated, we must establish that the sequence or the source from which the sequence was drawn is satisfactorily random. This is accomplished by subjecting the sequence and/or source to one or more randomicity tests. Such tests do not prove directly that a sequence is random; instead they determine whether there is any statistically significant evidence of bias or nonrandomness.

The sensitivity or capacity of these tests to do their job depends in part upon the number of targets being analysed. The target sequences in most psi tests are short and the randomicity tests correspondingly insensitive. Thus, although it is still important to evaluate actual target sequences for nonrandomness, a good deal of the burden falls upon demonstrating the general capacity of the source to produce random sequences.

In PK tests, of course, the burden falls entirely on such general or control sequences, since the point of the PK test is to make the sequence of events nonrandom in some prespecified way. The sequences in good random number tables such as the RAND (1955) tables have been prechecked for randomicity, but REGs should be checked frequently to be sure their output remains satisfactorily random. Fortunately, most REGs can generate large numbers of events in short periods of time and can even function in the researcher's absence, thus providing long sequences quite economically.

2.1 Equiprobability

There are two major characteristics that define any random sequence. The first is that each element (or target alternative, in our case) appear in the sequence a number of times closely proportional to its relative frequency in the population from which the sequence was drawn. Since in most situations this means that each target alternative should appear an approximately equal number of times, this characteristic is often called equiprobability*.

The equiprobability assumption can be tested simply by a chi-square goodness of fit test, using the formula:

$$\chi^2 = \sum_{i=1}^{m} \frac{(O_i - E_i)^2}{E_i}, \quad (1)$$

in which O_i is the number of times the ith target alternative appears in the sequence, m is the number of target alternatives, and E_i is the number of times the ith target alternative is expected to appear in the sequence. When E_i is the same for each target alternative, it is defined as n/m, where n is the number of targets in the sequence. The degrees of freedom are $n-1$.

2.2 Intertrial independence

The other major characteristic of a random sequence is intertrial independence*. This means that each target alternative has an equal opportunity of occurring after any other target or group of targets in the sequence. In a two-choice test, for example, a long sequence of the form 101010 would violate this rule, because, for instance, zeroes follow ones more frequently than ones follow ones.

This characteristic, as it applies to successive nonoverlapping pairs of targets (i.e. doublets) in a sequence, can be tested by constructing a matrix in which the rows represent the first members of each pair and the columns represent the second members. Each pair is then tallied in the appropriate cell of the matrix. For example, in Table 6.1, a ++ pair would add one to the count in the upper left cell of the matrix. A chi-square contingency test is then applied to the data. This test uses the same basic formula as (1) above, specifically,

$$\chi^2 = \sum_{j=1}^{l} \sum_{i=1}^{k} \frac{(O_{ij} - E_{ij})^2}{E_{ij}}, \quad (2)$$

in which O_{ij} refers to the frequency count in the cell intersecting the ith of k rows and the jth of l columns. In contrast to formula (1), the expected frequency of each cell (E_{ij}) is defined as the product of the marginal totals of the row and column it intersects, this product then being divided by the total number of pairs in the sequence. Thus in Table 6.1, E for the upper left cell is $\frac{(89 \times 119)}{500} = 21.2$. The degrees of freedom are $(k-1)(l-1)$.

Table 6.1: Matrix for chi-square contingency test of 500 target doublets

		Second members of doublets					
		Cross	Circle	Star	Square	Waves	
First members of doublets	Cross	20	18	22	16	13	89
	Circle	28	23	15	20	26	112
	Star	17	15	17	27	12	88
	Square	29	20	19	15	32	115
	Waves	25	12	11	28	20	96
		119	88	84	106	103	500

Formula (2) can be applied to the evaluation of intertrial independence beyond the doublet level, although computation becomes increasingly complicated the higher the level. Slight degrees of nonrandomness at these higher levels are unlikely to present a serious problem, unless one is conducting a lengthy ESP test with trial-by-trial feedback. On the other hand, if one is going repeatedly to use a given REG, an extensive analysis of the machine's output is strongly recommended.

A more complicated but also more sensitive test for nonrandomness has been developed by James Davis and Charles Akers (1974) in the form of a computer program that can evaluate sequences up to the septuplet level. For a more detailed discussion of randomicity testing, see Dudewicz and Ralley (1981).

2.3 Some hidden sources of bias

It is desirable to conduct general randomicity tests on an REG under conditions as similar as possible to those that pertain in the actual research. Such tests serve very much the same purpose as control conditions in psychological experiments. It is conceivable, for example, that an REG might be random at one rate of target generation but not at others. The burden of proof is on the researcher to show that the REG is ordinarily random under the conditions of his or her experiment.

It is also possible that a machine could oscillate between different manifestations of nonrandomness, such that the biases cancel. For example, a binary (two-choice) REG might produce 400 ones during the first 500 trials and only 100 ones during the next 500. The equiprobability assumption would be ideally met for the total 1,000 trials even though the REG was obviously biased. One way to detect such localized nonrandomness is to compute separate chi-squares for each of a prescribed set of subunits of the total sequence. These chi-squares can then be added together along with their degrees of freedom to provide a single estimate of nonrandomness.

3 Scores of individual trials

As mentioned at the beginning of the last chapter, the scientific study of parapsychology generally requires that we measure or represent quantitatively the amount or degree of psi reflected in our data. The building blocks for this quantification are the scores that we assign to individual trials, so let us turn to these next. The actual statistical analysis of these scores will be discussed in sections 4 and 5.

3.1 Levels of measurement

In order to understand how psi trials are scored, it is important to understand the different levels of measurement that such scores can reflect. The crudest level of measurement is called nominal* or categorical measurement, in which the trials are placed into discrete categories. Most commonly, these categories are 'hit' and 'miss.' The next most precise level of measurement is ordinal*, in which trial scores are expressed as ranks, i.e. they are ordered from the lowest to the highest, or worst to best. Finally, we have interval* measurement, in which the psi scores are numbers, each successive unit representing an identical increment in the assumed amount of psi. Total number of hits is a good example of an interval score, i.e. seven hits represent one more unit of psi than six hits, which represent one more unit than five hits, etc. Categorical measurement will sometimes be referred to as discrete*, and ordinal or interval measurement as continuous*.

It is important to keep in mind that these concepts refer to psi *scores* and not necessarily to psi itself. For example, classifying a trial as a hit does not necessarily mean that psi occurred; some hits are chance hits. Likewise, psi may not increment in equal intervals as psi scores do. This is simply to say that scores do not perfectly reflect the underlying reality. Yet these approximations are better than nothing, and they are essential to the scientific study of psi.

3.2 Restricted-choice tests

3.2.1 Discrete scoring methods

In discrete scoring, trials are classified as successful or unsuccessful, i.e. as hits or misses.

3.2.1a Direct hits

Most commonly, a trial is considered a hit in restricted-choice tests if the response matches the target for that trial. If you call 'star' and the target is 'star,' you are credited with a hit; otherwise it is a miss.

3.2.1b Between-trial displacement
There have been several parapsychological experiments in which subjects seemed to respond consistently to targets at particular locations in the sequence other than that designated for the trial in question (e.g. Fisk, 1951; Pratt, Martin and Stribic, 1974). This is called between-trial displacement*, or simply displacement. More precisely, if the subject's response matches the target for the next trial in the sequence (e.g. the response for trial two matches the target for trial three) we call it + 1 displacement, or a +1 hit. If it matches the target two trials ahead (trial four in our example) we call it a + 2 hit. Displacement ahead in the sequence can be referred to more generally as forward displacement*. In the same vein, if the response matches the target for the immediately preceding trial, the subject would be assigned a –1 hit, an example of backward displacement*. The degree of displacement can be as great as one minus the number of trials in the run (e.g. –24 to + 24 in a 25–trial run), or even in the whole test. But in most cases parapsychologists restrict their analyses to +1 and –1 displacements, as these seem to make the most sense psychologically.

3.2.2 Continuous scoring methods
Discrete scoring methods assume implicitly that psi functions on a given trial in an all-or-none fashion. It either works (hit) or it doesn't (miss). These methods are not very sensitive to partial hits or approximate hits. If we want to distinguish between degrees of psi manifesting on a given trial, we must use continuous scoring methods.

3.2.2a Clock-card tests
Perhaps the best example of restricted-choice targets designed for continuous scoring are clock cards*, introduced into parapsychology by George Fisk and A. M. Mitchell (1952). Drawn on each card is a clock face with a hand pointed to one of the twelve 'hours.' The subject's score is a function of how close in distance to the target number he or she draws the hand on the response card, which is identical to the target card except that no hand has been pre-drawn. The range of scores is from one to twelve. If the target is '12' and the subject draws a hand to '12,' he or she scores twelve points. (Note that this would be a direct hit were we using discrete scoring.) Responses of '11' or '1' would be the next closest, so we would want to give them the next highest scores, i.e. ten and eleven. But since they are equally good, we would rather not have to choose between them, so we interpolate and give each a score of 10.5. The same principle would apply to responses of '10' and '2,' '9' and '3,' etc. Finally, the worst response would be '6,' so this would receive a score of one.

In the above example, a partial hit was defined in terms of the spatial distance on the clock face between the target and response, and this assumption was reflected in the scoring scheme. However, we are free to make other assumptions. For example, we might want to say that '6' is the second-best response, because it bears a simple geometric relation to the target '12.' In this case, we might want to give this response a score of eleven and adjust the other possible scores accordingly. Scoring schemes are simply tools that allow us to express quantitatively our concept of a 'good' performance. They should be our servants, not our masters.

3.2.2b Weighting of ranks.

You may have noticed that in the clock-card test the scores are actually ranks. Expressing continuous scores as ranks has the important advantage of allowing us to analyse groups of such scores using statistical tests based on the mathematically derived distribution of ranks. On the other hand, there might be pressing reasons for adopting alternate schemes. One approach is to begin with ranks and then apply weights to them or transform them in some systematic way. For example, if we wanted to give progressively greater weight to scores as they approached a direct hit in the clock-card test, we could square each of the rank scores. Thus, instead of a set of scores '1,2,3, 4, . . . , 12,' we would have a set '1,4,9,16, . . . , 144.' Recently, Gerald Solfvin, Edward Kelly and Donald Burdick (1978) developed statistical tables that can be consulted if one wishes to evaluate weighted ranks for statistical significance in psi tests.

3.2.3 The majority vote technique*

In the last chapter, we noted that a problem called the stacking effect arises when more than one subject responds to the same target sequence. One solution to this problem is to calculate a single 'response' for each trial based on a count of how many subjects responded with each target alternative.

As another illustration, assume that 25 subjects each complete a standard card test, all responding to the same target sequence. On the first trial, let's say that eight subjects called 'star,' six called 'circle,' five 'cross,' four 'waves,' and two 'square.' If we choose discrete scoring, the trial would be a hit if 'star' was the target and a miss otherwise. If there had been a tie (e.g. eight subjects called 'circle' instead of six), we would award ½ hit to the trial.

If we choose rank scoring, we would rank the target alternatives according to how many subjects chose each one. If the target had been 'cross' in the previous example, the score for the trial would be three, because 'cross' received the third highest number of 'votes.'

The majority vote principle can also be applied to research with a single subject in ESP tests. In one successful application, for example, the target was defined as which side of a card, green on one side and white on the other, was uppermost inside an opaque envelope (Ryzl, 1966). Each envelope had a unique code number. The target sequence consisted of ten envelopes, which were reshuffled after each run. Because the location of the physical target in each run could be identified by its code, it was possible to calculate over a series of runs how many times the subject called each color for each target, thus allowing a majority vote. The subject need not know which envelope he or she is calling on a given trial.

1 The Fox sisters in 1848 (courtesy of Psi Search Exhibition and Book)

2 *(Left)* How an artist conceived an alleged levitation by D. D. Home, the Scottish-American medium (courtesy of Psi Search Exhibition and Book)

3 *(Below)* J. B. and Louisa Rhine examine galley proofs for an edition of the *Journal of Parapsychology* (from the archives of the Foundation for Research on the Nature of Man, Durham, North Carolina 27780–6847)

4 Julio, the alleged target person in the Miami disturbance, undergoing psycho-physiological measurement during a psi task (courtesy of Psi Search Exhibition and Book)

5 A subject in a ganzfeld experiment at the Psychophysical Research Laboratories, Princeton, New Jersey (courtesy of Mr Charles Honorton)

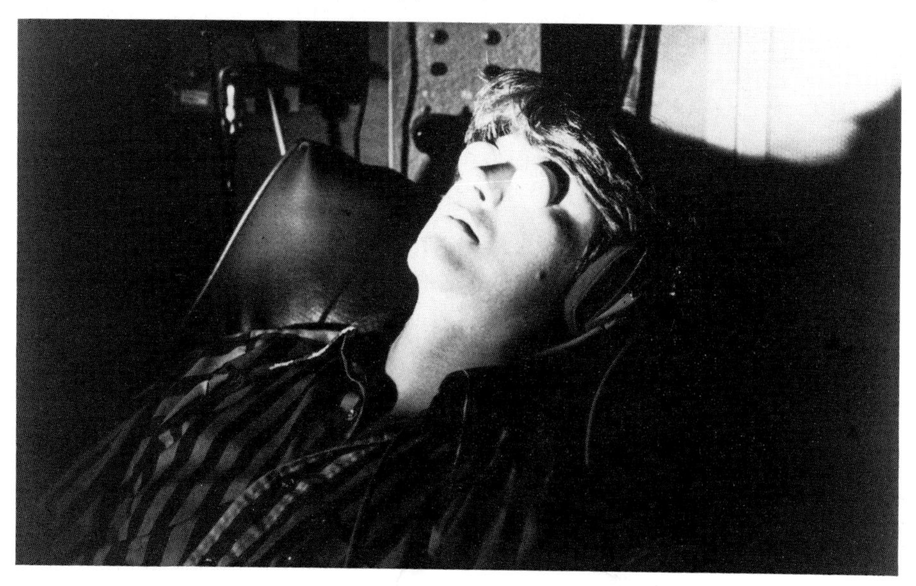

6 The Pratt-Woodruff experiment for using the screen touch matching procedure (from the archives of the Foundation for Research on the Nature of Man)

7 Dr Charles Tart operating his original ten-choice trainer. He is trying to telepathically influence a percipient in another room to press button no. 2 on the percipient's console (courtesy of Dr Tart)

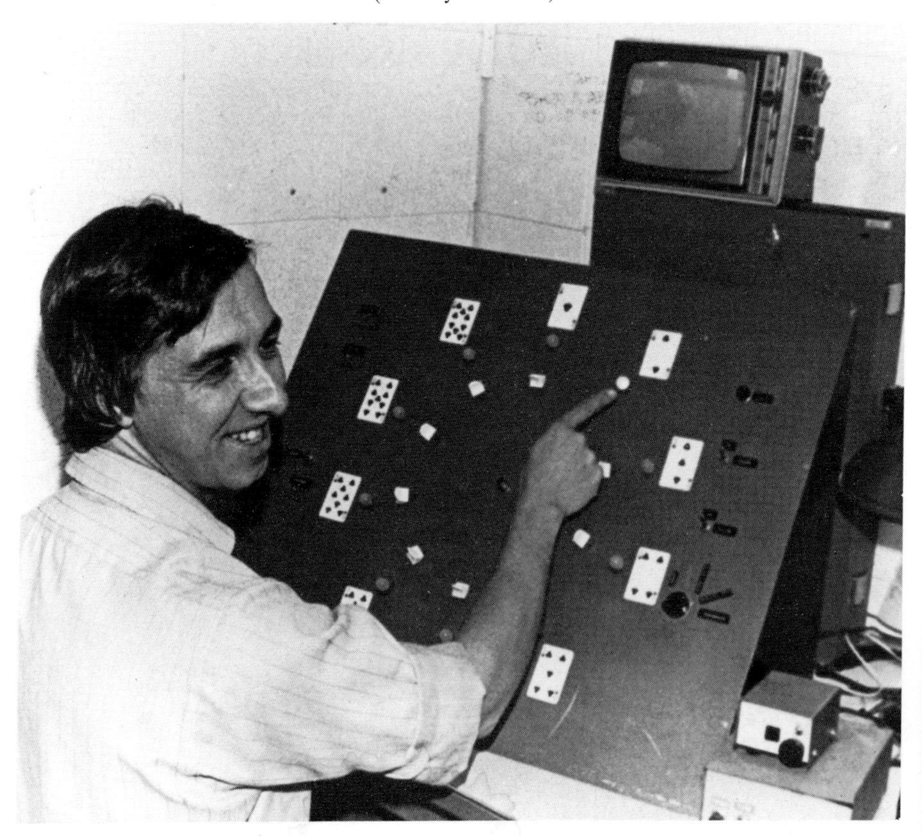

8 *(Above) The Descent from the Cross* by Max Beckmann, 1917. Oil on canvas, $59\frac{1}{2} \times 50\frac{3}{4}''$. Collection, The Museum of Modern Art, New York. Curt Valentin bequest. This picture was the target for a successful trial in dream research conducted at the Maimonides Medical Center, Brooklyn, New York. *(Below)* Multisensory materials given to the agent along with *The Descent from the Cross* to facilitate involvement with the target (courtesy of Dr Stanley Krippner)

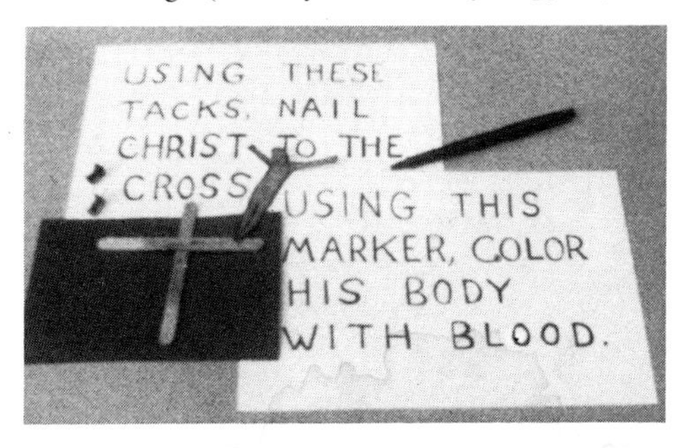

Pedestrian Overpass Target

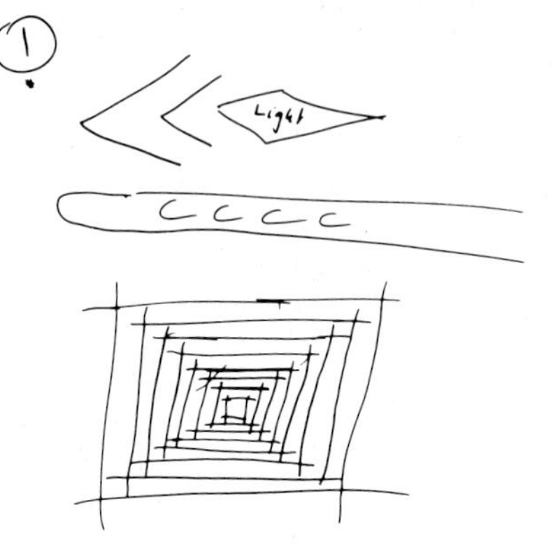

SUBJECT HAMMID DRAWING, DESCRIBED AS "SOME KIND OF DIAGONAL TROUGH UP IN THE AIR"

9 Remote viewing trial with pedestrian overpass as target (courtesy of SRI International)

10 Apparatus used in PK dice tests (from the archives of the Foundation for Research on the Nature of Man)

11 Dr Helmut Schmidt with the 'circle of lights' feedback device (REG) he has used in some PK tests (courtesy of Dr Schmidt)

12 *(Above)* Dome of the Church of Santa Maria di Loreto and Trajan's Column in Rome, from a photo in a book Eisenbud had just brought home and Serios had 'leafed through' rapidly immediately before the session (from *The Rome I Love* by P. Mollinard, G. Pilemont and F. Marceau, Tudor Publishing, New York, no date). *(Below left and right)* Polaroid photos produced by Serios during the ensuing test session (photos courtesy of Dr Eisenbud)

This is a very powerful procedure, based on information theory in psychology. If a subject is scoring consistently in the same direction (i.e. either psi-hitting or psi-missing) but psi is only operating on a small percentage of the trials, majority votes can still lead to a correct identification of the target. For example, Ryzl's subject was able to correctly decode a five-digit number by making repeated guesses of the same targets, even though only about 60 percent of those individual guesses were correct.

3.3 Free-response tests

Data from free-response tests must be reduced to a restricted-choice format before statistical analyses can be applied. There are two basic approaches to analysing free-response data. Holistic methods* require the judge to evaluate the subject's impressions as a unified whole, capitalizing upon the integrating powers of the human mind. Analytic methods* break down the subject's impressions into units that are evaluated separately.

3.3.1 Holistic methods

Holistic scoring methods can be illustrated most readily with an example using an open-deck target selection procedure in which a judge is presented with a set of four pictures, one of which is the target for the trial in question.

3.3.1a *Nominal scoring*

If nominal scoring is chosen, the judge simply picks on a 'blind' basis which of the four pictures corresponds most closely to the target. If he or she is correct, the trial is a hit, otherwise a miss. Alternatively, the judge might be asked to rank the pictures from one to four. If the target receives a rank of one or two, the trial is a hit. This method increases the probability of a hit from 0.25 to 0.50, a looser criterion of success.

3.3.1b *Ordinal scoring*

A more continuous and sensitive procedure is to have the judge rank the pictures (this time giving a rank of '4' to the closest correspondence), and treat the rank assigned to the target as the score for the trial. Such ranks can also be transformed or weighted, as discussed in section 3.2.2b.

3.3.1c *Interval scoring*

Although ordinal scoring is more sensitive than nominal scoring, a rank of '4' could mean anything from a marginal correspondence of the subject's response to the target, only slightly better than its correspondence to the other pictures, to a perfect correspondence obviously superior to the other possibilities. How can marginal and exceptional correspondences be distinguished in the scoring? One commonly used approach is to ask the judge to rate each of the four correspondences on a scale from, say, 0 to 30, in which 0 means no similarity and 30 means complete similarity.

These ratings are customarily converted to *z*-scores* (also called standard scores), which reflect how much the rating given to the target differs from the ratings given to the other pictures in the set. The formula is:

$$z = \frac{X_i - \bar{X}}{s_x}, \quad (3)$$

where X_i is the rating assigned to the target, $\bar{X}$ is the mean of all ratings in the trial, and s_x is the standard deviation of the ratings (a measure of how much they vary among themselves). These scores have an MCE equal to zero. Finally, note that although this formula is somewhat similar in structure to the one for the so-called *z*-test (to be discussed later), individual *z*-scores should not be analysed for statistical significance.

Although ratings are more sensitive than the other scoring methods, not all parapsychologists recommend them. Some believe that our measures of ESP are so crude that the added 'sensitivity' we get from ratings reflects little more than noise, or errors of measurement. In other words, if a direct hit on one trial gets a score of +1.23 and the direct hit on another trial gets a score of +0.56, the 'superiority' of the first score (according to this view) is probably a fluke due to the vagaries of judging. If this assumption is true, the rating methods may actually be less sensitive to real psi than the cruder nominal and ordinal methods.

Another problem with the rating method is that *z*-scores are potentially contaminated by the rating strategies of individual subjects. For example, a subject whose style is to 'go for broke' and give a much higher rating to one picture than the others will tend to get a more extreme *z*-score (hitting or missing) than a subject manifesting an equivalent amount of psi whose style is to distribute ratings more conservatively. Such problems can be minimized, although not entirely eliminated, by using independent judges (see chapter 5, section 3.6.2a).

3.3.2 Atomistic methods

In the last chapter, it was mentioned that psychic readings can be broken down into information units for analysis. This is one common example of an atomistic approach to the analysis of free-response data. A judge might be asked to assign a rating to each of these units according to a predetermined scheme, e.g. '2' if the assertion is completely true, '1' if it is partly true or somewhat true, and '0' if it is untrue. These ratings might then be added together to get the total score for the trial.

Two more refined atomistic scoring schemes have been published. In the last chapter, reference was made to Honorton's (1975b) pool of 1,024 pictorial slides, each representing a unique combination of the presence or absence of ten content categories (e.g. nature features, food, architectural features). Each slide has a ten-digit binary code representing its composition. For example a code of 1010000010 means that only categories one, three and nine are represented in the picture. A score can be obtained for a trial by having a judge (who could be the subject) code the subject's impressions in the same manner and then match the target and response codings. What we have in effect is a ten-trial restricted-choice test with two target alternatives. The subject's score for the actual trial can range from zero to ten, with MCE equal to five.

Although this method can be very sensitive, it is predicated on the assumption that the subject's ESP is oriented to the presence of content in the categories represented in the system. It may not be sensitive to more specific correspondences or to other kinds of correspondences. For example, in an experiment one of us conducted with the slides, the target for one trial included an image of Superman and the subject mentioned Superman in her response. However, her score by this method was only '4,' because her imagery did not correspond well to the overall structure of the target in terms of the content categories.

Robert Jahn, Brenda Dunne and E. G. Jahn (1980) have developed a coding scheme for remote viewing targets and responses consisting of 30 characteristics. The subject's score is the number of characteristics the response and the remote site share in common.

4 Statistical analysis of scores: descriptive methods

The next two sections discuss methods of evaluating for statistical significance the psi scores described in the last section. In this section, we will describe those tests which tell us whether a group of trials meets the criterion of significance. In section 5 we will briefly discuss techniques that allow us to draw more general conclusions about how psi might manifest in situations other than the immediate test.

As a general rule, we cannot determine the statistical significance of single trial scores; they simply give us too little information. The one exception is atomistically scored free-response trials, and this is because we break them up into subtrials which are treated as a group of trials statistically. In other cases, we must collect a group of trials before statistical analysis is possible.

4.1 Psi-hitting and psi-missing

4.1.1 Nominal scoring methods

When trials are scored as hits or misses, the evaluation of significance is based on the total number of hits (or the total score) over a group of trials. If the total number of trials is sufficiently large, the null or chance distribution of such total scores over a very large number of such tests will closely approximate the normal curve. This allows us to use a very simple statistical test which parapsychologists call the critical ratio, or CR^*. (This is an old term carried over from the 1930s; the more modern name for this test is the z-test.)

The formula is as follows:

$$CR(z) = \frac{H - np\ [\pm\ 0.5]}{\sqrt{npq}}, \quad (4)$$

where H is the number of hits, p is the probability of a hit (the reciprocal of the number of target alternatives), q is the probability of a miss (or $1-p$), and n is the number of trials. (± means adjust toward 0.)

Formula (4) should not be used if the product of n times p is less than ten. In such cases the chance distribution of scores departs too far from the normal curve, so we must fall back on a more complicated formula based directly on the underlying binomial distribution. The outcomes of such tests can often be determined directly from binomial or 'exact probability' tables found in many statistics texts.

4.1.2 Ordinal scoring methods

When individual trial scores are ranks and the number of independent trials exceeds ten, the total of the ten or more rank scores assigned to the correct targets will, over a very large number of tests, be distributed in a manner closely approximating the normal curve. This allows us to use another CR formula, which we will call the CR of summed ranks:

$$CR(z) = \frac{X - n\ [(R + 1)/2] \pm 0.5}{\sqrt{n(R^2 - 1)/12}}, \quad (5)$$

where X is the sum of the ranks assigned to the correct targets and R is the number of such ranks (equal to the number of target alternatives), and n is the number of trials.

If n is less than 13, the appropriate level of significance can be determined by consulting the table in Appendix A (page 383).

4.1.3 Interval scoring methods

In this section we will discuss statistical analysis of data where the trials are scored on a more-or-less interval scale. This situation occurs primarily in free-response tests in which ratings are made of the correspondences and also where cumulative trial scores are derived from atomistic analyses.

Analysis is generally quite straightforward in those cases for which MCE can be defined theoretically. Examples include ratings converted to either deviation scores or z-scores (MCE = 0) and Honorton's binary coding scores (MCE = 5). Groups of trials scored by such methods can be evaluated for statistical significance by a single-mean t-test, provided that the number of trials is large (at least ten), and the distribution does not depart too grossly from the normal curve.

The formula can be expressed as follows:

$$t = \frac{\bar{X} - \mu}{s_x/\sqrt{n}}, \quad (6)$$

where $\bar{X}$ is the arithmetic mean of the trial scores, μ is MCE, s_x is the unbiased standard deviation of the trial scores, and n is the number of trials. The degrees of freedom are $n-1$.

A complicated procedure designed to handle data with no theoretically defined MCE was developed by Thomas Greville (1944) and is described in detail in a technical but excellent review chapter on parapsychological statistics written by Donald Burdick and Edward Kelly (1977). However, it has not yet been established how this test behaves when the assumptions of the normal curve have not been met, which is likely to be the case in many of the situations in which we would want to use Greville's technique.

4.2 Analyses with closed decks

If the target sequence is a closed deck, analysis becomes more complicated because of the statistical dependency between trials. This dependency modifies the theoretical variance (or standard deviation) of the distribution of total scores, which is reflected in the denominators of the *CR* formulas. However, since the degree of bias depends upon the particular characteristics of each response sequence or score sequence, there is no general adjustment that can be made to the formulas that will be accurate in all instances.

One alternative is to use 'worst-case approximations,' in which the standard deviation you use is the largest possible. Such an adjustment can be applied to the discrete *CR* formula (4) by multiplying the denominator of the formula by $\sqrt{n/(n-1)}$. The corresponding adjustment for the rank *CR* formula (5) is to change -1 to $+2$ in the denominator, but this only adjusts the '1' ranks and thus must be used cautiously.

The only method discussed so far that can be used without modification in the closed deck case is the Greville technique.

4.2.1 Free-response matching procedures

In closed-deck free-response experiments, matching procedures are commonly used to obtain the subject's total score, which is then analysed by the methods described in the preceding section. The procedure that results in nominal scores is often called forced matching*. A 'blind' judge is given the targets and responses in random order and asked to match them up. The number of hits is the number of trials in which the target and response are matched correctly, with MCE always equal to one. In this case, the p-values can be obtained by consulting the table in Appendix B (page 384).

The matching method that yields ordinal trial scores is called preferential matching* or preferential ranking. Although these terms are sometimes applied to open-deck rankings, they are most commonly used in referring to closed decks. A 'blind' judge is given each response and asked to rank each of the targets according to its perceived degree of correspondence to it, or vice versa. The rankings can be expressed in a matrix such as that illustrated in Table 6.2, the total score being the sum of the ranks on the diagonal.

Table 6.2: Matrix of ranks for preferential matching

		Targets			
		A	B	C	D
Responses	a	*1*	4	2	3
	b	3	*1*	4	2
	c	3	4	*2*	1
	d	3	1	4	*2*

A possible means of avoiding the statistical problems ordinarily associated with closed deck target selection in preferential matching is to have a different judge do the matching for each target. However, it is important that each judge be 'blind' to the others' matchings.

4.3 The Pratt-Birge technique*

An adaptation of the Greville method designed to handle atomistically scored free-response data from psychic readings has been developed by Pratt and Birge (1948; Pratt, 1969). The method assumes that a psychic gives a reading to each of n clients. All these clients then rate all the statements from all the readings in random order, as described in section 3.3.2, without knowing which statements were intended for them. Alternatively, a group of judges can select out beforehand particular statements for rating that seem especially prone to psi influence according to some preset criterion such as specificity (Boerenkamp and Schouten, 1983). Such preselection makes the rating task considerably easier for the clients. In either case, a total score is then reconstructed for each reading as applied to each client by adding up the appropriate ratings. The scores can then be arranged in an $n \times n$ matrix as in Table 6.3.

Table 6.3: Matrix for Pratt-Birge analysis of psychic readings

		Clients					
		Bill	Dave	Jane	Beth	Alex	r
Judges	Bill	*58*	23	46	6	56	189
	Dave	25	*73*	14	45	53	210
	Jane	18	41	*67*	33	39	198
	Beth	61	22	40	*49*	30	202
	Alex	11	39	26	28	*72*	176
	c	173	198	193	161	250	

If row variances are homogeneous (i.e. the spread of scores within a row does not vary too much from row to row) and n is at least 10, the following formula can be applied:

$$CR(z) = \frac{X - (T/n)}{\sqrt{(T^2 + n^2\Sigma a^2 - n\Sigma r^2 - n\Sigma c^2)/n^2(n-1)}}, \quad (7)$$

where X is the sum of scores in the diagonal cells of the matrix, T is the sum of all scores, Σa^2 is the sum of the squared scores of all cells, Σr^2 is the sum of the squared row totals, Σc^2 is the sum of the squared column totals, and n is the number of clients.

In practice, a large enough n may be obtainable only by pooling the results of several small tables such as Table 6.3. In such cases, the expected mean (right-hand term in the numerator of formula (7)) is the sum of the individual table means, and the variance (square of the denominator of formula (7)) is the sum of the individual table variances.

4.4 Direct probability tests

There is a way out if we cannot meet the assumptions of independence, large enough sample size, and/or conformity to some specific distribution, but it often requires the use of a large computer. We begin with a matrix just like the ones illustrated in Tables 6.2 and 6.3 above. We then request the computer to rearrange the numbers inside the matrix in every possible way, computing each time a 'score' consisting of the sum (or the average) of the numbers that happen to be in the diagonal cells. If the number of possibilities is too large, we can ask the computer to select a random sample of them that is large enough to be representative. We then can claim statistical significance if the proportion of these scores that are more extreme than the real scores is less than our criterion *p*-value. For example, we would claim significant psi-hitting at the .05 level (one-tailed) for Table 6.2 if fewer than 5 percent of our sample scores were six or less. A readable article describing the application of this principle to preferential matching has been written by Michael Thalbourne (1979). Because of its flexibility and sensitivity, this method may well be the wave of the future in evaluating psi data, especially free-response ESP data.

4.5 Within-trial displacement

4.5.1 Restricted-choice methods

In section 3.2.1b, it was noted that sometimes psi is unintentionally displaced to another trial in the sequence, and this was called between-trial displacement. In restricted-choice tests, it is also possible for psi to be displaced to one of the other target alternatives on a given trial. If this within-trial displacement* occurs in the same manner over a series of trials (i.e. the same incorrect symbols are consistently called in place of the correct ones) it is called consistent missing* and can be evaluated statistically when trials are nominally scored.

The first step in the analysis of consistent missing is to set up a contingency table or confusions matrix. As illustrated in Table 6.4, the rows represent the responses and the columns represent the targets. The number of rows and columns is always equal and corresponds to the number of target alternatives. Each trial increments by one the total of one cell in the matrix, and the sum total of all the values inside the matrix is equal to the number of trials. For example, the number 15 in the upper left cell of the matrix means that there were 15 trials in which the target was 'cross' and the response was 'cross.'

Table 6.4: Confusions matrix for 250-trial card test

		Targets					
		Cross	Circle	Star	Square	Waves	
	Cross	*15*	26	4	5	7	57
	Circle	4	*10*	6	3	19	42
Responses	Star	23	6	*18*	7	10	64
	Square	0	4	22	*12*	6	44
	Waves	8	2	7	19	*7*	43
		50	48	57	46	49	250

You will note that the cells on the diagonal of the matrix represent direct hits. It is the other, 'off-diagonal' cells where consistent missing shows up. For example, if a subject frequently calls 'cross' when the target is 'circle,' then there would be a relatively large number in the second cell of the first row of the matrix, as illustrated in Table 6.4.

The principle behind the analysis of consistent missing is to determine whether the values in these off-diagonal cells differ significantly from the values expected on the basis of the number of times each symbol appears in the overall target and response sequences. A satisfactory method of achieving this was devised by Remi Cadoret and Gaither Pratt (1950). Unfortunately, it is too complicated to describe in this chapter.

4.5.2 Free-response methods

Within-trial displacement occurs in free-response tests when the subject's response corresponds to a picture in the judging set or pool other than the target. Although many an experimenter has groaned at the apparent occurrence of such displacement in his or her data, it is rarely evaluated statistically. Such analysis is feasible, however, if one is willing to assume that the displacement is confined to the other members of the target set. This assumption makes psychological sense in experiments where the subject is the judge and has contact with the control pictures of the target set during the judging process. As mentioned in chapter 5, section 3.6.2a, subjects could conceivably 'look ahead' precognitively to the judging task and have the control pictures contaminate their responses.

The one method that has so far been developed requires an open-deck target selection procedure and a reevaluation of the correspondences by outside judges (Palmer, Bogart, Jones and Tart, 1977). For each trial, each judge receives, say, eight pictures in random order. Four are the pictures in the target set for that trial, whereas the other four are from another set randomly selected from the pool. The judge 'blindly' rates the responses against each of the eight pictures, not knowing which are from the target set. The differences between the sums of the ratings of the two sets can then be converted to z-scores by dividing them by the standard deviation of all the ratings made by all the judges and evaluated for significance by using t-test formula (6).

4.6 Comparing groups of trials

The analyses discussed so far are appropriate if the direction of scoring (i.e. hitting or missing) is consistent throughout the test. But consider a standard four-run card guessing test in which the hit totals for the runs are 1,9,1,9. It looks as if psi may be present in the data, but the total number of hits is 20, exactly chance. In this section we will examine ways of evaluating these kind of results in restricted-choice tests in which the trials are scored nominally. Since free-response tests rarely accumulate large numbers of trials, this section generally will not apply to them, although there can, of course, be exceptions.

Before such analyses are possible, we must determine some basis for defining groups of scores. It really doesn't matter much from a statistical point of view how this is done (except that in definitive research it should be done prior to inspection of the scores), but a common procedure is to compare scores from individual runs, so we will begin with this breakdown.

4.6.1 Variance analyses

The most general approach to detecting fluctuations in the direction of scoring during a test is through variance analyses. When the groups being compared are runs, the analysis is called run-score variance* (Rogers, 1966). The principle is to compare the obtained variance of the run scores around MCE to the theoretically expected variance. The obtained variance is expressed as the sum of the squares of all the deviation scores around MCE. The greater the deviations the greater the variance, and since we are dealing with squares, the distinction between hitting and missing (and the possibility of their cancelling each other out) is eliminated. The formula uses the chi-square distribution:

$$\chi^2 = \frac{\sum_{i=1}^{N} (H_i - np)^2}{npq}, \quad (8)$$

where H_i is the number of hits in the ith run, n is the number of trials per run (or other unit of grouping), N is the number of runs, and p and q are as in formula (4). The degrees of freedom are $N - 1$.

An alternate approach is to analyse the variance around the empirical mean of all the run scores rather than around MCE. This is done by simply substituting this mean in place of np in formula (8). To appreciate this distinction, consider a series of run scores 9,9,9,9. These would have a high variance around MCE (=5), but a low (in fact, zero) variance around the empirical mean (=9).

Finally, if the number of trials in each group i is large enough that a separate CR can justifiably be computed for its total score by using formula (4), the variability of these group scores around MCE can be tested by squaring the CRs, computed without the I.5 adjustment, and summing them. The resulting sum is a chi-square with degrees of freedom equal to the number of scores summed:

$$\chi^2 = \sum_{i=1}^{N} CR_i^2, \quad (9)$$

4.6.2 Critical ratio of the difference

Variance analyses are appropriate if the change in scoring direction is unsystematic, or predicted to be so. An example would be a series of run scores 9,1,1,9,9,1,9,1. But what if this sequence were 9,9,9,9,1,1,1,1? In this case the scoring trend seems more orderly, which might justify the application of a more sensitive statistical test that takes this orderliness into account.

One such test is a variation of the critical ratio called the critical ratio of the difference, or CR_d*. It is used when the change in scoring can be represented as hit totals of two groups of trials. The formula is:

$$CR_d(z) = \frac{(H_1/n_1) - (H_2/n_2) \pm [0.5(1/n_1 + 1/n_2)]}{\sqrt{(pq/n_1) + (pq/n_2)}}, \quad (10)$$

where H_1 and H_2 are the total numbers of hits in each group, n_1 and n_2 are the corresponding numbers of trials, and p and q are as in formula (4).

4.6.2a Position effects

There are numerous ways in which trials can be grouped. Those groupings which reflect changes in scoring direction from one part of the test to another are called position effects*. The most common of these are the decline effect and the salience effect, and both have been found frequently in psi tests (J. B. Rhine, 1969).

In a decline effect, the scores tend to be above chance at the beginning of the test unit and decline to either chance or below chance as the test proceeds. It is also possible, of course, for scores to beçome higher during the test unit. Such incline effects may (but not necessarily) indicate learning, which some parapsychologists believe can be facilitated through trial-by-trial feedback of scores.

The salience effect* refers to more extreme hit totals (i.e. greater departures from MCE) at the beginning and end of the test unit than in the middle. When a salience effect is plotted graphically, it appears as a '*U*'-curve if overall scoring is above MCE and an 'Inverted U'-curve if it is below MCE.

Position effects can be evaluated either across runs or within runs. To illustrate the former, consider a series of run scores 9,4,5,8. To analyse for a decline effect between runs, we would compare the hit totals in the first two runs to the hit totals in the last two runs. Since both totals are 13, there obviously is no decline effect. To analyse for a salience effect, we would compare the hit totals of the first and fourth runs (= 17) to the hit totals of the second and third runs (= 9). A salience effect seems likely, so we would apply the CR_d formula (10) to determine if the trend reaches statistical significance.

To evaluate position effects within runs, we ordinarily divide the run into two parts, compute hit totals for each part, and then add up these hit totals for all the runs in the experiment. CR_d formula (10) is then applied as before.

Finally, it is possible to compare the variances of two sets of runs, e.g. evaluate the decline in run-score variance from the first to the second half of the test unit (Carpenter and Carpenter, 1967). To do this, we simply compute chi-square measures of run-score variance for each group of runs using formula (8) or its equivalent. The ratio of these two chi squares follows the *F* distribution with degrees of freedom equal to those used in computing the respective chi squares. The formula is:

$$F = \frac{\chi^2_1/(N_1 - 1)}{\chi^2_2/(N_2 - 1)}, \quad (11)$$

where N_1 and N_2 are the numbers of runs (or other units) in the two groups being compared. Note that since this formula requires that the larger of the two variances always appears in the numerator, the probability value we find in the *F* table must be interpreted as one-tailed. The degrees of freedom are N_1-1 for the numerator and N_2-1 for the denominator.

It is particularly important in assessing position effects to keep in mind that because there are so many possibilities it is not unlikely that one of them will turn up by chance in any individual case. Position effects are most evidential when they occur consistently over a series of tests.

4.6.2b Psi-prone trials

An alternate means of grouping trials is to select out those particular trials in a test that seem especially likely to be influenced by psi. A frequently used method of doing this capitalizes on the fact that the response sequences subjects generate in restricted-choice tests are often strongly nonrandom. Specific nonrandom response patterns are called response biases*. For example, a subject might have a tendency to avoid calling one of the five symbols in a standard card guessing test. A more common response bias is to avoid calling the same symbol twice in a row, which by chance should occur about 20 percent of the time in a standard card guessing test.

Rex Stanford (1967) has noted that to the extent ESP responses are governed by response biases they are not governed by ESP. Conversely, on those relatively rare occasions when subjects break their response biases, it is possible that the reason for the break was that psi overcame the biases. In other words, counter-bias responses* are relatively likely to be psi-mediated. Evaluations of this type have frequently revealed significant response-bias effects in ESP data (Stanford, 1975).

Before undertaking a response-bias analysis, it is a good idea if possible to show that a response bias in fact exists. If the number of trials per subject is sufficiently large, this can be done by applying simple randomicity tests of the type discussed in section 2 to the subject's response sequence.

Another way to isolate possible psi-prone trials is to have subjects make confidence calls* during the test. Customarily, this is done by having them indicate on each run about three to seven trials on which they feel their responses are especially likely to have been correct. Several studies have demonstrated elevated scoring rates on confidence calls (e.g. Fahler and Osis, 1966; Kanthamani and Kelly, 1974a).

The significance of scoring on psi-prone trials can be evaluated by CR formula (4) and compared to scoring on the other trials in the test by CR_d formula (10).

5 Statistical analysis of scores: inferential methods

The statistical methods discussed so far are appropriate if all we want to know is whether psi has occurred in a particular group of trials. They are most commonly used in evaluating the data from a single subject, but they may also be used in evaluating group experiments if it is not deemed important how the scoring is distributed among the members of the group.

This section is devoted to methods of analysis applicable to cases where we wish to generalize conclusions from the results of an experiment to a larger group or population of individuals. Such generalizations require that we meet two conditions. First, we must select as our experimental sample a group of subjects that can be taken to be representative of the larger population to which we would like our conclusions to apply. Second, we should never pool the trials of more than one subject to produce a single score (e.g. reflecting results in different experimental conditions or parts of the test). Each score must be unique to that subject.

The formulas discussed in the last section are not always appropriate for inferential purposes. In particular, the CR formulas should generally not be used in such cases unless each subject completes only one trial (Stanford and Palmer, 1972). The formulas and their applications which are appropriate for inferential purposes tend to be those stressed in textbooks of psychological statistics, so we will discuss them only briefly. This is in no way meant to minimize their importance in evaluating parapsychological data.

5.1 Proof versus process research

In most experiments where the methods of section 4 apply, the purpose is to show that psi occurred under a particular set of controlled conditions. As noted in chapter 2, such studies, which are more like demonstrations than experiments *per se,* are referred to by parapychologists as proof-oriented. On the other hand, an increasing number of psi experiments assume the existence of psi at least as a working hypothesis and focus upon understanding its nature. In this so-called process-oriented research, psi scores are generally treated as a dependent variable, and the purpose is to determine to what extent differences in these scores can be attributed to other factors represented as independent variables. Whereas proof research tends to seek uniformity in psi scores (e.g. consistent psi-hitting), process research tends to seek diversity in such scores, because it seeks to account for this diversity through the independent variable(s).

5.2 Experimenter psi assumptions

In the vast majority of cases in which we choose to apply inferential statistics to parapsychological data, we assume implicitly that the subjects are the source of any psi effects obtained. This may appear self-evident at first glance, but some parapsychologists have suggested that in many experiments it is the experimenter's psi that is really being measured rather than the subjects'. This hypothesis seems most plausible in PK experiments, but it can apply to ESP experiments as well. If the experimenter is in fact the psi source, then the methods of section 4 are the appropriate ones. Since we have no way of knowing at this stage of our understanding whether this hypothesis is correct in any given study, you are free to either accept or reject it. The only obligation is to use a statistical method that is compatible with your choice.

5.3 Specific inferential methods

5.3.1 Nominal methods

Nominal analyses generally require that the subject's score be classified as 'above MCE' or 'below MCE,' and these scores are then usually evaluated by some sort of chi-square test. If the purpose of the experiment is simply to determine if more subjects sampled from some population scored above (or below) MCE than expected by chance, chi-square formula (1) may be used, with *O* referring to the number of subjects in each category and *E* being defined as the total number of subjects (*N*) divided by two. Subjects who score right at MCE should be excluded from the analysis.

In process research where the independent variable is also defined nominally (e.g. sex), chi-square formula (2) may be utilized. In parapsychological jargon, this is often called a consistency test*. It is customary to include subjects who score right at MCE among those scoring below MCE, thus retaining the same two categories of ESP scores described in the preceding paragraph.

5.3.2 Ordinal methods

If subject scores are ranked from best to worst, there is no way to determine if the overall scoring level is significantly above or below MCE since the distribution of ranks is always the same. However, the relation between such ranks and an independent variable can be assessed by a variety of standard nonparametric statistical tests such as the Mann-Whitney *U*-Test, the Wilcoxon Test, and the Spearman Correlation.

5.3.3 Interval methods

If MCE can be defined for a group of scores and the distribution does not depart grossly from the normal curve, *t*-test formula (6) may be used to determine if the overall mean is significantly above or below MCE. Two-mean *t*-tests, analysis of variance (ANOVA), and multiple regression are among the other methods available to evaluate psi scores in relation to independent variables in process research.

6 Some cautionary notes

6.1 Selection of scoring and analysis methods

If we wish to draw a definitive conclusion from a psi experiment, it is important to specify in advance which of the myriad scoring and analysis methods we want to use in evaluating a given effect or hypothesis and stick with that decision. If we keep trying out different methods, sooner or later we are likely to find one that gives us statistical significance. But this will probably represent a so-called 'type-one error,' not psi. We may also wish to calculate the significance of relationships between variables in an experiment that were not explicitly hypothesized. Such data snooping can be very valuable in exploratory research or even for secondary, '*post hoc*' analyses in more definitive research. However, any significant effects uncovered by such exploratory analyses need to be replicated in follow-up research before they can be taken too seriously. Alternatively, one of several statistical methods can be applied which correct the *p*-values for the effects of multiple analyses. However, when a large number of such analyses is involved these methods virtually guarantee nonsignificance and may result in the loss of valuable information. Replication, although time-consuming, is thus often the better option.

6.2 Relation to MCE

When evaluating ordinal or interval scores in process research, it is important to keep in mind that these scores are on scales which do not take into account the relation of the scores to MCE. For example, in a standard card guessing test with MCE equal to five, the interpretation can be very different if the mean of the experimental group is 7.0 and the mean of the control group is 5.0 than if those respective means are 5.0 and 3.0, even though in both cases the experimental group scored significantly 'higher' than the control group. Such effects are especially obscured when correlational methods are used, because group mean scores do not enter into the computation and sometimes are not even reported. For a further discussion, see Palmer (1975b).

6.3 Within-subjects designs

When assessing the effect of an independent variable on ESP scores in process research, one must frequently decide whether to have the same subjects experience each condition (within-subjects design) or randomly assign different subjects to the conditions (between-subjects design). Although within-subjects designs are more economical, they have the important disadvantage that scoring in the latter condition may be influenced by subjects' experience of participating in the former one. This is especially true when they have already learned their scores in the first condition (e.g. studies with immediate feedback). A more uniquely parapsychological problem arises as a result of evidence suggesting that subjects tend to score in opposite directions more frequently than expected by chance when asked to take an ESP test in two different conditions, independently of the nature of these conditions. The evidence for this so-called differential effect* is discussed by Rao (1965).

Note

[1] My thanks to Dr. Edward Kelly for reviewing an earlier draft of this chapter.

Summary of terms

equiprobability
intertrial independence
nominal scale
forced matching
preferential matching
Pratt-Birge technique

ordinal scale
interval scale
discrete
continuous
between-trial displacement
forward (+) displacement
backward (−) displacement
clock-cards
majority vote technique
holistic scoring
analytic scoring
z-score
critical ratio (*CR*)

within-trial displacement
consistent missing
run-score variance
critical ratio of the difference
(CR_d)
position effect
salience effect
response bias
counter-bias response
confidence call
consistency test
differential effect

Thought questions

(1) In a restricted-choice ESP test with immediate feedback, you discover that your subject has demonstrated significant –1 displacement. Why would it be hazardous to assume that this is a real ESP effect? How could you test the validity of the 'normal' aiternate explanation?

(2) Why might it be especially advantageous to do a preliminary test prior to the formal test with a subject when you plan to analyse the results using the majority vote method?

(3) A practical problem with the use of the Pratt-Birge technique is that the raw sum-of-ratings scores in the matrix of Table 6.3 in many cases will not be distributed properly. Can you think of a way to solve the problem that would still allow you to use the method?

(4) In some PK dice tests (to be discussed in chapter 10), subjects scored above chance in the first part of the test and below chance to about an equal degree in the second part of the test. This result has traditionally been called a decline effect. Can you see a sense in which this label is misleading?

(5) In section 5.2, it was asserted that descriptive statistical methods are the ones to choose in 'process-oriented' research in which the experimenter is assumed to be the source of the psi. Explain why this is the case. Can you think of an experiment testing for experimenter psi for which this rule would not apply? How would the experimenters have to be selected in such a case?

Chapter 7
The ESP controversy

John Palmer

1 Introduction

The first question a critically oriented person is likely to ask when introduced to the concept of ESP is what 'hard' scientific evidence might exist for such a capacity. The controversy that has raged over this question throughout the modern history of parapsychology is the topic of this chapter. The subject will be approached through a discussion of ten separate research projects which some parapsychologists have claimed provide strong evidence for ESP and which have evoked at least some response from critics. They are grouped into restricted-choice and free-response categories, and within each category the projects are presented in roughly chronological order. Each will begin with a brief description of the methodology and results, followed by a discussion of how critics have attempted to demolish the evidentiality of the findings, and, finally, how the researchers or their colleagues have attempted to defend the research.

We should warn you at the outset that you should not expect clear-cut answers as to the 'right way' to interpret these findings. What you can expect is a fascinating glimpse of how the quest for knowledge is pursued on the 'wild frontier' of science, a region where the normal codes of conduct do not always apply. Some of the general strategies employed by the more extreme critics of parapsychology are critically discussed in chapter 12, section 5.3. You may find it useful to peruse this section before continuing in the present chapter.

Finally, the discussions in this chapter and the next assume mastery of the material in the preceding two chapters. You may find it helpful to refer back to this material from time to time as you read on.

2 Restricted-choice experiments

2.1 The Pearce-Pratt experiment

Hubert Pearce was a divinity student who participated in a number of ESP card-guessing experiments under both informal and formal conditions at Rhine's laboratory in the 1930s. The culmination of the research was an experiment of four series, comprising a total of 74 runs conducted during 37 sessions (J. B. Rhine and Pratt, 1954). There were generally two runs per session. The experiment was considered noteworthy at the time in that Pearce and the experimenter, Pratt, were located in buildings either 100 or 250 yards apart.

A modified BT procedure was used. Pearce and Pratt had synchronized their watches so that every time Pratt turned over a card, Pearce would record his guess for the corresponding trial. At the end of each run or pair of runs, Pratt recorded the target order on his record sheet. Both Pearce and Pratt made duplicate copies of the respective call and target sequences, and these were individually delivered to Rhine for independent counting of hits. During the last of the four series, Rhine was present with Pratt to observe the procedure at each session.

The mean number of hits per run throughout the entire experiment was 7.1, with an associated probability of $p < 10^{-22}$. Clearly the results could not be attributed to chance.

The attack on the experiment focused on the fact that no one was present with Pearce during the sessions. Hansel (1961a) noted that this allowed Pearce to leave the building and surreptitiously observe Pratt recording the target order before preparing his list of 'guesses,' thus allowing him fraudulently to obtain any number of hits he wished.

For three of the series, Hansel proposed that Pearce could have locked himself in an empty classroom across the hall from Pratt and observed the target order by looking through the glass transoms of the doors of the two rooms. In the remaining series, Pearce could have stationed himself in an attic above Pratt's room and peeked down onto the desk through a trap door. Hansel based his speculations on an examination of the rooms that he made during a visit to Duke in the 1960s. However, some of the rooms had been structurally altered since the 1930s, so some doubt remained about the viability of Hansel's hypothesis.

In the initial rebuttal, J. B. Rhine and Pratt (1961) argued that Hansel's hypothesis was precluded in the series where Rhine was present in the room with Pratt. Hansel countered that it did not necessarily follow from Rhine's presence that Pearce could have been detected, and that if Rhine had been focusing his attention on this possibility he would not have been able to observe if Pratt was cheating. A few years later, Stevenson (1967) was able to obtain blueprints of the rooms as they existed in the 1930s. They revealed that the classroom across the hall from Pratt did not in fact afford a direct line of sight onto Pratt's desk. Hansel (1980) countered by modifying his hypothesis to assume that Pearce had merely stationed himself in the hallway. Although, as Hansel noted, Pearce might have been able to arrange for testing times during which traffic in the hallway would be minimal, his revised scenario involved considerably greater risk of Pearce being detected than did his original one.

Finally, Hansel (1980) pointed to apparent inconsistencies in various official and unofficial reports of the experiment, the most telling of which concerned differences in the scores assigned to particular runs. A detailed rebuttal of these points has been offered by Rao (1981).

2.2 The Pratt-Woodruff experiment

This was another card guessing experiment conducted in the 1930s at Rhine's laboratory using the STM procedure (Pratt and Woodruff, 1939). (The actual setup of the experiment is illustrated in Plate 6.) In the more tightly controlled of the two series, 32 volunteer subjects completed a total of 2,400 runs. The mean number of hits per run was 5.21, which was highly significant statistically ($p < 10^{-5}$), although the significance was attributable to high scores by only five of the 32 subjects.

The testing procedure involved the subject on one side of the screen and the junior experimenter (E1) on the other side. The latter's role was to place each target card in the pile designated by the subject. The senior experimenter (E2) was seated behind the subject. His role was to take the five key cards off the pegs after each run, rearrange them, and return them to the subject with the instruction to replace them in an order unknown to E1. After each run, E1 copied down the identities of the target cards in each pile while E2 copied down the order of the key cards. E2 then counted the number of hits. Duplicates of the record sheets were subsequently scored by an independent checker.

Hansel (1961b, 1966) proposed an alternative hypothesis to ESP which involved cheating on the part of E1. He speculated that E1 might have been able to keep track of the key cards between runs, at least sometimes, and thus know on which pegs at least some of them were placed for the next run. It then would have been relatively simple to place one or two target cards in the wrong piles during that run so as to create bogus hits without being detected by either the subject or E2.

Hansel reasoned that it would be easiest to keep track of the key cards which occupied the extreme positions (1 and 5) on the screen during the preceding run. These cards can be referred to as E-cards and the middle cards as M-cards. To test his hypothesis, Hansel compared the numbers of hits on the E and M-cards for all the above-chance scoring runs completed by the five subjects whose scores for the entire series were significantly positive. (Remember, the E and M classifications refer to the locations of the key cards on the *preceding* run.) The hypothesis was confirmed, in that the number of hits on the E-cards significantly exceeded the number of hits on the M-cards. The confirmation was clear for the highest scoring subject, but some controversy arose about its confirmation for the other four subjects (Medhurst and Scott, 1974; Pratt, 1974). In any case, the effect Hansel found clearly accounted for the significance of the experiment; the successful outcome could have been due to E1 cheating.

As you might expect, Pratt and Woodruff (1961) did not react kindly to Hansel's allegation. A major point of contention was whether in fact the key cards were rearranged sufficiently by E2 to prevent E1 from keeping track of them. The procedure was not described in enough detail in the report to allow determination on that basis. In an effort to show that the rearrangement was not sufficient, Hansel demonstrated that, at least in the case of the two highest scoring subjects, the order of the key cards did not vary from run to run in a statistically random manner.

Pratt and Woodruff made two counterarguments. The first was that the rearrangements of the key cards did not need to meet the strict criteria of statistical randomness to be variable enough to keep E1 from keeping track of them. Their second counterargument was that even if the key cards had been thoroughly rearranged, a final systematic pattern could have resulted from the subject's preferring to place the key cards on the pegs in specific orders. In the final analysis, there simply is no way to determine whether the rearrangement was satisfactory or not.

Pratt (1974) proposed an alternative ESP interpretation of Hansel's finding. He reasoned that because of their locations, the E-cards would be more likely than the M-cards to be salient to the subject on the next run; i.e. subjects would be more likely to pay attention to the E-cards, perhaps even to the point of focusing their attention on them to the exclusion of the others. Such salience effects had been noted in other card-guessing experiments (e.g. J. B. Rhine, 1941), although not specifically in matching experiments, where they presumably had never been looked for.

Nonetheless, as George Medhurst (who had taken over from Hansel as the chief critic) pointed out, the hypothesis was *ad hoc* (Medhurst and Scott, 1974). Therefore, Pratt (1976) set about to test it experimentally. He reasoned that if a particular E-card were salient to the subject on a given run, the subject would be more likely to change its location for the next run than if it was not. Thus the scores should be higher on the E-cards whose locations had been changed. If anything, the fraud hypothesis would predict the opposite, i.e. it would be easier to keep track of those E-cards whose positions had remained the same.

Pratt tested his hypothesis on the data of the highest scoring subject. He found, as predicted, that the hit rate was 28.3 percent for the shifted E-cards and only 20.8 percent for the unshifted E-cards, a statistically significant difference. He thus concluded that the ESP salience interpretation of Hansel's effect was confirmed and the fraud interpretation was refuted.

Given the protracted nature of this particular controversy, it would be hazardous to conclude that Pratt's reanalysis is the last word. Suffice it to say that the ball is now in the critics' court.

2.3 The Soal-Shackleton experiment

Rhine's counterpart in Britain was the mathematician S. G. Soal. In an effort to replicate Rhine's results in the US, Soal carried out an extensive series of card-guessing experiments with no apparent success. Then another parapsychologist who had become interested in between-trial displacement effects encouraged Soal to look for such effects in his data. Soal indeed found two subjects who revealed +1 and −1 displacements to a marked degree: a photographer named Basil Shackleton and a housewife named Gloria Stewart.

Soal subsequently sought to confirm these effects in extensive series of tests with these two subjects. Both of them produced highly significant results. In the series with Shackleton, for example, there was a + 1 hit rate of 25.4 percent over 11,378 trials as compared to the MCE of 20.0 percent ($p < 10^{-35}$).

Most of the controversy has centered around the Shackleton experiment (Soal and Goldney, 1943), so I will restrict my attention to this. For the most part, a modified GESP procedure was used. The agent and percipient were located in separate rooms, each accompanied by an experimenter. The agent was seated in front of a cardboard box standing on its end in which five key cards were placed face-down. Each key card had the picture of a different animal printed on its face. Before each run, the agent shuffled the key cards and placed them inside the box in an order unknown to the agent's experimenter (EA). Before each trial, EA consulted a sheet of random numbers previously prepared by Soal and then displayed a card indicating the appropriate target number (1–5) to the agent. The agent then turned over the key card in the corresponding location and attempted to 'send' it to Shackleton, who recorded his response on a separate record sheet.

At the end of each session, which consisted of from four to ten 50–trial runs, all the participants and any outside observers who occasionally were present came together for the tabulation of the results. Shackleton's responses (which consisted of the first letters of the animals on the key cards) were converted to their numerical equivalents and recorded in the 'guess' columns of the target sheets. Then the number of direct and displacement hits were tallied. Finally, duplicate record sheets were made up to be mailed to a third party for safe keeping.

There were 40 sessions in all, some of which incorporated modifications of the above procedure. Sometimes the target order was determined by EA drawing a numbered counter from a large pool of such counters mixed together in a bowl. This seemed to have little effect on the results. Sometimes a clairvoyance procedure was used in which the agent did not look at the key cards. This procedure consistently produced chance results. Finally, there were runs for which Shackleton was instructed to increase his rate of responding. In these cases there was a corresponding tendency for the customary +1 hitting to be replaced by +2 hitting. This degree of lawful regularity is unprecedented in psi experiments, even with gifted subjects.

The identity of the agent also seemed to be important. Shackleton was successful with three agents but not with ten others who participated only briefly. With one of the successful agents, there was significant backward as well as forward displacement in the same runs.

Criticism of the experiment began with a famous article in the magazine *Science* by a research chemist, George Price (1955), who listed six ways Soal could have faked the results provided he had the collaboration of one or more of the other participants. For example, Soal could have made a deal with the agent to the effect that the latter would choose a particular ordering of the key cards in the box that maximized the number of hits for a given sequence of targets. Price's speculations were later extended and systematized by Hansel (1960, 1966), who claimed that the results of the entire 40 sessions could be accounted for by assuming trickery on the part of Soal in collaboration with Shackleton and two of the three successful agents.

These allegations led to a heated debate about their viability (Hansel, 1960; Soal, 1960). The points of dispute are quite technical, and fortunately they need not detain us because more serious allegations subsequently took center stage. During session 16, the third successful agent reported seeing Soal, who was then functioning as EA, altering figures on the target sheets during the tabulation of scores. Specifically, she said that he was changing 1s into 4s or 5s. This allegation was not officially published until 1960 and curiously enough was mentioned only briefly by Hansel. It was not until the 1970s that evidence began to appear confirming her charge.

The fireworks began when Medhurst (1971), who was seeking to vindicate Soal, conducted a computer analysis of all the target sequences used in the Shackleton experiment. These analyses revealed that Soal could not have obtained his target sequences from the sources of random numbers he claimed to have used. More importantly, it left open the possibility that the target sheets had been tampered with. Three years later, Christopher Scott reported a detailed analysis of the results of the crucial session 16 which confirmed in detail the agent's allegation, provided that the additional (and plausible) assumption was made that the record sheets Soal brought to the session contained an excess of 1s (Scott *et al.*, 1974). The hypothesis, then, was that during or immediately after the transfer of Shackleton's guesses to the target sheets, Soal changed some of the 1 targets into 4s or 5s so as to produce additional +1 hits. Had this in fact happened, one would expect to find certain tell-tale signs in the data. There would not only be large excesses of hits on 4s and 5s compared to 2s and 3s, but also a more modest excess of hits on 1s (because some of the misses on 1s had been removed). That is exactly what Scott found.

Soal was at this time too advanced in age to speak for himself, but no less than six other parapsychologists rallied to his defense (Scott *et al.*, 1974). The arguments ranged from an appeal to the fact that the anomaly could be found in only two other sessions in addition to session 16, to the observation that the scoring pattern resembled the familiar salience effect (an example of which we saw in the preceding section), to attacks on the agent's credibility as a witness. Yet none of the defenders were able to undermine the core of Scott's case: an observation of fraud had been confirmed in detail by an examination of the data.

The (apparently) final blow came four years later when Betty Markwick (1978) uncovered further anomalies in the data. By means of an extensive computer search, she found numerous instances where long sequences of target digits were duplicated in different runs. In many of these cases, one of the sequences was interrupted at one or more places by one or two extra digits. These digits proved very likely to correspond to hits; in fact, these hits proved to account for all the statistical significance in the runs to which the analyses applied. Although it has never been clear what specific mechanism of cheating this particular pattern could represent or what advantage Soal gained from duplicating the target sequences, the pattern hardly looked like an ESP effect. Viewed in the context of the earlier evidence, this new evidence of fraud on Soal's part appeared compelling. As Pratt, up to this point a staunch defender of Soal, concluded, 'we are compelled to consider all of the records to be invalid as evidence of ESP unless or until they can be shown to be otherwise' (Pratt, 1978, p. 28).

2.4 The Stepanek experiments

By far the most durable ESP subject in the history of parapsychology is a library clerk from Czechoslovakia by the name of Pavel Stepanek. Over a ten-year period he was the subject of 27 research reports co-authored by 18 investigators, not counting an overview by the most prominent of the researchers, Gaither Pratt (1973).

Stepanek was discovered by the Czech parapsychologist Milan Ryzl, who had been conducting a research project endeavoring to train ESP ability by means of hypnosis. Stepanek did not prove to be a very good hypnotic subject, but while in hypnosis he did demonstrate an unusual ability to guess whether the white or dark side of a thin piece of cardboard was facing upwards inside an opaque cardboard envelope. Stepanek was able to demonstrate this ability outside hypnosis as well, and it is doubtful that the hypnotic training made any substantive contribution to his abilities. During the period when these abilities were at their peak, Stepanek could make about 57 percent correct guesses.

In his overview, Pratt (1973) cited two experiments which he considered most evidential in terms of the results and the adequacy of the experimental controls (Blom and Pratt, 1968; Pratt, Keil and Stevenson, 1970). The Blom experiment provides a good illustration of the basic method. Blom was a physical scientist from the Netherlands who had no previous involvement with parapsychology. For the experiment, Blom and Pratt jointly prepared 40 envelopes with green/white target cards randomly inserted in such a way that neither researcher knew whether the green or white side was facing up. For each eight-trial run, Pratt randomized the order of eight of the envelopes and placed them inside opaque covers. This set of eight cards-within-envelopes-within-covers was then given to Blom, who presented them to Stepanek one at a time. Stepanek lightly placed his fingers on the upper surface of each cover and indicated whether he thought the green or white side of the card was facing up. Meanwhile, Pratt was busy preparing a new set of eight targets for the next run.

The experiment consisted of a total of 500 runs, 125 in each of four sessions. Since the target pool consisted of only 40 envelopes, this meant that each envelope was presented once every five runs, or 25 times per session. The cards were re-randomized inside the envelopes for every session. At the end of each session, Blom and Pratt jointly tabulated the results.

Stepanek's overall hit rate was 53.9 percent, which was highly significant statistically ($p < 10^{-6}$. The data were also analysed using a majority vote procedure. A separate 'guess' was computed for each of the 40 envelopes in each session, corresponding to the color Stepanek chose most frequently in his 25 calls of that envelope. Stepanek achieved hits on 96 (60 percent) of these 160 majority vote trials ($p <$ .002).

You may be wondering why the envelopes were further concealed in covers for this experiment. Apart from providing additional security against sensory cues, there was another reason. During the course of the investigations, the experimenters began to notice that Stepanek would consistently call certain envelopes, or certain sides of certain envelopes, either 'green' or 'white.' For example, envelope 7 might be called 'green' 20 out of 25 times in a session. So long as the envelopes were exposed to Stepanek, this effect was not very interesting from a parapsychological point of view: it could merely have been a habit based on Stepanek's recognizing sensorially unique characteristics of particular envelopes. However, it did become of parapsychological interest when this 'focusing effect'* on the envelopes continued after they were concealed inside covers. Later on, the effect migrated to the covers (a sensory effect) but persisted when the covers were further concealed by placing them inside jackets – a kind of Chinese box phenomenon. As the focusing effect evolved, Stepanek's success at guessing the green and white cards gradually dwindled. Much of the later work with Stepanek concentrated on attempting to verify and understand the focusing effect.

Surprisingly, the extensive work with Stepanek has received relatively little attention from critics either inside or outside parapsychology. Of course, as always, experimenter fraud is a possibility, although it has not yet been calculated what minimum number of researchers must have been involved in the conspiracy to account for all the results. The one semi-substantive criticism made so far concerns the possibility of Stepanek getting sensory cues from touching the outer coverings (Hansel, 1980). This, of course, is the logical place to attack. Pratt did take some precautions in this regard. With the exception of the first seven experiments, the envelopes were made of heavy cardboard apparently impervious to heat radiation. The target cards themselves were flexed to prevent warping.

Since Stepanek's success has been limited to this one particular procedure, the opportunity to touch the outer coverings would indeed seem to be important, for either psychological or physical reasons. But even if his abilities could ultimately be shown to have a sensory explanation, the degree of perceptual sensitivity he has demonstrated should be of scientific interest in its own right. Indeed, one might be able to think of several exotic sensory hypotheses that would be fascinating topics for research. Moreover, it should be noted that no current definition of ESP would rule out physical energies being involved indirectly in the transmission process, and according to some definitions physical energies could play a direct role. On the other hand, it should be kept in mind that no sensory explanation of Stepanek's results has ever been seriously proposed.

2.5 The Schmidt REG experiments

As indicated in chapter 5, a major advance in parapsychological methodology occurred with the advent of the REG, which was first introduced into parapsychology on a major scale by Helmut Schmidt. A large number of studies has demonstrated significant psi effects with such machines (Stanford, 1977c), and quite a few of these have been by Schmidt himself. As for ESP, attention has largely been focused on three simple experiments he conducted in the late 1960s (Schmidt, 1969a, 1969b).

All the experiments employed a four-choice REG with immediate feedback, the randomicity of the target sequence being partly determined by the random emission of electrons from a weak radioactive source. Two of the experiments utilized a precognition testing mode. The third was a clairvoyance experiment, for which a sequence from a random number table was fed into the machine in advance. Formal testing was restricted to a small number of subjects selected on the basis of their relative success in informal screening tests. Most were mediums or amateur psychics. They were tested at their homes, and Schmidt paid particular attention to providing a pleasant and supportive psychological atmosphere. Subjects were tested only when they were in the mood for it, and they could terminate a session whenever they wished.

Three subjects participated in the two precognition experiments, two of whom participated in both. The first experiment consisted of a total of 63,066 trials and yielded a hit rate of 26.1 percent ($p < 10^{-8}$). Two of the three subjects scored significantly above chance. In the second experiment, subjects could choose to aim for hits (high-aim, or HA) or for misses (low-aim, or LA). One subject chose all HA, one all LA, and the other some of each. With respect to the intended goal, the total hit rate was 27.0 percent over 20,000 trials ($p < 10^{-10}$). Each subject's score was independently significant. The HA-LA procedure was used again in the clairvoyance experiment. Six subjects were tested, two working individually and the remaining four in pairs, each performing some HA and some LA runs. Again with respect to the intended goal, the hit rate was 26.7 percent over 15,000 trials ($p < 10^{-5}$). Only the two subjects who worked alone produced independently significant scores, but this may simply have been because they completed the most trials.

Hansel's (1980) critique of this research was much more vague than those of the earlier experiments. He noted that in the two experiments using the HA-LA procedure the total number of actual hits was close to chance, and this was the only outcome recorded on the internal counters of the machine. However, the differential results were recorded on paper tape, also automatically. Exactly how this procedure was to have biased the experiments is unclear. Although Hansel complained that Schmidt worked alone with no one checking on him, he declined to explicitly accuse Schmidt of fraud.

A second weakness alluded to by Hansel concerns optional stopping. In his first precognition experiment, Schmidt specified in advance only a range of total trials to be conducted, and the range was rather wide (55,000–70,000). Although the high level of statistical significance argues against optional stopping being a likely explanation of the results, its likelihood is difficult to determine objectively. It can be safely ruled out in the other two experiments, where only two, widely divergent possibilities (e.g. 20,000 and 40,000) were permitted.

A third criticism, formulated in most detail by Ray Hyman (1981), concerns the adequacy of the randomicity tests on the REG. Although these criticisms were directed specifically at Schmidt's PK experiments, they would seem at least somewhat applicable to the first two ESP studies as well. The tests Schmidt used consisted of automatically activating one of the buttons of the machine at the rate of once a second. A total of five million targets were generated in this way on 100 separate occasions, usually right after the experimental sessions. No evidence was found of nonrandomness at either the singlet or doublet levels.

Hyman argued that these randomicity tests were not real controls in that they did not fully duplicate the conditions of the actual testing. For instance, nonrandomness might occur in short intermittent bursts to which Schmidt's more global tests were insensitive. However, Schmidt came at least partway toward meeting this criticism by analysing his randomicity tests in 1,000–trial blocks as well as *in toto*. The fact that there was no evidence of increasing levels of scoring over trials (i.e. 'learning') also argues against REG bias as an explanation of his results.

2.6 The Delmore experiments

Bill Delmore was a Yale law student at the time he participated in an extensive series of ESP and PK experiments at Rhine's laboratory in the early 1970s. Psychologically, he was distinguished by unusually vivid visual imagery, frequent lucid dreams, and a high degree of confidence in his psi abilities (Kelly and Kanthamani, 1972).

The most extensive series of ESP tests under well-controlled conditions used a card-guessing procedure (Kanthamani and Kelly, 1974b). A pool of 520 playing cards were thoroughly mixed and placed in desk drawers. (This method of randomization, which was used at Delmore's request, is not recommended, but extensive examination of the resulting target sequence revealed that it was satisfactorily random). For each trial, the experimenter, who was seated behind the desk, picked out a card and without looking at it placed it inside an opaque folder which was then shown to Delmore, although he was not allowed to touch it. The experiment consisted of a total of 46 runs of 52 trials each, usually one run per session. The results were analysed by several different statistical methods, all of which revealed significant evidence of psi. The strongest specific effect was an excess of 'exact hits' – getting the card correct with respect to both suit and number. Delmore obtained exact hits on 6 percent of the trials, whereas only about 2 percent (1/52) would be expected by chance ($p < 10^{-30}$). He was particularly successful on rare occasions where he made confidence calls. Out of 20 confidence calls, 14 were exact hits (Kanthamani and Kelly, 1974a). This experiment will be discussed further in the next chapter (section 2.1.1). Delmore was successful on other tasks as well, most notably a 'psychic shuffle' task (Kanthamani and Kelly, 1975) and trials with a four-choice Schmidt REG of the type discussed in the previous section (Kelly and Kanthamani, 1972). Over a period of eight sessions, he obtained 28.7 percent hits in 5,377 trials ($p < 10^{-9}$) on the REG.

The principal critic of the Delmore experiments has been Persi Diaconis (1978, 1979), a statistician who is also a magician. Diaconis accused Delmore of having used sleight-of-hand and other magician's tricks during an informal public demonstration of card guessing. Although he stated that the methodology of the experiments as described in the research reports cited above was 'beyond reproach' (Diaconis, 1978, p. 133), he nonetheless concluded that the experiments were worthless as scientific evidence because Delmore possessed conjuring skills and no conjuror was present to observe him during the sessions.

Kelly (1979) responded that it was unfair to extrapolate from a completely uncontrolled demonstration to controlled experiments, all the more since the tricks Diaconis said Delmore used were precluded in the latter and no deficiencies in the experimental procedures were cited. He also pointed out that even at the demonstration Diaconis had not actually observed tricks but only inferred them.

2.7 The Tart TCT experiment

This experiment was actually a component of a larger experiment that will be discussed in section 5.2 of the next chapter (Tart, 1976). The series of interest here incorporated a modified GESP procedure using a device called the ten-choice trainer (TCT). The subject was seated alone in front of a circular display panel of ten playing cards (ace through 10) with adjacent buttons and lamps. The experimenter/agent was seated in a partly electrically shielded room down the hall in front of a similar display panel. For each trial, the experimenter activated a separate ten-choice REG and then flicked the switch on the control panel of the TCT corresponding to the number displayed by the REG. This activated a warning light on the subject's console indicating that he or she should begin trying to identify the target. Subjects were encouraged to move their hands around the panel trying to 'feel' the correct target. The experimenter observed these hand movements on a video monitor and tried to telepathically guide the subject's hand toward the correct number. Subjects indicated their responses by pressing the appropriate button on their panel, after which the lamp corresponding to the target number was lit, thus providing immediate feedback. A chime sounded if the response was a hit. The experimenter then recorded the target and response on paper. The TCT automatically counted the number of hits, which the experimenter recorded at the end of each run. The device is illustrated in plate 7.

The experimenters were advanced undergraduate psychology students in an experimental psychology course taught by Tart. Ten subjects who had been screened for apparent psi talent each completed 20 runs of 25 trials each. The overall mean number of hits per run was 3.61 compared to an MCE of 2.50 ($p < 10^{-24}$). The scoring was not evenly distributed among the subjects, with five scoring markedly above chance and the other five close to chance. The five significant subjects were all tested by the same experimenter.

This experiment has probably evoked more controversy among parapsychologists than any other piece of research in the field. The majority of the criticisms have focused on evidence of nonrandomness in the target sequences. The most prevalent of these biases was a deficiency in the number of XX doublets (the same target appearing twice in a row), which Tart attributed to the possibility that the experimenters may sometimes have confused repetition of the same number by the REG with its failing to produce any number at all, thus leading the experimenter to generate another target. Some other, less pronounced biases were noted as well, and there was evidence that these biases tended to be greatest in the target sequences of the highest scoring subjects (Gatlin, 1979; J. E. Kennedy, 1980b). In a few cases, the same biases were found in both the target and response sequences.

These revelations triggered two distinct classes of alternative interpretations of Tart's results. Kennedy (1980b) noted that the experimenter could have cheated by activating a number on the console other than that given by the REG, perhaps even changing the target during the course of the trial based on feedback from the subject's hand movements. Such activity might have led to nonrandomness in the final target sequences, but not necessarily so. Kennedy did not go so far as to allege fraud outright, and he agreed with Tart that another possibility was a PK influence by either experimenter or subjects on the REG. Such an occurrence would differ little from the kind of nonintentional PK effects on REGs reported in other experiments (see chapter 10).

The other argument, made by both Kennedy and Lila Gatlin, was that the nonrandomness could have allowed subjects to consciously or unconsciously use logical inference to increase their ESP scores. Tart (1979, 1980) countered by noting that the important issue was not the randomicity of the target sequences, but their predictability. He demonstrated further that standard randomicity tests are not necessarily very good indicators of predictability.

In order to test whether the predictability of his target sequences was such that it could have accounted for the results obtained, an elaborate computer program was constructed (Tart and Dronek, 1983). The program was designed to model the behavior of a subject with perfect memory for how many times each possible target singlet, doublet, triplet, up to sextuplet had occurred previously in the sequence. The computer based its guesses exclusively on this information.

The intent, of course, was to see how well the computer would do in 'guessing' the actual target sequences from the experiment. The computer actually did not do badly, accumulating an average of 2.82 hits per run ($p < .005$). Three of the ten 'subjects' scored significantly above chance. On the other hand, the computer was not nearly as successful as the real subjects, and when the computer's score was substituted for the ordinary chance baseline of 2.50 hits per run, the subjects' scores were still highly significant. Moreover, the scores obtained by the computer and by the real subjects were uncorrelated with each other ($r = +.08$). Thus Tart concluded that unless someone could come up with a more powerful inference strategy, logical inference should not be preferred to psi as the explanation of his results.

Kennedy conceded that he could not describe such a strategy but argued that it was not necessary for him to do so, since such a strategy might still exist even if no one had yet devised it. (Of course, the same thing could have been said even if no evidence of nonrandomness had appeared in the randomicity tests.)

3 Free-response experiments

3.1 The Maimonides dream experiments

Largely due to the influence of J. B. Rhine, free-response testing procedures were uncommon in ESP research until the 1960s. Their current prominence is attributable in no small part to a successful series of investigations of ESP in dreams conducted at the Maimonides Medical Center in New York City during that decade. Orthodox dream research was experiencing a renaissance because of the discovery that periods of highly visual dream activity were strongly associated with a distinctive pattern of brain waves plus bursts of rapid eye movements (REMs). This discovery allowed researchers to awaken subjects during their dreams and thus obtain more accurate dream reports than could be obtained retrospectively.

The core experiments in the project have been described by the principal investigators, Montague Ullman and Stanley Krippner (1970; Ullman *et al.*, 1973), although important contributions were also made by Charles Honorton. The basic procedure can be described as follows. One trial was completed per night. The subject slept alone in a room at the laboratory with electrodes attached to measure brain waves and eye movements. The physiological recordings were monitored by an experimenter in another room. When these recordings indicated that the subject had been dreaming for several minutes, he or she was awakened by the experimenter and asked to give a description of the dream, which was tape recorded. This generally occurred between three and six times per night. The next morning, the experimenter played back the recordings of the dream reports, asking the subject for any elaborations or associations to the material and to guess what the target might be. These utterances were also tape recorded.

Before the subject went to bed, the agent used a random number table to select the target for the night from a pool of postcard-sized prints of famous paintings. The agent then went to spend the night in an isolated room. Off and on during the night, he or she concentrated on the art print, attempting to influence the subject's dreams.

Series consisted of from 7 to 12 trials each. Both the subject and one or more (usually three) outside judges were asked to rank each of the target prints for the series against typed copies of each of the dream protocols, an example of the preferential matching method. The trial was considered a hit if the rank assigned to the target was in the top half; i.e. $p = .5$. A more sensitive, rating procedure was also employed, and both rankings and ratings were made separately for the protocols with and without the morning-after elaborations. This procedure led to a large number of different analyses, but in all cases the majority of the results were either significant or nonsignificant, allowing a simple judgment to be made about the success or failure of the series.

The researchers began with a 12–trial screening study, in which 12 subjects selected for good dream recall and belief in telepathy participated for one night each. The overall results were positive but not significant by most of the analyses. However, two subjects showed sufficient promise to be invited back for further testing. One of these, a male psychologist named William Erwin, completed two separate series of seven and eight sessions each. Both series yielded clearly significant positive results. A novel feature of the second series was that the agent was given along with each target picture a matching set of 'multisensory materials,' small objects intended to help him dramatize or 'act out' the sending process.

The target picture from one successful trial of this series is reproduced in Plate 8a and the multisensory materials are presented in Plate 8b. Compare these to the following excerpts from the subject's 'guess for the night,' made the next morning, in which he tied together the common elements in his dreams, two of which had as major themes a speech by Winston Churchill and a native ceremonial sacrifice:

> In the Churchill thing there was a ceremonial thing going on, and in the native dream there was a type of ceremony going on . . . leading to whatever the ceremonial would be to sacrificing two victims. . . . I would say the sacrifice feeling in the native dream . . . would be more like the primitive trying to destroy the civilized. . . . It believed in the god-authority . . . no god was speaking. It was the use of the fear of this, or the awe of god idea, that was to bring about the control. Not that [the] god spoke. . . . (Ullman *et al.*, 1973, p. 123)

The pun represented by the name 'Churchill' is particularly noteworthy. Such 'primary process' associations are well known to characterize dream imagery, and they lend credibility to the target-protocol correspondences as reflecting genuine telepathic influence. At the same time, it should be noted that Erwin's dreams that night also included other elements, not cited above, that did not clearly relate to the target. The evidentiality of the experiment derives from the statistical analyses, which take such factors into account.

The second subject selected by the screening, a female secretary, failed to produce significant results in a followup series. A second screening study had meanwhile been conducted, which again yielded overall results that were positive but not significant. The most promising subject from this series, a female psychologist, gave nonsignificant results in a subsequent eight-night series. However, a male psychologist and parapsychologist named Robert Van de Castle, selected in part because of his successful performance in an informal confirmation of the Maimonides research at an independent laboratory (Hall, 1967), did produce significant results in an eight-night series. In this series, the subject was allowed to choose his own agent each night, and the target pool had been revised to capitalize on past indications that simple, emotional and colorful target pictures seemed most successful.

Subsequently, two statistically significant studies were completed using 'sensory bombardment' of the agent. In the first study, which included eight subjects, the agent viewed a slide of the art print while listening to thematically appropriate music played at a loud volume

(Krippner, Honorton, Ullman, Masters and Houston, 1971). In the second study, in which a psychic named Malcolm Bessent was the subject, the agents were the audience at a rock concert by the 'Grateful Dead' who viewed the target slide displayed on a large screen during one of the songs (Krippner, Honorton and Ullman, 1973). Two statistically significant precognition dream studies had previously been conducted with Bessent, although only the latter of them was adequately controlled (Krippner, Honorton and Ullman, 1972; Krippner, Ullman and Honorton, 1971).

In summary, although not all the series were significant, they nonetheless represent an impressive rate of success. It is perhaps noteworthy that the most successful subjects were males.

Attempted replications of the Van de Castle series and the first sensory bombardment experiment were later undertaken at the laboratory of dream researcher David Foulkes at the University of Wyoming (Belvedere and Foulkes, 1971; Foulkes *et al.*, 1972). Despite close collaboration with the Maimonides team, the results of both studies were nonsignificant. Markedly different and revealing speculations as to why the Maimonides and Wyoming results differed are offered by Van de Castle (1977b), who served as the subject in the Wyoming experiments, and Hansel (1980). Whereas Van de Castle stressed the adverse psychological impact of the skeptical orientation of the Wyoming investigators, Hansel praised them for taking more extensive precautions against experimenter fraud than did the Maimonides team. In any event, they deserve credit for their open-mindedness and courage in agreeing to collaborate with parapsychologists in such a replication attempt.

Hansel's other major criticism of the Maimonides experiments was that the agent may have had contact with one of the experimenters after learning the identity of the target in the Van de Castle series. This represents an incorrect reading of a possibly ambiguous statement in one of the experimental reports (Palmer, 1980). A more embarrassing misrepresentation of the procedure appears in a generally fair-minded critical book by Zusne and Jones (1982), who inform their readers on pp. 260–1 that the target picture shown to the subject the morning after the ESP session was instead shown to the subject before the session! The one clearly legitimate criticism of the Maimonides experiments has been by Child (in press) who notes that in the case of the preferential matchings the judges may not have succeeded in following the instruction to rank the targets independently of one another, thereby possibly violating the assumptions of the statistical test used (see chapter 6, section 4.2). However, Child demonstrates that the other analyses are sufficient to confirm the overall significance of the results.

3.2 The SRI remote viewing experiments

Perhaps the most widely publicized of all parapsychological research in the past decade have been the investigations of Hal Puthoff and Russell

Targ at a prestigious California research institute named SRI International. Although most of the publicity has accrued from their controversial experiments with the Israeli psychic Uri Geller (who contrary to popular belief was considered suspect by most parapsychologists from early on), their more orthodox studies of a free-response GESP procedure called remote viewing (RV)* have attracted more interest from psi researchers (Puthoff and Targ, 1979; Targ and Puthoff, 1977).

The first formal RV experiment was conducted with a former California city police commissioner named Pat Price as subject. For each trial, the 'outbound experimenter' drove to a randomly selected outdoor target location selected from a pool of 100 such locations by an SRI administrator. The locations in the pool were chosen because they had interesting architectural features. The experimenter was allowed 30 minutes' driving time, after which he observed the location for an additional 30 minutes. During the viewing period, Price was back at SRI with the 'inbound experimenter,' who was blind to the target pool and, of course, to the particular target location as well. Price was asked to both verbally describe and to draw what he 'saw,' with the experimenter asking questions that helped him to elaborate his descriptions.

This procedure was followed for a total of nine trials. Afterwards, the list of target locations and Price's drawings plus unedited transcripts were given to an independent judge who was asked to visit each site and to rank all the target pictures from 1 to 9 according to their similarity to the site as it looked to him. Seven of the nine transcripts were ranked first at the correct site ($p < 10^{-4}$). A second series of nine trials conducted with a photographer named Hella Hammid also yielded highly significant results ($p < 10^{-5}$). However, these p-values might be inflated because of failure to take account of possible dependencies between trials (J. E. Kennedy, 1979; see also chapter 6, section 4.2). An example of a successful trial in the Hammid series is given in Plate 9.

These experiments were evaluated as part of a larger series of 51 trials with nine different subjects. The net results remained significant ($p < 10^{-8}$). For twelve of the trials, the targets were pieces of office or laboratory equipment rather than geographical locations. Later, the basic RV procedure was extended to the precognitive mode and to distances up to thousands of miles (Puthoff and Targ, 1979; Targ, Puthoff, and May, 1979).

The most vigorous critics of the SRI experiments have been two psychologists named David Marks and Richard Kammann (1980). Their most serious and extensive criticisms concerned the Price and Hammid experiments. They actually came to California to discuss the experiments with Puthoff, Targ and the judge, as well as to examine the judging materials. They discovered that the unedited transcripts used for judging frequently included the date or other information indicating when the trial had taken place. There occasionally was even reference to the target on a previous trial. They concluded that this information could have easily compromised the blindness of the judge if the order in which the judge received the targets had not been randomized. Had it been?

In the case of the Price series, the answer seems to be no. Resolving this simple question for the Hammid series, however, has turned out to be remarkably complicated. In their critique, Marks and Kammann referred to a letter they received from the judge which they said confirmed that the judge had indeed received the targets in nonrandomized order, but this was explicitly denied by Puthoff and Targ (1981). In an effort to settle the matter, Robert Morris (1980) requested a copy of the judge's letter. According to Morris, the letter clearly stated that the judge had not been aware of whether the target list had been randomized or not. Marks (1981a) neither confirmed nor denied Morris's contention but cited indirect evidence which he claimed showed that supplementary information sheets describing the target locations had not been randomized. There the matter rests.

With regard to the Price series, Marks and Kammann set about to demonstrate empirically that their hypothesis could account for the results. Since descriptions of four of the nine trials had been published, they restricted their investigation to the five remaining trials. To begin with, they gave eight outside judges only the biasing cues present in the transcripts. On this basis alone, the judges were highly successful in placing them in the correct order.

But the really crucial question is whether judges could continue to succeed in matching with the biasing cues removed from the transcripts. Again working with the subsample of five transcripts, Marks and Kammann found that each of two outside judges, who were described only as 'research psychologists,' was unable to match the transcripts to the targets to a statistically significant degree.

Although Marks and Kammann are to be commended for subjecting their hypothesis to experimental test, their latter experiment can be criticized on several grounds. First, by reducing the sample size from nine to five they drastically reduced the sensitivity of their statistical evaluation. Moreover, since (as one would expect) the trials chosen for publication tended to be the most successful ones, the average quality of the trials selected for analysis was not truly representative of the whole. A better procedure would have been to use all nine trials and find some way reasonably to assure the blindness of the judges. Second, it is not clear who edited the transcripts. If this person already knew the experimental results, the editing could have been biased so as to favor the null hypothesis. Finally, we are not told anything about the motivation of the judges or what they knew about the authors' hypothesis. If the judges knew the hypothesis and either were skeptics or wanted to help out the authors, the judging quality might have suffered.

To counteract the above experiment, Charles Tart edited all nine transcripts and gave them to a judge of his choosing 'who was unfamiliar with the Price series' (Tart, Puthoff and Targ, 1980, p. 191). The judge succeeded at about the same level of significance as the original judges. Marks (1981b) criticized this study, first, because Tart knew the proper matches while doing the editing. Second, he criticized the use of all nine transcripts because, despite Tart's assurance, 'a "blind" judge may have some memory of previously seen target-transcript matchings or have access to the published material' (Marks, 1981b).

One clear lesson from all this is that it is important to describe the experimental procedure in as much detail as possible in the original report. If the various parties in the controversy had done this, much needless confusion could have been avoided.

Finally, a note should be included about the replicability of the RV procedure. Several successful RV experiments have been reported by parapsychologists (e.g. Bisaha and Dunne, 1979; Schlitz and Gruber, 1980, 1981). I know of two failures by outsiders. One was by Marks and Kammann (1980) themselves. The other (Karnes, Susman, Klusman and Turcotte, 1980) stimulated an extensive discussion over whether the researchers had replicated important aspects of the RV procedure (Commentaries, 1980).

3.3 The ganzfeld experiments

In chapter 5, section 3.4.2a, we briefly discussed a sensory isolation technique called the ganzfeld, which has been used to put subjects in a receptive mental state for free-response ESP. The ganzfeld has become quite popular among parapsychologists, and also quite successful. According to a recent survey by Charles Honorton (1978), 23 of 42 ganzfeld experiments have yielded statistically significant results for a success rate of 55 percent. Moreover, the successful studies came from nine independent laboratories.

Although this rate of success is far from perfect, it also is much greater than one would expect by chance. This observation has led to a new kind of claim for the reality of ESP. In the previous controversies that have been addressed, the focus was upon one experiment or integrated group of experiments from a single laboratory. The appeal in this case is rather to the consistency of the experiments as a group, not the 'conclusiveness' or 'fraud-proofness' of any one of them. Most used samples of more or less unselected subjects tested for one session each, and the issue of experimenter fraud has played a relatively minor role. For these reasons, the ganzfeld controversy resembles controversies in orthodox psychology to a much greater extent than do the others we have examined.

One of the very few critics who has been willing to play the game by these rules is psychologist Ray Hyman. Wanting to avoid placing undue attention on a handful of 'crucial' experiments but at the same time being unable critically to survey all the many hundreds of experimental reports in the parapsychological literature, Hyman chose the ganzfeld experiments as an integrated but representative sample of state-of-the-art psi research. He subsequently presented a critique in which he listed a series of purported flaws applicable to many of the ganzfeld experiments and which led him to conclude that collectively they do not provide a convincing case for ESP (Hyman, 1983, 1985).

Hyman's criticisms were challenged by Honorton (1983, 1985) in what has proven to be one of the most sophisticated critical exchanges in the history of parapsychology. The best that can be done here is to summarize briefly some of the key points of difference.

Hyman devoted most of his attention to attacking the claim that the replication rate was really higher than one would expect by chance. His major points can be summarized as follows.

(1) Experiments with small numbers of subjects may have been submitted for publication only if they were significant. This could explain why the experiments using larger samples of subjects were no more successful than the smaller ones, even though they were more powerful statistically. (It should be noted, however, that the larger and smaller studies differed in other respects as well and that these may have played a role.) Although a survey of unpublished ganzfeld experiments by Susan Blackmore (1980) showed that their rate of success was comparable to that of the published experiments, Hyman cited several reasons for believing that her survey may have overestimated the success rate of the unpublished studies.

(2) The ganzfeld studies varied widely in how the ESP data were scored (i.e. direct hits, binary hits, ratings, etc.). In some cases, more than one scoring method was used and it was not clear from the report which method was considered primary. When statistical corrections are applied to account for these and other secondary analyses conducted by the investigators, the number of significant studies drops drastically. This is an illustration of the multiple analysis problem discussed in chapter 6, section 6.1.

(3) Studies employing multiple experimental conditions were sometimes considered successful if only one of the conditions yielded a significant outcome. For example, in one experiment Honorton discounted data from two of the four experimental conditions because they involved a covert test procedure. The results of the remaining conditions were significant whereas those of the total experiment were not. Honorton argued that the omission was appropriate because all the other studies in the sample used intentional ESP only. Hyman objected on the grounds that there were many differences in procedure among the studies in the sample and that nonintentional ESP had been claimed in other experiments not involving the ganzfeld.

(4) One-tailed tests were often used even though psi-missing outcomes were accepted as successes. This criticism was not contested, but in fact only two of the 23 significant studies were in the psi-missing direction. This ratio of positive to negative outcomes is actually one of the strongest pieces of evidence that the distribution of outcomes is not a chance one.

Honorton's (1985) primary rebuttal to these points was to recompute his analysis using as a single criterion of significance a statistically significant ($p < .05$) excess of direct hits, the same criterion employed in the prototype experiment of Honorton and Harper (1974). Using the 28 studies for which such scores were available, he found twelve (43 percent) which were significantly above chance. When the number of direct hits in each study was converted to a critical ratio, a composite of these critical ratios proved to be highly significant ($p < 10^{-9}$). Moreover, Honorton calculated that it would require 423 unreported studies to bring this success rate down to a nonsignificant level. On the other hand, it is doubtful that Hyman would accept in all cases the appropriateness of these direct hit scores, with reference to criticisms such as number three above.

In conclusion, although it would appear that the originally claimed success rate of 55 percent is indeed too high, it is debatable whether Hyman has succeeded in reducing the 'real' rate sufficiently to make it consistent with the 'chance' hypothesis.

Hyman also criticized the ganzfeld studies on methodological grounds. The most important of these criticisms fall into two categories.

(1) *Sensory cues* In some of the experiments, the set of pictures given to the subjects for judging included the target picture handled by the agent. Research has shown that subjects are indeed able to detect such cues to a significantly better than chance degree when explicitly instructed to look for them (Palmer and Kramer, 1984). On the other hand, volunteer college students did not use such cues to raise their scores in an actual free-response GESP experiment in which presence of the cues was systematically manipulated and the judging procedure was modified to increase their salience (Palmer, 1983c).

(2) *Randomization* In some of the experiments, suboptimal methods of randomization were used to select the targets (e.g. hand shuffling) and/or determine its location within the set of pictures given to the judges. In other cases, the report did not adequately describe the methods used.

Honorton conceded that these flaws existed, but there was disagreement about how serious they were. In order to assess their impact, both authors undertook statistical comparisons of the success rates of the studies with and without particular flaws or categories of flaws. They both found that sensory cues *per se* did not distinguish the significant from the nonsignificant studies. However, whereas Honorton (1985) found that randomization also was not a significant discriminator, Hyman (1985) found that it was. Part of the reason for this discrepancy was that Honorton rated studies using shuffling methods higher than studies using 'other' methods (i.e. other than random number tables or REGs) or not reporting the method used. Hyman did the reverse.

An obvious problem with these 'box scores' is that Honorton and Hyman were aware of the outcomes of the studies when they made their classifications and could not help but be biased by this information in choosing what to count as flaws and how exactly to define them. It also should be pointed out that the research objectives of the authors of particular studies were not always the same as Honorton's. Despite these difficulties, such 'meta-analyses'* (Glass, McGaw and M. L. Smith, 1981) provide a much needed basis for assessing groups of experiments. Another application of this approach will be discussed in the next chapter.

4 Conclusion

So what are we to make of all this? A few things are clear. Parapsychologists have amassed an impressive number of demonstrations of ESP that satisfy the basic requirements of experimental control. Critics, on the other hand, have repeatedly been able to find flaws in these experiments, respects in which they were not watertight. Like most scientific experiments, these experiments, in retrospect, could have been improved. This is not to say they were bad, just not as good as they might have been. Finally, exaggerated claims have been made for some of the experiments. For example, whatever else one might think of Hansel's tactics, he was simply fulfilling his obligation as a critic to point out the fallacy in Rhine's claim that the results of the Pratt-Woodruff experiment 'could be explained by [the experimenter fraud] hypothesis only by assuming collusion between the two experimenters' (J. B. Rhine *et al.*, 1940/1966, p. 148). There has in fact been one conclusive case of experimenter fraud in parapsychology, the so-called Levy affair (J. B. Rhine, 1974), and the Soal experiments come close to fitting that description. However, these two cases represent a very small percentage of all psi research.

How much weight are we to attach to the flaws the critics have uncovered in the other cases? Are all the experiments worthless as evidence of ESP, as some critics have suggested (e.g. Alcock, 1981)? What about those cases where the flaw was shown not to be serious enough to actually account for the results? Does this settle the matter, or can the critic respond that the flaw is a sign of sloppiness in some other, unspecified aspect of the procedure – the 'Error Some Place' definition of ESP? It would seem that how much weight we attach to any experiment as evidence for ESP comes down in the final analysis to the likelihood we assign to the various alternatives, based on our past experiences and world views. Perhaps the biggest mistake both sides have made in the ESP controversy is to imply that it can be settled exclusively by appeal to objective criteria, unless we mean by objectivity the collective subjectivity of the community of scientists.

The futility of the ESP controversy is perhaps no better illustrated than by Diaconis's exchange with Kelly over the Delmore experiments. For Kelly, the important thing was the design and results of the experiments as reflected in the experimental reports. For Diaconis, the important thing was the credibility of the experimental team who conducted the research. According to Diaconis, without such credibility the reports are meaningless. But how can one determine the a priori credibility of researchers objectively?

The bottom line is that the apparent ESP demonstrated so far in controlled environments is simply not strong enough or reliable enough to *compel* acceptance of ESP as a fact of nature. Those who can be convinced by these kinds of demonstrations will find enough to satisfy them. Those who have not been convinced by them will probably not have their minds changed by more of the same, even if the controls are made tighter. There will always be that one more 'essential' control somebody overlooked, or as a last resort the researchers simply will not be trusted. Thus the value of the kinds of experiments discussed in this chapter is not that they 'prove' ESP, but that they define the alternatives that must be accepted if ESP is to be denied. In the next chapter we will consider a different approach to ESP research.

Summary of terms

focusing effect
remote viewing (RV)
meta-analysis

Thought questions

(1) Which of the research projects discussed in this chapter do you think provides the strongest evidence for ESP and which the weakest? Defend your choices.

(2) Do you think Hansel's insinuation of experimenter fraud in the Pratt-Woodruff experiment was justified (a) at the time it was made, and (b) in light of what has occurred since? Why or why not?

(3) We saw that despite the extensive randomicity tests Schmidt made on his REG their adequacy was still questioned. Apart from the kinds of control runs advocated by Hyman, can you think of something else Schmidt could have done (and perhaps could still do) to provide a more definitive check?

(4) Pretend that a government agency asked you to propose a methodology for a third reanalysis of the Price remote viewing series. What would you write?

(5) How much weight do you think should be attached to Hyman's criticism of some ganzfeld experiments because the agents handled the target pictures included in the judging sets? Should the critic be required to provide empirical evidence that such an artifact is likely to be a factor in experiments of the type criticized, or is it enough to point out that the artifact is a theoretical possibility?

Chapter 8
ESP research findings: the process approach

John Palmer

1 Introduction

The proof research discussed in the preceding chapter has received a disproportionate amount of attention from both the media and from scientific critics outside parapsychology. Yet much psi research is intended to do more than merely demonstrate psi. As noted previously, this so-called 'process-oriented' research is designed to increase the scientific understanding of psi anomalies by examining the characteristics of their manifestation and by exploring their relation to 'normal' psychological or physical processes. Palmer (1983b) recently conducted an informal survey of the major parapsychological journals during the decade of the 1970s in which he found that about 60 percent of the experimental reports had as an important objective the exploration of psi in relation to these other processes. This percentage would have been larger had process research directed toward the study of the internal characteristics of psi, e.g. decline effects, been included. This ignoring of process research by outside commentators has created a misleading impression about psi research, and particularly about the degree to which it conforms to research in other sciences.

But before we get too carried away, is process research in parapsychology really justified? One might argue that it is premature to study the characteristics of a process until it has been established that the process is real (e.g. Tobacyk, in press). Some scientists have criticized process research in parapsychology on the grounds that it unjustly presupposes the reality of psi. It is true that one occasionally comes across statements in the parapsychological literature of the sort, 'Now that we have proven the existence of psi it is time to begin studying its characteristics.' One can sympathize with the scientist who finds such statements annoying and arrogant. However, even though there may be process psi researchers who personally consider psi to be an established fact, such a belief is by no means a prerequisite for doing process research. It is only necessary that the existence of psi be accepted as a 'working hypothesis.' Indeed, looking at the matter from a broader perspective, one can easily conceive of process research designed to demonstrate that the process underlying 'psi' is a normal physical one.

But even from the narrower perspective, process research in parapsychology can be justified on the following three grounds.

(1) The demonstration of a significant and reliable relation between psi and some other variable is in itself evidence for the reality of psi. If the measure of psi were capturing only random variations from MCE, statistical theory tells us that such relations should not occur. Conversely, the fact that they do occur tells us that our psi test is measuring something real.

(2) To the extent that process research is successful in uncovering correlates of psi, this knowledge can help us to produce psi more reliably and thus lead to stronger and more easily obtainable demonstrations of it.

(3) Process research is a first step toward the development of empirically based theories or models of psi. It is the ability to rigorously conceptualize the process under study that is the ultimate goal of scientific inquiry.

1.1 Empirical generalizations

The bulk of process research in parapsychology has aimed either explicitly or implicitly at establishing empirical generalizations* or 'laws' of psi. Empirical generalizations refer to experimentally demonstrable relationships between psi and other variables. Examples of empirical generalizations might be: 'People who believe that ESP exists score higher on ESP tests than people who do not' or 'People score higher on ESP tests under hypnosis than in the normal "waking" state.'

The use of the term 'generalization' implies that we expect these relations to hold universally within a given domain. For instance, if hypnotized subjects score higher than 'waking' subjects in one experiment, we would expect to find the same thing in an attempted replication of that experiment. Likewise, we would expect to find the same thing regardless of the type of hypnotic induction and the type of ESP test we employed. If the latter proved not to be the case, we might be forced to state the law in a more circumscribed manner, i.e. to restrict its domain: e.g. 'Subjects hypnotized by the relaxation method score higher on restricted-choice ESP tests than do subjects in the "waking" state.'

A major problem we face in parapsychology is that relationships do not replicate to the extent that we would like. Because of this, our claims to have established any laws at all must be made tentatively and very cautiously.

How can this lack of repeatability be accounted for? One answer is the skeptical answer: there is no such thing as psi. According to this view, once positive results due to faulty methodology have been removed, the remaining significant results can be attributed to statistical flukes, which by their nature should not replicate. Psi proponents would counter by claiming that there are *enough* positive results from methodologically adequate research and *enough* replicability to render the skeptical hypothesis very unlikely. Unfortunately, it is very difficult if not impossible to settle this dispute by a rigorous objective analysis. But since we only need to accept psi as a working hypothesis in order to continue our inquiry, this dispute need not deter us. So let us assume that psi exists and see what other factors might lead to poor repeatability.

(1) The first of these is sampling error*. As discussed in chapter 5, the majority of hits in most ESP tests are not due to ESP at all but to 'chance,' and the number of chance hits can vary greatly from test to test. Thus a significant result in an initial experiment may fail to reappear in an attempted replication simply because the number of chance hits in the latter happened to be low. This problem can be minimized by using large numbers of trials, but this solution itself may carry disadvantages, such as tiring the subject.

(2) A probably more crucial problem, however, is that we do not yet have a very good idea of what factors determine how well or how poorly subjects perform in ESP tests. As was pointed out in chapter 5, it is difficult if not impossible to duplicate the procedure of an initial

experiment in all potentially important respects. This problem is greatly compounded, of course, when we cannot specify what those respects are. Even when we can we may not be able to duplicate them adequately in practice (e.g. interpersonal warmth). In other words, a replication attempt may fail because some such factor was left uncontrolled. Of course, it is precisely these factors which process research is intended to uncover.

All this puts us in a veritable 'catch–22:' we cannot identify these mediating factors without more reliable psi, but we cannot get more reliable psi until we identify the mediating factors. If psi were totally unreliable, the situation would indeed be hopeless. But as should become evident as we progress through the chapter, there are signs of regularity and lawfulness that emerge from the process ESP research that has been done up to this time. As these patterns emerge more clearly and become more precisely defined, they will lead to changes in our research procedures and/or selection of subjects that may well break through the catch–22. This is what the process approach to ESP research is really all about at this stage of the field's development.

(3) A final possibility is that psi is real but inherently unlawful or 'supernatural,' i.e. that it occurs arbitrarily, 'whimsically,' or in some way that is in principle unpredictable. Since the purpose of science is to uncover and conceptualize lawful regularities in nature, adopting this assumption would be tantamount to conceding that psi cannot be studied scientifically. The best we could do would be to put ourselves in position to observe psi as carefully and rigorously as possible whenever it decides to favor us with its presence. Parapsychology is based on the premise that psi is natural and lawful, and the field would cease to exist in its present form if this assumption were ever to be decisively discredited.

Even in the best of cases, it is unlikely that we will ever achieve absolute laws in parapsychology, i.e. laws that allow accurate prediction in each individual case. For example, even if we could consistently replicate an experiment which shows that subjects as a group score significantly higher on an ESP test under hypnosis than in the 'waking' state, it is unlikely that every subject would conform to this pattern. We can only say that subjects score better in hypnosis on the average. Another way of stating this is that we strive after statistical laws* rather than absolute laws. Statistical laws are both valid and useful scientifically, provided that we can specify reliably the nonchance probability that the law will hold in any individual case. Even statistical laws so defined have yet to be achieved in parapsychology, and they are not achieved very often in most areas of psychology either. Yet in both fields they represent a realistic and challenging goal.

The principles underlying statistical laws can also be exploited to help us extract what information exists in the relatively unreliable data we have at present in parapsychology. Just as we can draw conclusions about individual experiments when not every subject conforms to the general pattern, we can likewise draw conclusion about groups of experiments when not every experiment in the group conforms to the general pattern, i.e. incomplete replicability. Let's say, for example, that we have a group of 20 experiments exploring the relationship between ESP and hypnosis. By chance we would expect ten of these to show a positive relationship (higher scores among the hypnotized subjects) and ten to show the opposite. We also would expect an equal number of statistically significant outcomes in each direction. But let's say that we found that 17 of these experiments yielded positive relationships whereas only three yielded negative relationships, and furthermore, that all six of the statistically significant relationships were positive. We then might be tempted to conclude that there is a real positive relationship between ESP and hypnosis, even though the relationship was significantly confirmed in only six of the 20 experiments. This approach is another example of the 'meta-analysis' technique we encountered in our discussion of the ganzfeld research in the last chapter (section 3.3). It is one of the tools that parapsychologists use to assess what process research is telling us about psi.

However, meta-analysis must be used cautiously. It assumes that the experiments sampled are methodologically sound and that they are representative of all the relevant experiments conducted. The latter assumption is especially important in practice because not all experiments on a given topic find there way into the journals so they can be included in the samples. This is particularly true of studies with nonsignificant or 'negative' results. Because of the importance of negative results in assessing the overall status of the evidence for psi, the Parapsychological Association insists that its affiliated journals not turn down research reports for this reason, and many nonsignificant results can be found on the pages of these journals. However, this does not solve the problem of authors not submitting negative results for publication. Another difficulty, as we saw in the last chapter, is that deciding which studies should be considered significant or methodologically sound is not always a straightforward matter.

Fortunately, a publication bias in favor of significant results does not affect the kind of meta-analysis we have been discussing, which is concerned with the direction of relationships rather than their significance. But even though it is plausible to argue that the literature is not biased with respect to direction, we cannot actually verify that this is the case. For this and other reasons, the outcomes of meta-analysis in parapsychology are best used as guideposts for further research. Firm conclusions can only be drawn when our laws are more firmly pinned down.

1.2 Theory

The next step in the scientific process is to devise a network of more abstract generalizations to subsume, integrate, and explain the lower-level laws. Such networks are what we call theories*. Another important function of theories is to serve as the basis, ideally but not necessarily through the process of formal logical deduction, for the prediction of new lower-level laws. Such predictions are referred to as hypotheses* until confirmed by experimental tests.

Since parapsychology is for the most part preoccupied with establishing lower-level laws, theory development is in a rather primitive state. Strictly speaking, most 'theories' in parapsychology could more accurately be described as models or simply interpretations. From the point of view of the logical evolution of the scientific process, this relative lack of concern with theory at this stage is justifiable. On the other hand, theory has another important function to fulfil by helping the researcher to select which variables to study in his research, i.e. to decide which potential laws to look for. Such decisions are bound to be guided by implicit theories anyway, and the process might operate more effectively if the theories were made explicit, especially if these theories take account of the available data base. Of course, such theories must be entertained more tentatively than if they represented the integration of well established lower-level laws. This is not to say that there are no theories at all in parapsychology, and some attempts have been made to integrate the tentative laws that we do have. Nonetheless, we perhaps could benefit from more theorizing in parapsychology.

With respect to ESP, there are two broad categories of questions to which the theoretical process must address itself. The first of these is how information gets from the source to the receiver (or whether it is meaningful to talk about information transfer at all). The second is how the ESP 'stimulus' is processed by the mind or brain of the percipient before it appears (or fails to appear) as an observable response. The former category is most appropriately addressed by those parapsychologists trained as physicists (paraphysicists), whereas the latter category is more in the domain of those trained as psychologists.

The first category of theories will be discussed in chapter 11. With a couple of exceptions, these conceptualizations have yet to generate much research, particularly with respect to ESP. The great bulk of theory and hypothesis testing in parapsychology has occurred on the psychological side. In general, the strategy has been to borrow theories and models of varying degrees of scope from orthodox psychology and to adapt them to the needs of parapsychology.

1.2.1 The PMIR model

One of the best examples of formal theorizing and hypothesis testing we have in parapsychology is Rex Stanford's (1974) model of 'psi-mediated instrumental response,' or PMIR*. This model, which borrows its basic idea from learning theory in psychology, posits that humans psychically scan their environment for information relevant to the fulfillment of their biological and psychological needs. This information then leads to 'instrumental responses' to satisfy those needs.

A novel feature of the PMIR model is the proposition that ESP can occur without the person intending to use it or being aware of using it. Thus the model implies that ESP may be more widespread than is generally assumed.

The PMIR model arose out of attempts to integrate and partially explain anecdotal reports (i.e. 'real-life' experiences) and experimental data which seemed to reflect the nonintentional use of ESP or PK. With respect to ESP, Stanford expressed the model in terms of nine formally stated and experimentally testable postulates. He then set about to test these postulates (which thus became experimental hypotheses).

In one of these experiments (Stanford and associates, 1976), two hypotheses were tested.

(1) 'The strength of the disposition toward PMIR is directly and positively related to . . . the importance or strength of the need in question' (Stanford, 1974, p. 45).

(2) '. . . factors disposing toward misuse of PMIR are considered to include . . . a negative self-concept' (Stanford, 1974, p. 51). In other words, persons with a negative self-concept may use PMIR to their own disadvantage in order to confirm their self-concept.

Seventy-two male college students took a covert word-association ESP test in which they had to respond to each of ten stimulus words with the first word that came to mind. Unknown to the subjects, those who responded more rapidly to a randomly chosen key stimulus word than to the other words subsequently would get to engage in a presumably pleasant task, rating photographs of nude or semi-nude women. The other subjects got to engage in a boring task: tracking with a stylus a point on a rotating metal disk for 25 minutes.

Two experimental manipulations were incorporated in the experimental design, each representing one of the two hypotheses. Need strength was manipulated by having half of the subjects tested by one of three attractive female experimenters, whereas the other half were tested by male experimenters. The idea was that subjects tested by the female experimenters would be in a higher state of arousal and thus more motivated to engage in the picture-rating task than would the other subjects.

For ethical reasons, Stanford did not wish to induce a negative self-concept in his subjects, so the self-concept variable was manipulated indirectly. Half of the subjects in each of the previously defined groups were given a preliminary word-association test in which the experimenter praised the creativity of the subjects' responses and never corrected inappropriate responses (positive self-concept). The other subjects did receive correction and were given no praise (neutral self-concept).

The results confirmed the first hypothesis in that subjects tested by the female experimenters had significantly shorter response latencies to the key stimulus words than did subjects tested by the male experimenters. The second hypothesis was not confirmed, but the refutation is a weak one since a negative self-concept was not clearly induced in either group. Stanford and his colleagues have conducted several other experiments testing aspects of the PMIR model, sometimes confirming its predictions and sometimes not (Stanford and Rust, 1977; Stanford and Stio, 1976; Stanford and Thompson, 1974).

The PMIR model has since been superseded by another model called the conformance model (Stanford, 1978), but many of the assumptions of the PMIR model are still viable within this new framework and in any event can serve as a valuable stimulus for further research.

1.3 Things to come

In the remainder of this chapter, research in five distinct subareas where a relatively large amount of research has been done will be reviewed. This implies that a number of other topics will not be covered at all. Even within the topics considered, not all research will be included. For more comprehensive reviews, see Palmer (1978b, 1982) and Carpenter (1977).

The intent of this chapter is not to spoonfeed you a set of predigested facts but instead to give you some idea of how research, conceptualization and criticism interact in the gradual refinement of our knowledge. It will quickly become evident that this evolutionary process is only in its beginning stages. Although for ease of exposition we may sometimes write in this book as if ESP were an established fact, you should keep in mind that its existence is controversial. It is being construed in this chapter as a 'working hypothesis' for which the presently available evidence is inconclusive but nonetheless sufficiently encouraging to justify continued inquiry. Alternatively, one can view this chapter as a review of attempts to understand the psychological factors that interact with the anomalies we call ESP, independent of the assumptions one makes about the underlying nature of these anaomalies.

2 Cognitive processes

The most fundamental question confronting the psychological approach to the study of ESP is how the ESP 'message' interacts with, is distorted by, or is inhibited by ordinary cognitive processes. A rather ambitious attempt to describe this interaction has been made by Harvey Irwin (1979). His model is another example of how concepts from modern psychology, in this case cognitive psychology, can be applied to the subject matter of parapsychology.

2.1 Irwin's information processing model

The starting point of Irwin's model was a paper by William Roll (1966a), who speculated that the ESP stimulus does not input information into the receiving organism directly, but acts instead by evoking already existing long-term memories. Although there was and still is no direct empirical evidence supporting this view, several studies demonstrating relationships between ESP and memory processes indirectly suggest that this may be a promising approach (e.g. Feather, 1967; Stanford, 1970).

Irwin accepted Roll's basic idea and carried it further by proposing that the evoked memory trace goes through reprocessing comparable to the processing of perceptual stimuli from external sources. The model is most directly applicable to visual memory traces, but the basic ideas are meant to apply to memory traces of all kinds. Referring to ideas current in cognitive psychology, Irwin proposed three stages of processing, all occurring at the unconscious (or, more precisely, the preconscious) level. The first stage is called pattern recognition. Here the memory trace is compared to other memory traces to determine to which of these it most closely conforms. In the second stage, called semantic coding, the memory trace is provided with a code suitable for subsequent semantic analysis. Depending upon a number of factors, this code may be either a visual code (picture) or a verbal code (name), or both. Finally, the memory trace, mediated by this code, undergoes semantic analysis, through which its meaning is extracted. Only then does the ESP 'message' reach consciousness.

Irwin's model assumes that the memory traces activated by the ESP stimulus are those which represent the primitive sensory features, or form, of the target rather than its meaning. This emphasis was chosen because of observations by several investigators of free-response ESP that mentation reports are more likely to accurately represent the structure of the target than its verbal identity (Targ and Harary, 1984; Warcollier, 1948). For example, a pair of spectacles might be perceived as a bicycle.

2.1.1 Confusing kings and queens

Insight into how information is processed in the mind can often be gained by examining systematic errors in that processing. Because it proposes that the memory traces activated by the ESP stimulus are of a primitive nature that require multiple stages of preconscious processing, Irwin's model provides many opportunities for such errors to occur. An experiment designed to study such errors beginning at the level of pattern recognition was conducted with the subject Bill Delmore by Edward Kelly and associates (Kelly, Kanthamani, Child and Young, 1975). Kelly wanted to know whether Delmore would make the same kinds of mistakes when attempting to 'perceive' ordinary playing cards by means of ESP as when attempting visually to perceive slides of these cards presented for only 1/25 of a second by means of a tachistoscope. More specifically, Kelly wished to examine what he called 'confusions:' would specific cards be more frequently confused with some cards than others, and would these patterns of confusion be similar for the visual and ESP tasks?

The visual task consisted of 75 runs of 52 trials each, the 'cards' being presented in random order. The ESP test, which happens to be the one discussed in section 2.6 of the last chapter, consisted of 46 such runs. For each trial, the experimenter 'randomly' picked a playing card from a pool of 520 cards in a drawer and, without looking at it, placed it inside an opaque folder before presenting it to the subject.

As you might expect, when Delmore made mistakes in the visual task, he tended to confuse the face cards with each other rather than with the number cards. Second, he tended to consistently confuse the ace, deuce and trey (cards with small number of pips). Third, he tended to confuse suits of the same color with each other more than with suits of the opposite color. But the important point is that these same patterns of confusion appeared in the ESP data, especially in those runs in which the total ESP score was relatively high and thus some ESP was likely to have been operating.

Although more research will be needed to determine to what extent these results can be generalized to other persons, they do tend to support Irwin's proposition that ESP information is processed in much the same way as normal sensory information, and that the processing may well begin at the level of pattern recognition.

2.2 Altered states of consciousness

Another important proposition of Irwin's model borrowed from cognitive psychology has to do with processing capacity*. The theory is that the capacity available at any one time for processing normally acquired as well as extrasensory information at a given time is limited. Thus the more of this capacity that is taken up processing other kinds of material, the less will be available for processing the ESP input, and the less chance the latter has of reaching consciousness.

The concept of processing capacity has played a role in the development of a very extensive area of research in parapsychology, namely the exploration of the relationship between ESP and certain altered states of consciousness (ASCs). In an overview of relevant research conducted up to that time, Charles Honorton (1974b) proposed that ESP is facilitated by the reduction of competing sources of external and internal stimulation, or 'noise,' and the concomitant refocusing of attention on one's internal thought processes. To put this in terms of Irwin's model, the organism's processing capacity is relieved of competing obligations and can be devoted fully to the processing of the ESP input. Honorton's idea was developed further in a subsequent overview by William Braud (1975), who formally proposed a 'psi-conducive syndrome*' consisting of the following seven components: (1) physical relaxation, (2) reduced physiological arousal, (3) reduced sensory input and processing, (4) increased awareness of internal processes, (5) receptive-mode or 'right-hemisphere' functioning, (6) altered view of the natural world, and (7) the sense that psi is momentarily important.

2.2.1 Some relevant research

2.2.1a *Progressive relaxation*

Although component 3 of Braud's syndrome is most directly relevant to Irwin's model, many of the others are indirectly relevant. An example is physical relaxation, which has the effect of reducing extraneous proprioceptive stimulation from the external musculature. Braud and his wife Lendell have done an extensive amount of research exploring whether physical relaxation indeed facilitates successful performance on free-response ESP tests. Encouraged by the success of a series of pilot experiments (W. G. Braud and L. W. Braud, 1973), they proceeded to test their hypothesis in two more formal experiments (L. W. Braud and W. G. Braud, 1974). Both were free-response GESP experiments in which subjects were tested individually. The subject was seated and listened to a tape consisting of instructions for either muscular relaxation or tension. The tape was followed by a five-minute reception period during which the subject was encouraged to allow impressions of the target picture to enter consciousness. During this period, the experimenter/agent concentrated on the target, a magazine picture or art reproduction randomly selected from a pool of 120 such pictures that had previously been divided into 20 sets of six pictures each. To avoid contamination of the target picture by possible handling cues, it was covered by a sheet of glass during the sending period. Following the session, the subject was asked to rank on a 'blind' basis the target picture and the five other pictures in the appropriate set against his or her impressions.

Sixteen college students participated in the first experiment, all of whom experienced relaxation suggestions. Twelve obtained hits (the target given a rank of 1–3), a marginally significant outcome. More to the point, the eight best scorers rated themselves on the average as having been significantly more relaxed during the impression period than did the other subjects. The ratings were made on a simple ten-point scale before the subjects learned their ESP scores.

The second experiment introduced for the first time a comparison between a relaxation and control condition. Ten college students were randomly assigned to listen to a tape suggesting relaxation of the body, whereas the other ten listened to a similar tape suggesting bodily tension. The experimenter in contact with the subjects kept herself blind to which condition the subjects were in so as to not influence their attitudes toward the task. The effectiveness of the experimental manipulation was assessed not only by the kinds of self-ratings used in the previous experiment, but also by EMG (electromyograph*) measurements taken from the forehead (frontalis) muscle during the session. This use of convergent psychological and physiological measures is the recommended way to measure and verify alterations in state of consciousness (Stoyva and Kamiya, 1968). Finally, to control for the possibility that the results might be influenced by subjects in the two conditions having different expectations of success on the ESP task, subjects were asked immediately before listening to the tapes to rate their expectations and mood.

The results confirmed the experimental hypothesis in all respects. The mean rank assigned to the target by subjects in the relaxation condition was 2.0 compared to 3.4 in the tension condition, a statistically significant difference. Moreover, the subjects in the relaxation condition were significantly more relaxed during the impression period than were those in the tension condition on both the self-rating and EMG measures, and these measures were significantly correlated with each other. Finally, the groups did not differ significantly from each other on any of the expectation or mood items. Thus the authors concluded that relaxation did indeed facilitate ESP performances in this experiment.

2.2.1b *The ganzfeld*

An ASC induction technique which focuses on reducing meaningful external stimuli rather than internal proprioceptive stimuli is the ganzfeld procedure discussed in chapter 7, section 3.3. In chapter 7 these experiments were discussed in relation to the claim that a high proportion of them have provided significant evidence of overall psi-hitting. But even if we decide to accept this conclusion, it does not follow that the ASC presumably created by the ganzfeld is the factor responsible for the success.

The best way to test this latter hypothesis is through experiments like the second Braud experiment just described, in which a relaxation condition is compared to another condition made as similar as practicable except for the level of relaxation. Unfortunately, the overwhelming majority of ganzfeld experiments lack such control conditions. The one clear exception, an experiment by W. G. Braud, Wood, and L. W. Braud (1975), did, however, confirm the ASC hypothesis. The design of this experiment was very similar to Braud's relaxation experiment, except that a ganzfeld group was compared to a control group asked to sit quietly for the same period of time. The groups differed significantly on the ESP test, their mean ESP ranks happening to coincide identically to the comparable means in the relaxation experiment.

An alternative approach to testing the ASC hypothesis is the correlational approach exemplified by Braud's first relaxation experiment. We know that subjects differ in how they react to ASC induction procedures, the ganzfeld included. If the ASC hypothesis is correct, we would expect subjects who actually enter a pronounced ASC as a result of the induction to show more evidence of ESP than those who do not or who do so to a lesser degree. In order to test this hypothesis, several ganzfeld experimenters have had subjects complete versions of a rating scale originally developed by Rex Stanford after coming out of the ganzfeld but before learning their ESP scores. The results using this approach have not been particularly 'clean,' inasmuch as they consist of numerous *post hoc* analyses only a small percentage of which achieved statistical significance. What makes the results nonetheless worthy of some interest is the fact that the significant findings which have occurred are remarkably consistent, both with each other and with our theoretical expectations.

This correlational approach has been most fully exploited by Carl Sargent (1980b; Sargent, Bartlett and Moss, 1982). His overall ESP results with the ganzfeld have consistently been positive, usually significantly so. In these experiments he has found various rating-scale items reflecting changes in state of consciousness during ganzfeld to correlate significantly and positively with the ESP scores. The most successful of these items has been, reasonably enough, the most straightforward one: 'Compared to what you expected, how successful was the ganzfeld in altering your state of consciousness?' In five studies in which this item was used, it correlated significantly with ESP and positively in four of them, three by two-tailed test.

These findings are compatible with those of an earlier ganzfeld experiment by Palmer *et al.* (1977). In this experiment, the scoring was below chance, significantly so by one of the two judging methods. In order to simplify the rating-scale analyses, Palmer exploited a statistical technique called factor analysis to divide the pool of items into five mutually independent scales, each of which could be given a separate score for each subject. Inspection of the subscales prior to correlating them with the ESP scores revealed one which most clearly reflected the kind of ASC expected to be most ESP-conducive, one approximating the so-called hypnagogic state that people often experience just before falling asleep. The item which contributed the most heavily to this scale was the 'success' item discussed above. Both the scale and this item correlated significantly and *negatively* with the ESP scores. Although the direction of these relationships was the reverse of what Sargent found, this makes sense in view of the overall psi-missing in this study. In both Sargent's studies and Palmer's, the greatest deviations from MCE were produced, on the average, by those subjects who found the ganzfeld to be most successful for them.

The same pattern has appeared in numerous other studies involving ASCs ranging from relaxation (see above) to out-of-body experiences (Palmer, 1978a) and the state induced by a sensory isolation device called the 'witches' cradle' (Honorton, Drucker and Hermon, 1973). I am aware of one study where the classification is ambiguous (Stanford and Neylon, 1975), and no reversals. This ratio of significant confirmatory to disconfirmatory correlations forms a consistent pattern in support of the hypothesis that the kinds of ASCs implied by Braud's psi-conducive syndrome are conducive to free-response ESP. This of course does not mean that they are *necessary* for free-response ESP, a point illustrated by the apparent success of the remote viewing procedure.

2.2.2 Some alternative conceptualizations

2.2.2a *Lability**

Although much research has been directed toward establishing the effectiveness of ASC induction procedures, virtually no research has been undertaken to directly test Honorton's noise reduction model. A somewhat different formulation has been proposed by Stanford (1979), who suggests that such procedures, and particularly the ganzfeld, are ESP-conducive because they increase the lability of the subject's thought processes. The closely related notion that spontaneity is ESP-conducive has been a prominent feature of Stanford's theorizing since the 1960s, when he conducted a series of card-guessing experiments demonstrating that increases in run-score variance accompanied a reduction in subjects' tendencies to balance their calls (Stanford, 1975). This notion of spontaneity also plays a central role in his more recent conformance model (Stanford, 1978).

Stanford proposed that this cognitive lability is especially facilitated by the auditory component of the ganzfeld technique. To test this hypothesis, he conducted a ganzfeld experiment with 80 college students (Stanford, 1979). Half of them received standard auditory ganzfeld stimulation consisting of pink noise, whereas the other half listened to an organ note. For half of the subjects in each condition, this uniform stimulation was interrupted halfway through the 15-minute session by a brief 60 hz. hum. In addition to expecting the pink noise to be more ESP-conducive than the organ note in the uninterrupted conditions, Stanford also expected the interruptions to have different effects depending on the nature of the sound being interrupted. Specifically, with the organ note (which ordinarily would favor more structured mentation) the interruption was predicted to have a destabilizing, hence ESP-conducive effect. Its effect in the noise condition, however, was predicted to be just the opposite, i.e. to bring the subject 'back to reality.'

Two ESP scores were computed for each subject based on averaged ratings from three outside judges; one score was based on ratings of subjects' mentation from the three minutes following the interruption, whereas the other was based on the total mentation. The most positive scores tended to occur in the uninterrupted noise – traditional ganzfeld – condition, especially for the post-interruption period. Moreover, the interruptions had the predicted effects: facilitory with the tone and inhibitory with the noise.

Unfortunately, however, these trends did not reach significance (Stanford, 1979; Stanford and Sargent, 1983), so they can only be considered suggestive at best. Furthermore, research designed to confirm the model's predictions about the psychologically destabilizing effects of ganzfeld stimulation has so far yielded inconsistent results (Stanford and Angelini, 1983; Stanford and Roig, 1982). On the other hand, it would be a mistake to abandon this approach prematurely, especially since other research not involving the ganzfeld has offered more promising support for the lability hypothesis (e.g. W. G. Braud, Shafer and Mulgrew, 1983).

2.2.2b *Expectancy*

A third possible explanation of why ASC induction procedures might be ESP-conducive is simply that they increase subjects' confidence and expectation that ESP will occur, i.e. 'I feel something strange is happening to me so maybe they are really making me psychic.' Unfortunately, this hypothesis has rarely been tested directly. However, rating-scale data from both Sargent and Palmer (see above) suggest that perceived success of the ASC induction often coincides with expectation of success on the ESP test at the end of the session, which probably applies retroactively to part of the period during the session as well. On the other hand, in the Brauds' experiments involving relaxation (L. W. Braud and W. G. Braud, 1974) and the ganzfeld (W. G. Braud *et al.*, 1975) discussed above, subjects in the experimental conditions did not judge the induction procedures to be significantly more psi-conducive after the session than did subjects in the control conditions.

An area of ASC-ESP research which brings the possible role of subjects' expectations to the fore is that involving hypnosis. Meta-analyses have shown that hypnosis has rather consistently raised ESP scores in card-guessing experiments (Honorton and Krippner, 1969; Schechter, 1984; Van de Castle, 1969). There also are indications that among subjects who are highly susceptible to hypnosis, suggestions to have a 'hypnotic dream' about the target facilitate free-response ESP, but the pattern here is much less firmly established (e.g. Honorton, 1972; Parker and J. Beloff, 1970).

The induction of a hypnotic 'trance' nicely fulfills the requirements of the noise reduction model by promoting both relaxation and a focusing of attention. On the other hand, perhaps more so than other procedures, it incorporates implicit and often explicit suggestions that subjects can succeed in the task given them, whether it be raising their arm or scoring high on an ESP test.

Only one study so far has been designed to allow a systematic comparison of these influences. Lawrence Casler (1962, 1982) tested 48 subjects, of whom one subgroup was hypnotized and the other not. Each subgroup then received eight card-guessing runs using either a clairvoyance or GESP procedure. Four of these runs were preceded by suggestions that the subject 'believe, as intensely as he could, that ESP did exist and that he did possess it' (Casler, 1962, p. 79), whereas no suggestions preceded the other runs. Half of the subjects completed the suggestion runs first, the other half the opposite. Thus ASC (hypnosis vs. 'waking') and expectancy (suggestion vs. control) were manipulated independently, allowing a comparison of their effects. Since the subjects knew the suggestion and control runs were to be compared, it is unlikely that the normal implicit suggestion of success from the hypnosis *per se* applied to the control runs; indeed, there may even have been an expectation of failure on these runs.

As Casler did not conceptualize his study in quite the way referred to above, his analysis did not provide for a direct comparison between the ASC and suggestion factors. However, since he published the scores of his individual subjects (an excellent practice, if feasible), I was able to reanalyse his data using analysis of variance. This analysis revealed that although both hypnotic induction and suggestion were associated with higher ESP scores, the effect was only significant in the case of suggestion. The overall mean was also significantly above chance for the suggestion runs. These results highlight the important role of the suggestion component not only in hypnosis but also indirectly in other ASC induction procedures where suggestion might be present implicitly.

2.3 Brain hemisphere specialization

Another component of Braud's psi-conducive syndrome is the activation of cognitive processes associated with the right hemisphere of the brain. Research in psychology suggests that the right hemisphere is best suited for diffuse attending and holistic processing of information, whereas the preferred modes of attending and processing for the left hemisphere are focused and analytic. The preponderance of visual representation in ESP impressions also implicates right-hemisphere involvement.

The two parapsychologists who have done the most research on this topic are Richard Broughton and Michaeleen Maher. Both employed the same basic strategy: giving an ESP test designed to activate one hemisphere while simultaneously engaging the opposite hemisphere in a competing or distracting task. In choosing their ESP tasks, both researchers made use of the fact that the sensory and motor connections with each hand are with the brain hemisphere on the opposite side. This principle was exploited most fully by Broughton (1976), whose ESP test consisted of having subjects for each trial pick up with either the right or left hand one of five differently shaped objects (pyramid, cylinder, ball, cone or cube) without looking at it. Maher's procedure (Maher, Peratsakis and Schmeidler, 1979; Maher and Schmeidler, 1977) was somewhat different in that for each trial she had subjects reach into a bag with either the right or left hand and try to choose from among 25 tactilely identical plastic cubes one of the five that encased either a clover leaf ('right-hemisphere' stimulus) or the word 'clover' ('left-hemisphere' stimulus). In yet another adaptation, Broughton (1977) had subjects react to a warning tone by pressing a button with either the right or left hand, the idea being that the reaction time would be influenced by whether or not an agent also heard a warning tone immediately beforehand.

A variety of verbal, analytic tasks was used to distract the left hemisphere, such as reading law reports and solving syllogisms. Broughton could find no right-hemisphere distracting task he considered satisfactory, whereas Maher chose a pattern recognition task in which the subject was required to detect a simple pattern hidden in a complex one.

Each researcher was critical of the tasks chosen by the other (Broughton, 1978; Maher and Schmeidler, 1978). In neither of the ESP tasks involving object selection, for example, is it clear how the task would activate one hemisphere to the exclusion of the other hemisphere. For instance, the fact that the stimulus is a shape does not preclude verbal ('left-hemisphere') labeling of the stimulus prior to selecting the object or making the response. Nevertheless, the manipulations probably were at least partly successful.

The results of these experiments are complex and difficult to summarize briefly. Moreover, significant results were spotty and generally *post hoc.* Nevertheless, two patterns emerged which suggest a real effect. First, all the significant results occurred in those conditions where an ESP test of one hemisphere was combined with distraction of the other hemisphere (i.e. none occurred in the various control conditions included in the designs). Second, the significant effects were found to be almost entirely attributable to male subjects. Psychological research has shown that brain hemisphere specialization is more prominent in males than in females.

It would be premature to draw firm conclusions from these findings. The principal suggestion which seems to be emerging at this point, however, is not superiority for psi mediation by right-hemisphere processes so much as the possibly psi-conducive effect of creating a kind of 'dissociation' between the two hemispheres – as if the psi capacity of one hemisphere is ordinarily inhibited by the cognitive processes of the other, except when the processing capacity (to use Irwin's term) of the other is taken up with an irrelevant task. This dissociation bears some resemblance to automatic writing, a traditional mode of expression for spiritualist mediums. But if (as the data seem to imply) this dissociation is more readily achieved in males because of their greater brain hemisphere specialization, then why don't we find that males have more psi ability than females, and why are most mediums females? Obviously, a lot more thinking and research are needed on this interesting and potentially important topic.

3 Belief in ESP: the sheep-goat effect

Although expectancies can be influenced by experimental manipulations like hypnosis, they are also influenced by the beliefs which subjects bring with them about the existence of ESP and the likelihood of its occurrence in the experiment. This relationship between ESP and belief has come to be called the 'sheep-goat effect,' or SGE*. This does not mean that we are studying ESP in animals; the phrase was coined by the pioneer researcher on this topic, Gertrude Schmeidler, who metaphorically described her research as 'separating the sheep [believers] from the goats [non-believers].'

3.1 The correlational approach

Schmeidler began her extensive research on this topic by giving standard clairvoyance card tests to 151 subjects, each tested individually (Schmeidler and McConnell, 1958/1973). Prior to the testing, she determined by interview whether or not the subject accepted the possibility of ESP under the conditions of the experiment. The 111 subjects who did were classified as sheep, and their mean ESP score was 5.23 hits per run, which was significantly above chance. The 40 goats averaged 4.86 hits, significant psi-missing.

These results were confirmed in a series of classroom tests lasting over a period of six years. A total of 692 sheep had a mean of 5.10 compared to 4.93 for 465 goats. Both means differed significantly from MCE. The effect is of course quite weak in terms of magnitude, but it nonetheless demonstrates a tendency for belief to influence the direction of scoring on restricted-choice ESP tests.

Numerous studies since then have tested the SGE, using mostly restricted-choice testing procedures, and they by and large have confirmed Schmeidler's findings. In a review published about ten years ago (Palmer, 1971), it was found that 13 of 17 experiments yielded results in the predicted direction, of which five were statistically significant. There were no significant reversals. The trend seems to have been maintained over the last decade.

3.1.1 The problem of definition

There are two things to be noted about the particular way that Schmeidler defined the SGE. First of all, only firm disbelievers were classified as goats. Undecided subjects, even doubters, were classified as sheep. Indeed, a close inspection of her data reveals that the fence straddlers actually scored higher on the average than did the true believers. Other research suggests that these extreme sheep tend to show high between-subject variance, i.e. they tend to be either strong hitters or strong missers (Palmer, 1972).

Second, one often sees the SGE referred to as concerning whether or not subjects believe in the existence of ESP in the abstract. However, Schmeidler's definition refers only to the possibility of ESP occurring in the test situation. Admittedly these two definitions overlap considerably. Persons who believe that ESP does not exist will always be classified as goats. However, it is possible for a sheep who believes in ESP in the abstract to disbelieve that it can be demonstrated in experiments, especially card-guessing type experiments. Indeed, many fervent psychics are 'goats' in this respect.

Many researchers who claimed to be doing sheep-goat experiments did not adhere to Schmeidler's definition. Palmer distinguished four separate criteria that had been used in these studies. The first two criteria were impersonal: criterion 1 was belief that ESP could occur in the experiment (i.e. Schmeidler's), and criterion 2 was belief that ESP exists in the abstract. The other two criteria were personal. Criterion 3 concerned whether subjects believed themselves to be psychic or to have had genuine psychic experiences, whereas criterion 4 was subjects' estimates of how well they expected to score (or had scored) in the experiment they were participating in. In general, the impersonal criteria were found to be more reliable predicters of ESP scoring than the personal ones. Further research (e.g. Palmer, 1973) has tended to give the edge to criterion 1 as the best discriminator of the lot.

3.2 The experimental approach

So far, the evidence we have considered has been correlational in nature. The case for the SGE would be strengthened if we could also show that it occurs after experimental manipulation of belief. For example, this would help to rule out the possibility that sheep and goats tend to score differently on ESP tests because they differ in other respects besides their beliefs.

One example of this approach is the use of hypnosis to enhance ESP scoring, especially experiments like that of Casler (1962) in which belief in ESP was directly suggested. Another approach is simple persuasion. Two experiments (or, more precisely, pairs of experiments) of this type have been done, and they yielded markedly different results, a not uncommon occurrence in parapsychology. Judith Taddonio (1975) gave a sheep-goat questionnaire to 20 college students, on the basis of which she classified them as sheep, goats, or undecided. She then assigned half of the subjects in each category to a condition in which they were told that the ESP test they were about to take had been very successful in the past in producing significant psi-hitting and that she expected it to be just as successful this time. The other subjects were told that the test had a poor track record and that she expected chance results. All subjects were told that the purpose of the experiment was to determine why the test was good or bad, and they were asked to write down comments on this point after the test. All subjects then completed a 24–trial envelope test.

Subjects who received the positively worded instructions scored significantly above chance, whereas those who received the negatively worded instructions scored significantly below chance. Taddonio then conducted a strict replication of this study with a new sample of 40 college students and got the same significant result. In both experiments, the undecided subjects, who presumably were the most influenceable by the experimental manipulation, revealed the effect most strongly, but the sample sizes were too small to demonstrate their superiority statistically.

Rather different results emerged from two experiments by Bruce Layton and Bill Turnbull (1975). In their first study, 179 college undergraduates were tested in groups of 5 to 15. Some of the groups were told by an authoritative-looking experimenter that there was much scientific evidence for the existence of ESP and that he accepted this evidence. The other groups were given just the opposite message. All subjects then completed a 100–trial envelope test similar to that used by Taddonio. The one significant result was an interaction between the belief manipulation and the sex of the subjects; the SGE was confirmed for females but unexpectedly reversed for males. The authors then conducted a strict replication with 235 new subjects and found no evidence of ESP at all.

Although the results of the first study are sometimes cited as supporting the SGE, this is not quite accurate; such support would have required a significant difference between sheep and goats for both groups combined. Since the effect the authors did find was *post hoc,* of marginal statistical significance, and had no precedent in the research literature, it is not surprising that it failed to replicate.

The striking difference between the results of the Taddonio and Layton experiments is all the more remarkable when one considers that Layton used by far the larger numbers of subjects. It is doubtful that the divergence of results can be attributed to sampling error; some methodological difference must be responsible. We can only speculate at this point what it might be. The authoritative-looking experimenter in Layton's studies might have created a more tense atmosphere in the testing sessions than did Taddonio, thus leading to less spontaneity of responding on the ESP test. Also, how effective were the manipulations? A weakness of Taddonio's study was that no manipulation checks were made. Layton was very conscientious in this respect, and his measures showed strong between-group differences in belief. But in answering these questions, some subjects may have been influenced by 'demand characteristics*,' i.e. perceived pressure to tell the experimenter what they think he wanted to hear. This problem is a very difficult one to eliminate, and it is conceivably a biasing factor in all sheep-goat research. But this is not to say that one should necessarily accept Taddonio's results over Layton's. Other possibilities will be discussed in section 6.

3.3 Toward understanding the SGE

Despite the ever-present conflicting results, there is enough positive evidence for the SGE to justify exploring how it might be explained. A number of years ago Palmer (1972) offered the simple suggestion that sheep and goats score the way they do because of a need to 'vindicate' their prior beliefs about the existence of psi and the world view underlying that belief. An ingenious test of this hypothesis was recently reported by an undergraduate honors student, Barbara Lovitts (1981). Lovitts reasoned that if this hypothesis is correct and subjects were led to believe that successful performance on an ESP test actually would provide evidence against ESP, the standard SGE would be reversed. She accomplished this seemingly self-contradictory task by telling half of a group of 40 college students that the ESP test they were about to take was really a test of subliminal perception, and since subliminal perception is an alternative explanation to ESP, significant results in the experiment would actually count against the ESP hypothesis. The other subjects were told that they were to take a real ESP test.

Subjects in both conditions were asked to guess the identities of a sequence of slides presented by a tachistoscope for very brief durations that precluded accurate recognition. The slides in fact consisted of montages of the five ESP symbols, although subjects in the 'subliminal perception' condition were led to believe that they were individual symbols. All subjects were asked to record their responses on a blank sheet of paper pasted on the front of an opaque envelope which, unknown to the subjects, contained a target sequence inside (i.e. a standard envelope test).

At the beginning of the session subjects completed a sheep-goat questionnaire developed by Bhadra (1966). The scale has items reflecting all four sheep-goat criteria but is weighted in favor of the impersonal criteria. Subjects who scored above the group mean were classified as sheep and the rest goats.

The experimental hypothesis was confirmed by demonstration of a statistically significant interaction effect. As predicted, sheep scored higher than goats in the 'ESP' condition whereas goats scored higher than sheep in the 'subliminal perception' condition. Again, we cannot conclude too much from just one study, but Lovitts' experiment exemplifies the kind of research that will help us gain a theoretical understanding of the apparent tendency for sheep to score higher than goats on ESP tests.

4 Personality traits

In this section, we will consider the question of whether ESP test scores can be reliably predicted by measures of personality traits, i.e. relatively enduring characteristics of behavior or disposition for which people can be shown to differ along a continuum. Examples of such traits are 'dominance-submissiveness' and 'aggressiveness-docility.'

Would the demonstration of such relationships allow us to say that people with some personality traits are more 'psychic' or have more ESP ability than those with other traits? Unfortunately, not. First of all, people who have a lot of spontaneous ESP experiences are not necessarily the people who score well on ESP tests, for which voluntary control of ESP is important. Second, with the exception of a handful of 'gifted' subjects, there is little evidence that subjects who score well on an ESP test on one occasion will be able to repeat the performance at a later time. The reasons for this seem to be basically the same as those we have cited for the unreliability of ESP generally – sampling error and the fact that the psychological situation of subjects is different the second time around, especially if they have received feedback about how well they did on the first test. However, very little research has been done with repeated testing, and further inquiry may produce a more promising picture. Sargent (1980b), for example, has found encouraging results with repeated testing of subjects in the ganzfeld.

Finally, there is little evidence that gifted subjects, at least those who find their way into ESP experiments, conform to any common personality pattern that distinguishes them from the rest of us.

Thus in this section we will be discussing mainly how well certain personality traits predict how well a first-timer will do on ESP tests. Despite this limitation, such research has a good deal to tell us about the nature of ESP. We will focus on two examples representing two different approaches to personality measurement.

4.1 The theoretical approach: defense mechanisms

According to Irwin's model, the processing of ESP input can be either arrested or distorted at any of its stages by means of defense mechanisms. This concept obtained a prominent position in psychology through the writings of Sigmund Freud, who talked about the rational self or 'ego' preventing our more primitive sexual or aggressive impulses from reaching consciousness. Might such mechanisms also prevent ESP information from reaching consciousness? After all, knowledge that we really have psychic powers might be more than our egos really want to deal with. The concept of defense mechanisms also offers a plausible explanation for psi-missing. In a card test, for example, such defenses might suppress the target symbol at a preconscious level, forcing the overt response to be chosen from among the four incorrect alternatives.

4.1.1 The Defense Mechanism Test

From the point of view of the psychology of personality, the relevant question is whether some people use such defense mechanisms more than others. One way to approach this question is through the principle of perceptual defense*, the fact that we sometimes misperceive threatening external events in such a way that they do not seem threatening. A common example is failing to comprehend an unexpected insulting remark from someone you are talking to.

This principle has been incorporated in a personality test named, appropriately enough, the Defense Mechanism Test, or DMT (Kragh and G. W. Smith, 1970). Subjects are asked to identify a slide consisting of two people. The person in the foreground is a neutral-looking figure, called the 'hero,' with whom the subject is supposed to identify. The person in the background is a much more menacing-looking figure called the 'threat.' The slide is presented to subjects repeatedly for very brief periods by means of a tachistoscope or similar device, the duration of the exposure increasing with each presentation. Each time, subjects are asked to draw what they see, until the exposure time is so long that the slide is perceived accurately.

In scoring the subjects' responses, the scorer looks for various well-defined 'signs' that suggest the perceptual defense process. An example would be perceiving the threat as benign. These codings are then converted into a general score of perceptual defensiveness that can range from 1 to 9.

The DMT was introduced into parapsychology by Martin Johnson. He and various collaborators have now conducted ten separate experiments in which DMT scores have been compared to scores on a variety of restricted-choice ESP tests (Johnson and Haraldsson, 1984). The results have been encouraging in that there has been a positive correlation in every case between DMT and ESP, i.e. the lower the defensiveness, the higher the ESP score. On the basis of theory and pilot testing, the direction of the relationship was predicted in advance and the authors thus chose to evaluate the significance of the correlations by means of one-tailed statistical tests. By this criterion, seven of the ten correlations were significant, and four were significant by two-tailed tests as well.

As a general rule, Johnson, who scored the DMT protocols, kept himself 'blind' to the scores subjects obtained on the ESP tests, which in every case were administered by someone else. However, in the first two (preliminary) experiments and (accidentally) in one later experiment, Johnson was aware of the ESP scores of some of the subjects. Could this information have biased his DMT ratings in a way that helped 'confirm' the experimental hypothesis?

Favoring the artifact hypothesis is the fact that three of the four most statistically significant studies were the ones in which the artifact was possible. However, two other factors argue against this hypothesis. First of all, the results of the other seven experiments still show the same pattern to a lesser but still impressive degree. Second, in the case of the last of the biased experiments, Johnson took the all too uncommon step of actually testing the artifact hypothesis empirically. He did this by having Dr Ulf Kragh, the developer of the DMT, independently score the 12 DMT protocols of the subjects whose ESP scores Johnson saw, along with 12 protocols randomly selected from those remaining. Kragh's ratings correlated about 0.90 with Johnson's and also correlated significantly with the ESP scores of the 24 subjects in the subsample. Thus it does not seem likely that the artifact accounts for the results, but Dr Johnson would be the first to concede that the case would be stronger had blind scoring been used throughout.

4.2 The empirical approach: extraversion and neuroticism

The DMT represents a very theory-oriented approach to personality measurement. However, many personality scales have been developed using a more empirically oriented strategy which lets the data reveal what the traits are. One such approach is to begin with a large number of true-false items covering a multitude of personal characteristics, attitudes and behaviours. A large number of subjects are then asked to answer the items, and a statistical technique called factor analysis is applied to the results. The purpose of this technique is to identify clusters of items that seem to be measuring the same trait. By examining the nature of the items in each cluster, appropriate names can be assigned to the clusters representing the particular personality traits they seem to reflect.

4.2.1 The 16PF scale

One such scale is the so-called 16PF developed by psychologist Raymond Cattell (Cattell, Eber and Tatsuoka, 1970). The scale consists of 187 items which were classified by means of factor analysis into 16 clusters or 'primary source traits.' Through further factor analysis these source traits were themselves classified under two 'second-order' traits, which were labeled 'extraversion' and 'anxiety.' The anxiety scale was then modified by adding a few additional primary scales to form a 'neuroticism' scale. These same two basic traits, extraversion and either anxiety or neuroticism, frequently emerge from factor analytic studies of personality and are often considered as the fundamental underlying dimensions of personality.

Since the 1940s, parapsychologists have frequently conducted studies in which subjects are given some personality questionnaire along with a (usually restricted-choice) ESP test to see if reliable personality correlates of ESP could be discovered. The most extensive and systematic of these projects was a series of four experiments conducted by H. Kanthamani and Ramakrishna Rao (1971, 1972, 1973) with high school students in India. For their measure of personality, the authors chose a version of the 16PF designed for high school students called the High School Personality Questionnaire, or HSPQ (Cattell and H. Beloff, 1962). The structure of the extraversion and neuroticism scales of the HSPQ is similar but not identical to that of the 16PF. Subjects who score high on the extraversion scale of the HSPQ can be described as social, cheerful, adventurous and conforming, whereas low scorers (introverts) can be described as aloof, serious, withdrawn and self-sufficient. High scorers on the neuroticism scale can be described as emotional, excitable, shy, insecure, uncontrolled, tense, submissive, serious and esthetically sensitive. Low scorers are characterized by the opposites of these traits.

In their initial experiment the authors tested 22 female volunteers. The ESP test consisted of eight card-guessing runs using the blind matching procedure, four runs in each of two sessions. The HSPQ was administered in a third session. Subjects were divided into two groups on each scale at the scale's theoretical midpoint. The results revealed that extraverts scored significantly higher than introverts, and low-neurotic subjects significantly higher than high-neurotic subjects.

The authors proceeded to conduct three confirmatory experiments with 50 female, 36 male and 38 female subjects respectively. The procedure was essentially the same as in the first study, except that in the final experiment the HSPQ was given prior to the ESP sessions and a different experimenter administered the ESP test. The results of all three experiments completely replicated those of the initial experiment in terms of the direction of the effect. Moreover, the neuroticism-ESP and extraversion-ESP relationships were each statistically significant in two of the three experiments.

A meta-analysis of all relevant experiments published through the mid–1970s confirmed the trends for both variables, although neuroticism only seemed to be a successful predictor when subjects were tested individually (Palmer, 1977). Extraversion seems to be the more reliable of the two predictors. In a more recent survey, Sargent (1981) found that 18 of 53 reported extraversion-ESP correlations were statistically significant, with 17 of the 18 significant findings in the positive direction. Again, it is the directional consistency that is most noteworthy.

4.2.2 Theoretical considerations

Two competing but not necessarily mutually exclusive explanations have been proposed to account for the extraversion-ESP relationship. One is a social psychological explanation while the other is a physiological-cognitive explanation. According to the former view, extraverts score higher than introverts on ESP tests because they are more comfortable than introverts in social situations. An ESP test is, after all, a social situation, and a potentially stressful one at that. The introvert's discomfort could evoke defensive reactions, hence psi-missing. The other viewpoint is based on a theory of extraversion proposed by psychologist Hans Eysenck (1967b), who has accumulated a vast amount of evidence indicating that introverts are characterized by a generally higher level of arousal of the cerebral cortex than extraverts (Eysenck, 1967a). As psi is often construed as a very primitive ability that has been superseded in evolution by other cognitive and perceptual faculties, one might expect activation of these faculties (i.e. cortical arousal) to be psi-inhibitory. Note that Eysenck's theory implies that extraverts are intrinsically more psychic than introverts, whereas the social psychological explanation implies that the superiority of extraverts is really an artifact of the testing situation.

The social psychological explanation is consistent with other research, some of which will be discussed in section 6, which suggests that the nature of the subject-experimenter interaction affects scoring on ESP tests. Also, the measures of extraversion that have been the most successful predictors of ESP (e.g. the HSPQ) are somewhat correlated with neuroticism, i.e. the introverts on these scales tend to be somewhat neurotic as well, which suggests that they might indeed be anxiety-prone rather than just bored in social situations. In Kanthamani's experiments, for example, the extraversion-ESP relationship was heavily influenced by one primary scale on the HSPQ which was represented on the neuroticism as well as the extraversion factor.

Eysenck's explanation, on the other hand, has going for it the fact that some of the characteristics of successful ESP subjects, such as decline effects and the relative absence of rationally structured thought processes during the test, are typical of what one would expect from extraverts according to his theory. A weakness of his explanation, however, is that it is difficult to see how it would account for psi-missing rather than just chance scoring by introverts.

Regrettably, there has been little research directly testing either hypothesis – another task for the future.

4.2.3 A caution and an opportunity

We must end this section on another note of caution. Two significant reversals of the extraversion-ESP relationship have recently been reported from a major parapsychological laboratory (Thalbourne and Jungkuntz, 1983). Although the overwhelming proportion of the relationships are still positive, these latter findings are a sober reminder that anything we think we have found in parapsychology (or in any other science) can be overthrown by subsequent evidence. Eventually, we may find that the number of positive and negative correlations will balance out, implying that there was nothing there at all.

However, the fact that the findings are so out-of-balance at this point in time, plus the fact that these two reversals occurred back-to-back (in fact, the second could be considered as a replication of the first), suggests a more interesting possibility, namely that we have stumbled upon a boundary or limiting condition to the extraversion-ESP 'law,' the discovery of which could help us understand and explain it.

Are there any methodological differences between Thalbourne's studies and previous research that could account for the conflicting results? One possibility is that the targets Thalbourne used in his restricted-choice ESP test were brand names of consumer products. These are more meaningful than the more abstract targets normally used in such tests and thus may have evoked distracting thoughts that could have interacted with the processing of the ESP input. Subjects might also have had varying emotional reactions to certain product names. But how could such factors have differentially affected introverts and extraverts to produce the reversals Thalbourne found?

Thalbourne's results suggest that it may be naive to expect to find very many simple relationships between ESP and personality variables, and that it may be more profitable to explore the possibility that such relations are influenced by situational factors. A good example of this approach is a pair of experiments by James Carpenter (1971), who found that the relationship between ESP scores in a blind-matching test and personality test scores reflecting anxiety or guilt feelings about sex differed depending upon whether or not the envelopes containing the ESP key cards also contained erotic photographs. For example, the anxiety-ESP relationship was negative with the 'erotic' targets (i.e. the less anxious subjects got higher ESP scores) and positive with the neutral ones.

5 Can ESP be trained?

One of the most reliable – and frustrating– characteristics of ESP is for positive scores to decline to chance after repeated testing.[1] This so-called decline effect is especially apparent in restricted-choice tests. A number of years ago, Charles Tart (1966) offered an explanation for the decline effect based on elementary principles of learning theory in psychology. Psychologists have shown, for example, that you can train a pigeon to peck at a disk by giving it a food reward every time it makes such a pecking response spontaneously. The food in this case is called a 'positive reinforcement' and the increase in the rate of responding is considered an indication of learning. On the other hand, if you stop rewarding the pigeon, the pecking response will decline in frequency until it no longer occurs at all. This is called extinction.

Tart equated the decline in ESP scoring to this extinction effect in learning. In the typical restricted-choice ESP test, subjects receive no reward or immediate feedback after correct responses. Although they may get generalized feedback at the end of each run, this is a case of too little too late in terms of learning theory. Immediate feedback after correct responses can be construed as having both motivational and cognitive consequences. Being rewarded immediately after each correct response heightens the motivation for making more correct responses and is likely to help prevent boredom with the task generally. Perhaps even more importantly, immediate feedback helps subjects to identify subtle psychological cues that might help them to distinguish correct from incorrect responses. For example, with the aid of immediate feedback, a subject might eventually come to discern that correct guesses tend to be preceded by a fleeting visual image of an ESP symbol more often than incorrect guesses. Conversely, the absence of these factors can help to destabilize and eventually 'extinguish' psi-hitting by destroying motivation and failing to support good cognitive habits.

5.1 Research with unselected subjects: alternative possibilities

The above reasoning implies that immediate feedback might be used to train subjects to increase their level of scoring on ESP tests. The first systematic attempt to examine this possibility was by Charles Honorton. In his first experiment, Honorton (1970) tested 20 subjects, half of whom were randomly assigned to an experimental condition and the other half to a control condition.To provide a pre-training baseline measure of ESP, all subjects completed three standard DT runs without immediate feedback. Then subjects in the experimental condition received three DT training runs, this time with immediate feedback after each correct guess. Control subjects, on the other hand, received 'false feedback,' i.e. wrong information concerning the identity of the target, on the trial immediately following each hit trial. In other words, these subjects were given random feedback that should not facilitate learning. All subjects were encouraged during these training runs to identify any internal cues that might help them distinguish correct from incorrect guesses. Finally, subjects completed three post-training DT runs without feedback.

An added feature of the design was that during each pre– and post-training run subjects were asked to make about five confidence calls. Honorton reasoned that any learning effects on the post-training runs would be most likely to appear on those trials on which subjects felt that their calls were more than mere guesses. As predicted, subjects' rate of hitting on confidence calls was significantly greater in the post-training runs than in the pre-training runs in the experimental condition. This was not the case in the control condition.

Honorton (1971) then conducted a strict replication of this experiment and again found a significant increase from pre– to post-training in proportion of correct confidence calls, again restricted to the experimental condition. In a third study (McCallam and Honorton, 1973), the design was expanded. Two new experimental conditions were added, consisting of six and nine training runs respectively. Instead of false feedback, the control condition included a five-minute rest period in place of the training. The results *again* confirmed the significant 'learning' effect in the three-run training condition, but not in any of the other conditions. There were indications that subjects in the longer training conditions got bored, suggesting that if longer training is to be effective it should be dispersed over several sessions.

Be that as it may, Honorton was able to demonstrate the predicted effect with confidence calls in three successive experiments. In two of these, a significant increase in total ESP scores also occurred. Finally, a comparable result was found in a free-response ESP experiment using the ganzfeld (W. G. Braud and Wood, 1977). In this case, the pre– and post-training tests consisted of one trial per subject. There were six feedback training sessions, each held on a separate day, in which the subjects received feedback on each item of their mentation reports. However, the strength of these findings is weakened by the fact that the pre- to post-training increase was significant for only one of the three scoring schemes the researchers used.

An independent replication of Honorton's studies was later undertaken by Jackson, Franzoi and Schmeidler (1977). Although the trend in the experimental condition was clearly in the direction found by Honorton, it did not quite reach statistical significance. What interested the authors more, though, was the fact that the trend they did get was caused by significant psi-missing on confidence calls in the pre-training runs. It was as if the subjects, realizing that the hypothesis was that training should increase their scores, wanted to make it easy on themselves by starting out as low as possible.

Could this also have been a factor in Honorton's studies? When Honorton's data were examined more closely, it turned out that in two of his experiments the significant incline was indeed from significant psi-missing in the pre-training runs to near chance scoring in the post-training runs. This was not the case, however, in the other Honorton experiment and in Braud's experiment.

This example illustrates the importance of taking into account the relation of ESP scores to MCE when examining their relationship with other variables (see chapter 6, section 6.2). A simple model that can account for the type of result found by Jackson is to assume psi-missing on the pre-training runs, perhaps motivated by the factor mentioned above, and that the psi capacity merely 'burned out' by the time the post-training runs came about. Psychologists have known for a long time that performance on exacting tasks often deteriorates during the course of such 'massed practice.'

The problem with this model is that it does not account for the two cases where the incline went from chance scoring to hitting. Is there a model that can account for all the inclines? There is, but we lose some of the attractive simplicity of the first model. According to the more complicated model, there was a 'learning' factor that produced an element of psi-hitting in just the post-training runs (i.e. an incline effect) of all the studies. Then there was a second independent factor, presumably having something to do with the testing environment, which tended to produce psi-missing in both the pre– and post-training runs in three of the studies only. In the post-training runs of these three studies, these two factors tended to cancel each other out, with the net result being a mean close to MCE.

This same issue arises in the HSPQ studies of Kanthamani and Rao which were discussed in section 4.2.1. In one of their four studies, both the introverts and the extraverts scored below chance, although only the introverts did so to a significant degree. The two-factor model is particularly appealing in this case, because a different experimenter tested the subjects in this experiment than in the other three. Although the two-factor model is perhaps to be preferred for both the HSPQ and the training experiments because of its capacity to integrate all the relevant findings, a decisive answer, as we have said so often, must await more research. For a further discussion of these models, see Palmer (1975b).

If we can assume that the incline effects we have been examining in this section are caused by some genuine increase in a psi-hitting factor, are we justified to call this incline 'learning'? From an old-fashioned 'behavioristic' perspective, the answer is probably yes. However, if one adopts a more cognitive orientation things become less clear. Recall that Honorton's subjects received three runs – 75 trials – of feedback training. In each of these runs, we would expect these subjects to obtain an average of about five chance hits. As these hits are not due to psi, they constitute the equivalent of false feedback insofar as we are concerned with their capacity to provide useful information in identifying discriminating cues. Given the level of psi ability subjects demonstrated in the pre-training runs, we would expect, at best, no more than one or sometimes two true ESP hits per run. With this signal-to-noise ratio, was three runs enough to give such subjects useful information to help them improve their scoring on the post-training runs?

5.2 Research with selected subjects: the talent threshold

Tart (1966) was aware of this problem and proposed that learning was only likely to occur if subjects started out above a certain 'talent threshold.' For subjects with no psi talent, there is no psi to reinforce, and feedback should have no effect on performance. For subjects with moderate talent, the feedback should prevent declines but not actually improve scoring. Only with highly talented subjects would the ratio of real to chance hits be high enough to allow learning to take place. Tart could not specify what the various cutoff points are, leaving this as a question for empirical research to answer.

The experiment of Tart (1976) discussed in the preceding chapter (section 2.7) was actually designed primarily to test his learning theory. Most of the subjects who were tested in that experiment were selected by a two-stage screening process designed to find people who exceeded the hypothetical talent threshold. For the first stage, over 1,500 college students completed two standard card-guessing runs (one BT, one GESP) in classes ranging in size from 20 to 400 students. The 47 highest scorers, all of whom scored significantly above chance on one run or both runs combined, participated in the second stage, along with 23 other subjects considered promising by the student experimenters. This second stage consisted of six runs on the 10–choice trainer (TCT) and a 4–choice machine, at least two runs on each. The 42 best scorers, all of whom scored significantly above chance on one run or on the combined runs for one machine, graduated to the training study.

From the point of view of the learning hypothesis, the interesting question was whether the subjects would increase their levels of scoring during the training, which consisted of a total of 20 runs on the machine of the subject's choice, with varying numbers of runs per session. The progress of each subject's training was represented by a statistic called the regression slope, which reflects the linear increase (or decrease) in the level of scoring across the 20 runs. Of the 35 subjects who completed the training, only one showed significant learning by this measure, a result readily attributable to chance. However, there was one finding that did support the learning hypothesis, although other interpretations are possible as well. For the subjects who chose the TCT, there was a significant positive correlation between their mean scores on this machine in the second screening phase (a measure of their initial talent) and their regression slopes in the training study. Thus the more initial talent, the greater the relative increase in scoring in the training study. However, it should be noted that this effect was primarily attributable to the performance of one subject. The comparable relationship for the 4–choice machine was in the predicted direction but not significant.

This entire study was later replicated (Tart, Palmer and Redington, 1979). There was a much lower lower level of ESP scoring as compared to the first study, especially on the TCT. The learning correlation described above was not replicated, but this may have been due to the fact that no sufficiently talented subjects were found in the screening. Tart's learning theory and the evidence provided for it by his and other research have been the subject of an extensive debate (Stanford, 1977a, 1977d; Tart, 1977). A thorough discussion of the numerous points raised in this controversy is beyond the scope of this chapter.

5.3 Prospectus

Considering the difficulties parapsychologists face because of the low level and reliability of scoring on ESP tests, the possibility that we might eventually be able to train ESP cannot be abandoned lightly. Given the signal-to-noise problem discussed above, what we need to test adequately the learning hypothesis is the most initially talented subjects we can find spending not just several days, but several months, engaged in rigorous feedback training of the type pioneered by Honorton and Tart. Other kinds of feedback, especially biofeedback, could be used to help these subjects discriminate possibly relevant internal cues. The preliminary work described above and in a more comprehensive review by Tart (1976) provides enough rays of hope to encourage such an endeavor.

6 The experimenter effect

There is one important aspect of Tart's training study that we have not yet discussed. As noted in the last section, the significant results with the TCT were not evenly distributed among the subjects tested. It is particularly interesting that the five subjects who were responsible for the effect were all tested by the same experimenter. The five subjects whose results were close to chance were all tested by other experimenters. In fact when the results of the subjects tested by this one experimenter are removed, the results of the first training study prove to be remarkably similar to those of the replication, including the more modestly significant psi-htting on the 4–choice machine in both cases.

The above is but one of numerous examples of what has come to be called in parapsychology the experimenter effect, or EE* (J. E. Kennedy and Taddonio, 1976; White, 1976a, 1976b). It has been well known ever since the early Rhine days that some researchers consistently get significant results in their experiments, whatever the particular hypothesis they are testing, while others just as consistently do not. The existence of the EE is not in dispute, even among critics of parapsychology. On the other hand, there is a virulent controversy about how to interpret it. Three general hypotheses have been prevalent in the literature.

(1) *The experimenter error (E-error) hypothesis* Experimenters who get significant results in psi experiments do so either because their research procedures allow for artifacts or for cheating by their subjects, or because they cheat themselves. These problems are not necessarily reflected in the research reports.

(2) *The experimenter psychology (E-psych.) hypothesis* Experimenters who get significant results in psi experiments do so because, compared to other experimenters, they are more skilled at putting their subjects at ease, motivating them to score well, and inspiring confidence in them that they can score well.

(3) *The experimenter Psi (E-psi) hypothesis* Experimenters who get significant results in psi experiments do so because they are the source of the psi in those experiments. Unless the subjects are among the handful of 'gifted' subjects, they make no psychic contribution to the experimental outcome. Psi is not distributed generally in the population,

but is a special attribute of a small number of people, some of whom end up as psi experimenters or star subjects.

One thing we know about most, and probably, all established psi-conducive experimenters (PCEs) is that they are believers in psi. This is hardly surprising, considering that even if they started out as goats they would soon be converted by the success of their experiments, but it is likely that many of them started out as sheep as well. Does this mean that there is an actual relationship between belief in psi and success as an experimenter? Probably yes, but this has not been clearly established. One handicap is the fact that, since psi research is actively discouraged in a great many colleges and universities and most goats would not be motivated to conduct psi experiments in any case, it is difficult to generate a sufficiently large data base to adequately assess the hypothesis. On the other hand, experiments in which experimenters with differing beliefs were asked to conduct the same experiment (Parker, 1975) or the beliefs of the experimenters were manipulated in advance of testing (Taddonio, 1976) have so far tended to confirm the hypothesis.

Unfortunately, even if it is real, the belief-success relationship does not help us much in choosing among our three explanations of the EE, as it can easily be accommodated by all of them. The skeptic can argue that sheep experimenters are just the ones who would be most likely to make mistakes that would tend to 'confirm' ESP in order to vindicate their belief systems. From the standpoint of the E-psych. hypothesis, it is plausible to assume that sheep experimenters are the ones who would be most relaxed, motivated, and confident in the experimental setting themselves, and thus be best able to communicate these qualities, both explicitly and implicitly, to their subjects. Partisans of the E-psi hypothesis could argue that PCEs are sheep (at least in part) because they are psychic and aware of having this ability.

Are there other data that might be more helpful? Let's look at our three candidates one at a time.

6.1 The experimenter error hypothesis

The E-error hypothesis, unfortunately, is difficult to test experimentally for a number of reasons. Skeptics have frequently tried to argue for this view on a priori, philosophical grounds (see chapter 12, section 5.3). Attempts to test the hypothesis empirically have almost exclusively involved the case study method, usually attempts to show retrospectively that ESP researchers have cheated or been guilty of gross negligence.

Although this approach has met with occasional success (especially in the case of S. G. Soal), it suffers from inherent limitations that are likely to keep it from ever becoming decisive. An obvious problem is the difficulty in collecting the necessary information after the fact. Also, the 'subjects' will likely be reluctant to cooperate fully if they sense that the investigator is out to discredit them. A second problem has to do with generality. Unless one can collect a relatively large number of cases of demonstrated fraud or gross negligence (which is unlikely for the reasons cited above), it is not legitimate to extend one's conclusions to PCEs generally, especially if the investigator cannot show that the subsample was selected randomly. Even if it were, there might still be exceptions to the general rule. Finally, there are ethical issues involved. Insofar as the E-error hypothesis implies fraud or gross incompetence rather than the kind of normal criticism illustrated in this chapter, it is not just another scientific hypothesis, because its confirmation, or even its postulation, can seriously damage the welfare of the 'subject'. This does not mean that the E-error hypothesis should not be investigated or that relevant evidence should be suppressed, but it does mean that great care must be exercised in its exploration and, in particular, that insinuations of fraud or gross negligence must not be made without firm supporting evidence.

A better approach, albeit a less direct one, might be to adopt a more traditional methodology in which the focus is upon generalized scientific principles rather than individual personalities. The essence of the E-error hypothesis is that PCEs bias their results because they are so strongly committed to belief in psi. But commitment to one's hypotheses is obviously not unique to PCEs in parapsychology; it characterizes many scientists in all fields. This realization opens up the possibility of doing research with larger samples of subjects. For example, samples of graduate students with varying levels of commitment to a hypothesis (either naturally or by experimental induction) might be asked to conduct relevant experiments in which the possibility existed for certain kinds of experimenter error. This approach would be an extension of that used extensively by psychologist Robert Rosenthal and colleagues to study 'experimenter expectancy effects.' Although this research has not so far yielded evidence of experimenter fraud or gross incompetence (Rosenthal and D. R. Rubin, 1978), neither has it been directly focused on the issues raised by the skeptical hypothesis.

This approach eliminates the problem of retrospective analysis and allows the E-error hypothesis to be tested without getting into individual personalities. But it brings with it the opposite danger that whole classes of experimenters might be unfairly condemned by premature simplistic stereotypes. There is *no* approach to this topic that does not require a great deal of human sensitivity, something regrettably hard to find in the psi controversy up to this time. Finally, it should be noted that confirmation of the E-error hypothesis using this approach could have implications far transcending parapsychology.

The E-error hypothesis does not project a very flattering image of the scientific researcher. Is there any a priori reason to believe that dishonest manipulation of data, for example, is widespread in science? Historical analysis suggests that fraud in science indeed may be considerably more widespread than is commonly supposed (W. Broad and Wade, 1982). On the other hand, a powerful force operating against such deception is the vested interest that scientists have in exposing dishonest colleagues whose false claims both waste their time and discredit their profession. In parapsychology, for example, Levy was exposed not by outside critics but by his own co-experimenters. But we will never know how much weight to attach to the E-error hypothesis until it becomes the object of systematic research.

6.2 The experimenter psychology hypothesis

The traditional approach has characterized much of the research designed to provide experimental support for the E-psych. hypothesis. The question of whether the degree of rapport between subject and experimenter might influence ESP scoring was examined indirectly in a series of experiments by Margaret Anderson and Rhea White (1956). They commissioned seven high school teachers to give standard ESP envelope tests to their classes. In addition, the students and teachers anonymously expressed their liking for each other on rating scales. The combined results for the seven classes revealed significant psi-hitting among students when the mutual ratings were positive and significant psi-missing when they were negative. These results were significantly confirmed in a strict replication attempt with six new classes (Anderson and White, 1957). Subsequent replication attempts have produced mixed results (see Palmer, 1978b, p. 105). In general, the student evaluations seemed to be more important than those of the teachers.

A more direct approach to testing the E-psych. hypothesis was taken by Honorton, Ramsey and Cabbibo (1975), who gave 36 volunteer subjects a 200-trial precognition test on an REG. For half of the subjects, the experimenter intentionally behaved in a 'casual,' 'friendly' and 'supportive' manner, whereas for the other half the behaviour was 'formal,' 'unfriendly' and 'abrupt.' Honorton's two assistants each tested some of the subjects in each condition. Subjects who experienced the positively toned interaction scored significantly above chance on the ESP test, whereas those experiencing the negatively toned interaction scored significantly below chance.

An even more direct approach to testing the E-psych. hypothesis was taken by Schmeidler and Maher (1981a), who wanted to know if PCEs actually make a different impression on potential research subjects than do psi-inhibitory experimenters (PIEs). To test this hypothesis, they videotaped the presentation of papers (including responses to audience questions) from 27 parapsychologists at the 1979 Parapsychological Association Convention. From these they selected five-minute excerpts from the talks of five PCEs and five PIEs, who were matched for various physical characteristics. These tapes were played in counterbalanced orders to classes of New York college students, with the sound muffled so that the words could not be understood. Not knowing how the experimenters were classified, the students rated each one on 30 descriptive adjectives.

In line with the researchers' expectations, the PCEs were rated as significantly more flexible, friendly, free, likeable, warm, enthusiastic and playful than the PIEs. The PIEs were rated as more rigid, cold, overconfident, tense, excitable, egoistic and unfriendly than their PC counterparts. A similar breakdown occurred when tapes of three of the five pairs of experimenters were shown to a larger class of college students in Florida, but fewer of the adjectives yielded significant discriminations (Edge and Farkash, 1982).

In a critique of Schmeidler's experiment, Irvin Child (1981) pointed out that her method of analysis did not directly compare the two types of experimenters but rather the consistency of the students' ratings. As a consequence, we cannot properly generalize these findings beyond the individual experimenters examined. A related point is that no strict operational definitions were used to classify the experimenters. Could the researchers' classifications have been influenced in borderline cases by their preconceptions of what PCEs and PIEs should be like? Indeed, they later found that one of their PIEs was considered to be a PCE by two other parapsychologists they consulted.

Another potential difficulty with this type of experiment is that PCEs and PIEs may differ in relevant respects other than those addressed by the researchers. With reference to the E-error hypothesis, Brian Millar (Schmeidler and Maher, 1981b) suggested that PCEs may simply be less competent than PIEs. When Schmeidler reanalysed her data omitting two PCEs that her consultants considered a bit questionable in this respect, the discriminations by the student raters proved to be a little weaker than before but still clearly significant. But again, how objective were the classifications of competence? Better ways must be found for classifying experimenters and matching them on potential confounding variables if this valuable approach is to achieve its full potential.

Finally, the E-psych. hypothesis can claim indirect support from research in psychology that has shown that experimenters' expectations can be transferred to subjects by subtle, mostly nonverbal sensory cues, and thereby influence their behaviour in ways that help confirm their expectations (Rosenthal and D. R. Rubin, 1978). A caveat, however, has been pointed out by Kennedy and Taddonio (1976), who note that the experimenter expectancy effect in psychology tends to increase the more studies experimenters do, presumably because they get 'better' at biasing their subjects. If anything, the reverse is true in parapsychology.

6.3 The experimenter psi hypothesis

Relatively little research has been done to directly test the E-psi hypothesis, and most of what has been done has involved PK rather than ESP. The best single piece of support for this hypothesis, however, is an ESP experiment conducted by Donald West and George Fisk (1953). Prior to their collaboration, Fisk had the reputation of being a PCE while West had equally strong credentials as a PIE. For the experiment, they mailed 32 sealed packs of ESP clock cards to 20 subjects, each of whom was to guess the target orders. This testing procedure is not generally to be recommended, because subjects might be able to cheat by breaking the seals. However, in this particular case it is difficult to see how such cheating could have produced the effects the researchers were looking for. Unknown to the subjects, the target orders for ten of the packs were prepared by each researcher from a random number table, and each researcher scored the results from the packs he had prepared. (The checking was later verified by a third party.) As predicted, subjects scored significantly above chance on Fisk's targets and nonsignificantly on West's, with the difference between the two also being significant. Since the experimenters never had physical contact with the subjects and none of the subjects knew anything about the manipulation, it is difficult to see how these results could be explained by the E-psych. hypothesis.

Parapsychologists have also been guinea pigs in tests of the E-psi hypothesis. Adrian Parker (1977) got three parapsychologists to agree on the classification of 29 of their colleagues as PCEs or PIEs. These 29 experimenters were mailed an adjective checklist ostensibly intended as a personality test. Unknown to the 'subjects,' one of the responses on each item of the checklist was designated as a 'hit' on a covert ESP test. Since the checklist was such that some responses would likely be chosen more fequently than others, Parker based his prediction on the counter-bias (CB) responses (which were discussed in chapter 6, section 4.6.2b): specifically, he predicted that the fewer CB responses (i.e. the greater the response bias), the higher the ESP score on the CB responses, and that this effect would be significant only for the 14 PCEs. The prediction was confirmed. A comparable effect was later found by Sargent (1980a), who adopted the ingenious technique of using the relative frequency of certain letters of the alphabet in letters he received from various PCEs and PIEs as 'responses' in generating ESP scores.

A question raised by these findings is what would motivate the PCEs to confirm Parker's and Sargent's hypotheses. Most PCEs like to think of themselves as successful because they are skilled at handling their subjects, not because of their own psi. Could the results have reflected experimenter psi by the investigators? The difficulties discussed in the previous section of objectively classifying experimenters as PIEs or PCEs are also relevant. Nonetheless, these findings do seem to offer support for some kind of experimenter psi effect.

6.3.1 Interpreting experimenter psi

It is fairly easy to see how experimenter psi could determine the results of a PK experiment, but what about an ESP experiment? The most fully developed attempt to answer this question has come from the observational theories, to be discussed in chapter 11. According to these theories ESP is reduced to retroactive PK, i.e. PK backwards in time. Thus an observational theorist might explain the results of the West and Fisk experiment by proposing that the experimenters, as they observed the subjects' responses to the targets during the checkup of results, unconsciously tried to use PK retroactively to bias the brain processes of the subjects to call the correct targets. But only Fisk (the PCE) had enough psi ability to succeed.

However, one does not need to resort to the controversial observational theories to explain how experimenter psi could yield significant ESP effects. For instance, in cases where the experimenter or an assistant had been exposed to the target sequence before the test, one could propose that this person simply served unwittingly as a telepathic agent, and that some people are naturally better agents than others. There are other possibilities as well. Unfortunately, there has yet been no research on precisely how these experimenter psi effects actually might occur.

6.4 Implications of the experimenter effect

In conclusion, we can see that each of the three competing explanations of the EE have their talking points, and none has yet achieved a decisive victory. Indeed, the most likely possibility is that all three have some truth to them. What we can say with certainty is that all of them have important implications for how we must interpret all of the research discussed in this chapter. To make the points more clearly, let's see what the situation would be like in case each explanation were to achieve a total victory.

If the E-error hypothesis were to prevail, it would mean that all of the research, including that devoted to the EE, is worthless as evidence, not only for relationships between ESP and other variables, but for ESP itself. In other words, the E-error hypothesis is really the same as the skeptical explanation of psi generally.

If the E-psi hypothesis were to prevail, the research could still be accepted as evidence for psi, but most of its process-oriented implications would vanish. Sheep score higher than goats, for example, simply because that is what the experimenter wanted or expected. As you may already have noticed, this argument can be applied to some of the evidence for the E-psych. hypothesis as well. The triumph of the E-psi hypothesis would not argue for the abolishment of process research, but it would imply that we must direct such research toward answering such questions as why some experimenters are more psi-conducive than others.

Finally, if the E-psych. hypothesis were to prevail, our process-oriented conclusions would remain intact, but their generality would be severely limited. We would need to say, for example, that extraverts score higher than introverts, but only when tested by PCEs. Although this is a rather benign outcome compared to the two alternatives, it does not represent a satisfactory state of affairs. The principle of replication in science rightly demands of us that psi experiments be repeatable, at least in the statistical sense, by any qualified and fair-minded investigator, not just PCEs. What makes this problem solvable is that PCEs are not PCEs because they are PCEs, but because they share some attribute(s) that PIEs do not. Once we find out with sufficient exactitude what these attributes are, we likely will know how to turn PIEs into PCEs. One possibility might be to use hypnosis to temporarily transform certain goat experimenters into sheep.

For these reasons, the EE is the most important challenge facing modern experimental parapsychology. It may be that we will not be able to make too much progress in other areas of the field until the puzzle of the EE is solved.

Note

[1] A frequent point made by critics of parapsychology is that psi scores tend to decline after controls are tightened in later tests. Although this is true, psi scores also tend to decline if controls remain the same or are loosened. No evidence has ever been cited showing an actual relationship between the decline effect and tightening of controls.

Summary of terms

empirical generalization (law)
sampling error
statistical law
theory
hypothesis
psi-mediated instrumental response (PMIR)
processing capacity
psi-conducive syndrome
electromyograph (EMG)
lability
sheep-goat effect (SGE)
demand characteristics
perceptual defense
experimenter effect (EE)

Thought questions

(1) Even if we could succeed in making psi effects replicable on demand, it is still possible that 'normal' explanations could be proposed to account for them. Can you see how a process-oriented approach could be applied to overcome this 'hurdle'?

(2) In section 2.2.2b, evidence was cited suggesting that inducing expectancy of success on an ESP test by means of hypnosis seems to facilitate psi-hitting. In section 3.1.1, it was noted that in ordinary sheep-goat experiments personal expectancy of success has not proven to be a very successful predictor of ESP scoring. Assuming that both findings are valid, can you think of a simple way to reconcile them?

(3) In section 4.2.3, an experiment by Carpenter was briefly referred to in which a measure of anxiety was related to how well subjects scored on targets that were covertly associated with erotic pictures. With reference to Irwin's model and the concept of defense mechanisms, devise a possible explanation for this finding which addresses specific cognitive processes that might be involved.

(4) In section 5, reasons were discussed why some parapsychologists believe that immediate feedback should be ESP-facilitatory. Yet other parapsychologists believe that it should have just the opposite effect. What theoretical reasons do you think they would have for taking such a position?

(5) Take one of the sections 2–5 and review the experiments discussed in that section from the point of view of the experimenter effect, considering each of its three interpretations. Has your evaluation of any of this research been changed by this exercise? If so, how and why? Are there particular features of the results of any of these studies that seem to 'fit' one of these interpretations particularly well?

Chapter 9
Experimental methods in PK research

John Palmer (section 1 and 2)
Joseph H. Rush (section 3)

1 Introduction

In chapter 5, we discussed experimental methods for testing ESP in the laboratory. In this chapter, we will examine methodological issues pertaining to the other major branch of parapsychology, psychokinesis or PK. Thanks in large part to parapsychologists' increasing awareness of the revolutionary principles of modern physics plus the reemergence of seemingly talented PK subjects, PK research has enjoyed a tremendous renaissance in the last ten years, and PK methodology has become increasingly sophisticated.

The subject's task in a PK experiment is to paranormally influence the state or motion of a physical object or system. In so doing, the subject must be rendered incapable of exerting any physical effect on the object or system. This includes indirect influence by means such as magnets or the induction of air currents as well as by direct touching. As for the subject's psychological orientation to the task, most parapsychologists would recommend an attitude of passive volition. But the evidence on this point is by no means conclusive, and different strategies may work best for different people.

From the methodological standpoint, PK research can be divided into two broad categories. Micro-PK* refers to those PK effects that are weak or slight in magnitude, such as dice coming up 'six' more frequently than expected by chance. Micro-PK effects can rarely be identified as such by the naked eye and usually require the application of statistics for their detection. Macro-PK* or directly observable PK refers to PK effects which are large enough or strong enough to be detected as such by the naked eye and thus do not require statistics for their demonstration. The paranormal bending of a piece of metal would be an example of macro-PK.

Because micro-PK phenomena are readily adaptable to laboratory procedures, the methods for investigating them tend to become standardized and generally adopted. Reports of macro-PK are much rarer and the phenomena more varied. Moreover, because they are so rare, investigators must restrict themselves to the handful of subjects who seem able to produce them rather than select from pools of eager volunteers.

This chapter will be shorter than the chapter on ESP methods, not because PK is any less important than ESP, but because many of the principles discussed in chapter 5 apply to PK research as well. This is especially true of micro-PK research, which directly corresponds in many respects to restricted-choice ESP research. In particular, the sections of chapter 5 which cover the use of immediate feedback (2.4.1b), duration of testing (2.4.3), selection of subjects (3.1), and preparation of the subject (3.4) apply with equal force to PK research.

2 Micro-PK methods

2.1 Targets and testing procedures

In micro-PK research, it is important that the object or system to be influenced be sensitive or labile, i.e. it should require a minimal amount of physical energy to change it from one of its potential target states to any other one. This principle should become clear as we examine the kinds of targets used in micro-PK research.

2.1.1 The standard dice test*

The objective of the dice test, which was developed at the Duke Laboratory, is for the subject to make a falling die land with a predetermined face uppermost (J. B. Rhine and Pratt, 1957). In order to rule out the possibility of physical manipulation of the dice, an electromechanical device is used to release them. One or more dice are placed in a storage container at the top of the machine. The subject presses a button which opens a chute, allowing the dice to tumble down a beveled incline plane onto a level surface. The surface should be surrounded by siding to prevent the dice from falling on the floor. The bevels promote lability by helping to maximize the 'random' tumbling of the dice. The device is illustrated in Plate 10.

Any number of dice may be released at a time. In practice, the numbers have ranged from one to 96. Each individual outcome for a die customarily constitutes a trial, whereas each release of one or more dice is called a throw*. A run ordinarily consists of 24 trials. In the early dice tests, aggregates of runs were referred to as sets and aggregates of sets as pages, the latter representing the capacity of a single record sheet.

The die faces (normally six) represent the target alternatives. A hit is scored when the uppermost face of the die corresponds to the chosen target for the trial. The probability of a hit is one-sixth, thus MCE for a 24–trial run is four. The statistical significance of a given number of hits is determined exactly the same way as for a restricted-choice ESP test.

2.1.2 Placement tests

A more flexible approach to PK research is the placement test*. The dice machine can readily be modified for placement testing by dividing its surface lengthwise into two halves. The subject's task is to make the dice fall more frequently on one side than the other, the probability of a hit thus becoming one-half for each trial.

By having the subject aim for both a particular die face and a particular placement, a multiple-aspect test can be created. W. E. Cox (1951), for example, divided the bottom surface of a dice machine into 252 equal squares. Each square was labeled with a number from one to six, making 42 squares of each type. If the target were, say, a six, a subject could obtain a hit if the die either landed on a 'six' square or with the 'six' face uppermost. If both occurred, the trial would be classified as an exact hit.

Placement tests need not be restricted to dice. By comparing results with objects of differing sizes, shapes, weights and materials, the researcher can study the kinds of mechanical forces that might interact with the PK process (Forwald, 1969). Likewise, the device need not consist of an inclined plane. For example, Cox (1974b) created a machine in which hundreds of small metal balls are mechanically released into pairs of red and green chutes arranged in parallel columns. The number of hits is equal to the number of balls that land in chutes of the target color.

Alternatively, this test can be scored by the majority vote method (see chapter 6, section 3.2.3), a run being scored a hit if the majority of the balls land in the target chute of each pair. Cox has successfully utilized a number of different electromechanical devices for PK testing, thus demonstrating the flexibility of this approach (e.g. Cox, 1962, 1965).

2.1.3 Random event generators

REGs and their associated computer graphics (chapter 5, section 3.5.2) can readily be adapted for PK testing by having the subject aim for a given outcome to be generated on each trial or group of trials. Many REGs can produce sequences on their own without the subject pressing a button to activate each trial, often at very rapid rates (e.g. 300 per second) that allow large quantities of data to be accumulated in a short period of time. Some physicists are particularly interested in those REGs in which the outcomes are determined by the emission of electrons from a radioactive source, because the influence of such a subatomic process is especially relevant to quantum mechanics. More recent REGs use electronic noise sources such as Zener diodes which are sufficiently sensitive for PK testing.

The feedback capabilities of REGs, in addition to giving ongoing feedback, also provide the subject with a goal which is more comprehensible and psychologically captivating than the behaviour of the REG *per se*. In tests with one of Schmidt's machines, for example, the subject's task is to cause a light to 'walk' around a circular display of lamps in one direction rather than the other (see plate 11). The opportunities for providing motivating feedback displays are further enhanced when REGs are attached to computers with powerful graphics capabilities.

Another desirable feature of REGs is that they can be attached to peripheral equipment which can segregate test trials which are generated at moments when the subject is thought to be in a psi-conducive state. In one successful application of this principle (Honorton and Tremmel, 1979), trials were classified according to whether or not the subject's brainwaves at the time were in the alpha range. (Alpha is a brainwave of frequencey 8–13 hz which is often associated with a subjective state of nonattentive wakefulness.) As predicted, significant scoring was restricted to trials generated when alpha was present and subjects were given ongoing feedback of their brainwaves.

2.1.4 Ambient energy

A procedure based on physical principles similar to those governing the REG is to attempt PK influence on various forms of 'free' or ambient energy. The easiest of such energies to isolate experimentally is temperature. Gertrude Schmeidler (1973) asked subjects to use their PK to modify the temperature at a specific point in space and measured the result with a highly sensitive kind of thermometer called a thermistor, which was sealed inside a thermos container to eliminate the effect of outside room temperature. As an additional control, other thermistor units were placed elsewhere in the room. A trial was considered a hit if the temperature change recorded by the target thermistor was greater than the changes recorded by the controls.

2.1.5 Biological systems

The growing interest in the possibility of psychic healing has led many parapsychologists to explore PK effects on biological systems. The basic strategy is similar to that used by Schmeidler in her thermistor experiment. Separate target and control systems, initially in the same biological state, are assigned for each trial. The subject attempts to exert a PK effect on the target system. If the degree of change is greater in the target than in the control system at the end of a specified period of time, the trial is scored a hit. The target systems used in such experiments have ranged from enzymes (e.g. M. J. Smith, 1972) to plants (e.g. Grad, 1963) to animals (e.g. G. K. Watkins and A. M. Watkins, 1971). In another application similar in concept to the placement test, a subject attempted to use PK to cause tiny once-celled organisms called paramecia to migrate from the center of a Petri dish into one of its four quadrants (Richmond, 1952).

Although simplicity is generally the goal in selecting biological target systems, humans have occasionally been studied in such experiments. For example, William Braud (1978) successfully activated or suppressed the GSR of subjects participating in a free-response ESP test. You may recall that a similar kind of experiment was discussed in chapter 5, section 3.5.3, where psychophysiological responses such as GSR were treated as measures of ESP. This raises an interesting dilemma: did Braud's subjects respond to his telepathic messages by ESP or did Braud exert a PK effect on their autonomic nervous sytems? Unfortunately, we do not yet have the means to answer this theoretical question, so we must fall back upon the solution proposed in chapter 5 (section 2.4.1a) and approach the matter operationally: if we instruct the agent to send a telepathic message, we call it an ESP experiment; if we ask the agent to influence directly the subject's physiology, we call it a PK experiment.

2.2 Some adaptations of testing procedures

2.2.1 Hidden target and covert test methods

PK tests can be successfully conducted without subjects being given complete information about the task. For example, the researcher can decline to tell subjects the identity of the target, asking them simply to 'make it come out right' (e.g. Thouless, 1951; Fisk and West, 1958). This is analogous to the blind matching procedure in ESP testing and helps to make the test less cognitive for the subject. In most such tests the subject is informed of the general kind of effect desired (e.g. make the dice come up with a certain face uppermost) but not the specific effect (e.g. make them come up 'six'). However, it would be theoretically possible to deny the more general information as well (e.g. fail to tell the subject that you are scoring for placement of the dice as well as their faces).

The more extreme kinds of covert tests discussed in chapter 5 (section 3.5.5), where subjects are kept uninformed that they are participating in a psi test at all, can also be applied to PK research. REGs are excellent for this purpose because they can easily be left running while the subject is engaged in some other task. As in covert ESP tests, it is considered important to have some positive or negative consequence for the subject contingent upon whether the output of the REG is biased in the target direction. For example, Stanford, Zenhausern,

Taylor and Dwyer (1975) allowed subjects to escape a boring task at such time as the output of the REG departed from randomness to a statistically significant degree.

2.2.2 Time-displaced PK

If we are willing to assume that ESP can violate the conventional laws of time by extending into the future (i.e. precognition), then it is no less absurd to assume that PK can violate these same laws by extending backwards in time. Parapsychologists have recently begun to study the latter possibility, which they call retroactive PK, or simply retro-PK* (Schmidt, 1976). Methodologically, a retroactive PK experiment is conducted by generating the event sequence prior to the time that the subject attempts to influence it. For example, we might have an REG generate a sequence of binary numbers (e.g. ones and zeroes) and store electrical signals representing those numbers on magnetic tape such that no one observes them. Later a subject listens to the tape, on which the ones might be heard as clicks and the zeroes not heard at all, and tries to increase or decrease the number of clicks by, in effect, influencing the production of the numbers by the REG at the earlier time. If a covert test is desired, the subject can simply be told to listen to the clicks or to count them for some other purpose.

As you may have guessed, there is no conclusive way to rule out that the experimenter or even the subject might use PK to influence the sequence of numbers at the time they are generated. As we saw in the preceding section, a person need not be aware of the target or even consciously attempt a PK effect in order to exert one. So again, we must resort to defining retroactive PK operationally rather than theoretically.

Of course, PK might extend into the future as well as the past, and here our problem is a good deal simpler. All we need to do is measure the event some predetermined amount of time following the attempted PK influence. Such delayed PK effects are customarily called linger effects* or lag effects when they persist after attempted influence has ceased (e.g. Wells and G. K. Watkins, 1975) and release-of-effort effects* when they commence following attempted influence (e.g. Stanford and Fox, 1975). However, this distinction has not been rigorously applied.

2.3 Determining the event and target sequences

At this point it is necessary formally to introduce a terminological distinction between events and targets. Events* are the sequence of outcomes upon which the subject attempts to exert an influence. The targets are those particular outcomes the subject attempts to create.

The events in PK tests should be independent of one another, like open decks in ESP testing. This is automatically the case when different target objects or systems are used for each trial. It is also the case with properly functioning REGs. (REGs should always be checked for randomness in PK experiments just as in ESP experiments.) Lack of independence is most likely to be a serious problem in ambient energy or psychophysiological studies, in which the event sequence might be, for example, a series of GSR deflections. How can we be sure that one deflection did not somehow trigger a later deflection? Unfortunately, the answer is that we can never be absolutely sure, but we can be reasonably sure by not counting responses that occur together in bunches or 'bursts' as independent events.

It is also desirable that in the absence of PK influence each possible outcome in the event sequence occur an approximately equal number of times, according to the laws of randomness. One way to help assure this is to have unbiased target objects or systems. In dice tests, for example, the dice should be constructed such that no particular face is favored over the others. This is unlikely to be the case with pitted dice, because the 'six' face has more holes than the other faces. It therefore is slightly lighter in weight than these other faces and thus more likely to be uppermost. If the probability of a biased outcome can be specified precisely, it may be possible to adjust the statistical test to compensate for the bias, but it is best to avoid this kind of situation.

Another way to compensate for such biases, which should be used routinely in PK experiments, is to have each possible target alternative be the target for an equal number of trials. Thus in a standard dice test each die face should be the target an equal number of times, in a placement test each location should be the target an equal number of times, and on the Schmidt machine described in section 2.1.3 the target direction for movement of the lights should be clockwise and counter-clockwise an equal number of times. In other words, the sequence of targets should be a closed deck.

How exactly should the target sequence be determined? At least in overt tests, it is not a good idea to select a target separately for each trial. This forces subjects to shift their focus after each trial, which of course is impossible anyway in REG studies in which trials are being generated at a rapid rate. If the target sequence is selected randomly, the possibility is also enhanced that the person generating the target sequence might use his or her own psi to match the event sequence (see chapter 5, section 3.3.2).

A better solution is to have each target alternative be the target for a particular group of 'block' of trials. For example, a 60–trial dice test might be divided into six ten-trial runs with each face being the target for one run. But how do we determine the order of targets? The important principle here is to avoid sequences that might mimic a naturally occurring fluctuation in the system (which could mean that there is an intertrial dependency problem) or an internal scoring trend of possible interest. For example, if biased dice are used and the target sequence is 6,5,4,3,2,1, the overall score will be properly close to MCE if no PK is operative, but the scores might decline significantly from psi-hitting to psi-missing. This 'decline effect' would of course not be real evidence of PK, but simply an artifact of the biased dice. A better procedure is to randomize the order of the target alternatives and to use a different random order for each set or page.

In experiments with binary REGs, this effect can be accomplished by having subjects aim for high scores and low scores on different blocks of trials and determining the order of block designations (high or low) randomly. By then having an outside 'critical' observer generate the target sequence in a retro-PK experiment that allowed this target sequence to be registered in advance, Schmidt, Morris and Rudolph (1982) were able to utilize a research protocol that in principle eliminated the possibility of fraud on the part of the experimenter testing the subjects.

2.4 Recording the scores

When automated recording by REG or computer is not possible, as in traditional dice and placement tests, it is important to have two or more persons independently record the event sequences and then compare their records for possible discrepancies. In many cases it is possible to photograph the outcome of each event, which provides a permanent record that further enhances the reliability of scoring.

3 Macro-PK methods

Because of the rarity and the highly individual character of macro-PK manifestations, it is difficult to generalize as to investigative methods. However, some comments can be made with respect to the more frequently reported kinds of phenomena. We are concerned here only with effects that are sufficiently voluntary and repeatable to permit of at least a few controlled tests. Poltergeists and other transient, spontaneous phenomena are largely excluded (see chapter 3).

Physical mediums became prominent accessories of spiritualism; but investigative control methods were inadequate, and research interest shifted in the 1930s to statistical experiments (see chapter 2 and 10). When fresh reports of directly observable PK effects began to appear about 1960, they dealt with a generation of practitioners who no longer operated in darkness and seldom attributed their phenomena to spirits. Investigators also broke with the earlier tradition in their increasing application of sophisticated instrumental techniques and experimental designs. Because of these innovations we will consider here only investigations of macro-PK that have been reported since 1960.

The varieties of macro-PK effects are almost as numerous as the reports. (We will speak here of effects rather than targets because many macro-PK phenomena suggest greater complexity and a more variable kind of influence than is implied in a hit on such a standardized target as a die face or REG choice.) The purpose is not to review all of the alleged effects, but to mention some investigations that illustrate interesting methodological approaches.

3.1 The subject-collaborators

Again, a term derived from micro-PK and ESP experiments seems inappropriate here. Because of their rarity, macro-PK practitioners are self-selected, and they participate in experiments more as collaborators than as 'subjects'.

Almost all such subjects report that their PK abilities first manifested in spontaneous poltergeist disturbances, usually in adolescence. Most such episodes subside after a few days or weeks and do not recur, but in some cases they persist and are brought under voluntary control. Matthew Manning (1974) tells how he gained control of his unsought 'gift' by turning it to purposeful activities. Felicia Parise developed strong PK ability without prior experience (Honorton, 1974a). In at least one case a persistent investigator guided the development (Winther, 1928).

3.2 Experimental procedures and problems

The conditions of almost all recent macro-PK experiments contrast sharply with those reported in the heyday of the physical mediums. Gone are the darkened rooms, invocations of spirits, and other trappings of spiritualism. Instead, almost all such experiments are conducted in normal light in laboratories or other prosaic settings, with scientists and technicians in attendance. The new generation of PK practitioners clearly has shifted from religious to scientific orientation.

One might expect that this more accommodating attitude would have made the experimenter's task easy and the evidence for strong PK decisive; but that has not been the case. A macro-PK subject inevitably has more bargaining power than an ordinary volunteer, besides being usually a rather temperamental personality. Consequently, no standard procedure for such experiments is practicable. When gifted psychics have participated in routine ESP or micro-PK experiments, the results seldom have been remarkable. Each PK practitioner necessarily has developed a highly individual, frequently unique repertoire and usually is resistant to changing it. Consequently, a perceptive investigator must design an experiment around whatever effect the subject claims to produce, being sensitive to the subject's working habits and motivations. Yet the experiment must be designed to meet the essential scientific requirements: i.e. to observe and record unambiguously the events that occur, and particularly to exclude fraud and misinterpretation.

Recent developments in laboratory technology have contributed greatly to such designs. Various electronic devices, such as chart recorders, magnetometers, thermistors, strain gauges, oscilloscopes and video cameras, have been used as PK objects or recorders. Self-processing cameras have greatly simplified photographic experiments. Continuous monitoring of an experiment on film or videotape, sometimes accompanied by sound tape, is not uncommon, and a responsible magician can be helpful in some situations. Yet it is difficult to categorize the experimental methods that have evolved, because every experiment involves novel features and problems. One is reminded of physicist P. W. Bridgman's definition of scientific method as 'doing one's damnedest with one's mind, and no holds barred.'

For that reason, to discuss much of the methodology of macro-PK research would be to describe each individual experiment. However, several types of phenomena have been reported frequently enough or investigated persistently enough to justify some generalizations about methods.

3.2.1 Movements of objects

Most of the recent reports of this class of PK have come from investigations of a Soviet woman, Nina Kulagina. These are summarized in a review with original references by four of the investigators (Keil, Herbert, Ullman and Pratt, 1976). Controls consisted of such measures as close visual observation, detailed examination of equipment used, screening of test objects with various materials, introduction of new tests without notice, and sometimes still or motion picture records.

Most tests involved small objects at rest on a horizontal surface that were made to slide on the surface. Variable conditions included: material and texture of the surface; weight, size, shape, material, and number of objects; selective movement of one object in a group; and simultaneous movement of two objects in different directions. Similar tests were reported on floating objects and on a laboratory balance. A pendulum was used to test Kulagina's ability to start or stop it or to change the plane of its oscillation. Rotation of a compass needle was frequently observed. Concurrently with observations of PK effects, observations sometimes were made of Kulagina's heart rate, EEG pattern, weight loss, and other physiological parameters.

Harold Puthoff and Russell Targ (1975, p. 136) devised a pendulum PK experiment that is notable for its inherent security against fraudulent manipulation. A torsion (rotational) pendulum of the type used in some clocks was suspended inside a bell jar. A laser beam was reflected from a mirror on the pendulum bob to a photoelectric device that was sensitive to any displacement of the light beam. Thus, any rotation of the pendulum was detected and appeared in the trace on a chart recorder. It was found that the pendulum never came entirely to rest, but picked up enough energy from slight vibrations of the building to keep it oscillating through an almost constant small angle. Now, one can conceive of normal ways to increase the movement of the pendulum, though that would not have been easy in this case; but, short of placing a rather strong magnet near the pendulum, it is very difficult to imagine a way to stop the residual oscillation. Yet that is what a gifted subject was able to do, even from another room.

3.2.2 Metal bending

The vogue of paranormally bending and otherwise influencing metal objects that was initiated by Uri Geller about 1965 has produced many anecdotal reports but little well-controlled experimentation. In such tests, the investigator should identify the metal specimen to guard against possible substitution and also allow no opportunity for bending it by normal means. The latter condition has been difficult to meet, because the subject usually has insisted upon handling or at least touching the test specimen.

W. E. Cox (1974a) reported a test with Geller that is typical of such observations. He allowed Geller to examine briefly a flat steel key that Cox had brought. He then laid the key on a glass-topped table, noting that it lay flat, and held his finger on the large end while observing the under side of the key in a mirror he held underneath the table top. As Geller stroked the shank of the key, it bent upward. Cox verified the bend by rocking the key on the glass surface.

John Hasted (1981) and others have used electronic strain gauges to study very small deformations of objects. (A strain-gauge sensor cemented to a surface signals any stretching or compression of the surface.) This method allowed the experimenter to give full attention to the experimental situation while much more data than an observer could monitor were registered on a chart recorder. In these experiments the subjects' hands were kept at least several inches from the test objects. Further, Hasted relied on young subjects, mainly adolescents, on the dubious assumption that they would be less likely than adults to have developed fraudulent skills.

He also tried to identify the actual PK target by including dummy strain sensors and by using optical sensors also in some tests. He reasoned that, if the paranormal agency was acting upon the strain gauges instead of the metal specimen, it probably would affect the dummies similarly. (It did not.) Other adaptations of the versatile gauges were used to obtain clues to localizations and directions of the presumably paranormal forces.

3.2.3 Photographic effects: 'thoughtography*'

The most extensive investigations in this area were reported by Jule Eisenbud (e.g. 1967/1969, 1977). His reports concerned principally experiments with Ted Serios as subject. Almost all of the PK effects were obtained in Polaroid cameras working in normal indoor light. By eliminating darkroom processing and incidental handling of the film, the Polaroid camera greatly reduced opportunities for fraud. It also contributed to the procedure by revealing the result of each test immediately. Eisenbud took further precautions by buying his film at various stores and by routinely taking normal control exposures from each package when the subject was not 'trying.'

In a typical test, one of the several investigators present would sit with the camera in his lap aimed approximately toward Serios's head. Serios would stare at the camera and 'work himself up' until he felt ready. At his signal, the investigator would trip the shutter and develop and label the print immediately. A short paper cylinder that Serios liked to hold in front of the lens led to much controversy (chapter 10, section 3.5.4); but it was not used in all of the successful tests.

Eisenbud tried many successful variations of this basic method, tripping two cameras simultaneously, separating subject and camera by as much as 60 feet (18 meters), putting subject inside an electrical shield (Faraday cage) or shielded radiology laboratory with camera outside, or covering the camera lens with a hand or tape during the 'exposure.' Sometimes Serios was asked to produce a picture of a particular object; or such a request was written and sealed until the end of the session.

Experimenters have reported anomalous exposures of film incidentally to other PK effects that were of primary interest. Watkins and Watkins (1974), in an experiment with Parise, placed film in lightproof packets at the subject's focal point and at various distances from it. They obtained exposures that were strongest at the focal point. Similar procedures have been reported with Kulagina (Keil *et al.*, 1976). Much evidence of this kind suggests that it might be worthwhile in all PK experiments, or at least those involving macro-PK, to include sealed film packets near the target sites.

3.2.4 Effects on electronic apparatus

A few instances of macro-PK effects on electronic apparatus have been reported. These are not sufficient to permit any generalizations about methods, but the possibilities of such tests are so attractive that it appears worthwhile to mention these examples for their suggestive value.

Eisenbud (1972) mounted an electronic light sensor (photometer) inside a camera, so that operating the shutter in a lighted room produced a brief rise or 'blip' on the associated oscilloscope trace. Serios was observed in a series of trials to reduce the blip to zero and then below. He also produced pictures through a video camera. Puthoff and Targ (1975, p. 130) reported tests with gifted subjects on two types of magnetometers (instruments for measuring magnetic field strength). The subjects, in separate rooms but observing the readout devices, were able to alter the output readings.

Experiments such as these are relatively simple to control against fraud, since there are few ways to influence the apparatus without tampering with the circuitry. So long as PK phenomena are not understood or generally accepted, this aspect will remain prominent in all such experiments; and electronic devices offer an attractive combination of security, flexibility and convenience in registering results.

3.2.5 Acoustical effects

The literature of psychical research and spiritualism includes many accounts of paranormal 'direct voices' at seances, but no consideration of these effects is possible here because of the lack of recent scientific studies. With the advent of magnetic tape recorders, however, a succession of reports have told of voices and other sounds recorded apparently paranormally. These claims remain highly controversial even among parapsychologists. However, some comments on methods appear justified.

Raymond Bayless (1959; Rogo, 1976) recorded voices by placing an amplifier-recorder inside a dark cabinet while he and a gifted subject remained outside it. Konstantin Raudive (1971), the best-known such investigator, recorded through a microphone in a quiet room or from the output of a radio tuned between stations. His methods have been severely criticized (e.g. Ellis, 1974; Roll, 1982, p. 246; E. L. Smith, 1974) because of the possibility of recording extraneous sounds or weak, transient radio speech. His method of evaluating his recording by repeated listening for faint fragments in various languages also has been criticized as being too subjective.

Hans Bender (1972), working with Friedrich Jürgenson as subject, obtained a clear taped voice through only one channel of a stereophonic pair. Bayless (1976), in a variation of Raudive's method, recorded from a microphone in contact with a sounding board in a quiet room, obtaining otherwise inaudible raps and other sounds; but the problem of excluding normal sounds is obvious.

A methodologically promising study of normally audible rapping sounds obtained in a sitter-group experiment (section 3.2.6) was reported by Joel Whitton (1975). He compared analyses of the recorded wave forms of both the paranormal raps and normally produced raps of similar loudness, noting significant differences between them.

3.2.6 Sitter-group phenomena

An English psychologist, K. J. Batcheldor (1966, 1984; Isaacs, 1984) conceived a rationale for the reputed success of the traditional spiritistic seances that suggested a fresh approach to PK experimentation. He theorized that participants in a group are less inhibited than are individual subjects. A group member need not feel personally responsible for what may happen, and darkness shields the sitters from the shock of direct confrontation with incredible manifestations. Light conversation, laughter, and singing may relieve anxiety by distracting attention from the purpose of the session. Batcheldor also emphasized the importance of suggestion to induce confidence in the participants, even to the point of immediate belief. For this reason, he felt that ambiguous normal effects, such as slight movements of the experimental table by muscular impulses, are essential to develop such confidence.

In a series of sittings with two friends, Batcheldor put these principles to the test, reporting levitation of a table and other strong effects. A few other groups have reported success by similar techniques, some in normal light (Brookes-Smith and Hunt, 1970; Brookes-Smith, 1973; I. M. Owen and Sparrow, 1976).

Dark sessions obviously are difficult to control against trickery and malobservation. Batcheldor trusted his friends, but he recognized that impersonal controls are essential for scientific validation. Brookes-Smith, in an effort to meet this need, fitted the experimental table with strain gauges and other sensors and recorded their output signals and a sound track continuously on magnetic tape. He also introduced a novel psychological device, secretly designating one sitter to 'prime the pump' by judicious lifting of the table edge to raise confidence and expectancy in the group. The instrumental record was expected to indicate when such normal intervention had occurred.

Batcheldor's motivational concepts are so psychologically plausible and fit so neatly the traditional lore of the spiritistic seances that, despite some failures, they ought not to be lightly abandoned. Limited as they are, the sitter-group experiments that have been reported suggest a fertile alternative to the experimenter-subject dichotomy of the laboratory. The essential concepts also are adaptable to other experimental designs. Palmer (1983a) has reported such an experimental adaptation, in which hypnotic suggestion rather than environmental influences would be used to raise subjects' confidence and expectation.

Summary of terms

micro-PK
macro-PK
dice test (standard)
throw
placement test
retroactive PK
linger effect
release-of-effort effect
event
thoughtography

Thought questions

(1) In a psi test with dice, you toss the dice and call them while they are tumbling. You score significantly. Is this an example of ESP, or of PK? How can you tell?

(2) What kind and amount of evidence would be required to convince you of the genuineness of a macro-PK effect (e.g. metal bending): (a) if you were present; (b) if you were not?

(3) Experimental results indicate that certain experimenters consistently obtain significant PK scores by their subjects, while some others get consistently nonsignificant results. Can you suggest an experimental approach to determine whether the successful scoring is due to the experimenters' PK ability?

(4) Telepathy is commonly conceived as communication of thoughts. But clairvoyance implies the possibility that the percipient may be clairvoyantly 'reading' mental processes in a passive agent, and PK implies that the agent may be able to influence the mental processes of the percipient. Can you suggest any method for distinguishing between these possibilities? Does 'telepathy' have any independent meaning?

(5) Can you suggest a way to determine whether PK effects obtained in experiments with animals or plants as 'subjects' are actually produced by them and not the experimenter?

Chapter 10
Findings from experimental PK research

Joseph H. Rush

1 Introduction

All reports of physical psi effects (PK) before 1942 relate to macro-PK. The concept of standardized, statistically evaluable PK experiments emerged only as a derivative of J. B. Rhine's statistical ESP experiments during the 1930s. Reports of serious investigations of physical mediums (i.e. of macro-PK claims) practically ceased at about the same time. When reports of macro-PK demonstrations reappeared about 1960, the practitioners, their claimed effects, and the investigative methods that were applied all differed sharply from those of the pre–1940 period. For these reasons, it is convenient to discuss the work of the earlier period separately from the more recent findings. For background information on this period, see chapter 2; also Eisenbud (1977); Feilding (1963); Gauld (1968); Nicol (1977); Podmore (1902/1963, 1910/1975); Rogo (1975); Rush (1977).

Almost all investigations of macro-PK have attempted little more than to determine whether the observed effects were genuinely paranormal. That has been a sufficiently challenging task without trying to investigate more subtle aspects of the phenomena. The early statistical experiments with dice were similarly proof-oriented; but, as investigators gained confidence in the reality of PK, they increasingly turned to process-oriented research: i.e. to experiments designed to explore the influences of various physical and psychological variables upon PK manifestations and to test hypotheses.

These obviously are not distinct categories, since any good experiment that yields significant results contributes to the evidence for PK. However, in discussing the post–1940 research we will deal first with the primarily proof-oriented experiments and the criticisms they evoked, and then with the primarily process-oriented research. Experimental macro-PK in this period has been sparse and almost entirely proof-oriented. It will therefore be included in the discussion of proof-oriented research.

There is a principle of complementarity that applies to information: namely, quantity and reliability are inversely related. In almost any area of inquiry, if we ignore standards of reliability, the supply of information swells to overwhelming volume. But, if we insist upon absolute certainty, the supply shrinks toward zero. This principle is acutely relevant to the problem of evaluating psi research, particularly in the early investigations of macro-PK. The difficulties the investigators faced, and the reasons for them, have been discussed in chapter 2; see also Rush (1981). We are here concerned only with those investigations that involved enough controls and observational facilities to qualify as at least quasi-experimental. That restriction excludes most claims of macro-PK, including all spontaneous or anecdotal cases. Even so, there remains a great range of uncertainty in estimating the reliability of the remaining reports – uncertainty that is compounded by one's personal prejudices.

As to the following discussions of both early and recent macro-PK, the reader should keep in mind that this is not a comprehensive handbook, but an introductory text. The purpose is to present a representative group of findings for which there appears to be substantial experimental evidence. These findings must not be regarded as scientifically established, but neither should they be lightly dismissed.

2 Experimental PK findings before 1940

2.1 Mechanical effects

Movements of objects without evident cause, called telekinesis in the older literature, were reported from almost all sessions with physical mediums. Such movements, sometimes in normal light, were attested to by great numbers of witnesses.

Physicist William Crookes (1884, 1889; Medhurst, Goldney and Barrington, 1972; Tietze, 1973c), working with the medium D. D. Home, reported levitation of a table under good control conditions. He described also an experiment in which Home held an accordion by the end opposite the keys, the accordion hanging free inside a wire cage in good light. Under these conditions (abbreviated here) Crookes and others saw the accordion expand and contract while playing. The action continued even when Home removed his hand from the instrument.

Movements and levitations of objects and billowings of curtains occurred routinely in sessions with Eusapia Palladino (see chapter 2, sections 2.2, 3.2). The most persuasive account of these effects is that by Feilding, Baggally and Carrington (1909; Feilding, 1963), who were experienced, skeptical, and well aware of the medium's propensity to cheat if she could. Yet in a series of sittings at Naples in 1908 they were convinced by various effects that they observed repeatedly in light good enough to confirm their control of Palladino's hands and feet. Podmore (1909, 1910/1975), in a detailed analysis of the Feilding, Baggally and Carrington report, strongly contested their observations, alleging inadequate controls; Baggally (1910) responded.

Various mechanical effects produced repeatedly under much better conditions were reported by Harry Price (1925/1973). The young woman subject, Stella Cranshaw, was not a spiritualist or a professional medium. She was quiet and entirely compliant with controls during the sessions in Price's laboratory. Price conducted the experiments in the presence of several invited observers, some of whom were experienced investigators, in various levels of red light. Under these conditions small musical instruments inside a double cage under the experimental table were moved and played, and an electric bulb controlled by a switch inside a cell covered by a soap bubble film was lighted; the film was found intact. The table was repeatedly levitated and finally broke apart.

Price (1930) reported sessions with Rudi Schneider, a young Austrian PK subject, under ostensibly the best controls ever applied in such investigations. The sittings were conducted in darkness or near-darkness; but everyone present, including Price and Schneider, wore metallized mittens that were connected to small signal lights. Sitters all joined hands to complete an electric circuit to indicate if anyone in the circle broke hand contact. Under these conditions a wastebasket and other objects were moved and levitated (Besterman, 1932).

Price's reports of mechanical phenomena would be the strongest of the early period except for doubts cast on his integrity by later events.

Price (in a newspaper article) accused Schneider of fraud in a later investigation, but he had waited a year to report what amounted to negligent control on his part. Later developments in both this and the Borley Rectory haunting case provided grounds for questioning both his motives and his conduct (e.g. Dingwall, Goldney and Hall, 1955, 1956; Gregory, 1974, pp. 295–300, 1977; Hope *et al.*, 1933). However, it should be noted that none of the participants in Price's sessions with Cranshaw or Schneider published any serious criticism of them, and some confirmed Schneider's capabilities in independent, well-controlled experiments (see section 2.5.2).

Among the more impressive PK findings are the experiments with pendulums by Christian Winther (1928). These studies are notable for having been done in full light and for having concentrated on a narrow range of tests on pendulums, instead of encouraging the usual bewildering variety of effects. Winther's subject (not a medium) was able to increase or decrease the movement of a pendulum without disturbing an identical stationary pendulum hanging from the same support, thus implying the absence of any normal physical intervention.

Other examples of persuasive but inconclusive evidence for such movements of objects could be cited, but one more will suffice. A Polish investigator, Julien Ochorowicz, and several other scientists conducted tests of a young woman, Stanislawa Tomczyk, that were more like laboratory experiments than seances. In the presence of several investigators, under adequate lamplight, she levitated small balls between her open hands held a few centimeters apart. Investigators verified that no threads or other supports were attached to the ball while it was suspended (Hyslop, 1911; Ochorowicz, 1909; Tietze, 1974).

Several investigators tried to measure the force that could be applied to an object by a physical medium (Medhurst *et al.*, 1972). Crookes (1884, 1889; Tietze, 1973c) described several such experiments with Home in Crookes's dining room with various levels of gaslight. In the simplest version, one end of a 36–inch (91–centimeter) board rested on a table. The other end was suspended from a spring balance. While Crookes and several others observed, Home placed his fingers 'lightly' on the fixed end of the board, whereupon the balance indicated a downward force at the free end of up to 9 pounds (4 kilograms). Crookes noted that his full weight on the fixed end of the board moved the balance only 1.5 pounds (.7 kilogram).

During apparently well-controlled investigations of Palladino by a group of notable scientists at the Institut Général Psychologique in Paris, a lever balance was observed to register as much as 7 kilograms under her influence without direct contact (Courtier, 1908).

2.2 Sound effects: raps, voices, others

Sharp tapping or thumping sounds, generally called raps, were reported from practically all spiritistic seances and sessions with physical mediums. Yet good scientific evidence for their genuineness is meager, for two reasons. First, they may have been hallucinations. This possibility might seem to be negligible when several witnesses heard similar sounds at the same time. However, groups of ordinarily reliable persons repeatedly testified that in Home's presence the house shook and furniture rattled as in a moderate earthquake; but the damage that should have been expected from such a disturbance did not occur. Second, raps are easy to produce by normal means, and the source of a sound is difficult to locate, particularly if witnesses' attention is misdirected.

Crookes's (1874; Rogo, 1975, p. 47) account of observations in the presence of Kate Fox remains a fair example of the evidence for paranormal raps, except for the lack of multiple witnesses. He obtained raps on various objects and materials – a piece of glass, a tambourine, a tree, a sheet of paper suspended by a thread. However, the dubious record of the Fox sisters must be noted (see chapter 2, section 1.4).

During Price's sessions with Cranshaw (section 2.1), raps and pounding noises were frequently reported.

2.3 Photographic effects

Almost as soon as photography became generally available, some photographers began to display portraits that included images of persons who had not been physically present when the portraits were exposed. Some of these 'extras' were promptly claimed as likenesses of dead persons and eagerly embraced by spiritualists as evidence for survival of death. Thus technology opened up a fresh area of mediumship – one particularly tempting to fraud because of the esoteric process that it involved. The resulting claims and controversies persisted from about 1860 to the 1930s (Coates, 1911; Eisenbud, 1977). Today the spirit photographers' claims are as difficult to evaluate as those of the physical mediums.

A ten-year series of experiments by F. W. Warrick (1939), a British industrialist, yielded some of the better data of the period and at the same time posed clearly the problem of evaluating such evidence. His medium, Emma Deane, produced patterns and marks on photographic plates or even plain paper without a camera. Various constraints were used to preclude fraud, even to confining her hands in 'stocks'. Warrick did not publish his results until about five years after the last of the experiments. However, he stated that his paper comprised reports written within two days from notes made during each experiment. He also recognized that some of his results bore features that suggested fraud, but he was convinced that fraud had been impossible under the conditions he had imposed. Yet the essential question, as E. M. Sigdwick noted long ago, is not whether fraud could have occurred under the described conditions, but whether the conditions really were *as described.* One recalls Davey's slate-writing demonstrations (chapter 2, section 2.1) and wonders.

Fukurai's investigations of thoughtography (Fukurai, 1931/1975; Eisenbud, 1977, p. 416; Rush, 1977, p. 21) were well-conceived approximations to laboratory-type controlled experiments. His principal subject produced developable figures or symbols, frequently Japanese calligraphic characters, on sealed photographic plates. Usually these were patterns that Fukurai had prescribed before the test. Sometimes an exposure was obtained on a plate sandwiched between two others that were unaffected. Despite the compromises imposed by circumstances (the *pas de deux* between Fukurai and his subject is both entertaining and exasperating) he obtained good results in two tests that by his account were fully controlled. His results appear to be the most persuasive among the early photographic investigations.

2.4 Materializations

Undoubtedly the most controversial of paranormal physical effects is materialization, the apparent creation of tangible, physically substantial forms. Descriptions of these have ranged through a continuum of solidarity and definition, from opaque, foglike shapes to probing rodlike members to well-defined hands, faces, and even – rarely – full forms. However, the occurrence of materializations only in darkness or very dim light and the severe restrictions on touching or otherwise examining them detract from their credibility. From the many such accounts only a few of the better attested observations need be mentioned.

Fleeting appearances of apparent phantoms, from shapeless masses to fully formed hands, were frequent in Palladino's seances. The detailed report by Feilding, Baggally and Carrington (section 2.1), which represents one of the most competent and reliable investigations of Palladino, frequently mentions appearances of hands, arms, or other objects they could not explain. Nevertheless, their observations must share the uncertainties that attend all such reports.

Apparent materializations frequently were observed during Price's sessions with Rudi Schneider (see section 2.1). On one occasion an observer, Charles Hope, asked the medium's 'guide' to show herself. 'Immediately the wastepaper basket lifts, the sitters distinctly seeing the pseudopod supporting it. Some sitters saw the fingers, three in number, and part of an arm.' Twenty minutes later, 'The sitters all see a white seemingly shapeless mass form. . . . It seems luminous and fairly solid . . . about three feet high, remaining for perhaps two minutes' (quoted in Tietze, 1973b, p. 41). These incidents are typical of many that were observed under the electric-mitten controls mentioned earlier.

Ochorowicz and other investigators who observed Tomczyk's levitations of small objects in good light (section 2.1) reported that sometimes the object appeared to be supported on a threadlike strand between her hands. However, no thread was found, and when Ochorowicz 'cut' the strand it immediately reformed. Photographs sometimes showed it as an irregular stringlike filament.

The foregoing examples are representative of the better-attested observations of apparent materializations. Many other accounts exist (e.g. Crawford, 1921; Geley, 1927; Schrenck-Notzing, 1920) but they are evidentially weaker than those summarized here.

2.5 Miscellaneous effects

Several additional kinds of physical effects have been observed under good enough conditions to justify mention.

2.5.1 Influences on temperature

During the sessions with Cranshaw, Price kept a self-registering thermometer on the wall opposite the medium. This instrument was of the type that registers maximum and minimum readings. Decreases of up to 11 degrees Fahrenheit (6.1 Centigrade) from initial room temperature were noted by multiple witnesses, the magnitudes of the changes being roughly correlated with the violence of the mechanical effects that occurred during the sessions. However, the ostensible cooling effect would have been indistinguishable from direct PK influence on the minimum marker.

Winther (section 2.1) also reported lowering of thermometer readings in sessions with his subject, Anna Rasmussen.

2.5.2 Optical effects

Eugene Osty attended two of Price's sittings with Rudi Schneider and in 1931 brought the medium to his laboratory in Paris (Osty and Osty, 1932). As a control against fraud, he arranged a beam of infrared (IR) radiation to guard the object of PK influence. Any attempt to move the object by a hand or other material probe would interrupt the beam and trigger four cameras to photograph the intrusion. Several times during dark seances the cameras were triggered, but the photographs showed nothing intruding in the IR beam. Later the alarm was triggered during sittings in adequate red light, but the investigators saw nothing to account for the interruption of the beam. Osty concluded that something invisible but substantial enough to obscure the IR beam had been present on these occasions.

Lord Charles Hope (1933), who also had attended some of Price's sessions with Schneider, confirmed Osty's word with a similar IR apparatus designed by physicist Lord Rayleigh (1933). Their instrument registered interruptions of the IR beam even when a screen was placed between it and Schneider.

Both of these investigations appear to have been done under good controls. However, the conclusion that the IR beam was interrupted is dubious, since camera triggers or other parts of the apparatus may have been influenced paranormally.

2.5.3 Electrical effects

During the investigations of Palladino by scientists at the Institut Général Psychologique (section 2.1) a test was made with an electroscope, a simple instrument for indicating the presence of an electric charge stored in the instrument. Normally it would hold its charge with only very slow leakage, but in Palladino's presence it was quickly discharged (Courtier, 1908).

3 Proof-oriented experimentation since 1940

PK research of this recent period falls into two distinct classes: micro-PK experiments with dice, REGs, or other processes that require statistical evaluation; and directly observable macro-PK effects such as anomalous photography, metal bending, and movement of static objects. This research is summarized in Rush (1977, 1982), Schmeidler (1977, 1982), and Stanford (1977c).

The micro-PK work has been characterized by relatively good controls, widely repeated procedures, and statistically strong evidential value despite generally low scoring rates. Opportunities for experimental investigations of macro-PK effects have been limited by the rarity of credible subjects and, in most cases, the difficulties of designing procedures satisfactory to both subjects and experimenter. Consequently, though some of the macro-PK work is impressive, it inevitably lacks the evidential force of the more consistent and sustained statistical findings. For that reason, this section will be concerned principally with the statistical research.

The scope and variety of PK experiments have been presented in chapter 9. This section deals primarily with the findings from this research as evidence for the occurrence of PK effects. The discussion will therefore concentrate on a few selected experiments that combine good designs and procedures with statistically strong results. Comparison with similar surveys of ESP research (e.g. chapters 7 and 8; Palmer, 1978b) reveals many equivalent experimental designs and findings, implying that ESP and PK are alternative manifestations of the underlying principle that we call psi.

3.1 Statistical experiments with mechanical objects

The early PK experiments with dice, developed at Duke University by J. B. Rhine, were frankly exploratory, with more emphasis on psychologically congenial conditions than on rigorous controls. Experimental conditions gradually improved, particularly after published reports of the research began to rouse the interest of other experimenters and critics. A comprehensive summary of the research with mechanical objects is included in a critical review by Edward Girden (1962a).

3.1.1 The evidence: tests with dice

PK experiments with dice never produced such phenomally high scores as were reported for some ESP card tests, nor were the average PK scoring rates so high as those for ESP (Tart, 1983). Rather, the evidence

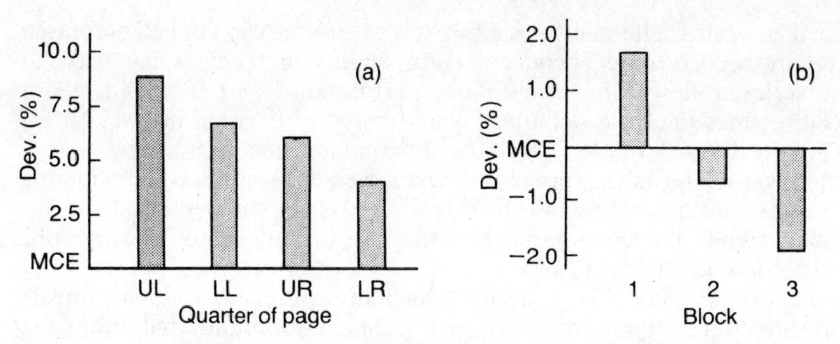

Figure 10.1: Decline effect in PK experiments with dice. (a) Decline by quarters of the record page, in terms of the mean percent deviation from MCE, of the composite score from 12 experimental series (J. B. Rhine and Humphrey, 1944a). The score in the upper left (UL) quarter was the highest in 10 of the series and lowest in only one. (b) Decline of mean scores through three successive blocks of 24 trials in each half-page run (McConnell, Snowdon and Powell, 1955). Note that the scoring tends to be positive in the first blocks, but almost equally negative in the third.

from extrachance scores has developed from modest departures from chance expectation that were maintained over long series of trials.

Many of the early experimenters with dice, at Duke and elsewhere, reported highly significant scores, but almost all of these results were compromised to various degrees by faults in experimental designs or procedures. The most pervasive defect was failure to compensate for dice bias. Many experiments were unwitnessed, and recording procedures were open to biased errors.

An example of the better work of the pre–1945 period is that of a husband-and-wife team (E. P. Gibson, L. H. Gibson and J. B. Rhine, 1944). Three dice were thrown in a motor-driven cage. The Gibsons and 13 others took turns as subjects, but one of the Gibsons always observed and recorded. Targets were rotated among the die faces. Under these conditions 33,696 die trials yielded a positive deviation of 171 over mean chance expectation (MCE) (p = .012), though the scoring rate was only 3 percent above MCE.

The evidential value of this early exploratory work was enhanced by the later discovery of a highly consistent internal decline effect in the data from many comparable experiments, a tendency for scoring rate to decline from beginning to end of a run or other unit independently of dice bias (Pratt, 1944; J. B. Rhine and Humphrey, 1944a, 1944b; J. B. Rhine, Humphrey, and Pratt, 1945). Actually, the analyses were done in terms of geometrical quarters of the record page on which trials had been recorded from top to bottom, in columns from left to right. On average, most hits occurred in the upper left quarter, next in the lower left, then upper right, and finally the lowest hit rate in the lower right quarter (see figure 10.1a). The difference between pooled first and fourth quarters from 18 experiments was highly significant ($p < 10^{-8}$). It was conjectured that, whatever the cause of the decline, the break before beginning a new record page had a refreshing or renewing effect on the PK subject.

The decline effect has not appeared consistently in later PK research. Many reports note a concentration of hits in the first few trials of a series, followed by near-chance performance (e.g. Forwald, 1969). Sometimes the hit distribution is a U-curve or even an incline; but, as Stanford (1977c) noted, declines are common, inclines rare.

Several later dice experiments met the essential criteria for evidential results: mechanical release or throwing of dice, compensation for dice bias, significant scores, and, in a few cases, duplicate or photographic recording of the die faces.

Laura A. Dale (1946) reported such an experiment with 54 subjects; results were significant (p = .005). She also found that individual subjects tended to score consistently high or low in alternate segments of the tests. However, three attempted replications (Dale and Woodruff, 1947) were nonsignificant.

R. A. McConnell used an automatic machine to tumble the dice for each trial and photograph the top faces; scores were recorded target-blind from the photographs (McConnell and Clark, 1983; McConnell, Snowdon and Powell, 1955). Of about 170,000 trials by 393 subjects, two-thirds were machine thrown and the remainder cup-thrown (see figure 10.1b). Scores were not significant, but a strong, consistent decline appeared (p = .002). Dice bias was irrelevant, since each record page used in the decline analysis had been run on a single target face.

G. W. Fisk in England conducted a series of five concealed-target PK experiments with a single subject – a woman physician, Dr Blundun – that rank among the better evidential tests with dice (Fisk and West, 1957, 1958; Mitchell and Fisk, 1953). Two of these experiments were especially well controlled. They also yielded the most significant scores of the series. In the first, Fisk displayed each day's target number at his home while each of ten subjects at various distances (including Blundun at 170 miles (274 kilometers)) tossed dice without normal knowledge of the target. This procedure disposed at once of concern with tossing methods and recording errors. Nine subjects' scores were marginal or nonsignificant, but Blundun's was much higher (in 10,000 trials, p = .0016, 2-t).[1]

In a later, similar test of 2,832 trials, targets were randomized and equalized. Fisk and West took turns as experimenter, each displaying the daily targets at his home during alternate weeks. Blundun's score on West's targets was nonsignificant, but on Fisk's it was significant (p = .013, 2-t). The difference, suggesting an experimenter effect, was weak (p = .05).

3.1.2 More evidence: placement PK tests

Placement tests (chapter 9, section 2.1.2; Rush 1977 p. 32; Stanford, 1977c, p. 326), which originated about 1950, led to highly significant scores in some cases. Cox (1974b) reported experiments with a device that allowed a large number of small steel balls to roll randomly into either of a pair of chutes. Scores were determined by counting the balls in target and nontarget chutes after each trial, or by recording a hit when the target chute of a pair intercepted more balls than the nontarget chute. This latter majority vote technique yielded highly significant scores for the pooled results of two confirmatory experiments ($p = .0006$). The same report summarized the results of two earlier similar experiments by Cox and a replication by Morris, all of which had yielded significant majority vote scores. A much more elaborate version of the parallel-chute device was reported by Roger Nelson, Brenda Dunne and Robert G. Jahn (1984) at Princeton University. In their apparatus, small plastic balls drop through an array of pins (a quincunx) into 19 chutes. If a large number of balls are dropped, the numbers in the successive chutes conform approximately to a normal (Gaussian) distribution. In a PK test, the subject tries to skew the distribution toward the right or left of the central chute. Highly significant results were reported (p approx. 10^{-4}).

Almost all of the placement tests that Cox reported had been witnessed. The persistent placement tests with cubes by Forwald present a more difficult problem of evaluation, since he conducted almost all of them alone (Forwald, 1969; Rush, 1971). He repeatedly (but not always) reported scores with extremely low probabilities: however, these resulted from modest scoring rates maintained through series of, typically, 10,000 to 40,000 trials. Forwald's experiments were well designed, except for being unwitnessed, and he was quick to note minor defects and correct them.

During a visit to the Duke laboratory in 1957, and after having participated in several exploratory placement series, Forwald scored significantly in a confirmatory series ($p = .0002$) with duplicate recording by a witness (Pratt and Forwald, 1958; McConnell and Forwald, 1967).

3.2 Statistical experiments with electronic random-event generators (REGs)

Helmut Schmidt, who developed the first practical REG, has reported several highly evidential PK experiments with it. In the first (Schmidt, 1970b), after preliminary tests had shown a tendency to negative scoring, he deliberately tried to discourage his 15 subjects during their sessions. The resulting negative deviation was significant ($p = .001$, 2-t). In a comparison of different rates of event generation (Schmidt, 1973) the overall score on 440,000 events was highly significant ($p = 10^{-9}$, 2-t). An experiment that compared simple versus complex REG machines (Schmidt, 1974) yielded a strong overall score (p approx. 10^{-7}, 1-t).

Many other experimenters have reported significant PK results with REG techniques as such machines have almost completely replaced mechanical devices. During this transitional period, in part because of the flexibility and other advantages of the REG, most such research has shifted from proof-oriented to process-oriented experimental designs. Consequently, many of the better experiments are cited in section 4. All of these, of course, have contributed to the cumulative evidence for PK to the extent that they have obtained significant scores, but they were designed for more subtle purposes. However, many attempted replications have failed.

3.3 Explorations of healing: PK experiments on chemical and biological objects

Parapsychologists generally have turned away from the investigation of unmanageable marvels in favor of less spectacular but more manageable effects that can be studied under laboratory conditions. Their approach to claims of psychic healing has followed this pattern. Cases of apparent healing are tantalizing and sometimes impressive, but they are even more difficult to establish scientifically than are most other macro-PK claims. Several investigators have taken a more fundamental, if less direct, approach to psychic healing by studying small, measurable effects of healers and others on chemical and biological processes.

PK effects have been reported on enzymes, bacteria, fungi and plants, and on both the behavior and physiological processes of animals (Rush, 1982, p. 99; Schmeidler, 1982, p. 120). The collective evidential value of this work is limited, however, because it consists largely of exploratory experiments that have not been sufficiently replicated to establish confidence. Some of these reports are discussed in section 4.

3.3.1 'Healing' experiments on animals and plants

A few investigators have conducted direct tests of healing effects in experimental animals. Psychologist Bernard Grad (1976) put mice on a diet that produced goiters (enlarged thyroid glands) and compared the rates of growth of the goiters in two control groups and in a group that a reputed healer, Oskar Estebany, 'treated' by holding their cages in his hands. One control group was put in heated cages during the treatment sessions to simulate the heating effect of the healer's hands on the experimental mice. Goiter growth rates in the two control groups did not differ significantly, but both were significantly greater than in the experimental group ($p = .001$).

Grad then conducted a more elaborate experiment on the rate of wound healing in mice (Grad, Cadoret and Paul, 1961). Three hundred mice were anesthetized and wounded by removing about 0.3 square inch (1.9 square centimeters) of skin from the back of each mouse. Three randomly selected groups of 100 mice then were assigned to control, to treatment by Estebany, and to similar handling by several medical students. The cage containing each treatment group of 10 mice was placed in a paper bag. In one mode, the healer put his hands inside the bag and around the cage. In the other mode, he held the bag, which was stapled shut, in his hands. Double-blind procedures were followed throughout the experiment.

The difference in healing rates between the control group and that handled by the students, determined by repeatedly measuring the areas of the wounds, never reached significance. But the difference between

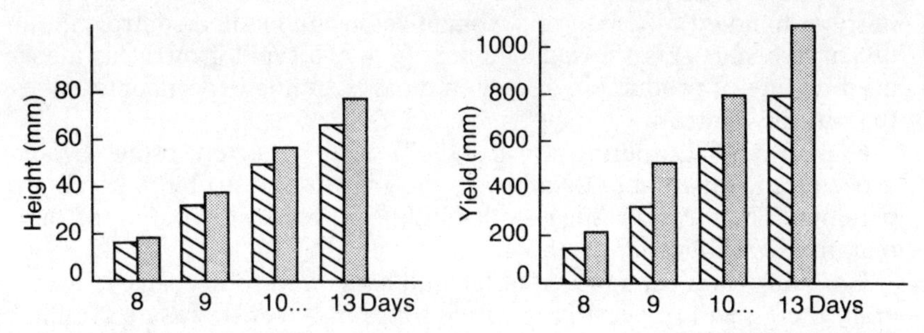

Figure 10.2: Healer's influence on growth of barley seedlings (Grad, 1965a, Experiment no. 4). Mean heights and yields of 'treated' plants (solid blocks) versus controls (hatched) at 8, 9, 10 and 13 days after planting. 'Yield' is the product of the mean number of viable plants per pot, and mean height

these groups and the group handled by the healer in the open bags became significant ($p = .01$) on the fifteenth day of recovery. Differences in the closed-bag mode were in the same direction but not significant. Grad noted that the mice in the closed bags became agitated, probably because they were too hot, and suggested that the healer may have been ineffective for this reason. But he also recognized that the closed bag may have been an effectual barrier to the healer's influence, whether chemical or paranormal.

G. K. and A. M. Watkins (1971; G. K. Watkins, A. M. Watkins and Wells, 1973) investigated the effects of healers and other subjects in hastening the recovery of mice from ether anesthesia (see also section 4.3.2). They repeatedly obtained significant results in the expected direction, as did Wells and Klein (1972); but lack of complete blinds leaves the interpretation uncertain.

In one of the stronger experimental series, Grad (1965a) tested Estebany's influence upon the growth of barley seedlings. In a fully blind procedure, the healer 'treated' (held in his hands) bottles of saline solution that later were used for the first watering of barley seeds. (The expected 'healing' effect was to be a reduction of the normally injurious effect of the salt on the seeds.) Three of four confirmatory series yielded significant results (p approx. .02–.05), based on number of seedlings, heights, and final weights, that indicated better germination and growth for the experimental seedlings than for control seedlings watered with saline that the healer had not handled (see Figure 10.2). Grad's results are impressive despite the generally modest level of significance because of good experimental design and consistently significant results in all but one test series.

3.3.2 PK experiments on microorganisms

Another group of experiments is impressive because it exhibits consistently significant results under similar, but not identical, procedures by three experimenters. All of these attempted to influence the growth rate of fungi. Grad (1965b), in a blind procedure similar to that described above, compared the effect on yeast growth of bottles of nutrient handled by a man or a woman versus unhandled controls. Four out of five such sets showed significantly more rapid growth, as measured by rate of production of carbon dioxide, in the experimental tubes than in the controls.

Carroll and Catherine Nash (1967) also reported using Grad's procedure in an attempt to influence the growth of yeast by 19 psychotic patients. Their results suggested inhibition of growth, but were only marginally significant.

Erlendur Haraldson (1973) of Iceland had seven subjects try to accelerate the growth of yeast in nutritive solution. Growth was determined by measuring the absorption of light passing through each culture tube. Comparison of each of 120 experimental tubes with its control tube yielded a marginally significant result (p = .02, 2-t). But the three subjects who were professional healers (two mental healers and a physician) produced most of the positive scoring (p = .00014, 2-t).

By contrast with these investigations, two experiments were intended to inhibit the growth of a disease-producing fungus, *Rhizoctonia solani*. A French physician, Jean Barry (1968), had ten subjects attempt such inhibition. In each trial the subject stood near five experimental and five control culture dishes, being told to try to influence only the former. After incubation of the dishes, the area of each fungus culture was measured under blind conditions. Differences between experimental cultures and controls were highly significant and in the expected direction. However, the method of measurement is not entirely clear.

William Tedder and Melissa Monty (1981) subjected the same parasitic fungus to attempts at growth inhibition by subjects one to 15 miles (1.6 to 24 kilometers) distant. Otherwise the design was similar to Barry's except for the use of two distinct groups of subjects: Tedder and six close acquaintances; and eight casual acquaintances or strangers. Experimental and control culture colonies were measured at the end of each trial period of about 72 hours. If the mean growth of a set of five experimental cultures was less than that of its five control cultures, the trial was scored as a hit. Scores of the second subject group were not significant; but the first group scored 16 hits and no misses (p = .00003, 2-t). Unfortunately, the method of measuring the culture colonies is not described, and some details of procedure are not clear.

A direct attempt to 'heal' chemically injured *Salmonella* bacteria was reported by Elizabeth Rauscher and Beverley Rubik (1980). They first had a reputed healer, Olga Worrall, 'treat' *Salmonella* cultures by holding the containers in her hands for several minutes. They then added enough phenol to the culture samples to stop all motility in a control sample in less than two minutes. They found about 5 percent of the bacteria in the healer-treated cultures still motile after 12 minutes. The effect of a growth inhibitor, chloramphenicol, on the bacteria also was moderated by the healer to a marginally significant degree. However, similar treatment of *Salmonella* in favorable culture medium without addition of injurious substances had no measurable effect on growth of the bacteria.

C. B. Nash (1984) had 52 unselected subjects try to influence the mutation rate of the common bacterium *E. coli.* This organism frequently mutates between a form that metabolizes lactose and one that cannot. Each subject tried to inhibit the lactose-positive mutation in three culture tubes and to promote it in three others; another three were controls. After incubation the proportions of the two mutant strains in each tube were determined. The difference between 'inhibited' and 'promoted' cultures was in the expected direction ($p = .005$); inhibition was more effective than promotion.

3.3.3 PK effects on an enzyme

All of the foregoing experiments afford some evidence for influence by certain persons on the physiological processes of living organisms, from mammals and green plants down to bacteria. However, only the most tentative efforts have been made to explore the physiological mechanisms through which the ostensible effects are mediated.

Enzymes – organic catalysts – are fundamental mediators and regulators of physiological processes. For this reason, M. Justa Smith (1972) undertook tests of the effect of a healer (Estebany) on the activity rate of the digestive enzyme trypsin. Her procedures compared in each trial the activities of four standardized lots of the enzyme: a control sample, a sample exposed to a strong magnetic field (which increased its activity); a sample irradiated by ultraviolet light (which reduced its activity) and then handled by Estebany: and a sample only handled by Estebany. The handling by the healer brought the activity of the irradiated sample back approximately to its normal rate, and that of the normal sample to a rate similar to that induced by the magnetic field.

However, Smith's attempts at replication a few months later were unsuccessful. A replication by Edge (1980) with another healer, Anne Gehman, conducted under essentially similar conditions, yielded marginally significant results only for normal trypsin handled by the healer.

3.4 Macro-PK experiments: directly observable effects

The highly varied experimental situations and procedures involved in recent macro-PK investigations have been developed in some detail in chapter 9, section 3.2, where the principal results are stated or implied. However, evidential evaluations of these highly individualistic investigations are difficult.

The evidential value of experimental findings generally depends upon several factors. A distinctly observable, unambiguous effect must be produced. It must be produced repeatedly under effective controls against observational error or fraud. It should be replicated by other experimenters and preferably by other subjects. It is questionable whether any macro-PK investigation entirely meets this standard, but a few approach it nearly enough to merit serious consideration of their findings.

One of the stronger cases is that of Kulagina. No adequate reports of investigations of her PK phenomena by Soviet scientists are available, but a succession of Western parapsychologists worked with her repeatedly (Keil *et al.*, 1976). Most of the effects they reported had been clearly observed. Controls were not so good as they could have been in a laboratory situation; but the investigators found little fault with them, particularly when they sometimes introduced new tests without warning. Some of the effects, particularly movements of objects, were observed repeatedly by various investigators.

The need for replication by another subject is met to some degree by Felicia Parise's demonstrations of movements of objects (Honorton, 1974a). Again, full laboratory controls were lacking, but several investigators observed repeated sliding movements of small objects under conditions that they considered reliable.

Another relatively strong case is Ted Serios's production of anomalous photographs. Eisenbud and several associates of various professional specialities investigated Serios's effects in many sessions during about three years. They obtained hundreds of anomalous exposures, many of which clearly were pictures of recognizable objects (see Plates 12a-c). Controls varied in quality among the various experimental situations. When Serios was far from the camera or inside a Faraday cage with the camera outside, or when he produced pictures corresponding to targets requested only at the session – or even concealed from him until the end of the session – it is difficult to identify any significant fault in the controls. Further evidence of paranormality appeared in the internal peculiarities of some of the pictures. Stevenson and Pratt (1968, 1969) reported similar, though less extensive, experiments with Serios, with similar results. Furthermore, his evidence for photographic PK is not unique (Eisenbud, 1977).

The most intriguing and vexing type of macro-PK that has been claimed in recent years is metal bending. It is an essentially novel claim rarely reported in the early literature. Since its introduction by Uri Geller about 1971, it has brought forth many claimants and endless controversy. What is has not brought forth is satisfactory evidence of its genuineness. Many credible observers and investigators now have reported witnessing demonstrations of the bending of keys, tableware and other objects (e.g. Panati, 1976). Cox's detailed account is one of the more impressive of these. Yet the evidence remains anecdotal. The sustained, well-controlled research that is essential to establish a phenomenon is lacking.

A variant of metal bending in which electronic strain gauges record microscopic distortions of a metal specimen appears to be more amenable to laboratory investigation than is the visible bending of gross specimens. Hasted (1981) and Julian Isaacs (1983) have developed apparatus that appears to be capable of distinguishing between paranormal distortion of the metal specimen and artifacts caused by electrical transients, vibrations, or other disturbances. However, it must be noted that this, like all other complex test devices, makes the site of PK influence ambiguous: the putative 'metal bending' may be an effect on the strain gauge or some other electronic component. Hasted took some steps to limit this uncertainty.

As to controls, Hasted did not describe his experimental procedures in as much detail as one would like, and he appears to have underestimated the possibilities for trickery by his young subjects. Statistical treatment of results is lacking, so that appraisal of their validity must rest largely upon one's confidence that artifactual signals had been eliminated. Yet Hasted did get positive effects with several subjects; and Isaacs and other investigators have essentially replicated his experiments.

3.5 Criticisms of the PK research

3.5.1 Dice and other mechanical techniques

The experiments with dice at the Duke University laboratory were first reported (L. E. Rhine and J. B. Rhine, 1943) soon after the climax of the ESP controversy (chapter 2, section 4.3) and in the midst of World War II. Probably for this reason, they did not provoke the storm of criticism that the ESP reports had encountered. Nevertheless, several critical readers soon called attention to deficiencies in the Duke experiments. In Britain attempts to replicate Rhine's results had almost uniformly failed, so that criticism from that quarter was particularly sharp (e.g. Mundle, 1950; Nicol, 1954; West, 1945).

However, it is not necessary to examine these criticisms in detail, because all of them and more were included in Girden's (1962a) comprehensive survey and critique of the statistical PK research. Girden considered both the early and later dice experiments and tests conducted by tossing objects other than dice, including placement experiments. His report is detailed and cogent, but it is seriously flawed in some respects. It should be read together with the rebuttal by Gardner Murphy (1962b), Girden's (1962b) rejoinder, a response by Pratt (1963), and comments by several other authors. All of these except Pratt are consolidated in a single review article (Girden *et al.*, 1964).

The principal faults that Girden cited were: inadequate compensation for dice bias; loose, unstandardized procedures; openness to recording errors; and lack of empirical control tests. That some of the early dice experiments were not rigorous is generally conceded; but, as Murphy noted, Girden magnified the faults by ignoring the experiments in which they had been avoided. His demand for empirical control series (i.e. dice trials under the same procedure as the experimental trials except that no one is 'wishing' for a particular face) is contrary to the generally accepted principle that the proper reference for evaluating a statistical anomaly is the theoretical mean chance expectation (MCE). Further, as his critics pointed out, comparison of the scores on a particular die face when it is the PK target and when it is not amounts to a valid empirical test.

The greatest evidence for PK in the early dice tests lies in the persistent decline effect. Girden attributed this finding largely if not wholly to dice bias. Subjects usually preferred the six-face as target. If targets were rotated casually, allowing the subject to begin with the six-face and progress to lower targets, the usual bias favoring the higher faces would produce a systematic decline in hits. However, this fault had been recognized and at least partially avoided by requiring 'that the same target face be used throughout the page or that it be so varied that the hit distribution could not be attributed to the favoring of any particular face' (J. B. Rhine and Humphrey, 1944a, p. 22). Records that did not meet this requirement were excluded from the decline analyses. Further, the decline appeared consistently even in long series run on a single target face. In an independent study (McConnell *et al.,* 1955) highly significant declines appeared in the scores on each target face separately.

Girden also criticized the decline findings as 'a new hypothesis subject to subsequent test.' But he did not recognize that the hypothesis was suggested by the first large series that was analysed and was confirmed by analyses of other series independently. The time order in which they had been done is irrelevant.

Much of Girden's criticism is valid, both in general and with respect to particular experiments. Most of the significant faults he noted had been recognized and corrected by the time his report appeared. One important requirement, however – provision for independent, blind recording of experimental data – continued to be neglected, though it could have been met with little additional effort by Fisk's device of concealed targets. But Girden's negative bias shows throughout his report. To appreciate the issues and the complexity of the arguments, one must read both it and the rebuttals by parapsychologists cited above.

3.5.2 The REG experiments

Responsible criticisms of psi experiments using random event generators have been remarkably sparse. These machines eliminate target bias, recording errors, and opportunities for fraud by a subject. They readily provide control runs; in fact, these are routinely produced for randomicity checks. In some experiments the REG is coupled to a computer that runs the experiment and processes the data. If the experimental procedure is properly designed, it leaves little to criticize.

The criticisms of REG ESP research (chapter 7, section 2.5) apply in principle to REG PK experiments as well. However, Hansel's (1980) two criticisms, of unreliable recording and optional stopping, relate only to certain experiments; they are not generally applicable. Hansel also asserted that there had been no significant replications of Schmidt's early results with REGs. This remarkable comment is refuted by the experiments mentioned here and in chapter 7, section 2.5, as well as others. Hyman's (1981) criticism of Schmidt's tests of randomicity is more serious. High significance usually was achieved by an extrachance scoring rate of the order of one percent of MCE that was sustained over very many trials. Consequently, a slight bias in the REG output would favor one or the other binary choice and thus reach significance in a sufficient number of trials. Schmidt's 1970 experiment appears to have been open to this possibility; but extensive tests of randomicity during control runs of the REG revealed no significant bias. Binary targets were balanced in the 1973 experiment, thus cancelling any systematic bias.

Hyman noted also that the REG output could be unbiased over the experimental run length and yet contain internal nonrandom patterns. These are irrelevant in PK trials for a fixed target, since the subject has no opportunity, as in an ESP test, to adapt individual trials to the pattern. Schmidt's 1974 report of a deviation of 4.5 percent is further evidence that his results were independent of statistical artifacts.

3.5.3 Criticisms of the biological experiments

G. F. Solfvin (1982a), in examining the difficulties of investigating paranormal healing, developed a detailed critical analysis of several experiments on plants and animals. His criticisms concern principally peculiarities in the data distributions that imply uncontrolled artifacts and improper treatment of data because of possible effects of incomplete blinds.

A simple example of the first type of problem is that the effect of injurious saline solution on barley seeds in Grad's plant experiments (section 3.3.1) varied with the weight of a seed. Another is the use of three handlers in the wound-healing experiments, who by slight differences in techniques may have produced systematic differences in healing rates among their groups. Such effects as these would be impartial as to experimental and control plants or animals, but they could interfere with analyses that depend on variance.

The second type of artifact could have occurred in the wound-healing experiments because the mice were 'treated' and handled in groups of ten. The handlers were of course blind as to which were experimental or control groups. But a handler who noticed apparently faster healing in one group than another might inadvertently, by subtly different handling, accelerate that group's healing relative to the other, so that a tentative and possibly insignificant difference would become decisive (Rosenthal, 1969). Solfvin notes that in such a case the appropriate unit for statistical treatment is not the individual animal or plant pot, but the group. The effect is to reduce or nullify the statistical significance of the result.

This criticism does not apply to Grad's later experiments with seedlings (section 3.3.1) because the person who tended and measured the plants did not know the group assignments of the individual pots. But it obviously applies to the wound-healing experiments. It applies also to the resuscitations of anesthetized mice (section 3.3.1), because the 'healing' effort was directed to the series of animals placed in one fixed location on the experimental table throughout a half-session; the other location was the control. Again, experimenter bias could have subtly favored one location or the other.

Solfvin also recognized the possibility of inadvertent paranormal influence (experimenter effect) by someone other than the ostensible healer (see also section 4.2.3). While not compromising the result as proof of psi, this alternative compounds the difficulties of investigating healers.

3.5.4 Criticisms of macro-PK claims

Controversy over Eisenbud's reports of Serios's thoughtography (e.g. Eisenbud, 1967; Eisendrath, 1967; Reynolds, 1967) focused inevitably upon the short fiber or paper cylinder that Serios liked to hold in front of the camera lens. Apart from possibly concealing something in the cylinder, it is very difficult to imagine any way in which Serios could have impressed any anomalous pictures on the film by normal means. The critics have responded by alleging that Serios used sleight-of-hand techniques to conceal inside the paper cylinder a device that projected a bit of a microfilmed picture into the camera. They ignore the many pictures that this assumption cannot account for.

Optically, the use of such a miniature projector is practicable in some circumstances, but concealing it from the scrutiny of several observers during hundreds of repetitious operations might be difficult. None of the magicians who have proposed this explanation has been willing to demonstrate it. However, it cannot account for pictures obtained at a distance from Serios, or in accordance with a request – sometimes concealed during the session – by an experimenter, or for 'exposure' of film behind a barrier placed over the lens or immediately in front of the film plane in the camera.

Macro-PK effects always threaten the scientific objectivity of both advocates and critics. When the practitioner is also a professional entertainer, the action inevitably spreads from scientific laboratories and journals into the public arena. It is therefore not surprising that most of the recent controversy over PK has focused on Uri Geller, or that it has been conducted largely in popular magazines and the news media. Neither is it surprising that the professional standards that ordinarily govern scientific controversy sometimes have been compromised or abandoned.

Because most recent demonstrations of metal bending have involved spectacular effects produced in circumstances of limited controls, their resemblance to stage magic is inescapable. They consequently have attracted the attention of professional magicians, who urge that any investigation of such claims should include a magician. Such assistance undoubtedly can be useful, but it is not infallible – magicians sometimes are fooled by other magicians. Only well-controlled experiments conducted repeatedly under varied conditions can begin to determine whether a claimed phenomenon merits confidence. In their absence, the timeworn battle of wits will continue.

An introduction to the character of much recent controversy may be found in an exchange relating to the most prominent group of critics

(Kurtz, 1978; T. Rockwell *et al.*, 1978a, 1978b). A more extensive examination of this and other controversies concerning parapsychology appears in chapter 12, section 5.

4 Process-oriented PK research

The rationale of process-oriented psi research and the justifications for pursuing it have been presented in the Introduction to chapter 8. Process-oriented PK research is conceptually similar to that in ESP, and the principal findings resulting from it tend toward similar implications. Comparison of these ESP and PK findings gives one a strong impression of the essential unity of these phenomena.

4.1 The mediation of PK influence

How PK is mediated, through what means or agency a subjective intention is expressed in a physical effect, remains an enigma. However, it is plausible that the process should be influenced by material barriers, distance, or time displacements as are such physical agencies as sound, light, or force fields. Few explicit tests of such dependence have been conducted, but some experiments have incidentally involved physical variables.

4.1.1 Shields: massive barriers and electromagnetic screens

Eisenbud (1977) obtained paranormal photographs when his subject, Serios, was inside an electrically and magnetically shielded room and the camera outside. Similarly, pictures were produced with lead-glass X-ray shielding between subject and camera.

In some other PK experiments subjects and PK objects have been in separate rooms, so that partition walls served incidentally as mass shields. However, such arrangements also involve distance as a variable. Puthoff and Targ (1975) obtained significant disturbances of a sensitive magnetometer while the subject was four meters distant in an adjoining room. In another experiment the subject tried to reduce the motion of a sealed torsion pendulum from a distance of about one meter and then from 12 meters, three rooms away (see chapter 9, section 3.2.1). Results were significant in both cases, but weaker in the second.

4.1.2 Distance as a variable

Apparently only three explicit quantitative investigations of the effect of distance on PK performance have yielded significant results. C. B. Nash (1946) compared scores with each subject alternately at 3 or 30 feet (0.9 or 9 meters) from the dice-tossing machine. Though the overall scores of nine subjects were highly significant, no significant dependence upon distance appeared. However, the experiment was flawed by the possibility that the experimenter, who always stood by the dice machine, could have been the effective PK agent.

A second, better designed experiment (Nash and Richards, 1947) with 48 individual subjects yielded only borderline significance overall, significant scoring at 30 feet, and no significant dependence on distance. Nash noted that some internal peculiarities in the data suggested again that the experimenter was the effective agent, though at the same location as the subject.

By far the most sophisticated test for dependence of PK performance on distance between subject and object was reported by Mark L. Dickstein and James W. Davis (1979). Taking full advantage of electronic techniques, they arranged for a computer to select randomly one of two REG machines for each trial. This selection meant that the output of the REG that was selected to generate the object event for a given trial would give the subject a feedback (success or failure) signal immediately after each trial. The other REG, though operating, would give no feedback. One REG was near the experimental room; the other was 7 miles (11 kilometers) distant. Thus a series of trial feedback signals came randomly from the near or the distant REG events, and neither the subject nor anyone else knew which was operative in a particular trial. A pilot series with 15 subjects revealed no significant dependence upon distance, though the difference between hits on the selected and the unselected REGs was marginally significant ($p = .02$). Results of a confirmatory experiment with 37 subjects were not significant.

In almost all PK experiments the subjects have been no more than a few feet from the dice or REGs. A few imply PK influence over substantial distances, though they did not test for dependence on distance. McConnell (1955) scored successfully on dice at about a mile (1.6 kilometers). Subjects in Tedder and Monty's (1981) tests of inhibition of growth of a fungus worked from distances of one to 15 miles from the fungus cultures. Eisenbud (1977) obtained pictures while his subject was at distances up to 62 feet (19 meters) from the camera. In other tests (Eisenbud, 1972) he obtained 'blackies' (i.e. apparently unexposed prints under conditions that should have produced normal photographs) while Serios was several miles from the camera.

Robert N. Miller and Philip B. Reinhart (1975) found that healer Olga Worrall could induce fog in their laboratory cloud chamber by placing her hands near it. (The device is used to detect ionizing particles, which leave tracks of fog droplets.) At a prearranged time two months later, while Worrall was at her home about 600 miles (970 kilometers) distant, the experimenters twice observed an anomalous cloud formation in the chamber a few minutes after Worrall began trying to influence it. This is the greatest distance over which a PK effect has been indicated. However, control observations of the normal behavior of the chamber were not reported, and the experiment was published only in a popular magazine and has not been repeated.

Collectively, these experiments on the effects of distance and barriers upon PK influence point to the same conclusion as do comparable ESP experiments (Palmer, 1978b, p. 73): i.e. that no consistent evidence of dependence of psi upon physical parameters has been discovered.

4.1.3 Across the time barrier (maybe)

Precognition is anomalous because it implies the transfer of information backward in time, from a future event to a present percipient (see chapter 7, section 2.5; Palmer, 1978b, p. 77). The PK analog of precognition is not the production of a future PK effect by present effort. Causes normally precede effects. To be analogous to precognition, a PK time anomaly must involve a reversal of cause-and-effect relations, i.e. a present influence on a past event.

Schmidt (1976) attempted in three experiments to demonstrate such a retroactive PK effect. In the first, 20 subjects in a pilot and 30 in a confirmatory series were not told they were doing a PK test. Instead, each was told to try to hear all of a series of faint clicks in headphones produced by an REG. Schmidt expected that the subjects' intent anticipation of the clicks would motivate them to increase the click frequency by PK influence on the REG. Such an influence was observed (p = .001, 1-t) in each experiment. A third series, with 30 subjects, was then conducted in the same way except that each subject listened to clicks from a magnetic tape on which the REG output had been recorded earlier. Scores in this series also were significant at the same level as the first two. Prerecorded tapes that had not been used in the tests, but held as controls, showed no significant increase in click frequency.

The 20 subjects for the second experiment tried consciously to develop extrachance scores on an REG, but they were not told that the trials were being alternated between the immediate REG output and earlier output that had been recorded, stored in computer memory, and punched in paper tape just before the test. Further, each recorded event was presented four times to the subject. Schmidt's theoretical model predicted that such repeated exposures should enhance the PK effect (see chapter 11, section 3.2.2).

An earlier experiment (Schmidt, 1973) had yielded reduced scores at a high REG output rate of 300 events per second, but Schmidt's model predicted that the generation rate for the prerecorded events would not matter. He therefore generated the stored record at 300 events per second, but presented all events in the test at only 10 per second.

The total score on the directly generated REG events was only marginally significant (p = .05, 1-t), but that on the prerecorded events was much higher (p = .0005, 1-t). Scoring rates on these binary events were 50.82 and 52.95 percent, respectively (each prerecorded event had been presented four times).

The third experiment in Schmidt's report is particularly interesting, because it ostensibly was a simple comparison of PK influence on two dissimilar REGs that offered hit probabilities of 1/8 and 7/8, respectively. However, one or the other REG was activated for each trial, in a random order dictated by a random binary REG sequence that had been stored in computer memory earlier. The subject could not know which REG was activated for any individual trial. The prestored sequence was used four times during the experimental run. Thus the design was similar to that of other experiments in which a test sequence is controlled by a stored computer program. In this case, however,

Schmidt expected that subjects' preference for the 'easier' REG with the higher hit possibility might result in retro-PK biasing of the prestored sequence to favor the easy REG. The scores confirmed this expectation, though not strongly (p = .01 in the pilot runs, .05 in the confirmatory tests).

A later retro-PK experiment (Schmidt, 1979) was highly successful (p = .0001), with scoring rates for current and prerecorded events nearly equal. Terry and Schmidt (1978) in another such experiment obtained significant scores (p = .005, 2-t) in the negative direction.

Several other experimenters have attempted to replicate Schmidt's retro-PK experiments, with mixed results. Houtkooper (1977) was successful. An elaborate set of five series (Davis and Morrison, 1978; Morrison and Davis, 1979), each of which involved currently generated events, prerecorded events presented once in the tests, and prerecorded events presented four times ran the gamut of positive, null, and negative results. The most notable observation was completely null results on the events that had been presented to subjects four times. Null retro-PK results were reported by Schouten (1977), Broughton, Millar, Beloff and Wilson (1978), and William Braud (1979).

In all of the reported experiments on retro-PK, the prerecorded sequences appear to have been used experimentally before anyone had examined them. From the standpoint of quantum theory, it is of interest to know whether such examination prior to the experiment would affect the retro-PK scoring; but no attempt to explore this question has been successful.

This body of experimental findings offers little evidence of dependence of PK influences upon physical variables, but it includes substantial positive evidence to the contrary. However, this indication must be considered highly tentative. In most experiments the subjects knew the essential conditions (distances, presence of shields), so that any apparent effects of physical conditions can as well be attributed to psychological influences. The only good double-blind distance experiment (Dickstein and Davis, 1979) yielded only marginally significant scores.

Some of the experimental findings can be plausibly attributed to experimenter effects. In others the locus of PK influence was ambiguous, e.g. in Puthoff and Targ's (1975) magnetometer and pendulum experiments, the agent was separated from the ostensible PK object but adjacent to the apparatus that recorded the effect.

Schmidt's and similar retro-PK experiments were double-blind, insofar as ESP does not vitiate the concept of a blind experiment. The only alternatives to retroactive influence (backward causation) appear to be PK influence by the experimenter or by the future subject while the tape was being recorded, requiring in either case the assumption of additional ESP/PK involvement. These ambiguities, plus the inconsistent results of attempts at replication, leave the question of time dependence of PK unresolved.

4.2 Object variables

Many different objects have been tried in PK experiments: dice, unmarked cubes, disks, balls, bubbles, pivoted needles, photographic film, plants and animals. Few well-designed experiments have been done, however, to investigate possible dependence of PK success upon physical or psychological properties of the objects. Some experiments will be mentioned despite flaws in design or procedure in order to indicate the trends in such work.

4.2.1 Mechanical objects

4.2.1a *Size and finish*

Two early experiments at the Duke laboratory (Hilton, Baer and J. B. Rhine, 1943; Hilton and J. B. Rhine, 1943) introduced among other variables three sizes of dice. Lack of blinds and inconsistent results suggest that psychological factors were responsible for the observed differences in scoring. George Cormack (Pratt, 1951) compared his scores on plastic dice of three different sizes thrown simultaneously. Scores were significant only for the largest dice.

Forwald (1955) compared his scores on smooth, rough, and very rough bakelite plastic cubes in placement tests (see chapter 9, section 2.1.2). He reported highly significant differences in scores on the smooth and the very rough cubes, but these unwitnessed tests were, like Cormack's, without blinds and therefore ambiguous as to physical versus psychological influences.

4.2.1b *Composition and density*

Forwald (1969; Rush, 1971) found no consistent differences in his placement scores for cubes of several different materials. However, when he experimented with cubes of wood covered with metal foils of various thicknesses, he found in his highly significant results two remarkably regular relations. First, the average PK energy apparently applied to the cubes (calculated from their lateral deviations from their original direction) increased with the thickness of the foil. This dependence fitted approximately an exponential relation of the form: $E = E_m (1 - e^{az})$, where E is the PK energy, E_m is a maximum PK energy corresponding to a foil thickness of about 0.7 millimeter, z is the foil thickness, and a is an empirical constant that was found to be the same for all of the metals tested. In further experiments Forwald found that the observed PK energy for a fixed foil thickness of various metals was approximately proportional to their atomic weights.

Because of the lack of blinds and the controversial nature of his determinations of PK energy, Forwald's results are of suggestive value only. He was an engineer who obviously anticipated and welcomed such orderly physical relations as he found in his data, so that these relations may only reflect his own psychological management of his PK ability. Apparently no one has attempted to replicate his experiments. His findings are noted here in some detail despite their weaknesses only because they constitute the sole experimental evidence for any detailed dependence of psi phenomena upon physical parameters.

Cox (1954) compared placement scoring on dice and marbles, 24 of each being released in each trial. In one series subjects were instructed to try to influence all of the objects indiscriminately; in a second, to influence the dice during the first half of the session and the marbles during the second; in a third, to choose which object they would try to influence. The outstanding result was consistently negative scoring on dice and positive scoring on marbles in all three series, the difference being significant ($p = .003$).

Apparently the only double-blind experiment on PK objects of different materials was reported by Cox (1971). He used an ingenious apparatus to compare scores of unselected subjects on lead and celluloid dice of the same size and color. Cox prepared the apparatus by placing each die in one of six channels of a tilting table, with glass and lead balls before and behind each die to prevent any visible differences in the tumbling of the heavy and light dice. Assistants conducted the tests. Neither they nor the subjects were told the real purpose of the experiment. In both pilot and confirmatory series, scores were positive on the celluloid and similarly negative on the lead dice, the differences being marginally significant ($p = .05$ and .027, respectively).

Because of the great difference between the densities of the lead and celluloid dice, subjects or experimenters may have detected some difference in their behavior despite the precautions Cox had taken to disguise them. The consistent scoring in opposite directions on the two materials, in agreement with the tendency in his earlier experiment comparing dice and marbles, suggests a psychological rather than physical influence; but its cause is obscure. Cox proposed, as some other experiments had indicated, that such differential scoring in a dual-aspect task may be a general tendency (see chapter 6, section 6.3).

4.2.2 Electronic and nuclear objects

Most recent micro-PK experimentation has been done on targets generated by random-event generators (REGs). In such an experiment the ostensible PK object is a naturally random fluctuation in the movement of electrons (random noise source) or the randomly occurring disintegration of an unstable atomic nucleus (radioactive source). Dice are tangible and familiar. These electronic or nuclear events are intangible, invisible, and unfamiliar to most experimental subjects.

Actually, a PK hit in such an experiment reduces to the registration of a desired (target) impulse on a counter or in the input to a computer. Several sensitive electronic processes mediate between the ostensible PK object and the trial record, and any or all of these are plausible loci for PK intervention. This ambiguity should be kept in mind in assessing the implications of PK results obtained on REG events.

Since the subject in such an experiment sees, not the crucial random event, but an arbitrary feedback display, an analytical approach suggests that the subject's task should be very difficult. However, some evidence indicates that psi is goal-oriented, i.e. that success depends upon clarity of intention rather than ease of manipulation of the PK object. Schmidt (1974) investigated this question in a test that involved two REGs, one of which employed a more complex decision-making process than the other. A prerecorded series of random binary choices automatically determined for each trial which REG would provide the object event for that trial. Thus, neither experimenter nor subject knew which REG was active in any trial. Overall scores were highly significant. Scoring rates in both pilot and confirmatory series were consistently higher on the simpler REG, but the difference was not significant.

In a related experiment, however, Schmidt (1973) obtained significantly higher PK scores on REG-generated binary events presented to the subjects at 30 per second than at 300 per second.

The conceptual ambiguity of PK and precognition has been mentioned, i.e. a coincidence between a present prediction and a rationally unpredictable future event can be attributed either to a backward transfer of information or to psychokinetic manipulation of the event to agree with the prediction. Schmidt and Lee Pantas (1972) reported an experiment that is at least obliquely relevant to this dilemma. In one mode, the REG was arranged for ostensibly precognitive trials (with PK as an unavoidable alternative interpretation). In its other mode, success ostensibly required PK influence on the REG. The experimenter switched the REG from one mode to the other between sessions. Again, highly significant scores were obtained, with no significant difference between the precognitive and PK modes.

4.2.3 Biological objects

Almost all PK experiments on biological objects have attempted only to demonstrate the occurrence of paranormal effects. At least one disclosed some process aspects, though not by design.

In his well-designed tests of the influence of a healer on the growth of seedlings (section 3.3.1), Grad discovered that the healer had little effect on seedlings that grew under normal, healthful conditions, but was influential in 'healing' seedlings that were handicapped by injurious conditions. He found also that it was sufficient for the healer to handle the bottle of injurious saline solution that was used later on the seeds, without seeing or touching the seeds at all. These findings suggested to Grad that the healer, accustomed to dealing with injury or disease rather than enhancing normal health, needed injured or handicapped specimens to demonstrate his influence. However, a more general principle may be involved, i.e. that organisms living under restrictive, marginal conditions will be more responsive to any improvement in those conditions than if they were living under optimal conditions.

Were the seedlings or the bottles of saline solution the recipients of the healer's influence? Grad found a consistent difference between the infrared (IR) absorption spectrum of the saline solution that had been 'treated' by the healer and that of untreated saline, but the effect appeared outside the reliable range of his spectrophotometer.

Further investigations by Douglas Dean (1983) appeared to confirm

Grad's tentative finding. Dean compared samples of distilled water from bottles held by healer Olga Worrall with control samples. Assisted in double-blind measurements by a specialist in chemical spectroscopy, he found in the healer's samples an absorption anomaly at a wavelength of about 3 micrometers, as Grad had reported. At King's College in London, Dean repeated the experiment with variations. Samples of distilled water held by another healer, Rose Gladden, for 2 to 30 minutes showed increases of 100 to 300 percent in the IR ratio (an index of absorption). Samples held by another person were not significantly affected.

This experimental evidence suggests that the healer's influence altered favorably the chemical properties of the saline solution in Grad's experiments and that the seedlings responded normally to the change. Obviously so potentially significant a finding needs further replication and investigation. Limited as Dean's experiments were, they nevertheless were done in part by two experimenters, they involved consistent effects by two subjects, the procedure was inherently simple and susceptible to excellent controls, and the effect was objectively measurable on a standard laboratory instrument. For these reasons, this exploratory work – including Grad's earlier observations – ranks as one of the more significant PK investigations.

In a healing situation, how much of the effect is due to the healer, and how much to the expectancy of the patient and other involved persons? G. F. Solfvin (1982b) explored this question in an experiment on mice inoculated with malaria, his purpose being to test the effects of expectancy in the subjects who handled the animals. These subjects, five veterinary students, were told that a distant healer would try to heal half of the mice in each subject's group after they had been inoculated with malarial culture; but actually no healer was involved. The subject-handlers did not know which mice Solfvin had designated for healing. Nevertheless, the results after seven days showed fewer damaged red blood cells in the 'healed' mice than in their cagemates. Each subject's animals showed a difference in this direction, the collective result being marginally significant ($p = .05$). This result suggests that a successful paranormal healing may be a joint venture of healer, patient, and concerned observers; and that healings attributed to shrines, relics, or other agencies may in fact be 'do-it-yourself projects.'

4.2.4 Labile versus inert PK objects

Almost all PK experiments have employed labile objects: tumbling dice or cubes, random electronic impulses, or the delicately balanced internal processes of plants or animals. Few investigators have asked ordinary subjects to influence inert objects – to affect photographic film, move stationary objects, or bend metal bars – and even fewer have reported success. Almost anyone would intuitively expect to influence rolling dice more readily than dice at rest. The question is whether the greater success in PK experiments with labile, easily affected objects is due to psychological or to physical causes. Does the subject score better on a labile object because it is inherently easier to influence, or because the subject believes it is easier?

William Braud (1980) has drawn on Stanford's concept of conformance behavior and Mattuck's ideas of noise reorganization (chapter 11, section 3.2.2) to develop a rationale of psi facilitation. In brief, he proposes that the susceptibility of a system to psi influence is proportional to its lability and inversely proportional to the constraints imposed upon it. He and his associates have developed an ongoing experimental program based upon this hypothesis that is remarkable for the strength and consistency of the effects.

An experiment designed to compare PK influence on labile and inert systems (a flickering candle flame and a stable electric lamp) yielded highly significant results on the flame alone, but in the comparison tests only marginal significance on the flame and no significant difference between effects on flame and lamp.

However, a series of 14 experiments on living material or organisms – movements of gerbils and electric fish, hemolysis of blood cells, and human electrodermal activity – resulted in significant effects in 11 cases (see also section 4.4). Braud attributes these successes to the extreme lability of living systems and sees in these findings significant implications for investigations of paranormal healing.

Stanford, Honorton and others have applied similar concepts to the design of ESP investigations, particularly in the ganzfeld experiments (see chapter 8, section 2.2). These also have succeeded with better than average consistency.

4.3 Psychological variables

4.3.1 Subject variables: attitudes and personality

The most obvious finding in psi research, after extra-chance scores, is that people differ widely in their psi capabilities (e.g. Dale, 1946; Fahler, 1959). The relations of scoring to measurable attitudes and personality traits have been explored extensively in ESP research, with some positive findings being reported (see chapter 8, section 3 and 4; Palmer, 1977). However, only a few experiments have been designed to clarify relations between PK performance and definable personal characteristics.

One of the most consistent correlations in ESP tests relates positive or negative scoring to subjects' attitudes of belief ('sheep') or skepticism ('goats') as to the possibility of experimental ESP. Palmer (1978b, pp. 153 ff.) noted that about one-third of the experiments that were comparable with Schmeidler's original design produced significant sheep-goat differences in scoring; however, all of these were in the expected direction.

Of the few tests of this relation in PK experiments (e.g. Dale, 1946; C. B. Nash, 1946; Van de Castle, 1958), the only one that produced significant results was reported by Lawrence Rubin and Honorton (1972). They evaluated the attitudes of 40 subjects and tested them with the ancient Chinese device for divination, the *I Ching*. The crucial step is the ritual tossing of sticks (or, in this case, coins) so that meaningful results imply PK intervention in the toss. The difference between the sheep's positive scores and the goats' negative scores was marginally significant ($p = .05$). However, this exploratory experiment has not been repeated.

Van de Castle (1958) subjected 31 subjects in dice PK tests to several types of personality evaluations. The strongest resulting correlation ($p = .05$) was between scoring level and a compressive-versus-expansive personality scale derived from subjects' freehand drawing styles. The expansive personalities scored more positively. Two different indices also related spontaneity consistently to PK success. The expansive-compressive correlation agrees with predominant findings in clairvoyance tests; but in GESP tests compressives have tended to score more positively than expansive subjects (Palmer, 1978b, p. 165 ff.).

Mischo and R. Weiss (1973) at Freiburg did a similar experiment with 50 subjects on an REG, but with an added element of frustration. PK control series run under normal test conditions before and after the experimental trials showed no significant correlations with the personality variables. However, the experimental PK tests, performed immediately after an exercise designed to induce frustration, correlated significantly with calmness and sociability (positive scoring) and with inhibition and depressive and neurotic tendencies (negative scoring).

4.3.2 Psychological states: can psi performance be facilitated?

Much evidence suggests that psi experiences are conditioned by mental states. Most spontaneous experiences occur in dreams or unfocused waking states, and several experimenters have tried to identify specific mental states that enhance or degrade PK performance. Their findings generally accord well with similar investigations of conditions affecting ESP (see chapter 8). Besides their obvious fundamental significance, such investigations hold out the promise of stronger and more consistent – and thus more convincing – experimental scores, which would afford a firmer basis for further process research.

4.3.2a Tension and relaxation: release-of-effort and linger effects

It is recognized that creative ideas or insights often emerge in consciousness during relaxation or distraction *after* intense concentration on a problem. Many incidental observations suggest that success in ESP or PK tasks follows a similar pattern, but few controlled experiments have been designed to investigate this possibility.

During tests of the ability of a reputed healer to hasten the waking of mice from ether anesthesia (Wells and G. K. Watkins, 1975) a lag or linger effect became apparent. For each trial, two anesthetized mice were placed on a table. The one on the right or the left was randomly designated for the subject's attention; the other served as control. Results were not significant. However, they became significant when the object mice were placed in the same location throughout the first half of a run (8 to 12 trials), then in the alternate location during the second half-run after a 30–minute break.

To test the linger hypothesis, the subject in a new series of tests left the building after the first half of each run, while the two experimenters (or two others blind to the first-half data) proceeded immediately with the second half-run. Scores were significant for each condition. Remarkably, they were stronger for the second half-runs, during which the subject was absent, than for the first halves.

Graham and Anita Watkins (1974) noted a strong linger effect in an experiment with Parise as subject. A compass needle was deflected 15 degrees and became unresponsive to steel or another magnet brought near it. The compass resumed normal functioning when it was removed from its original location, but 'froze' again at 15 degrees deflection when returned to it, thus suggesting a localized influence. The anomalous behavior persisted for about 30 minutes after Parise had stopped trying to influence the compass.

A few experiments suggest a tendency for PK effects to occur only after conscious intention or effort has ceased. Sometimes called the release-of-effort effect, this finding supports similar observations in mediumistic studies.

Stanford and Charles Fox (1975) studied PK effects on the electrical resistance of a light-sensitive device enclosed in a lightproof box. Each of 12 unselected subjects performed 30 10–second trials to influence the resistance reading, with 70-second intervals of relaxation of effort between trials. The changes in resistance from the normal (control) value were significantly greater during the rest periods than during active trials.

Palmer and Wim Kramer (1984) ran REG PK tests on a large number of unselected subjects. Each trial interval of 2.5 minutes was followed by a 2.5-minute rest period in which the REG output continued without the subject's knowing it. The results indicated that significant scoring had occurred only during the rest periods.

There is evidence that a tense, striving attitude may exert an inhibiting influence on PK effects measured during the test itself. Jeffrey Debes and Robert Morris (1982) found that college students randomly assigned to take an REG PK test with an 'active, competitive, striving' strategy scored significantly below chance (p = .02) while other subjects who were asked to adopt a 'relaxed, noncompetitive, nonstriving' strategy scored significantly above chance (p = .001). 'Focusing of willpower' also produced significant psi-missing in an earlier dice experiment by Steilberg (1975). These findings reinforce the traditional view that an attitude of 'passive volition' is most conducive to success in PK.

On the other hand, Honorton and Barksdale (1972) found that muscular tension led to significant positive scoring in an REG test when subjects were tested in a group but not when tested individually.

4.3.2b Altered states of consciousness: hypnosis and meditation

There are both theoretical and pragmatic reasons for expecting psi performance to be facilitated by suitable alteration of the subject's state of consciousness (chapter 8, section 2.2). A few PK experiments have attempted to explore this possibility.

Hypnosis is a familiar method for manipulating a subject's state of consciousness, but it has been almost entirely absent from PK research. A single report (J. B. Rhine, 1946a) noted significant but inconsistent effects among the scores of five subjects tested in dice trials before, during, and after hypnotic sessions. Among other conjectures, one may suspect that the wrong suggestions were given. Suggestions for quiet, passive awareness of the target might have been more favorable to PK success than were admonitions to try hard, to have great confidence, and to keep attention on the task. However, no one appears to have done anything further with hypnosis in PK work.

Meditation is another method for achieving quiet, detached awareness. Recently it has received some attention in PK research, but the results, though promising, are only suggestive. Francine Matas and Lee Pantas (1971) compared REG PK scores of 25 meditators with those of 25 nonmeditators. The difference between the group scores was highly significant ($p = .003$). However, the tests were not blind, and the substantial negative score of the nonmeditators suggests experimenter influence.

Honorton and Edwin May (1976; Stanford, 1977c, p. 343) had ten subjects, six of whom were meditators, try sometimes for high and sometimes for low scores in an REG PK task. Four of the six meditators achieved individually significant differences between high-aim and low-aim scores; only one of the four nonmeditators did so.

Schmeidler's (1973) tests for PK influence on an electronic thermometer included, besides psychic Ingo Swann, two students, one of whom was a meditator. Only Swann and the meditator attained significant results. One factor contributing to ambiguity is that persons who choose to practice meditation may in general differ from others in certain traits that themselves correlate with PK ability.

4.3.2c Cognitive modes: analytic versus holistic

Stanford (1969) had some unselected subjects do dice PK trials while visualizing as vividly as possible the target face. Others did the trials immediately after giving as many verbal associations to the target face as possible. He then tested each subject's tendency to think in visual imagery. Correlation analysis showed that visual thinkers scored better while visualizing, but that nonvisual thinkers did better under the verbal association condition ($p = .02$).

This and some other studies of psychological correlates of psi success (e.g. Maher and Schmeidler, 1977) suggest a relation to recently discovered distinctions between left-brain and right-brain functions (see chapter 8, section 2.3). In most persons, especially males, verbal and analytical processes are identified predominantly with the left hemisphere of the brain. Visualization, spatial relations, musical and artistic sensibilities are mainly right-hemisphere functions. Despite some inconsistencies, the meager experimental evidence suggests, as Stanford's results clearly indicate, that psi works best in the cognitive mode that is more congenial to the individual subject.

A team at the University of Houston addressed the question explicitly (W. G. Braud, G. Smith, Andrew and Willis, 1976). They compared PK scoring on an REG of subjects who were involved in logical, analytical activities with others who were engaged in visualization and other nonanalytical thinking. To induce the desired mental mode, each agent listened to an appropriate tape recording before and during the PK test. Two of three series of tests yielded significant results in the expected direction of higher scoring in the nonanalytical mode. However, in at least one of these two series the experimenter knew the mode that was in effect during each test, so that an experimenter effect may account for the results.

William Braud (1983) exploited this tentative finding by testing seven subjects before and after six weeks of intensive training and practice in visualization. Their collective scoring rate advanced from 50.5 percent to 53.9 percent, the difference being highly significant ($p = .0044$, 2-t). Thus it is evident that some evidence appears to favor the holistic mode for PK success. However, the subjects in these experiments were not tested for cognitive preference.

Other studies have sought to examine more specifically the kinds of imagery strategies most conducive to PK success. Ariel Levi (1979) randomly assigned 51 college students to one of three conditions: in the 'process-oriented' condition subjects were to imagine the process going on inside the REG during each trial; in the 'goal-oriented' condition they were simply to imagine the target numbers; in the control condition they listened to a taped lecture about the nature of random events. The goal-oriented condition was found to produce a significantly higher scoring rate than the other conditions, but only for those subjects who were shown an ongoing visual display of the results during the test.

These results were partially confirmed in an independent series of experiments by Morris, Nanko and Phillips (1982), who had college students attempt to influence an REG while watching a visual display somewhat different than that of Levi. Also in contrast to Levi, each subject attempted both imagery strategies. The first study produced significant hitting overall ($p = .05$) but although the goal-oriented strategy produced the higher scoring rate the results with this strategy were not independently significant. In the second experiment, the goal-oriented strategy did yield significantly higher scores ($p = .05$), which were found to be attributable to those subjects who had not previously practiced a 'mental development' technique. Subjects in this study were asked to practice one of the two strategies (whichever they wished) for two weeks and return for retesting. Those who chose the goal-oriented strategy scored significantly above chance on the retest ($p = .05$) and significantly higher than those who chose the process-oriented strategy.

In general, these results suggest that goal-oriented imagery may be superior for PK, at least when ongoing visual feedback is displayed.

4.3.3 Complex PK tasks

Some experiments have involved variables that are not directly concerned with the PK object or the mental state of the agent. Instead, they have involved distraction or competition, discrimination of alternate targets, variations of scoring during a session, or motivational factors.

4.3.3a Distraction and competition

An early PK experiment with dice (M. M. Price and J. B. Rhine, 1944) tested the effect on a subject's scoring of deliberate distraction by the experimenter. The subject had demonstrated significant positive results in the presence of a neutral observer a few days earlier. In the present experiment, the experimenter, with the subject's understanding and consent, continually tried to divert his attention and lower his confidence by disparaging remarks. His score was nonsignificantly negative, and the average of 80 runs declined from a high positive level at the beginnings to a still greater negative level toward the ends of the runs.

Can PK subjects influence scores by reinforcing or competing with each other? Another early dice experiment at Duke (Humphrey, 1947a) had two subjects try for the same target face in some runs, but for different targets in others. Scores in this 'help-hinder' series were positive under both conditions but significant ($p = .0001$) only in the 'help' modes; the difference between 'help' and 'hinder' scores was significant ($p = .02$). However, blinds were incomplete, so that interpretation of the result is uncertain. A similar experiment with both subjects blind to the 'help' or 'hinder' condition (Feather and L. E. Rhine, 1969) yielded lower 'help' than 'hinder' scores, the difference being marginally significant.

A competitive test format should be psychologically equivalent to the 'hinder' condition in the above experiments, since each contestant presumably wishes the other to score poorly. When four crap shooters were pitted against four ministerial students (Gatling and J. B. Rhine, 1946), on the implicit assumption that the students would not want to score well, both groups achieved phenomenally high scores, 13 percent above MCE ($CR = 9.97$). Dice were cup-thrown and target faces were equalized, but recording was done by several of the participants. It is impossible to know whether to attribute the uniformly high scores to biased recording errors or to the atmosphere of novelty and playful competition.

4.3.3b Target discrimination: multiple or concealed targets

Eisenbud (1969, p. 166) in his photographic studies of Serios sometimes found evidence of the fusion of competing target ideas in a single picture. At one session, for example, Serios was asked to duplicate a picture he was shown of buildings in a medieval village. A few days earlier he had visited a Colorado museum town, Central City, and had produced some pictures of it. After turning out a good approximation to the medieval buildings, he returned to the Central City theme. The resulting print accurately represented the old livery stable, except that the windows were blocked with recessed masonry and the walls, instead of being brick, appeared to be stone of a texture similar to that in the medieval buildings.

Humphrey (1947b) threw six red and six white dice at each trial, while mentally trying for hits on dice of one color and misses on the other. The target was always the one-face, and the colors for the high and low aims were alternated systematically. The results showed a significant difference ($p = .01$) in the expected direction between high-aim and low-aim scores.

Cox (1951) carried out a similar comparison of scoring on alternative targets (see chapter 9, section 2.1.2). The board onto which the dice tumbled when released was divided into squares numbered 1 to 6. Cox told each subject to concentrate, for example, on the die faces as primary targets and ignore the board numbers. After four throws for each face, the instruction was reversed. Results were highly significant, but hardly what Cox had anticipated. Scoring on primary targets was slightly positive, but scoring on the secondary, 'ignore' targets was strongly negative. The difference was significant ($p = 3 \times 10^{-7}$).

In a placement experiment mentioned earlier (section 4.2.1b) Cox (1954) combined cubes and spheres (dice and marbles) in each trial, but instructed the subject to concentrate on one or the other, in turn. Scores were negative on both primary and secondary targets, being nonsignificantly weaker on the former.

In another discrimination test, Forwald (1952) used in each placement PK trial three each of two kinds of cubes: steel and aluminum, or rough and smooth bakelite plastic, or wood and paper. He tried to influence the cubes of one kind in each pair – steel, rough plastic, or wood – while ignoring the other. Scores on the former were highly significant, while those he ignored scored near chance level, as did all cubes in control runs with no attempt at PK influence.

If diverting conscious attention from a target tends to enhance scoring on it (even though sometimes in the negative direction), may not concealing it entirely work even better? A few experiments have explored this possibility. Psychologist Robert H. Thouless (1951) reported PK success with concealed targets and speculated that being presented with an 'impossible' task might discourage the conscious effort that seems to inhibit success. Fisk's experiments (section 3.1.1), in which the subject threw dice for targets known only to the distant experimenter, yielded sustained high scores. Osis (1953), in an exploratory dice experiment with concealed targets, also obtained significant scoring at levels comparable to those found in tests with open targets. However, none of the foregoing experiments directly compared scores on both open and concealed targets.

4.4 Covert PK: goal versus process (just who is in the act?)

Arthur Foster (1940) noted that ESP card-matching tests with either open or concealed targets produced similar scoring levels, though concealing the target would seem to require a double ESP effort to identify both the target and object cards. On this evidence, he proposed that psi does not operate 'circumferentially' through a linear series of cognitive steps, but takes a 'diametric' shortcut to its goal. Evidence for the goal-oriented nature of psi has continued to accumulate, and some experiments have explored it explicitly.

Schmidt's theoretical model (chapter 11, section 3.2.2a) implies goal orientation. By assuming its validity, he avoided having to explain the REG circuitry or ask his experimental subjects to try to influence radioactive decay or other esoteric processes. Instead, he substituted a simple visual or auditory display of the REG output. The subject then could concentrate on the *goal* of influencing the display without being concerned with the *process* that actuated it. Several of Schmidt's experiments (section 4.2.2) as well as the concealed-target tests (section 4.3.3b) support the concept of psi as a goal-oriented manifestation.

If conscious knowledge of the details of a psi task is unnecessary, then what about the goal itself? If motivation is present, if psi can help to achieve some reward or satisfaction, may it intervene without conscious intention? Some evidence for such covert psi has been reviewed in chapter 8, and studies of RSPK incidents lend further support to the concept: so do several PK experiments, though with some inconsistencies.

One example is Schmidt's experiment (section 4.1.3) in which subjects given the task of trying to hear a random series of faint clicks from an REG actually biased the output to produce more clicks, though they had not been told that the experiment could involve PK.

In a similar experiment (Kuyper *et al.*, 1972) an REG controlled an unpleasant, distracting noise while subjects listened to music. However, only those who had been told that they might be able to turn off the noise by PK did so significantly. The others exhibited no evidence for covert PK.

Bert Camstra (1973) attempted to condition his experimental subjects to improve their PK scores by stopping an unpleasant noise for 10 seconds whenever the target number (with a probability of only .01) appeared in the REG output. Subjects who were told that the test was a PK test or were asked to concentrate on it improved significantly less than did others who did not know the nature of the task or did not concentrate. However, a second series with apparently minor modifications was not significant.

A few experimenters have tried to elicit covert PK in animals. Schmidt (1970a) shut a cat in a chilly room with a cushion under a 200-watt lamp. An REG turned the lamp on or off randomly at one-second intervals. During five half-hour sessions (until the cat refused to play!) the lamp was turned on consistently and significantly more often than not. But in a similar experiment with cockroaches that allowed them to influence electric shocks delivered by an REG, the frequency of shocks increased sharply. The experimenter noted that he is not fond of cockroaches.

William Braud (1976) arranged for a fish of a fighting species to see its image in a mirror, thus evoking a compulsively aggressive response. With an REG set to expose or suppress the image randomly every 20 seconds, he found that when the fish was present exposure periods dominated significantly.

Braud and Marilyn Schlitz (1983) reported an instance in which a need felt by a person who was the object of PK influence apparently facilitated that influence. They selected two groups of persons for unusually high and unusually low activation of the sympathetic nervous system, as indicated by the levels of electrodermal activity (EDA). On the premise that members of the first group would need and desire calming of their nervous activity, the experimenters expected that the EDAs of that group would decline more under PK influence than would the EDAs of the second, low-activity group. One or the other experimenter, acting as PK agent in a separate room from the object person, watched the EDA recorder while willing the reading to decline. The EDAs of the high-activity group declined significantly as expected, but those of the low-activity group did not. However, the difference may have resulted from agents' expectations, since blinds were not possible.

Consideration of these and other situations suggesting psi effects without conscious intent led Stanford (1977b, p. 839 ff.; also chapter 8, section 1.2.1) to formulate his PMIR hypothesis, which proposes that persons (and possibly other organisms) use psi much as they do sensorimotor processes to inform themselves of relevant elements in their situations and to influence them in accordance with their needs. His later modification, conformance behavior, is a more fundamental concept. It is to goal orientation as PMIR is to process orientation, i.e. needs tend, with some qualifications, to be fulfilled in ways that transcend both sensorimotor and psi efforts.

A PK experiment designed to test the PMIR concept (Stanford *et al.*, 1975) put each of 40 subjects through an overt REG PK test and then assigned each to a dull, boring task. The subject was not told that the REG was still running and that he could escape to a more interesting activity if the REG showed 7 or more hits in any block of 10 trials. Nevertheless, eight of the subjects, a significant number, escaped before the 45–minute time limit.

Another experiment (Palmer and Kramer, 1984) inadvertently provided another apparent example of PMIR. Their experimental sessions were matched with control runs of the REG. These were run by Palmer, who remained near the test room but was busy with other matters. Nevertheless, the variance of scores in the control series was significantly less than MCE – enough to provide a significant difference between it and the nonsignificant predicted high variance of the experimental scores, in effect 'salvaging' that aspect of the experiment.

These and many other observations of probable covert psi have intensified a nagging problem that has long worried parapsychologists. Eisenbud (1963a) put it clearly:

> Experiments are conducted on the curious assumption that the subjects in them will not use the very faculties they are being tested for . . . until they step across the threshold of the laboratory and hear the starting gong, and that then they will use these faculties only within the confines of their designated roles in the particular design employed. . . .
>
> By the same token it seems implicitly to be taken for granted that experimenters . . . will not, for whatever obscure reason, use any psi faculties *they* may have to muddy the field. (p. 258)

If psi can intervene without conscious awareness or intent, if it is an inherently need-serving, goal-seeking function, what is to preclude a complex interplay of psi among all of the participants in an experiment – or beyond it? After all, the experimenter usually has much more at stake than does a volunteer subject. Further, it has long been observed that some experimenters consistently get significant results, while others do not.

The evidence for such unscheduled psi interplay, called the experimenter effect but much broader in its implications, has been reviewed in chapter 8, section 6.3 ff., together with related evidence from ESP experiments. In some of the PK experiments that have been mentioned, an experimenter effect appears more probable than the ostensible interpretation. Schmidt's experiments with the cat and especially the cockroaches, which gave positive scores in the one case and negative in the other, seem more likely to have reflected his feelings about the animals than PK on their part. Similarly, his tests of retro-PK with prerecorded object tapes are open to alternative, admittedly tortuous, interpretation as experimenter influence.

The implications of such ambiguity are serious. The results of any process-oriented experiment are subject to alternative interpretations as need-serving patterns induced by the experimenter (or someone else) instead of the ostensible dependences upon the variables that are being tested. One parapsychologist has commented that the only thing the field has discovered is the experimenter effect!

That pessimistic estimate is obviously exaggerated. Consider an experiment (G. K. Watkins, 1972) in which lizards were put in an uncomfortably cool cage with an REG-controlled heater, as in Schmidt's cat experiment. Significant positive changes in the normally random output of the REG occurred. Further, they were correlated in a complex pattern with bright or dull days, barometric pressure, and humidity. Evidently low pressure or humidity increased the evaporative cooling of the lizards, so that their need for heat increased. Other correlations were noted between PK effects and sexes and social roles of the 'agent' animals. Such unanticipated internal evidence, relating much more intimately to the needs of the animals than to the experimenter's expectations, argues that the animals were the actual PK agents. However, a great many ingenious experiments will be necessary to clarify the obscure relationships that are involved in psi manifestations.

Note

[1] 1-t or 2-t indicates the one-tailed or two-tailed probability value; stated wherever given in the original report.

Thought questions

(1) A well designed PK experiment on an REG machine yields a positive score with an objectively determined probability. This probability is reported as being 'statistically significant.' Is this an objective conclusion? Why?

(2) In Grad's 'healing' experiments with seedlings, if the person who regularly watered and measured the seedlings had known which plants the healer-treated water had been used on, would this fact have affected the interpretation of the results? If so, how?

(3) Early experimental investigations, such as Crookes's experiment with Home, are generally neglected by parapsychologists. What reasons do you see for considering older reports unreliable or unimportant? Can you offer any arguments against such an attitude?

(4) Micro-PK experiments (REG, etc.) have been numerous but have yielded only modest extra-chance scoring rates. Macro-PK experiments have been relatively few, but their results have been obvious and sometimes spectacular. Which class of findings do you think offers the stronger evidence for the reality of PK, and why?

(5) Much experimental evidence indicates that ESP or PK scoring rates are independent of the complexity of the psi task. This finding is usually interpreted to mean that psi is goal-oriented – that it affects correlations of events without regard to the intermediate processes. Can you suggest an alternative explanation of the findings?

Chapter 11
Physical and quasi-physical theories of psi

Joseph H. Rush

1 What is a scientific theory?

The word *theory* often is used loosely to mean any degree of speculation. In legal or police work, for example, it usually refers to a provisional explanation of what happened in the commission of a crime. It is an imaginative structure based upon the available clues. It helps the investigation by suggesting other evidence and where to look for it.

In science a theory is more specifically defined. Like the crime theory, it must 'explain' the known facts – that is, relate them rationally to other facts; and it should predict new phenomena that can be sought through experiment or observation. But here the analogy ends. Science is concerned, not with proving an isolated event, but with establishing consistent relations, called laws of nature, that apply to large classes of events. Judicial law asks what happened; science asks what caused it to happen. Given certain conditions, what will result?

Science defines physical entities in operational terms. If asked to define or describe the color blue, one might refer to the clear sky or deep water or a piece of turquoise. But the physicist defines blue as the color perception induced by a certain range of wavelengths of light and prescribes experimental operations for measuring wavelengths. A scientific theory deals with such sets of operations and their effects. Usually it expresses relations in mathematical terms.

1.1 A theory must be testable

During the Middle Ages some religious philosophers held that each planet was guided in its orbit by an angel, or spirit. That was not a scientifically useful theory, because there was no way to prove or disprove (falsify*) it. (An English critic of spiritualism once remarked that a spirit is what is left if you subtract the sentence, 'The table moved,' from the sentence, 'A spirit moved the table.')

To say that gravity holds the planets in their paths is no improvement over angels or spirits. Gravitation also is an intangible concept that cannot be observed. But when Isaac Newton proposed the theory that a planet and the sun are attracted by a gravitational force that is proportional to the product of their masses and inversely proportional to the square of the distance between them, he offered a *relation* that could be tested against observations of the planets. By applying that relation he was able to calculate the planets' orbits and to show that they did agree with the observed orbits.

Note that the influence that Newton called gravitation remained as intangible and obscure as ever; he could just as well have said that spirits pulled the planets toward the sun. The essential feature of his theory was the mathematical relation involving masses and distances, which made possible operational tests of the implications of the theory against observational data.

Because Newton's theory was stated in exact mathematical terms, even slight disagreements with precise observations would have falsified it (as they actually did more than two centuries later). That is the power of mathematical theory: it enables scientists to discriminate between alternative theories that do not differ very much in their predictions. Other natural philosophers had recognized that the planets nearer the sun must be the more strongly attracted, but such a loose, qualitative relation seldom leads to useful predictions.

A theory never can be proved true for all possible situations. No matter how many phenomena it describes accurately, there is always the possibility (in the history of science, the near certainty) that a phenomenon will be discovered that contradicts the theory. Thus, scientific truth is relative – it never can amount to absolute certainty. A theory is considered valid so long as it is confirmed by observation and experiments, and confidence in the theory increases as such confirmations accumulate. In principle, a single well-established contradictory finding is enough to falsify the theory. It then must be modified to accommodate the troublesome new data or be used with caution until it is supplanted by a new theory.

1.2 Physical variables

It should be clear by now that a physical theory is primarily a statement of the effects that should be expected when certain influential factors in a situation are changed. Such factors are called *variables**. As a simple example, an experimenter might heat a metal bar and measure its length at various temperatures. Since the temperature is being varied arbitrarily by the experimenter, it is an independent variable*. The length, which changes in accordance with temperature changes, is the dependent variable*. Scientists advance in a new field by identifying the variables that dominate an effect that they are investigating and by measuring the changes produced in a given variable in response to changes in another. From such data a theory can be devised that explains these cause-and-effect relationships in terms of a unifying concept such as gravitation, heat, or an electromagnetic field. Theory is concerned with the causal relations, the process, rather than the entities themselves.

The application of these principles in parapsychology, and the great difficulties encountered in trying to identify significant variables, have been examined in chapter 8, section 1. A further difficulty, as in psychology and other complex fields, is that so many significant variables frequently are involved that it is impossible to control them even if they are identified. These are the principal reasons for the primary dependence upon statistical methods in parapsychological research. Such methods cannot evolve the exact causal relations that apply in much of physics, but they nevertheless are powerful analytic tools.

2 Physical concepts that constrain psi theories

Theories overlap, and some are more fundamental or general than others. Ideally they should not contradict each other. Actually some do, but are nevertheless too useful to discard.

Scientific theories are continually being revised or replaced. Certain ones, however, are so fundamental and so strongly confirmed by experience that they are regarded practically as being true for all situations. Any new theory or observation that appears to violate one of these basic principles is therefore severely challenged. In physics, the principal fundamental concepts are as follows.

2.1 The energy laws

The *first law of thermodynamics,* the law of conservation of energy, states that energy cannot be created or destroyed. It can only be transformed (e.g. a light bulb transforms electrical energy into heat and light energy). After Einstein showed that matter (mass) is a form of energy, the law was modified: energy can be transformed into matter, or matter into energy; but neither can be created or destroyed.

The *second law of thermodynamics* is more subtle and much more difficult to explain nonmathematically. In the succinct terms of physics, it states that the entropy of an isolated system continually increases. This means that, in a physical system – anything from an experimental apparatus to a galaxy – that is prevented from exchanging material or energy with any other system, the arrangements of matter and energy become continually more nearly random, more probable, more disorderly. Heat flows from warm to cold objects, so that all approach a uniform temperature. Machines wear out; hills erode and lakes fill with debris; organisms die and decay; orderly arrangements generally tend to become less orderly.

These energy laws are more fundamental then they might appear to be. They are intimately involved with the concepts of causation and the direction of time. Events are cause-and-effect sequences that always involve transfer of energy (subject to some modifications in quantum mechanics). The forward direction of time, from past to future, is the direction of increasing entropy in an isolated system.

2.2 The four physical agencies or 'forces'

Physicists have discovered only four kinds of force fields that mediate all of the known interactions between particles or objects in the physical world. The *strong nuclear force* binds the protons and neutrons that form the nucleus of an atom. This force is relatively very strong, much stronger than any force we ordinarily are familiar with; but it declines very rapidly with distance, so that it is insignificant beyond the nucleus even within the atom. The *weak nuclear force* is a contributing factor in the nuclear structure and radioactive decay, but it also is insignificant at greater distances.

The *electromagnetic force* is dominant in the electronic structure of the atom and in the molecular combinations of atoms that chemists are concerned with. It is a significant influence in many larger systems, from electrical machinery to stars and even galaxies. Everything in the human scale, all familiar objects and substances and even our own bodies are held together by electromagnetic forces.

Gravitation is far weaker than the other forces. The electrical force between two isolated protons (nuclei of hydrogen atoms), for example, is 10^{36} – a trillion trillion trillion – times as great as their gravitational attraction. Gravitation therefore is a negligible influence at the level of atoms and molecules. Even to an ant, the earth's gravitational force (the ant's weight) is less important than friction, adhesion and air resistance. But gravitational force depends upon the masses involved, so that among the vast masses and distances of the planets, stars and galaxies, where even electromagnetism is greatly weakened, gravitation becomes the dominant force.

Physicists know of no organizing influence in the universe except these four agencies. Consequently, they are extremely skeptical of any proposal to explain psi phemomena by postulating a new kind of force or field or 'vibration.'

2.3 Relativity and the speed limit of the universe

About 1915 Einstein's theory of relativity displaced Newton's gravitational theory as the preferred model for large-scale physics, the realm of great masses, distances and speeds. It implies consequences that violate commonsense experience in our familiar world. If, for example, the speed of any object is increased, a relatively stationary observer will see it shorten in the direction of motion and its inertia increase; but these effects become significant only at speeds approaching that of light or other electromagnetic radiation.

The theory also implies the now familiar equivalence of mass and energy ($e = mc^2$), so dramatically demonstrated by nuclear power plants and bombs. Further, it dictates that no material object or particle can be made to move faster than the speed of light, about 300,000 kilometers per second.

2.4 Quantum mechanics: the cosmic crap game, and the puzzling role of the observer

Quantum mechanics is complementary to relativity theory in that it concerns primarily the realm of the very small, from molecules on down. Like relativity, quantum theory violates outrageously our commonsense impressions of the world. It also is impossible to explain clearly except in terms of mathematics. However, some of its implications can be described.

Quantum mechanics grew out of the discovery about 1900 that certain basic physical quantities, such as energy and electric charge, cannot be subdivided indefinitely. Instead, they consist of very small units, called quanta*. Electrons, protons and other atomic particles do not behave according to the exact laws of causation that apply in familiar physical processes. Individually, their behavior is predictable only within a range of possibilities, but the behavior of large numbers of such particles can be predicted accurately by statistical methods. Thus quantum theory implies that the dependable order of cause and effect that we observe in our familiar world is really statistical order that arises from the individually unpredictable behavior of a vast population of atoms.

Further, quantum theory demonstrates that the ultimate accuracy of physical measurements is limited. To observe or measure anything is to disturb it, so that the very process of observation, however refined, is to some degree self-defeating. A few theoretical physicists even hold that the mental act of observing a quantum event, the conscious perception of it, itself reacts upon the physical event.

2.5 Implications for parapsychology

The foregoing principles and theoretical concepts are the very foundation of modern physics. They have been confirmed by countless observations and experiments. Obviously anyone who attempts to formulate a new theory of psi or anything else must treat them with great respect. That is one reason for the skepticism that most scientists feel toward parapsychological claims: psi phenomena appear to be indifferent to physical constraints.

Communication, for example, requires energy; yet no known energy appears to account for ESP. Suggestions have been made that the energy for some physical phenomena reported at seances may be heat energy concentrated from the air ('cold breezes' often are reported). But such a process would contradict the second law of thermodynamics. Materializations and dematerializations of objects are reported. Yet, by Einstein's equation, the dematerialization of a copper penny would require the sudden release of the energy of a small nuclear bomb! Quantum theory leaves open some possibility of accommodating psi phenomena, because it involves paradoxes and inconsistencies that are not yet resolved.

Ordinarily scientists explore a newly discovered phenomenon by varying the physical conditions under which it occurs and observing the effects on the phenomenon. Thus the mysterious radiations from radioactive ores were quickly found to be influenced by material barriers and by electric or magnetic fields. By studying the effects of measured changes in these variables, physicists soon defined the properties of the radiations and thus were able to identify them with already-known particles and wave phenomena.

That familiar procedure has not worked for psi phenomena because of one stark fact. *No physical variable has been shown to influence the scoring rate in psi experiments.* Few experiments have been designed explicitly to test the effects of distance, material barriers, or other physical variables upon scoring rates. Many experiments have implicitly tested some variations in such parameters, but the results are ambiguous because of confusion with known and unknown psychological variables. Most of these experiments have been discussed in chapters 5, 7, 8, 9 and 10. Consequently, theorists may speculate freely as to the relations of psi to the physical world; but their theories are difficult to test, because there is no way to isolate causal factors or define simple physical relationships. However, such speculative theories are sharply restricted by the very absence of known physical influences on psi phenomena.

This independence of physical influences confronts theorists with two distinct orders of theoretical difficulty. Telepathy, clairvoyance, or psychokinesis in present time conceivably might be explained by undiscovered radiation or other means of energy transfer. Unlikely as such an agency may be, it is not in principle impossible. But the concepts of precognition and retro-PK violate a most fundamental physical principle, that of causation and its irreversibility.

Despite these difficulties, a historical analogy may be relevant. Physicists a century ago postulated 'ether' permeating all matter and space, too subtle to be detected directly but serving as a medium for the transmission of light and other electromagnetic radiations. Consequently, it was believed that the observed speed of light should vary with the speed of an observer through the ether. However, delicate experiments designed to measure this 'ether drift' showed that the speed of light is independent of the motion of the observer, much as psi phenomena appear to be independent of physical variables. This paradoxical finding caused great puzzlement among physicists until Einstein stood the problem on its head by postulating that the speed of light in vacuum is necessarily constant and deducing the space-time relations that are required for that postulate to be true. His relativity theory did not reveal a means of detecting ether drift. Rather, it disposed of the imaginary ether and successfully predicted novel, unsuspected effects that revolutionized our conception of the world.

The quest for physical influences on psi phenomena may be as delusory as attempts to measure ether drift, while psi may be hinting of a new world view as bizarre as relativity appeared to Einstein's contemporaries. However, this analogy must not be pushed too far. Relativity grew out of anomalies *within* the structure of physics and derived from consistently observed dependences among physical entities, but psi phenomena have not been shown to accord with that structure, nor do they yet admit of exact measurements.

3 Approaches to a physical theory of psi

Theories tend to follow fashions, and a theory that works well in one field often is invoked to explain puzzling effects in another. Mesmer and other healers attributed their effects to 'animal magnetism,' trading on the concurrent physical discoveries in magnetism. Relativity theory was mimicked by 'fourth-dimension' hypotheses of psi, and the advent of radio broadcasting evoked an appealing concept of telepathy as 'mental radio.' A few theorists have tried to explain psi effects in terms of gravitation, and plasma physics has found its counterpart in theories of 'bioplasma.' Quantum mechanics has, with more justification, stimulated several quantum-theoretical approaches to paranormal phenomena.

Most theoretical efforts have been concerned primarily with ESP, especially telepathy, rather than PK. It is easier to conceive of an obscure medium of communication between two living brains than between a brain and an inanimate ESP target, to say nothing of precognition. The energy required for most PK effects presents a severe obstacle to theorists.

Further, nearly all attempts at physical theories of psi concern primarily the medium of information transfer – that is, the mechanism or process by which information is transferred from the ESP target to the brain of the percipient or from the brain of the PK agent to the PK object. This aspect of psi appears to be generally accepted as the primary problem. The difficulties arising from target complexity or subtlety (e.g. a stacked deck of cards or electron distributions in an REG), though formidable, have been regarded as secondary by most theorists.

Here we will comment upon only a few representative theories. More comprehensive summaries may be found in Chari (1974, 1977), Oteri (1975), and Rao (1978).

3.1 Quasi-physical theories

Most 'physical' theories of psi have postulated novel kinds of radiation, resonance, fields, or other agencies or effects that are analogous to known physical agencies or processes. However, such concepts in themselves explain nothing. To be useful as a model for organizing observed data, a theory must specify a set of orderly, quantitative relations among physical variables that can be tested in observations or experiments.

Consequently, theories that do not depend upon or relate to known physical agencies can hardly be considered physical theories. Rather, they are quasi-physical. They employ concepts that are formally similar to some that theoretical physicists have found useful, but they do not develop the specific quantitative relations that might reveal some connections with established physics. They have not proved useful in suggesting experimental tests.

3.1.1 Field theories

Regions of gravitational, magnetic, or other influences familiar to physicists are called fields. Such a field is precisely defined by the force or other effect it exerts at any point in it. Some theorists have tried to adapt the field concept to account for psi. However no known physical field has proved very useful for this purpose, so that theorists have had to postulate novel kinds of fields and ascribe to them the desired properties.

H. Berger (1940) advanced a hypothesis that is typical of many such. To explain telepathy, he proposed that some of the physical or chemical energy involved in thought processes in the brain is transformed into a new form he called psychic energy. He supposed this energy to be capable of radiating to great distances and affecting other brains; but such a form of energy is not recognized in physics. 'Psychic energy' really is little more than another name for telepathy. It suggests no mechanism for clairvoyance, precognition, or PK.

Adrian Dobbs (1965, 1967) proposed that certain mathematically imaginary terms in the equations of quantum mechanics represent physical particles that exist but are not impeded by distance or material barriers and therefore cannot be directly detected. He postulated that the brain sometimes emits showers of such particles, which he called psitrons, and that these can interact with neurons in another brain to induce thought patterns that resemble those that discharged the psitrons. He extended his argument to account for precognition. However, Dobbs's theory affords no good experimental test, nor does it provide for clairvoyance or psychokinesis.

An unusually sophisticated attempt to devise a novel physical psi field is due to G. D. Wasserman (1956/1966), a British mathematician. Wasserman disavowed nonphysical agencies, noting that physical fields can be formally derived from various members of a class of mathematical expressions called Lagrange functions. He maintained that, by suitable choices of such functions, he could devise physical fields to account for structural and behavioral patterns in organisms and also for psi phenomena. Though he developed this formal concept in schematic detail, he offered no evidence for the existence of such fields as he postulated, nor did he propose any experimental tests of their reality or properties.

William G. Roll (1966b) proposed a quasi-physical psi field that is similar to Wasserman's but elaborated somewhat differently in its details. He postulated psi fields attending both inanimate objects and living organisms and proposed that these individual fields can interact. These interactions are held to conform to the conservation-of-energy law and to be limited to some degree by distance; material barriers are not considered. The interactions are also dependent upon attention, motivation, and other psychological factors. This hypothesis, however, is like the other field hypotheses in postulating a physical field that is not identified with any of the four fundamental physical 'forces,' nor does it suggest any definitive experimental tests.

3.1.2 Multidimensional concepts

Einstein's relativity theory combined time with the three coordinates of space in the concept of a four-dimensional space-time continuum that is distorted ('curved') in still higher dimensions. This intriguing world picture has inspired much science fiction as well as serious theorizing as to the possibility that a higher dimension may provide a shortcut between events that are separated in the familiar world of space and time. Several such schemes have been proposed to account for psi phenomena (e.g. C. D. Broad, 1967; Dunne, 1927/1958; Hart, 1965; Smythies, 1967).

More recently Gertrude R. Schmeidler (1972) developed further the concept of virtual contact between isolated events through a fifth dimension. She conceived of this contact in terms of a 'topological fold' of space-time in a higher dimension and cited various aspects of experimental psi results that can be interpreted as supporting such a concept. The theory is entirely qualitative, however, and thus proposes no definitive experimental tests.

3.1.3 Resonance theory

Ninian Marshall (1960), to account for telepathy and precognition (but not other psi phenomena), invoked the physical principle of resonance*, familiar in the tuning of musical instruments or a radio. He proposed that two complex, similar systems (e.g. living brains), if nearly enough alike for one to resonate with the other, would tend to become more alike, to 'pull into synchronism' with each other. Thus a thought pattern in one brain might be reproduced in another.

However, Marshall did not suggest a physical process or energy. He simply postulated that similar complex systems will resonate and that this tendency will increase with the product of the complexities of the systems and decrease with the differences between them, independently of space and time. Since the hypothesis is not limited to living systems, it should be experimentally testable. In the absence of any such confirmation, however, it remains a quasi-physical speculation.

3.2 Physical theories

Proposals to account for psi phenomena by known physical agencies include several hypotheses involving radiation fields. These have invoked electromagnetic radiation (radio waves), neutrinos, and even tachyons – theoretically plausible particles that travel faster than light (Chari, 1974, 1977). But even the existence of tachyons has not been demonstrated; and neutrinos, which pass through the earth with little chance of interactions, are not a promising medium for communication. The only physical field hypotheses that have been developed and subjected to experiment to any serious degree are those that involve electromagnetic energy.

3.2.1 Electromagnetic theories

Early work on electromagnetic radiation as the medium for telepathy is summarized by Vasiliev (1963/1976, pp. 14–25). During the 1920s an Italian neurologist, F. Cazzamalli, reported experiments that seemed to indicate radio-frequency radiations from human subjects, and the discovery of 'brain waves' (actually voltage fluctuations, not radiation) lent a superficial plausibility to 'mental radio.' However, other investigators could not confirm Cazzamalli's findings, and Vasiliev found no significant difference in telepathic (actually GESP) scores with and without radio shields.

Recent work in Eastern Europe and the Soviet Union has concentrated on extremely-low-frequency (ELF) electromagnetic radiation. Oscillations of the order of ten per second accord with the brain wave frequencies, and radiation at such frequencies has interesting properties, including immunity to ordinary shielding. However, even its principal exponent, I.M. Kogan (1966, 1967), acknowledged that his ELF theory does not account satisfactorily for long-distance telepathy.

Objections to an electromagnetic mechanism for psi communication, as noted by Vasiliev, Rush (1943), and others, are formidable. These objections concern principally power and selectivity. The only known electrical oscillations in the brain are the brain-wave potentials with frequencies of the order of ten per second. The electrical power in these oscillations is minute, and the efficiency of radiation from the brain at such frequencies is extremely low. The problem of selectivity, of 'tuning in' one individual pattern among a chaos of biological transmitters, is obvious.

However, one common objection to communication theories of psi is based upon misconceptions. Frequently it is stated that, since the strength of any physical radiation declines proportionally to the square of the distance from the source – the 'inverse-square law' – then ESP test scores should decline with distance accordingly. However, as B. Hoffman (1940) noted, the inverse-square decline applies to the power of the carrier wave, but ESP scores would depend upon the *intelligibility* of the information. Radio reception is a familiar analogy: speech remains fully understandable over a wide range of distances. Further, the inverse-square law rarely applies in a practical situation, because of reflection, refraction, scattering and other effects, including intentional beaming. Spacecraft have transmitted picture signals over nearly a billion miles with power of only a few watts because the energy was concentrated in a narrow beam to earth.

Psychologist Michael A. Persinger (1979) proposed an ingenious variant of the ELF theory that avoids some of the usual objections, but encounters others. He made use of the fact that ELF radiation is continually generated by geomagnetic disturbances, lightning and other natural processes. A telepathic agent might somehow impress upon the existing ELF radiation a mental pattern of information that would affect a sensitive percipient so as to reproduce the information. Alternatively, Persinger suggested that, if two persons shared an emotionally charged experience during the passage of a distinctive pattern of ELF waves, then they might later, even if separated, experience similar emotions and imagery during the passage of a similar ELF disturbance. They then would attribute their coincidental experiences to telepathy. Despite its ingenuity, Persinger's hypothesis lacks plausible mechanisms and does not seriously address real psi experiences.

The gravest objection to all of the communication theories is that they account only for telepathy and, in some cases, a limited degree of precognition. Yet the experimental findings overwhelmingly indicate that all modes of ESP and PK are manifestations of a unitary principle. Even these modes are ambiguous, as has been noted. Any theoretical approach that does not encompass all modes of psi effects is inadequate.

3.2.2 Observational theories

Until recently the development of physical science had excluded mind and consciousness from its theoretical structure. The observer was considered to be just that, a spectator whose awareness had no effect upon physical processes. Einstein's relativity theory recognized that the perception of a physical event depends upon the situation of the observer relative to that event, but it did not imply any influence of the observer's mind upon the event. Quantum mechanics, which matured during the 1920s, explains and predicts fundamental physical events with impressive reliability, but it leads to a hiatus – the 'measurement problem' – that has not been satisfactorily resolved. This hiatus opens physics for the first time to the possibility that subjective mind may intervene significantly in the objective world of physics. Some physicists believe that the theory logically requires such interaction.

Quantum theory, supported by innumerable experiments, indicates that physical events at the fundamental level of atoms, electrons, and other particles are governed by statistical laws that can only state the *probability* that, for example, an electron will be observed in a specified location. The set of probabilities that the electron will be in any of a range of possible locations is represented by a mathematical expression called Schrödinger's equation.

In the actual event, however, the electron is observed to be in a particular location at the prescribed time. Here is the hiatus. What has 'decided' which of the range of potential locations will be realized in the actual event? No physical agency has been discovered that determines the individual event that will be observed when such a probabilistic situation is resolved. The most widely accepted view among physicists, the 'Copenhagen interpretation,' is that the electron, before its location is observed, is not merely in an unknown location; it is in an indeterminate state (in effect, it is nowhere in particular) until it is 'observed' by means of a suitable instrument. The act of observation somehow forces a decision (in technical terms it 'collapses the state vector').

Such an unresolved hiatus at the very heart of physical theory naturally has inspired fresh speculation on the ancient mind-body problem, the relation between the physical world and the world of consciousness and subjective experience. E. P. Wigner (1967, pp. 171–84) argued on quantum-theoretical grounds that the observer's perception of a physical event – not the instrumental or sensory detection of it, but the observer's awareness – must necessarily react upon the observed event or process and perturb it. Such interaction is at the quantum level, too minute to be directly significant. But in some circumstances it might trigger a diverging series of events that would become macroscopically significant. Physicist John A. Wheeler proposed that we not only discover the laws of nature but also may participate in making them (Misner, Thorne and Wheeler, 1973; Wheeler, 1974). Such intimations of involvement of mind in the physical world are profoundly important to science and philosophy.

This convergence of physical theory upon the crucial role of the observer has encouraged several theorists to try to explain psi phenomena in terms of quantum mechanics or other observer-centered concepts – the observational theories*. The possibilities are appealing. Quantum events are probabilistic, they are independent of time and distance, and they involve correlations of states rather than energetic communication. These are just the characteristics of psi that have been so resistant to explanation.

Some physicists have suggested that the indeterminate state of an atomic particle is resolved by hidden variables*, physical agencies that cannot be observed directly but are the missing link in a chain of causation that determines the particle's location or other condition (e.g. Bohm, 1952). To one who is not accustomed to mathematical theory, this concept of a hidden variable may be difficult to grasp.

A familiar analogy is pain. It cannot be directly measured, but we infer that a person is in pain by observing grimaces, cries, and other behavior that otherwise would be difficult to explain. Pain is thus the 'hidden variable' that largely determines the sufferer's behavior; but this is an analogy, not an example.

Evan Harris Walker (1974, 1975), a theoretical physicist, proposed that the hidden variable that determines the outcome of a probabilistic quantum situation is the consciousness of the observer. By that he meant that the intention or will of the observer determines which of the potential events represented by the Schrödinger equation will become the actual event. J. A. Donald and B. Martin (1976; Schmeidler, 1982, p. 138) developed a formalistic theory derived from thermodynamics that leads to a result that is mathematically equivalent to Walker's. However, they do not propose mechanisms, so that the practical implications of the theory are obscure.

Richard D. Mattuck (1977) proposed a direct action of mind (not brain) on macroscopic matter, through an informational interaction, to effect PK. In a later version (Mattuck, 1982) he attributed hidden variables (HVs) to mind and postulated mental capabilities amounting to ESP. He then proposed that by will (intention) the mind can 'skew,' or redistribute, the probabilities represented by the HVs so as to produce improbable events. By assuming that the distribution of HVs is stable for many minutes, he provides for improbable events accumulating on a macroscopic scale, thus accounting for large PK events.

W. von Lucadou and K. Kornwachs (1977) developed a variant concept that involves both quantum indeterminacy and the residual indeterminacy inherent in a complex system. Later they added a novel informational concept (von Lucadou and Kornwachs, 1983). However, their proposal has more the look of a qualitative analogy to physical theory than a testable hypothesis. The function of the observer is not clear.

Schmidt (1975) proposed a mathematical model of a fundamental psi process. Since his is a purely formal model that depends on postulating a 'psi source' and does not consider mechanisms, it really is quasi-physical. However, it is treated here because of its close relation to Walker's and other observational theories.

Several summaries of these theories and comments on them have been published (Houtkooper, 1983; Millar, 1978; Schouten, 1977). The following discussion will be limited to Walker's theory and Schmidt's model, since these have been the most developed and experimentally productive of the group.

3.2.2a Walker's theory and Schmidt's model

Walker's theory is not entirely *ad hoc,* but is a plausible extension of concepts that have evolved within quantum physics. It does not require a revolution in physics. Rather, if it proves to be valid, it will clarify physical theory by helping to resolve the hiatus of the measurement problem. The theory makes several quantitative predictions, so that it is subject to experimental tests and possible falsification.

The theory is developed mathematically in terms of hidden variables associated with brain activity and intention or will. Careful reading is required to understand it fully. To put it in the simplest descriptive terms, Walker proposes that conscious intention, or effort of will, can influence an indeterminate quantum situation so as to resolve it in a desired outcome. In the familiar case of an experimental REG actuated by random radioactive disintegrations, a PK subject wanting (+) outputs would influence the timing of each radioactive pulse slightly so as to produce the desired target. No analytical knowledge of how much to shift the timing or other details is required. What the theory proposes is that the subject's will brings about a correlation (agreement) between the imagined and the actual outcomes of the quantum process.

Recall that theorists hold that the indeterminate quantum state is resolved into an actual event when it is observed. For this reason, Walker considers it essential that the subject know the result of each trial, or at least the score of a run. This aspect carries the subtle implication that retro-PK is not only possible but inevitable, if the subject's effort is effective only upon observing the outcome of the *earlier* quantum event.

It also follows that PK can operate only upon an indeterminate (pure chance) situation, the outcome of which depends upon how quantum states are resolved. However, Walker notes that even gross mechanical processes, such as tumbling dice, involve minute quantum effects in individual atoms at each bounce. Slight changes in these events produce divergent effects on the dice, much as rain falling at points a few feet apart on a mountain ridge may run to different oceans. By Walker's theory, such divergence from microscopic effects is essential to explain macro-PK.

On the plausible assumption that some neural processes in the brain involve quantum indeterminacy, the theory can account for ESP as well as PK. In this case, the brain – or rather the mental process of formulating a guess of an ESP target – becomes the REG that is manipulated by the subject's will to score. Since quantum relations are nonlocal in space or time, precognition and long-distance ESP follow.

Schmidt's mathematical model amounts to precisely defining components and relations in psi experiments that qualitatively have been generally recognized. The experimenter, for example, is represented as a computer and REG. For the subject, Schmidt postulates a psi source, which is defined as an entity that changes the probability ratio of hits to misses (p/q) of the normal REG output by a factor that defines the strength of the psi source. Two or more psi sources act as additional factors, implying that two effective subjects trying for the same target should do better than one.

Though he does not get into mechanisms, Schmidt assumes quantum indeterminacy as the basis of psi. His model therefore requires indeterminate (pure chance) situations and feedback of results to the psi source. It is adaptable to both PK and ESP functions.

3.2.2b Predictions and experimental tests

Walker and Schmidt agree in most of their theoretical predictions. Relevant experimental tests of these predictions have been discussed in chapters 8 and 10; they will be only mentioned here.

Both predict independence of space and time for psi effects and emphasize that ESP and PK are aspects of a unitary phenomenon. In addition to the accumulated evidence for precognition, Schmidt's and other experiments appear to demonstrate retro-PK, though not unambiguously. Schmidt's experiment in which the task alternated between PK and precognition adds directly to the evidence for the unitary nature of psi.

Both models predict that psi effects, as basically quantum phenomena, should be independent of the kind of target or the complexity of the REG or other associated apparatus, or of the subject's detailed understanding of it. Again, Schmidt's experiment that compared scores on a simple and complex REG reinforces an accumulation of less explicit evidence of the goal-oriented character of psi.

Walker predicts that, under uniform conditions, the scoring rate will be proportional to the square root of the time the subject spends concentrating on each trial. But, since it is impractical to expect a subject's psychological condition to remain constant, the same effect can be had by conducting a retro-PK experiment in which the prerecorded REG output is presented to the subject repeatedly. Schmidt's model predicts that the scoring rate should be proportional to the number of such presentations. Schmidt's and other such experiments lend qualitative support to both his and Walker's predictions.

Walker's theory predicts a decline in scoring rate as the rate of presentation of trials (and feedback) increases, but Schmidt's is indifferent to the trial rate. Schmidt's experimental comparison of different trial rates showed a difference tending to support Walker's prediction; but a similar test (Pantas, 1971) with better allowance for psychological factors showed no significant difference.

Both theorists consider feedback of results to the subject or agent to be essential to psi performance. However, this crucial prediction is very difficult to test. 'Feedback' is an ambiguous idea. Schmidt requires feedback of the result of each trial, but Walker considers that feedback of only the score of a series is sufficient (though it would preclude such internal anomalies as decline effects). Further, no one can be sure who the effective subject is, or how many there may be. The predictions of additive psi effects by additional subjects further complicate the problem, implying that anyone who ever sees the results of a psi test becomes potentially a contributor to those results. This divergence problem* has been the subject of much inconclusive discussion (see below).

Walker has noted several examples of concordance between his theory and aspects of psi. Quantitatively, the most impressive of these is a mathematical tour-de-force by which he has reproduced with remarkable accuracy the relations Forwald found between placement scores and physical parameters of his cubes (see chapter 10, section 4.2.1b). There is reason to believe that Forwald's unique results reflected his expectations rather than physical dependencies; yet, if that is true, Walker's theoretical confirmation is indeed remarkable.

3.2.2c *Criticisms and evaluation of the observational theories*

The observational theories, particularly Walker's and Schmidt's, have been criticized on several grounds (e.g. Braude, 1979b; Chari, 1975; Houtkooper, 1983; Millar, 1978). Houtkooper and Millar were concerned particularly with the divergence problem, attempting both to analyse the effects of many future observers on an experimental result and to devise modifications of theory that would avoid or moderate such effects. Houtkooper predicted that the divergence effect would tend to produce abnormally large variances in experimental results. Schmidt (1978) argued that chance factors in the selection of observers of an experiment afford opportunity for PK influence that would avoid getting a neutral group as to psi ability. However, this argument does not appear to take account of later observers of the results. Walker (1982), responding to several criticisms, noted that Houtkooper's prediction of widely varying experimental results is 'exactly what we observe.'

Braude severely criticized the concept of 'backward causation' implied by the crucial role of feedback in the theories, arguing correctly that it logically implies a paradox, an event determined by an observation of the event after it has occurred. Walker replied that quantum theory implies correlation of events rather than classical causal relations, noting that recent physical experiments have confirmed this principle (Rohrlich, 1983).

Braude also attacked the entire concept of goal-oriented psi, offering some cogent arguments for the more traditional analogy to sensory and motor functions. However, he appears to assume mind as distinct from brain functions, with implied independence of space-time and fantastic information-processing capacity.

It is evident that Walker's and similar theories of psi meet their share of difficulties. Large-scale PK, particularly on static objects, is troublesome to the theorists. Walker requires conscious, willed attention to the psi goal; but both experiments and spontaneous cases indicate that such concentration is not essential to success and may be detrimental.

The observational theories are tentative gropings, not answers. They may prove to be a dead end. At best, they will require much further revision and development. Yet, despite their tentative character and obvious defects, these theories are a highly significant development in psi research. They mark a fundamental change of orientation, from hypotheses based on sensorimotor analogies to concepts that derive from the theoretical frontier of physics. Nor are they empty speculations. They make predictions, some of them quantitative, that accord with the principal experimental findings and suggest further empirical tests. They have inspired much of the process-oriented psi research of the past decade. Whatever the outcome, they signify a turning point in thought that may mitigate the concept of psi as a nonphysical agency.

Summary of terms

falsify
variable
independent variable
dependent variable
quanta
resonance
observational theories
hidden variable
divergence problem

Thought questions

(1) Which of the following items can be measured or operationally defined? (a) pitch of a musical tone; (b) intensity of pain; (c) scent of a flower; (d) brightness (or dimness) of light at a seance.

(2) Is the belief in spirit communication a testable hypothesis? Can you suggest any way to distinguish between a spirit's influence and ESP/PK by living persons?

(3) Keeping in mind the findings from psi experiments, what specific discrepancies do you find between the principal characteristics of psi effects and the implications of electromagnetic-wave ('radio') theories of psi? What discrepancies do you see between psi findings and the implications of Walker's theory?

(4) In what respects do Walker's observational theory and Schmidt's psi-source model agree in their predictions? In which do they differ? Can you suggest experimental designs to decide between them?

(5) What essential concept is common to all of the observational theories of psi? How do these theories, as a class, differ from other physical theories of psi?

Part III
Implications: scientific, philosophical and social

Chapter 12
Psi and science

Hoyt L. Edge (section 1 to 4)
Robert L. Morris (section 5)

1 Introduction

In 1982, parapsychology celebrated an important centennial event in its history as a science. The Society for Psychical Research was founded in 1882 (see chapter 2) for the purpose of investigating paranormal phenomena in a scientific way. As has been discussed in other chapters, parapsychology has always had a peculiar relationship with the rest of science. Its practitioners, who have been competent scientists (some of them have been leading scientists of their day, including Nobel Prize winners), have tried to use scientific approaches and methods in examining phenomena which seem by their nature to be excluded from the world view of normal science. In spite of parapsychologists' attempts to use scientific methods applied in a fairly rigorous way to very elusive phenomena, normal science has generally reacted with indifference, embarrassment, and even hostility. The acceptance of the Parapsychological Association as an Associate Member of the American Association for the Advancement of Science in December 1969 has not diminished this reaction.

This situation leads one to ask about the nature of science: what is science? What is the scientific method? What does objectivity mean? Do personal factors and prejudices play a role in science? Can parapsychology, studying the anomalous phenomena it does, receive an objective evaluation from traditional science? These are some of the questions we will be facing in this chapter.

Most researchers in the philosophy of science agree that our understanding of what science is and how it operates is changing in fundamental ways. This change is taking place for two reasons. The first is that the twentieth century has seen a revolution in physics which has altered some fundamental conceptions about the way the world works. The second reason is that we are paying more attention to the history of science and to how scientists actually practice their trade. What we are discovering is that science may not function in the way that we have thought it did for the last three centuries, and this perception is forcing us to come up with a better and more realistic version of what science is.

The traditional picture of science was developed in the seventeenth century at a time of the rise of modern science and the formation of the modern world in general, growing out of some very specific historical conditions in an attempt to answer some very specific questions. It served Western thought well for three centuries, but in the last thirty years we have begun to question the adequacy of this description of science, and it is too early for us to have achieved a new and consistent understanding of what science and culture should be like in such a world.

The first part of this chapter will focus on the traditional view of science, followed by another section in which this view is shown to be problematic. These two parts set the stage for what is the fundamental question of the chapter: is parapsychology a science, or better, in what ways can we say parapsychology is a science and in what ways is it not? This question obviously presumes that we understand what a science is, which is more difficult to define than may appear at first glance.

2 The classical view

Although dissatisfaction with the traditional Aristotelian description of the world had grown through the sixteenth century, the seventeenth was the century of genius which forged a new science. Unfortunately, we do not have time to consider the role in the development of the classical view of science played by Kepler, Bacon and Hobbes, all great seventeenth-century thinkers who owed a great deal to the Greek materialist, Democritus, in propounding their views of the nature of the world. All are important figures, but for our purposes we will focus on Galileo and Descartes as examples of the seventeenth-century movement.

2.1 The rise of science in Galileo and Descartes

Galileo is perhaps best known for his bringing empirical support to the Copernican heliocentric conception of the solar system. Galileo recognized that a Dutch toy which was a tube into which lenses had been inserted could be developed and used as a telescope. With the telescope, he was able to discover moons of Jupiter as well as other bodies which supported the Copernican view. While Galileo should be praised for his foresightedness in seeing the potential uses of the telescope, he was also influential in encouraging experimentation. Aristotelian science encouraged observation, but it did not encourage experimentation. Greek society was a stratified one in which the slaves did manual labor and worked with all machines. It was below the dignity of the Greek intellectual, in general, to set up experimental equipment and manipulate it to perform experiments, but Galileo was committed to experimentation as is seen in his experiments with balls rolling down an inclined plane. In addition, Galileo stressed quantification. An example of this can be seen in the story told about his discovery of the principle of the pendulum. At a medical school in Pisa, he noticed in the cathedral that after a lamp, which had been drawn to one side in order to light it, was released, it swung in decreasing arcs until it reached the point perpendicular to the floor. Using his pulse as a measuring device, he observed that although the arcs decreased, the amount of time it took to traverse a swing in the arc stayed constant, and thus he saw that the arc could be used as a way to keep time (which led to the development of the pendulum clock). The power of measurement and the ability to apply the results are hallmarks of science.

Although Descartes is known as the Father of Modern Philosophy, it must not be forgotten that there was no distinction between the philosopher and the scientist in the seventeenth century. His contributions to mathematics and to physics were influential. In some cases, it may be that it was Descartes's scientific interests that led him to develop the particular philosophy he did. As noted earlier, scientists in the sixteenth and seventeenth centuries were impressed with the materialism of Democritus, including Galileo, who asserted that the universe was nothing but atoms in motion, but such a view was difficult to reconcile with the medieval religious world view that predominated. Galileo's difficulties with the Church were well known in the seventeenth century, and the fact that he was forced to recant his views was not lost on Descartes. At this time, the areas of the religious and the moral were not in question; they were taken to be real and obvious. The practical problem, therefore (although it may not have been approached consciously), was how to carve out a space in which science could be independent of the influences of the religious and the moral. To solve this dilemma, Descartes proposed a bifurcation of the world, a division between mind and body. The area of the mind would be concerned with the religious, the moral, the personal, the subjective, and with free decisions. The material world would be concerned with the definition of the world developed by Democritus and popular in the seventeenth century. The division between these two worlds was absolute so that science, which could deal with the world as a machine, as a group of atoms in space whose motion was determined by prior motions, would be absolute in its own sphere and without the intrusion of religion. In this regard, the body was like any other material object, except that the mind had a special relationship to the body. The religious advantages of this separation were numerous, such as the ability of the mind to be immortal. The advantage to science was obvious in that it opened the way for science to be free of religious control as well as to specify what scientists should be concerned with, since 'matter' was given a very special definition.

2.2 Assumptions of seventeenth-century science

With the advantage of hindsight, it is possible to pinpoint a number of assumptions and explicit assertions that the new science was making about the world. This approach to nature did not spring full blown in the seventeenth century, having had precursors prior to the seventeenth century. However, it was the seventeenth century that gave impetus to this new world view which has been dominant until this century, and it is not possible to evaluate contemporary science without understanding its historical roots. We shall examine several of the more important points below.

2.2.1 The subject/object dichotomy

With the division of the world into mind and matter came the division between the subject and the object, which has developed into a division between the subjective and the objective. According to Descartes, the mind is an entity which thinks and it is actually the person. It is that which reasons and experiences, but matter is in no way conscious. The body is merely an automaton and the universe as a whole can be conceived as one great machine describable by a set of basic laws.

2.2.2 The primary/secondary distinction

The subject/object distinction gave rise to a second distinction. Matter is essentially atoms in motion whose dimensions, weight and velocity are measurable. What this implies is that there are some attributes of matter which are indigenous and essential to it – the primary qualities of solidity, extension, figure, motion, rest and number. On the other hand, there are secondary qualities which do not describe the inherent nature of the material world. For example, if two people stick their hands into a bucket of water, one having come from outside where it is freezing cold and the other having come from running laps in the gym, each experiences the same water as feeling different – the person having run laps will experience it as cool while the person coming from the outside will experience it as being warm. The secondary qualities (colors, sounds, tastes, smells) are more in the mind than in the material objects, and in that sense they cannot be the direct object of scientific investigation. It is only when science is able to roughly correlate secondary qualities with primary qualities which are quantifiable that they can become scientific. It is only when we substitute felt warmth with temperature that we have a term which science can successfully use. The primary/secondary distinction, therefore, comes out of the subject/object distinction in that it is only the primary qualities which are objective in an unqualified way and only they which can be successfully used, at least in the physical sciences.

2.2.3 Observation as mirroring

Another great seventeenth-century figure is John Locke, the philosopher who was first to clearly state the fundamentals of the empiricist epistemology. Empiricism is a view which says that all knowledge ultimately derives from sense experience, and as a result, it forms the epistemological basis of science, whose procedure is observation and experimentation. As opposed to Descartes, who worried about the problem of misperception, Locke virtually ignored the problem and asserted that perception was a kind of mirroring of the world. The mind is a blank tablet, a *tabula rasa**, and the tablet is written on by perception. The centrality of adequate perception is obvious, because if all knowledge is gained through sense perception, and if sense perception is not adequate to the task, it does not appear as if we could have science or knowledge in general. Today, perhaps we would want to use the analogy of the camera and say that perception is like taking a picture of what is in front of the eyes. The eyes are the lenses and the film is the mind, so what goes on film is an adequate representation of what is in the world (although we know that the camera does not reproduce true color or perspective). Furthermore, since material objects can be photographed by any number of cameras, they are public and open to inspection by anyone. As opposed to ideas, which are in the mind and are private to each person, material objects are public and open to the view of any observer. Indeed, a distinguishing feature of science as opposed to religion is that the latter is an internal affair, something that is concerned with subjective states and not directly observable. Science, on the other hand, is concerned precisely with those objects which can be viewed by anyone at any time, and since our perceptual apparatus is quite adequate to this process, any of us, so long as we are careful, can get a correct view of the material world.

2.2.4 Absolute deterministic laws

As this perception of the material world grew and science was more successful (particularly Newtonian mechanics in the eighteenth century), more and more faith was placed in the notion that matter was governed by a series of relatively simple deterministic laws which were absolute in that they applied to all material objects at all times. Every material object was causally determined by the preceding state of affairs, and every movement of a material object could be adequately described by laws. With the great strides made by Newtonian mechanics, so successful were the sciences that the physicist LaPlace said he could predict the state of the material world at any time in the future so long as he had the present complete description of the material world and knew the laws that governed the movement of matter. The world was a vast machine, totally predictable, totally determined, and totally material. The world was nothing but atoms in motion, the laws describing their movement being completely adequate for science, and any scientist could apply these laws to the world, as it was open to the observation of everyone.

2.2.5 Replication

Under this view of science, it is obvious not only why replication became important but why it was viewed as such a straightforward affair. So long as observation is straightforward and unproblematic, and so long as matter is describable by simple laws, there is no difficulty in describing an experimental procedure for anyone to replicate and for them simply to observe the process of nature before their eyes. Just as a camera is thought to picture only what is in front of it without affecting it, so the eye merely perceives what is in front of it and does not change it so that any individual, being in the right location, can perceive the appropriate public object. Simple laws and simple observation make replication simple and straightforward.

2.2.6 Atomism

Most of the important figures in the seventeenth century were quite explicit in stating that reality is best described in terms of material atoms in motion within space and time, both of which are absolute in Newtonian mechanics. But it was not just the material world that was atomistic but the whole epistemology of the time. Atomism* is the view that each atom (or unit) is separate and independent in itself, with no internal relationship to other atoms. The function of scientific laws is to describe how and under what circumstances the atoms will relate to each other, thus the basic procedure for science is to try to understand the basic atoms as well as one can, which means that one should first understand the basic building blocks of the world. The watchword in this kind of science becomes 'divide and conquer:' one should focus on the smallest bits of nature, the atoms, understand them first and then understand how they combine with each other. The world is to be understood as having some basic building blocks and one needs to understand them and their capacities before one can understand how they can fit together.

It was mentioned earlier that the epistemology of such a science was also atomistic. What was meant by that is that all knowledge is conceived around the principle of basic building blocks and in order to understand anything, one must understand the basic blocks. Implicit in the notion of building blocks is the notion that all knowledge can ultimately be reduced to the basic laws that describe the interrelationships among these building blocks. Reductionism is nothing but the urge to simplify, to describe every action in the world. Just as the world was viewed as ultimately simple by these seventeenth-century thinkers (as being composed of several basic atoms), so our system of laws of nature will be equally as simple, and we will be able to reduce all laws to a few simple and basic ones.

2.2.7 Recent views of science

Two points can be made about the relationship between parapsychology and this traditional view. The first is that parapsychology arose as a discipline in the nineteenth century in the context of this view of science. The founders of the Society for Psychical Research were individuals schooled in this version of empiricism, but they did not like the world view that seemed to develop from this science. Although it was taken for granted in the seventeenth century that the world of the subject, the religious and moral world, was true, by the end of the nineteenth century, with the successes of modern science, the faith in the truth of the religious and the moral began to fade. It did not take long to see that it was difficult to assert both an all-encompassing deterministic world, totally explicable in terms of mechanical laws, and at the same time assert that there was a free will which was efficacious in the material world. To put the point more directly, if the body is a machine, if it is totally self-sufficient, if there are laws that adequately explain every physical movement that it makes, where can the mind interfere with this complete system? Indeed, if it does, the system is *not* complete. Just as LaPlace retorted to Napoleon that he did not have need of the concept of God in his system, so one began to wonder whether or not one had need of the hypothesis of mind in science. Modern science germinated out of the need for the independence of science, and with the huge successes in science, its independence seemed assured. But the mind seemed to be lost, at best an epiphenomenon, an impotent by-product of physical processes which was in no way efficacious in the world.

It was this conclusion that the founders of the Society for Psychical Research, such as Myers and Sidgwick, could not accept, but being schooled in empiricism, they could not reject science. The alternative open to them was to use science to prove the efficacy of the mind. Although much knowledge had been gained by science, there remained a great deal about the world that we did not know, and it was hoped that parapsychology might bring the mind back into the realm of science. It was to restore the subject within the realm of the object (and thus to offer the possibility for survival after death) that parapsychologists in the nineteenth century devoted themselves to a plan of experimentation. It is questionable whether the main motivation of many parapsychologists today can be described in these terms, but parapsychology as a discipline was born as a reaction against this conception of science.

The second point is that many critics of parapsychology, perhaps knowing some of its history, criticize the field as if it were still in the nineteenth century with the motivations of the nineteenth century. Indeed, many of the critics of parapsychology seem to be staunchly defending the basic principles of this traditional view of science, and it is on the basis of faith in and commitment to this view of science that they reject parapsychology.

3 Problems with the Cartesian/Newtonian view

In the twentieth century, and particularly in the last thirty years, this traditional view of science has been questioned. Challenges essentially come from three fronts: from a more adequate view of perception, from a historical analysis of scientific development, and from the introduction of new ideas, particularly in physics. Let us see what some of these problems are.

3.1 The changing notion of perception

You will remember that the notion of observation used by traditional science was derived from seventeenth-century empiricism, particularly from the philosophy of John Locke. It was a view in which perception was thought to be analogous to the mind mirroring the world, or in more modern parlance, the mind taking a picture of physical reality. In this view, perception is simple, direct, and unmediated by any factors except the visual organ, which was assumed to be something like a mirror or a camera, i.e. an instrument which accurately represented what it was confronted with.

The view of science that one derives from this notion of perception is one in which there is an important distinction between theory and experience. What one does in experience is simply to perceive what is in the world, and then the imaginative element of science enters into the picture where one builds theories out of the raw experience, the sense data, but the two activities are absolutely separate in good science. The good observer is one who is unbiased, just as a camera is unbiased, and therefore simply mirrors what is in the world. The objectivity of science is thus guaranteed, and this view provides an ultimate foundation upon which objective scientific knowledge can be based. If there are questions about theory, if one wants to test a hypothesis, one simply turns to raw experience to perceive reality objectively.

Historically, this view of perception was already being questioned in the eighteenth century by the philosopher Immanuel Kant, who wanted

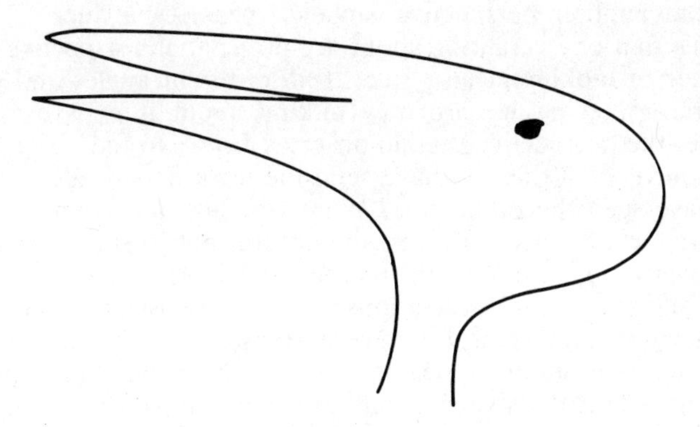

Figure 12.1: Gestalt switch of rabbit and duck

to defend Newtonian mechanics against the skepticism of David Hume, an empiricist who had drawn some skeptical conclusions from the empiricist philosophy. Hume argued that if one was a consistent empiricist who said that one gains knowledge only through experience and one knows only what has been experienced, then obviously one cannot know what will happen in the future, since that has not been experienced. Without discussing this problem (the problem of induction, as it is called), let us simply note that the optimism surrounding the introduction of Newtonian mechanics was undercut by this philosophy.

Kant argued that the mind should be viewed not as a blank tablet, nor as a mirror, nor as a camera. Perception was not a simple passive process whereby the eyes and the mind recorded what was seen, but perception should be viewed as an active process wherein the mind contributed as much as it received. Far from the mind being a blank tablet, it was something that had 'categories,' as Kant called them, or something like filters through which we perceive. For instance, if we wore rose-colored glasses, the world would invariably appear rosy; and in like manner, if the mind has structures through which we experience the world, we can know what the world will invariably be like since the structures determine our perception. Two of these 'filters' that Kant discussed were space and time, thought to be absolute constructs of the world as we know it, just as Newton asserted that space and time were absolute. The important point here is Kant's suggestion that perception is not purely passive, but it is active and that we bring something to experience. This revolutionary Kantian notion influenced generations of thinkers to begin to accept that mind may not be passive as the empiricists described it but may be a fundamental contributor to experience.

More recent discussions of this problem have referred to the gestalt switch*. Both R. Hanson (1965) and Thomas S. Kuhn (1962) made use of this notion in their influential books. The gestalt switch describes a sudden change in our perceptual experience as we are viewing a particular object. The most popular switch is the example shown in Figure 12.1. Viewed from one perspective, an observer sees a rabbit;

viewed from another perspective, an observer sees a duck. But the perspectives that one is talking about are not spatial perspectives. It is not a matter of looking at an object from different angles and seeing different things. What we are now talking about is a psychological perspective, the perspective that an observer brings to the observation. Some of you reading this will have seen the duck first, while others of you will have seen the rabbit first. What you saw first is not simply a matter of raw experience, of mirroring nature, but to some extent is a result of what you have brought to the experience, what your background is, and what your expectations are. The discussion of the gestalt switch has been important for several reasons in the literature of contemporary philosophy of science, but at this time, the important point is simply that the switch seems to show that perception is more than simple mirroring of nature.

Let us try a little experiment. The first thing that you should do is, without reading it, place your hand or a piece of paper on the indented sentence you find a few lines down. When you reach the end of these instructions, please read the sentence over quickly one time through. You may find the sentence to be a bit strange, but you will not be asked to memorize or repeat it, so now simply read the sentence over quickly and place your hand or a piece of paper back over the sentence.

> FINISHED FILES ARE THE RESULT OF YEARS OF SCIENTIFIC STUDY COMBINED WITH THE EXPERIENCE OF MANY YEARS.

To complete this experiment, you will be asked shortly to go back and read the sentence over again. This time, please count all of the occurrences of the letter 'F,' reading the sentence about as quickly as you read it the first time. Please do not ponder each letter but perform this task in a matter of three or four seconds. Now please go back and read the sentence and count the number of 'Fs.' How many did you count? Two? Three? Four? or more? Actually, there are six 'Fs,' but you may not have counted all of them. The reason is that most of us have learned to read phonetically, and the 'F' in the word 'of' sounds like a 'V' rather than an 'F.' We have a tendency to skip over those uses because they do not fulfill our expectations. What this demonstration shows is that we bring to our perceptual experience beliefs, expectations, and, in general, a whole set of background knowledge, which affect what we perceive. Perception is not a simple, unmediated, raw experience, but perception is mediated by what we bring to the experience.

What this means for science is that scientific perception, in the words of Hanson, is 'theory-laden.' No scientist comes to an experiment or an observation with a blank tablet, but the scientist comes with a set of expectations about how the world works, which has been developed in personal experience as well as more formal training. A scientist never merely observes but has goals in mind as well as background knowledge that affect the perception. What the scientist brings to the experiment not only influences what is perceived, but it also dictates what is worth observing, what is worth investigating, and what areas are worth pursuing. All of this background knowledge – the assumptions of the science, the important experiments within the discipline, the 'folklore' of experimental investigation that is gained working as an apprentice in graduate school – form what Thomas Kuhn first called a 'paradigm' and later a 'disciplinary matrix*.' Any scientist within a discipline approaches the experimental work with a disciplinary matrix, which affects to some degree what is perceived. The notion of the disciplinary matrix leads us to the second fundamental reason for questioning the traditional view of modern science, a historical analysis of how science has actually developed.

3.2 Radical discontinuity in the history of science

The traditional approach of modern science has viewed the development of science as a linear process, since science was perceived as achieving a better and more accurate set of observations about the world. Even when there was theory change, observations were neutral and one simply had to go back to observe things better and more closely to be convinced that one theory was superior to another. If observation is not theory-laden, to test one theory against another was a relatively simple process of going back to nature and observing how it behaved. Since perception was neutral, all the relevant factors could be perceived by an observer, just as a good mirror reflects all that is within its field. The notion that science works from disciplinary matrices, from structured world views, disrupted this version of the progress of science because observation was mediated by the assumptions which defined what one should observe, what problems were important, and where one should observe. When one views historical cases, one sees that scientific observation is not neutral and scientists are not machines.

Thomas Kuhn distinguishes two kinds of science. One is normal science in which the scientific community is unified around a disciplinary matrix (although the assumptions involved in the matrix may not be held consciously) and the job of the scientist is to solve problems, often very difficult and meaningful ones, within its framework. The other kind of science takes place at unique periods in the history of science, at times of 'scientific revolution*,' when one matrix is challenging another one or when one is being exchanged for another. At these times, changes may be so radical that what is accepted as interesting and important within one matrix is not viewed as interesting or important within another. Indeed, the program of research may differ so dramatically that whole lines of investigation which are viewed as central in one framework are viewed as unimportant in another. A particularly important point is that what may be taken as a problem to be solved within one matrix, as a fact to be dealt with, may be viewed by scientists in another one as proof that the first matrix is inadequate. At any time in science, there are facts that cannot be explained and observations which do not fit in fully with what is known. Proponents of the existing matrix have a faith that these facts can be explained by further research within the matrix while others may hold the anomalies to be so fundamental and so radical that they believe that only a change in the matrix ultimately can explain the facts.

A dramatic example of this difficulty occurred in the early nineteenth century when astronomers recognized that the orbit of Uranus, when computed on Newtonian principles, did not fit the observations. However, a reason for this discrepancy might be that another planet, unknown at the time, could be exerting a gravitational force on Uranus and causing it to deviate from its expected orbit in the same way that observation showed it in fact to be deviating. Based on this hypothesis, astronomers predicted the size of the unknown planet and its location and later observation in fact confirmed that this planet, Neptune, existed. Needless to say, this was a dramatic confirmation of Newtonian principles.

However, an exactly analogous situation occurred with Mercury in which it was noticed that there was a disparity between the theoretical orbit of Mercury and its actual observed orbit. Once again, astronomers took this as a puzzle case to be solved within the Newtonian framework, predicting another planet to be discovered. In this case, the faith that the problem could be solved within Newtonian mechanics was ill-founded, as it was with the introduction of the mathematics within the general theory of relativity that an accurate computation of Mercury's orbit could be made. There was nothing indigenous to the problem that could characterize the situation as a puzzle case or as a legitimate anomaly, unable to be solved within the framework. Only later research gave us the answer – in one case, faith was well-founded; in the other, it was not.

What Kuhn is trying to argue for and what these examples show is that science does not work by simple rules. There is no simple algorithm, there is no simple set of criteria by which we can decide whether or not a discrepancy is a puzzle case or an anomaly. Likewise, there is no algorithm or simple set of rules for deciding between competing world views.

Further, there is a problem in terminology between competing matrices. Key terms may be used in both matrices, but because the terms are partially defined in terms of the different theories within the matrices, they may have fundamentally different meanings. When one talks about motion as an Aristotelian, one is not using the word in the same way that Newton used it, and a Newtonian discussing 'matter' has an entirely different concept than we in the twentieth century after the Einsteinian revolution. This is why it is difficult to describe the progress of science as being unilinear, since it is so difficult to compare Newtonian science with Einsteinian science. While it seems obvious that we can do more things with Einsteinian science and that we can solve more problems that we feel are important, it is difficult to compare the two since, in fundamental ways, they are working on different problems and have different and sometimes conflicting definitions of key terms. Because a disciplinary matrix designates which problems are to be solved and how key terms are defined, and any scientist works out of this structured world view, science is not entirely neutral nor is observation. Both are matrix based, which means that many value judgments within science can be made only from that perspective.

3.3 The new physics

One of the reasons that we have been interested in revolutions in the history of science is that we have experienced such an upheaval in our own century. Einstein's relativity theory revolutionized our thinking about the macro-world, and quantum theory forced us to reconceptualize our understanding of the micro-world. But it is not simply the fact that we have experienced a revolution that has caused us to question the traditional explanations of science, but also in how science has described the world in relativity theory and quantum theory. If nature is not as we have taken it to be in Newtonian mechanics, if the world does not work according to the assumptions of that view, and if we have to devise a new science to describe the world, then it should come as no surprise that such a science will be a different kind of science from Newtonian science. Just as there were certain epistemological assumptions in the air during the Newtonian revolution, assumptions which contradicted the earlier Aristotelian notions and which supported Newtonian thought, so our view of the nature of knowledge and of science may have to accommodate the new physics.

3.3.1 Atomism questioned

The traditional view of science had its intellectual precursor in the thought of the atomist, Democritus, who felt that all reality could be reduced to atoms in motion. These atoms formed the basic building blocks out of which all things were made and if one explained the association of these atoms, one could explain all things in nature. This atomism has been questioned on several fronts in contemporary thought.

The old idea of a solid, indestructible atom has been rejected in the twentieth century with the advent of subatomic physics. Far from the atom being a solid bit of matter, atoms turned out to be vast reaches of empty space. An atom would have to be expanded to the size of the dome of St Peter's Cathedral in Rome for us to be able to see the nucleus with the naked eye, and even at that size, the nucleus would only be the size of a grain of salt. Even when physicists refer to elementary 'particles' they do not mean a solid, indestructible building block. Atoms are fields of energy, with different charges, and it is basically the relationship of these energies that define the atom. Einstein wrote:

> Before Clerk Maxwell, people conceived of physical reality – insofar as it is supposed to represent events in nature – as material points, whose changes consist exclusively of motions . . . after Maxwell,

> they conceived physical reality as represented by continuous fields, not mechanically explicable. . . . This change in the conception of reality is the most profound and fruitful one that has come to physics since Newton. (Margenau, 1959, p. 253)

In another place, Einstein (1959) writes, 'It therefore appears unavoidable that physical reality must be described in terms of continuous functions in space. The material point, therefore, can hardly be conceived any more as the basic concept of the theory' (p. 61). The movement from talk about atoms as basic building blocks to 'forces,' 'fields,' and 'continuous functions' is an important move, because it rejects traditional atomism.

With the rejection of atomism comes the concomitant rejection of reductionism. The classical notion of reductionism by which was meant the attempt to reduce in a deductive fashion all laws to a few basic ones is simply a failure. Galileo's laws cannot be deduced from Newtonian principles nor can Newtonian principles be deduced from relativity theory. That there are points of intersection cannot be denied, but classical mechanical laws and relativity theory do not give the same mathematical results for a moving body. The mathematics of the two systems yield different results, although in most cases the difference is insignificant.

> The physicist who uses classical mechanics for dealing with a low velocity situation is not making use of a special or limiting case of relativistic physics, but is taking advantage of a formal analogy in order to simplify computations. Let us remember that the use of Newtonian mechanics does not constitute simplification, for it is not literally true that the equations of relativity theory 'reduce' to those of classical mechanics for the case of a slowly moving body. The reduction is only complete in the case in which the velocity of the body in question is zero. For dynamical problems Newtonian and relativistic mechanics never gave the same results. The justification for using Newtonian mechanics in lieu of relativity is that for a certain range of cases and a permissible margin of error, the difference between the quantitative results supplied by the two theories can be ignored so that we might as well use the simpler equation of classical mechanics. (H. I. Brown, 1977, p. 125)

3.3.2 The rejection of absolutes

The impetus for seventeenth-century philosophy and science was the desire for absolute knowledge. Rather than faith being the road to absolute knowledge, it was felt that either reason (Descartes) or experience (Locke and Galileo) could provide absolute knowledge. We find the same desire for absoluteness in eighteenth-century Enlightenment and in Newtonian principles. Not only was Newtonian science thought to provide absolute knowledge, but it described things in absolute terms. A fundamental assertion of Newtonian mechanics was the absolute nature of space and time, which existed independently of any object or observer and were the containers and measurers of all events, providing an absolute yardstick by which events could be described.

Relativity theory, of course, has questioned the absoluteness of time and space. For instance, time is related to speed so that the closer an object approaches the speed of light, the more clocks and other rate processes slow down. Also, space and time are no longer containers by which an outside observer can uniquely describe an event, as the space-time continuum is inextricably linked to the observer.

Nor can we say that causation is an absolute, as it was in the Newtonian world view. LaPlace had argued that he could describe the movement of any object in space and be able to fix with precision its exact location any time in the future, giving the requisite description of the world. In subatomic physics, we know that such prediction is impossible. According to quantum theory, a position of an electron can only be given with probability. That is, we cannot give a unique coordinate of an electron (without increasing uncertainty in other coordinates) but only that there is such and such a probability that the electron will be found at that point at a specifiable time. The quantum physicist can still talk of causation, but the result is no longer an event describable in absolute terms but only one describable in probabilistic terms. In general, the use of statistics in science has grown, and most analyses in the social sciences are statistical. Parapsychology is similar to many other sciences in its heavy reliance on statistics, and it may be that psi phenomena may only be 'caught' statistically.

3.3.3 The reintroduction of consciousness

One of the hallmarks of Newtonian mechanics was the absolute separation between matter and mind. It was with the rejection of Aristotelian teleology that Galileo and Newton could assert their mechanism. Mind and matter were absolutely two realms of existence, and the world of the material was the world of the scientist. However, several contemporary physicists are suggesting that the notion of consciousness must be brought back into physics. The Nobel Prize-winning physicist Eugene Wigner (1967) suggested that it was consciousness which might be the 'hidden variable' proposed by Einstein in 1935. The Princeton physicist John Wheeler (Misner *et al.*, 1973) has suggested that we substitute the term 'participator' for the traditional term 'observer,' although he has cautioned that one can read too much into the term. David Bohm (1980), a collaborator of Einstein, has urged yet another theory in which consciousness has been introduced as a fundamental principle in nature. The main point here is not the detail of the various theories, and it is important to realize that the individual theories are products of speculation, but all imply that the absolute separation between the domains of the physical and of the mental is questionable. How far consciousness may be reintroduced into the system is anyone's guess, as many physicists reject this move, but one thing seems clear. With the denial of the traditional form of atomism, matter is no longer conceived in the same way as in the seventeenth century. Twentieth-century physics portrays a different picture of the material from the view developed by Galileo and Newton, and science and philosophy have not yet worked out what the implications of this change will be.

4 Is parapsychology a science?

It may not be too difficult to give a good definition of biology or chemistry or even psychology, but it is very difficult to give a good definition of science. A formal way of approaching the question would be to say that science is performed by people who belong to organizations which are affiliates of the American Association for the Advancement of Science (AAAS), but one cannot accredit science as one accredits colleges and universities. The approach is much too formal and legalistic. The question of what makes a science cannot be decided by a majority vote at a meeting in December 1969.

Nor is science a collection of facts, a compilation of 'truths.' Such an approach ignores the historical perspective that we have developed in the previous section. What is accepted as true at one period of science may not be accepted as true in another period.

Nor can we say that science is simply observing. The ancient Babylonians, who kept incredibly precise records of daily observations, were able to make unusually accurate predictions about the movement of heavenly bodies (see Toulmin and Goodfield, 1961), and might be viewed as just as good observers of the heavens as contemporary astronomers, given the difference in equipment. Although their successes may have been the precursor of legitimate science, simple observation and prediction are not science.

Additionally, in keeping with our understanding of the historical character of science, we must leave room for 'prematurity' in science. Gunther S. Stent (1972) defines prematurity in the following way: 'A discovery is premature if its implications cannot be connected by a series of simple logical steps to canonical, or generally accepted, knowledge' (p. 84). He gives the example of Oswald Avery's showing that DNA was genetic material, which was ignored by biologists for almost a decade. Likewise, after Alfred Wegener proposed the hypothesis of continental drift, the whole notion was viewed as rather crazy and not taken seriously for fifty years, until overwhelming evidence in favor of it accumulated. Simply because one body of knowledge conflicts with another which is generally accepted by science does not mean that the anomalous knowledge lacks scientific status. Premature science is simply that; it is a science that is premature. If science were defined solely in terms of accepted scientific knowledge, then Copernicus would not have been doing science before Kepler and Galileo gave legitimate empirical support for the Copernican theories. Therefore, science cannot be defined in terms of what is accepted by contemporary scientists, and if parapsychology conflicts with that body of knowledge, that does not mean in itself that parapsychology is less of a science.

There have been several attempts to solve this problem of demarcation, the problem of separating science from nonscience. Perhaps the best known of these attempts is the one by Karl Popper (1963), who argued that the criterion of demarcation was falsifiability, the ability to be put to empirical test.

In spite of the fact that the idea of falsifiability contains the truth that any scientific theory must be willing to specify the conditions under which it can be tested and it is a useful practical criterion for distinguishing between good and bad theories, falsifiability as a straightforward demarcation of science from nonscience is unacceptable. Not only is the principle of falsifiability itself unfalsifiable, but 'absolute falsification in science is a myth' (Rothbart, 1982, p. 98). Even if one specifies the conditions in which a theory can be tested and the experiment is performed and results are not arrived at which support the theory, all sorts of reasons can be given for that failure. We simply have to look at the history of science and see that predictions of Copernicus and Galileo and Newton were initially disconfirmed in some fundamental ways, but work continued on their theories and they were finally accepted.

There does not seem to be any simple way to define what science is and to demarcate it from nonscience. It seems obvious that science engages in testing, and it is a complex of theory and sensory data, but how to specify that complex is not clear. However, although there is no easy definition and although there are no hard and fast criteria by which we can easily judge whether a discipline is scientific, there do seem to be benchmarks of good science. Let us examine a number of these characteristics, not thinking of them in terms of absolute criteria by which we can easily divide work into either science or nonscience, but as benchmarks which, taken as a whole, can give indications of how scientific a discipline is.

4.1 Objectivity

One of the traditional hallmarks of science has been its objectivity, the notion that science has an objective procedure and deals with objective events in nature, open to scrutiny by any competent observer. This objectivity has been juxtaposed to religious faith which is not experimentally verifiable, and to pseudosciences which assert that knowledge is open only to those initiated into their craft. Unfortunately, the traditional notion of objectivity as it developed historically is now seen to be impossible in principle and not even an ideal of science. The idea of objectivity in science grew out of the traditional empiricist view of perception, in which the scientist was thought to be simply a mirror of nature or a camera photographing quite neutrally what lay in front of it. We have already seen that this idea of perception is inadequate and needs to be rejected. The scientist is no mere mirror and perception is not a process of photography; the scientist always works out of a world view and what he sees is to some degree dependent on that matrix. Science is not merely a process of observation and collecting data but a process of theory formation in which certain kinds of observations are taken to be important and others taken to be unimportant, so the process of science is not objective in the traditional sense because perception is theory-laden and the activities of the scientist are matrix-based.

Nevertheless, the thrust of the traditional notion of objectivity is important for science. Science is not being done when just any theory can be accepted and when knowledge is restricted to a select few. The notion of a disciplinary matrix or scientific world view does not undercut all notions of objectivity but it transforms the notion into one of inter-subjectivity*. There must be some agreement among the practitioners of the discipline as to what is important and what the data in the discipline is and how to test it. The practitioners in the discipline may be wrong in the sense that later science may accept a different and perhaps contradictory theory, but scientists are objective when they specify what they are studying and how they study it and offer the opportunity for others with the relevant background to participate in the study. In spite of complications introduced by the experimenter effect (chapters 8 and 10), parapsychology seems to meet these criteria.

4.2 Accepted theory

A disciplinary matrix consists of core knowledge and a set of core theories accepted by the practitioners within that discipline. A community cannot be united merely around a set of facts, but they must agree on theory and procedure. The Babylonians accumulated an impressive series of facts, but the Babylonians did not engage in science because they did not take the step to try to explain by theory how these facts fit together. Some may question whether or not parapsychology fulfills this benchmark of being a science, whether or not parapsychology has an accepted set of theories and procedures. If the situation in parapsychology is exhaustively described by the title of C. W. K. Mundle's 1972 Presidential Address to the Society for Psychical Research, i.e. 'Strange Facts in Search of a Theory' (Mundle, 1976), it does not seem that parapsychology can be called a science.

We must realize when talking about a matrix that we are not talking about a set of theories or a set of rules which are necessarily explicit. In fact, much of what binds a group together in a common search is not what is accepted explicitly but the implicit agreement on what problems are important and some procedures for attacking the problems. Kuhn goes so far as to say that not only may the disciplinary matrix be unconscious, but there may not be full agreement on the interpretation of the matrix and perhaps no set of explicit rules which bind the practitioners. Furthermore, the idea of a disciplinary matrix does not exclude the possibility of having competing theories on some level. There may be much disagreement within the discipline, with different practitioners offering different theories and different ways of solving problems, but the existence of a matrix suggests that there is a context for discussions about disagreements and a *general* agreement on what problems are important, what problems have been solved, and general procedures for attacking problems.

At this point, it must be admitted that there is no generally accepted theory or set of theories in parapsychology which explains most of the phenomena and ties them all together. There are no basic sets of laws, such as Newton's Three Principles, which form the basis for deducing other laws, and thus no full-scale disciplinary matrix. Perhaps this may be seen most dramatically in noting that the basic phenomena in parapsychology are defined negatively; that is, ESP is defined as gaining information without the use of known sensory channels. How the information is achieved, what 'energies' may be involved, exactly what conditions govern information reception are not described in an overarching theory. The failure to provide a set of explicit laws or theories, however, does not exclude parapsychology from the realm of scientific practice. There exists a network of core knowledge, accepted procedure, and some accepted lower-level theories which guide parapsychologists in their research. The earlier chapters discussing methodology in ESP and PK, as well as findings in these areas, show that there are core procedures which are accepted, as well as a core of knowledge. Furthermore, parapsychology does not lack for theories; the problem may be that there are too many theories! In the absence of an overarching theory to explain all the data, individual theories have been proposed to account for aspects of the data, and legitimate competing theories exist in a number of areas. Psychological models such as PMIR are generally accepted as providing models that guide research and provide hypotheses. Several physical theories proposed over the last decade attempt mathematical formulation of the ESP and PK processes and these are being tested extensively, although they are still in competition with more traditional theories. In fact, one of the most interesting phenomena in parapsychology over the past decade is the fact that so much research has been theory-driven, particularly by the observational theories and the conformance behavior model. Research programs dedicated to theory testing have dominated most of the research.

Another indication that parapsychologists are working with an accepted core of knowledge and procedure is the level of criticism found within the discipline among its practitioners. Experimental work is not only submitted to refereed journals but is hotly debated at parapsychological conferences. The level of critical acumen brought by one parapsychologist to the work of another is quite high, perhaps because parapsychologists know that their work will be viewed critically by those outside the field. But the point is that the internal criticism has been effective in changing research programs and sometimes in abandoning them. One could list a series of research programs which have been pursued in the past but now are only rarely engaged in as they are no longer seen by practitioners as productive, such as Kirlian photography (see chapter 14, section 4.1).

The fact that there is so much agreement on what parapsychologists should study and what they should not study, or what is interesting and what is not interesting, on what is included in the field and what is excluded, shows that there is significant agreement on the definition of the field, however difficult it may be to formulate that definition explicitly. At the same time, as should be obvious from the chapters on methodology, the procedures of parapsychology conform to the same procedures in relevant areas of the social and natural sciences. While there may be criticism from within the field at times about whether or not traditional procedures are adequate to study paranormal phenomena which seem to contradict many traditional assumptions about the world, there is no serious movement in parapsychology relinquishing these procedures.

In conclusion, it seems fair to say that parapsychologists have a set of core knowledge and core procedures, as well as an implicit understanding of what problems are important and should be tackled, and in that sense, there is theoretical agreement among the practitioners of the discipline. What parapsychology does not have, on the other hand, is a full-blown disciplinary matrix under which one can subsume all of the phenomena, a fact which becomes particularly acute when we examine the question of controls.

4.3 Controls

To have a science, one must be able to specify the relevant factors to control in an experiment, but if there is no generally accepted theory about how parapsychology works, then how can parapsychologists know what factors may affect the experiment? Obviously, if parapsychology is defined in terms of using something other than normal physical mechanisms, then one must exclude those sensory mechanisms, but if no positive definition of psi is given, then it is theoretically possible for anything to affect the experiment. Without knowing how ESP works, we do not really know whether the color of walls in the lab is a relevant factor, or if cold climates are more psi-inhibitory than warmer ones.

Although this problem in theory appears to be an overwhelming one, in practice it is not so great. While the definition of parapsychology is a negative one, still a great number of controls are implied in it. There are a great number of diverse means of normal sensory communication, and to exclude all of these provides a quite rigorous set of experimental requirements. Furthermore, parapsychologists have made advances in noting what other factors affect experiments, depending partially on a massive amount of anecdotal data which provide indications of the conditions under which paranormal phenomena appear spontaneously. While the anecdotal evidence does not meet the standards of rigor that parapsychology has set for itself, it is useful in giving indications of which factors are important and which ones are not.

Both in normal science and in parapsychology, our understanding of controls depends upon the level of knowledge at a particular time, and since scientific knowledge is constantly growing, our knowledge of what factors must be controlled is constantly improving. A great deal of process-oriented research has been performed over the past decades to inform us of what controls seem to be important in psi production and which do not seem to be important (see chapters 8 and 10). While parapsychologists cannot produce an exhaustive list of important factors, they are not without knowledge of what controls are relevant.

4.4 Connections with other fields of science

A scientific discipline cannot fruitfully exist in isolation, just as a person cannot. It must be nurtured by work in other fields, and just as the network of findings within a particular field forms interconnections, so the whole scientific enterprise forms a web of interrelated knowledge. An individual discipline is not merely a community within itself, but is part of a larger scientific community which interacts for the mutual benefit of all members of the community. If there are few points of connection between a group of scientists and the larger scientific community, then that discipline does not participate fully in the life of science. While avoiding the simplistic avenue of reductionism which attempts to reduce all disciplines to a fundamental set of laws, it is still important for the various disciplines to display interconnections. Indeed, some of these are so important that new specializations are formed working them out, such as biochemistry. Parapsychology has a particular problem with this benchmark of science as it defines its discipline as studying one set of phenomena which do *not* fit into the rest of science. Almost by definition, parapsychology excludes itself from the rest of the scientific enterprise in a fundamental way.

To stop with this analysis, however, would present too harsh a view on several counts. In fact, there are a number of connections between parapsychology and normal science. Some of the consistencies that we have found in our process work have been of a psychological nature, and they seem to work in an analogous way to normal psychological processes. Certain principles of motivation have been adapted from normal psychology, as well as results in attention and altered states of consciousness. The psychological factors that are at play in parapsychology seem, in many cases, to be the same ones that are at work in normal psychology. Others have taken models from normal science and have applied these to parapsychology, as, for example, the application of information processing to psi (H. J. Irwin, 1979) and word association tests (Stanford, 1982). The attempts by Walker (1975) and Schmidt (1975) to integrate parapsychology mathematically into subatomic physics are another example of the attempt at rapprochement, but not enough consistent positive results have been achieved to say that these attempts have been totally successful. Thus, our subject matter remains anomalous, even if our research methods follow main-line practices.

Let us consider this conclusion in light of some traditional criticisms against the field. One criticism is that psi phenomena are so anomalous that they should be rejected on a priori grounds. This criticism has a tradition coming from the Scottish philosopher, David Hume, and is grounded in the traditional notion of objective science (which we have seen to be inadequate, although there is a grain of truth in the criticism). Hume (1748/1962) first used this argument to dispute the possibility of miracles, saying: 'A miracle is a violation of the laws of nature; and as a firm and unalterable experience has established these laws, the proof against a miracle, from the very nature of the fact, is as entire as any argument from experience can possibly be imagined' (p. 119). In like manner, ESP should be rejected because it conflicts with what normal science takes to be the laws of nature. The inadequacy of the Humean argument stems from its presuppositions. For Hume, an empiricist, the mind merely reflected nature as a mirror, and observation was pure and unmediated. It was a relatively straightforward thing, therefore, to understand the absolute laws of nature, laws which were valid for all times and for all people, because all one had to do basically was to observe and calculate the weight of evidence. Hume's simplistic view of observation in science, of course, has been rejected along with his notion of objective calculation, but the force of the argument lives on. Certainly one wants to maintain that there are degrees of evidence and that evidence for one position is greater than another, giving reasons for rejecting the weaker position, but the process is not as simplistic as Hume thought. There is the constant danger of thinking that one knows 'the laws of nature' and of rejecting contrary evidence as being unscientific. The extreme of such a view can lead to a position that is purely prejudicial. D. O. Hebb (1951) recognized this when he wrote:

> Personally, I do not accept ESP for a moment, because it does not make sense. My external criteria, both of physics and physiology, say that ESP is not a fact despite the behavioral evidence that has been reported. I cannot see what other basis my colleagues have for rejecting it; and if they are using my basis, they and I are allowing psychological evidence to be passed on by physical and physiological sensors. Rhine may still turn out to be right, improbable as I think that is, and my own rejection of his views is – in a literal sense – prejudice. (p. 45)

Scientists invariably work out of a disciplinary matrix and view evidence from a perspective, but it does not logically follow that evidence amassed which contradicts the given matrix is not science. Such a condition merely displays the exciting characteristic of science, that it is not an activity which can be carried on by computer. It is a human enterprise, and has all of the problems and all of the glory associated with it. To make judgments about the adequacy of evidence, to make judgments about the amount of weight that should be given one set of evidence as opposed to another, to make judgments on scientific law is not an algorithmic process. As Walter B. Weimer stated:

> All theories are born refuted: None will agree with all the facts that are potentially available. Granting that all theories are 'lies,' some are 'blacker' than others, and our problem is to pick, and to attempt to improve, the least black lie from the alternatives available. (Mahoney, 1976, p. 172)

Anomalies may have to amass greater supporting evidence than other, more accepted phenomena, but they must not be rejected a priori, nor should the investigation of them fail to be recognized as scientific.

Parapsychology does not have a full-scale disciplinary matrix to explain all of its phenomena, and there is no theory which neatly connects its data with data from normal science. These failures present difficulties for parapsychology. It means that those within the field and those outside the field should look at the data with a greater critical eye; it means that parapsychologists must be constantly searching for greater controls; it means that parapsychologists must be striving to find an overarching theory or set of theories and to find as much rapprochement with normal science as possible. But it does not mean that parapsychology fails to be scientific, although it may not be a full-blown normal science.

4.5 Repeatability

It has been said that one of the chief hallmarks of science is the possibility of replicating experiments. It is generally thought that replication should be considered in the strong sense such that any competent experimenter will be able to duplicate in some sense the results of another experimenter if those results are valid. With repeatability, researchers are able to avoid sloppiness in research, reject results due to chance, as well as eliminate fraud. In addition, the urge to replication shows the social nature of science. Science is not done by an individual cloistered in some laboratory, but it is a social process which necessitates social interaction and intersubjective confirmation. There is no question that the notion of replication is central for science, and it is a particularly poignant one for parapsychology in that the field has been criticized for a failure to produce reliably replicable results. Unfortunately, the question of whether parapsychology has repeatable experiments is not an easy and straightforward question, and one of the reasons is the difficulty in knowing exactly what replication is and assessing its actual worth in the practice of science.

4.5.1 Problems in normal science

Replication forms the cornerstone of a larger context in science in which experimental data are subject to the evaluation by others in the field. From a number of studies in the past decade, it appears as if this process may be breaking down, if it ever worked well in the past. At the very least, we are beginning to see that the process is fraught with a number of difficulties. William Broad and Nicholas Wade (1982) approach the question of peer evaluation from the point of view of fraud. Their concern is with what appears to be the increasing amount of fraud among academic scientists, many at the top research institutions in the nation. The Association of American Universities has become so concerned about the problem of fraud that they have released what they call 'Guidelines for Integrity of Research' (Peterson, 1983). Broad and Wade (1982) point out that the problem is not recent. When Isaac Newton failed to convince certain rivals of his theory, later editions of *Principia* fudged some data, and the statistician Ronald Fisher has shown that the results of the geneticist Gregor Mendel were too good to be credible. But the problem seems to be compounded in recent years because of the pressures of publication brought on by a tight job market and decreased funding.

The policies of academic journals contribute to the problem. Mahoney writes: 'In the social sciences – where replication is barely tolerated – one's topic or approach must be sufficiently original to merit a distinction between 'new' and prior research. Replications are generally disfavored unless (a) they extend or refine a previous idea, or (b) they challenge it by obtaining opposite or different results' (p.92). In fact, very little replication work takes place in the sciences, where one's reputation and research funding are made on the basis of original work. All of the reinforcements are set up to reward those who do not perform straightforward replications. As a result, it is surprising how few experimental results are replicated in any direct way. Instead, what we find are so-called 'partial replications with extension,' experiments which do not try to replicate the original experiment in fundamental ways but rely on the results of the original experiment to probe further questions. It would be fair to say that the typical experiment, particularly in the social sciences, conforms to this description. Thus, much of what we accept as knowledge in social science is based on unreplicated (and possibly unreplicable) research.

4.5.2 Difficulty in defining 'replication'

While the concept of repeating someone else's work seems intuitively clear enough, in actual practice it becomes difficult to proceed with an exact replication. Such a replication would depend upon the experimenter knowing exactly what the first experimenter did. This assumes that the article describing the experiment reported all of the factors that the experimenter thought were relevant to conducting the experiment and described them sufficiently. While this idea may not be easily achieved, the difficulty I want to discuss is one that is far more pernicious. Any experiment entails a quite large assumption of '*ceteris paribus*,' the assumption that 'all other factors are the same.' When one is dealing with human subjects, this ideal can never be achieved. Humans are incredibly complex organisms, all of them having previous histories, and one can only hope that one has controlled factors that may affect the experiment.

H. M. Collins (1978) found the same problems in physical science when several institutions were trying to build a special laser machine first constructed by another university. What he found was that when universities tried to build the TEA laser on the basis of written reports or discussions with third parties, they were totally unsuccessful in their attempts to build a device which produced results that the original laser produced. The more directly the scientists worked with the original builders and the greater their contact, the more successful the replicating scientists were in building their own. Replication is not a process of following a formula, but there seems to be a great deal of 'tacit knowledge' necessary for a legitimate replication, and it is virtually impossible to make explicit all relevant considerations. We may have been misled by traditional science to an overly simplistic notion of replication – not just anyone with good vision (like a mirror) is a competent observer, but the observer must have a good deal of tacit background knowledge.

4.5.3 Parapsychology and replication

The degree of repeatability that exists in parapsychology is controversial and difficult to assess objectively, but there are several examples that can be cited where the replication rates appear on the surface at least to exceed what would be expected by chance. The most thoroughly evaluated case is that of the ganzfeld experiments, which have been discussed in detail in chapter 7, section 3.3. Other examples are REG PK (Honorton, 1976) and the relation of ESP to such psychological variables as hypnosis (Schechter, 1984), extraversion (Sargent, 1981), and belief in ESP (Palmer, 1971). There is no experimental procedure which has been found to produce significant results for any researcher at any time, but that is not an abnormal situation in human subject research.

Further, it is not the case that only a handful of experimenters get positive results. The typical researcher in parapsychology is well acquainted with both success and failure, although it does appear that there are only a handful of experimenters who get *consistently* positive results. However, the failure of more researchers to get more consistently positive results is not the kind of failure that one shrugs off lightly. There must be some sort of order in science, and replication attempts to establish that order. Despite the ambiguities of replication conceptually, and despite the difficulty of applying the notion in practice, replication is fundamental to science.

For a further discussion of the replicability issue in parapsychology, see Shapin and Coly (1984).

4.6 Concluding thoughts

We have seen that there is no easy definition of science, nor is there a clear demarcation between science and nonscience. One cannot deny scientific status to parapsychology on a priori grounds merely because it asserts the existence of phenomena which are incompatible with more established branches of science. What is more important to the scientific enterprise is not the set of knowledge espoused at any particular period in history, but it is the approach to the problem at hand that distinguishes science from nonscience. We have discussed a number of benchmarks of science and have seen that parapsychology does not fully meet a couple of these benchmarks, but it does not fail any of them.

Our problem is similar to the one described by the philosopher Ludwig Wittgenstein, who showed that it was not a straightforward matter to give a definition for the term 'game.' It is not possible to list a set of criteria which are necessary and sufficient conditions for something being a game; but rather it seems possible to list a number of characteristics such that some games share some of these characteristics while other games may share other characteristics. But there is no algorithmic way to say whether or not an exercise is a game. All we know is that games must have some of the criteria which are listed but not all.

We can use the same approach here. In general, the methodology of parapsychology, the experimental procedures and the attempts to control factors deemed to be relevant (at least in the best research) seem to be very good. In short, parapsychologists act just like any other scientists in setting up and controlling experiments, as well as in using the best information and the most sophisticated procedures at their disposal. They test theories, criticize each other's work, pursue their research with vigor and in openness to the results. In all these ways, one cannot distinguish a parapsychologist from a researcher in virtually any other discipline in science. One can say that, behaviorally, the parapsychologist acts like any other scientist.

William James (1907/1968) makes the distinction between two kinds of people, the tender-minded and the tough-minded (I prefer to call these people hard-headed). Tough-minded people are those whose love for the truth is so great that they want to be sure that truth is all they have, and so they exclude all information, all procedures which do not meet very strict criteria by which they can know they have the truth. On the other hand, the tender-minded are individuals whose love for the truth is so great that they are willing to risk error in taking a chance to grasp the truth. One approach is conservative, the other is liberal. One approach is restrictive, the other approach is expansive. As James points out, whether or not a person is one type or the other is very much a product of his temperament.

One can be tough-minded or tender-minded in one's approach to science. If one is particularly conservative and tough-minded, if a discipline does not live up to the highest standards in meeting all the benchmarks of science, it will be called a 'pseudoscience' or no science at all. But such an approach is debilitating and naive, failing to see the historical and human aspects of the scientific enterprise. Science progresses in its most exciting and interesting phases when it is open to new data and to new approaches, when it accepts challenges from all quarters which are open and honest in their search for the truth. As James pointed out, there may be some kinds of knowledge accessible only by the more open approach. If science seeks knowledge, and the history of science acquaints us with a wide variety of findings and disciplines which had difficulty initially in providing complete proof, the lesson we learn is to be open-minded to all competent research, even if (perhaps especially if) it seems to produce anomalies.

5 Advocacy and counteradvocacy

The implications of parapsychology are potentially far-reaching, yet at present uncertain. In the face of such great uncertainty, people with strong beliefs about the nature of the universe can be strongly motivated to interpret the phenomena as consistent with their own belief systems. Psi is inserted into their conceptual framework and regarded as having no new implications. With new implications comes new knowledge and consequent damage to the belief system. Thus strong believers often tend to discourage truly open scientific inquiry for fear such inquiry will uncover something new. They will support limited research, aimed at validating their beliefs.

Those with strong beliefs tend to function as advocates and counter-advocates. Several groups can be distinctly defined: (1) those who believe in nonmechanistic factors (such as God, or a pervasive life-force) and who advocate psi research as supportive of that view; (2) those with similar views but who are counteradvocates of psi research because they feel it will open us up to negative powers or who are worried that psi research will secularize the sacred; (3) those who believe in a universe governed by exclusively mechanistic factors and who are advocates of psi research because they feel such research will uncover new natural laws that will render the positing of nonmechanistic factors unnecessary; and (4) those with similar beliefs who are counter-advocates of psi research because they fear it encourages people to believe in supernatural causes or who feel that it is wasted effort that will not produce anything new. There are variants on each of the above. Their common characteristics are an emphasis on a priori assumptions more than scientific data gathering and hypothesis testing in their arguments.

Milder forms of advocacy and counteradvocacy also exist, more closely tied to an evaluation of the strength of the evidence itself. The present authors, for instance, advocate that the research, when considered in detail, does provide evidence for some yet unrecognized set of factors mediating between organisms and their environment, and we advocate further research to elicit the nature of these factors. If we are to be dissuaded it must be on the basis of new lines of evidence rather than argument from set assumptions. Certain counteradvocates have analogous positions (e.g. Truzzi, 1978).

5.1 Some characteristics of strong advocacy

The strong advocate starts with the conclusion and shapes the facts to fit it. Thus the advocate's writings will often attempt to draw extensive conclusions from relatively simple or sparse data. Support for one component of a theory will be generalized as support for the whole theory. Often the data will be alluded to, but not described in detail; little or no reference is made to the source of the data, for independent checking. Alternative explanations within present knowledge will either be ignored or dismissed casually.

5.2 Some characteristics shared by strong advocacy and counteradvocacy

Each is trying to persuade others and thus may make liberal use of the techniques of persuasion. Frequently used ploys include: emotional rhetoric; *ad hominem* arguments, including unsupported charges of incompetence; ridicule; guilt by association; generalizing to the whole from the faults of the part, including focusing on extremists in the 'opposing camp' and generalizing to those of moderation; obviously fallacious reasoning; and ignoring or superficially dismissing information counter to the strongly held position. Experimental research may occasionally be conducted, with unwarranted generalizations drawn from little data or from data that could obviously be affected by experimenter bias. Extreme advocates and counteradvocates may claim that their position needs no external support, that it is intuitively obvious to those willing to take it seriously; others are too biased or incompetent.

5.3 Some characteristics of strong counteradvocacy

Counteradvocacy can range from complete illogic to intelligent criticism. In this section we briefly consider some of the strategies of criticism that are independent of specific studies or sets of studies. A further discussion of these issues can be found in a spirited exchange between Palmer (1983b) and Alcock (1983).

A major strategy is to focus on very few, media-attractive studies and essentially ignore the bulk of the research, especially those sets of experimental studies that do show partial replicability. This is especially true of recent works by Abell and Singer (1981), Alcock (1981), Marks and Kammann (1980), and Zusne and Jones (1982). Hansel (1980) claimed that the Schmidt work with REGs is not replicable. Yet in a recent survey of the field mentioned by Hansel (Wolman, 1977), reference is made to a further 15 REG studies that found significant results, including four by Schmidt, four by others in Schmidt's laboratory, and seven from five other laboratories. In the years 1977 to 1979, at least 15 additional (and respectable) studies were reported, from nine separate laboratories. Although other research that failed to find evidence for a Schmidt effect has also been published, one can no longer assert that Schmidt's work cannot be replicated.

A second strategy is the reliance upon unfalsifiable criticisms of experimental studies. In a review of Marks and Kammann, Morris (1980) listed five such criticisms: (1) experimenter fraud in manipulating the data; (2) selective data reportage; (3) improper description of the experimental protocol in the research report; (4) undetected subject fraud; and (5) undetected alternate paths of information flow. We can never be certain that the data publicly presented by a researcher were not the product of one or more of these flaws. Such criticism can be very appropriate where replicability is essentially nil, as has been shown earlier in the text; however, parapsychology is quite beyond that stage. Obviously, researchers should guard as best they can against the presence of these flaws in their studies. In themselves, however, these criticisms do not constitute a refutation of research and should not be represented as such by those who assert them.

A third strategy is assertion of antecedent improbability, i.e. that new means of information exchange are inherently unlikely at this stage of our scientific knowledge. Yet science has always been a stream of new knowledge. Such knowledge need not conflict with the old; it may merely expand upon it or complement it, as has happened in the past. We have no firm basis for assigning any value to the likelihood of new knowledge of any sort, since by definition we are unable at present to specify the exact nature that that knowledge may have. One variant of the antecedent improbability assertion is that, if psi exists, we should see more evidence of it in our daily lives. Once again, the likelihood of its occurrence in any given facet of our daily lives depends upon its actual nature; as we come to understand that nature sufficiently to construct more detailed models of psi, we will be better able to specify its likelihood and the circumstances that increase that likelihood (e.g. Morris, 1981).

A fourth strategy is what might be called assertion of consequent improbability. This criticism essentially states that, given all the research that has been done in the past, we should have been able to observe a gradual building of knowledge about psi and its nature, resulting in increased replication, better theory construction, and signs of true application. As Alcock (1981) and Bunge (1982) note, a true protoscience becomes recognized as such when it starts to have consequences for other scientific disciplines, i.e. starts to contribute to the solution of problems in other disciplines and starts to integrate with existing bodies of knowledge to help them generate a fuller description of the phenomena they address. From the standpoint of Alcock and Bunge, parapsychology has been given adequate opportunity to show signs of becoming a true science. In their view it has failed to do so and that failure constitutes additional support for the improbability of its claims.

This argument is not without value. However, we would argue that in fact parapsychology has made progress in behaving like a science, in incorporating its findings into the body of knowledge extant in various disciplines. Recent conferences and papers have explored the implications of psi for such diverse fields as anthropology, medicine and theoretical physics, as well as various areas within psychology. Empirical research, as described in earlier chapters, has drawn liberally from models within other disciplines to generate hypotheses. The extent of integration, of course, is only apparent to those who take the trouble to familiarize themselves with the appropriate literature. We also regret that more has not been done to integrate psi with other fields and are encouraged that researchers from other disciplines are now attempting such integration themselves.

Strong counteradvocates who use the consequent improbability argument tend to minimize, or ignore, or be unaware of, any attempts of researchers to integrate their theory and concepts with the substance of other disciplines. Counteradvocates will be too quick to say, 'Time's up; you haven't proven your case.' The strong advocate, on the other hand, will either ignore this argument or ask for an endless amount of time, with an endless set of excuses.

In fairness to those named above in this section, each of them has left the door open to possible new developments that would improve their opinions of parapsychology. They are cited because their writings have illustrated some of the strategies of strong counteradvocacy. It is our hope that they and others who offer public statements will either take the time to familiarize themselves with the actual substance of parapsychological theory and research or else will state more clearly that their critiques are of certain individuals and claims rather than parapsychology as a whole.

Summary of terms

tabula rasa	disciplinary matrix
atomism	scientific revolution
gestalt switch	intersubjectivity

Thought questions

(1) Can you think of benchmarks of science not discussed in the chapter? How important are they compared to the ones mentioned? How does parapsychology fare in relation to them?

(2) Discuss the nature of observation. Does the questioning of the objectivity of observation result in a less valid science, or does intersubjectivity provide an adequate basis for science?

(3) Of what use is replication in science and how important is it? How often are replication studies performed and published in the various areas of psychology? Where would you put parapsychology in this list?

(4) Are you familiar with the introduction of other phenomena or theories into science – perhaps the theory of evolution, or immunization, or the theory of relativity or behavioral psychology? Were there arguments against these phenomena when they were introduced?

(5) How important have statistics become to science in general and to psychology in particular? How many findings display solely statistical relationships and cannot be counted on every time? What does it mean to say that statistical relationships hold? Does this view affect the acceptance of determinism in science?

Chapter 13
Survival and other philosophical questions

Hoyt L. Edge

1 Introduction

It should be evident from earlier chapters that there can be a great deal of controversy in science; indeed, to think otherwise would miss the dynamic and human nature of the scientific enterprise. Because of the nonempirical character of the subject matter dealt with by philosophy, there tends to be far more disagreement in philosophy than in science. This chapter provides one perspective and invites you to participate in the ongoing philosophical attempt to understand these unusual paranormal phenomena.

2 Philosophical psychology

2.1 Background

To set the stage for this section, let us quickly examine the analysis of mind given by Rene Descartes, who is known as the father of modern philosophy. Descartes was impressed by the rigor of mathematics, and as the developer of coordinate geometry, he understood both the method of geometric proof and the certainty of its results. He thought that if he could use the same method for arriving at conclusions as he employed in geometry, he could hold philosophical knowledge with the same degree of certainty he found in mathematics. If he could begin with an axiomatic first principle which was known with certainty and each step in the deduction was correct, then the conclusion of the argument must be known with as much certainty as the axiom. To arrive at such a first principle, Descartes employed the method of doubt, reasoning that if he could arrive at a statement which was impossible to doubt, it had to be known with certainty. Therefore, he began to examine all that he was supposed to know to see if it was logically possible to doubt it. He reasoned that since his memory had deceived him before, all information known through memory was dubitable, because any piece of memory could be a case of deception. Likewise, he could not depend on evidence from the senses and thus know anything about the physical world, as his senses had deceived him before. Further, he doubted the existence of his body because he could merely be dreaming that his body looked the way it did. Even reason itself could be doubted since it was possible that an evil genius could exist who might be creating in him the false belief that 2 + 3 = 5. It looked as if Descartes could doubt everything he thought he knew, doubting even that he was doubting; but notice that something strange has happened. Even in the act of doubting, at least one is doubting. One can say: 'I don't think that I am thinking,' but in denying that one is thinking, one is at least thinking. Thus, Descartes came to the conclusion: 'I think, therefore I am.' His description of the self as a thinking substance need not bother us here, but notice several other things. First, what Descartes concluded from the method of doubt was that mind indubitably existed. Further, he did not know that anything material existed, so that the mind must be conceived as being totally different from the body. Thus he arrived at a dualism* of mind and body in which the nature of mind was conceived to be radically different from the nature of the body, and it was known before and with more assurance than the body. Finally, what Descartes knew with certainty was his own mind. He was directly acquainted with his own thoughts, but this does not show that other minds existed any more than it does that the material world exists. Both of these categories of entities must be proven to exist independently of the proof of one's own mind.

Most of the problems that are faced in philosophical psychology are due to Descartes' approach and to his conclusions. Philosophy and science have been greatly influenced by his description of reality, and the sections that follow depend on familiarity with the outline of Descartes' argument given above. For instance, we will see that parapsychology has accepted the dualism of Descartes and some parapsychologists think that the existence of psi phenomena refutes any attempt to reject the existence of mind and establish materialism*. Further, the most widely accepted version of survival necessitates a dualism in which the mind is distinct from the body so that the mind can survive the demise of the body. Let us proceed to examine these two problems to see if parapsychology offers any unique insight in helping us solve them.

2.2 Parapsychology and dualism

It has been rather traditional to define parapsychology in terms of the mind. John Beloff (1978), one of the leading figures in the field, has argued that it is the mental component of phenomena that makes them parapsychological. He has defined parapsychology as 'the scientific study of psi phenomena, where "psi phenomena" are taken as a subclass of the paranormal which depends critically on the exercise of the subject's mental powers' (p. 291). Beloff admits that it is possible for the experimental data to prove him wrong, but he concludes: 'My own surmise here is that the Duke Laboratory had the right idea in supposing that psi was a function of mind rather than of life as such' (p. 301). There is no doubt that it is the historical view in parapsychology that the discipline deals with special mental powers, and it is to prove such powers that many have entered the field.

If parapsychology has been viewed as dealing with mind as separate from body, it should come as no surprise that key terminology is laced with dualistic overtones. It is not only that the popular, rough-and-ready definitions of PK as 'mind over matter' and telepathy as 'mind to mind communication' explicitly assume a dualism, but even the most careful definitions do. In the glossary published in every issue of the *Journal of Parapsychology* telepathy is defined as 'extrasensory perception of the mental state or activity of another person.' Psychokinesis is defined as 'a direct (i.e. mental but nonmuscular) influence exerted by the subject on an external physical process, condition, or object.' The separation of mind from body (and the rest of the material world) has been an implicit assumption of the discipline. That is why some have viewed parapsychology as being so important, because if one could prove the existence of telepathy or psychokinesis, one would therefore give scientific proof that the mind is distinct from the body. Let us turn to a careful analysis of this line of reasoning and examine how strong it is.

2.3 Materialism and parapsychology

Since its inception, parapsychology has been viewed as a bulwark against materialism (the view that only matter exists), perhaps the only scientifically acceptable one. The founders of the Society for Psychical Research were generally imbued with the spirit of empiricism and the methodology of science, but they did not want to accept the materialism that seemed to result from science. The only recourse they saw was to employ the methods of science to prove materialism wrong. However odd it may sound, these men wanted to use the methodology of science, which had seemingly denied a spiritual or mental realm and concluded that matter was the only casual reality, to undercut that conclusion and prove instead that a mental realm existed. Thus John Beloff (1962) writes:

> The radical attitude that psi phenomena exist holds not only that the facts must be accepted at their face value, but that they are necessarily incompatible with the postulates of scientific materialism. This has been the attitude that has inspired most of the actual research into the paranormal from the time of the founding-fathers of the Society for Psychical Research (SPR), e.g. Myers, Gurney, Sidgwick, etc., to that of outstanding pioneers of contemporary experimental parapsychology like Rhine in America. . . . (p. 214)

Parapsychology, he goes on to say, studies minds in isolation from bodies. Thus, a defining characteristic of parapsychology is that it is concerned with mental powers, powers which are a function of mind, rather than a function of the person as a whole or even of life in general. Organisms to which we cannot ascribe a mind would not normally be considered the objects of parapsychological investigation; minds have powers independent of their bodies, and that is what parapsychology deals with. To prove the existence of paranormal phenomena, therefore, would be to display the inadequacy of materialism because, e.g., telepathy is a property and power of an independently existing mind. So the philosopher H. H. Price (1949) urges: 'Telepathy is something which ought not to happen at all, if the Materialistic theory were true. But it does happen. So there must be something seriously wrong with the Materialistic theory, however numerous and imposing the *normal* facts which support it may be' (p.109).

J. B. Rhine, the prime mover of American parapsychology, argued in a number of places that materialism was refuted by psychic phenomena. In fact, he went so far as to say that 'the most distinctive finding of parapsychology as things now appear is the nonphysicality of its phenomena' (J. B. Rhine, 1972, p. 113). The thrust of his argument is that psi conflicts with physics in that physical energy attenuates with distance. Spontaneous cases of psi occur over long distances, and the experimental evidence tends to show that distance does not affect the production of psi. In other words, psi does not act like physical energy, so we must postulate another kind of energy, a psychic one, in which distance is not a factor. If one adds to this argument the fact that precognition and retrocognition seem to show that time is not a factor in the production of psi, it seems that the phenomena are bound neither by space nor time. Surely, then, the argument goes, parapsychology must be dealing with a nonmaterial force. Having proved that phenomena like telepathy and PK are real, parapsychology has scientifically shown that a full-blown materialism is inadequate to describe the world.

In evaluating this line of argument, the first thing that we must be clear about is that we are dealing with events which C. D. Broad (1969) would call *ostensibly* paranormal. In other words, it *appears* that they contradict some laws of science, at least in their general philosophical characteristics, since they have not been explained by contemporary physics; but it is a further step, one which is difficult if not impossible to make, to say that they actually do contradict the laws of science, not simply because it may be hard to point to a specific law which psi phenomena contradict but also because not all physical explanations of psi have been tried.

Further, it may be that psi can be explained not so much by our contemporary interpretation of existing laws, but the phenomena may be explained by a fairly simple extension of existing laws. The observational theories of E. Harris Walker (1975) and Helmut Schmidt (1975) are attempts in this direction. If they are correct, it is far from certain that any existing laws would be replaced, but the implications and range of these laws would be widened. There would be some change in the package of laws, some additions, and certainly we would want to say that progress in science had been made, but it is not clear what existing laws would be contradicted.

Perhaps Rhine's problem is not with materialism *per se,* but with two possible implications of materialism. The first is that if there are no minds, then there does not seem to be free will, but

> Without the exercise of some freedom from physical law, the concepts of character, responsibility, moral judgment, and democracy would not survive critical analysis. The concept of a spiritual order, either in the individual or beyond him, would have no logical place whatever. In fact, little of the entire value system under which human society has developed would survive the establishment of a thoroughgoing philosophy of physicalism (J. B. Rhine, 1954, p. 809).

The second problem materialism introduces is the impossibility of survival. If there is no mind existing independently from the body, then there seems to be no possibility of disembodied survival after biological death. If it is the case that the real problems with materialism are these hidden problems, we ought to confront them head-on. In a later section

(4.2), we will examine the problem of freedom and, by implication, morality. Let us turn now to the survival question.

2.4 Survival

2.4.1 Disembodied

Descartes argued on two grounds for the conception of a mind which is totally independent of the body. First, the mind is known before any material object, including the body, is known. The mind, therefore, is known with certainty apart from the body. The second reason is that the essential characteristics of each are different. Mind is not in space, while bodies are. For instance, it makes sense to ask how many inches long a table is or even a synapse in the brain, but it does not make sense to ask how many inches long the thought of fried chicken is. Conversely, we can ask without confusion how intense an emotion is, but it does not make sense to ask how intense a table is. We seem to talk about minds and bodies in different ways. Our language seems to refer to two kinds of objects which have incompatible characteristics, so they must be different objects.

Which of these objects provides the essential characteristic of personhood for Descartes? Since one's own existence is known independently of knowing the existence of the body, the mind must be what the person is. If that is true, then it is quite natural to talk about the survival of a disembodied person*. Minds are not physical, so when the body dies, a nonspatial mind, which is what the person essentially is, can survive. The modern view of survival mainly has been this one, and that is why the founders of the Society for Psychical Research were interested in mind-to-mind communication – to them it empirically proved that disembodied survival was conceivable and perhaps even probable.

There have been a number of philosophers, even those committed to the validity of parapsychology, who have argued that the concept of disembodied personal survival is a logical contradiction. For them the concept is as conceptually confused as is the idea of a 'married bachelor' and is confused in the same way. The problem has to do with making sense of 'disembodied persons.' How do we use the term 'person' in ordinary language? What are the persons of our ordinary experience? Antony Flew (1956) argues that 'People are what you meet. Person words refer to men and women like you and me and the other fellow. They are taught by pointing at people' (p.250). What if someone asked you to describe a friend? What kind of responses would be normal? Certainly, something like: six feet, one inch tall; fair complexion; intelligent; grew up in Idaho; sits next to me in class, etc. You will notice that most of these characterizations refer at least in part to your friend's body. Flew does not deny that we at times refer to people in ways that do not refer to the body; but the point is that if we want to look at all the ways we refer to people, we seem to include a good many bodily characteristics. People, then, are not minds isolated from their bodies, nor are they simply their bodies. People are the living, breathing entities that we run into every day. To talk about a person, then, seems to necessitate talk about something that is embodied. At this point, the argument is not that it is impossible for something or other to exist that is purely mental; rather, the argument is that what we mean by 'person' necessitates that *persons are embodied.* Therefore, it becomes logically contradictory to say that there is such a state as disembodied personal existence. Disembodiment is no more a possible state of the person than is a person's nonexistence. To use the phrase 'disembodied person' is really to say 'something that is embodied and is not embodied,' and that clearly involves a contradiction.

Lest you think that these philosophers are simply playing semantic games and that the problem is not genuine, ask yourself this question: 'Is it possible for you to imagine witnessing your own funeral?' Some people with active imaginations will want to respond in the affirmative, imagining themselves with a strange smile on their face, dressed in their Sunday best and lying in the coffin. Let me ask a further question, then: 'Can you imagine yourself seeing someone else witnessing their own funeral?' The full force of the argument comes out here, because seeing another person seems to necessitate that the other person has a body to see! What would it be like to see a totally disembodied entity? Even a ghostly figure has some sort of bodily outline, no matter how ephemeral its body may be described. It has form in a particular space, but can you see something that has *no* form at all?

Further, what could it possibly mean for a disembodied person to have experience? I know what it means to see, hear, smell and touch, but all of these feats seem to require a body. I see through my eyes, hear through my ears, etc., so that it does not seem to make sense to say that a disembodied person could have any experience without bodily senses.

One way to investigate this problem, it has been suggested (Penelhum, 1970), is to list what predicates we assign to a person and see whether it is conceivable for a disembodied entity to possess them. If we are successful in this project, then we may be able to talk about disembodied persons in a noncontradictory way. For instance, persons have abilities such as perception and agency. A disembodied person must be able to have the experiences of perceiving and affecting the world or we could not talk about any surviving entity as being a person and use the term in any meaningful way. Let us look at these two predicates and see if we can meaningfully attribute them to a disembodied entity.

Although it is obvious that an embodied person perceives using sense organs and thus to talk about an entity without them still perceiving seems odd, we can turn to the data of parapsychology to help solve this problem. Can we not say that clairvoyance is a type of perception in which one experiences the world, and if one is able to perceive without using sense organs, may we not extend the thought further and conceive of perception without a body at all? In some cases of clairvoyance, a person is able to get a better perspective at will, 'zooming in' on a target to read it more clearly. This may be a super form of clairvoyance, a form which is seldom achieved, but at least such abilities are conceivable. Thus, it looks as if we can say that a disembodied person could have perception.

Analogously, an embodied person has agency – he can, e.g., move something in the world. But in order to act on the world, it looks as if one must use the body. A disembodied person, of course, does not have a body to affect the world, so initially it seems that such an entity could not be assigned the predicate 'agency,' but again we can turn to parapsychology for rescue. Psychokinesis is the ability to affect things in the world without the intermediary of the body. If this is true, then there does not seem to be any problem in saying that a disembodied person has agency, so if these are the two essential predicates of personhood, we can make conceptual sense of calling a disembodied entity with these abilities a person.

However, that does not mean that Penelhum thinks a disembodied person could exist. As it turns out, the problem for Penelhum is not with the concept 'person' but with the unintelligibility of saying how we can identify the disembodied John Doe with the previously embodied John Doe. We want to know that the disembodied person is the same person as the previously embodied person, and we cannot do this without a principle allowing us to identify the two appearances as appearances of the same person. Under normal circumstances, we use the criterion of the continuity of the body, in which a person is the same person through time because of having the same body. Obviously, this criterion of identity will not be sufficient in the identity of a disembodied person.

Although there may be a way of meeting this criticism (see Edge, 1976a, 1976b; Wheatley, 1976), still it is difficult to describe what this self is which survives. To clarify this point, let us examine our understanding of telepathy. We can argue that telepathic ability seems to be a purely mental ability since, e.g., shielding does not seem to reduce its effectiveness, but the only way we know about telepathy is because of the experiences of an embodied person. Therefore, although the implications of paranormal abilities may point us away from emphasizing the body, the actual experience of paranormal occurrences draws us back. Penelhum is wrong, I think, in saying that the notion of a disembodied person existing through time is totally unintelligible, but his arguments point to a troublesome difficulty; an unembodied person is not someone that we have ever met.

2.4.2 The religious view

Perhaps it is this intuition which has prompted virtually all major religions that believe in survival to talk about it in some other terms than disembodiment. It is true that contemporary Christianity has a strong Platonic/Cartesian element, and many Christians today tend to think of an immaterial, unembodied mind or soul existing after death, but it is clear that St Paul conceived of survival in terms of embodiment when he talks about a resurrection body. After death and at the time of judgment, we would be resurrected with new bodies. Benjamin

Franklin had something like this in mind when he wrote his epitaph: 'The body of B. Franklin, Printer, Like the Cover of an Old Book, Its Contents torn out, And stript of its Lettering and Gilding, Lies here, Food for Worms. But the work shall not be lost; for it will, as he believe'd appear once more in a new and more elegant Edition Corrected and improved By the Author.' One way of conceiving this type of embodied survival is through the concept of the astral body*.

2.4.3 The astral way

To give us continuity through time, even after death, perhaps we need something else that endures, something that is not purely mental but has physical characteristics. Such is the attempt of the astral body view which asserts that we are essentially an astral body, an entity which has certain bodily characteristics (for instance, a ghost has the figure of a person), and yet we are not constituted by the matter of our regular bodies. There is, presumably, some 'finer' substance that constitutes an astral body. But the problem for this view is to give a positive characterization of what an astral body is. Flew (1956) thinks that this can be done by postulating some kind of instrument not yet invented which could detect astral bodies, since there must be some way of verifying their existence. Presumably, although astral bodies are not perceived by all of us all of the time now, they could be detected reliably with this postulated instrument and they could also be perceived routinely by other astral bodies, so that the afterlife would be agreeably like the present life in that you could know other persons by meeting them and engaging in social interaction much as you do now, although perhaps without as much difficulty or hindrance as happens with our material bodies. Communication and perception could be clearer and more direct without the encumbrance of the flesh.

However attractive this view is because it seems to solve the problem of personal identity, it has a basic problem – it is difficult to make the concept intelligible. This can be seen if we pay close attention to what we are talking about: astral bodies. It is clear that we want this entity to have bodily existence, to be material in an important respect – so much so that it can be detected by an instrument. On the other hand, the term 'astral' connotes a mental aspect. It is clear that we are not talking about something that is merely body, but it is a body with a difference. Tradition in philosophy has wanted to separate minds and bodies as different things, as seen in Descartes, but here we have an attempt to put them together. But how are they really put together? It is said that the astral body is of a finer stuff, but if the stuff is not material stuff, what kind of stuff is it? If it can be detected by some instrument of the future, why would we not want to call it material? Because astral characteristics are exactly those that are needed to solve the problem of personal identity – that which is mental enough not to have to depend on our normal bodies but which is physical enough to supply an easy quasi-bodily criterion of identity – and if no positive content can be given to specify the idea, then it seems to be merely the result of an ad hoc analysis and thus unacceptable.

2.4.4 Nonpersonal survival

Of course, it is not necessary that our survival be personal. Most of the difficulties that we have faced have revolved around personal survival and whether it is possible to assert that there could be a disembodied survival. Let us look at two alternatives to this view to see how attractive they are, although neither allows us to survive exactly as we are in our ordinary consciousness in this life.

The first one has been proposed by C. D. Broad (1958/1976), who talks about the possibility of a psi-component surviving, which is not a mind, but rather part of a compound which forms a mind. Although the psi-component usually accompanies a body, there is no a priori reason it could not survive the death of the body, much as the sound waves of a radio broadcast continue to exist as possible sounds after the station has gone off the air. However, the idea of a psi-component does not entail much, merely the dispositional basis of (or the potential for) consciousness, which may have no experiences unless united with an appropriate organism. Even when united, these experiences may be very low level (like an oyster), or they could range all the way to a unified memory of ante-mortem life along with post-mortem experiences. Only in the latter case could we talk about personality.

Broad is correct in showing that the concept of survival may not be as simple as we may have imagined. Survival may not be an all or nothing matter, with either a full person existing or nothing at all. Nor may it be an either/or situation, with everyone surviving (or surviving in exactly the same way). C. D. Broad (1958/1976) points out that the evidence is overwhelming in showing that 'the vast majority of dead men tell no tales and, so far as we are concerned, have vanished without trace' (p. 364). But the problem with Broad's suggestion is that it is not emotionally satisfying. Of what use is the survival of a bare dispositional basis of consciousness, and further, is there evidence for it? In both cases, the answers seem to be in the negative.

The second theory of nonpersonal survival is the more popular version in contemporary parapsychology. The psychologist Gardner Murphy made this theory popular several decades ago, and he called it the field theory* of survival. (In section 5.1.3, we will see that H. H. Price has a similar theory.) Murphy noticed that although we tend to think of the person as an individual, particularly because we seem to be so individuated by our bodies, the *relationship* among people is important for both normal and paranormal psychology. Paranormal events appear to be a function not only of individuals but they seem to be set free by the relationships among persons, and thus they are interpersonal. Studies in altered states of consciousness tend to show that paranormal events occur at times when the individuality of personality is not primary, when the ego is ill-defined. What these studies and some spontaneous cases seem to point to is that paranormal ability is hindered by psychological insulation. Since there is a similarity between this view and the scientific concern with the structure and organization of energy in general rather than having a primary concern for individual parts, Murphy proposes the term used in science to describe structural interdependence, a field. The psychological field does not seem to be particularly dependent on biological individuality, so the loss of such individuality does not necessarily imply a loss of the field. Individual personality, then, would not survive, but aspects of a field could. Just as the field in which you are involved constantly changes as interaction with the environment occurs, so a surviving field would be constantly changing. There is no changeless identity of personality either before or after death. Thus, the question for survival is not whether personality continues to exist but whether some kind of continuities can be observed, i.e. whether there are some points of functional comparability between those fields we call individuals and the interpersonal manifold which we may encounter in forms of mediumistic communication.

William Roll (1966b) has taken up the banner of the field theory approach to survival in the present decade. Like Murphy, one factor which leads him to this theory is the consideration that situations of ego-dissolution seem to enhance psi. Other aspects of parapsychology lead him in the same direction, however. He notes that it is possible for there to be mediumistic 'communication' without there being a communicator, either because the putative communicator is still alive or because there never was such a person (see sec. 3.2). Other factors that point toward a field relationship depend on a kind of focusing onto physical space. For instance, psychometry seems to be a phenomenon in which one has left 'traces' in the physical object. Hauntings are apparitional occurrences which are localized in a particular space, in a house for instance. The same figure is seen over and over again, perhaps by a number of people, and the figure is seldom if ever seen elsewhere. Even cases of reincarnation are spatially focused in that putative cases of reincarnation tend to occur in the same geographical area where the previous personality lived. What Roll is suggesting is that consciousness can become involved in a field relationship with a certain space or object, and it is that field which remains after the death of the biological system. While alive, the field seems to be primarily associated with the brain, but on death of the brain, the system may be associated with other physical systems. What would associate the system with one space rather than another would be described by the traditional laws of association, one of them being spatial contiguity. Just as two objects existing side by side tend to become associated in our minds so that when we think of one we naturally tend to think of the other (think of your house and you will tend to associate it with other houses around it), so consciousness literally sets up a field relationship with physical systems with which it comes into contact, and this field may survive. Mediumistic communication would be a contact with a 'charged' space or object in which some aspects of the field are described.

This theory is attractive in several ways. As a general observation, it appears that philosophy is moving away from conceptualizing mind or consciousness as being an individually isolated entity radically distinct from the material realm. Many will want to distinguish mental from physical functions, but the support for a dualism, particularly based on the mind being an entity, seems to be weakening. Further, on parapsychological grounds, the idea of telepathic awareness of another's thoughts and feelings undercuts the notion that we exist as enclosed, isolated systems. Our thoughts are no longer 'ours' as private possessions.

However, in the long run whether any real sense can be attached to the field theory remains to be seen. It certainly does not seem to be the kind of theory that Rhine was looking for to overcome materialism. Far from proving that consciousness is a distinct entity apart from matter, the field theory suggests that there is an intimate connection between consciousness and spatial objects.

3 Empirical evidence for survival

We have seen that although survival (disembodied or embodied) is logically possible, the concept is not a clear one. So far, our analysis has been mainly conceptual, yet many people look to parapsychology to provide empirical proof for disembodied personal survival. The founders of the SPR certainly did, and much time and effort have been spent seeking such empirical support. Leaving aside the philosophical questions, let us examine what empirical evidence can be brought to bear on the survival question. Bear in mind that in addition to the specific problems later enumerated, survival evidence is based on spontaneous cases and field studies in which it is more difficult to eliminate naturalistic explanations than in laboratory investigations.

3.1 Mental mediumship

Since we have already discussed physical mediumship in other parts of the book, we will focus on mental mediumship, a good example of which is provided in the case of Mrs Leonore Piper. In 1884, because of concerns about her own health, she visited a healer in Boston by the name of J. R. Cooke, and during the visit she went into trance and wrote a message. Her mediumship developed and she began holding sittings at her own home, with various spirit controls* coming through until Phinuit, purportedly a French doctor, became the dominant personality. Phinuit was able to give readings to sitters as well as diagnoses and prescriptions, but Phinuit did not seem to have much knowledge either of French or traditional medicine. However, the mother-in-law of William James, the Harvard psychologist, was so impressed with Mrs Piper that she recommended that James visit her, which he did anonymously and was so impressed by what he saw that he continued his own sittings. In 1887, he encouraged Richard Hodgson, the new secretary of the American Society for Psychical Research, a person skilled and experienced in detecting fraud, to continue the research. Again, the sittings were impressive, with Piper (at her best) giving detailed and accurate information – for instance, telling Hodgson that he had a half-brother (she was able to distinguish his being a half- from a full brother) by the name of John who died from a blow to the back of the head. In order to check her honesty, Hodgson had her and her family followed by detectives, and no evidence was uncovered to suggest that she engaged in collecting information.

In 1889, James arranged for her to go to England to be investigated by Myers and Sidgwick, of the SPR. Again, care was taken to minimize the possibility of fraud, with her mail and baggage being searched, and they also discovered that in her best sittings, she was able to give excellent information to sitters.

A couple of years later, her mediumship changed to be dominated by automatic writing, with information coming from a person with the pseudonym G. Pelham, who was able to give very detailed and accurate information to a number of sitters. Pelham had been killed in a riding accident only a short time before appearing through Piper, and of the 150 sitters who were introduced to him, he recognized and gave information about the 30 and only the 30 with whom the living Pelham had been acquainted. Not only the information but the style of conversation was remarkable, and only on occasion were there problems (although several of her failures are quite striking). Other controls appeared later, which were not so impressive, but what is extremely impressive about Mrs Piper is that she was investigated for the good part of 15 years and the records on her provide one of the best data bases on which to judge mental mediumship.

Another well-known trance medium was the British medium Mrs Gladys Leonard (S. Smith, 1964), whose principal control was an Indian girl by the name of Feda. Although Feda was the principal control, a broad range of voices issued from her, including a so-called 'independent voice' which seemed not to come from the lips of Mrs Leonard. The medium was also known for what is called a 'book test' in which Feda would identify a book by location, sometimes in a house where she had never been before, and would then describe the contents of a particular page of the book or indicate that it had particular relevance as a communication from a deceased friend or relative. She also participated in what are called 'proxy sittings' in which a person, many times a friend or relation, would sit in the place of the person about whom information was to be given. This experiment was tried in order to guard against the medium receiving the information telepathically from the sitter. This particular problem will be discussed in more detail in section 3.3.

Clearly, one is interested in asking the question about how accurate the information given in a mediumistic session actually is. In other settings we all have experienced lucky guesses, and this phenomenon could apply here, as well as the medium possibly having been able to pry information out of sitters in ways the sitters did not realize or remember. The conscious or unconscious reading of sensory cues such as body language also provides alternative explanations for some of the information (see chapter 4). Early investigators of Piper and Leonard conducted studies of the accuracy of the mediums' statements as well as the success of the book tests, but the methodology of these experiments was not as sharp as some contemporary methods. Bill Roll (1982, pp. 173–4) notes that he has conducted a number of mediumistic experiments without positive results. Usually the experiments done over the past decade have taken the following form: mediumistic readings for several sitters (given without the sitters having direct contact with the medium) are supplied to each of the sitters and they are asked to pick out items in each of the readings which apply to them and/or pick out which reading seems to apply most directly to them. Edge and Wright (1978) have had moderate success with this method, and one experiment with the Icelandic medium Hafsteinn Bjornsson was successful, but a second one was not (Haraldsson, Pratt and Kristjannson, 1978). Therefore, some evidence has been collected which supports the claim that some mediums are able to give on some occasions information that is detailed and specific enough for persons to separate their own reading from the readings of others. The literature, however, is not overwhelmingly positive in this regard.

3.2 An alternative explanation

When examining the empirical evidence for survival, we must ask two questions. The first is: how strong – how verifiable and reliable – is the evidence? The second question, a more complicated and difficult one, is: can the data be interpreted in only one way? Some people think that any data which can be presented as evidence for survival can also be attributed to psi on the part of the living. Even the early researchers into the survival question recognized that there was a possible alternative explanation to the spiritualistic hypothesis, one which has been called the 'this world ESP hypothesis*' or the 'super ESP hypothesis.' If this is true, and we have independent evidence that the living can display psi, it may be that the data should be explained by psi and not survival. At the very least, we need to suspend judgment until one explanation or the other gets adequate empirical support.

The problem is methodologically similar to the one encountered when parapsychology tries to investigate retrocognition. Let us say that an experimenter generates a series of random targets, and then a year later, a subject is able to guess successfully what they are. While on the surface this may seem to be a case of retrocognition, the only way to know whether the subject has been successful in the ESP task is to check the targets in the present. Yet, why would one want to think that the subject was viewing the targets as generated a year previous when the targets still exist in the present for the subject clairvoyantly to discern? Likewise, if a 'spirit' speaks through an entranced medium and gives information to a sitter which is specific and detailed enough to be evidential, the sitter must have that information in his or her mind or be able to verify it in another way. A classic example of a case which seems better explained by the 'this world ESP hypothesis' is the following (see Roll, 1974). While Dr Samuel Soal, a British researcher,

Myers was communicating through the mediums, a J. C. Piddington requested 'Myers' (through Mrs Piper) in Latin that he should provide evidence by giving fragmented information to two separate mediums, which would only make sense when explained by the scripts of a third medium. Within a month, Mrs Verrall talked about the use of an anagram which used the word 'stars,' made an allusion to hope, as well as an allusion to a Browning poem. Only six days later, Mrs Verrall made references in a script to stars as well as to another Browning poem. Not only was the word 'hope' used but it was especially emphasized since it came out in a misquote of a line from the Browning poem. Thereafter, Mrs Piper's 'Myers' indicated that he had fulfilled Piddington's request by referring to hope, star and Browning. In addition, Greek references were made in these scripts as well as a number of others, which have been taken to be evidential in that classical philosophy was a hobby of Myers.

While this 'test' is impressive, the evidence from cross-correspondences is not conclusive. In the first place, while Greek and Latin references are made by mediums such as Mrs Piper, who were not familiar with these languages, many of them were made by the Verralls, both of whom were acquainted with classical scholarship. The this-world naturalistic interpretation of cross-correspondence points out that the mediums could be receiving information telepathically from each other to orchestrate their individual responses; according to this interpretation, there is ample reason to think that the references to classical language would have come from the Verralls. Further, most of the correspondences are found in the scripts of the Verralls, and telepathy between mother and child is not as difficult to think of as telepathy among other people. Additionally, certain information in the scripts of Mrs Fleming, such as a description of a new dress that Mrs Verrall was currently being persuaded out of purchasing, seem undoubtedly to be due to ESP (Heywood, 1959, p. 71).

Finally, evidence based on allusions to the same theme and to the repetition of commonly used words make it difficult to be able to judge the material. The problem is the same as faced by those judging free response tests of ESP, trying to judge whether or not, e.g., one picture sufficiently mirrors another one in order to call the test a success. A study made by members of the SPR in which 'scripts' were created by individuals opening a book and writing down the first thing that came to their minds showed remarkable resemblances to each other (Moore, 1981, p. 104). When these problems are combined with the inconsistency of controls to prohibit collusion among the mediums, the evidence from the cross-correspondence cases does not seem to provide us with the overwhelming conviction that we would like to have.

3.3.3 Drop-in communicators*

There are cases in which a personality appears in mediumistic communication who is unknown either to the medium or to the sitters. In such a case, it is much harder to conceive of telepathy on the part of the living, or the medium being able to amass the specific information clairvoyantly from the divergent sources and from the wide variety of information available. The two most interesting reports have been given by Gauld (1971) and by Haraldsson and Stevenson (1975). Runolfur Runolfsson 'dropped in' during several sittings in the late 1930s with the Icelandic medium Hafsteinn Bjornsson. His story was both detailed and strange. He reported that while drunk he had been swept out to sea, only to be washed ashore later. Dogs, however, mutilated his body and he reported that his thigh bone was missing and could be found in the walls of a house of one of the sitters, who interestingly enough was not present during the first communication made by Runolfur. While the episode seems very impressive on first glance, Moore (1981) criticizes its evidential nature by pointing out that Bjornsson had visited the National Archives in which reports of the accident were found, although there is some question as to whether the visit was made prior to the communication. Haraldsson and Stevenson are quite fair in pointing out the difficulties of the case, investigated after the communication, so it is next to impossible to become clear on how strong the case is as evidence for survival.

Gauld investigated a series of communications produced by a private group using a ouija board. What is interesting about this case is that the 'sitters' made no attempt to verify the authenticity of the drop-in communicators, and so the case would have gone unnoticed if Gauld had not investigated it several decades later. In the latest report on them, Gauld (1977) noted that 38 of the several hundred communicators had been of the drop-in variety, and that he was able to verify wholly or partly 11 of them. Again, one can find very specific information, including little-known facts about World War I, a person's likes and dislikes, favorite authors and field of study in the university. Moore (1981) argues that half of the cases can be explained as cryptomnesia* (producing information which was normally received but forgotten by the conscious mind). The remaining cases are dismissed as possible cases of fraud or cryptomnesia, but his arguments are fairly weak. Admitting that all of the information given by the communicators was not found in one report, he argues that the information is of the type which could have appeared in print, although he provides no evidence that it had.

Deciding whether or not such drop-in cases could be instances of fraud or cryptomnesia is difficult enough, but these communications suffer a methodological flaw – since they are drop-in, a kind of control is lost over the session since their introduction is a surprise, and the investigation of the material is done at a later time, sometimes decades later.

3.3.4 Combination lock test

The early researchers experienced what appeared to be information coming through mediumistic sittings which directed the sitter to a hidden target or message. They decided to turn this situation into a type of experimental test, and so they developed the 'cipher' test in which living persons would write messages and place them in a sealed location, so that when they died, they could reveal the contents of the message through the medium. An inherent problem in the experiment was that if the medium reported having a message and the experimenter checked to see if the message was accurate, since a living person then knew the contents of the letter, one attempt to communicate the message would end the test. Ian Stevenson (1968), following up on a suggestion by Robert Thouless, created the combination lock experiment to overcome this difficulty. A living person would develop a code which could be translated into numbers, and then encode the message using a special lock such that the person was able to set its combination. While the person was alive, mediums would attempt to break the code, but if they were unsuccessful but were successful in breaking it on receiving a message from the then deceased person, evidence could be presented for survival. It may be possible to find methodological difficulties in this test, but in any case none of these cipher tests or combination lock tests have been particularly successful.

3.3.5 Out-of-the-body experience

OBEs have been taken by many, particularly those who have experienced them, as evidence for survival. A traditional spiritualistic interpretation of the OBE describes our having not only a physical body but a subtler spirit or astral body with which our mind or soul is connected and which leaves the physical body during these experiences. On one level all one has to go on, however, is the report of the subject – that the subject feels out of the body and reports being able to see his or her own body or other phenomena. However impressive these experiences may be to the person having them, they cannot provide evidence to others unless there is some public manifestation of these experiences. They could be due to an active imagination. The second aspect of the problem, therefore, is to ask whether veridical information can be obtained in the OBE state. While the experimental evidence is not conclusive, data nevertheless have been collected which seem to show that subjects reporting OBEs can bring back anomalous information (e.g. Osis, 1978; Palmer, 1978a; Tart, 1968). Yet Palmer (1975a) points out that 'The kinds of phenomena so far demonstrated in OBE experiments look suspiciously like phenomena obtained in non-survivalistic contexts' (p. 17).

3.3.6 Displaying skills

In normal ESP, there is virtually no evidence that one is able to acquire a skill, as opposed to information (knowing how rather than knowing that), so if one could provide strong evidence for the acquisition of a skill in a mediumistic setting or in a reincarnation case, good support for survival would have been produced. The type of skill most often investigated has been that of xenoglossy*, communicating in a language unknown to the person. There have been reported cases of recitative xenoglossy in which a person simply recites a passage in a foreign language, but also cases of the more impressive responsive xenoglossy, in which a person is able to respond coherently to questions in a foreign language. Stevenson (1974b) has reported cases of responsive xenoglossy in hypnotized persons, but the information given by the subjects did not appear to be accurate. Stevenson and Pasricha (1980) report on a relevant reincarnation case in India, but they come to the conclusion that it is possible for the subject to have learned words in Bengali at an early age. Because of the nature of the phenomenon, it is not possible to set up a well-controlled experiment testing xenoglossy, so investigation occurs after the fact and it is virtually impossible to rule out alternative explanations, such as unconsciously producing words heard in a foreign film years earlier.

3.4 Poltergeists

Another phenomenon which people have taken to be proof of survival is the poltergeist. The translation from the German is 'noisy spirit,' and poltergeist activity has traditionally been taken to be a sign that discarnate entities exist. Several good books have been published describing the poltergeist (A. R. G. Owen, 1964; Roll, 1976; Gauld and Cornell, 1979). The current explanation of these phenomena is that they are the result of a living agent. The agent involved in these activities is usually an adolescent not living with both natural parents, who has a great deal of hostility, usually toward the family unit, which he is unable to express in normal ways. The idea behind this theory is that whereas one of us, when we are angry, would pick up an object and throw it to vent our emotions, the RSPK agent is unable to do so, so that the agent unconsciously uses PK to 'pick up an object and throw it.'

A strong argument has been made recently by Gauld and Cornell (1979) that these naturalistic explanations of poltergeist cases are inadequate for two reasons. The first is that this approach tries to explain an unknown (poltergeist) in terms of an unknown (PK), especially since poltergeist activities bear little resemblance to documented dice throwing or REG experiments. The second reason is that the cases which seem easily explainable by PK on the part of the living form only a minority of the actual cases, either because the range of activities is so large (apparitions, hot objects, objects moving slowly through the air, hands seen or felt, etc.) or because the phenomena do not seem to revolve around an agent. In their words, cases are too diverse and complex for one simple theory to account for them. A more complete discussion of poltergeists can be found in chapter 3, section 2.2.

3.5 Apparitions and hauntings

Apparitions refer to reported citings of an embodied figure, whereas hauntings imply anomalous activity occurring at a particular place whether these activities be apparitional or not. Apparitions in particular seem to be good evidence for survival, as one perceives the figure of a deceased person (although apparitions of the living also occur).

However, apparitions present problems for an experimenter since they occur spontaneously, and so control of them is difficult. A traditional explanation for them accepted by many parapsychologists is that they are the result of hallucinations on the part of the living. In a classic study, Tyrrell (1942/1962) argued for this theory, although he did not exclude the participation of a discarnate entity in the production of the hallucination. A major reason for his adopting this theory was that apparitions act in a way that one would expect them to act if they were the products of our own thinking. For instance, if apparitions are really spirit entities, how could they not only appear clothed but be accompanied by dogs, walking sticks, or even a horse and carriage? If apparitions are taken to be proof of spirit persons, then surely they must be taken as proof of spirit shirts and trousers. For similar reasons, Louisa Rhine (1957) found no support for an external entity in apparitions. Therefore, the general agreement seems to be that apparitions do not provide dramatic empirical proof of survival.

There is a special category of apparitions, however, which provide particular difficulty for this theory – collective apparitions. Although they are less common than those seen by a single person, they do occur in a surprising number of cases. One classic study (H. Sidgwick *et al.*, 1894) found that when an apparition appeared to a person and another person happened to be present, in one-third of the cases the other person also saw the apparition. A second classic study (Hart and collaborators, 1956) found that 56 percent of the apparitional cases were collective when a second person was in a position to see the figure. A traditional explanation of collective cases has been mass hallucination, but that explanation fails to take into account the variety of conditions under which collective apparitions have occurred.

Perhaps the best naturalistic explanation of collective apparitions is provided by Tyrrell (1942/1962) who argues, as stated above, that apparitions are the product of hallucinations. He argues that the hallucinations are the result of our personality staging a drama, and further that a level of our personality is connected to the personality of other persons in a kind of collective unconscious, so when it is judicious in terms of making the drama as realistic as possible, the parts of our unconscious which are connected collaborate to produce the same kind of hallucination. For if both persons did not perceive the same apparition, the drama would not be realistic. Many parapsychologists are willing to accept this sort of naturalistic explanation, while others (e.g. Stevenson, 1982) find it inadequate.

3.6 Reincarnation

Reincarnation provides another approach to survival. There have been two methods of investigating reincarnation. One is the use of hypnosis in which a person is 'regressed' to a previous life, such as the well-known Bridey Murphy case. There is a great deal of dispute over whether Virginia Tigue through normal means could have acquired information about nineteenth-century Ireland and dramatized it to become Bridey Murphy, but it is clear that hypnosis is a state in which a person can be creative enough to invent a persona. Further, there has not been a great deal of success in tracking down persona described in regressions and verifying their existence. Two researchers in parapsychology, Ian Stevenson and Bill Roll, have had no success at all using hypnosis as a technique to produce evidential information of a previous life (see Roll, 1982).

The second approach is exemplified by Stevenson, who has produced the most systematic and most in-depth analyses of reincarnation type cases (see chapter 3, section 1.3.2). One of his books is entitled *Twenty Cases Suggestive of Reincarnation* (1974). However, even the title of the book points out the conservative evaluation that one should take in instances of this kind. At best, these cases *suggest* reincarnation, as evaluation is only *post hoc.* A researcher arrives on the scene of a reincarnation necessarily after the story becomes public, sometimes years thereafter. The difficulties with checking the stories and eliminating alternative natural explanations are obvious no matter how careful the investigator is. The two approaches to reincarnation, therefore, suffer from different problems. While the approach of hypnosis offers the opportunity for controlled experimentation and a degree of objective validation, it has not met with much success. The other approach, which consists of collecting and validating stories of people who report that they are really another individual and give details about their lives – the two individuals sometimes having remarkable psychological and physical similarities – does not allow for the controlled assessment that one would like in order to produce convincing evidence.

However, we should not be blind to the very interesting data which have been collected using the latter approach. While a child may report information about a previous personality or about a location of the country to which he has never been, a potentially more interesting set of data revolves around aspects of the situation which are less easily explainable by the use of ESP on the part of the child. We have already mentioned potential cases of xenoglossy in reincarnation, but unexpected behaviour also occurs. A child may suddenly display unusual personality characteristics, or she may have unusual likes or dislikes or phobias; she may have a special appetite for certain foods or appreciate certain books or have attractions to certain persons. Additionally, the child may display uncharacteristic attitudes or behavior such as appearing to have adult wisdom or a condescending attitude toward children. While all of these circumstances may occur in random instances among children, there seems to be an interesting connection between the unusual attitude or behavior of the child and the personality of the previous person. Further, Stevenson (1977) points out that 'in many cases, the subject has some birthmark or congenital deformity that corresponds in location and appearance to a wound (usually fatal) on the body of the related previous personality' (p. 638). While all of these correlations are important, perhaps more so than information given by the child, in giving evidence for reincarnation, consistency is hard to establish, and therefore these data must remain merely suggestive of reincarnation. There does not seem to be any difference in form between what may be veridical cases of reincarnation and merely cases of fantasy (Cook *et al.*, 1983) and so while the number of interesting correlations mount as reincarnation research continues, the evidence certainly is not conclusive.

3.7 Conclusions

The conclusion to our investigation of the empirical evidence for survival is that although there may be interesting evidence, there is no empirical proof. None of the data we have examined necessitate a discarnate entity in order to explain it; indeed, in virtually every instance, a naturalistic explanation is ready at hand. Even if the data indicate that there must be some mind behind the phenomenon, it may be the mind of a living person rather than a spirit.

One problem is that there has been no limit set empirically on ESP, and even the most complicated experiments have succeeded, giving us no indication that such a limit can be found. If none can be specified, then are we not forced to accept a more naturalistic explanation, the use of ESP or PK on the part of the living, to explain these phenomena? This conclusion seems sound in a general way.

However, two provisos must be noted. The first is that it is not an established fact that there are no limits to psi ability; we have simply not been able to establish what they are, if they exist. In order for the super ESP hypothesis to be falsifiable, it must accept the possibility of such a limit being found and thus of not being able to explain all of the data. The second is that many of the phenomena reported here – the ability to take information and divide it among several mediums, the ability to describe an apparition which is remarkably similar to a stranger who died in a hotel room sometime earlier, the ability to give intimate details about a person in another town who died months or years earlier – are *not* the kind of phenomena that are displayed typically in any experimental situation. What comes from our laboratories is less dramatic and, subjectively, less impressive. These two points should warn us against taking the issue of survival as being 'solved'. There is no doubt that survival has not been *proved,* as alternative explanations exist. That does not, however, negate the fact that there is interesting empirical evidence that can be interpreted as supporting the hypothesis. We can only say that we do not know that survival is the case. However, we are beginning to raise epistemological questions, questions about whether or not paranormal information gives us knowledge at all. Let us turn to that issue now.

4 Epistemology

4.1 Is ESP cognition?

On the surface, it certainly looks as if we would want to say that ESP is a form of knowing – precognition is knowing about the future, as telepathy is knowing what is in the mind of another person and clairvoyance is knowing about some state of the environment. Even the terminology implies a form of knowing, e.g. 'precognition' means literally to know before or have foreknowledge. Let us delve into the question of whether ESP is a form of knowledge by asking, first, what knowledge is. Traditional definitions posit three criteria which, combined, are necessary and sufficient conditions for saying that we know something (say, a proposition p). The first condition is that p must be true. This is a rather obvious consideration, for it seems absurd to say 'I know p but p is not true.' I cannot know that the earth is flat if it is not flat. While there may be problems with this criterion, nothing in parapsychology hangs on it, so let us go on to the second criterion: the person must believe p. To believe p and to know p are surely two different things; for instance, one can believe p without p being true. But although belief in p is not a sufficient condition of knowing p, it certainly is a necessary condition. What would it be like to say that you know that the sun is shining but you don't believe it? It would be very odd, indeed. But this condition gives trouble in arguing that ESP is knowledge, because many successful cases of ESP, particularly in the experimental setting, are not instances in which the subject has much belief or confidence in the calls.

But let's assume that we solve this problem; even then, we still may not have knowledge. Merely believing a true proposition is not enough to say that you know it. Let's speculate that you believe there are sentient beings on one of the recently discovered moons of Saturn and it happens to be the case that there are such beings, but you have no right to say that you *know* such a thing unless you can produce some sort of evidence. This, then, is our third criterion: not only must p be true and be believed, but some good evidence for the truth of p must be forthcoming. Do we have that in the case of ESP? It depends on what we mean by 'good evidence.' Success at ESP is notoriously slight; that is one reason parapsychologists have to turn to statistical analysis. Further, the decline effect and the question of repeatability both bring into question the strength of this evidence. I am not denying the existence of ESP, but I am pointing out the difficulty of saying that a particular case of ESP is an instance of knowing. Perhaps the biggest problem with presenting evidence is that the normal kinds of evidence we would present are ruled out almost by definition. I know that the sun is shining and I can present evidence by looking at the sun and having others do the same. I know that the earth is round and can give support to this belief by presenting all sorts of evidence, all of it deriving ultimately from sense experience. But if we are dealing with nonsensory functioning, I cannot present any normal sensory evidence when making an ESP claim.

Perhaps we are not dealing with knowing at all but merely guessing. Indeed, the literature is full of references to 'the guess' of a subject. In guessing, one does not *know* the object of the guess and therefore does not have to present proof for the correctness of the guess. Correct guessing is characterized by fulfilling the first (and perhaps the second) criterion of knowledge, but not the third.

Two philosophers who have made the suggestion that ESP is more like guessing than knowing are Harold Baldwin (1976) and Antony Flew (1953). Flew points out that a subject does not seem to know when he has a hit, and that ESP seems so unlike perception that we ought not to call it knowledge. He asks in a rhetorical manner whether we would say that a person who 'sees' something only six or seven times out of twenty-five is really seeing and, in turn, whether we would want to call such behavior knowing. Rather, he says, we ought to call it a special form of guessing. John Beloff (1962) takes up this last challenge and compares ESP to subliminal perception. It would be easy to flash a picture on a screen in such a short time that the subject is not only unable to perceive it consciously but is unable to respond behaviorly (perhaps through physiological measurements or picking which picture was shown from a pool of five) to more than six or seven of 25 pictures. In such a case, we would not want to call such responses 'guesses,' but we would attribute the lack of better success to the less than favorable viewing conditions, or to the weakness of the signal. Since it seems that information is transferred in ESP, to refer to it as mere guessing misdescribes what happens in an ESP task. If there is mere guessing, then it is difficult to see why extra-chance results are achieved. This argument suggests that ESP is not merely guessing; but, on the other hand, we have seen no good reason to call ESP cognition (an instance of knowing).

When we try to explain why predictions are correct, this explanation is usually in terms of a casual relationship between the prediction and the event or state of affairs predicted. Obviously a sensory explanation cannot be given in the case of ESP, but it is natural to seek and assume *some* sort of casual connection between giving the information and the state of affairs predicted. This is one reason that C. D. Broad (1969) made the distinction between telepathic cognition and telepathic interaction. There is every reason to think that telepathic interaction, e.g. the casual influence of one mind on another, takes place, even without there being telepathic cognition. The same analysis can be made in terms of precognition and clairvoyance, in that there is every reason to suspect that some sort of casual relation applies, but far less reason to use the term 'knowing.'

It is because of the problems mentioned above that H. H. Price (1940/1976) referred to telepathy once as being more like infecting than knowing. Much as catching another's cold, we seem to receive some sort of information which corresponds to the information another person has, but other marks of the knowing relationship seem to be missing. ESP is more like catching a disease than knowing it.

4.2 Precognition

Consider the following story told by a medium. Two women from Orlando, Florida, were visiting her for a reading in Cassadaga, a spiritualist retreat about 35 miles from Orlando. During the reading, she told them not to return by the interstate highway but to travel by a back road. Because one of the women had to return to Orlando quickly to pick up her son at the airport, they did not follow the medium's advice. On their return by the interstate, a car went out of control, crossed the median and crashed into the women's car killing both of them. If we suppose that the events really happened as the medium related them, this would seem to be a case of precognition, but the idea of precognition has seemed so strange to some people that they deny its possibility. Why?

There are two potential problems with precognition. The first concerns freedom. One may argue that if precognition is knowledge of the future, and one knows what is going to happen in the future, then the future in some way must be 'set' or fixed in such a way that excludes any free choices on my part. Also, precognition seems to require that the future event causes one to have information about the event in the present, so, in some sense, the future must cause the present. Thus the effect seems to occur before the cause.

Because of these troublesome problems, some people deny the possibility of precognition and try to explain what *seems* like precogniton as being really some other ability. For instance, rather than saying that the future events cause present information about them, one can say that a person guesses a target and then uses PK to affect the future to bring about the desired outcome. However plausible this approach may sound in an experiment using random event generators, it loses its attractiveness when applied to life situations. For instance, are we to say that the medium used her PK to cause a fatal automobile accident simply to have a prediction come true? This explanation seems just as problematic as taking precognition at its face value, even with all of the above-mentioned problems. But perhaps precognition does not really get us into the problems it seems to. Let us turn our attention to the cluster of problems revolving around precognition of a future event.

To get a better grasp of the strangeness of precognition and how it seems to land us into conceptual difficulties, let us first examine the process of memory. If you know an event through memory, say remembering having sausage and eggs for breakfast this morning, the event itself (your eating) was a casual factor in your remembering the event. One may want to explain it by memory traces so that your brain was structurally changed during the eating, and the changed state of the brain, combined with the desire to remember what you ate for breakfast, caused your memory of eating sausage and eggs. Although this analysis of brain traces may be both empirically and philosophically questionable, at least it points out that we want to say that the object of an information statement (in this case, your eating breakfast) was a causal factor in your having the information (remembering what you ate). If we take memory as an analog to precognition, we merely reverse the time direction. In both processes, we want to say that the object of information is a causal factor in having the information. Translated into precognition, it looks as if a future event is a causal factor in producing a present event, and what sense can we make of such backward causation*? I can understand how a past event can cause a present event, but is it not just plain nonsense to suppose that causation can go backwards, that the effect can occur before the cause? There are several problems here, so let us take care of them in order.

The first problem is a fairly easy one to resolve, and it is a verbal problem: isn't what is meant by 'cause' something that precedes an effect? Is not one of the characteristics of 'cause' a priority in time? This was the assertion of the philosopher David Hume, the first modern philosopher to focus on the idea of causation. There is no question that the way we ordinarily use language, we assume that the cause must come before the effect, but only because that is what we ordinarily experience. But surely, this does not resolve the main issue, which is concerned with whether it is *logically possible* for the effect to precede the cause. Aside from the unfamiliarity with typical cases of this variety, the real issue seems to be the following: the past is what it is. How can anything that you do now affect what has already gone before and is therefore 'set'? Backward causation seems to say that you must be able to change the past, to intervene in its workings so that something different would have happened, and the paradox that results from this is that you could change the past in such a way that you would never have been born. But how can you change the past to annihilate the empirical possibility of your existence? Not even H. G. Wells's time machine has that capability.

Robert Brier (1974) has introduced a basic distinction here that seems to resolve some of these issues. He says that we must distinguish between *changing* the past and *affecting* the past. There is no way that we can *change* the past, but there is no logical reason why we could not *affect* the past. What he means by 'affect the past' is that an event would not have happened in the past if it were not for some event happening in the present (or future). An example might be the promise made by a coal miner trapped in a mine that he would attend church every Sunday if he was rescued, and after being rescued, he did just that. A psychologist may want to say that it is superstitious behavior that he is engaging in by attending church. However much we may want to say that the miner was factually wrong in saying that his church attendance was part of what affected his rescue, he is not engaged in logical contradiction in saying this. At the most, we may want to smile and shake our heads at the credulity of the miner, but we would not say that he is talking nonsense in the same way that we would if he claimed that his married brother was a bachelor. Let us take another example, this one from Brier. What if every time you clapped your hands three times before opening a letter, you found a check in it for $1,000, and when you did not clap your hands, you did not find any money, and these correlations continued for several weeks. Do you think that the next time you received a letter you would not clap, even if you had no explanation for the correlation? Your clapping, of course, would not change anything in the sense of creating a check in the envelope when you clapped, but it could affect things in the sense that the check would not have been put into the envelope in the first place without your clapping.

Backwards causation does not necessitate the notion of changing the past, just as the same notion of change is not required when we say that we affect the future. Your actions now do not change a future event which already exists, but rather we think in terms of possible futures, and you merely bring about one possible future rather than another, depending on your choice. In other words, you affect the future in such a way that a future event depends on a present event for its instantiation. Likewise, affecting the past does not mean changing an already existing event but merely that the event depends on your doing something now. If this analysis is sound, there is nothing logically wrong with backward causation – a present event affecting a past event, or a future event affecting a present event – however *strange* the idea may be. Another reason to think that backward causation is logically possible is that quantum mechanical physicists such as Richard Feynman are postulating particles that go backward in time. Helmut Schmidt (1976) has also used quantum mechanics to explain his experiments in retroactive PK. Evidently some physicists do not see backward causation as an impossibility.

But there is another problem. If you know that there is a check in the letter, there is no reason for you to clap three times, and if you know that there is no check in the letter, no incantation or ritual is going to change that fact. To know that there is no check in the letter logically entails that there *is no* letter, so that there is nothing that you can do about it and your actions are futile. Likewise, in precognition, if you know the future, then it seems that there is nothing that you can do to prevent it. No amount of volition on your part will be able to affect it, so does not precognition imply that we live in a deterministic universe and therefore there is no free will? Far from precognition offering us possibilities, it implies that we are confined to our fate. On this analysis, the two women mentioned earlier really did not have any option about returning to Orlando by the back road, but they were condemned to death on the interstate. There was nothing that they could have done about it.

You will have noticed the continual reference to precognition as 'knowing the future.' Strictly speaking, in light of previous arguments as well as the following one, we cannot say that precognition is a form of knowing. But common parlance refers to precognition in this way, which leads us to an impossible situation. There is a sense of 'know' which refers to something necessarily being true. If you *know* that you had eggs for breakfast, you cannot be mistaken about it; if you did not have eggs, you could not know that you did. In other words, to use 'know' in the strongest epistemic sense is to say that something is known with certainty. It is this sense of 'know' which was implied above when it was said that if you know the future, then there is nothing you can do to prevent it. To know something in this strong sense means that it is necessarily true, so that if you know that there is no check in the envelope, then it is necessarily true that there is no check. However, it must be realized that you do not *know* whether there is a check in the envelope until you open the envelope. You may know that you had eggs this morning, and there is nothing that you can do about it, but notice that this sense of know seems to apply only to the past and present. You may know you had eggs this morning in this strong sense of 'know', but you do not know that you will have them tomorrcw, even if you have a firm resolution to have eggs every morning. Tomorrow, you may find that you have run out of eggs, or a burgler may have stolen them or farmers may be on strike, or any number of things may prevent you from having eggs tomorrow. Therefore, the description of knowing the future in this strong sense which requires that the precognized event necessarily happen is an inappropriate use of the term. We can never know anything in the future in this sense, whether it be through precognition or ordinary means. Because of this, precognition cannot mean knowing the future.

5 Metaphysics

5.1 Theories of expanded self

5.1.1 Myers

In his seminal book, *Human Personality,* Frederick Myers (1903/1975) introduces the notion of 'subliminal self*.' In addition to our 'conscious self,' as he calls our normal waking, integrated consciousness, the subliminal self exists and is a broader, more comprehensive consciousness which remains merely potential for the most part of our everyday lives. However, in dreams, hypnotic states and cases of split personality, we may have access to parts of the subliminal self not open to us in normal waking consciousness. Myers does not want to imply that there are two parallel selves, but that one shades into the other and that many kinds of 'upheavals' will cause fragments of the subliminal self to manifest in waking consciousness. The subliminal self has abilities similar to our conscious self, as well as a memory of its own. The postulation of such a subliminal self attempts to solve some problems in parapsychology in the following way. If there is such a subliminal self with powers of its own, then it is that self which takes control of the body in cases of automatic writing, trance, or other automatisms and can 'reassert itself in its plentitude after the liberating change of death.' Further, Myers states, telepathy suggests that we have abilities which are broader than those displayed by our normal conscious selves, and therefore we ought to extend our conception of self to include the broader abilities of the subliminal self. In support of this view, there is evidence which seems to indicate that we may have a good deal of information paranormally on the subliminal (or subconscious) level, but that we do not normally display it since it seems to be blocked in gaining conscious expression. Louisa Rhine (1962) has argued that ESP takes place in a two-step process, the first being the reception of the information on the subconscious level and then its expression consciously. Myers's concept of the subliminal introduces this two-step process and emphasizes the role of the subconscious in the production of psi.

Nevertheless, however interesting psychologically the concept of subliminal self is, it is not a concept that helps much parapsychologically. For one thing, it remains a vague concept. Myers is explicit about saying that the subliminal self is broader than our waking self, but how broad? Is it limited in any way? Is there communication between one subliminal self and another? Indeed, these questions point to an idea to which we must turn, one which appears to provide a bit more interesting possibilities.

5.1.2 Bergson

A variant on the idea of an expanded unconscious self was offered by Henri Bergson (1914) in his presidential address to the Society for Psychical Research. We assume that the brain has developed biologically for reasons of survival, thinking of it as an organ which has the main function of receiving information. However, it may be that the brain's main function is to *screen out* information in the service of biological survival. Bergson postulates that on a certain level of consciousness we are receiving a wide range of information paranormally. The mind, he says, 'overflows' the body in its information. The job of the brain, then, is to concentrate on the biological survival of the physical organism, and in doing so, it must exclude most of the information. Imagine trying to cross the street with your consciousness filled with the telepathically received thoughts of everyone present on the crowded street corner. You would not be safe! The brain must exclude a whole range of stimuli (normal and paranormal) so that you can focus on the task at hand. Bergson's view, then, allows for a subconscious mind filled with paranormal information, and gives a reason (one based on biological survival) for our not consciously knowing all of the information.

Bergson's proposal is intriguing, and it is a shame that it is not worked out in more detail. One still wants to ask, as we did concerning Myers's theory, for more information about this mind. How much is known? How does one describe the mind? How 'large' is it? Further, does Bergson's account solve the problems of ESP? If the brain is oriented toward biological survival, why does it not let into consciousness more information that would be of survival value? Furthermore, why is so much ESP information inconsequential – why do I dream of such useless (biologically speaking) things as which friend I will see the first thing in the morning? In other words, is the typical ESP message survival-related? Quite the opposite; it is irrelevant in many spontaneous cases (and more so in experimental conditions). Bergson does not seem to have solved a problem so much as he seems to have changed the focus: if we have all the information coming in, the interesting question concerns why certain information is *not* blocked out (as opposed to asking how a telepathic message could get from one mind to another). Such a question becomes a suggestion for an interesting change in research strategy (now we should look for what blocks ESP rather than how the message is carried), but without some empirical support, the theory is of little use in giving any better explanation of ESP. Finally, Bergson's proposal does nothing to help us to explain PK.

5.1.3 Price

H. H. Price (1940/1976) introduces the idea of the 'collective unconscious,' a notion similar to the last two, but it is a step forward in that Price attempts to discuss in more detail what he means by the unconscious. The advantage of the idea is obvious. If there is a level of self which is shared by all of us, then your knowing what a friend is thinking would be no stranger than your remembering what you had for breakfast. In both cases, you would simply be turning to the contents of 'your ' own mind. What is the mind? Price is adamant about denying that it is a thing; rather, it is simply a shorthand way of saying that unconscious events in one mind can affect unconscious events in another mind. The unity of the collective unconscious is merely a causal one. It is a '"field" of (purely mental) interaction.' Price admits that his theory of the collective unconscious is quite speculative and not well worked out. For instance, what is the difference between saying that one mind affects another causally and saying that there is one mind rather than two? Price seems to want to say both, but there seems to be a conceptual difference between the two concepts. It is not until LeShan that we have a fairly well worked out relationship between ESP and the unity of mind.

5.1.4 LeShan

Lawrence LeShan (1966) noticed in studying the medium Eileen Garrett that her state of consciousness and approach to the world seemed to be different when she was displaying psychic ability. In studying the matter further, he became convinced that parapsychology had gone wrong in thinking that the basic question was 'how does ESP work?' Rather, it ought to ask 'What is the structure of the whole situation when paranormal events occur?' or 'How does the sensitive view reality when producing paranormal results?' As opposed to the way we ordinarily perceive reality (which he designates as 'sensory reality') in which there is a dualism of subject and object, in which time and space are real and in which we gain information through the senses, he found that Garrett's conception of reality (called 'clairvoyant reality') was characterized in four ways: (1) there is a fundamental unity in all things,

(2) time is an illusion, (3) there is a better way of gaining information than through the senses, and (4) evil is mere appearance. There seems to be a direct contradiction between this way of viewing reality and the way we normally do, but which way is the correct way of viewing reality? Both, LeShan responds! To make this response intelligible, LeShan refers to the principle of complementarity in physics, which declares that light must be conceived to be both particles and waves. Light is both, depending on what you want to do with light and how you measure it. One is not more basic than the other, it being impossible to reduce the one to the other.

In the same way, reality can be conceived to be diverse. It is possible to take both attitudes toward the world, that of the sensory reality and that of the clairvoyant reality. Neither is more basic or a better description of the way the world really is; rather, the world really is both, just as light is both a particle and a wave. The importance of this assertion for LeShan is that different things are possible within one reality that are impossible within the other, and vice versa. Paranormal phenomena are impossible in the sensory reality, but they are normal in the clairvoyant reality. Depending on one's relationship to the world (or one's mode of being), one is able to perform feats called paranormal from the perspective of another mode of being.

If this is true, then it must be possible for anyone to perform paranormal phenomena by achieving the clairvoyant mode of being. LeShan reports training himself through meditation to achieve this view of the world, and then he reports that he successfully practiced paranormal healing. However, controlled experimentation has not shown that LeShan's approach provides the dramatic breakthrough that he may have hoped, but the results are encouraging enough to continue the work. What is important philosophically is twofold: first, it is the most detailed and thorough exposition of a Western theory relating parapsychology to a concept of universal mind, and second, LeShan is not satisfied with an untested theory. He actually puts his theoretical notions to experimental test, and as such, it is a good example of the practical use of theorizing found in the field.

5.2 Synchronicity

Among some people interested in psi phenomena, it has become popular to invoke Carl Jung's concept of synchronicity*. Jung used the term to describe 'meaningful coincidences', and as such, the term seems an apt description of many paranormal events, particularly spontaneous ones. Hans Bender (1977) relates the following episode in which he was a part:

> At the age of 14, Mrs G., her parents and her younger brother visited Mont Saint-Michel in Brittany. I [Bender] drove their car. While we visited the abbey, she and her brother examined the parked cars and she climbed into one of them which was

> particularly attractive. Its driver – so she reported with indignation – snapped at her in a foreign language and threw her out. Eight years later, she met her future husband, a Scandinavian engineer, in Munich. Once, when she was married, turning over the pages of his photograph album, she found a picture of Mont Saint-Michel with the same car and driver. She had climbed into her future husband's car.(p. 66)

This episode seems to fit aptly the description of a meaningful coincidence. Jung also had in mind such things as astrology and I Ching, but surely, Jung argued, there is no direct causal relationship between one's birth date and personality or between the fall of the yarrow stalks and one's personal problems. If there is no causal relationship, then there must be an *acausal* one, a relationship that is based on meaningfulness and not upon any spatial mechanism. Likewise, a successful instance of precognition would not be *mere* causal artifact, a coincidence to be dismissed as insignificant. Its meaningfulness is too apparent. Yet, for Jung, the meaning is not something that is simply a subjective aspect of the event, something ascribed to the event by an outside observer. Meaning is rather found in the very structure of the event, as objective a factor in the event as anything is.

In spite of the attraction of this theory to some people, it seems that the notion of synchronicity is confused when it asserts that meaning is an objective aspect of an event. There is no question that some events are meaningful, but meanings are not something inherent in the events any more than humor is inherent in a comment. A comment may be humorous to you but not to another – humor is found in the relationship between the comment and a person. If there were no person, there would be no meaning, so an event having an inherent meaning is an idea that does not make sense (see Braude, 1979a).

5.3 Conformance behavior model

Several years ago, Rex Stanford (1978) proposed a theory which some have thought to be more metaphysical than empirical. Since he began developing this theory as he was formulating his PMIR model, noticing some deficiencies in the latter, the best way to introduce the conformance behaviour model (CBM)* is to juxtapose it with the PMIR model. If you remember, the PMIR model says that all of us are constantly scanning the environment, consciously and unconsciously, using both our normal faculties as well as our paranormal faculties. If some sort of need is sensed (perhaps through ESP) we can use our paranormal abilities to find a solution to the need. The response that we make is instrumental in fulfilling our need and it is psi-mediated in that psi has been used to arrive at what needs to be accomplished to fulfill the need. The PMIR model is psychobiological in being perceptual, and it is cybernetic in depending on feedback. The PMIR model works in the following way. Let us say that you are walking home from work and, unconsciously using clairvoyance, you see a mugger around the corner. Something in a store window catches your eye, so you stop and look. Meanwhile, unconsciously, you are monitoring the location of the mugger, and when you see that he has left, you walk on home, entirely unaware consciously that you have used your ESP to avoid a mugging. What is important to understand the mechanics of the PMIR is that you are constantly monitoring the environment (perceptual model) and that you are getting feedback which directs your activity (cybernetic). In the same way, PK is thought of as your directing energy from yourself to the target and constantly getting feedback (perhaps through ESP) on your success so you could redirect your energies in light of the feedback. The PMIR model interprets psi functioning as analogous to normal sensory processes. They simply are *extra*-sensory in some ways.

In criticizing this theory, Stanford argued that if psi works in this psychobiological way, we ought to be able to make some predictions about psi functioning. For instance, the greater the complexity of the target, the less success one ought to have. The more complex a physical task one has – for instance, rubbing the stomach and patting the head at the same time as opposed to simply doing one of them – the less likely one is to be successful. However, there is a good deal of data which suggest that complexity is not a factor in reducing psi success. Likewise, the greater the speed of the task, one would expect less success. Imagine a production line at Ford that runs one mile an hour as opposed to 60 miles an hour! Yet the speed of target generation in a PK test does not seem to affect the score. Furthermore, the success rate does not seem to be affected if the target or the target direction is changed in a moment-to-moment way.

None of these considerations make the psychobiological or cybernetic models necessarily impossible, but they give enough grounds to formulate alternative models, and the CBM is such an alternative. The one thing from the PMIR model that Stanford retains is the concept of need – the CBM describes fulfilling the disposition or need of an organism. The CBM argues: (1) If the disposed organism is contingently related to a random process (usually an REG in a PK experiment or the brain in an ESP test) in which (2) an outcome that resolves the need of the organism is one of the options of the REG, the REG will be weighted toward this need-fulfilling option. It is almost as if the world is constructed such that our dispositions are served under appropriate circumstances. What this seems to imply is that teleological causation is an inherent part of the causal processes of the world. The world acts (not consciously, of course) toward certain ends – to fulfill needs. Notice that it is nature to which Stanford is ascribing this causation, it is not the person. Let us take Schmidt's original experiment with his cat (chapter 10, section 4.4) as an example. The cat was cold, and thus had a disposition or need. The heat lamp was hooked up to the REG so that the solution to its needs was possible. The traditional view of this experiment is that the cat focused some sort of energy on the REG, using its ESP to monitor its success with the subatomic particles. The cat is viewed as the active agent using PK. Under the CBM, the cat does not *do* anything; it merely has need. It is the contingent relationship between the cat in need and the REG which biases the REG so that the heat lamp comes on more (or less) than would be expected by chance.

There is no question that the CBM is a radical proposal. Science has made a great deal of progress by ignoring teleology as a causal principle in nature. There is virtually no other area of science in which such causation is accepted, so one must be careful in reintroducing it unnecessarily. To ascribe to nature what seems like a conscious, human quality seems to revert to primitivism rather than lead to progress. In itself, however, such fear should not disqualify the CBM from consideration, although it may be incumbent upon us to take a longer, more sober view of the empirical justification before accepting it. It must be remembered that the CBM has testable consequences. For instance, it does not eliminate lower organisms from the theory, so that if lower animals or plants are found to participate in the psi process, the CBM will become more likely. It also postulates that feedback is irrelevant, since feedback is what is necessary on the cybernetic model. The more feedback is shown to be unimportant, the more evidence the CBM will have in its favor (and vice versa). In the end, the CBM must live or die with its empirical consequences, not its philosophical radicalness. At this stage of research, it is not possible to point to unequivocal and overwhelming support for the theory, although a good deal of evidence has been amassed. (See Stanford (1977b) and Braud (1980) for some evidence supporting the theory.)

Summary of terms

dualism
materialism
disembodied person
astral body
field theory
spirit control
this world ESP (super ESP) hypothesis
drop-in communicator
crytomnesia
xenoglossy
backward causation
subliminal self
synchronicity
conformance behavior model (CBM)

Thought questions

(1) Dualism has meant that experimentally parapsychologists have been interested in asking how information can be transferred from one mind to another or from the world to a mind without the use of the senses. What kinds of questions will parapsychologists want to ask if one of the expanded theories of self is true?

(2) Do you think that it makes sense to speak of a disembodied person surviving? What are the conceptual difficulties with this view?

(3) Evaluate the 'this world hypothesis' as a theory. Can it account for all empirical evidence? Is it a scientific theory? Is there any evidence that could prove it wrong?

(4) Can you imagine a situation in which a person could say they know something through ESP? What 'good evidence' could be presented?

(5) Dualism pervades traditional parapsychology. Are there any theories in parapsychology which do not assume dualism?

Chapter 14
Sociocultural aspects of psi

Hoyt L. Edge

1 Anthropological data

1.1 Attitude of anthropologists and types of research

On the first glance, it would seem that anthropology would offer a fertile field for the exploration of psi phenomena, since reports of psi events seem to be widespread and common, but when one begins a serious study of the anthropological evidence, several problems arise. Most of the ethnological reports which contain anecdotal evidence for paranormal events are second-hand studies, where the anthropologist reports events which the natives describe but which are not themselves observed first-hand by the anthropologist. Naturally, as in all field work in parapsychology, one cannot take these reports at face value as evidence for paranormal events. At most, they indicate a belief that certain kinds of phenomena occur in the culture.

However, this leads us into a second problem – how anthropologists have traditionally viewed claims about paranormal or 'magical' events. One can either accept them as being possible events, and then proceed to the question of whether the events as reported really did happen, or one can take the skeptical stance adopted by most anthropologists and a priori reject the possibility of psi events. Such is the view of Edmund Leach (1969), past President of the Royal Anthropological Institute and of the British Humanistic Association. He writes: 'The anthropologist rejects the idea of supernatural forces' (p. 9). For instance, Frazer (1951) points out that the Papuans of Tumleo, an island off New Guinea, are careful with bandages removed from wounds, throwing them into the sea for fear that an enemy could get hold of the bandages and thereby injure the person. Frazer goes on to say, 'strained and unnatural as this idea may be, it is perhaps less so than the belief that magic sympathy is maintained between a person and his clothes, so that whatever is done to the clothes will be felt by the man himself, even though he may be far away at the time' (p. 50). Such a 'strained and unnatural' view will surely not be accepted by our culture, so we do not have to ask whether a person really could be injured by manipulation of clothes.

If this is one's stance, then anthropology is left merely to ask what demographic or economic or psychological value the purported practice may have in the culture. For instance, Nadel (1952) reports that in the African Nupe tribe, in which women have the economic dominance, only the women are accused of being witches. Others have asserted that witchcraft may be used as a form of social control, as a person may not act in certain ways for fear of being branded as a witch or out of fear of being bewitched by someone he has offended.[1] With such a tack, it is convenient to avoid asking about the reality of the phenomenon. One can stand back from the practice, view it from a Western perspective, fit it into the cultural matrix and stop there.

Although it is true that a few anthropologists have accepted the reality of psi events, nevertheless, these ways of avoiding even asking whether psi occurs in other cultures is widespread in anthropology and is seen as 'logical' from our cultural perspective. Thus, as R. Rose (1956) and others have pointed out, it takes years of cultivation and building of trust before natives will begin to divulge the secrets involved in their most sacred practices; and initiation of Westerners into their sacred traditions (called shamanism*), where one can most truly judge the practices, is rare indeed.

1.2 Reported psi events are widespread

One might think that reports of paranormal events in the anthropological literature are minimal, and thus one may safely ignore them, but the reverse is the case. In fact, such reports are widespread, occurring in virtually every culture and time that has been studied. Dean Shiels (1978) recently studied the Human Relations Area Files (HRAF), a set of data obtainable on microfiche containing ethnographic accounts of selected cultures which represent the variety of cultural diversity. He found that the out-of-the-body experience is widespread, being reported in 95 percent of the cultures. In spite of the fact that the study does not represent all cultures and it under-represents the European cultures around the Mediterranean, the great number of cultures reporting the OBE is impressive. Other studies (McIntosh, 1980) suggest that cultures not included in the HRAF literature report OBEs; for instance, all three cultures studied in New Guinea contain belief in out-of-the-body experiences (OBEs). Further, Shiels argues that since the reports are so widespread, they may be reporting an actual event. He supports this view by arguing that the two most widespread alternative explanations for the occurrence of OBE reports – that they are used for social control and that they are the result of dreams – seem inadequate, and Bouguignon (1976) reports that 74 percent of a sample of 488 societies believe in spirit possession. Of course, these statistics show only that certain beliefs are widespread and are not strong evidence in themselves for one interpretation of OBEs, but the fact that they are so widespread is interesting when combined with other data.

Joan Halifax-Grof (1974) notes that hex death has been reported in every major cultural area of the world and appears to have existed in every historical period, and yet the phenomenon has received little systematic attention in the anthropological literature. The main reason seems to be that it is treated as a superstition and therefore not worthy of study in itself, a position bolstered by instances of obvious trickery, such as the use of poison to induce death, and by psychological explanations of death being due to stress and shock. But such a view does not take into account those instances of hex death in which the victim does not know, at least by any normal means, that he is the object of a hex. Among the Jivaro, the person is intentionally not informed of the hex for fear that the person will take protective measures. The point of this discussion is not to argue that hex death necessarily occurs through paranormal determinants but it is to point out that there are enough moderating factors to suggest that an anthropologist, to be fair to the data, must at least entertain the possibility of psi being used and investigate that possibility in an objective way.

1.3 Individual anthropological reports

With our minds open to the possibility that psi may be a part of the explanation of some of the following events, let us quickly look at two reports of individuals as they have confronted other cultures.

Robert Boshier is an Englishman who has lived in Africa for two decades, living mainly in the bush off of the land. He has been accepted by several tribes as a fellow tribesman and has gone through twelve degrees of initiation as a witchdoctor. In his wanderings, he has encountered what he considers to be irrefutable instances of telepathy among the natives, particularly among the sangomas, probably the most common form of witchdoctor in Southern Africa. The sangoma is able to perform feats which we would describe as being accomplished through ESP, as well as diagnose illness and suggest a remedy. Traditionally, one does not come to a sangoma and ask a question or tell the sangoma symptoms of an illness; rather, one merely says, 'I want to know.' The sangoma is expected to be able to tell the person whatever it is that is sought. Boshier (1974) tells about his first encounter with a sangoma who described his earlier treks through Africa. On later returning from a trip, she correctly described that he had been underground in a mine and had encountered a leopard. In a more formal setting, Boshier tested the claims of a sangoma who appeared at the Museum of Man and Science in Johannesburg, where he is Operations Officer, by hiding the skin of a gemsbok. The sangoma, after kneeling and singing softly, was able to locate the skin hidden under a canvas sail outside of the building.

More dramatic events are described by Haraldsson and Osis (1977). On three trips to India, they observed what appeared to them to be cases of materializations. In discussions with Sri Sathya Sai Baba, it appeared that a rudraksha, a type of nut, materialized or was teleported into the hand of Sai Baba. He was discussing how the spiritual life and ordinary daily life should be 'grown together,' like a double rudraksha. To make his point clearer, he produced the double rudraksha, which is a rare specimen in nature. In the presence of the two researchers, Sai Baba also produced a ring and a necklace for a couple celebrating their 33rd wedding anniversary, and later he seemed to materialize some holy ash. Of course, these were not controlled tests, and Chari (1973) argues that mediums can regurgitate objects which are later assumed to be materialized. What is needed are good, controlled field studies and it is to this literature that we now turn.

1.4 Empirical studies

Generally speaking, we will present the following series of studies in chronological order. In this section, we will focus on the cases where traditional laboratory procedures have been attempted on natives in their cultures. All of these experiments seem to be pretty well controlled, but they are all field studies, carried out in the culture as opposed to the parapsychologists' own laboratories, and so controls are a bit more difficult to assure. Nevertheless, these seem to be good cases of well-controlled field experiments.

J. F. Laubscher, formerly Senior Psychiatrist, Union Mental Service, and Clinical Lecturer in Psychiatry, University of Cape Town, South Africa, made the acquaintance of Solomon Daba, a witchdoctor. Laubscher had several experiences in which Solomon Daba seemed to spontaneously give information that was paranormal, one time telling Laubscher that a planned trip to England would be delayed due to an illness at the last minute, and another time solving a local crime, the details of which were rather surprising. In one of a series of experiments done to test Solomon Daba, Laubscher (1938) bought and subsequently buried a cheap brown purse, putting on top of the spot a flat brown stone and a flat grey stone. Precautions were taken to assure that no one saw him buy the purse or bury it. He then drove the 60 miles from Cape Town to where Solomon Daba lived and requested a seance dance. During the dance, Solomon Daba was able to describe the spot in which the purse was buried in great detail, including the brown paper in which the purse was wrapped and the stones laid on top of the spot.

The rest of the studies will describe traditional card-guessing experiments. A. A. Foster (1943) trained a former pupil, who was then a teacher in an elementary school for Plains Indians in Canada, in card-guessing techniques. The test was conceived as a comparison between the traditional Screened Touch Matching (STM) techniques and a new one, something like the majority vote technique. While the latter technique did not produce significant results, the former did. About half of the children came from primitive or semi-primitive homes, while the other half came from relatively advanced homes. No separate analysis of the success of these two groups was made. However, overall significance was found in the STM part of the experiment, the odds being less than 700 to one that such a result would not occur by chance. This is probably the first successful report of ESP tests using Indians as subjects.

A very important series of experiments was conducted by Ronald and Lyndon Rose on Australian Aboriginals. In background papers and in a book (L. Rose, 1951; R. Rose, 1952b, 1956), they explain that the pattern of psi experiences as reported by the Aboriginals is very much like that experienced by Americans, although they believe that their 'clever men' can perform paranormal feats at will, and only these special persons can perform PK. The first set of experiments was carried out on the Woodenbong Aboriginal Settlement on the north coast of New South Wales in August 1949, when subjects from half– and lesser castes were tested. R. Rose either acted as agent or kept watch over the agent, while L. Rose recorded the calls. Care was taken to minimize possible sensory cuing and to double check the recording of the targets. Twenty-three subjects performed a total of 296 runs with a positive deviation of + 226, which gave highly significant results. Most of the significance in this series was due to one subject, Lizzie Williams, a half-caste who was diabetic and a cripple. At the time of the test, she was also caring for a rather active two-year-old great-grandson, and some of her best scores were when her attention was diverted to him. Another remarkable statistic was that not only was there highly significant hitting on the target, but there was significant missing on the targets immediately preceding and following the target. At the same time, the Rose team carried out PK tests, using specially made plastic colored cubes. No significance was found in the PK tests, and one naturally suspects a connection between this result and the belief that only clever men are able to perform PK.

The following year, the couple ran tests on a group of Aboriginals in Central Australia, using essentially the same procedures as before.

This time, part of the subjects were detribalized and part were still tribalized. There was no overall significance in the scores and no significant difference between the two groups, but when calculated independently, the tribalized group scored significantly while the detribalized group scored at chance. Neither of the groups scored above chance at the PK task, and, interestingly, clever men were unsuccessful at this task also (R. Rose, 1952a).

A final experiment was reported by R. Rose (1955) in which they returned to Woodenbong to retest the subjects who had been so successful in the first experiment. Twelve of the subjects were tested, using essentially the same procedure. Once again, the results were highly significant ($CR = 10.31$; $p < 10^{-22}$). Although Lizzie Williams again scored by far the highest, the overall pattern for the rest of the subjects was different. This time, more than half of the subjects obtained scores which were independently significant. However, again no PK was found.

Robert Van de Castle (1970, 1974,1977a) has reported on a series of experiments done with Cuna Indian students on the San Blas Islands, east of Panama. The experiments were carried out between 1968 and 1972 and tested 461 students, of which 96 were girls, using special cards made up of objects familiar to the culture (a jaguar in jungle setting, an underwater view of a shark, a conch shell on sand, a large canoe with a sail, and a propeller airplane in the sky). If one pools the total scores for all of the subjects for all of the years, one gets a nonsignificant score. However, Van de Castle noted a different attitude taken by the girls and the boys toward the test (the former gave more attention and effort), so he compared the scores of the boys and the girls (using only the scores of the first testing session if an individual had participated in more than one, in conformity with restrictions of the particular statistical analysis used) and found a significant difference ($p. <.01$). For the girls tested in more than one session, their scores declined significantly as a group from their first year's testing session to subsequent testing sessions, and they tended to retain their relative rank in scores from one year to the next.

The students displayed no PK ability in a series of tests. This finding relates to that of Rose and Rose, in that the Cuna had even more difficulty just conceiving of the PK task than of the ESP task. If anyone performed PK, in their view, it was their 'nele', one who could make contact with supernatural forces. Van de Castle was unable to test any of the neles in his visits.

The successes of the experiments described above should not imply that all tests done with native persons have been successful. Pope (1953) reports on a test carried out in 1952 on native pupils in New Guinea in which a card test was nonsignificant, although a free-response drawing test might be interpreted as suggestive of psi. Pope even concludes that the evidence for ESP is no stronger among native groups than among those in industrial Western societies. And certainly, the evidence from these tests do not point toward there being any more PK ability in these cultures than in our own.

1.5 Toward a new understanding of magic

In our culture, in which 'magic' refers merely to stage trickery, magic seems to be the antithesis of psi. Some of the leading critics of parapsychology are magicians, and their criticisms usually are directed toward showing that purported psi phenomena are or could be produced by magic. From this perspective, magic and psi are at opposite ends of the pole, and if magic is involved, then we have no right to believe in psi. In other words, magic is used as an alternative explanation to psi. However, anthropologists may also use the term in another way in which magical practices may be paranormal, but even these anthropologists sometimes shy away from more radical positions. R. Rose (1952b), for instance, talks about the clever men of the Australian Aboriginals producing through sleight of hand a bone from a subject's afflicted body. By doing this at the proper psychological moment, the clever man, according to Rose, is practicing a subtle form of suggestion, through which the placebo effect can take place. The clever men claim that it is the belief of the patient in the power of the clever men that produces the healing. Nevertheless, something more seems to be involved. Removing the bone is a symbolic gesture, but there must be more of a power involved than the placebo effect, and the clever men must believe this. When the shaman himself is sick, he goes to another shaman, knowing full well that the same sleight of hand will be performed, yet he has belief in the efficacy of the practice (R. Rose, 1956). In other words, the psychological explanation involving the placebo effect is too limiting. It may be, as R. Rose (1952b, p. 20) points out, that good care is taken to inform the victim of a 'bone pointing', the intent of which is to kill the victim, so that psychological explanations may be adequate to a degree, but the clever men must believe that other powers exist in the healing practice.

A related suggestion has been made by Reichbart (1978), who points out that magic may produce the conditions necessary for psi production. He argues that shamans are aware of the necessity of faith in the participants, and we know from the sheep-goat effect of the value of belief in the production of psi. What the shaman is doing, then, in using magic is to set the stage, to orchestrate the conditions – psychological and physical – necessary for the production of psi. The shaman is not omnipotent; rather, the belief of the participants may be just as important a part of the process as any power he has, so it is necessary for him to attend to this aspect. This idea has received some empirical attention lately from two Englishmen, Batcheldor and Brookes-Smith, who have deliberately used slight-of-hand procedures in table-tipping sessions to initially produce table movement. Batcheldor (1966) notes that people have a resistance to produce psi phenomena (especially macro-PK pheonomena), which he calls ownership resistance*, and they are even upset by witnessing them (called witness inhibition*). One way to break these resistances is to initially create an open environment with laughter and plenty of noise and introduce a bogus table movement. More stringent controls can be instituted at a later time when resistances have been overcome.

1.6 Psychic archaeology

Another point of linkage between parapsychology and other cultures can be found in psychic archaeology in which paranormal abilities are used as an aid in examining the past. The last decade has produced a good deal of interest in this method, although it has been used in the past, but the upsurge in interest is shown by the publication of three legitimate books exploring the use of psychics in archaeology (Goodman, 1977; Jones, 1979; Schwartz, 1978). For several years, Jones worked with four psychics in Central Florida. Jones is an anthropologist at a state university in Central Florida and had access to archaeological specimens. His usual procedure was to present to a psychic a concealed object, artifact or photograph. Many times Jones did not know the contents of the boxes containing the artifacts, as they had been selected and prepared by an assistant, a procedure which lessened the likelihood of leading questions on his part. The psychics would give a reading, usually using psychometry, on the object or the photograph. Jones would then compare what the psychics said with what he knew or could find out about the site or the object. A good deal of the book discusses what appear to be outstanding successes of description, some of which Jones had to research to confirm.

The material offered by Jones is fascinating, but it is only a first step. Jones admits that his work is only exploratory in nature, and as such it has a couple of shortcomings. For instance, Jones has extracted material from the readings which seem to be good descriptions, but does not discuss all of the 'misses.' Plus, at times it is unclear how much Jones has read into the material. In order to confirm the benefit of psychic archaeology, one needs a different type of study. Rather than dealing with artifacts that have been dug up and have psychics do readings on them, why not let the psychics give you information that no one knows but that is verifiable? If the psychic could describe a potential archaeological site not yet dug, perhaps one that is not even suspected as a good site, and describe what should be found, then we would seem to have something like a double-blind experiment.

Actually, such intuitive archaeology* has been practiced in the past, more by chance than as an experiment. Schwartz (1978) describes a number of these episodes, beginning with the uncovering of the Edgar Chapel at Glastonbury Abbey in England. Frederick Bligh Bond and a friend used automatic writing beginning in 1907 to discover the location of the chapel.

More usual is the case of J. Norman Emerson, a leading archaeologist in Canada and an expert in Iroquois culture of Eastern Canada. At his wife's insistence, Emerson met a psychic friend of hers who gave the archaeologist an interesting reading on his health. Emerson was impressed enough with this information that he later wondered what the psychic, McMullen, could do with an artifact. On being handed a chard, McMullen reported correctly that it was a pipestem, gave its age and the location of the site from which it came. He even sketched what the original pipe looked like. This encounter began an association which has lasted a decade. Sometimes he psychometrized objects and sometimes he visited sites and told about the life at the time and where artifacts could be found. Much of this information was not known and could be checked. At one site, McMullen said that Iroquois lived there but that they had not cultivated corn, beans or squash. Emerson could not believe this because not only were these crops staples of the Iroquois diet, but excavations had recovered an abundance of these vegetables. The psychic stuck to his story, however, so Emerson had soil samples taken and studied for pollen traces, and only one grain of corn pollen was found, implying that the psychic was probably right and that the Indians had obtained the vegetable by trade. This case provides an example of the contemporary use of psychics in archaeology, and Schwartz (1978) has argued that McMullen has located artifacts in locations where archaeologists have been unsuccessful in finding them.

Jeffrey Goodman (1977) used a psychic to locate a site for digging in Arizona and to predict what would be found. He claims that not only was the site an extremely unlikely one, but that the psychic was much more accurate in predicting what would be found at the site than two university professors who were familiar with the Flagstaff, Arizona area. The importance of these claims is due not only to their psychic origin, but, if true, they push back the entry of man into America by 25,000 years. The book is written for the popular audience and is therefore difficult to assess. David Barker (1978b), in the journal JASPR, is critical of it, and the two exchange views in a later issue of the journal (Barker, 1979; Goodman, 1979).

Psychic archaeology has been employed for a number of years, and there are indications that it may be used more by Europeans than it is by Americans. The work over the past decade seems to indicate that it may be a promising procedure, as Emerson claims that McMullen's accuracy on predictions is around 80 percent. This should not blind us to controversy surrounding the issue. Constance Cameron (D. R. Barker, 1978a) reports on a psychometry experiment in which wrapped and unwrapped objects were given to a total of 29 psychics. Cameron judged that the results were not accurate enough to make this approach a viable one in gaining archaeological data. The conclusion from all of this seems to be that the use of psychics in archaeology may be as good but also as risky as in other areas. Psychic information must be viewed as merely one source and ought to be part of a package of information utilizing all available sources. The important point, however, is that psychic archaeology seems to have reached a level of legitimization through the work of several archaeologists in the past decade.

2 What do surveys show?

We have spent a good deal of time discussing other cultures and the study of other cultures, asking whether there was belief in paranormal occurrences and how we can evaluate that belief as well as how we can use psi to gain information about other cultures. So far, we have not discussed belief concerning psi in contemporary Western culture. Let us turn to that question now, emphasizing that it is belief based on reported experiences that we are concerned with. One has to look at the empirical evidence for a discussion of the reality of psi events. Surveys can only tell us what a population believes to be the case. Because of the difficulty of performing follow-up work to determine whether the psi events that people claim to have happened to them actually did, one cannot accept the reports as totally accurate. Nevertheless, these surveys are important in telling us what the belief systems of our culture and certain subcultures are.

The most complete and up-to-date survey of the general American population was done by Palmer (1979) in the Charlottesville, Virginia area. He mailed his questionnaire to a random sampling of 300 students of the University of Virginia and to 700 other adult residents. A follow-up mailing procedure to those who failed to return questionnaires brought a very high 89 percent sampling from the students (S) and a reasonable 51 percent from the town (T) people. There was no straightforward question asking whether they believed in paranormal events, an item we will be concerned with in other surveys, but one can infer that the percentage of believers would be fairly high judging from the number of people who reported experiences. Over half of the sampling said that they had experienced some form of psi, with smaller percentages for the subcategories. For instance, 38 percent of the Ts and 39 percent of the Ss reported having at least one waking ESP experience, most of them being intuitive rather than visual. In a majority of cases, the confirming event occurred within 24 hours before or after the experience, and over a quarter of the persons reporting an ESP experience said that they had told another person of their experience before learning of the event through normal means. About the same percent of people had ESP dreams as waking ESP experiences, 36 percent of the Ts reporting them and 38 percent of the Ss. These dreams were rated as more vivid than ordinary dreams by two-thirds of the respondents. The percentages of those having waking ESP experiences and those having ESP dreams is similar to the proportions of high school students directly reporting some sort of psi experience (Haight, 1979) as well as of school children in India (Prasad and Stevenson, 1968). The similarities of all of these figures gives us some confidence in accepting these percentages as reliable. Eight percent of the T sample and 6 percent of the S sample experienced some sort of PK associated with poltergeist activity. In related subjects, 17 percent of both samples experienced, while awake, some sort of apparition, with an unusually large number of people reporting multiple experiences. Surprisingly, based on our preconceptions about apparitions being visual, most of those reported were auditory or tactile. Further, 8 percent of the Ts and 5 percent of the Ss reported communicating with the dead. A rather large percentage of the students reported an out-of-the-body experience (25 percent) as compared to the town population (14 percent). Palmer reports a tendency for those who had one psi experience to claim to have had multiple ones.

Surveys from the general population have been given in other Western cultures. Haraldsson *et al.* (1977) conducted a survey with a similar questionnaire in Iceland in 1974, with a return rate of an astounding 80 percent. In general, they found that Icelanders were greater believers in psi phenomena and more active in experiencing them than in the United States. Some psychic experience was reported by 64 percent of the sample, which is somewhat higher than in the Palmer study. Both of these figures, Haraldsson reports, are much greater than found in surveys in Europe, where only 11 percent of the Danes in 1958 and 19 percent of the Germans in 1959 claimed psychic experiences. Several figures were close to those in Palmer's survey, but some differed. For instance, 31 percent of the sample reported some sort of apparition of the dead, the second most common psi experience. Another suprisingly high figure was that 91 percent of the sample had visited a mental healer and had found the visit useful. While Haraldsson found that there was a decline in reported psychic experiences with greater education, education was not found to be a predicting factor in Palmer's survey.

When one examines the beliefs of college professors, the most skeptical seem to be psychology professors. In earlier studies, Warner and Clark (1938) found that only 8 percent of members of the American Psychological Association answering the questionnaire showed a favorable belief toward psi, while 50 percent said that ESP was only remotely possible or impossible. While the proportion of favorable responses rose in 1951 (Warner, 1952) to 17 percent, the unfavorable attitudes remained constant. Interestingly, most of those who expressed opposition to ESP did so on a priori grounds, thus showing the inadequacy of the skeptical argument that those who are most familiar with the literature and give an objective appraisal fail to be won over. Quite the contrary, the disagreement had nothing to do with the literature but with the a priori beliefs about how the world must operate. In contrast to these surveys among psychology professors, a survey conducted among the readership of the *New Scientist* (Evans, 1973) revealed that the sample (there is doubt about the randomness of the sample) of mainly scientists and technologists showed a high 67 percent positive attitude toward parapsychology.

Perhaps the best recent survey of college and university faculties was done by Wagner and Monnet (1979), who received replies from almost 50 percent of the 2,400 questionnaires sent. They conscientiously sampled faculty from all disciplines and found a belief in ESP among 66 percent of the respondents, a figure matching the one reported in a recent Gallup Poll. The main source of belief was newspapers, with a substantial proportion having become convinced because of reading either books by Rhine or journal articles. The high belief rate was not consistent among disciplines, however, with 73–79 percent of those in the humanities, arts and education as believers, but only 55 percent in the natural sciences and 53 percent in the social sciences expressing belief. This result is consistent with an earlier finding (Moon, 1975) that to a statistically significant degree more students studying the arts believe in ESP as compared to students in other areas. Again, in the Wagner and Monnet survey, psychology professors showed a greater reluctance to believe than professors in general. Of the social scientists stating that ESP was an impossibility, *all* were psychologists, a full third of the psychologists responding! Again, we see what appears to be an unusual reaction. The lower belief rate among psychologists seems not to be due to an evaluation of the evidence but to an a priori judgment. Their attitude seems to be that psi is impossible, not that the experiments are flawed.

It may come as a surprise to many that parapsychologists as a group may not differ in attitude too much from the general pool of college professors. Based on a survey of members and associate members of the Parapsychological Association, the international organization of parapsychologists, we find, as we would expect, a very high percentage of people expressing general belief in ESP. A 1975 survey (McConnell and Clark, 1980) puts it at 93 percent, while a 1980 survey which was conducted by the Parapsychological Association of its full members, puts the figure at 88 percent. Some interesting statistics, however, indicate that the organization is not filled just with 'true believers.' Of the people who had been members for five years or less, the proportion of believing members drops to 74 percent. McConnell found that 32 percent of those surveyed had less than complete belief in the reality of ESP, and 57 percent of the responding members began their careers without belief. Forty-eight percent experienced some sort of conflict with their belief system when they encountered the evidence, and a full 16 percent still experience that conflict. Clearly, a good number of parapsychologists still retain a healthy skepticism.

3 Psi in Western society: claims and difficulties

Given that such a high percentage of Americans believe in the existence of psi phenomena, it is not surprising that a number of organizations and programs have arisen claiming that they can teach techniques which will develop psi. Some of these, like Transcendental Meditation, view parapscyhology occurrences not as their central focus; rather, they have more spiritually oriented goals. Nevertheless, they have claimed that advanced courses teach practitioners to levitate. While all of the objective evidence, sparse and indirect as it is, contradicts this claim, the TM organization has not retracted its claim. Other organizations advertise greater life capacities, with ESP being one of the natural talents they develop with their special techniques. While these courses with their grandiose claims seem to be on the wane in contemporary culture, they were very popular in the mid-1970s and the organizations are still giving courses to a great number of people. At least two factors can be given for this decline. The first is an obvious change in our culture because of economic conditions towards thoughts of economic security and away from such popular efforts at entering a 'new age'. The other factor may be a mass disappointment in these organizations due to overinflated expectations of the populace based on their advertisements. The organizations do not seem to have produced new people overnight or with a weekend of meditation, and we do not seem to have millions of people who suddenly developed full-blown psychic ability. In other words, the organizations do not seem to have come through with what they were advertising.

What is wrong with these organizations is not that they fail to provide some benefit to the student. They may provide ways to increase imagery, concentration and relaxation, among other things, but the danger is in exorbitant claims about the production of psychic powers. Such claims, if believed, could produce unrealistic expectations of oneself, and if they are unfulfilled, cause serious harm to one's self-concept – 'if these abilities are so easy to develop, something must be wrong with me since I haven't developed them, even though I have tried.' Or, at the other extreme, they may think that they have developed certain abilities when they have not and this will lead to a faulty picture of themselves and the environment. They may suffer from a false sense of grandeur, or they may feel that they have healing ability and practice healing on themselves or others while not seeking proper medical attention. Further, these individuals may have a misperception of interpersonal relations, relying on false cues, and produce problems not only for themselves but for others. Finally, even if psychic abilities are produced in these organizations for those individuals who are ready to 'bloom' and techniques of imagery or relaxation provide the proper setting for these abilities to unfold, the individuals may not have an adequate world view for the proper use of the abilities and may use them in destructive ways, either of self or others. Perhaps it is too much to demand of popular organizations that they be more than popular, but in obscuring the difficulties involved in evaluating psi abilities, they do not give their students the techniques to test themselves; rather, they are told merely to believe, and too many of them do.

On the other hand, some people in our society who have not taken such courses may be having spontaneous experiences of psi in their lives, resulting in questioning their mental health. Parapsychologists often hear from people who report what appear to be legitimate cases of spontaneous psi. Undoubtedly, some of them claim parapsychological experiences out of pathology and some are deluded in their experiences, but enough empirical data has been amassed to assume that some of these individuals are really having spontaneous psi experiences. The problem is that, although a majority in our culture may give lip service to the belief in ESP, they have encountered the legitimate cases so rarely that in practical situations they disbelieve individual claims. After all, psi claims seem to contradict our normal world view, so they are hard to fit into our reality structure. Too often, those who experience psi have to make a choice between being silent about their experiences or being branded a deviant and being isolated from the culture. In such a situation, one begins to question one's self-identity and relationships with others. This may produce a recurrent pattern of dealing with others which ends in social rejection. In fact, one is placed in a double bind in which neither alternative is acceptable. And this may be happening much more often than we might think.

Some of these individuals may need rather radical help, but a great number of them merely need to be provided with information about the 'normalcy' of the paranormal and be assured that spontaneous experiences are not unusual, nor are they signs of mental problems. Such a process may come through attending classes in which legitimate research is discussed in a normal, nonmystical or nonspiritual way. It may come through reading, but it almost always requires the assurances of someone else who either has had such experiences or knows about them intimately and who is viewed as normal, so that the person can recognize that it is not strange, however unusual it may be, to have such experiences. Given the magnitude of this problem and the relative absence of knowledge about it, we need more research in the area, first into separating true from false claims for psi in individuals and second into finding if there is a typical pattern of responses to spontaneous psi that individuals display. Finally, there needs to be more understanding on the part of psychotherapists to the reality and dynamics of spontaneously occurring psi and more attention given to this potential mental health problem.

4 The future

4.1 Some speculation

What would it be like if, in the future, we were to understand psi well enough to bring it under control and teach it so that everyone in society could use psi to a high degree, although, much like basketball skill, presumably some people would have greater skill at it than others? Of course, it is pure speculation what it would be like, but it is instructive to engage in such speculation. Although many parapsychologists doubt that psi will ever be so controlled and so widespread, at least we can see a few possible uses and implications. Naturally, we must be cautious. Several years ago, a number of people were preaching the wonders of Kirlian photography as photography of the aura, but recent research has pointed toward naturalistic explanations for the effect (Stevens, L. Burton and Joines, 1974; L. Burton, Joines and Stevens, 1974; Dobervich, 1974; Konikicwicz, 1977). On the other hand, it may be that Kirlian photography may be of great use in the future, particularly in medical diagnosis, but it does not seem to be paranormal. Many of the claims today may turn out the same way. Further, the following speculation takes us far beyond what the laboratory evidence would lead us to believe possible. One should be careful not to oversensationalize these possibilities since they are mere speculations, but with these cautions in mind, let us proceed.

The kind of society we live in would probably function differently, and the widespread use of psi could be of benefit and detriment to society, depending on how widespread psi is and how it is used. For instance, our culture holds privacy as an important value and has a great fear of the possibility of an authoritarian control described in Orwell's *1984*. If government used the control to eavesdrop on the population, it could be a terrible world. But the way to overcome control is by countercontrol, and the way to avoid secrecy is to make the information public. If psi is widespread, presumably there could be no 1984 since everyone would have access by telepathy and clairvoyance to all information. Although there would be no privacy, at least there would be no control.

But there are potential benefits for society, some of which are already foreshadowed in contemporary research. Businessmen could use ESP to help them in supplying the right products and making decisions about future production. We might be able to use precognitive dreams to warn us of future disasters. The Central Premonitions Registry has already been established to test this possibility, and although there seems to have been a number of precognitive dreams (R. Nelson, 1976), they have not been of use yet in avoiding any disasters. Another similar potential for good is to use psychic ability to solve crimes. Martin Reiser, a staff psychologist of the Los Angeles Police Department, headed a group of people to investigate how well psychics could supply information about cases (Reiser, Ludwig, Saxe and Wagner, 1979). They tested 12 psychics using four cases, two solved and two unsolved, giving the psychics articles from the crimes and asking them to read them and give pertinent information. In no case did any of the psychics give information that showed that they could give the kind of information that would lead to the solution of a major crime, although there did seem to be some ability to detect to some degree the type of crime being investigated.

A great many people fear the military uses of psi, and there is speculation that we, along with other governments, are developing psi techniques for military use. There is some information that would support these claims (McRae, 1984; Wortz *et al.*, 1979), but how extensive and good the research is becomes questionable. There are indications that experiments have been done to test the feasibility of influencing human beings against their wills (LaMothe, 1972). There are other reports (LaMothe, 1972), difficult to assess, of a device that can store and amplify psychic energy and be used to run machinery. The macro-PK feats of Kulagina and others also have their implications for military use, perhaps being used to affect aircraft or the direction of missiles or even in defusing or detonating H-bombs. There is no good way to evaluate adequately military research in these areas, but the potentials for the military uses of psi are present.

We must not only keep in mind such direct uses, but also more indirect uses through individuals. Ehrenwald (1975a) has called Hitler the 'twentieth-century shaman,' arguing that our understanding of the power he had over others must take into account the parapsychological dimensions. Hitler believed in his special powers, having escaped from death in World War I by hearing a voice telling him to move, which he did, and he avoided a grenade that killed his comrades. His later escapes from assassination attempts reinforced his belief, and he seemed to use his paranormal powers 'on his underlings, transforming them into soulless robots' (p. 8). The influence of one person on another or even over masses of people may have a paranormal component which brings psi abilities out of the laboratory and destructively into the real world.

But if one person has such an influence over another, then our legal system would have to change to take this into account. At the present time, the law assumes that the mind can have no direct influence on the world, and a person cannot be held accountable for merely thoughts and wishes that he does not behaviorily act on (Reichbart, 1981). The law could not prosecute a witchdoctor who put a 'curse' on an individual who later died. Such causal relations are not accepted by the law. What we consider 'guilt' and 'innocence' would have to be modified to accept paranormal causation, and it may be that one could be arrested merely for thinking about a crime. On the other hand, juries would become obsolete if we have psychic judges who could use their abilities to mete out justice. In the meantime, psychic evidence or evidence of psychic ability would be accepted in court.

Technologically, there are a number of potential positive uses of psi. One could use ESP to find energy resources, possibly using PK to extract the energy. One could better control the weather, avoiding destruction caused by severe weather. Further, one might be able to solve the world food problem by using PK to help grow crops. Using precognition, the government and business communities could have greater insight into where they should put their resources for the greatest future benefit, and seeing into the future could bring us new technologies more quickly.

4.2 Cultural implications

All of the individual possibilities mentioned above mean that society will be changed, but the change may be greater than simple individual differences. The very foundation of culture may be redirected. Such a change might result from acceptance of psi phenomena as real, even if they are not well controlled.

Harman (1976) has suggested that there is already a paradigm shift going on in society, one that scientists, as members of society, are being affected by. Scientists are now moving from a feeling of discomfort to a feeling of comfort about a range of phenomena, and this change is not always a matter of rational argument or objectively examining the data to be convinced. The new image of the world, which Harman refers to as the perennial philosophy, seems to come from work in the human potential movement and from transpersonal psychology. At any rate, if Harman is right about such a change going on (see also Ferguson, 1980), most of the impetus for the change is coming from research in consciousness (biofeedback, altered states of consciousness) and in brain research. It does not appear that parapsychology could effect such a change alone, although psi research may be considered a part of consciousness research. Other areas of research that may be bringing about a shift in our understanding of the world comes from the 'hard' sciences, with the names of Bohm, Pribram, Wigner, Wheeler and Prigogine being mentioned often. The impact of such changes will have the effect of allowing for nonmechanistic explanations in science, if it turns out that paranormal phenomena have to be explained in those terms. It is in this sense that parapsychology may form part of the new paradigm, not itself forcing the acceptance of a new view, but being a part of the movement which may fundamentally change science and find a more conducive atmosphere in which unusual phenomena can be explained in unusual ways. Such a society promises much: a societal organization in which there will be less competition and more cooperation, and the feelings of the unity of society being greater than the assertions of the individual; less of a work ethic and more of a merging of work and play and learning; a greater tolerance of difference and experimentation; a greater respect for the potentials of consciousness; and institutions which will support these goals.

Parapyschology will not produce a panacea. Based on the continuing progress over the last century, we need to be realistic about the improbable prospects of achieving a complete understanding and control of psi so that it would, in itself, produce a fundamental change in culture. However, parapysychology, along with other disciplines, may advance so that the cumulative effect will cause us to question some fundamental scientific assumptions. Both because of the advances that parapsychology has made in comprehending psi and because of the potential of parapsychology contributing to a new understanding of nature, continuing research in the area is vital. It may be that parapsychology, in ways it has not in the past, will contribute in fundamental ways to the progress of science.

Note

[1] Other examples can be found in Van de Castle (1977a, p. 670). Among them are that in the Navajo culture less advantaged members tend to accuse more affluent members of witchcraft, and in another culture in which sex partners are relatively limited, witches are accused of sexual relations with secret partners, The diversity is so great in how paranormal practices are used in other cultures that one suspects few general statements of much quality can be made about cross-cultural practices. Furthermore, these practices seem to be so closely inter-

twined with specific cultural views that it does not seem that we can learn much about how psi may function in our culture, in which our world view is vastly different.

Summary of terms

shamanism	witness inhibition
ownership resistance	intuitive archaeology

Thought questions

(1) How would one go about testing the existence of psi in field situations using preliterate people? How much would you accept the world view of these people and their paranormal claims? What do you think of the research so far?

(2) What reasons could you give for psychologists having less belief in psi than other academics or than the population in general? Evaluate these reasons – are there some that are legitimate and others illegitimate?

(3) What is your evaluation of the relationship between psi production and magic? Should parapsychologists try to eliminate completely all forms of magic from our experiments?

(4) If psi is accepted scientifically, although it remains elusive and not practical in a widespread manner, what changes in society and our world view would result?

Part IV
Looking back

Chapter 15
A brief summary

Robert L Morris

By now it is evident that parapsychology is an interdisciplinary problem area. Its phenomena represent psychological anomalies of experience and behavior, plus physical and biological anomalies, as well as apparent anomalous interactions between the two. Our knowledge in these areas is meager but growing. We are still learning much about the nature of experience, about the full range of biological input and output systems, about cognition and memory, and about the strategies of deception. Much can be explained in ordinary terms if we consider the circumstances carefully. We must avoid the bias of assuming that such explanations can account for everything, that there are no truly new principles of nature to be learned. Conversely, we need to proceed with caution and not assume that each unexplained phenomenon is valid evidence for some major undiscovered force in the world around us.

Parapsychology has tried to apply the scientific method to learn whether some new factors are responsible for its observed anomalies. It has done so through a blend of strategies developed within existing disciplines, as well as some new strategies. It has done so with mixed success. Bad science and fraud have hampered legitimate investigation. Yet a sizeable body of data is emerging, with areas of partial replication and thematic consistency. The methodology is necessarily complex, and those with strong beliefs one way or the other have been reluctant to read original research reports in sufficient detail to evaluate them. We have tried to represent that literature as best we can, to give readers a reasonable picture of the actual strengths and weaknesses of parapsychological thought and research, as practiced by those we have come to respect.

Much has been left out, inevitably so. Students of broader areas of metaphysics and the occult will not find their philosophies and practices represented. Lines of research not well represented in refereed journals have also been omitted.

Parapsychology has strong potential implications, both philosophical and social. We regret the consequent polarization of many who value and devalue these implications. Advocate and counteradvocate alike have indulged in bad science and criticism. Yet we see encouraging signs that a middle ground is emerging, drawing from a variety of perspectives, and motivated to do some original problem solving. Hopefully our text will serve to clarify some of the myths and negate some of the extreme claims that have hampered active cooperation.

This book is a combination of text, progress report, personal and intellectual statement by four colleagues, and case study. There is much innovation yet to be done, much true exploration incorporating and expanding upon the tools of science. Perhaps by a fine blend of the art of experience and the science of procedure we can contribute to an understanding of ourselves that will transcend our present limited views, whatever they may be.

Appendix A
Critical values of sums of ranks (X) for open-deck analyses

Assignable	One-tailed *p*-values								
Ranks (*R*)	0.10	0.05	0.025	0.01	0.005	0.002	0.001	0.0005	10^{-4}
4	6	5	5	4	4				
5	10	9	8	7	6	6	5	5	
6	15	13	12	11	10	9	8	7	6
7	20	18	17	15	14	12	12	11	9
8	27	24	22	20	19	17	16	15	13
9	34	31	29	26	24	22	21	20	17
10	42	39	36	33	31	29	27	25	22
11	51	48	45	41	38	36	34	32	28
12	61	58	54	49	47	43	41	39	35

Note: Adapted from Morris (1972). The table assumes that the number of trials (*n*) equals *R*. For more complete tables, see Solfvin *et al*, (1978).

Appendix B
One-tailed *p*–values for forced matching

Trials (*n*)	Hits (*H*)			
	3	4	5	6
3	0.167			
4	–	0.042		
5	0.092	–	0.008	
6	0.078	0.022	–	0.001
7+	0.081	0.019	0.004	0.001

Note: Adapted from Scott (1972). Scott's full table provides *p*–values for up to 20 summed replications of the above.

Bibliography

Abbreviations

APR	S. Krippner (ed.), *Advances in Parapsychological Research* (3 vols). New York: Plenum Press, 1977, 1978, 1982.
EJP	*European Journal of Parapsychology* (RUU, Sorbonnelaan 1b, 3584 CA Utrecht, The Netherlands).
HB	B. B. Wolman (ed.), *Handbook of Parapsychology*. New York: Van Nostrand Reinhold, 1977.
IJP	*International Journal of Parapsychology* (222 East 71st St, New York, NY 10021).
JASPR	*Journal of the American Society for Psychical Research* (5 West 73rd St, New York, NY 10023).
JP	*Journal of Parapsychology* (Box 6847, College Station, Durham, NC 27708).
JSPR	*Journal of the Society for Psychical Research* (1 Adam and Eve Mews, London W8 6UG).
MAL	C. T. Tart, H. E. Puthoff and R. Targ (eds), *Mind at Large*. New York: Praeger, 1976.
PASPR	*Proceedings of the American Society for Psychical Research.*
PDP	J. M. O. Wheatley and H. L. Edge (eds), *Philosophical Dimensions of Parapsychology*. Springfield, IL: Charles Thomas, 1976.
PM	*Parapsychological Monographs.* New York: Parapsychology Foundation (228 East 71st St).
PPA	*Proceedings of the Parapsychological Association.*
	PR *Parapsychology Review* (228 East 71st St, New York, NY 10021).
PSPR	*Proceedings of the Society for Psychical Research.*
RIP 19XX	*Research in Parapsychology 19XX.* Metuchen, NJ: Scarecrow Press.
ZS	*Zetetic Scholar* (Box 1052, Ann Arbor, MI 48103).

Abell, G and Singer, B. (eds). (1981). *Science and the Paranormal.* New York: Scribners.

Adey, W. R. (1981). Tissue interactions with non-ionizing electromagnetic fields. *Physiological Review, 61,* 435–514.

Alcock, J. E. (1981). *Parapsychology: Science or Magic?*. Oxford: Pergamon Press.

Alcock, J. E. (1983). Science, psychology, and parapsychology: a reply to Dr Palmer. *ZS, 11,* 71–90, 104.

Anderson, M. and White, R. (1956). Teacher-pupil attitudes and clairvoyance test results. *JP, 20,* 141–57.

Anderson, M. and White, R. (1957). A further investigation of teacher-pupil attitudes and clairvoyance test results. *JP, 21,* 81–97.

Angoff, A. (1974). *Eileen Garrett and the World Beyond the Senses.* New York: William Morrow.

Baggally, W. W. (1910). Discussion of the Naples report on Eusapia Palladino. *JSPR, 14,* 213–28.

Baker, R. R. (1980). Goal orientation in blindfolded humans after long distance displacement: possible involvement of a magnetic sense. *Science, 210,* 555.

Baldwin, H. (1976). Conceptualizations of experimental clairvoyance. *JP, 40,* 136–44.

Barber, T. X. and Wilson, C. S. (1982). The 'fantasy-prone personality,' the psychic, and the excellent hypnotic subject ('somnanbule'): are they the same person? *RIP 1981* pp. 41–2.

Barker, D. R. (1978a). Parapsychological anthropology: growth toward interdisciplinary study. *PR*, 9(3), 18–19.

Barker, D. R. (1978b). [Review of Psychic archaeology]. *JASPR, 72,* 186–88.

Barker, D. R. (1979). [Correspondence]. *JASPR, 73,* 103–5.

Barker, J. C. (1967). Premonitions of the Aberfan disaster. *JSPR, 44,* 169–81.

Barnothy, M. F. (ed.) (1964). *Biological Effects of Magnetic Fields* (vols 1–2). New York: Plenum Press.

Barrett, W. F. (1911). Poltergeists, old and new. *PSPR, 25,* 377–412.

Barrett, W. F. (1926). *Death-bed Visions.* London: Methuen.

Barry, J. (1968). General and comparative study of the psychokinetic effect on a fungus culture. *JP, 32,* 237–43.

Batcheldor, K. J. (1966). Report on a case of table levitation and associated phenomena. *JSPR, 43,* 339–56.

Batcheldor, K. J. (1984). Contributions to the theory of PK induction from sitter-group work. *JASPR, 78,* 105–22.

Bayless, R. (1959). [Letter to the editor.] *JASPR, 53,* 35–8.

Bayless, R. (1976). Tape-recording of paranormally generated acoustical raps. *New Horizons, 2*(2), 12–17.

Becker, R. O. and Marino, A. A. (1982). *Electromagnetism and Life.* Albany, NY: SUNY Press.

Beloff, J. (1962). *The Existence of Mind.* London: MacGibbon & Kee.

Beloff, J. (1977). Historical overview [of parapsychology]. *HB* (pp. 3–24).

Beloff, J. (1978). The limits of parapsychology. *EJP, 2,* 291–303.

Belvedere, E. and Foulkes, D. (1971). Telepathy in dreams: a failure to replicate. *Perceptual and Motor Skills, 33,* 783–9.

Bender, H. (1971a). New developments in poltergeist research. *PPA, 6,* 81–102.

Bender, H. (1971b). Parapsychologie und spiritismus [Parapsychology and spiritism]. *Zeitschrift für Parapsychologie und Grenzgebiete der Psychologie, 13,* 1–23.

Bender, H. (1972). The phenomena of Friedrich Jürgenson. *Journal of Paraphysics, 6,* 65–75.

Bender, H. (1974). Modern poltergeist research. In J. Beloff (ed.), *New Directions in Parapsychology* (pp. 122–43). London: Elek Science.

Bender, H. (1977). Meaningful coincidences in light of the Jung-Pauli theory of synchronicity and parapsychology. In B. Shapin and L. Coly (eds), *The Philosophy of Parapsychology* (pp. 64–84). New York: Parapsychology Foundation.

Berger, H. (1940). *Psyche.* Jena, DDR: Verlag Gustav Fischer.

Bergson, H. (1914). [Presidential address]. *PSPR, 27,* 157–75.

Bertini, M., Lewis, H. and Witkin, H. (1969). Some preliminary observations with an experimental procedure for the study of hypnogogic and related phenomena. In C. T. Tart (ed.), *Altered States of Consciousness* (pp.93–111). New York: Wiley.

Besterman, T. (1932). The mediumship of Rudi Schneider. *PSPR, 40,* 428–36.

Besterman, T., Soal, S. G. and Jephson, I. (1931). Report of a series of experiments in clairvoyance conducted at a distance under approximately fraud-proof conditions. *PSPR, 39,* 375–414.

Bhadra, B. H. (1966). The relationship of test scores to belief in ESP. *JP, 30,* 1–17.

Birge, W. R. (1948). A new method and an experiment in pure telepathy. *JP, 12,* 273–88.

Bisaha, J. P. and Dunne, B. J. (1979). Multiple subject and long-distance precognitive remote viewing of geographical locations. *MAL* (pp. 107–24).

Bjerre, P. (1947). *Spökerier* [*Hauntings*]. Stockholm: Centrum.

Blackmore, S. J. (1980). The extent of selective reporting in ESP ganzfeld studies. *EJP, 3,* 213–19.

Blom, J. G. and Pratt, J. G. (1968). A second confirmatory ESP experiment with Pavel Stepanek as a 'borrowed' subject. *JASPR, 62,* 28–45.

Boerenkamp, H. G. and Schouten, S. A. (1983). Estimating the potential paranormal value of verbal statements. *JP, 47,* 121–30.

Bohm, D. (1952). A suggested interpretation of the quantum theory in terms of 'hidden' variables: Parts I and II. *Physical Review, 85* (2), 166–93.

Bohm, D. (1980). *Wholeness and the Implicate Order.* London: Routledge & Kegan Paul.

Boshier, A. K. (1974). African apprenticeship. In A. Angoff and D. Barth (eds), *Parapsychology and Anthropology* (pp. 273–93). New York: Parapsychology Foundation.

Bouguignon, E. (1976). Spirit possession belief and social structure. In A. Bharati (ed.), *The Realm of the Extra-human* (pp. 17–26). The Hague: Mouton.

Bozzano, E. (1920). *Les phénomènes de hantise* [*The phenomena of haunting*]. Paris: Alcan.

Braud, L. W. and Braud, W. G. (1974). Further studies of relaxation as a psi-conducive state. *JASPR, 68,* 229–45.

Braud, W. G. (1975). Psi-conducive states. *Journal of Communication, 25,* 142–52.

Braud, W. (G.) (1976). Psychokinesis in aggressive and nonaggressive fish with mirror presentation feedback for hits. *JP, 40,* 296–307.

Braud, W. (G.) (1978). Allobiofeedback: immediate feedback for a psychokinetic influence upon another person's physiology. *RIP 1977* (pp. 123–34.

Braud, W. (G.) (1979). Conformance behavior involving living systems. *RIP 1978* (pp. 111–15.

Braud, W. (G.) (1980). Lability and inertia in conformance behavior. *JASPR, 74,* 297–318.

Braud, W. (G.) (1983). Prolonged visualization practice and psychokinesis: a pilot study. *RIP 1982* (pp. 187–9).

Braud, W. G. and Braud, L. W. (1973). Preliminary explorations of psi-conducive states: progressive muscular relaxation. *JASPR, 67,* 24–46.

Braud, W. (G.) and Schlitz, M, (1983). Psychokinetic influence on electrodermal activity. *JP, 47,* 95–119.

Braud, W. G., Shafer, D. and Mulgrew, J. (1983). Psi functioning and assessed cognitive lability. *JASPR, 77,* 193–208.

Braud, W. G., Smith, G., Andrew, K. and Willis, S. (1976). Psychokinetic influences on random number generators during evocation of 'analytic' vs. 'nonanalytic' modes of information processing. *RIP 1975* (pp. 85–8).

Braud, W. G. and Wood, R. (1977). Influence of immediate feedback on free-response GESP performance during ganzfeld stimulation. *JASPR, 71,* 409–27.

Braud, W. G., Wood, R. and Braud, L. W. (1975). Free-response GESP performance during an experimental hypnagogic state induced by visual and acoustic ganzfeld techniques: a replication and extension. *JASPR, 69,* 105–13.

Braude, S. E. (1979a). *ESP and Psychokinesis: A Philosophical Examination.* Philadelphia: Temple University Press.

Braude, S. (E.) (1979b). The observational theories in parapsychology: a critique. *JASPR, 73,* 349–66.

Brenner, D., Williamson, S. and Kaufman, L. (1975). Visually evoked magnetic fields of the human brain. *Science, 190,* 480–2.

Brian, D. (1982). The Enchanted Voyager. Englewood Cliffs, NJ: Prentice-Hall.

Brier, R. (1974). *Precognition and the Philosophy of Science.* New York: Humanities Press.

Broad, C.D. (1967). The notion of 'precognition'. In J. R. Smythies (ed.), *Science and ESP* (pp. 165–9). New York: Humanties Press.

Broad, C. D. (1969). Religion, Philosophy and Psychical Research. New York: Humanities Press.

Broad, C. D. (1976). Personal identity and survival. *PDP* (pp. 348–65). (Original work published 1958.)

Broad, W. and Wade, N. (1982). *Betrayers of the Truth.* New York: Simon & Schuster.

Brookes-Smith, C. (1973). Data-tape recorded experimental PK phenomena. *JSPR, 47,* 69–89.

Brookes-Smith, C. and Hunt, D. W. (1970). Some experiments in psychokinesis. *JSPR, 45,* 265–81.

Broughton, R. S. (1976). Possible brain hemisphere laterality effects in ESP performance. *JSPR, 48,* 384–99.

Broughton, R. S. (1977). Brain hemisphere differences in psi-influenced reaction time. *RIP 1976* (pp. 86–8).

Broughton, R. S. (1978). Comments on 'Cerebral lateralization effects in ESP processing'. *JASPR, 72,* 384–9.

Broughton, R., Millar, B., Beloff, J. and Wilson, K. (1978). A PK investigation of the experimenter effect and its psi-based component. *RIP 1977* (pp. 41–8).

Brown, E. L. and Deffenbacher, K. (1979). *Perception and the Senses.* Oxford: Oxford University Press.

Brown, H. I. (1977). *Perception, Theory and Commitment.* Chicago: Precedent.

Brown, S. (1972). *The Heyday of Spiritualism.* New York: Hawthorne.

Bunge, M. (1982). Demarcating science from pseudoscience. *Fundamenta Scientiae, 3,* 369–88.

Burdick, D. S. and Kelly, E. F. (1977). Statistical methods in parapsychological research. *HB* (pp. 81–130).

Burton, J. (1948). *The Hey-day of a Wizard.* London: Harrap.

Burton, L., Joines, W. and Stevens, B. (1974). Kirlian photography and its relevance to parapsychological research. *RIP 1973* (pp. 107–12).

Cadoret, R. and Pratt, J. G. (1950). The consistent missing effect in ESP, JP, 14, 244–56.

Camstra, B. (1973). PK conditioning. *RIP 1972* (pp. 25–7).

Carington, W. W. (1933–1934). The quantitative study of trance personalities: Part I. *PSPR, 42,* 173–240.

Carington, W. W. (1935). The quantitative study of trance personalities; Part II. *PSPR, 43,* 319–61.

Carington, W. W. (1936–1937). The quantitative study of trance personalities: Part III. *PSPR, 44,* 189–222.

Carington, W. W. (1940). Experiments on the paranormal cognition of drawings. *JP, 4,* 1–129.

Carpenter, J. C. (1971). The differential effect and hidden target differences consisting of erotic and neutral stimuli. *JASPR, 65,* 204–14.

Carpenter, J. C. (1977). Intrasubject and subject-agent effects in ESP experiments. *HB* (pp. 202–72).

Carpenter, J. C. and Carpenter, J. E. (1967). Decline of variability of ESP scoring across a period of effort. *JP, 31,* 179–91.

Carrington, H. (1920). *The Physical Phenomena of Spiritualism.* New York: Dodd, Mead. (Original work published 1907.)

Carrington, H. (1954). *The American Seances with Eusapia Palladino.* New York: Garrett.

Carrington, H. and Fodor, N. (1951). *Haunted People.* New York: New American Library.

Casler, L. (1962). The improvement of clairvoyance scores by means of hypnotic suggestion. *JP, 26,* 77–87.

Casler, L. (1982). [Letter to the editor]. *JP, 46,* 289–90.

Cattell, R. B. and Beloff, H. (1962). *Handbook for the Junior-Senior High School Personality Questionnaire.* Champagne, IL: Institute for Personality and Ability Testing.

Cattell, R. B., Eber, H. W. and Tatsuoka, M. M. (1970). *Handbook for the Sixteen Personality Factor Questionnaire.* Champagne, IL: Institute for Personality and Ability Testing.

Cavanna, R. and Servadio, E. (1964). ESP experiments with LSD–25 and psilocybin. *PM no. 5.*

Chari, C. T. K. (1973). Regurgitation, mediumship and yoga. *JASPR, 47,* 156–72.

Chari, C. T. K. (1974). The challenge of psi: new horizons of scientific research. *JP, 38,* 1–15.

Chari, C. T. K. (1975). Comments [on physical theories of psi]. In L. Oteri (ed.), *Quantum Physics and Parapsychology* (pp. 252–63). New York: Parapsychology Foundation.

Chari, C. T. K. (1977). Some generalized theories and models of psi: a critical evaluation. *HB* (pp. 803–22).

Child, I. L. (1981). Remarks on 'Psi-conducive and psi-inhibitory experimenters'. *JASPR, 75,* 360–3.

Child, I. L. (1985). Psychology and anomalous observations: the question of ESP in dreams. *American Psychologist*, *40*, 1219–30.

Christopher, M. (1970). *ESP, Seers, and Psychics.* New York: Crowell Press.

Coates, J. (1911). *Photographing the Invisible.* London: Fowler.

Cohen, D. (1975). Magnetic fields of the human body. *Physics Today,* no. 8, pp. 34–43.

Collins, H. M. (1978, February). Science and the rule of repeatability. Paper presented at the annual meeting of the American Association for the Advancement of Science, Washington.

Commentaries on the paper by Professor Karnes *et al.* (1980). *ZS, 6,* 77–89.

Cook, E. W., Pasricha, S., Samararatne, G., Maung, U. W. and Stevenson, I. (1983). A review and analysis of 'unsolved' cases of the reincarnation type: II. *JASPR, 77,* 115–35.

Coover, J. E. (1975). *Experiments in Psychical Research at Leland Stanford Junior University.* New York: Arno Press. (Original work published 1917.)

Courtier, J. (1908). *Rapport sur les séances d'Eusapia Palladino à l'Institut Général Psychologique en 1905, 1906, 1907 et 1908* [*Report on Eusapia Palladino's Seances at the General Psychological Institute in 1905, 1906, 1907, and 1908*]. Paris: Institut Général Psychologique.

Cox, W. E. (1951). The effect of PK on the placement of falling objects. *JP, 15,* 40–8.

Cox, W. E. (1954). A comparison of spheres and cubes in placement PK tests. *JP, 18,* 234–9.

Cox, W. E. (1956). Precognition: an analysis, II. *JASPR, 50,* 99–109.

Cox, W. E. (1961). Introductory comparative analysis of some poltergeist cases. *JASPR, 55,* 47–72.

Cox, W. E. (1962). Five-tier placement PK. *JP, 26,* 35–46.

Cox, W. E. (1965). Effect of PK on electromechanical systems. *JP, 29,* 165–75.

Cox, W. E. (1971). A comparison of different densities of dice in a PK task. *JP, 35,* 108–19.

Cox, W. E. (1974a). Note on some experiments with Uri Geller. *JP, 38,* 408–11.

Cox, W. E. (1974b). PK tests with a thirty-two channel balls machine. *JP, 38,* 56–68.

Crawford, W. J. (1921). *The Psychic Structures at the Goligher Circle.* New York: Dutton.

Crookall, R. (1961). *The Study and Practice of Astral Projection.* Hackensack, NJ.: Wehman.

Crookes, W. (1874). *Researches in the Phenomena of Spiritualism.* London: J. Burns.

Crookes, W. (1889). Notes on seances with D. D. Home. *PSPR, 6,* 98–127.

Cumberland, S. (1975). *A Thought-reader's Thoughts.* New York: Arno Press. (Original work published 1888.).

Dale, L. A. (1946). The psychokinetic effect: the first A.S.P.R. experiment. *JASPR, 40,* 123–51.

Dale, L. A. (1951). A series of spontaneous cases in the tradition of *Phantasms of the Living. JASPR, 45,* 85–102.

Dale, L. A., White, R. (A.) and Murphy, G. (1962). A selection of cases from a recent survey of spontaneous ESP phenomena. *JASPR, 56,* 3–47.

Dale, L. A. and Woodruff, J. L. (1947). The psychokinetic effect: further A.S.P.R. experiments. *JASPR, 41,* 65–82.

Davis, A. J. (1847). *The Principles of Nature, her Divine Revelations, and a Voice to Mankind.* London: John Chapman.

Davis, J. W. (1978). The stacking effect: its practical significance in parapsychology. JP, 42, 67.

David, J. W. and Akers, C. (1974). Randomization and tests for randomness. *JP, 38,* 393–408.

David, J. W. and Morrison, M. D. (1978). A test of Schmidt's prediction concerning multiple feedback in a PK task. *RIP 1977* (pp. 163–8).

Dean, (E.) D. (1983). Infrared measurements of healer-treated water. *RIP 1982* (pp. 100–1).

Dean, E. D. and Nash, C. B. (1967). Coincident plethysmograph results under controlled conditions. *JSPR, 44,* 1–14.

Debes, J. and Morris, R. L. (1982). Comparison of striving and nonstriving instructional sets in a PK study. *JP, 46,* 297–312.

Devereux, G. (ed.). (1971). *Psychoanalysis and the occult.* New York: International Universities Press. (Original work published 1953.)

Diaconis, P. (1978). Statistical problems in ESP research. *Science, 201,* 131–6.

Diaconis, P. (1979). Rejoinder to Edward F. Kelly. *ZS, 5,* 29–31.

Dickstein, M. L. and Davis, J. W. (1979). A blind PK test over two distances. *JP, 43,* 41–2.

Dingwall, E. J. (1968). Hypnotism in France 1800–1900. In E. J. Dingwall (ed.), *Abnormal Hypnotic Phenomena* (vol. 1). New York: Barnes & Noble.

Dingwall, E. J., Goldney, K. M. and Hall, T. H. (1955). *The Haunting of Borley Rectory.* London: Duckworth.

Dingwall, E. J., Goldney, K. M. and Hall, T. H. (1956). The haunting of Borley Rectory: a critical survey of the evidence (with index and diary of events). *PSPR, 51,* i-xiv, 1–181.

Dingwall, E. J. and Hall, T. H. (1958). *Four Modern Ghosts.* London: Duckworth.

Dixon, N. F. (1971). *Subliminal Perception.* New York: McGraw-Hill.

Dobbs, H. A. C. (1965). Time and ESP. *PSPR, 54,* 249–61.

Dobbs, H. A. C. (1967). The feasibility of a physical theory of ESP. In J. R. Smythies (ed.), *Science and ESP* (pp. 225–54). New York: Humanities Press.

Dobervich, C. (1974). Kirlian photography revealed? *Psychic,* pp. 34–9.

Dodds, E. R. (1971). Supernormal phenomena in classical antiquity. *PSPR, 55,* 189–237.

Dommeyer, F. C. (1975). Psychical research at Stanford University. *JP, 39,* 173–205.

Donald, J. A. and Martin, B. (1976). Time-symmetric thermodynamics and causality violation. *EJP, 1*(3), 17–36.

Dudewicz, E. J. and Ralley, T. (1981). *Handbook of Random Number Generation and Testing with TESTRAND Computer Code.* Syracuse, NY: American Sciences Press.

Dunne, J. W. (1958). *An Experiment with Time.* New York: Hillary. (Original work published 1927.)

Duval, P. and Montredon, E. (1968). ESP experiments with mice. *JP, 32,* 153–66.

Edge, H. L. (1976a). Do spirits matter? Naturalism and disembodied survival. *JASPR, 70,* 293–301.

Edge, H. L. (1976b). Rejoinder to Dr Wheatley's notes on 'Do spirits matter?'. *JASPR, 70,* 397–401.

Edge, H. (L.) (1980). The effect of laying on of hands on an enzyme. *RIP 1979* (pp. 137–9).

Edge, H. (L.) and Farkash, M. (1982). Further support for the psi-distributed hypothesis. *RIP 1981* (pp. 171–2).

Edge, H. L. and Wright, A. M. (1978). A possible case of displacement effect. *New England Journal of Parapsychology, 1*(2), 28–43.

Ehrenwald, J. (1975a). Hitler: shaman, schizophrenic, medium?. *PR, 6*(2), 3–9.

Ehrenwald, J. (1975b). *New Dimensions of Deep Analysis.* New York: Arno Press (Original work published 1955.)

Ehrenwald, J. (1977a). Psi, psychotherapy, and psychoanalysis. *HB* (pp. 529–40).

Ehrenwald, J. (1977b). Therapeutic applications [of psi in psychotherapy]. *APR:* vol. 1 (pp. 133–48).

Einstein, A. (1959). Autobiographical notes. In P. A. Schlipp (ed.), *Albert Einstein: Philosopher Scientist* (pp. 1–95). New York: Harper.

Eisenbud, J. (1955). On the use of the psi hypothesis in psychoanalysis. *International Journal of Psychoanalysis, 36,* 1–5.

Eisenbud, J. (1963a). Psi and the nature of things. *IJP, 5,* 245–73.

Eisenbud, J. (1963b). Two approaches to spontaneous case material. *JASPR, 57,* 118–35.

Eisenbud, J. (1967, November). The cruel, cruel world of Ted Serios. *Popular Photography,* pp. 31–2, 34, 134, 136.

Eisenbud, J. (1969). *The World of Ted Serios.* New York: Paperback Library. (Original work published 1967.)

Eisenbud, J. (1970). *Psi and Psychoanalysis.* New York: Grune & Stratton.

Eisenbud, J. (1972). The Serios 'blackies' and related phenomena. *JASPR, 66,* 180–92.

Eisenbud, J. (1977). Paranormal photography. *HB* (pp. 414–32).

Eisenbud, J. (1982). *Paranormal Foreknowledge.* New York: Human Sciences Press.

Eisendrath, D. B., Jr (1967, October). An amazing weekend with the amazing Ted Serios: part II. *Popular Photography,* pp. 84–7, 131–3, 136.

Ellenberger, H. F. (1970). *The Discovery of the Unconscious.* New York: Basic Books.

Ellis, D. (1975). Listening to the 'Raudive voices'. *JSPR, 48,* 31–42.

Epstein, R. A. (1967). *The Theory of Gambling and Statistical Logic.* New York: Academic Press.

Estabrooks, G. H. (1961). A contribution to experimental telepathy. *JP, 25,* 190–213. (Original work published 1927.)

Evans, C. (1973). Parapsychology – what the questionnaire revealed. *New Scientist, 57,* 209.

Eysenck, H. J. (1967a). *The Biological Basis of Personality.* Springfield, IL: Charles Thomas.

Eysenck, H. J. (1967b). Personality and extrasensory perception. *JSPR, 44,* 55–71.

Fahler, J. (1959). Exploratory 'scaled' PK placement tests with nine college students with and without distance. *JASPR, 53,* 106–13.

Fahler, J. and Osis, K. (1966). Checking for awareness of hits in a precognition experiment with hypnotized subjects. *JASPR, 60,* 340–6.

Feather, S. R. (1967). A quantitative comparison of memory and psi. *JP, 31,* 93–8.
Feather, S. R. and Rhine, L. E. (1969). PK experiments with same and different targets. *JP, 33,* 213–27.
Feilding, E. (1963). *Sittings with Eusapia Palladino and Other Studies.* New Hyde Park, NY: University Books.
Feilding, E., Baggally, W. W. and Carrington, H. (1909). Report on a series of sittings with Eusapia Palladino. *PSPR, 23,* 306–569.
Ferguson, M. (1980). *The Aquarian Conspiracy.* Los Angeles: Tarcher.
Fisk, G. W. (1951). Home-testing ESP experiments: second report. *JSPR, 36,* 518–20.
Fisk, G. W. and Mitchell, A. M. J. (1952). ESP experiments with clock cards: a new technique with differential scoring. *JSPR, 37,* 1–14.
Fisk, G. W. and West, D. J. (1957). Psychokinetic experiments with a single subject. *Newsletter of the Parapsychology Foundation, 4*(6), 3–7.
Fisk, G. W. and West, D. J. (1958). Die-casting with a single subject. *JSPR, 39,* 277–87.
Fitzkee, D. (1944). *The Trick Brain* (2nd edn). Oakland, CA: Magic Limited.
Flammarion, C. (1971). *Haunted Houses* (trans. E. F. d'Albe). Detroit: Gale. (Original work published 1923.)
Flew, A. N. G. (1953). *New Approach to Psychical Research.* London: Watts.
Flew, A. N. G. (1956). Can a man witness his own funeral?. *Hibbert Journal, 54,* 242–50.
Fodor, N. (1948). The poltergeist – psychoanalyzed. *Psychiatric Quarterly, 22,* 195–203.
Fodor, N. (1966). *Encyclopedia of Psychic Science.* New Hyde Park, NY; University Books. (Paper, Secaucus, NJ: Citadel, 1974: original work published 1933.)
Fodor, N. (1968). *The Haunted Mind.* New York: New American Library. (Original work published 1959.)
Forwald, H. (1952). A continuation of the experiments in placement PK. *JP, 16,* 273–83.
Forwald, H. (1955). A study of psychokinesis in relation to physical conditions. *JP, 19,* 133–54.
Forwald, H. (1969). Mind, matter, and gravitation: a theoretical and experimental study. *PM no. 11.*
Foster, A. A. (1940). In ESP diametric?. *JP, 4,* 325–8.
Foster, A. A. (1943). ESP tests with American Indian children. *JP, 7,* 94–103.
Foulkes, D., Belvedere, E., Masters, R., Houston, J., Krippner, S., Honorton, C. and Ullman, M. (1972). Long-distance 'sensory-bombardment' ESP: a failure to replicate. *Perceptual and Motor Skills, 35,* 731–4.
Frazer, Sir J. G. (1951). *The Golden Bough.* New York: Macmillan.
Fukurai, T. (1975). *Clairvoyance and Thoughtography* (trans.). New York: Arno Press. (Original work published 1931.)
Garrett, E. J. (1949). *Adventures in the Supernormal.* New York: Garrett.
Gatlin, L. L. (1979). A new measure of bias in finite sequences with applications to ESP data. *JASPR, 73,* 29–43.
Gatling, W. and Rhine, J. B. (1946). Two groups of PK subjects compared. *JP, 10,* 120–5.
Gauld, A. (1968). *The Founders of Psychical Research.* New York: Schocken.
Gauld, A. (1971). A series of 'drop in' communicators. *PSPR, 55,* 273–340.
Gauld, A. (1977). Discarnate survival. *HB* (pp. 577–630).
Gauld, A. and Cornell, A. D. (1979). *Poltergeists.* London: Routledge & Kegan Paul.

Geldard, F. (1972). *The Human Senses* (2nd edn). New York: Wiley.

Geley, G. (1927). *Clairvoyance and Materialization* (trans.). New York: Doran.

Gibson, E. P., Gibson, L. H. and Rhine, J. B. (1944). The PK effect: mechanical throwing of three dice. *JP, 8,* 95–109.

Girden, E. (1962a). A review of psychokinesis (PK). *Psychological Bulletin, 59,* 353–88.

Girden, E. (1962b). A postscript to 'A review of psychokinesis (PK)'. *Psychological Bulletin, 59,* 529–31.

Girden, E., Murphy, G., Beloff, J., Eisenbud, J., Flew, A., Rush, J. H., Schmeidler, G. and Thouless, R. H. (1964). A discussion of psychokinesis. *IJP, 6,* 25–137.

Glass, G. V., McGaw, B. and Smith, M. L. (1981). *Meta-analysis in Social Research.* Beverly Hills, CA: Sage.

Goodman, J. (1977). *Psychic Archaeology.* New York: Putnam's.

Goodman, J. (1979). [Correspondence]. *JASPR, 73,* 100–3.

Gould, J. L. and Able, K. P. (1981). Human homing: an elusive phenomenon. *Science, 212,* 1061.

Grad, B. (1963). A telekinetic effect on plant growth. *IJP, 5,* 117–33.

Grad, B. (1965a). Some biological effects of the 'laying on of hands': a review of experiments with animals and plants. *JASPR, 59,* 95–127.

Grad, B. (1965b). A telekinetic effect on yeast activity. *JP, 29,* 285–6.

Grad, B. (1976). The biological effects of the 'laying on of hands' on animals and plants: implications for biology. In G. R. Schmeidler (ed.), *Parapsychology: Its Relation to Physics, Biology, Psychology, and Psychiatry* (pp. 76–89). Metuchen, NJ: Scarecrow Press.

Grad, B., Cadoret, R. J. and Paul, G. I. (1961). The influence of an unorthodox method of treatment on wound healing in mice. *IJP, 3*(2), 5–24.

Green, C. E. (1960). Analysis of spontaneous cases. *PSPR, 53,* 97–161.

Green, C. E. (1968). *Out-of-the-body Experiences.* Oxford: Institute for Psychophysical Research.

Gregory, A. (1974). Ethics and psychical research. *JSPR, 47,* 283–305.

Gregory, A. (1977). Anatomy of a fraud. *Annals of Science, 34,* 449–549.

Greville, T. N. E. (1944). On multiple matching with one variable deck. *Annals of Mathematical Statistics, 15,* 432–4.

Gurney, E., Myers, F. W. H. and Podmore, F. (1970). *Phantasms of the Living.* Gainesville, FL: Scholars' Facsimiles and Reprints. (Original work published 1886.)

Haight, J. M. (1979). Spontaneous psi cases: a survey and preliminary study of ESP, attitude, and personality relationships. *JP, 43,* 179–204.

Halifax-Grof, J. (1974). Hex death. In A. Angoff and D. Barth (eds), *Parapsychology and Anthropology* (pp. 59–79). New York: Parapsychology Foundation.

Hall, C. (1967). Experiments with telepathically influenced dreams. *Zeitschrift für Parapsychologie und Grenzgebiete der Psychologie, 10,* 18–47.

Hansel, C. E. M. (1960). A critical review of experiments with Mr Basil Shackleton and Mrs Gloria Stewart as sensitives. *PSPR, 53,* 1–42.

Hansel, C. E. M. (1961a). A critical analysis of the Pearce-Pratt experiment. *JP, 25,* 87–91.

Hansel, C. E. M. (1961b). A critical analysis of the Pratt-Woodruff experiment. *JP, 25,* 99–113.

Hansel, C. E. M. (1966). *ESP: A Scientific Evaluation.* New York: Scribners.

Hansel, C. E. M. (1980). *ESP and Parapsychology: A Critical Re-evaluation.* Buffalo: Prometheus.

Hanson, N. R. (1965). *Patterns of Discovery.* Cambridge: Cambridge University Press.

Haraldsson, E. (1973). Psychokinetic effects on yeast: an exploratory experiment. *RIP 1972* (pp. 20–1).

Haraldsson, E., Gudmundsdottir, A., Ragnarsson, A., Loftsson, J. and Jonsson, S. (1977). National survey of psychical experiences and attitudes towards the paranormal in Iceland. *RIP 1976* (pp. 182–6).

Haraldsson, E. and Osis, K. (1977). The appearance and disappearance of objects in the presence of Sri Sathya Sai Baba. *JASPR, 71,* 33–43.

Haraldsson, E., Pratt, J. G. and Kristjansson, M. (1978). Further experiments with the Icelandic medium Hafsteinn Bjornsson. *JASPR, 72,* 339–47.

Haraldsson, E. and Stevenson, I. (1975). A communicator of the 'drop in' type: the case of Runolfur Ronolfsson. *JASPR, 69,* 33–59.

Harman, W. W. (1976). The societal implications and social impact of psi phenomena. *RIP 1975* (pp. 225–42).

Hart, H. (1965). Toward a philosophical basis for parapsychological phenomena. *PM no. 6.*

Hart, H. and collaborators (1956). Six theories about apparitions. *PSPR, 50,* 153–239.

Hartwell, J. W. (1978). Contingent negative variation as an index of precognitive information. *EJP, 2,* 83–103.

Hasted, J. (1981). *The Metal-benders.* London: Routledge & Kegan Paul.

Haynes, R. (1970). *Philosopher King.* London: Weidenfeld & Nicolson.

Haynes, R. (1982). *The Society for Psychical Research, 1882–1982.* London: Macdonald.

Hebb, D. O. (1951). The role of neurological ideas in psychology. *Journal of Personality, 20,* 35–55.

Heseltine, G. L. and Kirk, J. H. (1979). EEG activity of a trance medium. Unpublished manuscript.

Heywood, R. (1959). *Beyond the Reach of Sense.* New York: Dutton.

Heywood, R. (1964). *ESP: A Personal Memoir.* New York: Dutton.

Higbee, K. L. (1977). *Your Memory: How It Works and How To Improve It.* Englewood Cliffs, NJ: Prentice-Hall.

Hilton, H., Jr, Baer, G. and Rhine, J. B. (1943). A comparison of three sizes of dice in PK tests. *JP, 7,* 172–190.

Hilton, H., Jr, and Rhine, J. B. (1943). A second comparison of three sizes of dice in PK tests. *JP, 7,* 191–206.

Hodgson, R. (1892). Mr Davey's imitations by conjuring of phenomena sometimes attributed to spirit agency. *PSPR, 8,* 253–310.

Hoffman, B. (1940). ESP and the inverse-square law. *JP, 4,* 149–52.

Honorton, C. (1970). Effects of feedback on discrimination between correct and incorrect ESP responses. *JASPR, 64,* 404–10.

Honorton, C. (1971). Effects of feedback on discrimination between correct and incorrect ESP responses: a replication study. *JASPR, 65,* 155–61.

Honorton, C. (1972). Significant factors in hypnotically induced clairvoyant dreams. *JASPR, 66,* 86–102.

Honorton, C. (1974a). Apparent psychokinesis on static objects by a 'gifted' subject. *RIP 1973* (pp. 128–31.

Honorton, C. (1974b). Psi-conducive states. In J. White (ed.), *Psychic Exploration* (pp. 616–38). New York: Putnam's.

Honorton, C. (1975a). 'Error some place!'. *Journal of Communication, 25,* 103–16.

Honorton, C. (1975b). Objective determination of information rate in psi tasks with pictorial stimuli. *JASPR, 69,* 353–9.

Honorton, C. (1977). Psi and internal attention states. *HB* (pp. 453–72).

Honorton, C. (1978). Psi and internal attention states: information retrieval in the ganzfeld. In B. Shapin and L. Coly (eds), *Psi and States of Awareness* (pp. 79–90). New York: Parapsychology Foundation.

Honorton, C. (1983). Response to Hyman's critique of psi ganzfeld studies. *RIP 1982* (pp. 23–6).

Honorton, C. (1985.) Meta-analysis of psi ganzfeld research: a response to Hyman. *JP, 49,* 51–91.

Honorton, C. and Barksdale, W. (1972). PK performance with waking suggestions for muscle tension versus relaxation. *JASPR, 66,* 208–14.

Honorton, C., Davidson, R. and Bindler, P. (1971). Feedback-augmented EEG alpha, shifts in subjective state and ESP card-guessing performance. *JASPR, 65,* 308–23.

Honorton, C., Drucker, S. A. and Hermon, H. (1973). Shifts in subjective state and ESP under conditions of partial sensory deprivation: a preliminary study. *JASPR, 67,* 191–6.

Honorton, C. and Harper, S. (1974). Psi-mediated imagery and ideation in an experimental procedure for regulating perceptual input. *JASPR, 68,* 156–68.

Honorton, C. and Krippner, S. (1969). Hypnosis and ESP: a review of the experimental literature. *JASPR, 63,* 214–52.

Honorton, C. and May, E. C. (1976). Volitional control in a psychokinetic task with auditory and visual feedback. *RIP 1975* (pp. 90–1).

Honorton, C., Ramsey, M. and Cabibbo, C. (1975). Experimenter effects in extrasensory perception. *JASPR, 69,* 135–49.

Honorton, C. and Tremmel, L. (1979). Psi correlates of volition: preliminary test of Eccles' 'neurophysiological hypothesis' of mind-brain interaction. *RIP 1978* (pp. 36–8).

Honorton, C. and Tremmel, L. (1980). PSITREK: a preliminary effort toward development of psi-conducive computer software. *RIP 1979* (pp. 159–61).

Hope, C. *et al.* (1933). Report of a series of sittings with Rudi Schneider. *PSPR, 41,* 255–330.

Houtkooper, J. M. (1977). A study of repeated retroactive psychokinesis in relation to direct and random PK effects. *EJP, 1*(4), 1–20.

Houtkooper, J. M. (1983). *Observational Theory: A Research Programme for Paranormal Phenomena.* Lisse, The Netherlands: Swets & Zeitlinger.

Hugard, J. and Braue, F. (1974). *Expert Card Technique.* New York: Dover. (Original work published 1944.)

Hume, D. (1962). An inquiry concerning human understanding. In A. Flew (ed.), *Hume on Human Nature and the Understanding* (pp. 23–163). New York: Collier. (Original work published 1748.)

Humphrey, B. M. (1947a). Help-hinder comparisons in PK tests. *JP, 11,* 4–13.

Humphrey, B. M. (1947b). Simultaneous high and low aim in PK tests. *JP, 11,* 160–174.

Hyman, R. (1981). Further comments on Schmidt's PK experiments. *Skeptical Inquirer, 5*(3), 34–40.

Hyman, R. (1983). Does the ganzfeld answer the critics' objections?. *RIP 1982* (pp. 21–3).

Hyman, R. (1985). The ganzfeld/psi experiment: a critical appraisal. *JP, 49,* 3–49.

Hyslop, J. H. (1908). *Psychical Research and the Resurrection.* Boston: Small, Maynard.

Hyslop, J. H. (ed.). (1911). Experiments of Dr Ochorovics (sic) [trans. of reports of experiments with S. Tomczyk, including report of investigative commission]. *JASPR, 5,* 678–720.

Inglis, B. (1977). *Natural and Supernatural.* London: Hodder & Stoughton.

Irwin, C. P. (1980). The implications of subject familiarity with free-response target pools. *JASPR, 74,* 183–90.

Irwin, H. J. (1979). *Psi and the Mind.* Metuchen, NJ: Scarecrow Press.

Isaacs, J. (1983). A twelve-session study of micro-PKMB training. *RIP 1982* (pp. 31–5).

Isaacs, J. (1984). The Batcheldor approach: some strengths and weaknesses. *JASPR, 78,* 123–32.

Jackson, M., Franzoi, S. and Schmeidler, G. R. (1977). Effects of feedback on ESP: a curious partial replication. *JASPR, 71,* 147–55.

Jacobson, E. (1974). *Progressive Relaxation* (rev. edn). Chicago: University of Chicago Press. (Original work published 1938.)

Jahn, R. G., Dunne, B. J. and Jahn, E. G. (1980). Analytic judging procedures in remote perception experiments. *JP, 44,* 207–31.

James, W. (1960). Frederic Myers' service to psychology. In G. Murphy and R. O. Ballou (eds), *William James on Psychical Research.* (pp. 213–25). New York: Viking. (Original work published 1901.)

James, W. (1968). The present dilemma in philosophy. In J. J. McDermott (ed.), *William James: A Comprehensive Edition* (pp. 362–76). New York: Modern Library. (Original work published 1907.)

Jephson, I. (1929). Evidence for clairvoyance in card-guessing: a report on some recent experiments. *PSPR, 38,* 223–68.

Johnson, M. (1973). A new technique of testing ESP in a real-life, high motivational context. *JP, 37,* 210–17.

Johnson, M. and Haraldsson, E. (1984). The Defense Mechanism Test as a predictor of ESP scores: Icelandic studies IV and V. *JP, 48,* 185–200.

Jones, D. E. (1979). *Visions of Time.* Wheaton, IL: Theosophical Publishing House.

Kanthamani, H. and Kelly, E. F. (1974a). Awareness of success in an exceptional subject. *JP, 38,* 355–82.

Kanthamani, H. and Kelly, E. F. (1974b). Card experiments with a special subject. I. Single-card clairvoyance. *JP, 38,* 16–26.

Kanthamani, H. and Kelly, E. F. (1975). Card experiments with a special subject. II. The shuffle method. *JP, 39,* 206–21.

Kanthamani, B. K. [H.] and Rao, K. R. (1971). Personality characteristics of ESP subjects. I. Primary personality characteristics and ESP. *JP, 35,* 189–207.

Kanthamani, B. K. [H.] and Rao, K. R. (1972). Personality characteristics of ESP subjects. III. Extraversion and ESP. *JP, 36,* 198–212.

Kanthamani, B. K. [H.] and Rao, K. R. (1973). Personality characteristics of ESP subjects. IV. Neuroticism and ESP. *JP, 37,* 37–50.

Kappers, J. (1964). Spontaneous paranormal phenomena in Amsterdam. *JP, 28,* 283–4.

Karger, F. and Zicha, G. (1971). Physical investigation of psychokinetic phenomena in Rosenheim, Germany, 1967. *PPA, 5,* 33–5.

Karnes, E. W., Susman, E. P., Klusman, P. and Turcotte, L. (1980). Failures to replicate remote viewing using psychic subjects. *ZS, 6,* 66–76.
Keene, M. L. (1976). *The Psychic Mafia.* New York: Dell.
Keil, H. H. J. (1965). A GESP test with favorite music targets. *JP, 29,* 35–44.
Keil, H. H. J., Herbert, B., Ullman, M. and Pratt, J. G. (1976). Directly observable voluntary PK effects. *PSPR, 56,* 197–235.
Kelly, E. F. (1979). Reply to Persi Diaconis. *ZS, 5,* 20–8.
Kelly, E. F. and Kanthamani, B. K. [H.] (1972). A subject's efforts toward voluntary control. *JP, 36,* 185–97.
Kelly, E. F., Kanthamani, B. K. [H.], Child, I. L. and Young, F. W. (1975). On the relation between visual and ESP confusion structures in an exceptional ESP subject. *JASPR, 69,* 1–32.
Kennedy, J. E. (1979). Methodological problems in free-response ESP experiments. *JASPR, 73,* 1–15.
Kennedy, J. E. (1980a). Information processing in ESP: a survey of forced-choice experiments using multiple-aspect targets. *JP, 44,* 9–34.
Kennedy, J. E. (1980b). Learning to use ESP: do the calls match the targets or do the targets match the calls?. *JASPR, 74,* 191–209.
Kennedy, J. E. and Taddonio, J. L. (1976). Experimenter effects in parapsychological research. *JP, 40,* 1–33.
Kennedy, J. L. and Uphoff, H. F. (1939). Experiments on the nature of extrasensory perception: the recording error criticism of extrachance scores. *JP, 3,* 226–45.
Kline, M. (ed.) (1956). *A Scientific Report on 'The Search for Bridey Murphy'.* New York: Julian Press.
Kogan, I. M. (1966). Is telepathy possible?. *Telecommunication and Radio Engineering, 21*(1, part 2), 75–81.
Kogan, I. M. (1967). Telepathy – hypotheses and observations. *Telecommunication and Radio Engineering, 22* (1, part 2), 141–4.
Konikicwicz, L. W. (1977). Kirlian photography in theory and clinical application. *Journal of the Biological Photographic Association, 45,* 115–34.
Kotik, N. (1908). *Die Emanation der Psychophysichen Energie* [*The Emanation of Psychophysical Energy*]. Wiesbaden, West Germany: J. F. Bergmann.
Kragh, U. and Smith, G. W. (1970). *Percept-genetic Analysis.* Lund, Sweden: Gleerups.
Krippner, S. (ed.) (1977, 1978, 1982). *APR.*
Krippner, S., Honorton, C. and Ullman, M. (1972). A second precognitive dream study with Malcolm Bessent. *JASPR, 66,* 269–79.
Krippner, S., Honorton, C. and Ullman, M. (1973). A long-distance ESP dream study with the 'Grateful Dead'. *Journal of the American Society of Psychosomatic Dentistry and Medicine, 65,* 468–75.
Krippner, S., Honorton, C., Ullman, M., Masters, R. and Houston, J. (1971). A long-distance 'sensory bombardment' study of ESP in dreams. *JASPR, 65,* 468–75.
Krippner, S., Ullman, M. and Honorton, C. (1971). A precognitive dream study with a single subject. *JASPR, 65,* 192–203.
Kübler-Ross, E. (1969). *On Death and Dying.* New York: Macmillan.
Kübler-Ross, E. (1975). *Death: The Final Stage of Growth.* Englewood Cliffs, NJ: Prentice-Hall.
Kuhn, T. S. (1962). *The Structure of Scientific Revolutions.* Chicago: University of Chicago Press.
Kurtz, P. (1978). The *Humanist*'s crusade against parapsychology: a

discussion. Part I. On the art of quoting out of context: a response to the Rockwells' critique. *JASPR, 72,* 349–57.

Kuyper, O. *et al.* (1972). The conditioning of PK responses. *JP, 36,* 253–4.

Lambert, G. W. (1955). Poltergeists: a physical theory. *JSPR, 38,* 49–71.

Lambert, G. W. (1960). The geography of London ghosts. *JSPR, 40,* 397–409.

LaMothe, J. D. (1972). Controlled offensive behavior. A report of the Defense Intelligence Agency prepared by the US Army.

Laubscher, B. J. F. (1938). *Sex, Custom and Psychopathology.* New York: McBride.

Layard, J. (1944). Psi phenomena and poltergeists. *PSPR, 47,* 237–47.

Layton, B. D. and Turnbull, B. (1975). Belief, evaluation, and performance on an ESP task. *Journal of Experimental Social Psychology, 11,* 166–79.

Leach, E. (1969). *Genesis as Myth and Other Essays.* London: Cape.

LeShan, L. (1966). *The Medium, the Mystic, and the Physicist.* New York: Random House.

Leuret, F. and Bon, H. (1957). *Modern Miraculous Cures.* London: Peter Davies.

Levi, A. (1979). The influence of imagery and feedback on PK effects. *JP, 43,* 275–89.

Lovitts, B. E. (1981). The sheep-goat effect turned upside down. *JP, 45,* 293–310.

Lucadou, W. V. and Kornwachs, K. (1977). Can quantum theory explain paranormal phenomena?. *RIP 1976* (pp. 187–91).

Lucadou, W. v. and Kornwachs, K. (1983). On the limitations of psi – a system-theoretic approach. *RIP 1982* (pp. 85–9).

Luria, A. R. (1968). *The Mind of a Mnemonist* (trans. L. Solotaroff). New York: Avon Books.

McCallam, E. and Honorton, C. (1973). Effects of feedback on discrimination between correct and incorrect ESP responses: a further replication and extension. *JASPR, 67,* 77–85.

McConnell, R. A. (1955). Remote night tests for PK. *JASPR, 49,* 99–108.

McConnell, R. A. and Clark, T. K. (1980). Training, belief, and mental conflict within the Parapsychological Association. *JP, 44,* 245–68.

McConnell, R. A. and Clark, T. K. (1983). Progressive organization and ambivalence within the psychokinetic testing session. In R. A. McConnell (ed.) *Parapsychology and Self-deception in Science* (pp. 55–70). Pittsburgh: R. A. McConnell.

McConnell, R. A. and Forwald, H. (1967). Psychokinetic placement. I. A re-examination of the Forwald-Durham experiment. *JP, 31,* 51–69.

McConnell, R. A., Snowdon, R. J. and Powell, K. F. (1955). Wishing with dice. *Journal of Experimental Psychology, 50,* 269–75.

McIntosh, A. I. (1980). Beliefs about out of the body experiences among the Elema, Gulf Kamea and Rigo peoples of Papua New Guinea. *JSPR, 50,* 460–77.

McMahan, E. A. (1946). An experiment in pure telepathy. *JP, 10,* 242–62.

McNulty, P. J., Pease, V. P. and Bond, V. P. (1975). Visual sensations induced by Cerenkov radiation. *Science, 189* 453–4.

McRae, R. (1984). *Mind Wars.* New York: St Martin's Press.

Maher, M., Peratsakis, D. and Schmeidler, G. R. (1979). Cerebral lateralization effects in ESP processing: an attempted replication. *JASPR, 73,* 167–77.

Maher, M. and Schmeidler, G. R. (1975). Quantitative investigation of a recurrent apparition. *JASPR, 69,* 341–52.

Maher, M. and Schmeidler, G. R. (1977). Cerebral lateralization effects in ESP processing. *JASPR, 71,* 261–71.

Maher, M. and Schmeidler, G. R. (1978). The authors' reply to Mr Broughton. *JASPR, 72,* 389–92.

Mahoney, M. J. (1976). *Scientist as Subject.* Cambridge, MA: Ballinger.

Manning, M. (1974). *The Link.* New York: Holt, Rinehart & Winston.

Margenau, H. (1959). Einstein's conception of reality. In P. A. Schlipp (ed.), *Einstein: Philosopher Scientist* (pp. 243–68). New York: Harper.

Marks, D. (1981a). On the review of *The Psychology of the psychic:* a reply to Dr Morris. *JASPR, 75,* 197–203.

Marks, D. (1981b). Sensory cues invalidate remote viewing experiments. *Nature, 292,* 177.

Marks, D. and Kammann, R. (1980). *The Psychology of the Psychic.* Buffalo: Prometheus.

Markwick, B. (1978). The Soal-Goldney experiments with Basil Shackleton: new evidence of data manipulation. *PSPR, 56,* 250–77.

Marshall, N. (1960). ESP and memory: a physical theory. *British Journal for Philosophy of Science, 10* 265–86.

Matas, F. and Pantas, L. (1971). A PK experiment comparing meditating versus nonmeditating subjects. *PPA, 8,* 12–13.

Mattuck, R. D. (1977). Random fluctuation theory of psychokinesis: thermal noise model. *RIP 1976* (pp. 191–5).

Mattuck, R. D. (1982). Quantum mechanical 'skewed hidden variables' model of large-scale psychokinetic phenomena. Unpublished manuscript.

Mauskopf, S. H. and McVaugh, M. R. (1980). *The Elusive Science* [with an afterword by J. B. and L. E. Rhine]. Baltimore: Johns Hopkins University Press.

May, E. C., Targ, R. and Puthoff, H. E. (1979). EEG correlates to remote light flashes under conditions of sensory shielding. *MAL* (pp. 125–36).

Medhurst, R. G. (1971). The origin of the 'prepared random numbers' used in the Shackleton experiments. *JSPR, 46,* 39–55.

Medhurst, R. G., Goldney, K. M. and Barrington, M. R. (1972). *Crookes and the Spirit World.* New York: Taplinger.

Medhurst, R. G. and Scott, C. (1974). A re-examination of C. E. M. Hansel's criticism of the Pratt-Woodruff experiment. *JP, 38,* 163–84.

Millar, B. (1978). The observational theories: a primer. *EJP, 2,* 304–32.

Miller, R. N. and Reinhart, P. B. (1975, June). Measuring psychic energy. *Psychic,* pp. 46–7.

Mills, J. (1979). *Six Years with God.* New York: A & W Publishers.

Mischo, J. and Weis, R. (1973). A pilot study on the relations between PK scores and personality variables. *RIP 1972* (pp. 21–3).

Misner, C. W., Thorne, K. S. and Wheeler, J. A. (1973). *Gravitation.* San Francisco: Freeman.

Mitchell, A. M. J., and Fisk, G. W. (1953). The application of differential scoring methods to PK tests. *JSPR, 37,* 45–60.

Montagno, E. de A. and Roll, W. G. (1983). A neurological model for psychokinesis. *RIP 1982* (pp. 272–3).

Moody, R. A., Jr (1975). *Life After Life.* Covington, GA: Mockingbird Books.

Moon, M. L. (1975). Artists contrasted with non-artists concerning belief in ESP: a poll. *JASPR, 69,* 161–6.

Moore, B. N. (1981). *The Philosophical Possibilities Beyond Death.* Springfield, IL: Charles Thomas.

Morris, R. L. (1968). Obtaining non-random entry points: a complex psi task. In J. B. Rhine and R. Brier (eds), *Parapsychology Today*. New York: Citadel.

Morris, R. L. (1970). Psi and animal behavior: a survey. *JASPR, 64,* 242–60.

Morris, R. L. (1972). An exact method for evaluating preferentially matched free-response material. *JASPR, 66,* 401–7.

Morris, R. L. (1978). A survey of methods and issues in ESP research. *APR:* vol. 2 (pp. 7–58).

Morris, R. L. (1980). Some comments on the assessment of parapsychological studies: a review of *The Psychology of the Psychic* by D. Marks and R. Kammann. *JASPR, 74,* 425–43.

Morris, R. L. (1981). Developing 'extreme case' causal models for synchronistic phenomena. In B. Shapin and L. Coly (eds), *Concepts and Theories of Parapsychology* (pp. 80–90). New York: Parapsychology Foundation.

Morris, R. L. (1982). Mainstream science, experts, and anomaly: a review of *Science and the Paranormal* edited by George O. Abell and Barry Singer. *JASPR, 76,* 257–81.

Morris, R. L., Nanko, M. and Phillips, D. (1982). A comparison of two popularly advocated visual imagery strategies in a psychokinesis task. *JP, 46,* 1–16.

Morrison, M. D. and Davis, J. W. (1979). PK with immediate, delayed, and multiple feedback: a test of the Schmidt model's predictions. *RIP 1978* (pp. 117–20).

Morton, R. C. (1892). A record of a haunted house. *PSPR, 8,* 311–32.

Mundle, C. W. K. (1950). The experimental evidence for PK and precognition. *PSPR, 49,* 61–78.

Mundle, C. W. K. (1976). Strange facts in search of a theory. *PDP* (pp. 76–97).

Murphy, G. (1945). *Three Papers on the Survival Problem.* New York: American Society for Psychical Research.

Murphy, G. (1962a). A qualitative study of telepathic phenomena. *JASPR, 56,* 63–79.

Murphy, G. (1962b). Report on paper by Edward Girden on psychokinesis. *Psychological Bulletin, 59,* 520–8.

Myers, F. W. H. (1886). On telepathic hypnotism, and its relation to other forms of hypnotic suggestion. *PSPR, 4,* 127–88.

Myers, F. W. H. (1975). *Human Personality and its Survival of Bodily Death* (2 vols). New York: Arno Press. (Original work published 1903.)

Nadel, S. F. (1952). Witchcraft in four African societies: an essay in comparison. *American Anthropologist, 54,* 18–29.

Nash, C. B. (1946). Position effects in PK tests with twenty-four dice. *JP, 10,* 51–7.

Nash, C. B. (1984). A test of psychokinetic control of bacterial mutation. *JASPR, 78,* 145–52.

Nash, C. B. and Nash, C. S. (1967). Effect of paranormally conditioned solution on yeast fermentation. *JP, 31,* 314.

Nash, C. B. and Richards, A. (1947). Comparison of two distances in PK tests. *JP, 11,* 269–82.

Nelms, H. (1969). *Magic and Showmanship.* New York: Dover.

Nelson, G. K. (1969). *Spiritualism and Society.* New York: Schocken.

Nelson, R. (1976). From the Central Premonitions Registry. *PR, 7*(3), 22–4.

Nelson, R. D., Dunne, B. J. and Jahn, R. G. (1984). A psychokinetic experiment with a random mechanical cascade. *RIP 1983* (pp. 86–9).

Nicol, J. F. (1954). The design of experiments in psychokinesis. *JSPR, 37,* 355–7.

Nicol, J. F. (1961). Apparent spontaneous precognition: a historical review. *IJP, 3*(2), 26–39.

Nicol, J. F. (1977). Historical background [of PK research]. *HB* (pp. 305–23).

Ochorowicz, J. (1909). Un nouveau phénomène mediumique [A new mediumistic phenomenon]. *Annales des Sciences Psychiques, 19,* 1–10, 45–51, 65–77, 97–106, 129–33. (Trans. by J. H. Hyslop: *JASPR,* 1911, *5,* 678–720.)

Osis, K. (1953). A test of the relationship between ESP and PK. *JP, 17,* 298–309.

Osis, K. (1961). Deathbed observations by physicians and nurses. *PM no. 3.*

Osis, K. (1978). Out-of-the-body research at the American Society for Psychical Research. In D. S. Rogo (ed.), *Mind Beyond the Body* (pp. 162–9). New York: Penguin Books.

Osis, K. and Bokert, E. (1971). ESP and changed states of consciousness induced by meditation. *JASPR, 64,* 17–65.

Osis, K. and Haraldsson, E. (1977). *At the Hour of Death.* New York: Avon Books (paper).

Osty, E. and Osty, M. (1932). *Les pouvoirs inconnus sur la matière: premières étapes d'une recherche* [*Unknown Powers Over Matter: First Stages of an Investigation*]. Paris: Felix Alcan.

Oteri, L. (ed.). (1975). *Quantum Physics and Parapsychology.* New York: Parapsychology Foundation.

Owen, A. R. G. (1964). *Can We Explain the Poltergeist*?. New York: Garrett.

Owen, I. M. and Sparrow, M. H. (1976). *Conjuring up Philip.* New York: Harper & Row.

Pagenstecher, G. (1923). Past events seership. *PASPR, 16,* 1–136.

Palmer, J. (1971). Scoring in ESP tests as a function of belief in ESP. Part I: The sheep-goat effect. *JASPR, 65,* 373–408.

Palmer, J. (1972). Scoring in ESP tests as a function of belief in ESP. Part II: Beyond the sheep-goat effect. *JASPR, 66,* 1–26.

Palmer, J. (1973). ESP scoring as predicted from four definitions of the sheep-goat variable. *RIP 1972* (pp. 37–9).

Palmer, J. (1975a). Some recent trends in survival research. *PR, 6*(3), 15–17.

Palmer, J. (1975b). Three models of psi test performance. *JASPR, 69,* 333–9.

Palmer, J. (1977). Attitudes and personality traits in experimental ESP research. *HB* (pp. 175–201).

Palmer, J. (1978a). ESP and out-of-body experiences: an experimental approach. In D. Rogo (ed.), *Mind Beyond the Body* (pp. 193–217). New York: Penguin Books.

Palmer, J. (1978b). Extrasensory perception: research findings. *APR:* vol. 2 (pp. 59–243).

Palmer, J. (1979). A community mail survey of psychic experiences. *JASPR, 73,* 221–51.

Palmer, J. (1980). Parapsychology: science or pseudoscience? [Review of *ESP and Parapsychology: A Critical Re-evaluation*]. *Contemporary Psychology, 26,* 9–10.

Palmer, J. (1982). ESP research findings: 1976–1978. *APR:* vol. 3 (pp. 41–82).

Palmer, J. (1983a). Hypnosis and psi: a research program related to the theory of Kenneth Batcheldor. *RIP 1982* (pp. 55–8).
Palmer, J. (1983b). In defense of parapsychology: a reply to James E. Alcock. *ZS, 11,* 39–70, 91–103.
Palmer, J. (1983c). Sensory contamination of free-response ESP targets: the greasy fingers hypothesis. *JASPR, 77,* 101–13.
Palmer, J., Bogart, D. N., Jones, S. and Tart, C. T. (1977). Scoring patterns in an ESP ganzfeld experiment. *JASPR, 71,* 121–45.
Palmer, J. and Kramer, W. (1984). A study of internal state and temporal factors in psychokinesis. *JP, 48,* 1–25.
Palmer, J. and Kramer, W. (1984). Sensory identification of contaminated free-response ESP targets: return of the greasy fingers. *JASPR.*
Panati, C. (1976). *The Geller Papers.* Boston: Houghton Mifflin.
Pantas, L. (1971). PK scoring under preferred and nonpreferred conditions. *PPA, 8,* 47–9.
Parker, A. (1974). ESP in gerbils using positive reinforcement. *JP, 38,* 301–11.
Parker, A. (1975). A pilot study of the influence of experimenter expectancy on ESP scores. *RIP 1974* (pp. 42–4).
Parker, A. (1977). Parapsychologists' personality and psi in relation to the experimenter effect. *RIP 1976* (pp. 107–9).
Parker, A. and Beloff, J. (1970). Hypnotically-induced clairvoyant dreams: a partial replication and attempted confirmation. *JASPR, 64,* 432–42.
Penelhum, T. (1970). *Survival and Disembodied Existence.* New York: Humanities Press.
Persinger, M. A. (1979). ELF field mediation in spontaneous psi events: direct information transfer or conditioned elicitation?. *MAL* (pp. 190–204).
Peterson, I. (1983, 30 April). Preventing fraud in research. *Science News,* p. 279.
Pfungst, O. (1965). *Clever Hans* (ed. R. Rosenthal). New York: Holt, Rinehart & Winston.
Podmore, F. (1897). *Studies in Psychical Research.* New York: Putnam's.
Podmore, F. (1909). The report on Eusapia Palladino. *JSPR, 14,* 172–6.
Podmore, F. (1963). *Mediums of the 19th century* (2 vols). New Hyde Park, New York: University Books. (Original work published as *Modern Spiritualism,* 1902.)
Podmore, F. (1965). *From Mesmer to Christian Science.* New Hyde Park, New York: University Books. (Original work published as *Mesmerism and Christian Science,* 1908.)
Podmore, F. (1975). *The Newer Spiritualism.* New York: Arno Press. (Original work published 1910.)
Pope, D. H. (1953). ESP tests with primitive people. *Parapsychology Bulletin, 30,* 1–3.
Popper, K. (1963). *Conjectures and Refutations.* New York: Basic Books.
Prasad, J. and Stevenson, I. (1968). A survey of spontaneous psychical experiences in school children of Uttar Pradesh, India. *IJP, 10,* 241–61.
Pratt, J. G. (1944). A reinvestigation of the quarter distribution of the (PK) page. *JP, 8,* 61–3.
Pratt, J. G. (1951). The Cormack placement PK experiments. *JP, 15,* 57–73.
Pratt, J. G. (1963). The Girden-Murphy papers on PK. *JP, 27,* 199–209.
Pratt, J. G. (1964). *Parapsychology: An Insider's View of ESP.* New York: Doubleday.
Pratt, J. G. (1969). On the evaluation of verbal material in parapsychology. *PM no. 10.*

Pratt, J. G. (1973). A decade of research with a selected ESP subject: an overview and reappraisal of the work with Pavel Stepanek. *PASPR, 30,* 1–78.

Pratt, J. G. (1974). Comments on the Medhurst-Scott criticism of the Pratt-Woodruff experiment. *JP, 38,* 185–201.

Pratt, J. G. (1976). New evidence supporting the ESP interpretation of the Pratt-Woodruff experiment. *JP, 40,* 217–27.

Pratt, J. G. (1977). Soviet research in parapsychology. *HB* (pp. 883–903).

Pratt, J. G. (1978) [Statement]. *PSPR, 56,* 279–81.

Pratt, J. G. and Birge, W. R. (1948). Appraising verbal test material in parapsychology. *JP, 12,* 236–56.

Pratt, J. G. and Forwald, H. (1958). Confirmation of the PK placement effect. *JP, 22,* 1–19.

Pratt, J. G., Keil, H. H. J. and Stevenson, I. (1970). Three-experimenter ESP tests of Pavel Stepanek during his 1968 visit to Charlottesville. *JASPR, 64,* 18–39.

Pratt, J. G., Martin, D. R. and Stribic, F. P. (1974). Computer studies of the ESP process in card guessing. III. Displacement effects in the C. J. records from the Colorado series. *JASPR, 68,* 357–84.

Pratt, J. G. and Woodruff, J. L. (1939). Size of stimulus symbols in extra-sensory perception. *JP, 3,* 121–58.

Pratt, J. G. and Woodruff, J. L. (1961). Refutation of Hansel's allegation concerning the Pratt-Woodruff series. *JP, 25,* 114–29.

Presman, A. S. (1970). *Electromagnetic Fields and Life* (trans. F. L. Sinclair; ed. F. A. Brown). New York: Plenum Press.

Price, G. R. (1955). Science and the supernatural. *Science, 122,* 359–67.

Price, H. (1930). *Rudi Schneider: A Scientific Explanation of his Mediumship.* London: Methuen.

Price, H. (1973). *Stella C.: An Account of Some Original Experiments in Psychical Research.* London: Souvenir Press. (Original work published 1925.)

Price, H. H. (1949). Psychical research and human personality. *Hibbert Journal, 47,* 105–13.

Price, H. H. (1976). Some philosophical questions about telepathy and clairvoyance. *PDP* (pp. 105–32). (Original work published 1940.)

Price, M. M. and Rhine, J. B. (1944). The subject-experimenter relation in the PK test. *JP, 8,* 177–86.

Prince, W. F. (1921). Psychometric experiments with Senora Maria de Z. *PASPR, 15,* 189–314.

Puthoff, H. E. and Targ, R. (1974a). PK experiments with Uri Geller and Ingo Swann. *RIP 1973* (pp. 125–8).

Puthoff, H. E. and Targ, R. (1974b). Psychic research and modern physics. In J. White (ed.), *Psychic Exploration* (pp. 524–42). New York: Putnam's.

Puthoff, H. and Targ, R. (1975). Physics, entropy, and psychokinesis. In L. Oteri (ed.), *Quantum Physics and Parapsychology* (pp. 129–44). New York: Parapsychology Foundation.

Puthoff, H. E. and Targ, R. (1979). A perceptual channel for information transfer over kilometer distances: historical perspective and recent research. *MAL* (pp. 11–76).

Puthoff, H. E. and Targ, R. (1981). Rebuttal of criticisms of remote viewing experiments. *Nature, 292,* 388.

RAND Corporation (1955). *A Million Random Digits and 100,000 Normal Deviates.* Glencoe, Illinois: Free Press.

Rao, K. R. (1964). The differential response in three new situations. *JP, 28,* 81–92.

Rao, K. R. (1965). The bidirectionality of psi. *JP, 29,* 230–50.

Rao, K. R. (1978). Theories of psi. *APR:* vol 2. (pp. 245–95).

Rao, K. R. (1981). [Letter to the editor]. *JSPR, 51,* 191–3.

Raudive, K. (1971). *Breakthrough.* New York: Taplinger.

Rauscher, E. A. and Rubik, B. A. (1980). Effects on motility behavior and growth rate of Salmonella typhimurium in the presence of a psychic subject. *RIP 1979* (pp. 140–2).

Rayleigh, Lord (1933). On a method of silhouette photography by infra-red rays for use in mediumistic investigation. *PSPR, 41,* 89–98.

Reichbart, R. (1978). Magic and psi: some speculations on their relationship. *JASPR, 72,* 153–75.

Reichbart, R. (1981). Western law and parapsychology. *PR, 12*(2), 9–11.

Reiser, M., Ludwig, L., Saxe, S. and Wagner, C. (1979). An evaluation of the use of psychics in investigations of major crimes. *Journal of Police Science and Administration, 7,* 18–25.

Resch, A. (1969). Der Fall Rosenheim [The Rosenheim case]: Part IV. *Grenzgebiete der Wissenschaft, 18,* 1–15.

Reynolds, C. (1967, October). An amazing weekend with the amazing Ted Serios: Part I. *Popular Photography,* pp. 81–3, 136–40, 158.

Rhine, J. B. (1937). *New Frontiers of the Mind.* New York: Farrar & Rinehart.

Rhine, J. B. (1941). Terminal salience in ESP performance. *JP, 5,* 183–244.

Rhine, J. B. (1946a). Hypnotic suggestion in PK tests. *JP, 10,* 126–40.

Rhine, J. B. (1946b). The psychokinetic effect: a review. *JP, 10,* 5–20.

Rhine, J. B. (1947a). Pierre Janet's contribution to parapsychology. *JP, 11,* 155–9.

Rhine, J. B. (1947b). *The Reach of the Mind.* New York: Sloane.

Rhine, J. B. (1948). The value of reports of spontaneous psi experiences. *JP, 12,* 231–5.

Rhine, J. B. (1954). The science of nonphysical nature. *The Journal of Philosophy, 51,* 801–10.

Rhine, J. B. (1969). Position effects in psi test results. *JP, 33,* 136–57.

Rhine, J. B. (1972). Parapsychology and man. *JP, 36,* 101–21.

Rhine, J. B. (1973). *Extrasensory Perception* (rev. edn). Boston: Bruce Humphries. (Original work published 1934.)

Rhine, J. B. (1974). Comments: a new case of experimenter unreliability. *JP, 38,* 215–25.

Rhine, J. B. (1977). History of experimental studies. *HB* (pp. 25–47).

Rhine, J. B. and associates (1965). *Parapsychology from Duke to FRNM.* Durham, North Carolina: Parapsychology Press.

Rhine, J. B. and Feather, S. R. (1962). The study of cases of psi-trailing in animals. *JP, 26,* 1–22.

Rhine, J. B. and Humphrey, B. M. (1944a). The PK effect: special evidence from hit patterns. I. Quarter distributions of the page. *JP, 8,* 18–60.

Rhine, J. B. and Humphrey, B. M. (1944b). The PK effect: special evidence from hit patterns. II. Quarter distributions of the set. *JP, 8,* 254–71.

Rhine, J. B., Humphrey, B. M. and Pratt, J. G. (1945). The PK effect: special evidence from hit patterns. III. Quarter distributions of the half-set. *JP, 9,* 150–68.

Rhine, J. B. and Pratt, J. G. (1954). A review of the Pearce-Pratt distance series of ESP tests. *JP, 18,* 165–77.

Rhine, J. B. and Pratt, J. G. (1957). *Parapsychology: Frontier Science of the Mind.* Springfield, Illinois: Charles Thomas.

Rhine, J. B. and Pratt, J. G. (1961). A reply to the Hansel critique of the Pearce-Pratt series. *JP, 25,* 92–8.

Rhine, J. B., Pratt, J. G., Stuart, C. E., Smith, B. M. and Greenwood, J. A. (1966). *Extra-sensory Perception after Sixty Years.* Boston: Bruce Humphries. (Original work published 1940.)

Rhine, J. B., Smith, B. M. and Woodruff, J. L. (1938). Experiments bearing on the precognition hypothesis: II. The role of ESP in the shuffling of cards. *JP, 2,* 119–31.

Rhine, L. E. (1951). Conviction and associated conditions in spontaneous cases. *JP, 15,* 164–91.

Rhine, L. E. (1957). Hallucinatory psi experiences: III. The intention of the agent and the dramatizing tendency of the percipient. *JP, 21,* 186–226.

Rhine, L. E. (1962). Psychological processes in ESP experiences. Part I. Waking experiences. *JP, 26,* 88–111.

Rhine, L. E. (1965). *Hidden Channels of the Mind.* New York: William Morrow.

Rhine, L. E. (1967). *ESP in Life and Lab.* New York: Macmillan. (Paper, New York: Collier, 1969.)

Rhine, L. E. (1969). Case study review. *JP, 33,* 228–66.

Rhine, L. E. (1970). *Mind over Matter.* New York: Macmillan.

Rhine, L. E. (1981). *The Invisible Picture.* Jefferson, North Carolina: McFarland.

Rhine, L. E. and Rhine, J. B. (1943). The psychokinetic effect: I. The first experiment. *JP, 7,* 20–43.

Richet, C. (1975). *Thirty Years of Psychical Research* (trans. S. de Brath). New York: Arno Press. (Original work published 1923.)

Richmond, N. (1952). Two series of PK tests on paramecia. *JSPR, 36,* 577–88.

Rockwell, T. (1979). Pseudoscience? Or Pseudocriticism. *JP, 43,* 221–31.

Rockwell, T., Rockwell, R. and Rockwell, W. T. (1978a). Irrational rationalists: a critique of *The Humanist*'s crusade against parapsycholgoy. *JASPR, 72,* 23–34.

Rockwell, T., Rockwell, R. and Rockwell, W. T. (1978b). *The Humanist*'s crusade against parapsychology: a discussion. Part II. Context vs. meaning: a reply to Dr Kurtz. *JASPR, 72,* 357–64.

Rogers, D. P. (1966). Negative and positive affect and ESP run-score variance. *JP, 30,* 151–9.

Rogo, D. S. (1975). *Parapsychology: A Century of Inquiry.* New York: Taplinger.

Rogo, D. S. (1976). *In Search of the Unknown.* New York: Taplinger.

Rogo, D. S. (1980). The poltergeist and family dynamics: a report on a recent investigation. *RIP 1979* (pp. 108–9).

Rohrlich, F. (1983). Facing quantum mechanical reality. *Science, 221,* 1251–5.

Roll, W. G. (1966a). ESP and memory. *International Journal of Neuropsychiatry, 2,* 505–21.

Roll, W. G. (1966b). The psi field. *PPA, 1,* 32–65.

Roll, W. G. (1974). Survival research: problems and possibilities. In J. White (ed.), *Psychic Exploration* (pp. 397–424). New York: Putnam's.

Roll, W. G. (1976). *The Poltergeist.* Metuchen, New Jersey: Scarecrow Press.

Roll, W. G. (1977). Poltergeists. *HB* (pp. 382–413).

Roll, W. G. (1982). The changing perspective on life after death. *APR:* vol. 3 (pp. 147–291).

Roll, W. G., Burdick, D. S. and Joines, W. T. (1973). Radial and tangential forces in the Miami poltergeist. *JASPR, 67,* 267–81.

Roll, W. G. and Montagno, E. de A. (1983). Similarities between RSPK and motor epilepsy. *RIP 1982* (pp. 270–1).

Roll, W. G. and Pratt, J. G. (1971). The Miami disturbances. *JASPR, 65,* 409–54.

Roll, W. G. and Solfvin, G. F. (1976). Meditation and ESP. *RIP 1975* (pp. 92–7).

Roll, W. G. and Stump, J. P. (1971). The Olive Hill poltergeist. *PPA, 6,* 57–8.

Rose, L. (1951). Psi patterns amongst the Australian Aborigines. *JASPR, 45,* 71–6.

Rose, L. and Rose, R. (1951). Psi experiments with Australian Aborigines. *JP, 15,* 122–31.

Rose, R. (1952a). Experiments in ESP and PK with Aboriginal subjects. *JP, 16,* 219–20.

Rose, R. (1952b). Psi and Australian Aborigines. *JASPR, 46,* 17–28.

Rose, R. (1955). A second report on psi experiments with Australian Aborigines. *JP, 19,* 92–8.

Rose, R. (1956). *Living Magic.* New York: Rand McNally.

Rosenthal, R. (1969). Interpersonal expectancies: the effects of the experimenter's hypothesis. In R. Rosenthal and R. Rosnow (eds), *Artifact in Behavioral Research* (pp. 181–277). New York: Academic Press.

Rosenthal, R. and Rubin, D. R. (1978). Interpersonal expectancy effects: the first 345 studies. *The Behavioral and Brain Sciences, 3,* 377–415.

Rothbart, D. (1982). Demarcating genuine science from pseudoscience. In P. Grim (ed.), *Philosophy of Science and the Occult* (pp. 94–105). Albany: SUNY Press.

Rubin, L. and Honorton, C. (1972). Separating the yins from the yangs: an experiment with the *I Ching. PPA, 8,* 6–7.

Rush, J. H. (1943). Some considerations as to a physical basis of ESP. *JP, 7,* 44–9.

Rush, J. H. (1964). New directions in parapsychological research. *PM no. 4.*

Rush, J. H. (1971). [Review of *Mind, matter, and gravitation: a theoretical and experimental study.*] *JASPR, 65,* 223–7.

Rush, J. H. (1976). Physical aspects of psi phenomena. In G. R. Schmeidler (ed.), *Parapsychology: Its Relation to Physics, Biology, Psychology, and Psychiatry* (pp. 6–39). Metuchen, New Jersey: Scarecrow Press.

Rush, J. H. (1977). Problems and methods in psychokinesis research. *APR:* vol. 1 (pp. 15–78).

Rush, J. H. (1981). Sensory deprivation and seance phenomena. *Theta, 9*(4), 7–9.

Rush, J. H. (1982). Problems and methods in psychokinesis research. *APR:* vol. 3 (pp. 83–114).

Ryzl, M. (1961). Research on telepathy in Soviet Russia. *JP, 25,* 75–85.

Ryzl, M. (1966). A model of parapsychological communication. *JP, 30,* 18–30.

Sabom, M. B. (1982). *Recollections of Death,* New York: Harper & Row.

Salter, W. H. (1938). *Ghosts and Apparitions.* London: G. Bell.

Saltmarsh, H. F. (1975). *Evidence of Personal Survival from Cross-correspondences.* New York: Arno Press. (Original work published 1938.)

Sannwald, G. (1963). On the psychology of spontaneous paranormal phenomena. *IJP, 5*(3), 274–92.

Sargent, C. L. (1980a). A covert test of psi abilities of psi-conducive and psi-inhibitory experimenters. *RIP 1979* (pp. 115–16).

Sargent, C. L. (1980b). Exploring psi in the ganzfeld. *PM no. 17.*

Sargent, C. L. (1981). Extraversion and performance in 'extra-sensory' perception tasks. *Personality and Individual Differences, 2,* 137–43.

Sargent, C. L., Bartlett, H. J. and Moss, S. P. (1982). Response structure and temporal incline in ganzfeld free-response ESP testing. *JP, 46,* 85–110.

Schechter, E. I. (1984). Hypnotic induction vs. control conditions: illustrating an approach to the evaluation of replicability in parapsychological data. *JASPR, 78,* 1–27.

Schlitz, M. and Gruber, E. (1980). Transcontinental remote viewing. *JP, 44,* 305–17.

Schlitz, M. and Gruber, E. (1981). Transcontinental remote viewing: a rejudging. *JP, 45,* 233–37.

Schmeidler, G. R. (1964). An experiment in precognitive clairvoyance. Part I. The main results. *JP, 28,* 1–14.

Schmeidler, G. R. (1972). Respice, adspice, prospice. *PPA, 8,* 117–45.

Schmeidler, G. R. (1973). PK effects upon continuously recorded temperature. *JASPR, 67,* 325–40.

Schmeidler, G. R. (1977). Research findings in psychokinesis. *APR:* vol. 1 (pp. 79–132).

Schmeidler, G. R. (1982). PK research: findings and theories. *APR:* vol. 3 (pp. 115–46).

Schmeidler, G. R. and Maher, M. (1981a). Judges' responses to the nonverbal behavior of psi-conducive and psi-inhibitory experimenters. *JASPR, 75,* 241–57.

Schmeidler, G. R. and Maher, M. (1981b). [Letter to the editor.] *JASPR, 75,* 364–5.

Schmeidler, G. R. and McConnell, R. A. (1973). *ESP and Personality Patterns.* Westport, Conn.: Greenwood Press. (Original work published 1958.)

Schmidt, H. (1969a). Clairvoyance tests with a machine. *JP, 33,* 300–6.

Schmidt, H. (1969b). Precognition of a quantum process. *JP, 33,* 99–108.

Schmidt, H. (1970a). PK experiments with animals as subjects. *JP, 34,* 255–61.

Schmidt, H. (1970b). A PK test with electronic equipment. *JP, 34,* 175–81.

Schmidt, H. (1970c). A quantum mechanical random number generator for psi tests. *JP, 34,* 219–24.

Schmidt, H. (1973). PK tests with a high-speed random number generator. *JP, 37,* 105–18.

Schmidt, H. (1974). Comparison of PK action on two different random number generators. *JP, 38,* 47–55.

Schmidt, H. (1975). Toward a mathematical theory of psi. *JASPR, 69,* 267–291.

Schmidt, H. (1976). PK effect on pre-recorded targets. *JASPR, 70,* 267–92.

Schmidt, H. (1978). A remark on the 'divergence problem'. *EJP, 2,* 163–6.

Schmidt, H. (1979). Use of stroboscobic light as rewarding feedback in a PK test with prerecorded and momentarily generated random events. *RIP 1978* (pp. 115–17).

Schmidt, H., Morris, R. L. and Rudolph, L. (1982). Channeling evidence to 'critical' observers. *RIP 1981* (pp. 136–8.)

Schmidt, H. and Pantas, L. (1972). Psi tests with internally different machines. *JP, 36,* 222–32.

Schouten, S. A. (1972). Psi in mice: positive reinforcement. *JP, 36,* 261–82.

Schouten, S. A. (1976). Autonomic psychophysiological reactions to sensory and emotive stimuli in a psi experiment. *EJP, 1*(2), 57–71.
Schouten, S. A. (1977). Testing some implications of a PK observational theory. *EJP, 1*(4), 21–31.
Schouten, S. A. (1979). Analysis of spontaneous cases as reported in *Phantasms of the Living*. *EJP, 2,* 408–54.
Schouten, S. A. (1981). Analysing spontaneous cases: a replication based on the Sannwald collection. *EJP, 4,* 9–48.
Schouten, S. A. (1982). Analysing spontaneous cases: a replication based on the Rhine collection. *EJP, 4,* 113–58.
Schouten, S. A. and Kelly, E. F. (1978). On the experiment of Brugmans, Heymans, and Weinberg. *EJP, 2,* 247–90.
Schrenk-Notzing, A. (1920). *The Phenomena of Materialization* (trans.). London: Kegan Paul, Trench, Trübner & Co.
Schwartz, S. A. (1978). *The Secret Vaults of Time.* New York: Grosset & Dunlap.
Scott, C. (1972). On the evaluation of verbal material in parapsychology. *JSPR, 46,* 79–90.
Scott, C. *et al.* (1974). The Soal-Goldney experiments with Basil Shackleton: a discussion. *PSPR, 56,* 43–131.
Shapin, B. and Coly, L. (1984). *The Problem of Repeatability.* New York: Parapsychology Foundation.
Shiels, D. (1978). A cross-cultural study of beliefs in out-of-the-body experiences. *JSPR, 49,* 697–741.
Sidgwick, E. M. (1900). Discussion of the trance phenomena of Mrs Piper. *PSPR, 15,* 16–38.
Sidgwick, E. M. (1913). A reply to Dr Joseph Maxwell's paper on 'Cross correspondences' and the experimental method. *PSPR, 26,* 375–400.
Sidgwick, E. M. (ed.) (1918/1975). *Phantasms of the Living* [1-vol. abridgment of Gurney, Myers and Podmore, same title]. (Bound with E. M. Sidgwick, 1923.) New York: Arno Press.
Sidgwick, E. M. (ed.) (1923/1975). *Phantasms of the Living* [cases from the *Journal* of the SPR]. (Bound with E. M. Sidgwick, 1918.) New York: Arno Press.
Sidgwick, H. (1882). [President's address.] *PSPR, 1,* 7–12.
Sidgwick, H., Johnson, A., Myers, F. W. H., Podmore, F. and Sidgwick, E. M. (1894). Report of the Census of Hallucinations. *PSPR, 10,* 25–422.
Sinclair, U. (1962). *Mental Radio.* Springfield, Illinois: Charles Thomas. (Original work published 1930.)
Smith, E. L. (1974). The Raudive voices – objective or subjective?. *JASPR, 68,* 91–100.
Smith, M. J. (1972). Paranormal effects on enzyme activity. *Human Dimensions, 1*(2), 15–19.
Smith, S. (1964). *The mediumship of Mrs Leonard.* New Hyde Park, New York: University Books.
Smythies, J. R. (1967). Is ESP possible?. In J. R. Smythies (ed.), *Science and ESP* (pp. 1–14). New York: Humanities Press.
Soal, S. G. (1948). [Review of *The Reach of the Mind.*] *JSPR, 34,* 183–5.
Soal, S. G. (1960). A reply to Mr Hansel. *PSPR, 53,* 43–82.
Soal, S. G. and Goldney, K. M. (1943). Experiments in precognitive telepathy. *PSPR, 47,* 21–150.
Solfvin, G. F., Roll, W. G. and Kelly, E. F. (1977). A psychophysiological study of mediumistic communicators. *PR, 8*(3), 21–2.

Solfvin, G. F. (1982a). Expectancy and placebo effects in experimental studies of mental healing. Unpublished doctoral dissertation, University of Utrecht, The Netherlands.

Solfvin, G. F. (1982b). Psi expectancy effects in psychic healing studies with malarial mice. *EJP, 4,* 159–97.

Solfvin, G. F., Kelly, E. F. and Burdick, D. S. (1978). Some new methods of analysis for preferential-ranking data. *JASPR, 72,* 93–109.

Sondow, N. (1979). Effects of associations and feedback on psi in the ganzfeld: is there more than meets the judge's eye? *JASPR, 73,* 123–50.

SPR Committee (1922). Report on a series of sittings with Eva C. *PSPR, 32,* 209–343.

Stanford, R. G. (1967). Response bias and the correctness of ESP test responses. *JP, 31,* 280–9.

Stanford, R. G. (1969). 'Associative activation of the unconscious' and 'visualization' as methods for influencing the PK target. *JASPR, 63,* 338–51.

Stanford, R. G. (1970). Extrasensory effects upon 'memory'. *JASPR, 64,* 161–86.

Stanford, R. G. (1974). An experimentally testable model for spontaneous psi events. I. Extrasensory events. *JASPR, 68,* 34–57.

Stanford, R. G. (1975). Response patterns in extrasensory performance. *Journal of Communication, 25,* 153–61.

Stanford, R. G. (1977a). The application of learning theory to ESP performance: a review of Dr C. T. Tart's monograph. *JASPR, 71,* 55–80.

Stanford, R. G. (1977b). Conceptual frameworks of contemporary psi research. *HB* (pp. 823–58).

Stanford, R. G. (1977c). Experimental psychokinesis: a review from diverse perspectives. *HB* (pp. 324–81).

Stanford, R. G. (1977d). The question is: good experimentation or not? A reply to Dr C. T. Tart. *JASPR, 71,* 191–200.

Stanford, R. G. (1978). Toward reinterpreting psi events. *JASPR, 72,* 197–214.

Stanford, R. G. (1979). The influence of auditory ganzfeld characteristics upon free-response ESP performance. *JASPR, 73,* 253–72.

Stanford, R. G. and Angelini, R. F. (1983). The noise-silence and target-encodability variables in a ganzfeld word-association ESP task: the application of methods based upon signal detection theory. *RIP 1982* (pp. 185–7).

Stanford, R. G. and associates (1976). A Study of motivational arousal and self-concept in psi-mediated instrumental response. *JASPR, 70,* 167–78.

Stanford, R. G. and Fox, C. (1975). An effect of release of effort in a psychokinetic task. *RIP 1974* (pp. 61–3).

Stanford, R. G. and Neylon, A. (1975). Experimental factors related to free-response clairvoyance performance in a sensory uniform setting (ganzfeld). *RIP 1974* (pp. 89–93).

Stanford, R. G. and Palmer, J. (1972). Some statistical considerations concerning process-oriented research in parapsychology. *JASPR, 66,* 166–79.

Stanford, R. G. and Palmer, J. (1975). Free-response ESP performance and occipital alpha rhythms. *JASPR, 69,* 235–43.

Stanford, R. G. and Roig, M. (1982). Toward understanding the cognitive consequences of the auditory stimulation used for ganzfeld: two studies. *JASPR, 76,* 319–40.

Stanford, R. G. and Rust, P. (1977). Psi-mediated helping behavior: experimental paradigm and initial results. *RIP 1976* (pp. 109–10).

Stanford, R. G. and Sargent, C. L. (1983). Z-scores in free-response ESP methodology: comments on their utility and correction of an error. *JASPR, 77,* 319–26.

Stanford, R. G. and Stio, A. (1976). A study of associative mediation in psi-mediated instrumental response. *JASPR, 70,* 55–64.

Stanford, R. G. and Thompson, G. (1974). Unconscious psi-mediated instrumental response and its relation to conscious ESP performance. *RIP 1973* (pp. 99–103).

Stanford, R. G., Zenhausern, R., Taylor, A. and Dwyer, M. (1975). Psychokinesis as psi-mediated instrumental response. *JASPR, 69,* 127–34.

Steilberg, B. J. (1975). 'Conscious concentration' versus 'visualization' in PK tests. *JP, 39,* 12–20.

Stent, G. S. (1972). Prematurity and uniqueness in scientific discovery. *Scientific American, 227*(6), 84–93.

Stevens, B., Burton, L. and Joines, W. (1974). Charge build-up on the body as a basis for the 'human aura' and certain PK events. *RIP 1973* (pp. 77–80).

Stevenson, I. (1960). A review and analysis of paranormal experiences connected with the sinking of the *Titanic. JASPR, 54,* 153–71.

Stevenson, I. (1965). Seven more paranormal experiences associated with the sinking of the *Titanic. JASPR, 59,* 211–25.

Stevenson, I. (1967). An antagonist's view of parapsychology. A review of Professor Hansel's *ESP: A Scientific Evaluation. JASPR, 61,* 254–67.

Stevenson, I. (1968). The combination lock test for survival. *JASPR, 62,* 246–54.

Stevenson, I. (1970a). [Letters and comments.] *JP, 34,* 143–9.

Stevenson, I. (1970b). *Telepathic Impressions.* Charlottesville: University Press of Virginia. (Original work published as *PASPR, 29,* 1970.)

Stevenson, I. (1974a). *Twenty Cases Suggestive of Reincarnation.* Charlottesville: University Press of Virginia.

Stevenson, I. (1974b). Xenoglossy: a review and report of a case. *PASPR, 31,* 1–268.

Stevenson, I. (1975). *Cases of the Reincarnation Type. Volume 1. Ten Cases in India.* Charlottesville: University Press of Virginia.

Stevenson, I. (1977). Reincarnation: field studies and theoretical issues. *HB* (pp. 631–63).

Stevenson, I. (1982). The contribution of apparitions to the evidence for survival. *JASPR, 76,* 341–58.

Stevenson, I. and Pasricha, S. (1980). A preliminary report on an unusual case of the reincarnation type with xenoglossy. *JASPR, 74,* 331–48.

Stevenson, I. and Pratt, J. G. (1968). Exploratory investigations of the psychic photography of Ted Serios. *JASPR, 62,* 103–29.

Stevenson, I. and Pratt, J. G. (1969). Further investigations of the psychic photography of Ted Serios. *JASPR, 63,* 352–65.

Stoyva, J. and Kamiya, J. (1968). Electrophysiological studies of dreaming as the prototype of a new strategy in the study of consciousness. *Psychological Review, 75,* 192–205.

Stuart, C. E. (1945). A classroom ESP experiment with the free response method. *JP, 9,* 92–105.

Swann, I. (1975). *To Kiss Earth Goodbye.* New York: Dell. (Paper.)

Taboas, A. M. (1980). The psychopathological model of poltergeist phenomena: some criticisms and suggestions. *PR, 11*(2), 24–7.

Taddonio, J. L. (1975). Attitudes and expectancies in ESP scoring. *JP, 39,* 289–96.

Taddonio, J. L. (1976). The relationship of experimenter expectancy to performance on ESP tasks. *JP, 40,* 107–14.

Targ, R. and Harary, K. (1984). *The Mind Race.* New York: Villard Books.

Targ, R. and Puthoff, H. (1977). *Mind-reach.* New York: Delacorte.

Targ, R., Puthoff, H. E. and May, E. (1979). Direct perception of remote geographical locations. *MAL* (pp. 77–106).

Tart, C. T. (1963). Physiological correlates of psi cognition. *IJP, 5,* 375–86.

Tart, C. T. (1966). Card guessing tests: learning paradigm or extinction paradigm?. *JASPR, 60,* 46–55.

Tart, C. T. (1968). A psychophysiological study of out-of-body experiences in a selected subject. *JASPR, 62,* 3–27.

Tart, C. T. (1976). *Learning to Use Extrasensory Perception.* Chicago: University of Chicago Press.

Tart, C. T. (1977). Towards humanistic experimentation in parapsychology: a reply to Dr Stanford's review. *JASPR, 71,* 81–101.

Tart, C. T. (1979). Randomicity, predictability, and mathematical inference strategies in ESP feedback experiments. *JASPR, 73,* 44–60.

Tart, C. T. (1980). Are we interested in making ESP function strongly and reliably? A reply to J. E. Kennedy. *JASPR, 74,* 210–22.

Tart, C. T. (1983). Laboratory PK: frequency of manifestation and resemblance to precognition. *RIP 1982* (pp. 101–2).

Tart, C. T. and Dronek, E. (1983). Mathematical inference strategies versus psi: initial explorations with the Probabilistic Predictor Program. *EJP, 4,* 325–55.

Tart, C. T., Palmer, J. and Redington, D. J. (1979). Effects of immediate feedback on ESP performance: a second study. *JASPR, 73,* 151–65.

Tart, C. T., Puthoff, H. E. and Targ, R. (1980). Information transmission in remote viewing experiments. *Nature, 284,* 191.

Tedder, W. H. and Monty, M. L. (1981). Exploration of long-distance PK: a conceptual replication of the influence on a biological system. *RIP 1980* (pp. 90–3).

Terry, J. C. and Harris, S. A. (1975). Precognition in water-deprived rats. *RIP 1974* (p. 81).

Terry, J. (C.) and Schmidt, H. (1978). Conscious and subconscious PK tests with pre-recorded targets. *RIP 1977* (pp. 36–41).

Thalbourne, M. A. (1979). A more powerful method of evaluating data from free-response experiments. *JSPR, 50,* 84–107.

Thalbourne, M. A. and Jungkuntz, J. H. (1983). Extraverted sheep vs. introverted goats: experiments VII and VIII. *JP, 47,* 49–51.

Thouless, R. H. (1951). A report on an experiment in psycho-kinesis with dice, and a discussion on psychological factors favoring success. *PSPR, 49,* 107–30.

Tietze, T. R. (1973a). *Margery.* New York: Harper & Row.

Tietze, T. R. (1973b, April). The mystery of Rudi Schneider. *Psychic,* pp. 38–43.

Tietze, T. R. (1973c, February). Phenomena [Crookes-Home experiments]. *Psychic,* pp. 30–1, 55.

Tietze, T. R. (1974, February). Great physical mediums, Part II. *Psychic,* pp. 30–5.

Tischner, R. (1925). *Telepathy and Clairvoyance* (trans.). New York: Harcourt, Brace.

Tobacyk, J. J. (in press). Some consideration on the Alcock-Palmer exchange. *ZS.*

Toulmin, S. and Goodfield, J. (1961). *The Fabric of the Heavens.* New York: Harper & Row.

Tripplett, N. (1900). The psychology of conjuring deceptions. *American Journal of Psychology, 11,* 439–510.

Truzzi, M. (1978) On the extraordinary: an attempt at clarification. *ZS, 1,* 11–22.

Tversky, A. and Kahneman, D. (1973). Availability: a heuristic for judging frequency and probability. *Cognitive Psychology, 5,* 207–32.

Tversky, A. and Kahneman, D. (1974). Judgment under uncertainty: heuristics and biases. *Science, 185,* 1124–31.

Tyrrell, G. N. M. (1938). The Tyrrell apparatus for testing extrasensory perception. *JP, 2,* 107–18.

Tyrrell, G. N. M. (1962). *Apparitions.* New York: Macmillan. (Original work published 1942.)

Ullman, M. (1952). On the nature of resistance to psi phenomena. *JASPR, 46,* 11–13.

Ullman, M. (1959). On the occurrence of telepathic dreams. *JASPR, 53,* 50–61.

Ullman, M. (1975). Parapsychology and psychiatry. In A. M. Freedman, H. I. Kaplan and B. J. Saddock (eds), *Comprehensive Textbook of Psychiatry* (2nd ed, vol. 2, pp. 2552–61). Baltimore: Williams & Wilkins.

Ullman, M. and Krippner, S. (1970). Dream studies and telepathy. *PM no. 12.*

Ullman, M., Krippner, S. and Vaughan, A. (1973). *Dream Telepathy.* New York: Macmillan.

Van de Castle, R. L. (1958). An exploratory study of some personality correlates associated with PK performance. *JASPR, 52,* 134–50.

Van de Castle, R. L. (1969). The facilitation of ESP through hypnosis. *American Journal of Clinical Hypnosis, 12,* 37–56.

Van de Castle, R. L. (1970). Psi abilities in primitive groups. *PPA, 7,* 97–122.

Van de Castle, R. L. (1974). An investigation of psi abilities among the Cuna Indians of Panama. In A. Angoff and D. Barth (eds), *Parapsychology and Anthropology* (pp. 80–100). New York: Parapsychology Foundation.

Van de Castle, R. L. (1977a). Parapsychology and anthropology. *HB* (pp. 667–86).

Van de Castle, R. L. (1977b). Sleep and dreams. *HB* (pp. 473–99).

Vasiliev, L. L. (1976). *Experiments in Distant Influence* (trans.). New York: Dutton. (Original work published as *Experiments in Mental Suggestion,* 1963.)

Wagner, M. W. and Monnet, M. (1979). Attitudes of college professors toward extra-sensory perception. *ZS, 5,* 7–16.

Walker, E. H. (1974). Consciousness and quantum theory. In J. White (ed.), *Psychic Exploration* (pp. 544–68). New York: Putnam's.

Walker, E. H. (1975). Foundations of paraphysical and parapsychological phenomena. In L. Oteri (ed.), *Quantum Physics and Parapsychology* (pp. 1–53). New York: Parapsychology Foundation.

Walker, E. H. (1982). A response to criticisms of the quantum theory of psi phenomena. *RIP 1981* (pp. 68–72).

Warcollier, R. (1948). *Mind to Mind.* New York: Creative Age Press.

Warcollier, R. (1975). *Experimental Telepathy* (trans.). New York: Arno Press. (Original work published 1938.)

Warner, L. (1952). A second survey of psychological opinion on ESP. *JP, 16,* 284–95.

Warner, L. and Clark, C. C. (1938). A survey of psychological opinion on ESP. *JP, 2,* 196–301.

Warrick, F. W. (1939). *Experiments in Psychics.* New York: Dutton.

Wasserman, G. D. (1966). An outline of a field theory of organismic form and behavior. In G. E. Wolstenholme and E. C. P. Millar (eds), *Extrasensory Perception: A CIBA Foundation Symposium* (pp. 53–72). New York: Citadel. (Original work published 1956.)

Watkins, G. K. (1972). Possible PK in the lizard Anolis sagrei. *PPA, 8,* 23–5.

Watkins, G. K. and Watkins, A. M. (1971). Possible PK influence on the resuscitation of anesthetized mice. *JP, 35,* 257–72.

Watkins, G. K. and Watkins, A. M. (1974). Apparent psychokinesis on static objects by a 'gifted' subject: a laboratory demonstration. *RIP 1973* (pp. 132–4).

Watkins, G. K., Watkins, A. M. and Wells, R. A. (1973). Further studies on the resuscitation of anesthetized mice. *RIP 1972* (pp. 157–9).

Wells, R. (A.) and Klein, J. (1972). A replication of a 'psychic healing' paradigm. *JP, 36,* 144–9.

Wells, R. (A.) and Watkins, G. K. (1975). Linger effects in several PK experiments. *RIP 1974* (pp. 143–7).

West, D. J. (1945). A critical survey of the American PK research. *PSPR, 47,* 281–90.

West, D. J. (1948). The investigation of spontaneous cases. *PSPR, 48,* 264–300.

West, D. J. (1957). *Eleven Lourdes Miracles.* New York: Garrett.

West, D. J. (1960). Visionary and hallucinatory experiences: a comparative appraisal. *IJP, 2*(1), 89–97.

West, D. J. and Fisk, G. W. (1953). A dual ESP experiment with clock cards. *JSPR, 37,* 185–9.

Wheatley, J. M. O. (1976). A note on Hoyt L. Edge's 'Do spirits matter?'. *JASPR, 70,* 397–401.

Wheeler, J. A. (1974). The universe as a home for man. *American Scientist, 62,* 683–91.

White, R. A. (1976a). The influence of persons other than the experimenter on the subject's scores in psi experiments. *JASPR, 70,* 133–66.

White, R. A. (1976b). The limits of experimenter influence on psi test results: can any be set?. *JASPR, 70,* 333–69.

Whitton, J. L. (1975). Qualitative time-domain analysis of acoustic envelopes of psychokinetic table rappings. *New Horizons, 2*(1), 21–4.

Wigner, E. P. (1967). *Symmetries and Reflections.* Bloomington: Indiana University Press.

Winther, C. (1928). Experimental inquiries into telekinesis. *JASPR, 22,* 25–31, 82–99, 164–80, 230–9, 278–90.

Wolman, B. B. (ed.) (1977). *HB.*

Wortz, E. C., Bauer, A. S., Blackwelder, R. F., Eerkens, J. W. and Saur, A. J. (1979). An investigation of Soviet research. *MAL* (pp. 233–60).

Zorab, G. (1964). A further comparative analysis of some poltergeist phenomena: cases from continental Europe. *JASPR, 58,* 105–27.

Zusne, L. and Jones, W. H. (1982). *Anomalistic Psychology.* Hillsdale, New Jersey: Lawrence Erlbaum.

Name index

A bold page number indicates an extensive or significant reference.

Subject index